VERDI'S
MACBETH

Car[o] Suocero

Milano 25 Marzo 1847.

Da molto tempo era ne' miei pensieri
d' intitolare un opera a Voi che m'è
stato e padre, e benefattore, ed amico.
Era un dovere, cui doveva soddisfare prima
d' ora, e l'avrei fatto se imperiose
circostanze non l'avessero impedito —
Ora eccole questo <u>Macbeth</u> che io amo
a preferenza delle altre mie opere, e che
quindi stimo più degno d'essere presentato a
Voi. — Il cuore l'offre : l'accetti di cuore,
e le sia testimonianza della memoria
eterna, della gratitudine, e dell' affetto
che le porta

Il suo aff
G. Verdi

Verdi's letter dedicating Macbeth. *"which I love in preference to my other operas," to his father-in-law, Antonio Barezzi. A transcription and a translation appear on page 57.*

VERDI'S

MACBETH

A Sourcebook

EDITED BY

DAVID ROSEN

AND

ANDREW PORTER

CAMBRIDGE UNIVERSITY PRESS
CAMBRIDGE
LONDON • NEW YORK • NEW ROCHELLE
MELBOURNE • SYDNEY

Published by the Press Syndicate of the University of Cambridge
The Pitt Building, Trumpington Street, Cambridge CB2 1RP
32 East 57th Street, New York, NY 10022, USA
296 Beaconsfield Parade, Middle Park, Melbourne 3206, Australia

© 1984 by W.W. Norton & Company, Inc.

FIRST PUBLISHED 1984

PRINTED IN THE UNITED STATES OF AMERICA

Library of Congress catalogue card number: 81-1495

BL   British Library Cataloguing in Publication Data
Verdi's Macbeth.
1. Verdi, Giuseppe. Macbeth
I. Rosen, David   II. Porter, Andrew
782.1'092'4   ML410.V4
ISBN 0 521 26520 7

Acknowledgments

Centre College, Danville, Kentucky,
was host to the congress
that gave rise to this book.

Its publication was made possible
by a generous grant from the Courier-Journal
and Times Foundation
of Louisville, Kentucky.

A handsome gift from those ardent
supporters of Verdi scholarship and performance,
Brena and Lee A. Freeman, brought it
safely to conclusion.

Further assistance was provided
in the form of a research grant
from the National Endowment for the Humanities.
The findings and conclusions presented here
do not necessarily represent
the views of the Endowment.

Contents

In this Macbeth,
*the more one thinks about it,
the more one finds ways
to improve it.*

Verdi to Piave
3 December 1846

How to Use This Book

Cross-references within this volume are indicated by the author's name in small capitals preceded by "at" (e.g., "see DEGRADA at 158").

Bibliographical abbreviations used throughout are:

Abbiati   Franco Abbiati: *Giuseppe Verdi* (Milan: Ricordi, 1959)

Alberti   Annibale Alberti: *Verdi intimo: carteggio di Giuseppe Verdi con il conte Opprandino Arrivabene (1861-1866)* (Verona: Mondadori, 1931)

Carteggi   Gaetano Cesari and Alessandro Luzio, eds.: *Carteggi verdiani* (Rome: Reale Accademia d'Italia, 1 and 2, 1935; 3 and 4, 1947)

Copialettere Alessandro Luzio, ed.: *I copialettere di Giuseppe Verdi* (Milan, 1913)

Garibaldi   Luigi Agostino Garibaldi: *Giuseppe Verdi nelle lettere di Emanuele Muzio ad Antonio Barezzi* (Milan: Fratelli Treves, 1931)

References by author and short title (e.g., Gerhartz: *Auseinandersetzungen;* Lawton and Rosen: "Non-definitive revisions") point to a full listing in the alphabetical BIBLIOGRAPHY at 464.

...   Verdi frequently punctuated his letters with three (and sometimes two or four) dots. These have been regularized as three dots, unspaced, and do not represent an omission.

. . .   Three spaced dots have been used to indicate omissions.

Technical terms, chiefly formal (*cavatina, tempo di mezzo*) and metric (*strofetta, versi lirici*), are italicized and left untranslated. Where necessary, the particular sense in which Verdi and his contemporaries used them is defined or explained in the GLOSSARY at 459-60.

Persons to whom no more than a passing reference or two is made are identified in footnotes. Those who appear several times or in widely separated contexts are included in the PERSONALIA at 461-63.

Musical references are, when not otherwise specified, to the current Ricordi vocal score of the 1865 *Macbeth* (p.n. 42311) and to the Kalmus reprint of it (#6738), and are made by "page.system.measure" (e.g., 112.1.4); if only two numbers are shown, they refer to page and system. A "conversion table" to the G. Schirmer score (p.n. 46438) and to other editions appears at 465-68.

Preface:
The Danville Congress

The *Macbeth* Congress held at Danville, Kentucky, 10–12 November 1977 was an unforgettable experience. The fifth in the series of international Verdi congresses, it was hosted by an old and distinguished liberal arts college, Centre College of Kentucky. The lovely bluegrass region of that state, cooperative weather, and in particular the warmth of Kentucky hospitality combined to make an ideal setting for the first major event of the newly-founded American Institute for Verdi Studies. The previous congresses had been held in Venice (1966), Verona, Parma, and Busseto (1969), Milan (1972), and Chicago (1974). Centre College offered a beautiful and flexible Regional Arts Center, seating as the occasion demands three hundred, a thousand, or fifteen hundred people, with a stage wider than that of the Metropolitan Opera House, and with stunning acoustics. It serves Americans from five states (Kentucky, Tennessee, West Virginia, southern Ohio and southern Indiana). This regional center, designed by the Taliesin Associates of the Frank Lloyd Wright Foundation, which opened in 1973 with a performance of Verdi's *Otello,* allowed the Verdi Institute, which has its base in New York, to demonstrate that it is indeed an American institute.

Consonant with the primary aim of the Institute, i.e., to bring performers, scholars, and listeners more closely together, an integral part of the planning for the event was a performance during the congress of the original version of *Macbeth,* Verdi's most significant early opera. Andrew Porter made a new English translation. At my suggestion, David Lawton, a member of the Institute's advisory board, prepared a new edition of the score and acted as musical advisor for the Kentucky Opera Association and its conductor, Moritz Bomhard. This kind of cooperation established a precedent for future Verdi congresses.

Mary Jane Phillips Matz, an AIVS executive board member, first suggested the Regional Arts Center as the setting for the congress, and brought me and Floyd Herzog, its managing director, together in the spring of 1976 at New York University's Bobst Library. Hard work combined with friendship did the rest. The planning committee was expanded to include Andrew Porter and Mario Medici, the founder and at that time the director of the Istituto di studi verdiani at Parma. Maestro Medici also allowed materials from the Parma Institute to be shipped to the United States for use in a major Verdi exhibition mounted in the Regional Arts Center's spacious foyer. Some forty-five individuals and as many institutions in Italy, England, and the United States contributed to this splendid exhibition. The largest group of items, mainly photographs, was gathered by Mrs. Matz, and many of them are now in the AIVS archive. At the congress, working sessions alternated with visits to historic locations commemorating Kentucky's early history, social events, and a moving Convocation at Centre College at which honorary doctorates were awarded to Moritz Bomhard, Martin Chusid, Joseph Duffey, Alexander Heard, Mary Jane Phillips Matz, and Mario

Medici. The National Endowment for the Humanities made a major grant toward the cost of the congress, for which we are deeply grateful. Through the efforts of President Thomas A. Spragens of Centre College, a substantial and much appreciated subvention was also received from the Courier-Journal and Times Foundation of Louisville to help W. W. Norton publish this volume. A further generous gift from Brena and Lee A. Freeman brought it to conclusion.

On behalf of everyone who attended the congress, we should like to acknowledge the uniformly cheerful and gracious assistance of both the staff at the Regional Arts Center—Joyce Jackson, James Peterson, Roberta Crawford, Peggy Frisbie, Katherine Nichols, John Kriz, Henry Lewis, Stephen Martin, and David Trapp—and of the Istituto di studi verdiani, Marisa Casati and Lina Re. We should like to acknowledge the strong support of the American Institute's staff at New York University—Rena Mueller, John Nádas, Luke Jensen, Mary McCarthy, and Jane Wozniak—before, during, and after the congress.

We hope the *Macbeth* Sourcebook will prove as enlightening and enjoyable for scholars, performers, and Verdians throughout the world as was the congress for its fortunate participants.

MARTIN CHUSID
Director, American Institute for Verdi Studies

Introduction

Verdi dedicated *Macbeth*, in 1847, to his benefactor and father-in-law, Antonio Barezzi, as "this *Macbeth* that I love in preference to all my other operas." In 1875, when he was in Vienna to conduct the *Requiem*, a journalist interviewed him and (in the *Neue Freie Presse*) reported a remark of his made after some tactful replies to questions about Wagner: "I, too, have attempted the fusion of music and drama, and that in *Macbeth*." Verdi's *Macbeth* was by no means the first opera with a plot drawn from Shakespeare, but is the first that can justly be described as Shakespearean. He took unusual care over its composition and its first performance. He strove to create something new, serious, and exciting. That has long been recognized. The full evidence of it is collected in this volume.

In 1969, the Istituto di Studi Verdiani, in Parma, held its second international congress, with *Don Carlos* as the subject and around a performance of *Don Carlos* in the Verona Arena. The *Atti*, filling a fat volume of 611 pages, contain much that is valuable and important to Verdi studies. However, the most important discoveries about *Don Carlos* were probably those made after the congress—and as a direct result of it. For at such gatherings—it is one reason for traveling to hear what could in many cases more conveniently and profitably be read—information and ideas are generously shared. A fact brought forward by one scholar, whether in a formal paper or during informal conversation, may spur another to new researches. A spark from one speaker's critical or analytical observation may fire another's thinking. This happened at the *Don Carlos* congress, with the result that a student of that opera must now consult not only the *Atti* but also, for post-1969 congress fruits—the *Revue de Musicologie, Analecta Musicologica*, and several other publications containing basic *Carlos* material.

When the American Institute for Verdi Studies planned its first international congress, to be held in Centre College, Danville, Kentucky, in November 1977,[1] on the subject of *Macbeth* and around a production, by the Kentucky Opera, of the 1847 score, I suggested to Martin Chusid, the AIVS director, that its "proceedings" might profitably be expanded to become something more than a collection of the papers read there. In addition, a *Macbeth* volume derived from such a congress might aim to contain not only all the new information, facts, documents, etc. that an international assembly of *Macbeth* scholars would certainly command, but also any post-congress treasure unearthed as a result of following up clues planted at Danville. The information would most concisely and usefully be presented by setting the previously unknown in the context of the known. Other features might be a collection of the contemporary reviews of *Macbeth*, in 1847 and 1865; contemporary iconography; and early performance annals. The response of the *congressisti* was enthusiastic

---

1. For an account of the congress, see the AIVS *Verdi Newsletter* No. 4 (January 1978), 7–11.

and generous. They brought us rich hoards of documents, reviews, and illustrations. They readily agreed to let us lift unpublished material from their individual papers and range it in an impersonal chronological context. And during the next three years they sent us their further discoveries.

I had dreamed of a volume that would gather and order *all* the material related to *Macbeth* that a student of Verdi, a conductor, director, or singer, an historian, or an ordinary enthusiast might like to consult. The time seemed ripe for compiling a *Macbeth* sourcebook. In general, Verdi's music and all that bears on it had at last begun to receive close, serious attention such as Josquin's, Mozart's, Beethoven's, and Wagner's works have long received. The congresses and publications of the Parma Istituto, founded in 1959, provided a focus for the new scholarship, and its archive amassed under one roof what could previously be read only after much travel. The American Institute for Verdi Studies, founded in 1976, then gave Verdi scholarship a bifocal, or transatlantic, vision, and its archive, housed in the Bobst Library of New York University, is now even richer than that of the Parmesan fellow institute. (For some account of the holdings, see the AIVS *Verdi Newsletters* Nos. 7 and 9/10.) Many of the documents are here published for the first time (for example, Verdi's rich letter to Léon Escudier of 11 March 1865, which was turned up by Martin Chusid and John Nádas in the films of the AIVS archive. Most of those already in print could be newly checked against the originals or facsimiles.

What matters most about Verdi is, of course, his operas. When inviting contributions to the Danville congress, we tried to insure that all the kinds of approach that can lead to a clearer understanding and fuller enjoyment of *Macbeth* would be represented. Verdi's thoughts and feelings about and his knowledge of Shakespeare; his sense of musical forms; his theatrical instinct and flair; his understanding of human character and his sense of individual personality; his insistence upon cogent, revealing words; his harmonic structures; his orchestration; his command of meters poetic and musical; his ideas about singing and acting and his very practical ideas about staging; his relation to progressive Italian thought, cultural and political, at the mid-century; his business dealings with impresarios, librettists, and publishers and his practical dealings with singers, directors, and designers; his changing ideas and his revisions; his drafts, autographs, the first and subsequent printed editions—these and more were among the diverse topics of the congress, and they are some of the diverse yet linked topics of this volume.

Francis Jeffreys, the formidable first editor of the *Edinburgh Review,* warned his contributors that he took "the unquestioned and unlimited power of alteration and rejection . . . into his own hands," and advised them "not to be surprised if their best efforts be . . . published so changed that they cannot recognize their own offspring, or only recognize them so much as to be horrified by the change of their dress, manners, and opinions." We were less stern. An AIVS editorial committee—Claire Brook, Martin Chusid, Philip Gossett, David Rosen, and I—was formed, to read and reread the Danville papers and decide which should be included, which not, and to assist in the preliminary editing. Requests and suggestions for alteration were submitted to the authors. David Rosen was persuaded to edit the volume, with me to help him, and then the huge task began of assembling and refining the documentary material and relating it to the Danville papers. At Martin Chusid's suggestion, John Nádas, the AIVS archivist, amassed a first compilation of relevant letters. Our contributors produced and continued to produce far, far more information, far more documents, than we had at first envisaged. The book grew, and so did the time it took to put it together. A new document would suddenly confirm, refute, or amplify something that had been suggested at Danville. Then it had to be sent to the authors of whatever papers it might affect so that they could take account of it and appropriately rewrite their contributions. Our decision to present the letters in both the original language and English translation further slowed things down. So did checking and rechecking against films in the AIVS archive and originals in European libraries. At "home base," so to speak, a vast, complicated jigsaw puzzle of all that had gone into the making of *Macbeth* slowly took shape. Piece fitted into piece. One thing explained another. As the detailed picture began to emerge, we felt mounting excitement, and we hope that some of that excitement may also be felt by our readers. We were torn between, on the one hand, letting them put the pieces together for themselves and discover how they fit, and, on the other hand, pointing out the connections by means of footnotes and cross-references. We decided on not a middle course but—since a chief purpose of the book is to make information readily accessible—a good deal of cross-reference. Nevertheless, a reader who pursues the documents in sequence should not miss the "detective-story" element.

Macbeth was composed in response to a commission from the Teatro della Pergola, in Florence, for performance in 1847. At that date, Shakespeare's play, it seems, had not been staged in Italy. Within a decade, Verdi's version of it had been heard in nearly a hundred towns. Florence was a liberal center. In Papal Rome, references to the supernatural were expunged from Verdi's libretto. In regal Naples and Palermo, references to regicide were expunged. In Austrian-occupied Milan, the chorus did not sing of a *patria oppressa*. But everywhere, although not by everyone, the ambition, power, and originality of *Macbeth* were recognized. It was and is a key work in the career of a great dramatic composer; and the written evidence for what Verdi intended to achieve in it—musically, theatrically, and as an interpretation, cast for the lyric stage, of Shakespeare's play—makes important reading.

Eighteen years later—two years after *La forza del destino*, two before *Don Carlos*—Verdi revised his 1847 *Macbeth* for a production at the Théâtre-Lyrique, in Paris. Paris, with its long rehearsal periods and stable, salaried companies, was a magnet for nineteenth-century opera composers distressed by the hurly-burly of Italian operatic life, but a magnet whose poles could repel as well as attract: bureaucracy, singers' vanity, a peculiarly Parisian emphasis on novelty and "sensation," and a lack of due seriousness were among the things composers complained of. An ambiguous relation with Paris opera runs through Verdi's career; there were things about it that he valued, others that he despised, and things that by means of his compositions for Paris he tried to reform. The Théâtre-Lyrique, where *Faust*, *Roméo et Juliette*, *Les Pêcheurs de perles*, and *Les Troyens à Carthage* had their premieres, was a "progressive" house. It put on the revised *Macbeth* in conscious rivalry to Meyerbeer's *L'Africaine*, the Opéra's novelty of 1865. Verdi poured fine, strong new music into this work but—he who had rehearsed the Florence premiere so intently—did not go to Paris to supervise its production, and was not altogether surprised at its lukewarm reception.

Some of the new things that appear in this volume and some of the dominant themes that emerged during its compilation are perhaps worth singling out here. On the detailed level, there is Francesco Degrada's edition of the manuscript "working libretto" in Verdi's and Andrea Maffei's hands—the first publication of its kind. Read in conjunction with the Piave-Verdi correspondence about the text and with the 1847 libretto itself (reproduced in facsimile at pp. 471-76), the transcription provides a view into that Verdian workshop where getting the words of a new opera right often seems to have been a more arduous—and longer—task than composing the music. (One must remember, however, that many of Verdi's verbal sketches but very few of his musical sketches have been made public; examination of the latter may one day change our ideas considerably.) Another such detailed and intimate study is provided by the intricate drafts in Verdi's and Giuseppina Strepponi's hands of the text for the 1865 finale, and the Verdi-Piave correspondence about it. Among general themes, the high seriousness with which Verdi approached Shakespeare, the influence of August Wilhelm Schlegel on his thinking, his ambition to capture new ground for the lyric theatre of his day emerge again and again in several contexts. Through the nineteenth-century writers and thinkers represented in this book we can encounter *Macbeth* freshly, discover it as it broke upon ears and eyes that did not know *Otello* and *Falstaff*. We find much concern for an aspect of the piece that hardly bothers us today: the representation and significance of the supernatural. In a letter of 8 February 1865, Verdi says that "the witches dominate the drama; everything derives from them," and the witches also dominate a good deal of the contemporary criticism. These things—and also the practical details of staging set out by a composer who had stage pictures in his mind while he composed—are important to current interpreters of *Macbeth*, whether they work in the theatre or as commentators and critics.

Many hands have contributed to the volume besides those of the individual authors. Specific acknowledgments of special contributions appear in introductions to various sections. Francesco Degrada and Marcello Conati contributed material, knowledge, and time beyond even what numerous specific acknowledgments suggest. John Nádas and Luke Jensen, AIVS archivists, cheerfully met our requests for further checking of texts. Claire Brook, the music editor of W. W. Norton, combined rare patience with tactful encouragement and eased our task in every possible way. Elizabeth Davis, Norton copy editor of this volume, was sometimes asked to determine our intended final reading from palimpsests in several hands and various colors. Dorle and Dario Soria, David Hamilton, and Edward Schneider provided English translations of some of the Danville papers; Charlotte Greenspan helped in editing others. Finally, on a personal note, since I am writing this introduction, I would say simply that working on this book with David Rosen, being in contact with his scholarship, acuity, precision, industry, and wit, has been one of the most enjoyable experiences of my life.

ANDREW PORTER

LETTERS

and Other Documents

This is an attempt to present in chronological sequence all the surviving letters, etc., relating to the commission, conception, composition, and first performances of the 1847 Macbeth; to some of its revivals; and to the 1865 revision for Paris. Some of these letters are already famous, but new lights are shed on them when they are read in the context of hitherto unpublished letters.

The initial compilation was undertaken by John Nádas, first from a wide variety of published sources and then from the rich archive of unpublished letters, on film or in photostatic copies, in the American Institute for Verdi Studies. New documents brought to light at the 1977 Danville congress were incorporated. During the next three years, many more letters were added as colleagues in Italy—notably Marcello Conati and Francesco Degrada—sent us whatever they found.

We have aimed to check the text of Verdi's letters against the originals or photographs thereof; and there are several differences, some of them startling, between the texts here printed and those published before. These differences are not signaled with a [sic]; nor are the grammatical slips Verdi committed in haste or his misspellings of proper names. (But the latter are silently corrected in the English translation.) The intention is, so far as possible, to reproduce what Verdi wrote, slips of the pen and all; "silent corrections" are limited to the occasional addition of a period when before a new line, paragraph, or page, Verdi omitted it, and the assigning of a slope to some French accents that he penned more or less vertically. Sic is reserved to indicate a word that without it might seem to be a misprint.

Such checking—in which we were much helped by Messrs. Conati and Degrada in Italy, by Ursula Günther in Paris, by Mr. Nádas and Luke Jensen in the AIVS archive—was, of course, impossible where a published text was the only available source. The cases where this was so are made plain in what follows. Beneath the Italian or French text of each letter there appears, where applicable, first the location of the original letter and then a reference to its publication (limited, as a rule, to a single citation). Where only a location is given, the letter is previously unpublished. Where only a bibliographical reference is given, we have been unable to trace and see the original and have had to rely on a published text. (There are just two or three exceptions to this: documents culled from the appendix of the Copialettere which, hopefully, we "located" at Sant'Agata but have not yet managed to turn up.)

In the case of letters written to Verdi, our procedure has been slightly less rigorous. Many, indeed most, of them were checked by some member or other of our team. And such things as Piave's letters about the text of the libretto are, for obvious reasons, reproduced as accurately as possible. Verdi's slips seemed worth preserving; they can be vivid and even revealing. But we hardly felt that Verdian scholarship would be seriously jeopardized if, say, in some everyday, ordinary French word Escudier, writing in haste, had possibly omitted a letter and we failed to reproduce his error exactly. If the sense was affected, then, of course, the original was reconsulted.

A working draft of the English translation was prepared by John Nádas. What appears here is sometimes the product of a tenth or even later draft, the result of three years' toing-and-froing— sometimes across a table, sometimes across continents—between two editors determined to tease out so far as possible the precise sense of what Verdi wrote. (Sometimes, the meaning of a phrase which had baffled us became clear only a year or so later when a new letter that explained it came to light.) In general, the degree of formality implied by the writer's choice of second-person form (e.g., tu, voi, or Ella) is reflected by an avoidance or not of contractions in the English. It may be worth repeating here that technical terms relating to the forms and metrics of Italian opera, for which the apparent English "equivalents" could be misleading, are left untranslated and are explained in the GLOSSARY *at 459–60. The "main characters of the drama" are listed in the* PERSONALIA *at 461–63; the* comprimarii *who put in but fleeting appearances are, where possible, identified in footnotes. Three close dots* (...) *represent original punctuation; omissions are shown by three spaced dots* (. . .).

Only passages relating directly to Macbeth or to circumstances around it are included; in the case of published letters, the bibliographical citation can lead a reader to the whole letter or, at least, to the fullest version of it in print. Conventional salutations and valedictions are omitted; a few that are unconventional and revealing are retained. Dating and city of provenance are regularized.

We would thank, besides those mentioned above, Claire Brook, Hans Busch, Martin Chusid, Ursula Günther, Mary-Jane Phillips Matz, Carol Rosen, Donatella Stocchi, William Weaver, and Piero Weiss for help in compiling the documents and with points of translation; Gabriela Carrara-Verdi, whose generous opening of Sant'Agata to the AIVS camera immensely simplified the tasks of discovering and checking these letters; and the staffs of the many libraries and institutes whose names appear below. The manuscript had been delivered to the publisher—but, fortunately, not yet set—when Dr. Philip B. Clements sent us the text of an important, unpublished letter of Verdi's to Escudier now in his possession.

1846

VERDI TO LANARI
Milan, 17 May 1846

... Ora che siamo perfettamente d'accordo sul genere fantastico[1] dell'opera che devo scrivere per Firenze[2] bisognerà che tu procuri di sapermi dire più presto che potrai i sogetti:[3] perchè ho in vista due argomenti entrambi fantastici e bellissimi che sceglierò quale sarà più adatto ai sogetti. Sta tranquillo che non mancherà tempo: una volta trovato l'argomento tutto il resto si trova più facilmente. Circa all'andare in scena in Quaresima io veramente avrei diverse cose che me lo impedirebbero, ma cercheremo di superarle tanto più se tu mi darai mano ...

Abbiati 1, 636

... Now that we are perfectly agreed on the fantastical[1] genre for the opera that I have to write for Florence,[2] you must undertake to let me know as soon as you can who the performers will be[3]: because I have two plots in mind, both of them fantastical and very fine, and I'll choose whichever is better suited to the performers. Don't worry, there will be time enough: once the subject is found, all the rest will go easily. As for putting it on in Lent, there really would be several things to stop me from doing so, but we'll try to overcome them, all the more if you give me a hand ...

1. The *genere fantastico* had fascinated composers and critics (see REVIEWS section 381–86, and BASEVI, 421–22) since the Italian premieres of Meyerbeer's *Robert le diable* (Florence, 1840) and Weber's *Der Freischütz* (Florence, 1843). On this and, equally, on the subject of Shakespeare as matter meet or not for opera, the Avvertimento with which Giovanni Peruzzini introduced his *Amleto*, a libretto he wrote for Antonio Buzzola, throws curious light. *Amleto* came hard on the heels of *Macbeth*; it had its first performance at the Fenice, Venice, on 24 March 1848, two months after the Venice premiere of Verdi's opera; Varesi, the original and also the Fenice Macbeth, sang Claudius, and Anna de La Grange, the Lady Macbeth of the Fenice production, sang Gertrude. The Avvertimento reads:

"Whoever knows *Hamlet,* Shakespeare's sublime creation, can easily see that it is not in the least adaptable to the restricted form of a dramma per musica. And even if it were, I should have abstained from laying hands on it, as a profanation. So I declare that from the great Englishman's *Hamlet* I have taken almost nothing but the name, both because of the prestige that invests it and because it is a history almost lost in legend; so I felt free to imagine for myself dramatic situations suited to the somewhat grandiose and fantastical genre of modern music."

For another example of an un-Shakespearean treatment of a Shakespearean theme, see the scenario of Luigi Henry's *Macbetto* at pp. 359–61.

2. In 1845, Verdi had engaged himself to compose an opera for Alessandro Lanari's son, Antonio, at Teatro Sociale in Mantua, for the 1846–47 Carnival season. Alessandro Lanari took over this contract: see Giovanni Ricordi's letter to Lanari of 16 November 1846.

3. Abbiati reads "sogetti"—the sense requires something like "the singers you have engaged."

MUZIO TO BAREZZI

... Il signor Maestro si occupa del libretto per Firenze; i soggetti sono tre: l'*Avola*,[1] i *Masnadieri*[2] e *Macbeth*.—Se avrà Fraschini farà l'*Avola*, se invece di Fraschini gli danno Moriani, come sembra, allora fa il *Macbeth*, e non abbisogna più di un tenore di grande forza. Se Moriani fosse ancora ne' suoi mezzi gli si potrebbe dare una parte di protagonista, ma si dice che sia diventato *un arrosto*.[3] Il signor Maestro però lo sentirà a Bergamo e poi deciderà ...

Garibaldi, 258–59.

... The Maestro is considering the libretto for Florence. There are three possible subjects: *Avola*,[1] *Masnadieri*,[2] and *Macbeth*.—If he has Fraschini, he will do *Avola*; if instead of Fraschini they give him Moriani, as seems likely, then he will do *Macbeth* and a powerful tenor is no longer needed. If Moriani were still in voice, he could be given a leading role, but they say that he is burned out.[3] But the Maestro will hear him in Bergamo and then decide ...

1. Grillparzer's play *Die Ahnfrau*. It figures high on Verdi's list of possible opera subjects (*Copialettere*, plate XI, between pp. 422 and 423). There is an *Avola* scenario in Verdi's hand in Sant'Agata (film in the AIVS archive).

2. *I masnadieri*, libretto by Andrea Maffei after Schiller's *Die Räuber*, was composed for Her Majesty's, London (first performance, 22 July 1847).

3. See the letters of 24 August and 3 September 1846.

VERDI TO LANARI

Sono mortificato e sorpreso che tu non abbia risposto alla lettera in cui mi lagnavo delle esigenze di Moriani.[1] Ma se tu non hai risposto avrai avute le tue ragioni e di questo non se ne parli più. Il tempo stringe e sogna pur decidere qualche cosa: per fa ° un lavoro di qualche importanza i mesi che restano sono appena sufficienti. Orbene, s'hai fissato e stabilito il contratto con Fraschini, niente di meglio ed allora farò uno dei due sogetti che t'accennai: nel caso non abbia fissato Fraschini io non voglio arrischiarmi con altri tenori, ne voglio tremare per gli altri: così ho in vista di trattare un sogetto in cui si possa risparmiare il tenore. In questo caso avrei bisogno assolutamente dei due artisti che ti nomino: La Loewe, e Varesi.

Varesi è il solo artista attuale in Italia che possa fare la parte che medito e per il suo genere di Canto, e per il suo sentire, ed anche per la stessa sua figura. Tutti gli altri artisti anche i migliori di lui non potrebbero farmi quella parte come io vorrei senza nulla togliere al merito di Ferri[2] che ha più bella figura più bella voce, e se vuoi anche migliore cantante non mi potrebbe certamente fare in quella parte l'effetto che mi farebbe Varesi. Cerca adunque di far un cambio cedendo Ferri e tutto così è accomodato. Il sogetto non è ne politico ne religioso, è fantastico. Decidi adunque: o prendi Fraschini (ed allora mi farebbe più a caso la Barbieri) o se

I am mortified and surprised that you haven't answered the letter in which I complained about Moriani's demands.[1] But if you haven't answered you probably had your reasons, and we'll leave it at that. Time is pressing and something really must be decided; to do a work of some importance the months that are left are only just sufficient. Well, if you have arranged and settled the contract with Fraschini, nothing could be better, and I'll do one of the two subjects I mentioned to you. But if you have not signed up Fraschini, I don't want to take a chance with any other tenor, nor do I want to have worries about the others; so I'm thinking of using a subject in which we could do without [a lead] tenor. In this case I would absolutely need the following two artists: *Loewe and Varesi.*

Varesi is the only artist in Italy today who is able to do the part I have in mind, both because of his style of singing and his feeling—and even because of his appearance. All other artists, even those better than he, couldn't do that part for me as I'd like—not to detract from the merits of Ferri,[2] who is better looking, has a more beautiful voice, and, if you like, is even a better singer, but in that role certainly couldn't give me the effect that Varesi would. So try to make an exchange, ceding Ferri, and then everything's taken care of. The subject is neither political nor religious: it is fantastical. So decide: either you get Fraschini (and in that case I'd find

non puoi Fraschini fa il possibile di prender Varesi. Io stesso se credi tratterò (con Varesi) questa cosa per facilitarla purchè tu me ne autorizzi. Il resto della compagnia dovrà esser composto di buone seconde parti, ma mi abbisogna un buon coro...ma di questo ne parleremo più tardi. Presto presto rispondimi a posta corrente e fa che tutte le mie cure i studii fatti per questi maleditissimi [sic] sogetti non restino infruttuosi.

Sant'Agata; Copialettere, 25–26

Barbieri rather more suitable), or, if you can't get Fraschini, do all you can to engage Varesi. I myself, if you think it a good idea, will negotiate with Varesi on this to make things easier, provided that you authorize me to. The rest of the company should be composed of good secondary singers, but I'll need a good chorus...but we'll talk about that later. Answer me *at once* by return mail, and don't let all the pains I've lavished on these damned subjects come to nothing.

1. Moriani was certainly making extraordinary demands; see the letter of 3 September 1846.

2. Gaetano Ferri, the Nabucco of La Scala's spectacularly successful autumn 1842 reprise of *Nabucco* (Giorgio Ronconi had "created" the role at eight Lenten performances that year), and later the first Egberto in *Aroldo* (1857). He sang Macbeth in Barcelona in 1848, in Bologna in 1850, etc. See "A Hundred Years of *Macbeth*," at 428–30 where an initial distinguishes him from the C. Ferri who also sang Macbeth.

MUZIO TO BAREZZI

Milan, 24 August 1846

... A Bergamo gli affari del Teatro vanno poco bene; Moriani non ha piaciuto come si aspettava; e soddisfa poco; la *Linda* non piace niente affatto quantunque eseguita dalla Tadolini; il fatto è che il teatro è poco frequentato, e l'impresa si duole. Dimani a Cremona va in scena l'*Attila* ...

Garibaldi, 260

... Affairs at the theater are not going well in Bergamo; Moriani was not liked as expected; he pleases little; [Donizetti's] *Linda* [*di Chamounix*] is not liked at all, notwithstanding Tadolini in the role; the fact is that the theater is poorly attended, and the administration is unhappy. *Attila* goes on tomorrow in Cremona ...

VERDI TO VARESI

[Milan,] 25 August 1846

Carissimo,

Vuoi dunque venire a Firenze in Quaresima?...Se lo vuoi io scriverò per te il *Macbet!*...

Poche parole, e risposta prontissima: dimmi quando sarai a Firenze, quando andrai in scena: ricordati che non devi cantare (per obbligo) che nella mia opera espressamente scritta. In poche parole scrivimi tutte le condizioni e le tue pretese pecuniarie; e ti prego stringerle più che puoi perchè tu sai che Lanari ha Ferri e certamente non vuol fare grandi sacrifici. Rispondimi a posta corrente ne dimenticarti nulla.

Addio, addio, di fretta.

P.S.—Rispondi subito, subito, e tieni la cosa segreta.

[P.P.S.] Tieni la cosa molto segreta, poichè capirai che non è non [sic] facile combinarsi. Scrivimi sinceramente le tue intenzioni e lascia

Carissimo,

So, do you want to come to Florence during Lent? If you do, I'll write *Macbeth* for you!

Few words, and an immediate answer: tell me when you'll be in Florence and when you'll be performing; remember that you're not contractually obliged to sing except in the new opera I've written for the season. Send me a few words about all the conditions and financial terms; and, please, keep them down as much as possible, because you know that Lanari [already] has Ferri and certainly doesn't want to make great sacrifices. Answer me by return mail, and don't forget anything.

Addio, addio in haste.

P.S.—Answer *quickly* and keep the thing secret.

[P.P.S.] Keep it *very* secret, for you'll understand that it's not an easy thing to arrange. Tell me frankly what your plans are and leave it to me,

fare a me, ma ti raccomando abbia riguardo.[1]

Siena: Archivio dell'Accademia Chigiana;
Nuova Antologia 281 (1932), 436;
Quaderni dell'Accademia Chigiana 27 (1953), 7

but I urge you to be considerate.[1]

1. Varesi's contract with Lanari is dated 24 September 1846 (de Angelis, *Le carte*, p. 116; original in Florence: Biblioteca Nazionale, Fondo Lanari 13[1].44, a. 2). He was to receive 3600 lire, payable in four *quartali*, for singing in Verdi's new opera.

MUZIO TO BAREZZI   *Milan, 27 August 1846*

... Forse a Firenze nell'opera del signor Maestro non canterà nè Moriani nè Ferri. Adesso tutto dipende da una risposta di Varesi; se Varesi accetta di cantare nella Quaresima a Firenze, allora scrive il *Macbeth*, ove vi sono due sole parti principali: Cordelia[!] e Macbeth: la Löwe e Varesi; le altre sono seconde parti. Nessun attore, al presente, in Italia può fare più bene il *Macbeth* di Varesi, e per il suo modo di canto, e per la sua intelligenza, e per la sua stessa piccola e brutta figura. Forse egli dirà che stuona, questo non fa niente perchè la parte sarebbe quasi tutta declamata, ed in questo vale molto. Sono persuaso che entro la settimana tutto si deciderà; perchè per fare un lavoro di qualche importanza il tempo stringe ...[1]

Garibaldi, 261-62

... Perhaps, in Florence, neither Moriani nor Ferri will sing in the Maestro's opera. Now everything depends on an answer from Varesi; if Varesi agrees to sing in Florence in Lent, then he writes *Macbeth*, in which there are only two principal roles: Cordelia[!] and Macbeth—Löwe and Varesi. The others are secondary roles. No actor in Italy today can do *Macbeth* better than Varesi, both because of his way of singing, and because of his intelligence, and even because of his small and ugly appearance. Perhaps you will say he sings out of tune, but that doesn't matter since the part would be almost totally declaimed, and he is very good at that. I feel sure that everything will be decided within the week, because in order to create a work of some importance time is pressing ...[1]

1. Muzio often echoes Verdi's opinions and very words (sometimes with some garbling). Cf. this letter with Verdi's of 19 August 1847: Muzio's last sentence with Verdi's third, and the remarks about Varesi.

VERDI TO VARESI   [*Milan,*] *2 September 1846*

Ho ricevuto la carissima tua. Se la cosa è combinabile in quanto al prezzo cercherò di farti dare una paga conveniente; forse vi saranno difficoltà sulle tre recite, e mi pare sarebbe necessario proprio farne quattro etc...Se si potranno sormontare le altre difficoltà (che ti dirò a voce) spero che pel resto si combineremo... Quando vieni a Milano appena arrivato fammi sapere dove ti devo trovare perchè allora avrò forse ricevuta la risposta decisiva di Lanari ...

P.S. Ti raccomando sempre la segretezza e dimmi anche se ci sarebbe mezzo di fermarsi a Firenze oltre il 18 marzo. Perchè è vero che Egli ha altri bassi[1] ma montando l'opera con te bisogna seguitare con te ...

Siena: Archivio dell'Accademia Chigiana;
Quaderni dell'Accademia Chigiana 27 (1953), 7

I have received your precious letter. If the thing can be arranged so far as money is concerned I'll try to see that you are paid suitably; perhaps there will be difficulties about the three performances, and it seems to me that it would really be necessary to have a fourth, etc...If the other difficulties (which I'll tell you about in person) can be overcome, I hope that we can work out the rest. When you come to Milan, as soon as you arrive let me know where I can find you, because by then I may have received the definite answer from Lanari ...

P.S. Let me stress again the need for secrecy, and tell me also if there is any way for you to stay on in Florence after March 18. Because it's true that he [Lanari] has other basses,[1] but mounting the opera with you, we must continue with you ...

1. *Basso* is a term that was commonly used to include baritones; in 1872, Verdi referred to the Posa-Philip duet in *Don Carlos* as the "Duetto dei due Bassi."

VERDI TO PIAVE

[2-3 September 1846]

Sono dolentissimo della tua disgrazia![1]...Procura di farti animo, e cercare tutte le distrazioni possibili!...Ti mando li 100 fiorini. Domani o dopo ti manderò lo schizzo del *Macbet.* Io te lo raccomando coll'anima!...

Abbiati 1, 642-43

I'm very sorry about your misfortune![1] Try to cheer up and look for things to take your mind off it! I'm sending you the 100 *fiorini.* Tomorrow or the day after I'll send you the draft for *Macbeth.* I beg you with all my heart to take great pains with it!

1. Piave's misfortune is probably that mentioned in Muzio's letter of 17 September 1846.

MUZIO TO BAREZZI

Milan, 3 September 1846

... Non si sa nulla di decisivo per Firenze, entro la settimana ventura tutto sarà finito. O vi sarà Fraschini ed allora fa i *Masnadieri,* o non vi sarà, ed allora farà il *Macbeth* con Varesi, che sarebbe meglio, perchè è un soggetto conosciuto da tutto il mondo.

A Bergamo sempre teatro vuoto. Moriani non può più. È facile però che lo scritturino per il Carnevale alla Scala; ma esso per fare che l'impresa abbandoni il pensiero gli ha detto che a meno di 40 mila franchi non canta ...

Garibaldi, 268

... Nothing definite is known about Florence; by the end of next week everything will be settled. Either there'll be Fraschini and then he'll do *Masnadieri,* or there won't be, and then he'll do *Macbeth* with Varesi, which would be better, because it is a subject known the whole world over.

At Bergamo, the theater is always empty. Moriani can't make it any more. Yet he could easily be signed up for the carnival season at La Scala; but he, in order to make the administration abandon the idea, has said that he won't sing for less than 40,000 francs ...

VERDI TO PIAVE

Milan, 4 September 1846

Eccoti lo schizzo del *Macbet.* Questa tragedia è una delle più grandi creazioni umane!...Se noi non possiamo fare una gran cosa cerchiamo di fare una cosa almeno fuori del comune. Lo schizzo è netto: senza convenzione, senza stento, e breve. Ti raccomando i versi che essi pure siano brevi: quanto più saranno brevi e tanto più troverai effetto. Il solo atto primo è un po' lunghetto ma starà a noi tenere i pezzi brevi. Nei versi ricordati bene che non vi deve essere parola inutile: tutto deve dire qualche cosa, e bisogna adoperare un linguaggio sublime ad eccezione dei cori delle streghe: quelli devono essere triviali, ma stravaganti ed originali.

Quando avrai fatta tutta l'introduzione ti prego di mandarmela, la quale è composta di piccole quattro scene e può stare in pochi versi. Una volta fatta questa introduzione io ti lascierò tutto il tempo che vorrai perchè il carattere generale e le tinte le conosco come se il libretto fosse fatto. Oh ti raccomando non trascurarmi questo *Macbet,* te ne prego inginocchiato, se non altro, curalo per me e per la mia salute che ora è ottima ma che diventa subito

Here is the draft of *Macbeth.* This tragedy is one of the greatest creations of man! If we can't do something great with it, let us at least try to do something out of the ordinary. The draft is clear: unconventional, simple, and short. I beg you to make the lines short, too; the shorter they are, the more effect you'll make. Only the first act is a shade long, but it will be up to us to keep the numbers short. In your lines, remember well, there should be not one useless word: everything must say something, and you must adopt a sublime diction, except in the witches' choruses, which must be trivial, yet bizarre and original.

When you've done the whole *introduzione,* please send it to me; it is composed of four small scenes, which need only a few lines. Once this introduction is done I'll let you have all the time you want, because I know the general character and the *tinte* as if the libretto were already finished. Oh, I beg you, don't neglect this *Macbeth* of mine; I beg you on my knees, if nothing else, treat it well for me and for my health, which at the moment is excellent but

cattiva se mi fai inquietare...Brevità e sublimità...[1]

Abbiati 1, 643

gets worse at once if you upset me. Brevity and
sublimity.[1]

1. The need for conciseness becomes a leitmotif of Verdi's correspondence with Piave.

MUZIO TO BAREZZI

Milan, 10 September 1846

Il signor Maestro è ancora a Varese . . .

Stamattina è arrivata una lettera di Lanari da
Firenze, e credo che conterrà la decisione se vi
sarà Fraschini o no.[1] Era fissato che tutto si
dovesse decidere entro questa settimana e sicuramente questa lettera finirà tutto. Io lo saprò
stassera. Egli giovedì prossimo . . .

Garibaldi, 269

The Maestro is still in Varese . . .

This morning a letter from Lanari arrived
from Florence, and I think it will include the
decision as to whether it's Fraschini or not.[1] It
was agreed that everything had to be decided
this week, and surely this letter will settle
everything. I'll know tonight; you, next Thursday . . .

1. So work on *Macbeth* was already under way before it had been established which subject would be that of the
Florence opera.

VERDI TO PIAVE

Milan, 14 September 1846

Spero che ti sarai rimesso; però non affaticarti
per il *Macbet*, perchè c'è tempo, ed ho piacere
che tu scriva soltanto nei momenti d'ispirazione
. . .

Morazzoni, 27

I hope that you've recovered; but don't tire
yourself over *Macbeth*, because there's time, and
I'd like it if you wrote only in moments of
inspiration . . .

MUZIO TO BAREZZI

Milan, 17 September 1846

. . . Il signor Maestro attende tuttora la risposta
da Lanari per sapere se vi è Fraschini o no. Egli
incomincia a impazientirsi.

Dica a Giovanni[1] che l'amorosa di Piave an-
dando a Verona la diligenza si rovesciò ed essa
ne ebbe schiacciata una mano che gliela han
dovuta tagliare. Il povero poeta ne è desolatis-
simo . . .

Garibaldi, 273-74

. . . The Maestro is still waiting for Lanari's
reply, to learn whether it's Fraschini or not.
He's beginning to get impatient.

Tell Giovanni[1] that Piave's *amorosa*, on the
way to Verona, had one of her hands crushed
when the stage-coach overturned, and they
had to amputate it. The poor poet is terribly
upset . . .

1. Giovanni (or Giovannino) Barezzi, Antonio's eldest son.

VERDI TO PIAVE

Milan, 22 September 1846

Ricevo la cavatina che va meglio dell'Introduzione. Nonostante come sei sempre prolisso!!
per esempio la lettera che legge Lady sono pro-
priamente parole in verso: poca energia nel resto
del recitativo—e pochissima nella prima quartina dell'adagio—il verso *'vieni su questo core'* è
così comune che toglie tutta l'energia della
strofa: la cabaletta va bene: coreggi addunque di
questo pezzo la lettera che si può accorciare
senza nulla omettere: troppe parole hai ado-
perato per esprimere *'Ma tu abbastanza non sarai*

I've received the *cavatina*, which goes better
than the *introduzione*. Nevertheless, how wordy
you always are!! For example, the letter that the
Lady reads is just so many words cast in verse;
little energy in the rest of the recitative—and
very little in the first quatrain of the *adagio*—the
line "come to this heart" is so commonplace
that it removes all energy from the strophe; the
cabaletta is fine; so, in this number, correct the
letter, which can be shortened without omitting
anything: you've used too many words to ex-

malvaggio...' troppe parole anche: 'Chi a congiurarsi non si sente forte e vi si addentra infamia aspetti e morte.' Le stesse cose con uno stile più elevato si dicono con metà parole! Aggiustami anche la prima quartina dell'adagio etc...

In quanto all'Introduzione bisogna fare molte cose. Le prime strofe delle streghe devono per aver carattere essere più strane: io non ti so indicare il modo ma so che così non sono belle: per esempio se tu avessi fatti tanti versi tronchi tutti forse forse era meglio, insomma sperimenta e trova il modo di fare della poesia bizzarra, almeno nella prima strofa l'ultima strofetta può andar bene facendo una sola quartina (ABBIA SEMPRE IN MENTE DI DIR POCHE PAROLE...POCHE PAROLE...POCHE POCHE MA SIGNIFICANTI) dopo accorcierai più che potrai il tempo di mezzo e ridurrai a versi endecasillabi i tre saluti delle streghe. Riduci con sei versi per cadauno il duetto tra Macbet e Banco e leva cioè tutti quei versacci che t'ho indicato nell'altra mia. (TI RIPETO POCHE PAROLE). Se io dovessi levare via tutte le parole che dicon niente e che son fatte soltanto per la rima o per il verso bisognerebbe levarne un buon terzo: da questo capirai se lo stile è conciso come dovrebbe essere.

Prima d'andar avanti ti prego d'aggiustarmi questi due pezzi e fà in modo che io non abbia da credere questo lavoro buttato là tanto per finirlo come mi pare di vedere finora. Dell'ultima aria ti rimando le cancellature dei versi che vanno più concisi e più belli...Del pezzo che hai mandato prima bisognerebbe che cancellassi quasi tutto sicchè pensa tu ad accomodare e finire questi pezzi prima d'andare avanti onde io possa cominciare a scrivere...STILE CONCISO!...POCHE PAROLE...hai capito?...

... Ora che ci penso un poco mi pare che fare nel primo coro versi tutti tronchi darà un suono strano che sarà caratteristico. Guarda anche nella scelta delle parole...Addio...Quando avrai fatte quelle correzioni mandami tutto disteso in netto ma di tuo carattere.

Abbiati 1, 644–45

press "But you will be insufficiently malevolent"; too many words also in "Who does not feel himself strong for a conspiracy yet enters upon it, let him expect infamy and death." The same thing in a more elevated style can be said in half the words! Also fix the first quatrain of the _adagio_ for me, etc.

As for the _introduzione_, many things need doing. To have character, the witches' first strophes should be stranger; I can't tell you how to do it, but I do know that they are not good the way they are. For example, if you had used many _versi tronchi,_ then maybe, maybe it would have been better; in short, experiment and find a way of writing bizzare poetry, at least in the first strophe; the last _strofetta_ will be fine as just one quatrain (ALWAYS BEAR IN MIND; USE FEW WORDS...FEW WORDS...FEW, FEW BUT SIGNIFICANT) then you will shorten the _tempo di mezzo_ as much as you can and you will reduce the witches' three salutations to _endecasillabi._ Reduce the duet between Macbeth and Banquo to six lines apiece and, that is to say, take out all those awful lines that I pointed out in my other letter to you. (I REPEAT, FEW WORDS.) If I had to take out all of the words that say nothing and that are put in just for the rhyme or the meter, I'd have to take out a good third of them; from that you'll understand whether the style is concise as it should be.

Before going any further, I'd like you to fix these two numbers for me and do it in a way that doesn't force me to think of it as work tossed off just to get it done—which is what it seems to me to be, so far. I'm sending the last aria back to you, the lines crossed out that ought to be briefer and better. As for the number you sent before, I'd have to cross out almost everything, so you've got to get these numbers into shape before going any further, so that I can get on with composing...CONCISE STYLE!...FEW WORDS...got it?

... Now that I think about it a little, I believe that making all the lines in the first chorus _versi tronchi_ will produce a strange sound that will have character. Watch the choice of words, too. Farewell. When you've made these corrections, send everything to me, copied out clearly, but in your own handwriting.

MUZIO TO BAREZZI   _Milan, 24 September 1846_

... Per Firenze è quasi cosa certa che vi sarà Varesi, ed allora l'argomento dell'opera sarà il _Macbeth_, poesia di Piave ...

Garibaldi, 274

... It's almost a sure thing that it'll be Varesi for Florence, and so the subject of the opera will be _Macbeth_, libretto by Piave ...

VERDI TO CLARA MAFFEI

Milan, 26 September 1846

... Le mie faccende sono oramai finite, e finito è pure il mio carteggio maledetissimo [*sic*] con Firenze che m'ha impedito di venire a Clusone.[1] A Firenze farò il *Macbet*, ed i *Masnadieri* li farò per l'opera di Lucca.[2] Maffei è tornato sabato sera e sta bene. Io farò una visita breve breve ai Fontana,[3] e poi non mi muoverò più da Milano se non per andare a Firenze ...

Quartetto Milanese Ottocentesco, 63–64

... My business affairs are finished now, and finished too my damnable correspondence with Florence, which kept me from coming to Clusone.[1] I'll do *Macbeth* for Florence, and I'll do *Masnadieri* as Lucca's opera.[2] [Andrea] Maffei returned Saturday night and is well. I'll pay a very quick visit to the Fontanas,[3] and then I won't move from Milan again except to go to Florence ...

1. I.e., to Clara Maffei's villa in Clusone about 20 miles from Bergamo.
2. Verdi was under contract to write an opera to be premiered at Her Majesty's and published by Ricordi's chief rival, the Italian publisher Francesco Lucca and his wife Giovannina Strazza.
3. Venetian friends of Verdi, probably dating from his stay in Venice to produce *Ernani* (March 1844); at this time they were apparently living in Como.

MUZIO TO BAREZZI

Milan, 4 October 1846

Il signor Maestro è a Como con Piave; ritornerà forse stassera. Se Piave aveva più tempo da fermarsi venivano a fare una improvvisata a Giovannino ed a lei; ma deve partire subito e manca solamente il tempo ...

Garibaldi, 278

The Maestro is in Como with Piave; he'll return perhaps this evening. If Piave had time to stay longer, they'd pay a surprise visit to Giovannino and you; but he must leave immediately and there's just no time ...

MUZIO TO BAREZZI

Milan, 15 October 1846

... A Firenze scrive il signor Maestro il *Macbeth*. Gli esecutori saranno la Löwe, Varesi, non Ferri, perchè il signor Maestro non l'ha voluto; Ferri ignora che sia scritturato Varesi, e non sa neanche che non canterà nelle nuove opere. Si tiene celato fino alla Quaresima, e poi gli si rivelerà che nell'opera il *Macbeth* canterà Varesi. La scrittura di Varesi non sarà annunciata in nessun giornale affinchè non arrivi a saperlo Ferri ...

Garibaldi, 283

... For Florence, the Maestro is writing *Macbeth*. The singers will be Loewe and Varesi; not Ferri, because the Maestro didn't want him. Ferri doesn't know that Varesi has been engaged, and he doesn't even know that he won't sing in the new operas. It will be kept secret until Lent, and then he'll be told that Varesi will sing *Macbeth*. Varesi's contract won't be announced in any papers until Ferri has learned of it ...

VERDI TO LANARI

Milan, 15 October 1846

Eccoti lo schizzo del *Macbet* e capirai di che si tratta. Tu vedi che mi abbisogna un eccellente coro: specialmente il coro delle donne sia buonissimo perchè vi saranno due cori di Streghe della massima importanza. Bada anche al machinismo. Insomma le cose da curare molto in quest'opera sono: *Coro e Machinismo*.

Tutto il resto sono persuaso che lo monterai con quella splendidezza che tanto ti distingue e che non baderai ad economia. Osserva anche che mi abbisognano anche le ballerine per fare

Here's the outline of *Macbeth*, and you'll understand what we're dealing with. You see I'll need an excellent chorus, in particular the women's chorus must be very good, since there'll be two witches' choruses of the utmost importance. Also pay attention to the stage machinery. In short, the things that need special care in this work are: *Chorus and Machinery*.

I'm convinced that you'll mount all the rest with that splendor which you're so celebrated for and that you won't try to economize. Note also that I'll need dancers for a graceful little

un piccolo ballabile grazioso sul finire del terzo atto. Non badare (te lo ripeto) a spese che ne avrai, io spero, un compenso, e poi sarai benedetto da me mille volte al giorno, e bada bene che le mie benedizioni valgono quasi quasi come quelle d'un papa.

A monte gli scherzi, ma veramente ti raccomando di fare in modo che tutto vadi bene e che io non abbia a tremare per gli altri. Se poi vorrai che io ti faccia fare [gli] schizzi delle scene ed i figurini per i vestiarj, li farò fare ma con comodo perchè ora bisogna che vadi avanti a scrivere e non ho tempo da perdere.

Abbiati 1, 650–51

ballet at the end of Act III. Don't worry (I repeat) about expenses, because you'll be rewarded, I hope, and what's more, you'll be blessed by me a thousand times a day and I assure you that my blessings are almost as valuable as a pope's.

But really, all joking aside, I urge you to see that everything goes well and that I don't have to worry about the other people. Then if you want me to have designs of the scenes and costumes made for you, I'll have them done, but not in any hurry, because now it's time for me to get on with composing and I have no time to lose.

MUZIO TO BAREZZI

Milan, 22 October 1846

... Il signor Maestro scrive adagio adagio e sta bene ...

Garibaldi, 285

... The Maestro is writing slowly—very slowly—and is well ...

VERDI TO PIAVE

Milan, 25 October 1846

Mettiti subito in relazione con Lanari per la messa in scena del *Macbet*. Scrivi subito una lettera e descrivi le ordinazioni, attrezzi, figurini, scenari, vestiario, comparseria ecc. ecc...Non dimenticare nulla e fà tutto con amore se non vuoi che vadi in furore. Lanari è disposto a far tutto quello che abbisogna. Pensaci bene, e fà le ordinazioni giuste: niente di più nè di meno di quanto abbisogna.[1]

Nel *Macbet* al principio del secondo fà che Lady nel soliloquio non scriva la lettera a Macbet sull'uccisione di Banco—Non mi piace farle scrivere una lettera in quell'atrio, d'altronde con poche parole si può fare egualmente senza far scrivere la lettera.

"Banco, e suo figlio vivono...ma la natura non li creò immortali...Oh Macbet...Un nuovo delitto!...Le imprese cominciate ecc. ecc..."[2]

Addio...ti raccomando le ordinazioni. Ora sto bene.

Abbiati 1, 651

Get in touch with Lanari at once about the staging of *Macbeth*. Write a letter at once and describe the special requirements, the props, the costume designs, the sets, the wardrobe, extras, etc. etc...Don't forget anything and do everything *con amore*, if you don't want me to fly into a rage. Lanari is willing to do everything that's needed. Think it over carefully, and state exactly what's needed: neither more nor less than what's required.[1]

At the beginning of the second act of *Macbeth*, don't have the Lady, in her soliloquy, write the letter to Macbeth about the murder of Banquo. I don't like having her write a letter in that hall; instead, it can be done just as well in a few words, without having her write the letter.

"Banquo and his son live...but Nature did not create them immortal...Oh Macbeth...a new crime...Enterprises begun, etc..."[2]

Farewell. Be careful about the stage requirements. I'm well at the moment.

---

1. In mid-nineteenth century Italy, the librettist of a new opera was generally responsible for supervising the requirements of the staging; the actual stage direction was generally worked out by the librettist, the composer and the impresario.

2. With two small exceptions, these lines come directly from Rusconi's translation; Rusconi has "Banquo e Fleance sono ancor vivi," and Verdi adds the exclamation "Oh Macbet." This scene is discussed further in letters of 29 October and 3 December 1846 and in DEGRADA at 160–63.

PIAVE TO LANARI

Venice, 28 October 1846

L'amico Verdi mi scrive che mi metta teco in relazione per mandarti le note relative alla messa in scena del *Macbeth*. Io farò ciò quanto prima, non potendolo al momento, perchè mi resta da far qualche studio, e desidero fartele esatte affinchè non debbano poi esservi pentimenti. Caro Lanari, questo *Macbeth* sarà pur la gran cosa; io ne sono entusiasmato. La parte della Loewe specialmente sarà la parte più altamente sentita che mai comparisse sulle melodrammatiche scene italiane, così pure quella del baritono. Io credo che quest'opera, piacendo, sia per dare nuove tendenze alla nostra musica ed aprir nuove strade ai maestri presenti e avvenire; e tu sarai quello che avrà dato per primo un tale spartito all'Italia. Lo meriti ...

Copialettere, 444–45

Our friend Verdi writes me that I should get in touch with you to send you the notes about the staging of *Macbeth*. I'll do it for you as soon as possible, not being able to at the moment, because I still have to study it a bit, and I want to make them exact to avoid later changes. Dear Lanari, this *Macbeth* really will be something great; I'm excited about it. Loewe's part in particular will be the most loftily conceived that has ever appeared on the Italian operatic stage; the baritone's likewise. I believe that this opera, if it is well received, will give new directions to our music and open new paths to present and future composers. And you'll be the first to have given Italy such a score. You deserve to be ...

VERDI TO PIAVE

Milan, 29 October 1846

... Ho ricevuto lettera da Lanari sull'affare della Loewe. Io non ci penso! Sarà quel che sarà! Sono assuefatto a queste contrarietà che non mi sorprendono più. Lascia correre e scrivi.

Mi parli già del terzo atto? Ed il secondo è finito? Perchè non lo mandi?...Fai troppo presto e prevedo dei guai! Basta! Come si può in sì poco tempo un atto di quella sublimità come il 2° atto del *Macbet*?

P.S. Nella prima scena di Lady del 2° atto non farle dire che una semplice frase indicante l'uccisione di Banco..."Oh Macbet è necessario un'altro delitto!"

P.S. Che diavolo non sai cosa far dire alle Streghe quando Macbet è svenuto?...Non c'è in Shaespeare? Non c'è una frase che aiuti li *Spiriti aerei* a ridonare i sensi perduti?[1]...Oh povero me!!...Addio! Addio!

Abbiati 1, 652

... I received a letter from Lanari about the Loewe business. I'm just not going to think about it! *Che sarà sarà!* I am accustomed to these setbacks, which no longer surprise me. Let things go their own way, and write on.

You're already talking to me about Act III? And is Act II finished? Why don't you send it? You're going too fast and I see trouble ahead! Enough! How can an act so sublime as Act II of *Macbeth* get done in so short a time?

P.S. In the Lady's first scene in Act II have her say just one simple sentence alluding to the murder of Banquo..."Oh Macbeth, another crime is needed!"

P.S. Why the devil don't you know what to make the witches say when Macbeth has fainted? Isn't it in Shakespeare? Isn't there a sentence that helps the *aerial spirits* to restore his lost senses?[1]...Oh poor me!!...Farewell! Farewell!

1. There is: IV.1, 127ff., a passage generally considered to be a non-Shakespearean interpolation. But there, Macbeth does not faint; the direction "Macbeth, colpito d'orrore, cade privo di sensi" is an addition of Rusconi's (or of the edition he used to make his translation from).

LANARI TO PIAVE

Florence, 2 November 1846

È anche mio desiderio che allorquando mi mandi le note relative alla messa in scena del *Macbeth*, esse siano precise. Tuttavia pregoti di sollecitarle, perchè più si ha tempo e meglio si fanno le cose. Sono molto contento che questo soggetto dia tanto a sperar bene, e già avevo

It's my wish too that when you send me the notes about the staging of *Macbeth* they should be precise. Nevertheless, I ask you to hurry up with them, because the more time one has, the better things are done. I am very pleased that this subject should give such cause for high

visto anch'io ch'è molto grandioso e di genere straordinario. Vi è qualche dubbio che la Loewe non sia in grado di eseguire quest'opera,[1] come avrai inteso dal sig. Giuseppe Berti;[2] ma qualora questa cosa si verifichi, io ho la Barbieri da mettere a disposizione di Verdi, alla quale si attagliano. meravigliosamente anche le parti create per la Loewe, come l'*Ernani* e l'*Attila* ne fanno prova . . .

Copialettere, 445

1. See the following letter.
2. Functionary at the Teatro La Fenice (Venice).

hopes, and I too had already perceived that it is very grand and of an extraordinary nature. There is some doubt whether Loewe is in a condition to perform this work,[1] as you will have heard from Mr. Giuseppe Berti;[2] but if that turns out to be true, I have Barbieri to put at Verdi's disposal, to whom the parts created for Loewe are marvelously well suited, as *Ernani* and *Attila* have shown . . .

MUZIO TO BAREZZI   *Milan, 2 November 1846*

. . . La Loewe si ritira dalle scene. Essa è apparsa a Firenze nell'*Ernani,* nel quale ha fatto fiasco. Essa era gravida ed ha voluto abortire, e dicesi questo essere stato causa di aver perduta quasi la voce. Fin da quando era a Livorno non andava troppo bene. Al signor Maestro rincresce questa cosa, perchè per fare la parte di Lady nel *Macbeth* nessuna donna delle attuali lo potrebbero fare con l'effetto della Loewe. Invece canterà la Barbieri . . .[1]

Garibaldi, 289–90

. . . Loewe is retiring from the stage. She appeared in Florence in *Ernani,* in which she had a fiasco. She was pregnant and decided to have an abortion, and it's said that this is the cause of her having almost lost her voice. She hasn't been doing too well since she was in Leghorn. The Maestro regrets this, since no woman today could do the part of the Lady in *Macbeth* with the same effect as Loewe. Barbieri will sing instead . . .[1]

1. Marianna Barbieri-Nini (see PERSONALIA), Verdi's first Lucrezia in *I due Foscari* (Rome, 1844). She made her London debut in 1851 as Donizetti's Lucrezia Borgia, her most celebrated role, and Henry F. Chorley left a vivid account both of her appearance and of vocal qualities apt for Lady Macbeth: "In her youth, Madame Barbieri-Nini must have possessed one of the most splendid organs ever born into an Italian throat—a *soprano* voice, sonorous, even ample, and still not heavy, with a geniality of tone rare in German voices of the same quality . . . But Nature had done no more for her. Unsightly is a gentle adjective as applied in her case.—There is an expressive ugliness which may be turned to a certain account on the stage—an unmarked meanness of feature which Genius can light up and animate; but Madame Barbieri-Nini's uncomeliness was at once large and mean—a thing not to be escaped from—and unvarying . . . [Her Lucrezia Borgia] was throughout careful—in a point or two more—being grand.— She sang the florid *largo* in the last scene superbly:—with that mixture of breadth of phrasing, pompous execution, and measurement of time, which belongs to the best school of Italian vocal art—now all but extinct—and she made a real impression on her audience, in spite of her rare physical defects.—But the last were too strong for her.—She arrived too late to habituate her audience to them . . ." *Thirty Years' Musical Recollections,* 1 (London: Hurst & Blackett, 1862), 141–42. De Angelis (*Le carte,* p. 116) reports that Barbieri-Nini was already under contract to Lanari, from 1 April 1846 to 31 March 1847.

VERDI TO MARIE ESCUDIER   *[Milan,] 5 November 1846*

Nissuno più di me desidera di veder Parigi, ma voi sapete che io sono troppo occupato.[1] Io non posso rubar tempo ai miei lavori tanto più che a Firenze scriverò il *Macbet,* e voi sapete di quanta importanza è quell'argomento e quanto studio richiede. Del resto poi se si metterà impegno le mie opere potranno andare anche senza di me. Si fanno dapertutto, ed io non vado mai a metterle in scena; fino nella stessa Milano, dove

No one wants to see Paris more than I do, but you know that I'm too busy.[1] I cannot steal time away from my work, especially since for Florence I'll write *Macbeth,* and you know how important that subject is and how much study it requires. Moreover, if my operas are treated with care, they can make their way even without me. They get done everywhere, and I never go to put them on; even in Milan itself, where I

Marianna Barbieri-Nini

io sto abitualmente, non vado mai alle prove delle mie opere ...

Abbiati 1, 654

usually am, I never go to the rehearsals of my operas ...

1. Escudier wanted Verdi to assist with the Théâtre-Italien production of *I due Foscari*; see *Abbiati* 1, 653.

VARESI TO LANARI
Milan, 15 November 1846

Fui da Verdi il quale mi ha mostrato l'orditura del suo Libbro [*sic*] e tante cose indispensabili a sapersi da me, e mi ha promesso di darmi metà della mia parte cioè il primo e secondo atto prima della mia partenza per Roma.[1] Io intanto ho fatto scrivere a Londra e ad Edimborgo per avere il costume e le nozioni storiche tutte necessarie per il personaggio di *Macbeth*.

Florence: Biblioteca Nazionale, Fondo Lanari 18II.138; de Angelis: *Le carte*, p.119

I was at Verdi's place and he showed me the scheme of his libretto and many things that I absolutely must know, and he promised to give me half my part—that is, the first and second acts—before I left for Rome.[1] Meanwhile, I sent to London and to Edinburgh for the costumes and the historical information all needed for the character of Macbeth.

1. To sing in *Maria di Rohan* and *I due Foscari* (de Angelis's note)

GIOVANNI RICORDI TO LANARI
Milan, 16 November 1846

Rilevo dalla cara vostra 7 corr.e che voi avete assunti i contratti che aveva in corso il vostro Sig. Figlio Antonio, e mi invitate a mandarvi una modula di scrittura da rispettivamente firmarsi per il contratto di cessione dell'opera che

I gather from your esteemed communication of the 7th inst. that you have taken over the current contracts of your son Antonio, and you request me to send you a form of agreement, for mutual signature, for the contract ceding

M.º Verdi, obbligato, a scriverla per vostro Figlio nel venturo Carnevale,[1] va invece a scrivere per voi a cod.º I. e R. Teatro della Pergola nella p.a vent.a Quaresima.

Mi affretto quindi di rispondervi che voi versate in un innocente equivoco, in quanto che il contratto che voi credete che fosse ancora a stipularsi è già sino dallo scorso anno deffinitivamente [sic] conchiuso tra me e vostro figlio, come rileverete dalla copia del contratto stesso firmata dal vostro Figlio che vi compiego, ed a cui si riferiscono appunto le mie lettere di accettazione.

Che anzi non solo il contratto stesso fu conchiuso ed è in ogni parte perfetto, ma è in pieno corso di esecuzione, giacchè vennero da me fatti successivamente al vostro Figlio tutti i noleggi degli spartiti nei modi appunto stabiliti nel contratto suddetto e qual altro dei correspettivi ivi convenuti, come potrete rilevare agevolmente dalla corrispondenza tra me e vostro Figlio. Per il che voi ben vedete che nulla rimane a stipularsi in proposito, e che solo ci resta a continuare nella reciproca doverosa esecuzione del contratto stesso.[2]

Il S.r M.º Verdi vi ha già communicato il suo vivo desiderio ch'egli avrebbe che le parti di questa sua nuova Opera fossero copiate qui come già si fece coi Foscari.[3] Questa cosa che è di tanto aggradimento al Maestro non riesce per voi di disturbo, anzi di utile, perché mandandovi io le parti già cavate, il vostro copista non avrà che a raddoppiarle senza avere la pena più grave di cavarle dalla partitura. Se ci saranno poi delle mutazioni da farsi alle parti in causa di cambiamenti che il M.º vi praticasse all'Atto delle prove costì, voi me ne darete debito, come pure mi darete debito di que' pezzi che mai per caso il M.º non avesse istrumentati qui, e di cui voi dovreste far estrarre le parti per completare l'orchestra che mi rimanderete, tenendo per voi quelle che avrete raddoppiata su questa. Appena in scena poi voi mi manderete lo spartito autografato col corriere per potervi io dal mio conto far avere la copia entro i venti giorni pattuiti ed anche prima. Siate dunque compiacente di far avere subito al S.r M.º Verdi la chiestovi autorizzazione per dar principio a questo lavoro delle parti.

De Angelis: *Le carte*, pp. 228–29

the opera that M.º Verdi, who was engaged to write it for your son during the forthcoming carnival season,[1] will instead compose for you at the aforesaid Imperial and Royal Teatro della Pergola during the forthcoming Lent season.

I hasten therefore to reply to you that you are under an innocent misapprehension, in that the contract that you believe still needs drawing up has already—since last year—been definitively concluded between me and your son, as you will discover from the copy of the aforesaid contract, signed by your son, which I enclose, and to which my letters of acceptance [of, presumably, terms for the Florence *Macbeth*] specifically refer.

Moreover, not only has the same contract been concluded and completed in every detail, but it is in full course of being carried out, since, in succession to your son, I have made all the rental arrangements for the score, precisely as established in the aforesaid contract and in that other one about the compensation therein agreed, as you can readily ascertain from the correspondence between me and your son. From which you see clearly that nothing remains to be stipulated on this head, and that it remains only to continue the reciprocal, punctilious execution of the aforesaid contract.[2]

M.º Verdi has communicated to you his strong desire to have the parts of this his new opera copied here, as was done in the case of *I due Foscari*.[3] This matter, on which the composer sets such store, will cause you no trouble, and will even be useful to you, since, if I send you parts already extracted [from the full score], your copyist will need only to make further copies without having the heavier task of extracting them from the score. If there should then be alterations to be made to the parts in consequence of changes effected by the composer while rehearsals are in progress there, you will set them to my charge, as you will also set to my charge whatever numbers the composer may possibly not have orchestrated here and for which you would have to have the parts extracted, to complete the set of orchestral material, which you will return to me, keeping for yourself the parts you will have had copied from it. As soon as the opera is produced, you will send me the autograph score, by courier, so that I for my part can have the complete copy within the stipulated twenty days or even earlier. Please be good enough to let M.º Verdi

have the requested authorization at once so that this work on the parts can be put in hand.

1. Alessandro Lanari's son Antonio was active at the Teatro Sociale of Mantua in the Carnival season of 1846–47 (De Angelis, *Le carte*, p. 117).

2. Ricordi was evidently determined to hold Alessandro Lanari to the precise terms of the contract signed with Antonio Lanari.

3. *I due Foscari* was first performed in Rome, at the Teatro Argentina, on 3 November 1844.

LANARI TO VARESI

[Florence, November 1846]

Mi fa piacere grande di vedere l'interesse che ti prendi pel Macbet, e sarà per me un vero piacere se potrò per tempo avere tutte le possibili nozioni onde disporre vestiario, e decorazicni tutte su di che ne ho premurosamente scritto a Piave di darmi per tempo esatte e dettagliate ordinazioni, e così fai tu per ciò che ti riguarda.

De Angelis, *Le carte*, p.117

It gives me great pleasure to see the interest you are taking in *Macbeth*, and it will be a real pleasure if I can have in good time all possible information to prepare the costumes and all the decor, about which I have written pressingly to Piave to ask him to give me exact and detailed staging requirements in good time, and you do the same for what concerns you [i.e., for the role of Macbeth].

PIAVE TO LANARI

17 November 1846

Quanto al libretto del *Macbeth,* non te lo posso spedire perchè non l'ho ancora finito; e poi sarà bene che ti rivolga al Verdi, poichè a lui solo devo mandarlo. Circa poi alla messa in scena, leggi le unite note e vedrai con precisione e chiarezza indicato quanto può occorrervi: queste, unite alla selva che già possiedi, possono dare più che bastanti lumi al bravo Romani per fare il tutto approntare . . .

Copialettere, 445

As for the libretto of *Macbeth*, I can't send it to you because I haven't yet finished it; and then, it would be good if you got in touch with Verdi, since he is the only person I may send it to. Then with regard to the staging, read the enclosed notes and you'll see everything that you might need indicated with precision and clarity. These notes, along with the plot summary you already have, can give the good Romani more than enough light to have everything gotten ready . . .

LANARI TO PIAVE

[Florence,] 23 November 1846

In quanto alle note di ordinazioni che mi hai rimesse del *Macbeth,* sono troppo concise, ed è necessario che tu dia il numero rispettivo dei corpi di comparseria, come intendi disporli, sia i paggi ecc.: calcola un palcoscenico come quello della Fenice. Tu dici che la selva che mandasti e la nota che ora dai può servire a Romani; ma senza il libro positivo, questi non può conoscere a quai punti di azione succedono apparizioni, movimenti e come s'agiti l'azione; e dovendo da questa dipendere, da macchine, ecc., bisogna bene vederci chiaro, prima di ordinare per tempo, per ottenere precisa esecuzione. Già ne ho scritto anche a Verdi, interessandomi assai di mandarla bene. Ti osservo poi che i spiriti aerei, che tu noti *devono ballare,* bisogna toglierli,

As for the notes on the staging you sent me for *Macbeth,* they are too concise; you must state the respective numbers of the groups of extras and how you intend to arrange them, how many pages, etc. Reckon on a stage like the Fenice's. You say the plot you sent, and the notes you now send, are all Romani needs, but without the actual libretto he can't tell at what points in the action the apparitions and movements are to take place, and how the action is to be effected. And having to depend on this, on the stage machinery, etc., we must be absolutely clear about it, before placing orders in good time, to achieve a precise performance. I've already written about it to Verdi, too, since I'm much concerned to do it well. Then, let me

come ne scrissi anche in addietro a Verdi, poichè in quaresima sono proibite le danze di qualunque specie e non sono ammissibili. Quindi bisogna, finchè c'è tempo, variar l'idea in quel punto di scena per non esser poi costretti di lasciare la cosa mozza. Come ho detto, Verdi stesso ti scriverà per mandarmi copia del libro, e però non tardarmela: se brami accurata *mise en scène*, fai quelle più late spiegazioni che ti ho detto nelle ordinazioni, e mandami le tracce dei costumi se puoi. Vedrai da te che tutt'altro che irregolare è il mandare copia del libro all'Impresario per cui si scrive l'opera nuova, e che deve disporre le decorazioni . . .

Copialettere, 446

point out to you that the aerial spirits, which you say *must dance,* have to be taken out—as I wrote some time ago also to Verdi—because dancing of any kind is forbidden during Lent, and so they are inadmissible. Therefore, the idea at that point in the staging must be changed while there's still time, so that we won't then be [forced to cut them out and be] left with a stump. As I've said, Verdi himself will write to you to tell you to send me a copy of the libretto, so don't delay sending it to me. If you want a careful mise-en-scène, let me have the fuller explanations of the scenic requirements which I have asked you for, and, if you can, send me the sketches for the costumes. You can surely see for yourself that it is anything but improper to send a copy of the libretto to the impresario for whom one is writing a new opera, and who has to make arrangements for the decor . . .

VERDI TO PIAVE

Milan, 3 December 1846

In questo *Macbet* tanto più ci si pensa tanto più si trova di far qualche cosa di meglio. Nel principio del secondo c'è un inconveniente ed è che Lady medita, e fissa di uccider Banco ed appena sortita sortono subito i Sicarj per eseguire l'ordine di Lady. È vero che cambiando scena pel coro de' Sicarj si può suporre che passi un po' di tempo, ma in ogni modo non stà bene perchè si può ripiegare molto meglio nel seguente modo...

In this *Macbeth*, the more one thinks about it, the more one finds ways to improve it. In the beginning of Act II there's a drawback, and that is that the Lady ponders and decides upon Banquo's murder, and no sooner has she gone off, than the assassins come on to execute the Lady's order. It's true that in changing the scene for the chorus of assassins one can suggest that a little time passes, but in any case it's not good, since one can fall back on a far better solution, as follows:

ATTO SECONDO

SCENA I[1]

MACBET, *seguito da* LADY

LADY
Perchè ora mi fuggi?...
Perchè sempre assorto in tristi pensieri?. . .
Inutile è pensare all'irrevocabile.
Ora sei Re, come ti predisser le streghe.
Il figlio di Duncano fuggendo in Brettagna
Parricida fu detto e vuoto il soglio
A te lasciò.

MACBETH
Ma le spirtali donne
Banco padre di regi han profetato.
Dunque i suoi figli regneran?...Duncano
Per costor sarà spento?...

ACT II

SCENE I[1]

MACBETH, *followed by* LADY

LADY
Why do you flee me?...
Why always rapt in sad thoughts?...
No use to think on what cannot be called back.
You are King now, as the witches foretold.
The son of Duncan, fleeing into Britain,
Was declared a parricide and left the throne
Vacant for you.

MACBETH
But the daemonic women
Predicted Banquo the sire of kings.
So will his children reign?...Will it be for them
That Duncan was slain?...

LADY
Egli e suo figlio
Vivono, ma la natura non li creò immortali.

MACBETH
Ciò mi conforta: ei non sono immortali.
LADY
Quindi se un altro delitto?...
MACBETH
Un'altro delitto?...
LADY
È necessario...
MACBETH
Quando?...
LADY
Appena annotti!...
MACBETH (finge)
Un nuovo delitto!!!...
LADY
Ebbene?...
MACBETH
È deciso!...
Banco fra pochi istanti
Per te comincia l'eternità. (parte)

SCENA II[2]

LADY (sola)
S'allarghi ora il core alla speranza che po-
tremo alfine regnar sicuri sul trono.
Tra misfatti ha fin l'impresa
Se un misfatto a lei fu culla
La regal corona è un nulla
Se può in capo vacillar!...

È inutile che ti dica che tutta la scena fra
Macbet e Lady và in Recitativo e che i versi
siano forti e concisi specialmente sul finire del
Recitativo sul genere d'Alfieri. Quando Lady
resta sola bisogna farne due quartine ma non
possono più stare le vecchie, e la prima specialmente bisogna cambiarla, così invece d'un adagio farò un Allegro che sarà anche meglio.

Dopo viene il Coro dei Sicarj, e qui va la
scena assai avanti per preparare il Banchetto.
Lanari si lagna di te perchè li hai mandato uno
schizzo che non si capisce niente (e lo credo) ed
io pure mi lagno perchè non mi mandi mai
questo benedetto coro del terzo atto. Tu ti sei
adossato troppo lavoro[3] ed ora tocca a me a
sopportare.

Fammi intanto la scena che ti mando che

LADY
He and his son
Live, but nature did not make them immor-
tal.

MACBETH
That comforts me: they're not immortal.
LADY
So if a second crime...?
MACBETH
A second crime...?
LADY
It is needed...
MACBETH
When?...
LADY
This very evening!...
MACBETH (feigns)
A new crime!!!...
LADY
Well?...
MACBETH
'Tis decided!...
Banquo, ere long
Eternity begins for thee. (exit)

SCENE II[2]

LADY (alone)
My heart overflows at the hope that at last
we can reign secure on the throne.
An enterprise is brought to
conclusion by misdeeds
If in a misdeed it was cradled,
The royal crown is nothing
If on the brow it is insecure!...

I needn't tell you that the entire scene between Macbeth and the Lady should be in recitative, and that the lines, especially at the end
of the recitative, should be strong and concise,
in the manner of Alfieri. When the Lady remains alone, two quatrains are needed; but the
old ones can no longer be used, and the first one
in particular must be changed; so instead of an
adagio I'll write an Allegro, which will be even
better.

Then follows the assassins' chorus, and here
the scene goes on a good bit in order to set up
the banquet scene. Lanari is complaining about
you because you sent him a sketch in which
nothing is clear (and I believe it), and I too am
complaining because you never send me the
blessed chorus from Act III. You've taken on
too much work,[3] and now I'm the one who has
to bear the burden.

In the meantime, write me the scene I am

puoi farla subito subito e mandala al più presto possibile, e manda presto anche il resto.

Avverti ti ripeto che dopo la scena fra Lady e Macbet non può più stare il pensiero tetro della prima quartina perchè è già detto nel Recitativo.[4] Sia conciso. Addio.

Guarda che tutto sia ben legato, che non vi siano i soliti pasticci. Fa presto se non vuoi che vadi in furia.

Abbiati 1, 656–58

sending you, which you can do *immediately*, and send it to me as soon as possible; and send the rest soon too.

Note, I repeat, that after the scene between the Lady and Macbeth, the gloomy idea of the first quatrain can no longer stand, because it's already said in the recitative.[4] Be concise. Farewell.

Make sure that it all holds together, that there aren't the usual muddles. Be quick about it if you don't want me to fly into a rage.

1. This scene is based closely on Rusconi's translation of III.1 and 2. However, in Shakespeare, with her insinuating "But in them nature's copy's not eterne" the Lady seems to be hinting at the crime, but since Macbeth in the previous scene (III.1) has already ordered it, he can reply "There's comfort yet . . . Ere the bat hath flown . . . there shall be done/ A deed of dreadful note." And to her "What's to be done?" he can answer, "Be innocent of the knowledge, dearest chuck,/ Till thou applaud the deed." In both scenes set out in this letter, it should be noted, Verdi drew upon lines already prepared according to his instructions and transcribed into the Scala manuscript libretto (see DEGRADA at 160–63 and the edition of this libretto at 321–22).

2. The Lady's speech is drawn from two of Macbeth's, again in Rusconi's translation: III.1 ("Regnare è nulla; mestieri è regnar sicuri") and III.2 ("le imprese incominciate col delitto, mestieri è pur che coi delitti si compiano"). The quatrain is an intermediate version between that transcribed in the Scala libretto and the definitive version, but all three resemble one another closely.

3. *Tutti amanti*, an opera by Carlo Romani (Pietro's young nephew, b. 1824), libretto by Piave, was premiered at the Pergola in January 1847; Federico Ricci's *Griselda*, again on a Piave libretto, was premiered at La Fenice on March 13—the day before *Macbeth*'s premiere.

4. The reason offered earlier seems more likely: that Verdi had first planned to write a *romanza* (adagio), but then decided for a triumphant *cabaletta* (allegro). He found the gloomy images of the first quatrain unsuitable for this new plan (although the second quatrain could fit either adagio or allegro) and asked for the new text. In replacing this aria with "La luce langue" in 1865, Verdi carries out both plans in a single aria.

PIAVE TO GIOVANNI RICORDI   *Venice, 7 December 1846*

Signor Giovanni Ricordi Amico Pregiatissimo,

Solo oggi ho ricevuto la cara vostra 30 fuggito, in calce d'altra dell'amico Lanari. Per regolarità della cosa, avendo io avuto la commissione del Macbet dal M.° Verdi, ed essendo da lui pagato e non dal Lanari, così non posso farne una cessione che a sua richiesta, e con sua autorizzazione. Oggi stesso dovendo mandare allo stesso Maestro de' versi appunto del Macbet gli ho scritto in proposito, e appena ricevutane risposta, vi manderò la lettera che mi chiedete. Scusatemi, ma si tratta d'ordine, del quale Lanari me ne dà continue lezioni. . . .

Milan: Archivio Ricordi

Signor Giovanni Ricordi Most Esteemed Friend,

I received your valued letter of the 30th of last month only today, on the heels of another from friend Lanari. To keep things in order, since I received the commission for *Macbeth* from M.° Verdi, and since I am paid by him and not by Lanari, I can only yield it up at his request, and with his authorization. As I have to send the Maestro some verses for *Macbeth* this very day, I have written to him about this, and just as soon as I receive an answer from him, I will send you the letter you request. Forgive me, but it is a matter of procedure, on which subject Lanari lectures me all the time. . . .

VERDI TO PIAVE   *Milan, 10 December 1846*

Di qui in avanti daremo sempre ragione a Lei Sig. Poeta: sì sì *hai ragione, hai ragione, hai ragione* sempre sempre...

Henceforth, Signor Poet, we will never venture to disagree with you again; yes, yes, *you're right, you're right, you're right* always always.

Quantunque non mi sia piaciuto niente affatto questo Coro di Streghe,[1] nonostante ho riso assai leggendo nell'intestazione della scena..."Streghe in abito di cerimonia"...Le Streghe in abito di cerimonia?...È questa l'intenzione di Shaspeare? Hai capito bene cosa ha voluto fare *Shaspeare* di queste Streghe?...

Che difficoltà mi fai sulli spiriti aerei che non possono ballare?...Falli come è indicato. Il poema e la musica devono essere così e così bisogna farli. Avverti che intanto che gli Spiriti danzeranno intorno allo svenuto Macbet, le Streghe dovranno dire due stroffette etc...etc... Mandami subito la fine di questo terzo Atto. Spero che domani riceverò quella scena del 2° Atto tra Macbet e Lady. Almeno almeno fa presto. In quanto a Lanari ed a Ricordi ci penso io. Tu non puoi né devi consegnare niente a nissuno senza essere autorizzato da me.

Io vorrei che mi facesti capire bene l'ultimo Atto. Vorrei che s'aprisse la scena con un grandioso Coro patetico che descrivesse lo stato miserabile della Scozia sotto il dominio di Macbet. Il Coro dovrebbe essere di profughi Scozzesi in Inghilterra, sia poi gente del popolo, siano poi Thani, siano poi e l'uno e l'altro non importa: fa come credi bene. In questo Coro vorrei (come Shaespeare ha fatto in un dialogo tra Rosse e Macduff) una pittura caratteristica sublime patetica della miseria della Scozia. La scena dovrebbe essere in Inghilterra ma sui confini della Scozia. In somma io ti dico le mie intenzioni, ma se trovi di far meglio, fallo: quello che è assolutamente necessario pel dramma è di far una descrizione o in un modo o nell'altro della tirannia di Macbet e quindi della miseria della Scozia. Eccoti lo schizzo.

ATTO IV

SCENA I

Landa in Inghilterra sui confini colla Scozia vedrassi in distanza la foresta di Birman.
Profughi di Scozia. Uomini, fanciulli e donne.

CORO

Oh patria nostra infelice chè mal ti chiameremo madre, dacché ora sei solo tomba de' tuoi figli. Sospiri e gemiti il pianto non trovano più che irrisione e disprezzo. Ogni gioia il tiranno sbandò. Lo squillo funebre indice ad ogni istante le esequie d'un estinto senza che uomo osi chiedere perchè morì.[2]
(Sia questo un Coro grandioso. Poesia bella e

Although I didn't like this chorus of witches at all,[1] I nevertheless had a good laugh reading at the head of the scene..."Witches in ceremonial dress"...The witches in ceremonial dress? Is this Shakespeare's intention? Have you really understood what *Shakespeare* wanted to do with these witches?

What's all this trouble you're giving me about the aerial spirits who aren't supposed to dance? Do them as indicated. The poem and the music must be that way, and in that way they must be done. Note that while the aerial spirits are dancing around Macbeth in his faint, the witches have to say two *strofette* etc. etc. Send me the end of this third act at once. I hope that I'll receive that second-act scene between Macbeth and the Lady tomorrow. At least get a move on. As for Lanari and Ricordi, I'll take care of it. You may not, and must not, hand over anything to anyone without my authorization.

I'd like you to make the last act very clear for me. I'd like the scene to open with a grandiose, affecting chorus, which would describe Scotland's wretched state under Macbeth's rule. The chorus should be made up of Scottish refugees in England, either common people or thanes, or both; it's not important, do as you think best. In this chorus I'd like (as Shakespeare did in a dialogue between Ross and Macduff) a genre scene, a sublime, affecting picture of Scotland's misery. The scene should be in England, but on the Scottish border. In short, these are my ideas, but if you find a better way of doing it, do it; what's absolutely essential for the drama is to give a description, in one way or another, of Macbeth's tyranny, and thus the misery of Scotland. Here's the sketch for you:

ACT IV

SCENE I

A moor in England, on the Scottish border; in the distance, Birnam Wood is seen. Scottish refugees.
Men, children, and women.

CHORUS

Oh, our unhappy country, which we cannot rightly call mother, since now thou art only the tomb of thy children. Sighs and groans and weeping now call forth only derision and scorn. Every joy the tyrant has banished. The funeral knell indicates at every instant the exequies of one who has died without anyone's daring to ask why

patetica di quel metro che vorrai ad eccezione del decasillabo)

he died.[2] (*Let this be an imposing chorus. Beautiful and affecting poetry, in any meter you want except* decasillibi)

SCENA II

MACDUF *e detti*

MACDUF

Miei figli! Miei figli!...

CORO

Che avvenne?...

MACDUF

Tutti il tiranno uccise!...E moglie, e figli, e servi, e quanti abitavano nel mio castello!...(*Recitativo*)

CORO

Oh sventura!

MACDUF

Me sconsigliato!! Io solo fui cagione della loro morte. L'improvviso mio bando segnò la loro morte! Ma tu, giusto Cielo, pormi [probably "pommi"] di fronte al mio nemico, e se ei mi sfugge, tu pure allora gli perdona[3] (8 *versi—Due stroffette patetiche*)

SCENA III[4]

MALCOLMO *con soldati Inglesi Thani e detti*

MALCOLMO

Qual foresta è quella?

CORO

Di Birman.

MALCOLMO

Ogni soldato sfrondi un ramo e lo porti avanti di sé per ascondere all'inimico la massa del nostro esercito. (*A Macduf*) Sopporta la tua sventura che fra poco ti vendicherai...

MACDUF

Ah! ei non ha figli!!

MALCOLMO *al Coro*

Chi di voi ama la patria prenda l'armi e mi segua!...(*versi lirici—tempo di mezzo*)

TUTTI *con entusiasmo*

S'imbrandisca la spada vendicatrice e si liberi la patria nostra dalla tirannia di quel mostro. Da valorosi gloriamo le ombre di mille vittime innocenti. (6 *od* 8 *versi lirici forti, ed entusiasmo*)

La scena del sonnambulismo va bene come è nello schizzo che hai, se non che bisogna fare qualche piccolo cambiamento. Tutto il principio va bene ed attaccherai...[5]

SCENE II

MACDUFF *and the preceding*

MACDUFF

My children! My children!...

CHORUS

What happened?...

MACDUFF

The tyrant killed them all!...Wife, children, servants, and all who lived in my castle!... (*Recitative*)

CHORUS

Oh, misfortune!

MACDUFF

Rash Macduff!! I alone was the cause of their death. My sudden banishment signed their death warrant! But thou, O righteous heaven, bring me to face my foe, and if he escape me, then mayst thou pardon him too.[3] (8 *lines—Two affecting* strofette)

SCENE III[4]

MALCOLM *with the English soldiers, thanes, and the preceding*

MALCOLM

What wood is this?

CHORUS

The wood of Birnam.

MALCOLM

Let every soldier hew a branch and bear it before him to conceal from the foe the numbers of our host. (*To Macduff*) Bear your misfortune, which soon you will avenge...

MACDUFF

Ah! he has no children!!

MALCOLM

Whoever of you loves his fatherland, let him take up arms and follow me!...(*versi lirici— tempo di mezzo*)

ALL *with enthusiasm*

Let the avenging sword be brandished, and our fatherland be liberated from that monster's tyranny. As men of valor, we glorify the shades of a thousand innocent victims. (6 *or* 8 *powerful and enthusiastic* versi lirici)

The sleepwalking scene is fine as it is in the sketch you have, except that a few small changes are needed. All the beginning goes well, and then continue...[5]

LADY

Macduf aveva moglie e figli: dove sono ora?...
Ma queste mani non diverranno mai terse?...

MACDUF [sc. MEDICO]

Qual'orribile segreto!

DAMA

Ella ha detto ciò che non doveva.

LADY

Quest'odore di sangue dappertutto mi segue...
Tutti i profumi dell'Arabia non varrebbero
a lenire l'odore di questa piccola mano...
Ohimè!...

MEDICO

Quale sospiro!!...

LADY

Tergi quelle mani, indossa la tunica da letto,
né mostrarti sì pallido. Sì te lo ripeto.
Banco è sepolto e non uscirà dal suo sepolcro.

MEDICO

E questo ancora?...

LADY

A letto a letto: picchiano!...Vieni vieni...
dammi la mano: il fatto è irreparabile...an-
diamo...a letto...a letto...(Esce)

MEDICO e DAMA

Gran Dio abbi pietà di Lei!...(Sarà ottima cosa
se farai tutta questa scena in versi ottonari
perchè siccome Ella ripete in sogno le idee già
dette nel dramma, così io non[6] farei note in
più)

L'ultima scena di Macbet va bene fino al
racconto che va alla battaglia e lì vorrei che si
sentissero trombe interne, tamburi grida dei
soldati tutto internamente fino al momento che
resta ferito Macbet...

. . . .
. . . . ed in groppa va
pure va cadavere
generoso coperto di ferro[7] (Corre via frettoloso)

SCENA

*La scena è vuota ed internamente sentesi in
diversi punti trombe e tamburi, strepito di spade e
le scolte che gridano
'All'armi...All'armi...Guerra...Guerra
Morte...Morte...etc...etc...'*

LADY

Macduff had a wife and children: where are
they now?...But will these hands never become clean?...

MACDUFF [sc. DOCTOR]

What a horrible secret!

LADY-IN-WAITING

She has spoken what she should not.

LADY

This smell of blood follows me everywhere...All
the perfumes of Arabia would not serve to
sweeten the smell of this little hand...Alas!...

DOCTOR

What a sigh!!...

LADY

Wash those hands, put on your nightgown, and
do not show yourself so pale. Yes, I tell you
again. Banquo is buried and will not leave
his tomb.

DOCTOR

And that too?...

LADY

To bed, to bed: someone's knocking!...Come,
come...give me your hand: what's done cannot be undone...let's go...to bed...to bed...
(Exit)

DOCTOR and LADY-IN-WAITING

Great God, have pity on her!... (It will be best if
you cast all this scene in ottonari, because, as
the Lady repeats in her dream themes already
stated in the drama, that way I would not[6] have
to add notes)

Macbeth's last scene is fine until the speech
that leads to the battle, and there I would like
offstage trumpets, drums, soldiers' shouts, all
offstage, until the moment when Macbeth is
wounded...

. . . .
. . . . .and on into the fray
at least we'll die
with harness on our back[7] (He rushes off in
haste)

SCENA

*The stage is empty, and offstage from various
points are heard trumpets and drums, the clash of
swords, and the sentries crying
"To arms...To arms...War...War...
Death...Death...etc...etc..."*

MACBET *inseguito da* MACDUF

MACBET

Non voglio combattere teco fuggi

MACDUF

Fuggire?...

MACBET

Io sono fatato!...nissun mortale nato da donna può uccidermi!...

MACDUF

Dispera e muori—Io non nacqui: fui strappato col ferro dal fianco di mia madre...

MACBET

Maledetta la tua lingua...S'abbia l'inferno chi prima griderà m'arrendo...(*Combattono; Macbet resta ferito e cade: odonsi internamente le grida: 'Vittoria Vittoria' ed entrano... armati Malcolm con soldati e Thani etc.*)

MACDUF *dice a* MALCOLMO

Ecco il tiranno!...(*E inutile che ti dica che questi vanno versi lirici, e che questo dialogo tra Macduf e Macbet sia detto con pochissime parole se no raffredda l'azione*)

MACBET *s'alza lentamente e dice:*

Maledetto chi crederà agli oracoli!...Oh quanto felice era quando prode guerriero non aveva nell'animo il delitto...Ed ora?... Eccone il frutto!...Ma oimè!...Quali tenebre! L'eternità m'attende!...Io muoio!...Maledetto chi crederà nei loro oracoli!...

TUTTI

È spento!! Viva Malcolmo! Viva il Re di Scozia! (*Fa due stroffette cerca di darle un po' di patetico ma non dimenticare però il carattere di Macbet*)

Fai presto e cerca di far meglio che non hai fatto in questo coro delle streghe. Mandami subito il terzo atto: e poi cerca che tutto sia finito entro l'anno...

Abbiati 1, 667–73

MACBETH *followed by* MACDUFF

MACBETH

I do not wish to fight with you. Flee.

MACDUFF

Flee?...

MACBETH

I bear a charmed life!...no mortal born of woman can slay me!...

MACDUFF

Despair and die—I was not born: I was ripped by iron from my mother's womb...

MACBETH

Cursed be your tongue...Let hell have him who first cries I surrender...(*They fight; Macbeth is wounded and falls: offstage, cries of "Victory Victory" are heard, and there enter... armed, Malcolm with soldiers and Thanes, etc.*)

MACDUFF *says to* MALCOLM

Behold the tyrant!...(*These, of course, are versi lirici, and this dialogue between Macduff and Macbeth should be expressed in few words, or else it cools the action*)

MACBETH *raises himself slowly and says:*

Cursed, he who puts his faith in oracles!...Oh, how happy was I when, a brave warrior, I had no crime in my soul...And now?... Behold the fruits of it!...But alas!... What darkness! Eternity awaits me!...I die!...Cursed, he who puts his faith in oracles!...

ALL

He is dead! Hail, Malcolm! Hail, King of Scotland! (*Make two strofette, try to give them some touching quality, but don't then forget Macbeth's character*)

Get a move on and try to do better than you did with this witches' chorus. Send me Act III without delay: and then try to get everything done by the end of the year.

1. Maffei subsequently rewrote this chorus, according to Verdi's letter of 11 April 1857.

2. This is very close to Rusconi's translation of Ross's speech, IV.3, 164–71; for the two central strophes of the chorus, Piave turned to Macduff's speech earlier in the scene, lines 4–8.

3. Close to Rusconi's version of IV.3, 223–26 ("l'improvviso tuo bando segnò la loro sentenza" is his addition to Shakespeare) and 231–34

4. Verdi moves to V.4, but at "Ah! ei non ha figli" returns to IV.3.

5. All the wording that follows is close to Rusconi's V.1.

6. The "non" is an addition, proposed by Degrada, to Abbiati's reading. See DEGRADA at 170. The passages or numbers in *ottonario* meter in which Lady has participated thus far are both *tempo di mezzo* and *cabaletta* of the Act I duet, her aria "Trionfai," and three passages from the Act II *finale*: the opening quatrain, the conversation with the murderer and continuation up to the appearance of Banquo's ghost, and the concluding *concertato* "Sangue a me".

7. Difficult to translate! Rusconi's version of "Blow, wind! come, wrack!/At least we'll die with harness on our back" (V.5) is: "soffino aridi i venti: e tu, distruzione, vieni; apprèstati a un lauto pasto, e ingoia me pure, ma cadavere di generoso, tutto coperto di ferro." Although Piave versified this passage—Verdi quotes a fragment of Piave's lines in his letter of 22 December 1846 to Piave—this text has no counterpart in the definitive libretto or in the Scala manuscript libretto; it suggests that Verdi may have planned to provide a *cabaletta* with chorus at this point.

MUZIO TO BAREZZI   *Milan, 14 December 1846*

....Tutti sono a pregare il signor Maestro che vada a metterlo [*Attila*][1] in scena, e che ciò è un desiderio di tutta Milano, la quale ammirerebbe uno dei suoi capi lavori. Pare che si sia cominciato a piegare un poco; ed anzi ieri sera si è fatta una prova in casa della Tadolini, alla quale assisteva il signor Maestro; ed io stavo al cembalo ad accompagnare per non farlo affaticare tanto ... Se sentisse la Tadolini! Canta la cavatina e il duetto con Moriani come un angelo. Che bella voce! Che magnifica voce! ...

Oggi porterò alla copisteria un atto quasi del *Macbeth*.[2] Non può farsi un'idea della originalità, della bellezza di quella musica; quando il signor Maestro me la fa sentire, sto due o tre ore senza poter scrivere, tanto è l'entusiasmo che mi mette nell'animo. Sono ben fortunati i Fiorentini che saranno i primi a gustarla!

Il signor Maestro è stato un po' incomodato nei giorni passati. Ha avuto dei dolori intestinali, i quali gli produssero una diarrea che non lo lasciava quieto un momento; aveva fatto un'assai cattiva cera. Non si può immaginare qual pena mi faceva a vederlo così; Egli poi si metteva in testa delle malinconie, dicendo che faceva una malattia peggio dell'anno scorso, e tante altre cose che quasi mi faceva piangere.

Quando Dio ha voluto ha cessato quell'incomodo mercè le cure del dottor Belcredi,[3] e sono tre giorni che sta bene e che lavora ...

Sono due giorni che lavoriamo dalle 9 fino alle 12 della sera, fuori delle ore d'andare a pranzo; ed è forse un po' troppo già, ma ancora per alcuni giorni e poi ripiglieremo le nostre passeggiate e i nostri piccoli divertimenti. Io scrivo in casa sua sullo stesso tavolo, ed ho sempre così i suoi consigli; e ce ne stiamo assieme tanto bene ...

Garibaldi, 300–1

...Everyone is begging the Maestro to go and prepare it [*Attila*][1] for performance, that being the wish of all Milan, which would admire one of his masterpieces. It seems that he has begun to give in a little; in fact, yesterday evening there was a rehearsal in Tadolini's house which the Maestro attended; and I stood in at the keyboard to accompany so as not to tire him so much ... If you could only hear Tadolini! She sings the *cavatina* and the duet with Moriani like an angel. What a beautiful voice! What a magnificent voice! ...

Today I'll take almost a whole act of *Macbeth* to the *copisteria*.[2] You can't imagine the originality, the beauty of this music; when the Maestro plays it to me, I can't write for two or three hours, so great is the enthusiasm with which it fills my spirit. Lucky Florentines, to be the first to enjoy it!

The Maestro was somewhat unwell in the past few days. He had intestinal pains, which produced a diarrhea that did not leave him calm for a moment; it made him look rather terrible. You can't imagine how it grieved me to see him looking thus; then he abandoned himself to melancholy, saying that his illness was worse than last year's, and so much else that it almost made me weep.

When God willed it, this illness ended, thanks to the treatment of Dr. [Gaspare] Belcredi,[3] and for the last three days he has been well and working ...

For the past two days we've been working from nine [in the morning] until twelve at night, except for when we went out to eat; and maybe already we've been overdoing it a bit; but a few more days to go and then we'll resume our walks and our little amusements. In his house I write at the same table and so I always have his advice; and we get along together so well ...

1. *Attila* had its Milan premiere on 26 December 1846.

2. At this stage, Verdi would have written vocal lines and bass; for a discussion of the stages in Verdi's compositional process, see pp. 210–11; for David Lawton's and Francesco Degrada's reconstruction of the chronology of the composition, see pp. 211–15 & 171–73 respectively.

3. Milanese doctor; one of the two doctors who had provided Verdi with certificates attesting to his ill health earlier that year (*Copialettere*, 19)

MUZIO TO BAREZZI

Milan, 19 December 1846

... Lanari ieri ha fatto pagare al signor Maestro da un banchiere 225 marenghini[1] per il primo quartale dell'Opera di Firenze.

Macbeth progredisce di bene in meglio; che musica sublime! Le so dire che vi sono cose che fanno rizzare i capelli in testa! Gli costa una gran fatica a fare di questa musica, ma gli riesce bene assai assai!! I due primi atti sono quasi finiti e, meno le arie, il resto è già alla copisteria e nella ventura settimana sarà mandato ai rispettivi esecutori.

Varesi, quando partì per Roma, ha portato seco il *Convito* e la *Visione* ed ha fatto un gran fracasso per tutta Milano, dicendo che quella era la musica più bella e drammatica del Verdi. A Piacenza ha detto ancor di più. In tutti i paesi dove è passato—a Parma, Bologna, Firenze—gridava a tutti come un pazzo che aveva con sè la più sublime musica di Verdi ...

... Yesterday Lanari had a banker pay the Maestro 225 *marenghini*[1] for the first quarter of the fee for the Florence opera.

Macbeth is progressing from good to better; what sublime music! I can tell you that there are things that will make your hair stand on end! It is a great effort for him to compose this music, but it is turning out very well for him—very well!! The first two acts are almost finished and, except for the arias, the rest is already at the *copisteria* and will be sent next week to the respective performers.

Varesi, when he left for Rome, took the *Convito* and *Visione* with him, and he made a big ruckus all over Milan, saying that it was Verdi's most beautiful and dramatic music. He said even more in Piacenza. In all the towns he passed through—Parma, Bologna, Florence—he yelled like a lunatic to everyone that he had with him Verdi's most sublime music ...

Garibaldi, 302–3

1. a *marengo*, a gold coin worth twenty francs; if Verdi was paid in four equal installments, his total fee would have been 18,000 francs, equivalent to about 19,500 Austrian lire. Demaldé reported compensation as 19,800 (see MATZ at 134).

VERDI TO PIAVE

Milan, 22 December 1846

Non t'ho mai autorizzato ad adoperare li 20 Napoleoni d'oro che m'appartengono.[1] Ora te ne autorizzo: prendi i Napoleoni d'oro, va da un cambista e fatteli ridurre (col maggior agio possibile) in L. aus. effettive: mi scriverai cosa ne hai ricavato. Queste svanziche unite alle altre trecento che t'imprestai[2] e alle altre che ti darò dopo in scena il *Macbet*, serviranno a pagarti il *Macbet* stesso. Mi scriverai poi cosa te ne devo dare a compimento ed appena in scena sarai soddisfatto.

Intanto ti prego di fare presto l'ultimo Atto; di più aggiungo che essendomi provato a fare il primo Coro non mi riesce grandioso anche perchè il metro è troppo breve. Quindi mi farai il piacere di fare quattro strofette di versi ottonarj.

Io vorrei fare un Coro dell'importanza di quello del *Nabucco*: non vorrei adoperare però lo stesso andamento ed è perciò che ti prego dei versi ottonarj.[3] Non lasciarti sfuggire questo momento che è il solo che sia patetico in tutta l'opera. Quindi fallo con passione, e che vi siano più pensieri (starei per dire) che parole.

I never authorized you to use the 20 gold Napoleons [400 francs] that belong to me.[1] Now I do authorize you: take the gold Napoleons and go to a currency exchanger and have them changed (at the best possible rate) into current Austrian lire; write me what you got from it. These *svanziche* [Austrian lire], together with the other three hundred I lent you[2] and with the rest that I'll give you once *Macbeth* is produced, will serve to pay you for *Macbeth*. So you'll write to me, telling me what I still owe you, and as soon as the opera is on you'll receive the rest.

Meanwhile please do the last act quickly; moreover, let me add that I've tried to set the first chorus but haven't been able to make it turn out grandiose because, among other things, the meter is too short. So do me the favor of making four *strofette* of *ottonari*.

I'd like to do a chorus as important as the one in *Nabucco*; but I wouldn't want it to move along in the same way, and that's why I ask you for *ottonari*.[3] Don't let this moment slip by, the only one in the entire opera that's affecting. So do it with passion, and let there be more thoughts (I was about to say) than words.

Ricordati anche dell'Aria del Tenore di fare ben patetico l'Adagio—La cabaletta falla *tutti* insieme[4] ma non versi endecasillabi. Procura di far presto e addio. Ti raccomando il Sonnambulismo. Stà attaccato bene all'ultimo schizzo.

Un'altra idea: Vorrei che dopo l'Aria di Macbet nell'ultimo atto...'*un cadavere / armato almen cadrà...*' Macbet col Coro fuggisse e si cambiasse scena: Una vasta pianura e far vedere in fondo tutti i soldati (che sono comparse) portanti avanti di loro il ramo d'albero: dovrebbero essere ben in fondo e muoversi a suono di Banda a poco a poco. Macduff dicesse le parole:

'*Ecco il castello: Coraggio: la fortuna ti secondi: suonino le trombe foriere della battaglia'*. Tutti partono e lasciano vuota per un momento la scena mentre odesi internamente lo strepitio della battaglia, poi viene la scena tra Macbet e Macduff etc. Così sarebbe più ragionato ed avressimo un altro effetto di scena.

Abbiati 1, 674–75

Remember also to make the *adagio* of the tenor aria quite affecting. As for the cabaletta, make it a general tutti,[4] but not with *endecasillabi*. Try to work quickly; farewell. Take care with the sleepwalking scene. Stick closely to the last sketch.

Another idea: after Macbeth's aria in the last act..."at least I'll fall/with harness on my back..." I'd like Macbeth to flee with the chorus and there to be a scene change—a vast plain showing all the soldiers in the distance (they're supers) carrying a tree branch in front of them. They should be well in the background and be moving little by little to the sound of a band. Macduff should say the words:

"Behold the castle: Courage: may fortune second you: let the trumpets sound as harbingers of battle." All depart and leave the stage empty for a moment while the din of the battle is heard offstage; then comes the scene between Macbeth and Macduff, etc. In that way it makes more sense, and we'd have another striking scenic effect.

1. Verdi had lent 800 francs to Nani Mocenigo, a mutual friend in Venice; in late October he told Piave that 400 had been paid and authorized him to collect the rest on his behalf (*Abbiati* 1, 652).

2. See letter of 2 or 3 September 1846.

3. The chorus "Va pensiero" in *Nabucco,* as well as similar patriotic choruses in *I lombardi* and *Ernani,* have *decasyllabic* lines.

4. "La patria tradita" is indeed sung by everyone (Macduff, Malcolm, and chorus), an unusual feature in the *cabaletta* of an aria.

VERDI TO LANARI   *Milan, 22 December 1846*

... Stò bene di salute: ma come ti dissi nell'ultima mia sono un poco stanco. La *Barbieri* abbia un po' pazienza che se il genere le piace, è trattata assai bene ...

P.S. Guarda che l'ombra di Banco deve sortire sotterra: dovrà essere l'attore istesso che rappresentava Banco nell'Atto 1°,[1] dovrà avere un velo cenerino ma assai rado e fino che appena appena si veda, e Banco dovrà avere i capelli rabbuffati e diverse ferite nel collo visibili.

Tu[tte] queste nozioni io le ho da Londra[2] ove si rappresenta continuamente questa Tragedia da 200 anni e più.

Florence: Biblioteca Nazionale;
Copialettere, 446–47

... I'm in good health, but as I told you in my last letter, I'm a little tired. Let Barbieri show a bit of patience, for if she likes the genre, then she has been handsomely done by ...

P.S. Note that Banquo's ghost must make his entrance from underground; it must be the same actor that played Banquo in Act I.[1] He must be wearing an ashen veil, but quite thin and fine, and just barely visible; and Banquo must have ruffled hair and various wounds visible on his neck.

I've gotten all of these ideas from London,[2] where this tragedy has been produced continually for over 200 years.

1. And Act II, of course, but Banquo's appearance there is a later addition. (See DEGRADA at 172, and LAWTON at 212.)

2. In Macready's production, "The ghost entered through a trap, hidden by the gathering servants. When the servants moved away, Lennox pointed to the chair in which the ghost sat, requesting Macbeth to sit down. Banquo, 'pale as chalk,' with a gash across his throat, turned slowly to face Macbeth." Bartholomeusz, *Macbeth and the Players,* p. 166.

VERDI TO GIOVANNI RICORDI   *Milan, 29 December 1846*

Approvo il contratto[1] dell'opera mia *Macbeth* che andrà in scena nella prossima quaresima in Firenze, e dò la mia adesione perchè tu ne faccia uso colla condizione però che tu non permetta la rappresentazione di questo *Macbeth* all' I. R. Teatro la Scala.

Ho troppi esempi per essere persuaso che qui non si sà o non si vuole montare come si conviene le opere specialmente le mie. Non posso dimenticarmi della pessima *mise en scene* dei Lombardi, dell'Ernani, dei Foscari etc...Un'altra prova ho sotto gli occhi coll'Attila.[2] Domando a te stesso, se quest'opera, ad onta di una buona compagnia, può essere nel complesso eseguita, e messa in scena più malamente?

Ti ripeto addunque che io non posso ne devo permettere la rappresentazione di questo *Macbeth* alla Scala almeno fino a che io le cose non siano cambiate in meglio[3] e che stesso le approvi. Mi credo in obbligo anche di avvertirti per tua norma che questa condizione che ora metto pel *Macbeth* da qui in avanti la metterò per tutte le opere mie.

> Milan: Archivio Ricordi;
> *Copialettere,* 34–35 (draft)

I approve the contract[1] for my opera *Macbeth,* which will be produced during the next Lenten season in Florence, and I agree to your making use of it on the condition, however, that you do not allow any performance of this *Macbeth* at the Imperial and Royal Scala Theater.

I have more than enough examples to persuade me that here they do not know how, or do not want, to mount operas—my operas in particular—in a suitable manner. I cannot forget the wretched staging of *I lombardi, Ernani, I due Foscari,* etc. I have another proof of this before my eyes with *Attila.*[2] I ask yóu yourself whether this opera, in spite of a good cast, could overall be performed and staged any worse?

I repeat to you, therefore, that I cannot and must not permit the performance of this *Macbeth* at La Scala, at least until there has been a change for the better,[3] and I myself give approval. I also feel obliged to advise you, for your guidance, that this condition which I now place upon *Macbeth,* I shall place upon all my operas from now on.

1. contratto ... *Macbeth:* (draft) contratto che hai fatto per l'Opera mia nuova *Macbeth* (contract ... *Macbeth:* (draft) contract you have drawn up for my new opera *Macbeth*).
2. *Attila* had opened the Scala season three days earlier. Muzio raved about the singers, but described the mise-en-scène as *perfida:* the sun rose before the proper moment; the sea and sky were serene throughout the storm scene; etc. (27 December 1846 letter to Barezzi, in *Garibaldi,* 303–4).
3. meglio ... Mi credo in obbligo: [draft] meglio. Mi credo in obbligo (better ... I also feel obliged: [draft] better. I feel obliged.) The added clause insures that Verdi, rather than Ricordi, would be the judge of when there has been a change for the better at La Scala. (*Macbeth* was first performed at La Scala on 24 February 1849.)

1847

VERDI TO BARBIERI-NINI   *Milan, 2 January 1847*

Lanari le avrà, credo, scritto ch'Ella canterà nella mia nuova opera per Firenze. Io me ne chiamo veramente fortunato e le mando alcuni pezzi, pei quali mi permetterà di fare alcune osservazioni.

Lanari, I believe, will have written to tell you that you will sing in my new opera for Florence. I count myself truly fortunate, and I send you some numbers about which you will permit me to make some observations.

Prima di tutto il carattere della parte e risoluto, fiero, drammatico estremamente. Il soggetto è preso da una delle più grandi tragedie che vanti il teatro ed io ho cercato di farne estrarre tutte le posizioni con fedeltà, di farlo verseggiare bene e di farne un tessuto nuovo e di fare della musica attaccata, il più che poteva, alla parola ed alla posizione; ed io desidero che questa mia idea la comprendano bene gli artisti, in somma desidero che gli artisti servano meglio il poeta che il maestro.[1]

Il primo suo pezzo è la cavatina. Sorte leggendo una lettera, poi un recitativo largo... Viene un adagio d'un genere grandioso e cantabile, ma d'un cantabile non sdolcinato: la prego di riflettere bene alla frase nelle parole:

Che tardi? accetta il dono
Ascendimi a regnar

di fare che la voce si rinforzi non tutta in una volta, ma a poco a poco e di marcare con significato tutte le volte la parola: *che tardi,* nel tempo che viene prima della cabaletta badi bene alle parole....*qui ...qui... la notte?* Queste parole hanno un altissimo significato di molta importanza da levare insomma un applauso. La prima parte della cabaletta va detta grandiosa, con fierezza, ma in mezzo a questa fierezza vi deve essere della gioia. Nella seconda parte, forse sarà bassa la frase nelle parole: *tu notte ne avvolgi,* ecc., ma è mia intenzione di farla appunto cupa e misteriosa (nel caso questa frase è subito cambiata) per avere poi tutto lo slancio sul finire... *Qual petto percota,* ecc. ecc.

Il finaletto[2] del primo atto, badi bene che è quasi tutto a voci sole, quindi ci vuole molta sicurezza, specialmente nelle due parti principali.

Troverà unito a questo il finale del secondo atto in cui Ella ha un brindisi. È inutile che le dica che questo va detto leggero, brillante, con tutte le appoggiature, gruppetti e mordenti, ecc. Io non ricordo bene se Ella fa facilmente il trillo: io l'ho messo, ma nel caso è subito levato. Il tempo di questo brindisi è ampio, ma non troppo. Nel seguito viene una visione di *Macbet* in cui Ella ha dei passi magnifici per *controscena.* L'atto si chiude con un pezzo concertato in cui Ella parla quasi sempre sotto voce a *Macbet.*

First of all, the character of the part is resolute, bold, extremely dramatic. The plot is taken from one of the greatest tragedies the theatre boasts, and I have tried to have all the dramatic situations drawn from it faithfully, to have it well versified, and to give it a new texture, and to compose music tied so far as possible to the text and to the situations; and I wish this idea of mine to be well understood by the performers; indeed, I wish the performers to serve the poet better than they serve the composer.[1]

Your first number is the *cavatina.* You come out reading a letter, and then there is a broad recitative. There follows an *adagio* of a grandiose and cantabile kind, but not too sugary a cantabile; I would ask you to consider carefully the phrase at the words:

Che tardi? accetta il dono
Ascendimi a regnar

and to do it in such a way that the voice does not swell up all at once, but gradually; and to give meaningful emphasis each time to the words "Che tardi." In the passage that comes before the *cabaletta,* pay careful attention to the words "qui ... qui ... la notte?" These words have tremendous significance; in short, they should arouse applause. The first part of the *cabaletta* is to be uttered in a grandiose manner, with pride, but mingled with the pride there should be joy. In the second part, the phrase at the words "Tu notte ne avvolgi," etc. will perhaps be low; but it is precisely my intention to make it dark and mysterious (if necessary, this phrase can be changed at once) so as then to have all the brilliance at the end... "Qual petto percota," etc. etc.

Note well that the *finaletto*[2] of Act I is almost all unaccompanied, and so great security is called for, especially in the two principal parts.

You will also find enclosed the second-act *finale,* in which you have a *brindisi.* There is no need to tell you that this should be uttered lightly, brilliantly, with all the appoggiaturas, gruppetti, mordents, etc. I do not well recall whether you trill with ease; I have included a trill, but if necessary it can be taken out at once. The tempo of this *brindisi* is broad, but not too broad. In what follows, there is a vision scene for Macbeth in which you have splendid passages of byplay. The act closes with an ensemble in which you address Macbeth almost always sotto voce.

Presto le manderò un duetto. Un'altra aria composta però d'un recitativo e di una sola cabaletta brillante. Indi la gran scena in cui Ella è *sonnambula* e svela nel sogno tutti i delitti commessi. È una gran scena nel dramma: se la musica riesce appena appena buona, l'effetto vi sarà.

Nei pezzi che le mando ora badi semplicemente alla tessitura (non alla musica, la quale difficilmente si potrà capire dalla sua particella) mi sappia dire qualche cosa e se vi fosse qualche passo incomodo me lo accenni prima d'istromentare.

La posta parte e non posso più trattenermi, con tutta stima ed ammirazione.

> Present location unknown; date and most of second paragraph taken from J. A. Stargardt, Catalogue 603 (1974), No. 559; the remainder from *Musica: Settimanale di Cultura e di Cronaca* (Rome), 23 November 1911 [*recte* 1913]

Soon I shall send you a duet. Another aria consisting, however, of a recitative and a single brilliant *cabaletta* ["Trionfai"]. And then the *gran scena* in which you *sleepwalk* and reveal in your dream all the crimes committed. It is a great scene in the play; if the music is any good at all, the effect will be made.

In the numbers that I am sending you now, pay attention simply to the tessitura (not to the music, which is difficult to grasp from your particella [score consisting of vocal line and bass]), and let me have some comment; and if there should be some passage that lies badly, let me know before I do the orchestration.

The mail is leaving, and I cannot go on any longer. With all esteem and admiration.

---

1. Verdi tells Varesi the same in his 7 January 1847 letter.
2. Verdi calls it a *little* finale because it lacks a separate stretta movement.

VERDI TO VARESI

[*Milan,*] *7 January 1847*

Sono stato un po' tardivo a mandarti musica perchè aveva bisogno d'un po di riposo. Or eccoti un Duettino, un Duetto grande ed un finale.[1]–Io non cesserò mai di raccomandarti di studiare bene la posizione, e le parole; la musica viene da se. Insomma ho più piacere che servi meglio il poeta del maestro. Nel primo Duettino tu potrai cavare molto partito (meglio che se fosse una cavatina). Abbia bene sott'occhio la posizione che è quando s'incontra con le streghe, che gli predicono il trono. Tu resti a tal annunzio sbalordito, ed atterrito; ma ti nasce nello stesso tempo l'ambizione d'arrivare al trono. Perciò il principio del Duettino lo dirai *sotto voce* e bada di dare tutta l'importanza ai versi. *Ma perchè sento rizzarsi il crine?* Bada bene ai cenni alli accenti al pp. e F...accennati nella musica. Ricordati che devi cavare anche un altro effetto sulle note

I've been a little late in sending you music because I needed a bit of rest. Now here are a *duettino,* a grand duet, and a *finale* for you.[1] I'll never stop urging you to study the dramatic situation and the words well; the music will come by itself. In a word, I'd rather you served the poet better than you serve the composer. You'll be able to do well for yourself with the first *duettino* (more than if it were a *cavatina*). Bear well in mind the dramatic situation, which is when he meets the witches who predict the throne for him. You are stunned and terrified by this prophecy; but, at the same time, there is born in you the ambition to reach the throne. Therefore you'll sing the beginning of this *duettino* sotto voce, and be sure that you give real importance to the lines "Ma perchè sento rizzarsi il crine?" Pay careful attention to the indications, the accents, and to the *pp*'s and *f*'s marked in the music. Remember that you must achieve still another effect on the notes

Nel Duetto grande i primi versi del Recitativo vanno detti senza importanza quando dà l'ordine al servitore. Ma dopo che resta solo a poco a poco si trasporta e gli pare di vedersi un pugnale nel mani [?] che gl'indichi la strada per uccidere Duncano. Questo è un bellissimo punto drammatico e poetico e tu lo devi curar molto. Bada che è di notte: tutti dormono; e tutto questo Duetto dovrà esser detto sotto voce, ma con voce cupa da incutere terrore. Macbet solo (come in un momento di trasporto) dirà alcune frasi a voce forte e spiegata: ma tutto questo lo troverai spiegato nella parte. Perchè tu bene intenda le mie idee ti dico anche che in tutto questo Rec° e Duetto l'istromentale consiste nelli istromenti d'arco colle sordine in due fagotti, in due Corni ed un timpano.[2]— Tu vedi che l'orchestra suonerà estremamente piano e voi altri dovete cantare pure colle sordine. Io ti raccomando di fare risaltare molto le idee poetiche seguenti che sono estremamente belle!

1.a   *Ah questa mano*
          Non potrebbe l'Oceano
          queste mani a me lavar!

poi l'altra

          Vendetta tuonarmi come Angeli d'ira
          Udrò di Duncano le sante virtù

Il primo tempo 6/8 del Duetto và piuttosto presto. Il secondo tempo 3/8 và andantino mosso—L'ultimo tempo $\math01{C}$ va prestissimo, sotto voce e sul finire dovrà appena appena sentirsi la parola mentre Macbet (quasi fuori di se) è trascinato da *Lady*

Il finale 1° è chiaro per se. Bada soltanto che dopo le prime battute c'è uno squarcio a voci sole e bisognerà che tu e la Barbieri siate ben sicuri per sostenere gli altri—

Scusa la chiaccherata. Presto ti manderò il resto. Addio!...

Nel finale del convito cambia alcuni versi che ti mando che sono più giusti e poetici. *In principio*

Mac.   Prenda ciascun l'orrevole
        Seggio al suo grado eletto!
        Lieto son io d'accogliere

In the grand duet the first lines of the recitative—when he gives the orders to the servant—should be said without emphasis. But after he's left alone, little by little he gets carried away, and he thinks he sees a dagger in his hands [?], pointing the way to the murder of Duncan. This is a most beautiful moment, both dramatically and poetically, and you must take great care with it. Note that it's night; everyone is asleep, and this whole duet will have to be sung sotto voce, but in a hollow voice such as to arouse terror. Macbeth, alone (as if momentarily transported), will sing a few phrases in full, expansive voice. But all of this you will find set out in [your] part. So that you'll understand my ideas clearly, let me tell you that in the entire recitative and duet, the orchestra consists of muted strings, two bassoons, two horns, and a kettledrum.[2] You see, the orchestra will play extremely softly, and therefore you two will have to sing with mutes too. I urge you to bring out strongly the following poetic ideas, which are extremely beautiful!

1)   Ah, this hand—
          The Ocean could not
          wash these hands of mine

and then

          Like Angels of wrath, I shall hear
          Duncan's holy virtues thundering
            vengeance

The *primo tempo* 6/8 of the duet is rather fast. The *secondo tempo* 3/8 is sung andantino mosso. The final *tempo* $\math01{C}$ is prestissimo, sotto voce, and at the end one should only barely hear the words while Macbeth (almost beside himself) is dragged off by the Lady.

The first finale is self-explanatory. Only note that after the first few measures there is an unaccompanied passage for solo voices, and you and Barbieri will have to be very secure, to sustain the others.

Excuse the chit-chat. I'll send you the rest soon. Farewell!...

In the finale of the banquet scene, change a few lines to these which I send you; they are more appropriate and poetic. *At the start*

Macbeth   Let each one take his honored
            Seat according to his rank!
            I am happy to welcome

Tali ospiti a banchetto	Such guests to the banquet.
La mia consorte assidasi	Let my consort seat herself
Nel seggio a lei sortito	In the seat ordained for her,
Ma pria le piaccia un brindisi	But first, may it please her to launch
Sciogliere a vostro onor!...	A toast in your honor.

Più avanti   *Further on*

Non dirmi ch'io fossi!...le ciocche cruente	Do not tell me that it was I!... your gory locks
Non scuotermi incontro!...Macbetto è soffrente	Do not shake against me!...Macbeth is afflicted.
*Và...spirto d'abisso!...spalanca una fossa*3	Hence...spirit from hell!...may the earth gape3

Siena: Archivio dell'Accademia Chigiana;
Nuova Antologia 271 (1932), 437;
Quaderni dell'Accademia Chigiana 27 (1953), 7–8

1. These three numbers include virtually everything that Macbeth sings in Act I. The music Verdi sent would have consisted of the vocal line and bass line (perhaps with some cues to other parts) written on two staves. For a facsimile of such a score, see p. 42.

2. On the orchestration of the duet, see BUDDEN at 229.

3. Both these passages correspond to the final layer of text in the Scala manuscript libretto (that is, *after* Maffei's corrections), establishing that Maffei had at least begun his work on the libretto by 7 January 1847, the date of this letter.

VERDI TO MARIE(?) ESCUDIER   *Milan, 12 January 1847*

... Presto presto il *Macbeth* sarà finito, e così avrò un'opera di meno sulle spalle ... Per Londra ho fissato i *Masnadieri* di cui è già terminato il libretto ...

British Library;
Rassegna Musicale 21 (1951), 258

... Very, very soon *Macbeth* will be finished, and so I'll have one opera less on my back ... for London, I've settled on *I masnadieri*, whose libretto is already finished ...

MUZIO TO BAREZZI   *Milan, 18 January 1847*

... Il Maestro lavora molto al *Macbeth*; oggi e domani finirà il terzo atto; non gli rimane più che il quarto e così forse alla fine del mese avrà finito tutto ...

Garibaldi, 307

... The Maestro is working hard at *Macbeth;* today and tomorrow he'll finish Act III. All that's left for him to do is Act IV, and so maybe by the end of the month he'll have finished everything ...

VERDI TO TITO RICORDI   [*Milan, mid-January 1847*]

Fammi il piacere di far sapere al *Perrone*1 che l'epoca di *Macbet* è di molto posteriore ad *Ossian* ed all'*Impero Romano*.

Macbet assassinò Duncano nel 1040: ed egli fù poi ucciso nel *1057.–*

In Inghilterra nel 1039 regnava *Aroldo* detto *Re di lepre*2 re di stirpe danese: gli successe nell'anno stesso *Ardecanuto* fratello uterino d'*Odoardo* il confessore et...

Non mancare di dar a Perrone subito queste

Do me the favor of letting Perrone1 know that the period of *Macbeth* is much later than *Ossian* and the *Roman Empire*.

Macbeth assassinated Duncan in 1040; and then he was killed in *1057*.

In England in 1039 the king was *Harold—* called *King of Hares,*2 a king of Danish origins. In the same year *Hardicanute, Edward* the Confessor's half-brother, succeeded him, etc.

Don't fail to give Perrone this information

notizie perchè credo s'inganni circa l'epoca—

Florence: Biblioteca Nazionale;
Copialettere, 448

immediately, because I believe he's mistaken about the period.

1. Presumably Filippo Peroni, Scala designer, and probably the "Perroni" mentioned in Verdi's 1879 biographical sketch as having assembled scenes for the *Nabucco* premiere (Arthur Pougin, *Giuseppe Verdi, vita anedottica* ... [Milan: Ricordi, 1881] p. 46). *Macbeth* designs were prepared in Milan; see the following letter.

2. Verdi perhaps intended to write "Piè di lepre" ("Harefoot"). He had evidently been boning up on his British history. His facts are essentially right: Malcolm invaded Scotland (for a second time) in 1057, but the date now generally assigned to the end of the campaign, and Macbeth's death, is 1058. Harefoot was an illegitimate son of King Canute, who was also King of Denmark; Hardicanute claimed the English crown in 1035.

VERDI TO LANARI
Milan, 21 January 1847

Diffatti non t'ho scritto perchè sono eccessivamente occupato. Senza dubbio presto presto scriverò a Romani pregandolo anzi perchè s'adopri per la *mise en scène;* ma siccome io non voglio vedere *brutti musi* dal poeta così aspetto ancora a scriverli qualche giorno. Bisogna anche che ti prevenga che parlando giorni fà con Sanquirico[1] del *Macbet* ed esternandoli il mio desiderio di montare[2] assai bene il terzo Atto delle apparizioni egli mi suggerì diverse cose, ma la più bella è certamente la *fantasmagorìa.*[3] Egli mi assicurò che sarebbe stata cosa estremamente bella ed adattissima: ed Egli stesso s'è incaricato di parlare all'ottico Duroni[4] onde preparare la macchina. Tu sai cosa è la *fantasmagorìa* ed è inutile te ne faccia descrizione. Per Dio se la cosa riesce bene come me l'ha descritta Sanquirico sarà un'affare da sbalordire, e da far correre un mondo di gente soltanto per quello. Circa la spesa m'assicura che sarà poco più d'una altra macchina...Che ne dici?...Entro la settimana avrai tutto il terzo Atto, il principio del quarto: il libretto terminato, e spero anche i figurini. Io desidero che i figurini sieno eseguiti bene: Puoi esser certo che saran fatti bene: perchè ho mandato a prenderne diversi a Londra, ho fatto consultare da letterati di primissimo ordine l'epoca e i costumi, e poi saranno esaminati da Hayez[5] e dalli altri della comissione etc. etc.

Vedrai quando riceverai la musica che vi sono due Cori di grandissima importanza: non risparmiare nel corpo dei Coristi e ne sarai contento: Bada che le streghe devono essere sempre divise in tre drapelli e sarebbe ottima cosa che fossero *6. 6. 6.* in tutto *18.*[6] etc...Ti raccomando il tenore che deve fare il Macduff e poi sieno buone tutte le seconde parti perchè i pezzi concertati hanno bisogno delle buone

True, I haven't written to you, because I'm excessively busy. Very soon, without fail, I'll write to Romani asking him to help with the mise-en-scène; but since I don't want to see any scowls on the face of the librettist, I'm still waiting a few days before writing to him. I must also inform you that, having spoken to Sanquirico[1] a few days ago about *Macbeth,* and expressing my desire to do a very good job of staging[2] the third act, the one with the apparitions, he suggested various things to me, but the most beautiful is certainly the *fantasmagorìa.*[3] He assured me that it would be extremely beautiful and effective, and he himself has taken on the responsibility of speaking to the optician Duroni[4] to have the machine built. You know what the *fantasmagorìa* is, and so there's no need for me to describe it to you. By God, if this turns out well, as Sanquirico has described it to me, it will be astonishing and bring a flock of people running just for that alone. As for the cost, he assures me that it will be little more than for another machine. What do you say? Within the week you'll have all of the third act, the beginning of the fourth, the completed libretto, and, I hope, the costume designs as well. I want the costume designs to be well realized; you can be sure that the designs will be well made, because I had a number of them sent from London. I've had eminent scholars do research on the epoch and costumes, and then they will be looked over by Hayez[5] and the others from the Commission, etc., etc.

When you receive the music, you will see that there are two choruses of the greatest importance; don't scrimp with the size of the chorus and you'll be pleased with the result. Note that the witches must always be divided into three groups, and it would be excellent if these were 6, 6, and 6—18 in all,[6] etc. I urge you to take care in choosing the tenor to do Macduff, and all the secondary singers should be

parti. E questi pezzi concertati mi premono molto.

Non ti sò dire precisamente quando sarò a Firenze perchè voglio quì quietamente finire tutta l'opera. Stà certo che sarò là a tempo. Dispensa di mano in mano le parti dei cori e cantantanti [sic] affinchè quando io arrivo si possa con due o tre prove andare in Orchestra: poichè saranno necessarie molte prove d'Orchestra e di scena. Anzi mi spiace che chi farà la parte di Banco non voglia far l'ombra![7] E perchè?...I cantanti devono essere scritturati per cantare ed agire: d'altronde queste convenienze è tempo di abbandonarle. Sarebbe una cosa mostruosa che un'altro facesse l'ombra poichè Banco deve conservare precisamente la sua figura anchè quando è ombra. Addio Addio. Scrivimi subito...Ti ripeto che spero di mandarti presto altra musica con et...Ad[dio]. Salutami Romani intanto e le scriverò presto.

Florence: Biblioteca Nazionale;
Copialettere, 447–48 (draft)

good, because the ensembles need good ones. And these ensembles are very important to me.

I can't tell you precisely when I'll be in Florence, because I want to finish the entire opera in peace here. Rest assured that I'll be there in time. Give out the chorus and solo parts as they become ready, so that when I arrive we can start orchestra rehearsals after two or three [piano] rehearsals, for many orchestral and stage rehearsals will be necessary. Furthermore, I'm sorry to hear that the singer who will do Banquo's part doesn't want to do the Ghost as well.[7] And why not? Singers must be hired to sing and act; moreover, it's high time these "traditions" were abandoned. It would be monstrous for someone else to do Banquo's ghost, because Banquo should look exactly the same, even when he's a ghost. Farewell, farewell. Write to me immediately. I repeat that I hope to send you more music soon with etc. Farewell. In the meantime give my regards to Romani and I'll write to him soon.

1. Alessandro Sanquirico (1777–1849), celebrated scene designer and painter, active at La Scala 1805–32 (from 1817 their sole *scenografo*); also some decorations for the Duomo (1838) and various gardens and courtyards in Milan

2. Verdi first wrote "desiderio di fare qualche cosa di bello nel montare" (desire to do something beautiful in staging).

3. For a description of the *fantasmogorìa* see CONATI at 235–36.

4. Alessandro Duroni (1807–70), *cavaliere* of the SS. Maurizio e Lazzaro, scientist, patriot, optician, astronomer, physicist, inventor of the negative-positive photographic method (1853), founder of the Tecnomasio italiano (first scientific organization for optical equipment). All this comes from his "Our Founder" photo hanging in the firm's office, in the Milan Galleria. The firm was founded in 1837.

5. Francesco Hayez (1791–1882), the Italian painter, president of an artists club founded in 1845 that included Verdi, Sanquirico, Gustavo Modena, Grossi, Carlo Cattaneo, Andrea Maffei, Carcano, and the Belgiojosos (according to Carlo Castellaneta and Sergio Coradeschi, *L'opera completa di Hayez* [Milan: Rizzoli, 1971], p. 84). Member of La Scala's supervisory committee on set and costume designs.

6. The chorus (male and female) numbered 48 at the Florentine premiere, according to the 9 March 1847 issue of the *Gazzetta di Firenze*.

7. See Verdi's 22 December 1846 letter to Lanari on this point. Two points should be made here: 1) the bass in question may or may not have been Benedetti, for the assignment of Banquo's role seems to have been made rather late (see ROSEN at 303); (2) the 1847 Florence libretto lists Banquo's ghost as a separate character, giving N. N. (Anonymous) as the performer. However this may be interpreted, in the 1865 Paris production Petit certainly played Banquo dead as well as alive (see Paul Smith's review at 403).

VERDI TO PIAVE

Milan, 21 January 1847

Oh certamente tu non hai nissun torto salvo quello d'avermi trascurato in modo incredibile questi due ultimi atti. Pazienza! S. Andrea [Maffei] ha aiutato te e me; e me più ancora perchè se devo parlarti francamente, io non avrei potuto metterli in musica, e tu vedi in quale imbarazzo mi sarei trovato. Ora tutto è accomodato cambiando però quasi tutto.

Oh no indeed, you're not at fault at all—except for having taken so incredibly little trouble with these last two acts of mine. But never mind! St. Andrew [Andrea Maffei] came to your aid and to mine. Especially to mine, because—if I must be frank with you—I couldn't have put them to music, and you can see what a mess I'd have found myself in. Now every-

Manderò io il libretto a Lanari ed ora non c'è bisogno delle tue ordinazioni.

Fammi il piacere di mandare a corso di posta a Ricordi quello che ti ha chiesto, cioè l'autorizzazione di stampare etc. etc...Saluta la Loeve tanto tanto ...

Abbiati 1, 676–77

thing is fixed up, but just about everything had to be changed. I'll send the libretto to Lanari, and now there's no need for your description of the staging requirements.

Do me the favor of sending to Ricordi, by mail, what he asked you for; that is, the authorization to publish, etc. etc. Give my very best to Loewe ...

PIAVE TO GIOVANNI RICORDI

Venice, 23 January 1847

Troverete qui unita la cessione come mi chiedevate colla vostra 30 9mbre.[1] Ho voluto in essa variare una frase perchè si sappia ch'io ho scritto per commissione del M.*ro* Verdi non già di Lanari.

Ora interesso la vostra amicizia a dirmi se riceveste dallo stesso Verdi una specie di prefazione al detto libro, perchè s'egli si fosse scordato di darvela, m'affretterei io stesso a spedirvene copia poichè intendo assolutamente che la vostra edizione sia preceduta da tale mio avvertimento.

In ogni modo aspetto a posta corrente un riscontro su tale proposito, al quale io metto molta importanza ...

Milan: Archivio Ricordi

1. See his letter of 7 December 1846.

You will find here attached the cession which you requested in yours of November 30.[1] I decided to change a sentence in it to make it known that I wrote on M.° Verdi's commission and not Lanari's.

I now appeal to your kindness by asking you to let me know whether you received from Verdi a kind of preface to the said book, for if he should have forgotten to give it to you, I should myself hasten to send you a copy, since it is absolutely my intention that your publication should be preceded by this note of mine.

I await in any case, by return of post, a response on the said matter, to which I attach a great importance ...

VERDI TO LANARI

Milan, 24 January 1847

[... Macduff non è una][1] gran parte, ma è sempre un carattere importante, d'altronde ti ripeto che ha l'Aria la quale (per esempio) se fosse cantata da Guasco[2] farebbe furore.—

È inutile che ti dica che nel vestiario non vi deve essere mai nè seta nè veluto etc...

Scriverò presto a Romani, intanto pregalo pure di occuparsene che gliene sarò gratissimo come, ti ripeto, le scriverò io stesso.

P.S. Non ti dico precisamente quando sarò a Firenze perchè desidero terminare bene tutto, ma stà sicuro che tutto sarà terminato a tempo ed ch'io sarò la prima che arrivino Varesi e la Barbieri—Mi sono sempre scordato di dirti che ho ricevuto l'intero primo quartale[3]—

Ti raccomando di nuovo tutto. Cerca di far fare presto tutto, e fà in modo che tutto sia pronto anche per risparmiare a me della fatica,

[... Macduff isn't][1] a big part, but he's still an important character. Besides, as I told you, he does have that aria, which, if it were sung by, say, Guasco,[2] would cause a furor.

There's no need to tell you that there mustn't ever be any silk or velvet in the costumes, etc.

I'll write to Romani soon. Meanwhile go ahead and ask him to take care of this, and I'll be very grateful to him, as, I repeat, I'll tell him by letter myself.

P.S. I'm not telling you exactly when I'll be in Florence because I want everything to be good and finished, but rest assured that everything will be finished in time and that I'll be there before Varesi and Barbieri arrive. I keep forgetting to tell you that I've received the entire first *quartale*.[3]

Again, please take care of everything. Try to get everything done quickly, and see to it that everything is ready—also to save me exertion,

perchè tu sai che non ho salute da gettare.

Florence: Biblioteca Nazionale

because you know that I haven't any health to spare.

1. The first part of this letter is missing.
2. Carlo Guasco (1813–76) sang the leading tenor roles in the premieres of *I lombardi*, *Ernani*, and *Attila*.
3. See letter of 19 December 1846, Note 1.

VERDI TO VARESI

[*Milan, c.23–30 January 1847*]

Ecco l'Atto terzo che, come vedrai, è riuscito meno faticoso di quello che credeva—La scena rappresenta una caverna in cui le streghe fanno i loro stregamenti in un coro: poscia tu entri ad interrogarle in un breve Recitativo poscia vengono le apparizione [*sic*] in cui tu non hai che poche parole ma, come attore, accompagnerai tutto colle controscene—Poscia tu hai il cantabile quando ti si presentano gli otto Re: in principio èspezzato per accompagnare le apparizioni: ma poscia c'è un cantabile (*sui generis*) in cui tu devi trarre molto effetto: è inutile che ti dica che un effetto c'è sulle parole (*muori fatal progenie*) poi un altro in ultimo sulle parole (*Ah che non hai tu vita*) questo passo c'è in due maniere fallo come ti vien meglio e scrivimi quale debbo istromentare—

La cabaletta[1] te la raccomando: osservala bene: non ha la forma comune perchè dopo tutto il precedente una cabaletta colle solite forme e coi soliti ritornelli riesciva triviale. Io ne aveva fatto un'altra che mi piaceva quando la provavo isolatamente, quando la univo a tutto quello che precedeva mi riesciva intollerabile. Questa m'accomoda assai e spero accomoderà a te pure. Bada bene che non va troppo presto ma piuttosto grandiosa. Dopo la cadenza c'è una frase

Here's Act III and, as you'll see, it turned out to be less tiring than I had thought. The setting is a cavern where the witches carry out their witcheries in a chorus; then you come in to question them in a brief recitative. Then come the apparitions, during which you have but few words, but, as an actor, you'll accompany everything with your by-play. Then you have the cantabile when the eight kings appear before you; at first it is broken up, to accompany the apparitions, but then there is a cantabile sui generis with which you have to make a big effect. I don't need to tell you that there is one effect on the words "muori fatal progenie," and then another on the words "Ah che non hai tu vita." There are two versions of this passage; do the one that suits you best, and write to tell me which one I should orchestrate.

I urge you to pay special attention to the *cabaletta;*[1] mark it well; it isn't in the usual form, because, after all that has gone before, a *cabaletta* in the usual mold and with usual ritornelli would sound trivial. I'd made another one that I liked when I tried it out by itself, but when I joined it to all that went before, I found it unbearable. This one suits me fine, and I hope it will suit you too. Note that it shouldn't be too quick, but, rather, grandiose. After the cadenza there's a phrase

la quale desidero quasi saltellante e sotto voce riserbando tutta la forza al maggiore che vien dopo

which I'd like done in an almost bouncy manner and sotto voce, reserving full force for the major-mode section that follows

e qui si può un poco stringere.

Spero che avarai ricevuto anche il primo Atto: dopo avrai ricevuto questa scrivimi subito: Sono persuaso che la tessitura ti va bene, ma forse ti potrebbe essere qualche nota qualche passo incomodo e scrivimi prima che io istromenti.

and here it can go a little faster.

I hope that you have received the first act too; after you have received this [letter], write to me at once. I'm convinced that the tessitura suits you well; but there could be some notes or passages that are uncomfortable for you, so write to me before I orchestrate.

Ora non manca che l'ultima scena la quale consite per te in un Adagio[2] quieto cantabile, ed in una morte brevissima: ma non sarà una di quelle morti solite, sdolcinate etc... Tu capisci bene che *Macbetto* non deve morire come muojono *Edgardo*[3] e simili—

In somma bada alle parole, ed al sogetto: io non cerco altro: Il sogetto è bello, le parole anche etc...

> Siena: Archivio dell'Accademia Chigiana;
> *Nuova Antologia* 281 (1932), 438;
> *Abbiati* 1, 661–62

All that's missing now is the last scene, which for you consists of an *adagio*,[2] quiet and cantabile, and a very brief death scene—but it won't be one of those usual death scenes, oversweet, etc. You'll well understand that *Macbeth* shouldn't die as *Edgardo*[3] and *his like* do.

In short, pay attention to the words, and to the subject—that's all I ask. The subject is beautiful, and so are the words, etc.

1. The text of this *cabaletta,* "Vada in fiamme," appears at 504–8.

2. "Pietà, rispetto ..."

3. In Donizetti's *Lucia*

MUZIO TO BAREZZI

Milan, 28 January 1847

... Stamattina poi, quando ha ricevuto la Sua lettera e quella di Giovannino, ha detto che sono gente che hanno paura di un po' di neve e di ghiaccio. Essi sono sani, robusti, forti, con uno stomaco di ferro, ed hanno paura di un po' di neve, mentre io (diceva il signor Maestro) da qui a quindici giorni dovrò andare a Firenze anche se venissero dei fulmini, e passare gli Apennini coperti di neve, col pericolo di essere coperto da una qualche frana di monte, come nel ritorno che feci da Roma.[1] Essi se la godono; io lavoro dalla mattina alle 8 fino alle 12 di notte, e mi consumo la vita nel lavorare. Che destino perfido che è il mio! Queste ed altre cose diceva il signor Maestro, che non me le sono tenute tutte in mente. Ma credo che quello che non han fatto lo faranno ed andranno a trovarlo a Firenze.

Domenica il signor Maestro avrà finita tutta l'opera e lunedì incomincerà ad istrumentare e finita l'istrumentazione[2] andrà a Firenze.

La musica del *Macbeth* è immensamente bella. Non v'è un pezzo scadente, tutti sono belli. I tempi di mezzo, le stesse parti accessorie sono riuscite bellissime. Io credo che nessuno può fare della musica più bella di quella del *Macbeth*. Se l'effetto della *mise en scène* è bello, non vi è sicuramente in nessun'opera moderna uno spettacolo sì grandioso e solenne ...

> *Garibaldi*, 308–9

... Then this morning, when [Verdi] received your letter and Giovannino's [announcing that they were not coming to Milan after all] he said that you're people who are afraid of a little snow and ice. They're healthy, robust, strong, with iron stomachs—and they're afraid of a bit of snow; while I (the Maestro said) have to go to Florence in two weeks, even if there's thunder and lightning, and I have to cross the Apennines, which are covered with snow, and risk being buried in some avalanche, as when I returned from Rome.[1] They enjoy life—I work from 8 in the morning to midnight, and use up my life with work. What a horrible destiny is mine! The Maestro said these and other things—I can't remember them all. But I believe that you *will* do what you *didn't* do, and you'll come to see him in Florence.

By Sunday [January 31] the Maestro will have finished the entire opera, and Monday he'll begin the orchestration, and once the orchestration is finished,[2] he'll go to Florence.

The music of *Macbeth* is immensely beautiful. There isn't one inferior piece; they're all beautiful. The *tempi di mezzo*, even the subsidiary parts, have turned out beautifully. I don't believe anyone can compose more beautiful music than that of *Macbeth*. If the mise-en-scène makes a good effect, then there surely won't be such a grand and solemn spectacle in any other modern opera ...

1. The reference is probably to the return trip to Milan after Verdi supervised the production of *I due Foscari* at the Teatro Argentina in November 1844.

2. Verdi regarded composition and orchestration as separate processes; see pp. 210–11 and 227. He preferred (according to Ricordi's letter of 16 November 1846) to have the orchestral material prepared in Milan.

PIAVE TO GIOVANNI RICORDI

Venice, 28 January 1847

Eccovi caro Ricordi la dichiarazione firmata, e scusatemi se mi scordai di mandarla prima in carta bollata.

Troverete anche qui unita la prefazione che vi prego di far tenere anche a Lanari, perchè sia pure preposta all'edizione fiorentina, e sono certo che voi non lascierete poi d'inserirla nella vostra. Ciò è indispensabile alla piena intelligenza della nostra riduzione. Addio. Non dubitate che mi farete tenere qualche copia di questo mio libretto ...

Ai Lettori

Edoardo il Confessore teneva il trono d'Inghilterra, quando verso la metà dell'undecimo secolo il buon re Duncano a quello ascendeva di Scozia. Difficili volgevano i tempi, poichè Scozia era internamente commossa dalle rivolte de' turbolenti suoi thani (baroni), ed assalita frequentemente ai confini da' popoli di Danimarca e Norvegia. Trovandosi re Duncano incapace a sedare e respingere cotesti interni e stranieri nemici, affidonne a Macbet, suo valoroso capitano, la cura. Costui, secondato da Banco, raggiunse l'intento, e, non pago degli onori e delle ricompense dal re suo impartitegli, osò aspirare alla regal potestà. A tanto lo incoraggivano le scozzesi leggi, portanti, che ove il re morto fosse senza lasciar figli maggiori, passar dovea la corona sul capo del più prossimo parente. Macbet era tale, e Duncano già vecchio non avea che due teneri figli, Malcolmo e Sivardo. Camminavano su tal piede le cose, quando Duncano con regale decreto si nominò il primogenito suo Malcolmo a successore. Macbet allora, che così svanir vedeva ogni sua legittima speranza alla successione, sdegnatosene, pensò ottener col delitto quello che più pervenire non gli poteva per giustizia; tramò co' thani amici suoi, tra' quali erano Banco e Macduffo, ed una notte che re Duncano nell'anno settimo del suo regno, venuto era ospite in Ivernesso, castello di lui, spintovi anche dall'ambiziosa moglie, lo trucidò. Malcolmo rifuggì in Inghilterra presso Edoardo, Sivardo in Irlanda, e Macbet, corso a Scona, vi si fece coronare re di Scozia. Poichè egli ebbe lo scettro, si diede a sostenere con ogni guisa di vessazioni la sua usurpazione, e, sospettando perfino de' propri complici, trucidar fece Banco, e perchè Macduffo riuscito era a fuggirgli, ne fece perire i figli e la moglie. In tal guisa regnò ben 17 anni, alla fine de' quali, Malcolmo, ottenuti dal re Edoardo 10000 soldati inglesi, secondato dai thani istigati da Macduffo, e dalle popolazioni scozzesi stanche della tirannica oppressione di Macbet, lo vinse, lo uccise, e ricuperò il trono avito.

Questa è la storia. Le cronache poi e le nazionali tradizioni, da cui l'immortale Shakspeare [ha] tolto il

Here, dear Ricordi, you have the signed declaration, and forgive me if I forgot to send it sooner on *carta bollata* [officially-stamped paper].

You will also find herewith attached the preface which I ask you also to let Lanari have, so that it can also be placed at the front of the Florence edition, and I am sure you will not fail to insert it in your own. It is indispensable for a full understanding of our treatment [of Shakespeare's play]. Farewell. Doubtless you will let me have some copies of this libretto of mine ...

To the Readers

Edward the Confessor was on the throne of England when, toward the middle of the eleventh century, good King Duncan ascended that of Scotland. Times were difficult, because Scotland was internally racked by the revolts of its turbulent thanes (barons) and frequently assailed on its borders by the peoples of Denmark and Norway. King Duncan, finding himself incapable of quelling and rebuffing these internal and foreign enemies, entrusted the task to Macbeth, his valorous captain. The latter, seconded by Banquo, attained the objective and, not satisfied with the honors and rewards imparted to him by his king, dared to aspire to the royal power. To this aspiration the Scottish laws lent support, for they stipulated that, if the King should die leaving no sons of age, the crown should pass to the next of kin. Macbeth was that, and Duncan, being of an advanced age, had but two young children, Malcolm and Siward. Matters were at this stage when Duncan, by royal decree, named his firstborn, Malcolm, as his successor. Then Macbeth, who thus saw his every legitimate hope for the succession vanish, waxed indignant and decided to obtain criminally that which would no longer become his by law; he conspired with the thanes his friends, among whom were Banquo and Macduff, and one night, when King Duncan, in the seventh year of his reign, was a guest at Inverness, Macbeth's castle, Macbeth, impelled to it also by his ambitious wife, murdered him. Malcolm fled into England, to Edward, Siward into Ireland, and Macbeth, having hastened to Scone, had himself crowned there as King of Scotland. Once the scepter was his, he took to upholding his usurpation with all manner of harassment, and, having become suspicious even of his accomplices, he had Banquo murdered; and, as Macduff had succeeded in escaping him, he had his children and wife killed. In this wise he reigned for all of 17 years, at the end of which Malcolm, having obtained from King Edward 10,000 English soldiers, with the support of the thanes incited by Macduff and of the Scottish peoples weary of Macbeth's tyrannous oppression, conquered him, killed him, and recovered the hereditary throne.

So much is history. The later chronicles and national traditions, from which the immortal Shake-

soggetto della presente tragedia che ho ardito a ridurre a melodrammatica forma, accompagnano cotesti fatti con istrane e favolose circostanze, quali sono quelle delle streghe. "Shakspeare, egregiamente dice il chiarissimo G. Niccolini,[1] fece delle streghe tante ministre d'inferno in una impresa ordinata al sacrificio dell'innocenza e alla rovina dello stesso colpevole; venendo così a salvare in qualche modo l'onore della specie umana, e riducendo ne' termini del terribile ciò che altrimenti sarebbe stato orrendo e insopportabile, e diede grandezza e solennità ad un'azione per sè stessa non altro che atroce."

Siccome poi egli scriveva a' tempi di Giacomo I, discendente di Banco, così si è compiaciuto farlo vedere innocente, mentre le storie ce lo addimostrano correo dell'usurpatore Macbetto.

Tanto m'era duopo ricordare ai lettori per la più facile intelligenza del presente lavoro.

Milan: Archivio Ricordi

speare derived the subject of the present tragedy, which I have been so bold as to arrange in operatic form, accompany these facts with strange and fabulous circumstances, such as those of the witches. "Shakespeare," as the celebrated G. Nicolini[1] so admirably says, "made the witches ministers of Hell in an enterprise destined to sacrifice innocence and ruin the guilty one himself; thus managing somehow to save the honor of the human race, and reducing within the bounds of the terrible what would otherwise have been ghastly and unbearable, and lending grandeur and solemnity to an action which, of itself, was only atrocious."

Since, besides, he was writing in the days of James I, Banquo's descendant, he therefore was pleased to portray him innocent, whereas the histories prove he was an accomplice of the usurper Macbeth.

This much it was incumbent upon me to bring to the reader's attention for his better understanding of the present work.

---

1. For Niccolini [*recte* Nicolini] see WEAVER and PORTER at 146 and 351–52, respectively. Piave's citation from Nicolini's preface is essentially accurate, although he joins two sentences into one ("venendo così" for "E così venne") and changes "orribile" to "orrendo." As DEGRADA has noted (at 156n), Piave has drawn extensively from Nicolini's "Notizia ai lettori" in preparing this prefatory note.

VERDI TO BARBIERI-NINI   *Milan, 31 January 1847*

Le spedisco li altri pezzi del Macbet; ora a completare la sua parte non manca che una sola cabaletta la quale gliela farò a Firenze onde le sia perfettamente nelle sue corde e di sicuro effetto—

Dalla sua lettera ho visto quanto Ella desidererebbe un cantabile in genere di quello della *Fausta*.[1] Ma osservi un po' bene il carattere di questa parte e vedrà che senza tradirlo e far guerra apertamente al buon senso non si potrebbe fare. D'altronde sarebbe una profanazione alterare un carattere così grande, così energico, così originale come si è questo creato dal gran tragico Inglese. Credo di averglielo detto altra volta questo è un dramma che non ha nulla di comune cogli altri, e tutti dobbiamo fare ogni sforzo per renderlo nel modo più originale possibile. Io credo poi che sia ormai tempo di abbandonare le formule solite, ed i soliti modi, e credo che se ne possa trarre un maggior partito, con Lei poi che ha tanti mezzi.

In quanto alla lettera è impossibile levarla perchè sù questa ha fondamento il dramma, ma se a Lei rincresce recitarla la metteremo in musica.[2]

I am sending you the other numbers of *Macbeth*; now all that is needed to complete your part is a *cabaletta* ["Trionfai"], which I shall write for you in Florence so that it will suit your voice perfectly and be sure to make an effect.

From your letter, I saw how much you would have wanted a cantabile of the type in *Fausta*.[1] But observe well the character of this role and you will see that that could not be done without betraying it, and declaring open warfare on good sense. Moreover, it would be a profanation to alter a character so great, so energetic, so original as this one created by the great English tragedian. I believe I told you already that this is a drama that has nothing in common with the others, and we must all make every effort to render it in the most original way possible. Furthermore, I believe that it is high time to abandon the usual formulas and the usual procedures, and I think that by doing so one could make much more of it—especially with you who have so many resources.

As for the letter, it is impossible to take it out, because the drama is built upon it, but if it would displease you to speak it, we shall set it to music.[2]

Le raccomando questi due pezzi: le note sono semplici, e sono fatte per la scena; sopratutto la scena del Sonna[m]bulismo che come posizione drammatica è una delle più alte creazioni teatrali;[3] badi bene che ogni parola ha un significato, e che bisogna assolutamente esprimerlo e col canto e coll'azione. Tutto và detto sotto voce ed in modo da incutere terrore e pietà. La studij bene e vedrà che le farà effetto se anche non ha uno di quei canti filati, e soliti, che si riscontrano dappertutto e che tutti si somigliano—

In questi pezzi e nelli altri ricevuti mi sappia dire se c'è qualche nota incomoda prima che io li istromenti. Nel brindisi c'è un passo a due maniere; mi dica quale le stà meglio[4]—In questo Duetto nel Adagio 3/8 in fine c'è una scala semitonata

Let me stress the importance of these two pieces. The notes are simple and created with the action in mind, especially in the sleepwalking scene, which, so far as the dramatic situation is concerned, is one of the most sublime theatrical creations.[3] Bear in mind that every word has a meaning, and that it is absolutely essential to express it both with the voice and with the acting. Everything is to be said sotto voce and in such a way as to arouse terror and pity. Study it well and you will see that you can make an effect with it, even if it lacks one of those flowing, conventional melodies, which are found everywhere and which are all alike.

Let me know if there are any uncomfortable notes in these numbers, as well as in those you have already received, before I orchestrate them. In the *brindisi* there is a passage written in two ways; tell me which suits you better.[4] In the 3/8 *adagio* of this duet there is a chromatic scale at the end:

bisogna dirla rallentando e terminare in un pianissimo: se questa Le riescisse difficile me lo sappia dire—[5]

Il Sonnambulismo va molto adagio—Mi favorisca dirmi quando sarà a Firenze. Le raccomando poi di venire là colla parte quasi a memoria perchè desidero fare poche prove di cembalo e molte di scena e d'Orchestra.

Probabilmente io verrò a riverirla prima a Parma; ma in ogni modo mi scriva intorno la cosa che ho domandato.

Con tutta la stima mi dico

it must be sung rallentando and end in a pianissimo; if this proves difficult for you, let me know.[5]

The sleepwalking scene goes very slowly. Please tell me when you will be in Florence. I urge you, moreover, to come with the part almost memorized, because I want to have few piano rehearsals and many stage and orchestral ones.

I shall probably come to pay my respects to you in Parma before then, but, in any case, write to me about what I have asked.

With the greatest esteem I remain

Suo Ammiratore ed Amico

Your admirer and friend

Photostat in the Istituto di Studi Verdiani, Parma; J. A. Stargardt, Catalogue 606 (1975), No. 867 [original, Max Reis, Zurich]; published in *Musica: Settimanale di Cultura e di Cronaca* [Rome], 23 November 1911 [*recte* 1913]

1. Opera by Donizetti (1832). The cantabile in question is probably Fausta's death scene ("Tu che voli già spirto beato"), a famous excerpt, and in the 1830s, incorporated into many other scores. Tadolini made a furor with it at La Scala in 1841. See Guglielmo Barblan, *L'opera di Donizetti nell'età romantica* (Bergamo, 1948), pp. 62–63 (musical examples 20–21).

2. Verdi did not set it to music, but according to Casamorata (pp. 387–88n), Barbieri-Nini sang the lines anyway.

3. Twenty years later, after reading some of the French critics' reviews of *Don Carlos*, Verdi wrote: "Infine sono un wagneriano quasi perfetto. Ma se i critici avessero fatto un po' più d'attenzione avrebbero visto che le stesse intenzioni vi sono nel terzetto dell'*Ernani*, nel Sonnambulismo del *Macbet* ed in tanti altri pezzi etc. etc..." ("So in the final analysis, I'm a near-perfect Wagnerian. But if the critics had paid a bit more attention, they would have seen that the same goals are to be found in the final trio of *Ernani*, in the sleepwalking scene in *Macbeth*, and in

many other pieces, etc. etc...") 1 April 1867 letter to L. Escudier, in *Abbiati* 3, 131–132

4. See LAWTON at 222.

5. This passage was replaced, but only after Verdi had scored it. See LAWTON and DEGRADA at 223–25 and 170–71 respectively.

VERDI TO VARESI   [*Milan,*] *4 February 1847*

Sono sorpreso che tu non abbia mai risposto a due mie lettere le quali accompagnavano sempre qualche pezzo del Macbet. Ora eccoti l'ultimo pezzo che tu farai trascrivere in largo da un copista per poterlo studiare e così avrai tutta la parte:[1] mi raccomando di impararla bene prima d'essere a Firenze onde poter far subito prove di scena.—Questa scena finale la metto nelle tue mani. C'è un Adagio in *re b.* che bisogna miniarlo cantabile ed affettuoso— Nell'intermezzo i versi

> *La vita!...che importa!*
> *È il racconto d'un povero idiota:*
> *Vento e suono che nulla dinota*

Ti raccomando di dirli con tutta l'ironia e lo sprezzo possibile—Dalla morte[2] potrai trarre molto partito se unita, al canto, farai l'azione ragionata. Tu capirai benissimo che *Macbet* non deve morire come *Edgardo, Gennaro,*[3] etc... quindi bisogna trattarla in un modo nuovo—Sia patetica, ma più che patetica, terribile. Tutta sotto voce, ad eccezione dei due ultimi versi chè anzi qui l'accompagnerai anche coll'azione prorompendo con tutta forza sulle parole... *Vil...corona...e sol per te!...*Tu sei (già s'intende) per terra, ma in quest'ultimo verso ti solleverai quasi ritto nella persona e fare tutto l'effetto possibile...Addio...Sia presto a Firenze e colla parte a memoria.

Siena: Archivio dell'Accademia Chigiana;
Nuova Antologia 281 (1932), 438–39

I'm surprised that you've never answered two of my letters, which I sent along with the numbers from *Macbeth*. Now here's the last piece for you. Have a copyist write it out in full so that you can study it, and then you'll have your entire part.[1] I urge you to learn it well before arriving in Florence, so that you can go straight into stage rehearsals. This final scene I put into your hands. There's an *adagio* in D flat, every detail of which needs coloring, cantabile and *affettuoso*. As for the lines in the intervening passage

> *Life!...What does it matter!*
> *'Tis a tale told by a poor idiot:*
> *Wind and sound, signifying nothing*

I want you to declaim them with all the irony and contempt possible. You'll be able to make much of the death scene[2] if, together with your singing, your acting is well thought out. You can see very well that Macbeth mustn't die like Edgardo, Gennaro,[3] etc., therefore it has to be treated in a new way. It should be affecting, yes; but more than affecting, it should be *terribile*. All of it sotto voce, except for the last two lines, which, in fact, you'll also accompany with acting, bursting out with full force on the words "Vile...crown...and only for you!..." You're on the ground, of course, but for this last line you'll stand almost straight up and will make as great an impression as possible. Farewell. Be in Florence soon and with your part memorized.

1. Verdi enclosed three pages, headed "Scena Aria e Morte di Macbet," vocal line and bass (with a few cues) for all of Macbeth's role in Act IV. See overleaf for a facsimile.

2. This scene is reproduced in "Selected Passages from the 1847 Version," at 517–19.

3. In Donizetti's *Lucia di Lammermoor* (1835) and *Lucrezia Borgia* (1833)

VERDI TO PIAVE   *Milan, 14 February 1847*

Sono contento che tu abbi capito la cosa pel suo verso. T'assicuro ch'io non vorrei il tuo dramma per tutto l'oro del mondo. Parto domani! Addio! Ho molto da fare. Addio.

Abbiati 1, 680

I'm glad that you've understood things for what they are. I assure you that I wouldn't take your drama for all the gold in the world. I'm leaving tomorrow! Farewell! I have a lot to do. Farewell.

The first page of Macbeth's final scenes, vocal line and bass, sent by Verdi to Varesi on 4 February 1847

VERDI TO LANARI

Florence, [c.18 February 1847]

Eccomi in Firenze—

Spero che jeri avrai ricevuta l'ultima mia in cui ti ringraziavo delle gentili offerte fattemi di alloggiare in casa tua: io sono in compagnia[1] e non posso approfittarne, ma sii però certo che te ne sono grato egualmente.

Più tardi io verrò da te; ma se adesso mi potessi mandare qualcuno dei tuoi, tu mi faresti cosa grata, perchè ho bisogno di diverse istru-

Here I am in Florence.

I hope yesterday you received my last letter in which I thanked you for your kind offer to put me up in your house; I'm in company[1] and can't take advantage of it, but rest assured that I am grateful just the same.

I'll come to see you later, but if you could send me one of your people now, you would be doing me a favor because I need various pieces

zioni: quale albergo mi convenga scegliere per alloggiare e che sia comodo anche pel teatro.— Addio! a rivederci più tardi.

of information: which hotel I should choose to stay at, one that would be convenient for the theatre. Good-bye! I'll see you later.

Florence: Biblioteca Nazionale;
Copialettere, 449

1. Although Giuseppina Strepponi was in Florence at the time of the *Macbeth* premiere, the reference here is merely to Muzio, with whom Verdi shared an apartment—see Muzio's letter of 25 February 1847.

VERDI TO CLARA MAFFEI

Florence, 20 February 1847

Sono qui da Giovedì mattina, e non le ho scritto jeri perchè non era giorno di posta. Ho fatto un viaggio felicissimo e stò bene anzi stò meglio, perchè come mi succede sempre il viaggiare mi giova.

Jeri ho dato all'ingrosso un'occhiata a Firenze che mi piace assai. La preferisco a tutte le città d'Italia salvo Roma. Oh è pur bella questa nostra Italia!...

Il Macbeth andrà in scena piuttosto tardi. Intanto si fà la Sonnambula, poi si rifanno alcune recite dell'Attila indi il Macbeth.

No ho ancora visto nissuno delle mie conoscenze, nè ho ancora fatte visite, ma oggi andrò ...

P.S. ... Ho visto con gran giubilo a Piacenza i miei parenti ed ho passato tre ore felicemente.[1] Emanuele è fuor di sè dalla gioja ...

Quartetto Milanese Ottocentesco, 71

I've been here since Thursday morning [February 18], and I didn't write to you yesterday because it wasn't a mail day. I had a very pleasant trip, and I'm well—in fact, I'm better— because, as is always the case with me, traveling does me good.

Yesterday I had a general look at Florence, which I like very much. I like it best of all the cities of Italy, except for Rome. Oh, this Italy of ours is indeed beautiful!...

Macbeth will be produced rather late in the season. In the meantime they're doing *Sonnambula*, then there will be a few more performances of *Attila*, and afterwards *Macbeth*.

I haven't seen any of my acquaintances yet, nor have I made any visits; but today I shall ...

P.S. ... At Piacenza I saw my relations with great delight, and I spent three happy hours.[1] Emanuele is beside himself with joy ...

1. Verdi had Uttini and Carotti relations living in Piacenza, which he passed through on his journey to Florence.

STREPPONI TO LUCCA

Paris, 23 February 1847

... Li Escudier sono ancora colla bocca aperta e la *Lunette* appiccicata all'occhio incerti se leggano bene o male, la cifra che avete domandata pei Masnadieri (10/m franchi!!). Tanto più sono meravigliati di tale domanda, inquantochè tutte le opere di Verdi comperate da Ricordi, non oltrepassano la somma di tremila franchi cadauna, non eccettuato il Macbet, che ha tutte le probabilità di una gran riuscita in Italia, ed è uno dei soggetti più adatti alla scena Francese ...

Brescia: Biblioteca Queriniana;
Carteggi Verdiani 4, 252–53

... The Escudiers are still open-mouthed with their lorgnettes pressed to their eyes, uncertain whether they are reading rightly or wrongly the amount that you've asked for *Masnadieri* (10 thousand francs!!). They are all the more astonished at such a demand since none of Verdi's operas bought by Ricordi go over the sum of three thousand francs each—not excepting *Macbeth*, which has every probability of being a great success in Italy, and is one of the subjects that's best suited to the French stage ...

MUZIO TO BAREZZI

Florence, 25 February 1847

Ieri sera è arrivata la Barbieri. Oggi le prove dell'*Attila*, che anderà in scena domenica. Il Maestro non vuole assistere a nessuna prova e

Barbieri arrived yesterday evening. Today the rehearsals for *Attila*, which goes on on Sunday [February 28]. The Maestro doesn't want to

invece me ne ha dato a me l'incarico. Sabbato poi incominceranno le prime prove di cembalo del *Macbeth*. Nella settimana ventura forse gli potrò scrivere il giorno preciso che anderà in scena. Si ricordi che lo aspettiamo con Giovannino il quale è desiderato da alcuni suoi conoscenti. Noi alloggiamo alla *Pensione Svizzera*, ove abbiamo un magnifico appartamento, con aria di paradiso, ed *una tavola da re;*[1] e ci pensi a pagare il Maestro..., cioè l'impresario.

Il dirle che il Maestro è idolatrato, cercato e ricercato da tutti è cosa che Egli se la sarà di già immaginata. Gli uomini più celebri hanno desiderato di conoscerlo; Niccolini, Giusti, Bartolini, Dupré, ecc.;[2] e perfino il Gran Duca lo ha mandato ad invitare di andare da Lui, e ieri sera ci è andato un po' malvolentieri. Il Gran Duca gli ha saputo raccontare tutta la sua vita. Financo che non lo volevano a Busseto. Insomma egli sapeva tutto.

Si ricordi che presto li aspettiamo. Lunedì Le scriverò l'esito dell'*Attila*.

Garibaldi, 311

attend any of the rehearsals and instead has given me the job. Then Saturday [February 27], the first piano rehearsals for *Macbeth* begin. Maybe next week I'll be able to write you the exact date that it goes on stage. Remember that we are expecting you, along with Giovannino [Barezzi]—some of his acquaintances want to see him. We are staying at the Pensione Svizzera, where we have a magnificent apartment—it seems like paradise—and *food fit for a king.*[1] And the Maestro is taking care of the bill... that's to say, the impresario is.

To tell you that the Maestro is idolized, in demand over and over again by everyone, is something you've probably already imagined. The most celebrated men have wanted to meet him; Niccolini, Giusti, Bartolini, Dupré, etc.;[2] even the Grand Duke sent him an invitation to visit Him, and yesterday evening he went, somewhat unwillingly. The Grand Duke was able to narrate his [Verdi's] entire life to him. Even the fact that in Busseto they didn't want him. In short, he knew everything.

Remember that we expect you soon. Monday I'll write you about the reception of *Attila*.

1. The Hôtel Suisse was situated on the corner of the Via Strozzi and the Via della Vigna Nouva. There is a plate of it in de Angelis, *Le carte,* following p. 94.

2. Giovan Battista Niccolini (1782–1861), Florentine playwright, historian, essayist, and ardent republican. For the poet Giuseppe Giusti and the sculptor Giovanni Dupré, PERSONALIA. Giuseppina's son Camillo was apprenticed to the sculptor Lorenzo Bartolini; see MATZ at 130. In connection with Verdi's round of visits, see the excerpt from Dupré's memoirs, which follows.

FROM GIOVANNI DUPRÉ'S MEMOIRS

In quel tempo venne a Firenze Giuseppe Verdi per mettere in scena il *Macbeth*. Se non isbaglio, era la prima volta ch'ei veniva fra noi; la sua fama lo aveva preceduto; nemici, com'è naturale, ne aveva dimolti; io era partigiano dei suoi lavori allora conosciuti, il *Nabucco*, i *Lombardi*, l'*Ernani* e la *Giovanna D'Arco*. I nemici suoi dicevano che come artista era volgarissimo e corruttore del bel canto italiano, e come uomo lo dicevano un orso addirittura, pieno d'alterigia e d'orgoglio, e che sdegnava di avvicinarsi a chicchessia. Volli convincermene subito; scrissi un biglietto in questi termini: "Giovanni Dupré pregherebbe il chiarissimo maestro G. Verdi di volersi degnare a tutto suo comodo di recarsi al suo Studio, ove sta ultimando in marmo il *Caino*, e desidererebbe mostrarglielo prima di spedirlo."—Ma per vedere fino a che punto era orso, volli portar la lettera io stesso e presentarmi come un giovane di Studio del professore.

At that time, Giuseppe Verdi came to Florence to stage *Macbeth*. If I am not wrong, this was the first time that he had visited us. His fame had preceded him. Naturally, he had enemies in plenty; I was a champion of the works of his already known—*Nabucco, I lombardi, Ernani,* and *Giovanna d'Arco*. His enemies declared that as an artist he was very vulgar, and a corrupter of Italian bel canto, and as a man they declared him a veritable bear, filled with arrogance and pride, one who kept himself aloof from everyone. I wanted to find out the truth at once; I wrote a note as follows: "Giovanni Dupré would like to request the eminent Maestro G. Verdi to deign at his convenience to visit his studio, where he is bringing to completion a marble statue of *Cain,* and he would like to show it to him before dispatching it." But to see just how much of a bear he was, I decided to deliver the letter myself and present myself as a

M'accolse con molta urbanità, lesse la lettera, e poi con volto nè ridente nè serio mi disse:

—Dica al professore che lo ringrazio molto, e il più presto che mi sarà possibile andrò a trovarlo, giacchè io avevo in mente di conoscere personalmente un giovane scultore, che...ec.—

Risposi:—Se Ella, signor maestro, ha voglia di conoscere il più presto possibile quel giovane scultore, può soddisfarsi subito, giacchè sono io.—

Sorrise piacevolmente, e stringendomi la mano disse:—Oh! questa è proprio da artista.—

Parlammo a lungo, e mi mostrò alcune lettere di presentazione ch'egli aveva pel Capponi, pel Giusti e pel Niccolini; quella pel Giusti era del Manzoni.[1] Tutto il tempo ch'egli restò in Firenze ci vedemmo quasi ogni giorno; facemmo qualche gitarella nei dintorni, come a dire alla Fabbrica Ginori, a Fiesole e alla Torre del Gallo. Eravamo una brigatella di quattro o cinque: Andrea Maffei, il Manara che poi morì a Roma, Giulio Piatti,[2] il Verdi ed io; la sera ei ci permetteva di andare or l'uno or l'altro alle prove del *Macbeth;* la mattina spessissimo egli e il Maffei venivano al mio Studio. Gustava assaissimo la pittura e la scultura, e ne parlava con acume non ordinario; preferiva singolarmente Michelangelo . . .

Del mio *Caino* parve contento; quella fierezza quasi selvaggia gli andava a sangue, e mi ricordo che il Maffei si studiava persuaderlo che dalla tragedia *Il Caino* del Byron, che appunto in quel tempo ei traduceva, potea levarsi un dramma di molto effetto per le situazioni e i contrapposti, nei quali il genio e l'indole del Verdi amano spaziare.[3]

Giovanni Dupré: Pensieri sull'arte e ricordi autobiografici (Florence: successori Le Monnier, 1879), 166–68

young man from the professor's studio. He welcomed me most politely, read the letter, and then, with an expression neither smiling nor serious, he said to me:

"Tell the professor that I am most grateful and that I will come to visit him as soon as possible, for I had intended to make the personal acquaintance of a young sculptor who ...etc."

I replied: "Signor Maestro, if you have a wish to make that young sculptor's acquaintance as soon as possible, you may gratify it at once, for I am he."

He gave a pleasant smile, and clasping my hand said: "Oh! You managed that like a true artist."

We spoke for a long time, and he showed me some letters of introduction he had to Capponi, Giusti, and Niccolini; the one for Giusti was from Manzoni.[1] All the time he remained in Florence we saw one another almost every day; we made some excursions into the surrounding country, for example to the Ginori factory, to Fiesole, and to Torre del Gallo. We were a band of four or five: Andrea Maffei, Manara (who later died in Rome), Giulio Piatti,[2] Verdi, and I; in the evenings he allowed one or another of us to attend the *Macbeth* rehearsals; in the mornings he and Maffei very often came to my studio. He was extremely fond of painting and sculpture and spoke about them with uncommon acuteness; he especially favored Michelangelo . . .

He seemed pleased with my *Cain;* that almost savage pride stirred him, and I recall that Maffei tried to persuade him that from Byron's tragedy *Cain,* which in fact he was translating at that time, a drama could be drawn that would be very effective because of situations and contrasts such as Verdi's genius and natural disposition loved to explore.[3]

1. See the following item.
2. For Piatti see MATZ at 132 and 135–36.
3. *Caino* appears in the list of possible subjects for operas that Verdi drew up (*Copialettere,* Plate XI).

ALESSANDRO MANZONI TO GIUSEPPE GIUSTI   [*Milan, February 1847*]

Caro Geppino,

Due versi, e inutili. Il Sig.ʳ Maestro Verdi desidera, e qui ha ragione, ma con moltissimi, di conoscerti, e s'immagina, e qui ha torto, d'aver

Dear Geppino,

Two lines, and useless ones. Maestro Verdi wishes, and in this he is right, but along with very many others, to make your acquaintance;

bisogno d'esserti raccomandato. Ma non saranno affatto inutili, perchè ti richiameranno alla memoria

Il tuo Sandro

Leghorn: Biblioteca Labroconiana

and he imagines, and in this he is wrong, that he needs a recommendation to you. But the lines will not be altogether pointless since they will recall to you

Your Sandro

GIULIO CARCANO TO ANDREA MAFFEI

Milan, 27 February 1847

... Vorrei invece scriverti qualche novità; ma in questa nostra pettegola Milano c'è ben poco di nuovo; e ho detto pettegola, perchè le ciancie le più ridicole sono moneta corrente. Ieri in un palco mi venne domandato se fosse vero ch'io avessi scritto una parte del *Macbeth*. Che sciocchi! ho dovuto protestare che non c'era sillaba del mio, e ch'io non feci altro che parlare di questa tragedia coll'amico Verdi.[1] Il quale, chi sa che non potesse prendersela anche con me, perchè gli oziosi vanno a dire la prima cosa che loro viene in mente! ...

Opere complete di Giulio Carcano, (Milan, 2nd ed., 1896) 10, 37

... Instead, I wish I could send you some news, but in this gossipy Milan of ours, there is very little that's new, and I say "gossipy" because the most ridiculous tittle-tattle is accepted at face value. Yesterday in a box [at the theater] I was asked if it was true that I had written a part of *Macbeth*. What fools! I had to protest that there wasn't one syllable of mine, and that I didn't do anything besides discuss this tragedy with our friend Verdi.[1] Who knows if he won't become cross with me too, just because these idlers go around saying the first thing that comes into their heads! ...

1. Forty years later, a few months after the premiere of *Otello*, Giovanni Rizzi declared in an address, "Oh how happy Carcano would have been had he been able to be present at the recent triumphs of his friend—he who, by continually speaking and writing to Verdi about Shakespeare, by sending him his *King Lear* translation in 1843, by reading *Macbeth* to him at Clusone in 1847 [*recte* 1846], by dedicating *Anthony and Cleopatra* to him in 1875, brought him to love [Shakespeare] even more..." (*op. cit.,* p. 36)

VARESI TO BRENNA[1]

Florence, 7 March 1847

Avendo io in questi ultimi giorni ricevute varie inchieste per l'autunno e pel Carneval venturo, e richieste tali ch'io non debbo trascurare, così te ne do avviso e ti chiedo una risposta all'ultima mia. Ora siamo quasi pronti col Macbeth, che ci ha sbalorditi tutti quanti alle prove d'orchestra. Per me sono innamorato di quella Musica e massime della mia parte che è la più grandiosa che sia mai stata scritta per Baritono.

L'andata in scena è fissata a Venerdi e te ne saprò dare le notizie.

Venice: Fenice archives

Having received in the past few days various inquiries for the autumn and for the next Carnival season, and offers of a kind that I cannot disregard, so I am hereby advising you of this and ask you for a reply to my last letter. We are now almost ready with *Macbeth*, which has astonished us all at the orchestra rehearsals. As for me, I'm in love with that music, and most of all with my part, which is the most grandiose that has ever been written for baritone.

The premiere is set for Friday [March 12] and I'll be able to give you a report.

1. Guglielmo Brenna was the Secretary of La Fenice, Venice.

A VERDI MEMORANDUM

[Florence, 7 March 1847]

Dire a Lanari che sarà bene andare in scena Venerdi e perchè tutto andasse perfettamente bene fare riposo Domani (Lunedi) e fare una gran prova; Martedì fare la *Sonnambula*; Mercoledì, e Giovedì fare riposo e quindi le prove

Tell Lanari that it will be good to have the first performance on Friday [March 12] and, so that everything will go perfectly, have no performance tomorrow (Monday) and have a big rehearsal; on Tuesday, do *Sonnambula*;

d'orchestra alla sera, ed alla mattina fare la prova del solo terzo atto colle coriste, Varesi, le apparizioni, le ballerine etc. etc...

N.B. Questa prova della mattina si può fare senza l'orchestra, soltanto due violini, oppure un cembalo etc...

Abbiati 1, 685–86

MUZIO TO BAREZZI

Le scrivo del brillante successo che ha avuto *Attila* per la terza volta sulle scene della *Pergola*. Domenica il teatro era pieno zeppo di gente, e tutti erano accorsi per festeggiare il Maestro. Cominciarono dopo la cavatina della Barbieri a chiamar *fuori Verdi* ed avranno seguitato un quarto d'ora; finalmente si presentò l'avvisatore, e tutti tacquero; e disse: il Maestro Verdi non si trova in teatro. Allora si sentì rispondere da tutte le parti: *Si vada a prenderlo, si vada a prenderlo;* ed urlavano più forte di prima. Fu calato il sipario e non si continuava lo spettacolo. Allora si tacquero e lo spettacolo andò fino alla fine. Fu fatto ripetere il finale dell'atto terzo, ed anche qui si voleva il Maestro; ma poi si persuasero e tacquero. Ma però vi era una *mormorazione?!* un malcontento generale; e se ne ebbero a male, perchè il Maestro non andò a teatro.

Ieri, lunedì, cominciai a seccarlo dalla mattina alla sera per indurlo a venire a teatro, ma ei non voleva venire. Finalmente mi venne in mente uno stratagemma, e gli dissi che il capobanda aveva bisogno di sue istruzioni, e gli dissi ancora che si era rotta una lente della fantasmagoria, e che bisognava andare ad ordinare un ripiego, e che io non ero buono per fare tutte queste cose, e che la Barbieri aveva bisogno d'un cambiamento d'un passo, e che se egli non faceva tutte queste cose alla sera stessa, si sarebbe perduta la prova ed anche quella della sera. Allora egli mi promise di venire, ma tardò quando lo spettacolo era cominciato. Andammo a teatro dopo il prologo. E ci volle andare per una porticina segreta, che conduce al palcoscenico senza farsi vedere da anima vivente. Quando fu in teatro io andai in platea ed avvertii alcuni amici che Verdi vi era. Le voci passarono al terzo ed al quarto, ed in un momento, dopo il duetto, si misero ad urlare tutti: *Fuori il Maestro!*

I write you about the brilliant success *Attila* had, for the third performance at the Pergola. Sunday, the theatre was packed with people, and everyone had come to honor the Maestro. After Barbieri's *cavatina*, they began to shout "Fuori Verdi" [Come out and take a call], and went on for fifteen minutes; finally a spokesman came out, and everyone fell silent, and he said: "Maestro Verdi is not in the theatre." Then from every corner people answered: "Go get him, go get him"; and they shouted louder than before. The curtain was lowered, and the performance came to a halt. Then they became quiet, and the performance went on to the end. The finale of the third act had to be repeated, and here again the audience wanted the Maestro; but then they were persuaded and they became quiet. But then there was a *murmuration?!* a general discontent; and they took it badly because the Maestro did not go to the theatre.

Yesterday, Monday, I began to needle him from morning until evening to persuade him to come to the theatre, but he did not want to come. Finally, a trick came into my mind, and I told him that the leader of the *banda* needed instructions from him, and then I told him that a lens of the fantasmagoria had been broken, and that he had to go to order the replacement, and that I was not up to doing all these things, and that Barbieri needed to have a passage changed, and that if he did not do all these things that same evening, both the rehearsal [of *Macbeth*] and the evening [performance of *Attila*] would be ruined. Then he promised me he would come, but he delayed until the show had begun. We went to the theatre after the Prologue. We decided to go by way of a small secret door that leads directly to the stage, so that not a living soul can see you. When he was in the theatre, I went into the *platea* [orchestra] and advised some friends that Verdi was there.

Allora egli voleva partire, ma venne la Direzione e lo pregò a presentarsi. Egli dovette comparire otto volte di seguito in mezzo ai plausi più frenetici. Io ero contento più di un principe. Dopo il finale fu chiamato ancora e gli gettarono un'immensità di mazzi di fiori. Finalmente mi domandò dov' era questo capobanda, questa macchina, questo cambiamento della Barbieri, ma io gli dissi che intanto che esso si presentava al pubblico io avevo accomodato tutto; ma egli non volle credere e mi disse: *Sono in collera con Lei;* ma non era vero. Non l'ho mai visto in collera con me. Stamattina, appena svegliato, gli ho domandato se era in collera con me. E mi ha detto: *Sei un mattone!* Questa è la storia, un po' lunga; ma abbia pazienza di leggerla ...

F. T. Garibaldi, *Verdi,* 262-63

The word was passed from one to another, and in a moment, after the duet, everyone set about shouting "Fuori il Maestro!" Then he wanted to leave, but the management came and begged him to show himself. He had to appear eight times in a row, in the midst of the most frenzied applause. I was happier than a prince. After the finale, he was called out again, and they threw him an enormous number of bouquets. Finally, he asked me where this *banda* leader was, this machine, this alteration for Barbieri, but I told him that while he was showing himself to the audience I had taken care of everything, but he wouldn't believe it, and said to me: "I am angry with you"; but it was not true. I have never seen him angry with me. This morning, the first thing on waking, I asked him if he was angry with me. And he said to me: "You really are a crazy one!" That's the story, a bit long, but have the patience to read it...

VERDI TO CLARA MAFFEI

Florence, [*11 March 1847*]

... Mi continua a piacere sempre più Firenze; e ... stò benissimo di salute: l'opera continua bene alla prove: tutti trovano assai bene, ma non c'è da badare perchè alle prove si fanno tutti un dovere di trovare bello tutto quello che vi scrivere [*sic*], a viceversa del pubblico che ordinariamente si fà un dovere di trovare tutto brutto. Dopo la prima sera le scriverò genuinamente l'esito, e francamente le dirò anche la mia opinione su tutto come se giudicassi cose altrui. Il cavaliere[1] stà perfettamente ma ognuno tende a fatti suoi vale a dir che fuori dell'ora di pranzo ci troviamo poco insieme ...

Quartetto Milanese Ottocentesco, 72

... I continue to like Florence more and more, and ... I'm in very good health. The opera continues to go well at the rehearsals. Everyone thinks highly of it, but that doesn't mean much, because at rehearsals everyone feels obliged to find everything one's written beautiful, as opposed to the audience, which normally feels obliged to find everything awful. After the first night I'll write and tell you the result honestly, and I'll also give you my own opinion about everything frankly, just as if I were judging someone else's work. The *cavaliere*[1] is quite well, but we all go about our own concerns—which means that except at meal times we are seldom together ...

1. Andrea Maffei

MUZIO TO THE BAREZZI FAMILY

Florence, 12 March 1847

Or ora è arrivato alle ore 3 il signor Antonio che sta bene ed ha fatto buon viaggio, e l'Opera anderà in scena Domenica e non Sabbato ...[1]

Garibaldi, 311

Just now, at 3 o'clock, Signor Antonio [Barezzi] has arrived; he's fine, and had a good journey; and the opera goes on on Sunday [March 14], not Saturday ...[1]

1. Originally planned for Friday, March 12, the performance had to be postponed because of Varesi's indisposition (see Verdi's memorandum of 7 March 1847 and the March 13 communication to the *Gazzetta Musicale di Milano* at p. 372).

BARBIERI-NINI'S RECOLLECTIONS

Barbieri-Nini's recollections of the rehearsals are usually cited from the unreliable Gino Monaldi's Verdi: 1838–1898 *(Turin: Bocca, 1899), 79–82; second edition (1926), 74–77. We give them here as they appeared in Eugenio Checchi's* Giuseppe Verdi: il genio e le opere *(Florence: G. Barbera, 1887), 64–68, together with some paragraphs, before and after, that are evidently based on Florentine memories.*

Andrea Maffei che, per antica amicizia al Verdi, rivedeva un po' le buccie ai versi dei librettisti, e poi s'irritava se una sua correzione non era accettata dal maestro, al quale piaceva di più, per ragioni musicali, una sconcordanza grammaticale del Piave, il Maffei, dicevo, era quello che conduceva l'amico negli studi dei più celebrati pittori e scultori, e lo iniziava alla gioconda vita di qualche casa patrizia. Fra una passeggiata e l'altra il poeta cedeva finalmente alla preghiera tante volte ripetutagli dal Verdi, e scriveva per lui il libretto dei *Masnadieri:* Opera che un anno dopo con poca o punta fortuna fu rappresentata a Londra.

Ma intanto le prove del *Macbeth* si succedevano con regolare lentezza, e il Verdi, che pur voleva in qualche modo mostrarsi grato agli amici che gli tenevano compagnia il giorno, li faceva assistere uno per sera alle prove: ed era questa una delle più grandi testimonianze d'amicizia, perchè egli ebbe sempre grandemente in uggia di chiamar gli altri in teatro, dove veramente egli si trasformava al punto da parere un altro uomo. Così la figura di rustico e di rude che si attribuisce al Verdi, è dovuta a un certo suo modo d'essere che aveva in teatro soltanto, e di cui si armava per star sempre in guardia contro le esorbitanze stravaganti, contro le singolarità e le bizzarrie di una classe rispettabile di persone, le quali non conoscono altra logica all'infuori della parte che devono eseguire, e altro ragionamento all'infuori degli applausi che, a sentir loro, non sono mai troppi.

Vive oggi in Firenze, ritirata dal teatro, ma con la memoria ancor fresca dei ricordi del tempo, la singolare cantatrice per la quale il *Macbeth* ebbe un così clamoroso successo: quella Barbieri-Nini della quale si disse allora che aveva, meglio di qualsiasi più grande e celebrata attrice, interpretata la parte della terribile protagonista nel dramma dello Shakespeare. Poche settimane fa un amico carissimo, da me inviato, risvegliò nella mente della grande artista quei ricordi, ed essi ebbero virtù di riportarla con la fantasia ai giorni indimenticabili in cui il *Macbeth* si studiava, si rappresentava, e diffondeva per il mondo un altro raggio della luce divina del genio.

Andrea Maffei who, because of his long friendship with Verdi, would tend to find fault with the librettists' verses and then be irritated if one of his corrections was not accepted by the Maestro, who, for musical reasons, preferred a grammatical disagreement by Piave—Maffei, as I was saying, was the one who introduced his friend into the studios of the best-known painters and sculptors and initiated him into the cheerful life of some patrician homes. Between strolls the poet yielded at last to the request so often repeated by Verdi and wrote for him the libretto of *I masnadieri:* an opera that was produced in London one year later with little or no success.

But meanwhile the rehearsals of *Macbeth* followed one upon the other with slow regularity, and Verdi, who after all wanted to show his gratitude to the friends who kept him company during the daytime, let them—one at a time—attend the evening rehearsals. This was one of the greatest tokens of friendship, because he very much disliked inviting people to the theatre, where he truly underwent a transformation to the point of seeming a different man. Thus Verdi's reputation of being a rustic and rough man is due to a certain way of his which he had only in the theatre, with which he armed himself in order to be always on guard against the extravagant excesses, against the peculiarities and caprices of a respectable class of person, who know no logic beyond the roles they are to perform, and no argument beyond applause which, if we are to believe them, is never too much.

There lives today in Florence, retired from the stage, but with memory still fresh with recollections of those days, the unique singer through whom *Macbeth* obtained such a clamorous success: that Barbieri-Nini about whom it was said at the time that she had interpreted the part of the terrible protagonist in Shakespeare's drama better than any great and celebrated actress. A few weeks ago, a very dear friend, sent by me, awakened those recollections in the mind of the great artist, and they had the power of taking her back in her imagination to the unforgettable days when *Macbeth* was being studied, being performed, and when it spread

Racconta dunque la Barbieri-Nini che una singolarità del Verdi durante le prove era di non dir quasi mai una parola. Questo non significava già che il maestro fosse contento: tutt'altro. Ma finito un pezzo, egli faceva cenno al Romani . . . e al cenno del Verdi il Romani gli si accostava, andavano in fondo al palcoscenico, e col quaderno sotto gli occhi l'autore accennava col dito i punti in cui l'esecuzione non era quella voluta da lui.

"Dimmi tu come devo fare," replicava con molta pazienza il Romani.

Ma il Verdi raramente spiegava quel benedetto come. Si aiutava con gesti, con grandi percosse sul libro, rallentando con la mano o rafforzando i tempi, e poi, come se avesse avuto luogo fra i due una lunga e persuasiva spiegazione, il Verdi tornava addietro dicendo:

"Ora hai capito: così."

E il povero Romani doveva mettere a tortura l'ingegno acutissimo per capire, anche quando non aveva capito nulla, e per fare da interprete con l'orchestra e con i cantanti.

Le prove del Macbeth, tra pianoforte ed orchestra, furono più di cento: il Verdi implacabile non badava a stancare gli artisti, a tormentarli per ore e ore col medesimo pezzo: e finchè non fosse raggiunta quella interpretazione, che a lui pareva si accostasse il meno peggio all'ideale della sua mente, non passava ad un'altra scena. Non era troppo amato dalle masse, perche non uscì mai dalle sue labbra una parola d'incoraggiamento, mai un bravo di convinzione, neppure quando e professori d'orchestra e coristi credevano d'aver fatto il possibile per contentarlo; e la sboccata vena di quegli arguti Fiorentini, un po'impermaliti, si sfogava in epiteti, qualcheduno dei quali somigliava a capello a quella parte del violino che serve a stringere e allentare le corde.[1]

Ma i direttori dello spettacolo, Pietro Romani concertatore e Alamanno Biagi direttore d'orchestra, e gli artisti che avevano un nome giustamente celebre come la Barbieri-Nini e il Varesi, subivano a poco a poco il fascino di quella volantà ferrea, di quell'indomita fantasia non mai contenta di sè, e che tornava ogni giorno a suggerire qualche nuova interpretazione, magari cozzante con quella del giorno avanti, ma più perfetta, più artisticamente efficace.

into the world another ray of the divine light of genius.

Barbieri-Nini, then, tells us that it was a peculiar characteristic of Verdi during rehearsals almost never to utter a word. This by no means signified the Maestro was pleased: quite the opposite. But when a piece was finished, he would make a sign to Romani . . .; and at Verdi's sign, Romani would approach him, they would walk upstage, and, notebook in hand, the composer would indicate with his finger the places where the execution had not been according to his wishes.

"Well then, tell me how I'm to do it," Romani would reply with the greatest patience.

But Verdi rarely explained that blessed "how." He made use of gestures, banging on the book, slowing down or urging on the tempos with his hand, and then, as if there had taken place between them a lengthy, persuasive explanation, Verdi would come back, saying:

"Now you've got it: that's how."

And poor Romani was forced to rack his very capable brain to understand, even when he had not understood a thing, and to act as interpreter to the orchestra and the singers.

The rehearsals of Macbeth, counting both piano and orchestral, came to more than one hundred. Verdi, implacable, did not care if he wearied the artists and tormented them for hours on end with the same piece: and until that interpretation was attained which, to his mind, approximated as closely as possible the ideal he had envisioned, he did not proceed to the next scene. He was not too well liked by the masse [i.e., the chorus and orchestra], because a word of encouragement never escaped from his lips: never a wholehearted bravo, not even when both the members of the orchestra and the chorus thought they had done their best to please him. And the rather uninhibited temper of those witty Florentines, who were somewhat hurt, found vent in epithets, one of which bore a striking resemblance to that part of the violin which serves to tighten and slacken the strings.[1]

But the directors of the spectacle, Pietro Romani, concertatore, and Alamanno Biagi, leader of the orchestra, and those artists who had a justifiably celebrated name such as Barbieri-Nini and Varesi, gradually came under the spell of that iron will, that untamed imagination never satisfied with itself, that every day suggested some new interpretation, possibly at variance with that of the day before, but more perfect, more artistically effective.

Così i Cori delle streghe, che lo scandalizzato Andrea Maffei diceva il più grande delitto letterario commesso dal Piave, perchè erano una vera caricatura della poesia shakespeariana, furono dal Maffei per consiglio del Verdi rifatti, e così anche ne fu riscritta in gran parte la musica. E qui volentieri lascio parlare la Barbieri-Nini, che animandosi a poco a poco nella evocazione dei ricordi, così diceva non è molto all'amico mio, inviato da me ad interrogarla:

"Di tutto lo spartito il maestro ebbe grande cura durante la prova, e mi ricordo che, mattina e sera, nel *foyer* del teatro o sul palcoscenico (secondo che le prove erano a pianoforte o in orchestra) guardavamo con trepidazione il maestro appena compariva, cercando d'indovinare dai suoi occhi, o dal modo suo di salutare gli artisti, se ci fosse per quel giorno qualche novità. Se mi veniva incontro quasi sorridente, e diceva qualche cosa che potesse parere un complimento, ero certa che per quel giorno mi si serbava una grossa aggiunta alla prova. Chinavo rassegnata la testa, ma a poco a poco finii anch'io per prendere una gran passione per questo *Macbeth*, che usciva in modo tanto singolare da tutto quello che s'era scritto e rappresentato fino allora.

"Mi ricordo che erano due, per il Verdi, i punti culminanti dell'Opera: la scena del sonnambulismo, e il duetto mio col baritono.[2] Durerete fatica a crederlo, ma la scena del sonnambulismo mi portò via tre mesi di studio:[3] io per tre mesi, mattina e sera, cercai di imitare quelli che parlano dormendo, che articolano parole (come mi diceva il Verdi) senza quasi muover le labbra, e lasciando immobili le altre parti del viso, compresi gli occhi. Fu una cosa da ammattire.

"E il duo col baritono che incomincia: *Fatal mia donna, un murmure*, vi parrà un'esagerazione, ma fu provato più di centocinquanta volte: per ottenere, diceva il maestro, che fosse più *discorso* che *cantato*. Sentite questa, ora. La sera della prova generale, a teatro pieno, il Verdi impose anche agli artisti d'indossare il costume, e quando lui s'impuntava in una cosa, guai a contradirlo! Eravamo dunque vestiti e pronti, l'orchestra in ordine, i Cori sulla scena, quando il Verdi, fatto cenno a me e al Varesi, ci chiamò dietro le quinte: disse che per fargli piacere andassimo con lui nella sala del *foyer* per fare un'altra prova a pianoforte di quel maledettissimo duo.

Thus the witches' choruses, which the scandalized Andrea Maffei called the greatest literary crime committed by Piave, because they were an outright caricature of the Shakespearean poetry, were done over by Maffei following Verdi's advice, and thus, too, much of their music was rewritten. And here I gladly yield to Barbieri-Nini, who, growing more and more animated as she called forth her recollections, spoke as follows to the friend I had sent to interrogate her not long ago:

"The whole score came under the Maestro's solicitous care throughout the [period of] rehearsal, and I remember that, morning and evening, in the *foyer* of the theatre or on stage (according to whether the rehearsals were with the piano or orchestral), we looked at the Maestro with trepidation as he made his appearance, trying to guess by his eyes, or from the way he greeted the artists, whether that day there would be something new. If he came towards me almost smiling, and said something that might seem a compliment, I was sure that on that day he had some big addition in store for me at the rehearsal. I bowed my head in resignation, but gradually I, too, became enamored of this *Macbeth*, which differed in such a singular way from anything that had ever been written and performed until that time.

"I remember that for Verdi there were two climactic points in the opera: the sleepwalking scene and my duet with the baritone.[2] You won't believe this, but the sleepwalking scene cost me three months' study:[3] for three months, morning and evening, I tried to imitate those who talk in their sleep, uttering words (as Verdi would say to me) while hardly moving their lips, leaving the rest of the face immobile, including the eyes. It was enough to drive one crazy.

"As for the duet with the baritone that begins: "Fatal mia donna, un murmure,"—you may think I am exaggerating, but it was rehearsed more than a hundred and fifty times so that it might be closer to *speech* than to *singing*, the Maestro would say. Now listen to this. On the evening of the final rehearsal, with the theatre full, Verdi insisted that even the soloists should be in costume, and when he set his mind on something, woe if you opposed him! And so we were dressed and ready, the orchestra in place, the chorus on stage, when Verdi made a sign to me and Varesi, and called us backstage: he asked us—as a favor to him—to go with him into the foyer and rehearse that dammed duet again at the piano.

" 'Maestro,' dissi io atterrita, 'siamo già in costume scozzese: come si fa?'

" 'Vi metterete un mantello.'

"E il Varesi baritono, stufo della singolare richiesta, si provò ad alzare un po' la voce dicendo:

" 'Ma l'abbiamo provato centocinquanta volte, perdio!'

" 'Non dirai così fra mezz'ora: saranno centocinquantuna.'

"Bisognò per forza obbedire al tiranno. Mi ricordo ancora delle truci occhiate, che gli scagliava addosso il Varesi avviandosi al *foyer;* col pugno sull'elsa della spada pareva meditasse di trucidare il Verdi, come avrebbe dovuto più tardi trucidare il re Duncano. Peraltro si piegò, rassegnato anche lui; e la centocinquantunesima prova ebbe luogo, mentre il pubblico impaziente tumultuava in platea.

"E voi saprete che quel duo, chi dicesse che destò entusiasmo e fanatismo non direbbe nulla: fu qualche cosa d'incredibile, di nuovo, di non mai successo. Dappertutto dove ho cantato il *Macbeth,* e tutte le sere durante la stagione della Pergola, il duo bisognò ripeterlo perfino tre volte, perfino quattro: una volta dovemmo subire la quinta replica![4]

"La sera della prima rappresentazione non dimenticherò mai che, prima della scena del sonnambulismo, che è una delle ultime dell' Opera, il Verdi mi girava attorno inquieto, senza dir nulla: si vedeva benissimo che il successo, di già grande, non sarebbe stato definitivo per lui se non dopo quella scena. Mi feci dunque il segno della croce (è un'abitudine che si conserva anch' oggi sul palcoscenico per i momenti difficili) e andai avanti. I giornali di quel tempo vi diranno se io interpretai giustamente il pensiero drammatico e musicale del grandissimo Verdi, nella scena del sonnambulismo. Io so questo: che appena calmata la furia degli applausi, rientrata tutta commaossa, tremante e disfatta nel camerino, vidi spalancarsi l'uscio (ero già mezzo spogliata) e il Verdi entrò, agitando le mani e movendo le labbra, come volesse fare un gran discorso: ma non riuscì a pronunziare una sola parola. Io ridevo e piangevo, e non dicevo nulla neanch'io: ma guardando in faccia il maestro mi avvidi che aveva gli occhi rossi anche lui. Ci stringemmo le mani forte forte, poi lui, senza dir nulla, uscì a precipizio. Quella forte scena di commozione mi compensò ad usura di tanti mesi di assiduo la-

" 'Maestro,' said I, aghast, 'we are already dressed in our Scottish costumes: how can we do it?'

" 'You'll put on a cloak,'

"And the baritone Varesi, fed up with this extraordinary request, tried raising his voice a little, saying:

" 'For God's sake, we've already rehearsed it a hundred and fifty times!'

" 'You won't be saying that in a half hour's time: it will be one hundred and fifty-one by then.'

"We were forced to obey the tyrant. I still remember the threatening looks Varesi shot at him on the way to the foyer; with his fist on the hilt of his sword, he seemed to be about to slaughter Verdi, as he would later slaughter King Duncan. However he yielded, resigning himself too; and the one hundred and fifty-first rehearsal took place, while the impatient audience made an uproar in the theatre.

"And, as you probably know, anyone who says that duet was received enthusiastically is saying nothing; it was something unbelievable, something new, unprecedented. Wherever I sang *Macbeth,* and every evening during the season at La Pergola, that duet had to be repeated up to three even four times. Once we had to undergo even a fifth performance of it![4]

"The night of the first performance I will never forget that, before the sleepwalking scene, which is one of the last in the Opera, Verdi prowled around me anxiously, without saying anything: it was very plain that the success, already great, would not seem definitive to him until after that scene. So I crossed myself (a theatre custom that is still today practiced in the most difficult moments) and went on. The papers of the time will tell you whether, in the sleepwalking scene, I interpreted our great Verdi's dramatic and musical thought correctly. I know this: that the turmoil of applause had hardly died down, and I had just returned to my dressing room, all trembling and distraught, when I saw the door fly open (I was already half out of my costume) and Verdi entered, gesturing with his hands and moving his lips, as if he wished to make a great speech: but he could not get out a single word. I was laughing and weeping, and I, too, said nothing: but looking at the Maestro's face I noticed that his eyes were red, too. We clasped hands tightly, and then, without a word, he rushed out. That striking emotional scene rewarded me with interest for so many months of hard labor and

voro e di trepidazioni continue.". . .

L'Accademia dunque dei signori Immobili, proprietari del teatro posto in via della Pergola (così veramente si ha da dire, come l' illustre amico mio Alessandro Ademollo mi avverte, e non già teatro della Pergola che non avrebbe significato alcuno),[5] l'Accademia dei signori Immobili (per emblema un mulino a vento, col motto: *In sua movenza è fermo*), per attestare la gratitudine della città all'insigne autore del *Macbeth*, gli offrì una corona di lauro con foglie d'oro, e in ciascuna foglia stava scritto il titolo d'un'opera di Giuseppe Verdi . . .

ceaseless trepidation."

The gentlemen of the Accademia degli Immobili, proprietors of the theatre situated in Via della Pergola (for that is the proper appellation, as my illustrious friend Alessandro Ademollo advises me, rather than Teatro della Pergola, which has no meaning at all)[5], the gentlemen of the Accademia degli Immobili (its emblem a windmill, with the motto: *"In motion it stands firm"*), in token of the city's gratitude to the eminent composer of *Macbeth*, presented him with a laurel wreath made of golden leaves, and on each leaf there was inscribed the title of an opera by Giuseppe Verdi. . .

1. In Tuscan dialect "bischero" (tuning-pin in standard Italian) means "prick."

2. See Verdi's letter to Cammarano of 23 November 1848.

3. This is clearly an exaggeration, as is the number of rehearsals Barbieri-Nini claims there were: Verdi did not send her the music of the sleepwalking scene until January 31. Barbieri-Nini did not arrive in Florence until February 24, and the first piano rehearsals did not take place before February 27 (according to Muzio's 25 February 1847 letter to A. Barezzi).

4. As the Florentine reviews demonstrate, Barbieri means the *primo tempo* of the duet (the F-minor, 6/8 section beginning "Fatal mia donna"–the one movement of the duet that Verdi left unrevised in 1865), not the entire number. See the reviews of the Padua and first Florence productions and Muzio's 23 August 1847 letter for evidence that "Fatal mia donna" was indeed sometimes performed four and five times.

5. The Accademia degli Immobili, founded in 1648, inaugurated its theater in the via della Pergola in 1656. It was—*pace* the illustrious Ademollo—and still is commonly referred to as the Teatro della Pergola. By adding "signori" to the title of the venerable institution, Checchi plays with its literal meaning, "the Academy of Immovable Gentlemen."

MUZIO TO THE BAREZZI FAMILY *Florence, 16 March 1847 at 7 A.M.*

Non ho scritto ieri per mancanza di tempo perchè ebbimo a vedere tante cose da sbalordire qualunque grand'uomo; e tutto questo lo racconterò in persona.

Ieri sera fu la grande rappresentazione del *Macbeth*, quale, secondo il solito delle opere di Verdi, ha prodotto un immenso fanatismo, avendo dovuto comparire sul palco nel corso della rappresentazione 38 volte, e posso assicurarvi che il *Macbeth* è una grand'opera, estremamente grande e magnifica.

Nel sortire che feci con Verdi dal teatro fossimo attorniati da un'immensità di popolo e questi ci accompagnarono in mezzo agli evviva sino al nostro albergo essendo distante dal teatro quasi un miglio; Verdi di quando in quando dovette fermarsi a ringraziare la popolazione fiorentina, quale era composta della prima gioventù.

Mi dimenticavo di dirvi che alla prima sera vi fu una calca terribile; aprirono il teatro alle 4 e dopo pochi minuti il teatro era pieno, avendo io dovuto prendere i posti riservati per me e Giovannino, che costano un *pisis*[1] per ogni

I didn't write yesterday for want of time because we had so many things to see such as would dumbfound even the high and mighty; all this I'll tell you in person.

Last night was the great performance of *Macbeth*, which, as usual with Verdi's operas, produced tremendous enthusiasm, [Verdi] having to appear onstage thirty-eight times in the course of the performance. I can assure you that *Macbeth* is a great opera, extremely great and magnificent.

Upon leaving the theatre with Verdi, we were surrounded by an immense crowd, who accompanied us with hurrahs up to our hotel, almost a mile away from the theatre. Verdi, from time to time, had to stop and thank the people of Florence, made up of young people.

I forgot to tell you that on opening night there was a terrible crush. The theatre opened at four, and within a few minutes the theatre was full so I had to get reserved seats for me and Giovannino, which cost a *pisis*[1] for every

posto riservato oltre il biglietto.

L'opera incominciò alle 8 precise e subito fu applaudita l'introduzione e chiamato fuori il Maestro, indi fu replicato il coro delle streghe e parimenti e freneticamente chiamato fuori il Maestro. Fu pure replicato il duetto fra la Barbieri e Varesi,[2] come anche altri due cori, ed il Maestro in tutto il corso dell'opera fu chiamato fuori 27 volte.

Questa è la pura storia della prima sera. I minuti aneddoti ve li racconterò personalmente, come pure racconterò ciò che succederà dimani a sera, ultima della presenza di Verdi, perchè questa sera vi è riposo, e per conseguenza giorno libero di divertimento, aspettando a momenti la carrozza del barone Ricasoli per andare tutt'oggi a vedere queste delizie di vero paradiso ...Non posso esprimervi la sensazione che mi ha fatto Firenze! Credevo dalle descrizioni ricevute anteriori che fosse bella, ma non al punto che da me è stata ritrovata ...

place reserved, in addition to the price of the ticket itself.

The opera began at eight precisely, and the *introduzione* was immediately applauded and the Maestro called out. Then the witches' chorus was encored, and the Maestro was similarly and frenetically called out. The duet between Barbieri and Varesi was likewise encored,[2] as were two other choruses, and in the course of the whole opera the Maestro was called out twenty-seven times.

These are the basic facts about opening night. The minor details I'll tell you in person, just as I'll tell what happens tomorrow evening, the last [performance] with Verdi present, because tonight there's no performance, and so the day is free for diversions, and we're expecting Baron Ricasoli's carriage any moment, to spend the whole day seeing the delights of true paradise ...I can't tell you what an effect Florence has had on me! I thought from the descriptions I'd received before that it was beautiful, but not to the extent that I discovered for myself ...

Garibaldi, 312–13

1. A Florentine *pisis* (or *francescone*) was worth about 6.30 Austrian lire.
2. In fact, only the *primo tempo* of the duet was repeated, as the reviews indicate.

VARESI TO RANZANICI   *Florence, 17 March 1847*

Con questa dò risposta alla tua dell'11 corrente, colle nuove che mi chiedi del Macbeth. Questo nuovo lavoro di Verdi ha ottenuto un'esito straordinario, e sebbene la 1ª sera non fosse capito interamente (come avevamo previsto) pure il M.º fu chiamato sulla scena più di 24 volte e furono ripetuti tre pezzi di Musica. La Seconda sera fu un fanatismo inaudito, il M.º fu chiamato innumerevoli volte e poscia condotto a casa da una folla di gente che urlava come i dannati. Nel Macbeth Verdi ha adottato un nuovo stile adatto al genere fantastico della Tragedia di *Sheackspear* e secondo me quel suo spartito è il più accurato ed il più bello in Arte ch'egli abbia scritto. I pezzi veramente di Genio e d'inspirazione sono; Un coro di Streghe d'introduz[ione,] Il Duetto, durante l'assassinio del Re fra me e la Barbieri (che è una cosa veramente divina), Il Finale del 2.º Atto. Un coro di sgherri, La scena del Sonnambulismo della Barbieri, e l'aria ultima e la *Morte mia*.

L'esito che ho ottenuto colla Parte di Macbeth è il più bello il più importante ch'io abbia

I hereby reply to your letter of the eleventh, with the news about *Macbeth* which you ask for. This new work by Verdi has had an extraordinary reception, and although it wasn't completely understood on opening night (as we had foreseen), the Maestro was still called onstage more than twenty-four times and three numbers were repeated. On the second night there was wild, unheard-of enthusiasm; the Maestro was called out innumerable times and was then accompanied home by a crowd of people who yelled like the damned. In *Macbeth* Verdi has adopted a new style suited to the fantastical nature of Shakespeare's tragedy and in my opinion this score of his is the most careful and the most artistically beautiful that he has written. The numbers of true genius and inspiration are a witches' chorus in the *introduzione*, the duet for me and Barbieri during the assassination of the King (which is a truly divine thing), the *finale* of Act II, a chorus of murderers, Barbieri's sleepwalking scene, and the last aria and *my death scene*.

The success that I obtained with the role of Macbeth is the finest, the most important that

The witches' cavern: a sepia drawing presented by Countess Clara Maffei to Verdi for his album (*Collection Carrara-Verdi, Sant'Agata*)

conseguito nella mia Carriera[.] Le difficoltà per rappresentare questo personaggio erano immense e tante che dalle prime prove m'ero quasi scoraggiato: ma poi radoppiai di lena e volli riuscirvi ed ora mi veggo ben compensato per tanto studio e tante fatiche. La Barbieri ha cantato ed Agito per eccellenza così chè l'altra sera si può dire che tutto il Macbeth fu un solo e prolungato applauso[.] Quest'opera richiede una gran Messa in scena ed un doppio Numero di Cori, il Tenore vi ha pochissima parte.

Riguardo alla Domanda pel Carnevale di Venezia io l'ho già fatta coll'altra mia diretta all'Amico Brenna, ed il maggiore ribasso ch'io potrò fare sarà di limitarmi alle 20 Mille Lire effettive[.][1] Rispondimi presto in proposito perchè Lanari vorrebbe fare un contratto d'un anno con me, e Jacovacci[2] mi ha già scritto per avermi ancora il Carnevale: io però preferirei di andare a Venezia ma senza mio discapito;[3] Jacovacci quest'anno pel solo Carnevale mi diede 2,400 collonati[4] che fanno 15,500 . . .

Ronzani mi scrisse per avermi dopo Vienna per Padova per dare Il Macbeth. Ma io l'ho

I've attained in my career. The difficulties in portraying this character were immense, to the point where from the first rehearsals I was nearly discouraged, but then I redoubled my efforts, wanting to succeed, and now I see myself well rewarded for so much study and so much hard work. Barbieri sang and acted so excellently that one could say the other night that the entire *Macbeth* was one single, prolonged ovation. This opera calls for an elaborate mise-en-scène and twice the usual number of choristers. The tenor has a very small part.

As for the question of the Carnival season in Venice, I have already answered in another letter addressed to our friend Brenna, and the biggest reduction I could make would be to limit myself to twenty thousand current lire.[1] Answer me about this soon, because Lanari would like to make a year's contract with me, and Jacovacci[2] has already written about having me for Carnival too. However, I would prefer to go to Venice, but without making a financial sacrifice.[3] This year Jacovacci gave me 2,400 *colonati*[4] for Carnival alone, which makes 15,500 . . .

Ronzani wrote asking to have me, after Vienna, to do *Macbeth* in Padua. But I thanked

ringraziato tanto dicendogli che volevo riposare due mesi d'Estate.

him very much, telling him that I wanted to rest for two months in summer.

Venice: Fenice archives

1. If Varesi refers to *lire Venete* (lire of the Veneto provinces, including Venice), the equivalent in Austrian lire would be about 11,500.

2. Vincenzo Jacovacci (1811–1881), impresario and manager of the Apollo and Argentina theaters in Rome

3. Varesi did go to Venice during Carnival for one of his rather surprisingly few appearances as Macbeth (see "A Hundred Years of *Macbeth*", at 428).

4. I.e., 2,400 pontifical *scudi*, the equivalent of about 14,650 Austrian lire (one *scudo* equals about 6.11 Austrian lire)

GIUSTI TO VERDI

Pescia, 19 March 1847

Lunedì passato, mi dispiacque di non trovarti in casa, perchè dovendo assentarmi da Firenze per quattro o sei giorni, avrei desiderato di vederti prima di partire.

Il tuo lavoro, più sarà riprodotto più sarà inteso e gustato, perchè il buono di certe cose, non s'afferra alle prime. Prosegui che non ti può fallire un bel nome, ma se credi a uno che vuol bene all'arte e a te, non ti togliere l'occasione d'esprimere colle tue note quella dolce mestizia nella quale hai dimostrato di poter tanto. Tu sai che la corda del dolore è quella che trova maggior risonanza nell'animo nostro, ma il dolore assume carattere diverso a seconda del tempo e a seconda dell'indole e dello stato di questa nazione o di quella. La specie di dolore che occupa ora gli animi di noi Italiani, è il dolore d'una gente che si sente bisognosa di destini migliori; è il dolore di chi è caduto e desidera rialzarsi; è il dolore di chi si pente, e aspetta e vuole la sua rigenerazione. Accompagna, Verdi mio, colle tue nobili armonie questo dolore alto e solenne; fa di nutrirlo, di fortificarlo, d'indirizzarlo al suo scopo. La musica è favella intesa da tutti, e non v'è effetto grande, che la musica non valga a produrre. Il fantastico, è cosa che può provare l'ingegno; il vero, prova l'ingegno e l'animo. Vorrei che gl'ingegni italiani contraessero tutti un forte e pieno connubio coll'arte italiana e s'astenessero dalla vaga venere dei congiungimenti forestieri. Queste cose te le dico per cenni e in punta di penna, perchè le sento molto e le so dir poco, e perchè al buono intenditore poche parole bastano.

Tornerò a Firenze Lunedì o Martedì alla più lunga, e desidero d'abbracciarti prima del tuo ritorno a Milano; ma se mai il caso facesse che io non ti trovassi più costà, sii certo che hai lasciato qua un altro amico, uno che fino a qui

Last Monday I was sorry not to find you at home, because, having to be away from Florence for four or six days, I would like to have seen you before leaving.

The more your work is performed, the more it will be understood and enjoyed: the excellence of certain things is not grasped at once. Continue, for you cannot help but be successful. But, if you will trust someone who loves both art and you, do not lose the occasion to express in your strains that sweet sadness in which you have shown you can achieve so much. You know that the string of pain is that which finds the greatest resonance within our soul, but pain assumes a different character according to the times and according to the nature and state of this or that nation. The kind of pain that now fills the souls of us Italians is the pain of a people who feel the need of a better future; it is the pain of one who has fallen and wishes to rise again; it is the pain of one who repents, and awaits and wills his regeneration. Accompany, my Verdi, this lofty and solemn pain with your noble harmonies; nourish it, fortify it, direct it to its goal. Music is a language understood by all, and there is no great effect that music is not capable of producing. The Fantastic is something that can challenge the intellect; truth challenges both the intellect and the soul. I would like all Italians of genius to contract a strong and full marriage with Italian art, and to shun fair siren songs of foreign liaisons. I am only touching on these things, lightly sketching them, for I feel them very strongly but cannot express them well, and because a word to the wise is sufficient.

I will return to Florence on Monday or Tuesday [March 22–23] at the latest and would like to embrace you before your return to Milan, but if it should turn out that I do not find you there, know that you have left behind

voleva un gran bene alle cose tue e ora lo vuole alle cose tue e a te.[1]

Sant'Agata (Verdi's autograph album);
Copialettere, 449–50

another friend, one who previously greatly admired your works and now admires both your works and you.[1]

---

1. In a letter to Andrea Maffei of 29 June 1847, Giusti said: "Salutami anco il Verdi se è costà, e pregalo di non darmi di pedante per la lettera che gli scrissi" ("Give Verdi my greetings too, if he's there, and beg him not to think me a pedant for the letter that I wrote him"). The letter to Maffei is printed in Ferdinando Martini, *Epistolario di Giuseppe Giusti* rev. ed.; (Florence, 1932) 2, 551–52. Verdi replied to Giusti on 27 March 1847; see below.

In late May 1897, Verdi sent a transcription of Giusti's letter to Martini along with a brief covering letter including this comment: " 'Il fantastico' Egli dice 'può provare l'ingegno; il vero prova l'ingegno e l'animo.—Vorrei che gli ingegni italiani … s'astenessero dalla vaga venere di congiungimenti fantastici [thus in *Abbiati* 1, 69; a slip of his or of Verdi's for "forestieri"?]. Speranze vane, ma ha ben ragione!" ("Vain wishes—but he is certainly right!") For Martini's and Verdi's exchange, see *Copialettere,* 408–9 and *Abbiati* 4, 600–1. According to *Abbiati* 1, 690, Verdi copied the remark about the *fantastico* and the *vero* into Clara Maffei's personal album.

VERDI TO CLARA MAFFEI

Bologna, 21 March 1847

… L'opera non ha fatto fiasco. Non posso raccontare le particolarità perchè, a dir vero, i Fiorentini hanno fatto più di quello che si doveva: le dimostrazioni sono state eccessive e gliele dirò a voce …

Quartetto Milanese Ottocentesco, 74

… The opera was not a fiasco. I cannot recount the details because, to tell the truth, the Florentines did more than was justified: the demonstrations were excessive, and I'll tell you about them in person …

VERDI TO BAREZZI

Milan, 25 March 1847

Cariss° Suocero

Da molto tempo era ne' miei pensieri d'intitolare un'opera a Lei che m'è stato e padre, e benefattore, ed amico.[1] Era un dovere, cui doveva soddisfare prima d'ora, e l'avrei fatto se imperiose circostanze non l'avessero impedito.

Ora eccole questo *Macbeth* che io amo a preferenza delle altre mie opere, e che quindi stimo più degno d'essere presentato a Lei. Il cuore l'offre: l'accetti il cuore,[2] e le sia testimonianza della memoria eterna, della gratitudine, dell'affetto che le porta

Il suo aff

G. Verdi

Fidenza, Private Collection of Alba Caraffini;
Copialettere, 451

Dearest Father-in-law,

For a long time it has been an intention of mine to dedicate an opera to you who have been to me at once father, benefactor, and friend.[1] It was a duty that I should have fulfilled before now, and I would have done so had not impelling circumstances prevented it.

Here now is this *Macbeth*, which I love in preference to my other operas, and thus deem more worthy of being presented to you. The heart offers it; may the heart receive it,[2] and may it be a witness to the eternal memory, the gratitude, and the love felt for you by your affectionate

G. Verdi

---

1. As early as March 1846 Verdi expressed the desire to dedicate an opera to Barezzi; see *Abbiati* 1, 686–87. The vocal score was published by Ricordi with the dedication: "per grata memoria dedicata / al / suo amatissimo suocero / Antonio Barezzi." Barezzi's name is in larger letters than the composer's.

2. Cf. "Vom Herzen—Möge es wieder—zu Herzen gehen!," Beethoven's superscription to the *Missa Solemnis.*

VERDI TO PIAVE

Milan, 26 March 1847

Le notizie del *Macbet* le sai, ha fatto furore: m'han regalato una corona d'oro del valore di

You'll have heard the news about *Macbeth*: it was an enormous success. They gave me a gold

57

200 zecchini,[1] la bella Barbieri[2] me l'ha presentata alla 3ª recita: I FIORENTINI A G. VERDI. Amen.

Ti mando il compimento di 900 Lire austriache a totale pagamento del Macbet; altra volta mi dicesti che avevi ricevute L. au. 733; ti mando ora 55 fiorini, e perciò ti darò due L. austriache alle prime volte che ci vedremo.[3] Nel farmi la ricevuta dirai: "Ricevo il compimento delle 900 L. austriache a totale pagamento del Macbet il quale resta di proprietà di G. Verdi."

Salutami tanto tanto la famiglia Fontana. Mille cose alla Loeve: dille che sarebbe stata forse contenta della parte di Lady.

Abbiati 1, 689

crown worth 200 *zecchini;*[1] the fair Barbieri[2] presented it to me at the third performance: "The Florentines to G. Verdi." *Amen.*

I'm sending you the remainder of the 900 Austrian lire, payment in full for *Macbeth.* You told me before that you had received 733 Austrian lire; now I'm sending you 55 florins, and so I'll give you two Austrian lire the next time we see each other.[3] In writing a receipt for me, you'll write: "I have received the remainder of the 900 Austrian lire, full payment for *Macbeth,* which remains the property of G. Verdi."

Give my very best wishes to the Fontana family. Many regards to Loewe—tell her that she would perhaps have been happy with the part of Lady Macbeth.

1. A *zecchino* is a gold coin worth about 13.5 Austrian lire, so the crown would be valued at about 2,700 Austrian lire, three times what poor Piave received for the libretto.

2. Barbieri-Nini was no beauty. Giuseppina Strepponi's comment on learning of her marriage: "Oh, if *she's* found a husband, no one need despair of finding one anymore." (Letter to Lanari, January 1842; in *Abbiati* 1, 382). And see Henry F. Chorley's account of her, in the note to Muzio's letter of 2 November 1846.

3. The arithmetic is as follows: Verdi had lent Piave 300 Austrian lire, and Piave exchanged Verdi's 20 gold Napoleons (400 French or Piedmontese francs) for 433 more, a total of 733 (see Verdi's 2 September and 22 December 1846 letters). Verdi sent the equivalent of 165 more (a florin was equal to 3 lire), for a grand total of 898.

VERDI TO GIUSEPPE GIUSTI

Milan, 27 March 1847

Grazie, mille volte grazie della tua carissima lettera; m'hai compensato in parte del dispiacere di non averti potuto abbracciare prima di lasciare Firenze.

Sì: tu dici benissimo: *la corda del dolore è quella che trova maggior consonanza nell'animo nostro:* tu parli dell'arte da quel grande che sei ed io seguirò certamente i tuoi suggerimenti chè intendo cosa vuoi dire.

Oh se avessimo un poeta che ci sapesse ordire un dramma come tu l'intendi! Ma sgraziatamente (tu stesso ne converrai) se vogliamo qualche cosa che almeno almeno faccia effetto bisogna a nostra vergogna ricorrere a cose non nostre. Quanti argomenti nelle nostre istorie! . . .

Abbiati 1, 691

Thanks, a thousand thanks for your dear letter; you have compensated in part for my regret in not having been able to embrace you before leaving Florence.

You put it very well: *the string of pain is that which finds greatest consonance within our soul:* you speak of art as the great man that you are, and I will certainly follow your suggestions, for I understand what you mean.

Oh, if only we had a poet who knew how to devise such a drama as you have in mind! But unfortunately (you yourself will agree) if we want something that is at the very least effective, we must then, to our shame, resort to things not ours. How many subjects in our own history! . . .

PIAVE TO LANARI

Venice, 30 March 1847

Ti ringrazio del libretto del Macbetto cui mi sarebbe piaciuto avessi unito due righe. Ho sottochio lettera di Verdi che mi scrive tanto delle accoglienze Fiorentine. Firenze deve essere ben grata anche a Lanari, se un lavoro quale si è il

I thank you for the *Macbeth* libretto; it would have pleased me had you sent two or three lines with it. I have before me a letter of Verdi's, and he writes much to me about the warm Florentine reception. Florence must be most grateful,

Macbetto si scriveva per la Pergola, e tu pure ne sarai contento. Tutti sono contenti fuorchè il poeta del quale per puntigli si ommise il nome.

Florence: Biblioteca Nazionale,
Fondo Lanari 20^{II}.128;
De Angelis, *Le carte*, p.119

too, to Lanari, if such a work as *Macbeth* is was written for the Pergola, and you, too, must be happy about it. Everyone is happy except the librettist whose name through scruples was omitted.

VERDI TO ANDREA MAFFEI

[*Milan?, early April 1847?*]

Ti prego d'accettare per mia memoria questa bagatella: è ben poca cosa in confronto a quello che tu hai fatto per me, ma valgami almeno la volontà, ed il desiderio d'esserti grato.—

Riceverai anche 50 Napoleoni d'oro per i *Masnadieri* . . . [1]

Milan: Biblioteca Nazionale Braidense;
Quartetto Milanese Ottocentesco, 74

I beg you to accept this trifle as a souvenir; it is quite a small thing in comparison with what you have done for me, but let it at least serve to express my wish and desire to thank you.

You will also receive 50 gold Napoleons for *Masnadieri* . . . [1]

1. Equivalent to about 1,083 Austrian lire (judging from the exchange rate that Piave obtained), about twenty percent more than the 900 lire Piave received for *Macbeth*. Maffei's reply (see next item) began with the complaint that he had been paid more than the amount agreed upon—"what you've always given to Piave and Solera"—and his insistence that the excess should be returned to Verdi.

MAFFEI TO VERDI

11 April 1847

. . . Perchè m'invii il regalo magnifico d'un oriolo e d'una catenella d'oro? Che cosa ti ho fatto per questo? Vuoi forse pagarmi quei miserabili tapelli che ho messo al libretto del Piave? Quanto essi valgano dimandalo alla Rivista fiorentina.[1] Il tuo cuore che dovrebbe conoscermi non può avere avuta questa intenzione, che mi farebbe morir di vergogna. Rimandarti il tuo dono? ma come farlo senza offenderti? Ed io vorrei pure attaccarmi a te come al più caro, al più nobile, al più glorioso de' miei amici. Non ne ho dunque il coraggio. Ma s'io lo debbo tenere, non negarmi almeno la grazia di accettare anche da te [*sic*] le due povere memorie che tu vedi . . .

Sant'Agata; *Gatti* (1931) 1, 288

. . . Why do you send me the magnificent gift of a watch and gold chain? What have I done for you to deserve this? Do you perhaps want to pay me for those wretched little patches which I put on Piave's libretto? Ask the *Rivista fiorentina*[1] how much they are worth. Your heart, which should know me, could not have had this intention, which would make me die of shame. Send back your gift? But how, without offending you? And yet I want to attach myself to you as the dearest, the noblest, the most glorious of my friends. And so I lack the courage to do it. But if I must keep it, at least do not deny me the favor of accepting from me the two insignificant souvenirs that you see . . .

1. Maffei probably meant Montazio's *La Rivista di Firenze*, especially his article *"Macbeth:* Profanazione in quattro atti di F. M. Piave" in the 27 March 1847 issue (see "Reviews" at 382 and Verdi's 11 April 1857 letter to Tito Ricordi).

MUZIO TO BAREZZI

Milan, 12 April 1847

. . . Il *Macbeth* viene contrastato da tre impresari, di Venezia, Padova, Vicenza, i quali lo vorrebbero prima di tutti gli altri; cioè Venezia lo vorrebbe prima di Padova e Vicenza; Padova prima di Venezia e Vicenza; e Vicenza prima di Venezia e Padova; perchè avendo la strada di

. . . *Macbeth* is being fought over by three impresarios, from Venice, Padua, and Vicenza, and each would like to get it before the others; that is, Venice would like it before Padua and Vicenza; Padua, before Venice and Vicenza; and Vicenza, before Venice and Padua; for

ferro la gente vi accorre con facilità e poca spesa.[1]

Lumley paga cinque volte il nolo a Ricordi, basta che Ricordi non dia il *Macbeth* al teatro di Covent-Garden, ove canta Ronconi,[2] ma Ricordi non può perchè ha già fatto il contratto. Tutti i giornali francesi grandi e piccoli, e così gli Inglesi, hanno parlato molto bene del *Macbeth*, fuori di uno: la *Gazette des Theatres* di Parigi che ne ha detto male, ed è stato un fiorentino che ha scritto l'articolo.[3]

La *Gazzetta Musicale* di Ricordi ha incominciato ieri a parlare del *Macbeth* con la critica,[4] ma siccome fino ad ora non parla che del libro, così in avvenire quando parlerà della musica ce la manderò, ma si ricordi che è un articolo assai severo perchè me lo ha detto Ricordi . . .

Garibaldi, 314

now, having the railroad, people can get [from one place to the other] easily and cheaply.[1]

Lumley will pay five times the rental price to Ricordi, provided that Ricordi doesn't give *Macbeth* to the Covent Garden Theater, where Ronconi is singing;[2] but Ricordi can't do this because he's already made the contract. All the French newspapers, big and small, and likewise the English ones, have spoken very highly of *Macbeth*, except for one: the *Gazette des Théâtres* of Paris, which spoke badly of it, and it was a Florentine who wrote the article.[3]

Ricordi's *Gazzetta musicale* began yesterday to review *Macbeth*,[4] but since so far it has dealt only with the libretto, in the future, when they deal with the music, I'll send it to you. But remember that it's a very stern article, for Ricordi has told me so . . .

1. The Paduan impresario won this battle; see "A Hundred Years of *Macbeth*," at 428.

2. Benjamin Lumley, impresario of Her Majesty's, London; *I masnadieri* was composed to his commission. Giorgio Ronconi (the first Nabucco) was engaged at the rival London house. In fact, *Macbeth* was done at neither theater (it did not reach Covent Garden until 1960); see Muzio's letter of 29 June 1847.

3. Although this critic is generally assumed to be Enrico Montazio (e.g., Mila, *La Giovinezza di Verdi*, p. 276), Muzio must be referring to Alessandro Gagliardi's quite nasty review in the *Revue et Gazette Musicale* of 28 March 1847 (see Reviews at 376–79). The *Gazette des Théâtres* did not exist in 1847, and neither of the two Parisian journals with titles at all similar to Muzio's "Gazette des Théâtres" (*Revue et Gazette des Théâtres* and *Journal des Théâtres*) even carried a review of the Florence *Macbeth*.

4. Muzio refers to the first installment of Casamorata's long essay, reprinted at 385–95.

MUZIO TO BAREZZI
Milan, 14 April 1847

A quest'ora avrà già ricevuta un'altra mia lettera. Il signor Maestro sta bene e lavora molto; ma non ho ancora potuto parlargli nè di Londra, nè di nessun'altra cosa; perchè ci vediamo poco, ed ognuno sta nella sua stanza, essendo anch'io tanto occupato delle riduzioni del *Macbeth* che non posso quasi tener dietro agli incisori,[1] e Ricordi ne ha una premura del diavolo.

Quando arrivai a Milano trovai il Maestro arrabbiato, perchè ho tardato. Ricordi anch'esso perchè le stampe del *Macbeth* sono sortite scorrette e piene di errori di stampa, e toccava a me, avendole ridotte, assistere alla stampa; di più trovai i miei scolari infedeli, e questi non li ho più, essendosi provvisti di altro maestro . . .

Garibaldi, 314–15

By now you've probably received another letter of mine. The Maestro is well and is working hard; but I haven't been able to speak to him about London or anything else; because we see little of each other, and each of us stays in his own room, I myself being so busy with the arrangements of *Macbeth* that I can hardly keep up with the engravers,[1] and Ricordi is in a fiendish rush.

When I arrived in Milan I found the Maestro angry because I was late. Ricordi was, too, because the prints of *Macbeth* came out incorrectly and full of printing errors, and it fell to me, having made the arrangement, to help in the printing; moreover, I found my students disloyal, and I don't have them any more, for they found themselves another teacher . . .

1. According to the *libroni* (see pp. 302–03), Ricordi's engravers had begun work just the day before on the last installment of the piano solo arrangement, scheduled for publication on April 17. Muzio then turned to the piano-duet arrangement, as his April 22 letter indicates.

Frontispiece of first piano-vocal score, 1847

MUZIO TO BAREZZI

Milan, 22 April 1847

. . . Il *Macbeth* trova a Milano grandi fautori, in tutte le case si suona, ed i pezzi sono sopra tutti i cembali.[1] Ho finito stamattina la riduzione del primo atto a quattro mani,[2] che è riuscito bene molto, e quando la suoniamo col Maestro sembra l'effetto d'un'orchestra. Quando sarà stampata intera gliene manderò una copia, perchè dovendo ridurre qualche cosa per banda od orchestra, vi si trova tutto l'effetto che si vuole e tutta l'istrumentazione come nell'originale.[3]

Il *Macbeth* è fissato per la fiera del Santo a *Padova,* mediante 3.000 Lire Austr. di nolo; la Barbieri e Colini[4] sono gli esecutori principali. Coro di donne n. 24, ed uomini n. 30. La fiera succede in luglio, e se io sarò a Milano forse anderò a metterlo in scena, avendomi cercato.[5]

Finita la stagione di Mantova, Lanari farà ancora il *Macbeth* a Firenze con De-Bassini e la Boccabadati o la De la Grange.[6] Egli, che vuol guadagnare, sa quali opere vogliono esser fatte. Tutti i fiorentini desiderano di sentirlo ancora; ma manca la Barbieri, e questo è un gran vuoto.[7]

. . . *Macbeth* is finding enthusiastic supporters in Milan; it's played in all homes, and the numbers are on every piano.[1] This morning I finished the piano-duet arrangement of Act I,[2] which turned out very well, and when I play it with the Maestro it seems to have the effect of an orchestra. When it's printed in full I'll send you a copy, so that, when you have to arrange something for band or orchestra, you'll find in it all the effect you could want and all the instrumentation, as in the original.[3]

Macbeth is scheduled for the festival of the Saint [St. Anthony] in Padua, for 3,000 Austrian lire rental fee. Barbieri and Colini[4] are the principal singers. Chorus: twenty-four women and thirty men. The festival falls in July, and if I'm in Milan maybe I'll go and stage it, since they asked me to.[5]

Once the season in Mantua is over, Lanari will do *Macbeth* in Florence again, with De Bassini and Boccabadati or De la Grange.[6] He wants to make money, and knows what operas they want to hear done. All the Florentines want to hear it again, but Barbieri is missing and that's a big gap.[7]

Anche a Brescia e Bergamo hanno cercato il *Macbeth;* ma Ricordi, prima di darlo, vuol sapere i cantanti ed il numero dei cori.

A Venezia si darà in Carnevale alla Fenice il *Macbeth.* ...

... Anche Lumley vuol fare il *Macbeth* nel suo Teatro,[8] e ha scritto al Maestro che porti seco lo spartito, come se il Maestro fosse ancora padrone dello spartito ...

Ieri hanno dichiarato in contravvenzione Varesi perchè ha cantato un'aria del *Macbeth* a Vienna in un concerto in teatro, e chi sa quanto gli faranno pagare il gusto di aver cantato questa aria ...

They've asked for *Macbeth* at Brescia and Bergamo too, but Ricordi wants to know who the singers are, and the size of the chorus, before giving it to them.

Macbeth will be performed during Carnival at the Fenice in Venice ...

... Lumley, too, wants to do *Macbeth* in his theatre,[8] and has written to ask the Maestro to bring the score with him, as if the Maestro were still the proprietor of the music ...

Yesterday, they declared Varesi at fault for singing an aria from *Macbeth* at a theater concert in Vienna, and who knows how much they'll make him pay for the pleasure of having sung that aria ...

Garibaldi, 316–17

1. From April 17, the entire opera was available in both piano-vocal and piano-solo arrangements.

2. Ricordi's engravers began work on this edition two days earlier, so Muzio must already have turned in part of his arrangement. According to the *libroni,* work on other numbers began on April 26, 27, 28, May 3, May (unspecified)—one can picture Muzio trying desperately to keep ahead of the engravers. The edition was announced as ready in the May 19 issue of Ricordi's *Gazzetta Musicale di Milano,* a week before Muzio and Verdi departed for London.

3. Muzio surely means that a piano-duet reduction keeps most of the *material* of the orchestral score (as compared to a piano-solo reduction, for example), not the actual instrumentation; he is more specific in his letter of ?23 May 1847.

4. Filippo Colini (1811–63). Italian baritone, debut 1835. Created principal baritone roles in *Giovanna d'Arco* (La Scala, 1845), *Battaglia di Legnano* (Argentina, Rome, 1849), and *Stiffelio* (Teatro Grande, Trieste, 1850). Other Verdian operas in his repertory included *Oberto, Nabucco, Lombardi, Ernani, Macbeth,* and *Luisa Miller.* Only two productions of *Macbeth* have been documented thus far: Padua in 1847 and Rome's Teatro Argentina in 1854.

5. Muzio spent July in London and Paris with Verdi, but he did have an opportunity to stage *Macbeth* at Lodi and Mantua in the 1847–48 Carnival season.

6. For De Bassini, see PERSONALIA. Augusta Boccabadati (?–1875) made her debut in Parma in 1844 and, after appearances in various Italian theaters, eventually settled in Santiago, Chile. She sang Lady Macbeth in the June 1847 production in Florence, in Rome three months later, in Venice (1851), Terni (1852), and Messina (1853). Not to be confused with her more celebrated mother Luigia or sister Virginia (a noted interpreter of Violetta). Anna de la Grange (who was New York's first Violetta, in 1856, and Leonora in the 1863 Madrid *Forza*) sang the role of Lady Macbeth only once, at La Fenice in December 1847, without much success. One gathers from the review in the *Gazzetta Privilegiata di Venezia* that she was a singer more of the Rossinian stamp.

7. According to Montazio's review of this revival, in the 23 June 1847 number of his *La Rivista di Firenze* (see "Reviews" at 396), the opera was as well received as before, showing the "stubborn *anti-verdisti*" the falsity of their claim that the triumph of the opera had been due solely to Barbieri. Although Boccabadati was not the sublime singer Barbieri was, she won the favor of the audience "with intelligent and animated acting, always an impossible desire with Barbieri." (If this last is correct, perhaps Verdi *needed* to make Barbieri rehearse the duet "151" times.)

8. I.e., as well as *I masnadieri,* which Verdi was composing for Her Majesty's

PIAVE TO GIOVANNI RICORDI   *Venice, 27 April 1847*

Voi foste a Venezia ed io non vi ho veduto! Credetemi che ne ho vera bile; ma io era malato, e alla forza maggiore convien piegare il capo.

Ho pregato il celebre Dottor Fario [?] a farvi capitare la presente, che serve a chiedervi la manutenzione d'una vostra promessa, quella

You were in Venice and I didn't see you! Believe me, I'm most upset; but I was ill, and we must bow before force majeure.

I have asked the famous Dr. Fario [?] to convey to you this note, which will serve to ask that you keep a promise you made, namely that

cioè di farmi avere qualche copia del libretto *Macbet*. Potrete consegnarla allo stesso gentile porgitore della presente, che s'incaricherà di portarmele ...

P.S. Essendo partito l'amico senza ch'io giungessi a consegnargli la presente la imposto, e vi prego a mandarmi sotto fascia le copie del *Macbet* ...

Milan: Archivio Ricordi

you would have a few copies of the *Macbeth* libretto sent to me. You might entrust them to the same kind bearer of the present note who would undertake to bring them to me ...

P.S. Since the friend left before I could give him this, I am posting it, and beg you to send me the copies of *Macbeth* under separate cover ...

MUZIO TO BAREZZI

[Milan, 21 May 1847]

Eccogli le marce. Vi è quella del *Macbeth*, che è molto bella e graziosa. Lunedì gli manderò entro una lettera in carta da musica sottilissima l'Adagio, non avendolo ancora potuto fare per mancanza di tempo.

Nel fare lo spartito ho fatto in maniera che si possano fare le piccole parti, collo stesso spartito, cioè tagliando in piccole liste ciascuna parte e con un poco di *colla* attaccarle sopra una carta bianca e così sono già fatte le parti. Vedrà che per questo io non ho scritto che sul davanti della facciata.

L'Oficleid vuol essere trasportata secondo il solito.

Tanto le marce del *Macbeth* che le altre due vogliono essere suonate (per esserci l'effetto sicuro) brillanti, staccate e il tempo piuttosto mosso.

... Entro la ventura settimana avrà la riduzione a quattro mani del *Macbeth*, che gli servirà molto per le sue riduzioni ...

Garibaldi, 319–20

Here are the marches for you, including the one from *Macbeth*, which is very beautiful and graceful. Monday I'll send you the *adagio*, on very fine music paper, in a letter, not having yet been able to do this through shortage of time.

In making the score I made it possible to prepare the instrumental parts from the score itself, i.e., by cutting out each part in small strips and sticking them on a blank page with a little glue. And that way the parts are ready made. For that reason, I wrote on only the front side of the page, as you'll see.

The ophicleide part should be transposed in the usual way.

The marches from *Macbeth* as well as the other two are to be played (to be of surefire effect) brillante, staccato, and with a rather fast tempo.

... By the end of next week you'll have the piano-duet arrangement of *Macbeth*, which you'll find very useful for your own arrangements ...

MUZIO TO BAREZZI

[Milan, 23 May 1847?]

Quando riceverà questa mia io sarò già in viaggio col Maestro per Londra.—Andiamo prima a Parigi, ma non ci fermeremo che un giorno o due, e poi continueremo il viaggio per Londra. Noi partiremo mercoledì alle undici della mattina e passiamo per la Svizzera, Basilea, Strasburgo, Parigi, Londra.

La decisione così precipitata del Maestro mi ha rubato il tempo per farci l'adagio ...

Dimani mando a Cremona la riduzione a quattro mani del *Macbeth*; essa le può servire per ridurre; ma alle volte gli effetti sono trasportati in altra maniera, e bisogna essere molto guardinghi ed accorti nel rilevarli. Ad ogni modo la riduzione per canto è più utile nelle arie e duetti; ma nei cori, nei pezzi concertati, e

When you receive this letter I'll already be on the way to London with the Maestro. We go to Paris first, but we'll only stop there for a day or two, and then we'll continue on to London. We'll leave Wednesday [May 26] morning at eleven and we go through Switzerland, Basle, Strasbourg, Paris, London.

The Maestro's sudden decision robbed me of the time to do our *adagio* ...

Tomorrow I'll send the four-hand arrangement of *Macbeth* to Cremona. You can use it for [your own] arrangements, but sometimes the effects [of the original] are rendered in a different way, and one must be very cautious and shrewd in reconstructing them. At any rate, the piano-vocal arrangement is more use-

massime in questi, troverà gli accompagnamenti ed i movimenti come vi sono nell'orchestra.—Si ricordi della battaglia che ci vogliono due trombe in re, le quali facciano sempre un sol fino a quando passa in maggiore, che allora si fermano.

Garibaldi, 320–21

ful for the arias and duets; but in the choruses, the ensembles, and especially in these, you'll find [in the four-hand arrangement] the accompaniments and the figurations as they are in the orchestra [score]. Remember that two trumpets in D are needed for the battle, and they should keep playing a [written] G up to the change to major, and then they stop.

MUZIO TO BAREZZI

London, 29 June 1847

... Alla Opera vorrebbero mettere in scena il *Macbeth*, e se il Maestro lo vuol mettere in Francese, gli darebbero i diritti di autore che gli potrebbero fruttare un ventimila franchi; e così riposando guadagnerebbe questi denari; se tutto questo si potrà combinare, l'affare è tre volte vantaggioso ... [1]

Sabbato al Covent-Garden va in scena l'*Ernani* e Carlo V sarà l'*Alboni* (contralto). A Londra contralto e basso è lo stesso. Il *Macbeth* pare che non si faccia più[2] perchè Ronconi dice che non gli sta bene la parte; ma è per un puntiglio, e perchè già sa che a Parigi gettò a terra l'*Ernani* l'anno passato.[3] Orbene, appena Verdi fu qui a Londra, gli mandò a dire da Marini[4] che avrebbe piacere di passare i *Foscari* con lui per intendersi sopra certe cose che non gli stavano bene; ma Verdi gli fece rispondere che l'*Ernani* glielo avrebbe insegnato, perchè fece fiasco a Parigi, ma che i *Foscari* non glieli insegnerebbe, perchè, se vuole, ha talento bastantemente per fare quella parte e per trovargli l'effetto; per questo Ronconi non vuol più fare il *Macbeth*, ma l'impresa lo vuole ... vedremo chi vincerà ...

Garibaldi, 335–37

... They would like to produce *Macbeth* at the [Paris] Opéra, and if the Maestro wants to present it in French, they would give him author's rights, which would bring him about twenty thousand francs, and so, he'd earn this money by taking a rest. If all of this can be arranged, the business is triply advantageous ... [1]

Ernani will be produced at Covent Garden on Saturday, and [Marietta] Alboni (contralto) will be the Carlo V. Contralto or bass— in London it's all the same to them. It seems that they won't do *Macbeth* after all,[2] because [Giorgio] Ronconi says that the part doesn't suit him well. But it's really for a personal petty grudge; and because, as you know, he ruined *Ernani* in Paris last year.[3] Well, as soon as Verdi arrived here in London, [Ronconi] sent word through Marini[4] that he'd like to run through *Due Foscari* with him to work out certain things that didn't suit him well, but Verdi sent back the reply that he would have taught him *Ernani*, since he made a fiasco with it in Paris, but wouldn't teach him *Due Foscari*, because, if he wants to, he has enough talent to do that part and to find out by himself how to make it effective. And so Ronconi no longer wants to do *Macbeth*, but the management wants him to ... we'll see who wins ...

1. Nothing came of this; *Macbeth* was not done in French until the 1865 premiere of *Macbeth II*, and it was not performed at the Opéra during Verdi's lifetime.

2. In a letter of 16 June 1847 (*Garibaldi*, 331) Muzio had said that the work would be performed later with Ronconi and Giulia Grisi. This was Covent Garden's first season as the Royal Italian Opera, in rivalry to Her Majesty's, where Verdi was preparing *I masnadieri*.

3. This fact, as well as an anecdote that Muzio goes on to relate, explains why Ronconi rejected the role of Carlo V; Antonio Tamburini, Covent Garden's other baritone that season, had already rejected it as lying too high for him.

4. Ignazio Marini, creator of Oberto and Attila, and Covent Garden's principal bass that season

MUZIO TO BAREZZI

Milan, 23 August 1847

... Il *Pirata*[1] non ha parlato del *Macbeth?* ... io non lo sapevo, perchè non leggo mai alcun

... The *Pirata*[1] hasn't discussed *Macbeth?* ... I didn't know that because I never read a news-

giornale. Gli dirò però che il *Macbeth* ha fatto un furore a Padova, di cui non se ne ha alcun esempio. Basta il dirle che in 8 sere che fu dato il *Macbeth,* il famoso duetto si ripetè 25 volte, e nell'ultima sera si fece ripetere 5 volte ... [2]

Garibaldi, 352

1. Milanese theatrical journal, edited by F. Regli

paper. I'll tell you, however, that in Padua *Macbeth* made an unparalleled furor. It's enough to tell you that in [the] eight evenings that *Macbeth* was given, the famous duet was done twenty-five times, and on the final evening it had to be done five times ... [2]

2. See "Reviews" at 396–97.

1848–1857

TITO RICORDI TO VERDI

Milan, 6 October 1848

... è già qualche tempo che Lanari mi scrisse di essere stato eletto per unico agente al servizio di quella impresa [San Carlo of Naples], e in tale qualità mi aveva chiesto il prezzo di nolo del Macbeth, facendomi però rimarcare che in Napoli esisteva già questo spartito, probabilmente istrumentato sulla riduzione stampata. Avendogli io fatto la mia dimanda in 300 Ducati (Per un Macbeth e per un teatro come il S. Carlo di Napoli è forse troppo?), Lanari mi risponde d'aver scritto a Napoli la mia dimanda, ma credere egli che non sarà facile il combinare, poichè gli era stato scritto che ne esisteva colà una copia, e che se ciò fosse vero non preferiranno certo di spendere questa somma a fronte di quella copia che avranno a meno anche a rischio di *qualche alterazione d'istrumentatura!!!* che non farà gran risalto ove non si conosce l'originale. Per cui tu vedi che la morale di quella Impresa non ha punto migliorato, e che il rispetto dovuto agli autori cade dinanzi al risparmio di qualche ducato. E ciò trattandosi d'un'opera come il Macbeth! Quello che è certo è che la stagione si apre coi Lombardi, che non diedi io, e che probabilmente sarà uno spartito fatturato nello stesso modo; mentre avrebbero potuto dimandare la Gerusalemme per un teatro come quello; e poi si è già annunciato il Macbeth ...

Sant'Agata

... It's already some time ago that Lanari wrote me that he had been chosen as the sole agent serving that theatrical administration [San Carlo of Naples], and in that capacity he asked me the *Macbeth* rental fee, bringing to my attention, however, that in Naples there already was a score of the work, probably orchestrated from the printed [piano-vocal] reduction. After I quoted him a price of 300 ducats—for a *Macbeth* and for a theatre like the San Carlo of Naples is that too much to ask?—Lanari replied that he had conveyed my price to Naples, but that he believed that the deal wouldn't be easy to arrange since they had written to him that there was already a copy there, and, if this is true, they certainly won't choose to spend that amount instead of using the copy they have, even at the risk of *some changes in the orchestration!!!* which won't be very obvious where the original isn't known. From which you see that the ethics of that administration hasn't improved a bit and that the respect owed to authors yields to the saving of a ducat or two. And this with an opera like *Macbeth!* What's certain is that the season will open with *Lombardi,* which I haven't rented to them, and which will probably be a score concocted in the same way; while they could have asked for *Gerusalemme* for a theater like that; and then *Macbeth* has already been announced ...

GIOVANNI RICORDI TO VERDI

Como, 15 October 1848

... Ora sappia che Flauto[1] fù sì indelicato da mandarmi il prospetto d'appalto stampato, in cui sono annunciate 4 opere nuove p[er] Napoli, cioè i Lombardi, Macbeth, Roberto il Diavolo, ed i Martiri di Donizetti. Del Macbeth poi non ebbi più da Lanari alcuna risposta p[er] cui mi sembra che si vogliono proprio servire della copia istrumentata che colà esiste!!! Mentre invece con altra lettera Flauto venne a chiedermi lo spart[it]o de' Martiri, senza far cenno alcuno nè dei Lombardi nè del Macbeth! cosa ne dici? ...

Sant'Agata

1. See note to following letter.

... Now learn that Flauto[1] was so tactless as to send me the printed prospectus, in which four operas new to Naples are announced, namely *I lombardi, Macbeth, Roberto il diavolo,* and Donizetti's *I martiri.* I've had no answer from Lanari about *Macbeth,* from which it seems to me that they really do want to use the copy orchestrated [from a piano-vocal score] that exists there!!! Meanwhile in another letter Flauto proceeded to ask me for the score of *I martiri,* without making any mention either of *I lombardi* or of *Macbeth!* What do you say to that? ...

VERDI TO VINCENZO FLAUTO[1]

Paris, 23 November 1848

... Scrivo a Cammarano[2] per diverse cose sul *Macbeth;* assistete anche voi alle prove e non vi rincresca farne fare una di più: è un'opera un po' più difficile delle altre mie ed importante per la *mise en scene.* Vi confesso che ci tengo a quest'opera a preferenza dell'altre mie e mi rincrescerebbe vederla andare a precipizio. Avvertite che appartiene ad un genere che generalmente o vanno benissimo, o vanno a *rompicollo.* Quindi è necessario una estrema cura nell'esecuzione.[3]

Sant'Agata (draft); *Copialettere,* 59–60

... I am writing to Cammarano[2] about various matters concerning *Macbeth;* attend the rehearsals yourself, too, and do not object to calling an extra one: it is an opera a little more difficult than my others, and important for the mise-en-scène. I confess to you that I hold this opera in greater regard than my others, and I would regret seeing it fall to pieces. Note that it belongs to a genre that generally either does very well or is a *disaster.* So, extreme care is needed with its execution.[3]

1. Impresario of the San Carlo, Naples; *Macbeth* was performed there on 22 January 1849. See the following letter, to Cammarano.

2. See note to following letter.

3. In a passage subsequently crossed out in this draft letter, Verdi makes some observations on operatic practice at the Paris Opéra: "You know that they have here six to seven, and even eight, months of rehearsals. Do not think that this is useless; I once thought so, but now that I have had experience of it I can see that it is necessary, because here, you might say, a good part of the opera needs to be created on stage, while the rehearsals are actually in progress. The mise-en-scène is perhaps the principal thing here, and many operas are sustained in this way ... "

VERDI TO SALVATORE CAMMARANO[1]

Paris, 23 November 1848

... So che state concertando il Macbeth e siccome è una opera a cui m'interesso più che alle altre così permettete che ve ne dica alcune parole. Si è data alla Tadolini la parte di Lady Macbeth ed io resto sorpreso come Ella abbia accondisceso fare questa parte. Voi sapete quanta stima ho della Tadolini, ed Ella stessa lo sa, ma nell'interesse comune io credo necessario farvi alcune riflessioni. La Tadolini ha troppo grandi qualità per fare quella parte! Vi parrà questo un assurdo forse!!...La Tadolini ha una

... I know that you are rehearsing *Macbeth,* and since it's an opera that interests me more than the others, permit me to say a few words to you about it. The role of Lady Macbeth has been assigned to Tadolini, and I'm surprised that she should have deigned to undertake this role. You know how highly I regard Tadolini, and she herself knows it; but I believe it's necessary—for the interest of all concerned—to make a few observations to you. Tadolini's qualities are far too good for that role! This

figura bella e buona, ed io vorrei Lady Macbeth brutta e cattiva. La Tadolini canta alla perfezione; ed io vorrei che *Lady* non cantasse. La Tadolini ha una voce stupenda, chiara, limpida, potente; ed io vorrei in Lady una voce aspra, soffocata, cupa. La voce della Tadolini ha dell'angelico;[2] la voce di Lady vorrei che avesse del diabolico. Sottomettete queste riflessioni all'Impresa, al M.° Mercadante, che egli più delli altri approverà queste mie idee, alla Tadolini stessa, poi fate nella vostra sagezza quello che stimate meglio.[3]

Avvertite che i pezzi principali dell'Opera sono due: il Duetto fra *Lady, ed il marito* ed il Sonna[m]bulismo; Se questi pezzi si perdono l'opera è a terra: e questi pezzi non si devono assolutamente cantare:

bisogna agirli, e declamarli
con una voce ben cupa
e velata: senza di ciò non
vi può essere effetto. (L'orchestra *colle sordine*.)

La scena estremamente scura—Nel terzo atto le apparizioni dei re (io l'ho visto a Londra)[4] si devono fare dietro un foro nella scena, con avanti un velo non spesso *cenerino*. I *re* devono essere non fantocci ma otto uomini in carne ed ossa: il piano su cui devono passare deve essere come una montagnuola, e che si veda ben distintamente montare e discendere. La scena dovrà essere perfettamente scura specialmente quando la caldaja sparisce e soltanto chiaro [*sic*] ove passano i *re*. La musica che è sotto il palco scenico, dovrà essere (per il gran Teatro di S. Carlo) rinforzata ma badate bene non vi siano nè trombe nè tromboni. Il suono deve apparir lontano e muto quindi dovrà essere composta di clarini bassi, fagotti, contrafagotti e nient'altro.[5]

Sant'Agata; *Copialettere*, 60–62

may perhaps seem absurd to you!!...Tadolini has a beautiful and attractive appearance; and I would like Lady Macbeth to be ugly and evil. Tadolini sings to perfection; and I would like the Lady not to sing. Tadolini has a stupendous voice, clear, limpid, powerful; and I would like the Lady to have a harsh, stifled, and hollow voice. Tadolini's voice has an angelic quality;[2] I would like the Lady's voice to have a diabolical quality! Submit these remarks to the management, to Maestro Mercadante, who will approve these ideas of mine more than the others will, and to Tadolini herself. Then do in your wisdom what you think best.[3]

Note that there are two principal numbers in the opera: the duet between the Lady and her husband and the sleepwalking scene. If these numbers fail, then the opera is ruined. And these pieces absolutely must not be sung;

They must be acted out and declaimed
with a very hollow and veiled
voice; otherwise, they won't
be able to make any effect. (The orchestra with *mutes*.)

The stage is extremely dark. In the third act, the apparitions of the kings (I've seen it done in London)[4] must take place behind an opening in the scenery, with a fine, *ashen* veil in front of it. The *kings* should not be puppets, but eight men of flesh and blood. The floor over which they pass must resemble a mound, and they must be seen clearly to ascend and descend. The scene must be completely dark, especially when the cauldron disappears, and lighted only where the *kings* pass. The music beneath the stage must be reinforced (for the large San Carlo Theatre), but be sure there are neither trumpets nor trombones. The sound must seem distant and muted, and must therefore be composed of bass clarinets, bassoons, contrabassoons, and nothing else.[5]

1. Librettist, but also stage director, etc., at the San Carlo. For Verdi, he had already written *Alzira* (1845), and at the time of this letter he was busy with *La battaglia di Legnano*; *Luisa Miller* and *Il trovatore* were still in the future.

2. Cf. Muzio's comment, "She sings . . . like an angel," in his letter of 14 December 1846, above.

3. Tadolini did sing the part.

4. Probably the production of Macready at the Princess's Theatre, on either 7 or 14 June 1847. See WEAVER at 144.

5. As noted in CONATI at 236n, neither bass clarinets nor contrabassoons appear in the 1847 score. At one point, Verdi had included trumpets, however; see LAWTON at 225–26.

GIOVANNI RICORDI TO VERDI   *Milan, 19 January 1849*

. . . Seppi poi con vero piacere dai De Rossi il p[ieno][1] entusiasmo che ottenne il tuo Macbeth

. . . Then I learned from the De Rossis—with real pleasure—about the [completely][1] enthusi-

messo da te i[n scena;] pareva tutt'altra opera di quella che si era rappresent[ata prima(?).] Sento anche che questa circostanza ha per naturale consequenza ritardato l'andata in scena della nuova opera ... [2]

astic reception of your *Macbeth* in your [staging;] it seemed a totally different work from the one perform[ed before(?).] I also hear that this fact has naturally delayed the production of the new opera ... [2]

Sant'Agata

1. Readings in brackets are conjectural; the letter is torn.

2. Verdi was in Rome to stage *La battaglia di Legnano*, which was finally produced on January 27; *Macbeth* had been performed on January 10.

VERDI TO NESTOR ROQUEPLAN[1]   *Paris, 2 February 1852*

J'ai bien reflechi à toutes les offres que vous m'avez faites ces jours derniers, et à ce que vous m'avez dit ce matin: je m'empresse à vous communiquer ma réponse definitive. C'est vrai: moi même je vous ai proposé autrefois de traduire Macbeth, à la condition cependant d'écrire éxpres l'année suivante une partition pour l'Opéra. Malheureusement le seule époque que j'ai exceptée (l'hiver 1852–53) c'est précisement la seule que [vous] pouvez m'accorder. Plus: je vous ai laissé le choix de l'année pour donner l'Africaine de M.ᵣ Meyerbeer[,] disposé à donner mon opéra avant, ou après comme mieux vous conviendrait: mais il fallait absolument fixer une époque. Vous ne le pouvez pas!: Par consequence je renonce à l'idee d'écrire un opéra nouveau, et aussi de traduir Macbeth.

Sant'Agata; *Copialettere*, 134

I have given much thought to the offers you have made to me these last few days, and to what you told me this morning; I hasten to convey to you my definitive reply. True, I myself once suggested that I should make a French version of *Macbeth*, but on condition that the following year I should compose a work expressly for the Opéra. Unfortunately the only period that I excepted (the winter of 1852–53) is precisely the only period that you can offer me. Moreover, I left it up to you to decide which year M. Meyerbeer's *L'Africaine* should be given, being prepared to give my opera either before or afterward as it suited you: but it was absolutely necessary to fix the period. You cannot do so! As a result, I give up the idea of writing a new opera, and also of translating *Macbeth*.

1. Director of the Paris Opéra. This forceful letter produced a result. On February 28 Verdi signed a contract with Roqueplan to compose a new work for the Opéra, to be produced in 1854–55; *Les Vêpres siciliennes* was the subject eventually chosen.

VERDI TO ALBERTO TORRI[1]   *Paris, 14 February 1852*

Sarà come tu dici! ma le notizie che ricevo da cento parti intorno alli spettacoli della Scala sono scoraggianti. Sarà come tu dici! ma è certo che si è fatto o si voleva fare il Macbet per *opera di ripiego*.[2] Domando a chi ha soltanto ombra di buon senso se è possibile dare uno spartito di quel genere come opera di *ripiego*. Capirai che a me poco importa se *Miller, Attila, Macbet* rappresentate in tanti paesi ed in Milano stessa abbiano ora, o non abbiano successo, ma per tutti i Diavoli io non scriverò mai per un teatro ove si assassinano le opere in quel modo.

Sant'Agata; *Copialettere*, 136

Just as you say! but the news that I receive from a hundred sources about the performances at La Scala is discouraging! Just as you say! but it is certain that *Macbeth* was or was going to be done as an *opera di ripiego*.[2] I ask anyone with even a shadow of good sense if it's possible to present a score of that type as an *opera di ripiego*. You understand that it doesn't much matter to me if *Miller, Attila,* and *Macbeth,* which are played in so many countries, and even in Milan, have a success now or not; but by all the devils in hell, I'll never write for a theatre where they assassinate operas that way.

1. Theatrical agent in Milan

2. An opera to "fall back upon," usually with very little preparation, as when the regularly scheduled opera is not ready in time or is a fiasco. According to a note in the *Copialettere*, in this Milan production (20 January 1852)

neither the doctor nor "Dama di Lady" bothered to appear in the sleepwalking scene, Macbeth's part was too high and Banquo's too low for the respective singers, the women's chorus (including non-singing extras) numbered thirteen, etc.

VERDI TO ANTONIO SOMMA[1]

Busseto, 9 September 1853

... In quanto ai recitativi, se il momento è interessante, possono essere anche lunghetti. Io ne ho fatto dei lunghissimi, per esempio il soliloquio nel duetto del primo atto del *Macbeth:* e l'altro soliloquio nel duetto del primo atto del *Rigoletto.*[2]

Pascolato: *Re Lear e Ballo in maschera*
(Città di Castello: 1902), p. 56

... As for the recitatives, if the situation is interesting they can even be on the long side. I have done some very long ones, for example in the soliloquy in the Act I duet of *Macbeth,* and in the other soliloquy in the Act I duet of *Rigoletto.*[1]

1. The librettist of an uncomposed *King Lear* and then of *Un ballo in maschera;* Verdi's letters to him, collected in the Pascolato volume, form a veritable correspondence course in libretto writing.

2. The dagger speech and "Pari siamo," each formally the first stretch of a *scena e duetto.* These remarks are among the "instructions to a librettist" sent to Somma while he was writing a *King Lear* libretto for Verdi.

VERDI TO TITO RICORDI

Sant'Agata, 11 April 1857

... Torelli[1] di Napoli mi scrive di mandargli il libretto [del *Simon Boccanegra*] ... Egli mi domanda inoltre se la poesia ne è veramente così orribile come si dice: e pare sia opinione universale!! Cosa curiosa! a me pare la poesia migliore che in tanti altri libretti di Piave. Ma basta che un libretto porti il nome di questo povero diavolo perchè la poesia venga giudicata cattiva, anche prima di leggerla: ed a questo proposito bisogna che ti racconti una storiella— Son or dieci anni mi venne in capo di fare il *Macbet:* ne feci io stesso la selva, anzi più della selva feci distesamente il dramma in prosa colla distribuzione di atti, scene, pezzi etc. etc...poi lo diedi a Piave da verseggiare. Come io trovai a ridire su questa verseggiatura, pregai Maffei, col consenso dello stesso Piave, di ripassare quei versi, e di rifarmi di peso il *Coro* delle streghe Atto III, ed il *Sonnambulismo.* Ebbene, lo crederai! quantunque il libretto non portasse il nome di poeta, ma creduto di Piave, il citato *Coro* ed il *Sonnambulismo* furono i più maltrattati, e messi anche in ridicolo!![2] Forse si può in quei due pezzi far meglio, ma tali e quali come esistono son sempre versi di Maffei, ed il Coro specialmente ha molto carattere. Così è: ecco l'opinione pubblica! ...

Milan: Archivio Ricordi (65);
Copialettere, 444

... [Vincenzo] Torelli[1] in Naples has written to me asking me to send him the libretto [of *Simon Boccanegra*] ... Moreover, he has asked me whether the poetry is really as horrible as is said; and it seems to be a universal opinion!! What a curious thing! It seems to me to be better poetry than in many other librettos by Piave. But a libretto need only bear the name of this poor devil for the poetry to be judged bad, even before reading it; and with regard to this I've got to tell you a little story. Ten years ago I got it into my head to do *Macbeth;* I wrote the scenario myself and, indeed, more than the scenario; I wrote out the whole drama in prose, with divisions into acts, scenes, numbers, etc., etc. then I gave it to Piave to put into verse. Since I found things to criticize in the versification, I asked Maffei, with the consent of Piave himself, to go over those lines, and rewrite entirely the *witches' chorus* from Act III, as well as the *sleepwalking scene.* Well, would you believe it? Although the libretto did not bear the poet's name, it was believed to be by Piave, and the said *chorus* and *sleepwalking scene* were treated the worst and even held up to ridicule!![2] Perhaps those two pieces could be done better, but as they stand they're nonetheless Maffei's lines, and the chorus in particular has a lot of character. So, there's public opinion for you! ...

1. Joint-secretary of the San Carlo

2. See, for example, Montazio's *"Macbeth: Profanazione in quattro atti di F. M. Piave,"* in the 27 March 1847 issue of *La Rivista di Firenze,* reprinted at 381–82.

1864

LEON ESCUDIER TO VERDI[1]   *Paris, 13 March 1864*

... Carvalho veut monter [*Macbeth*] l'hiver prochain avec un grand éclat. Pour cet opéra, comme pour Rigoletto il pourrait évidemment se passer de moi et de vous, mais il ne le fera pas. Je lui demanderai une nouvelle prime,[2] mais cette fois plus forte du double que la première; et elle vous appartiendra personnellement. Je ne veux pas qu'il soit dit en ce qui me concerne que vous êtes déshérité en France du produit de votre génie ...

... Carvalho wants to stage [*Macbeth*] next winter in great style. For this opera, as for *Rigoletto*, he could obviously bypass both of us, but he won't do that. I will ask him for another "premium,"[2] but this time twice as large as the first; and it will belong to you personally. I don't want it said that in France you are deprived of the fruits of your genius through any fault of mine ...

Sant'Agata; *Carteggi* 4, 136

1. For a discussion of the Verdi-Escudier correspondence, see GÜNTHER at 174–81.

2. By French law, Carvalho (as Escudier explains in the earlier part of this letter) could have done *Rigoletto* without paying royalties to the composer, but, "like a gentleman," he assigned a *prime personelle* (a personal compensation) to Verdi.

ESCUDIER TO VERDI   *Paris, 27 September 1864*

Les rossignols ne chantent plus. La brise froide commence à souffler ...

Au lyrique on répète depuis un mois la *Traviata*. Je crois à un *grand* succès ...[1] Carvalho du reste ne néglige rien pour l'ouvrage. Il n'y a pas encore eu de répétitions d'orchestre. Je vous tiendrai au courant. Pendant qu'on répète la Traviata les rôles de Macbeth sont distribués. C'est Ismaël qui jouera Macbeth; il y sera très beau. J'ai fait engager pour Lady Macbeth la seule artiste qu'il y ait peut'être en france pour interpréter dignement cette grande création. C'est Mme Rey-Balla qui a chanté avec un immense succès tous vos opéras et que l'opéra de Paris eut la maladresse de laisser partir il y a cinq ans. Carvalho fait pour Macbeth une mise en scène splendide. Permettez-moi de vous rappeler cher maître que fait de la promesse que vous avez bien voulu me faire,[2] j'ai promis à mon tour trois airs de ballet à Carvalho. Voici le moment de vous exécuter. Vous seriez tout à fait aimable si vous vouliez me les envoyer car ils doivent être composés. Ainsi tout va très bien de ce côté. Vous trouverez votre compte je ne

The nightingales sing no more. The cold wind begins to blow ...

At the Lyrique, they have been rehearsing *Traviata* for a month. I think it will be a great success ...[1] Carvalho, moreover, has spared no pains over the production. There has not yet been an orchestral rehearsal. I will keep you posted. While *Traviata* is being rehearsed, the parts for *Macbeth* have been given out. Ismaël will play Macbeth; he'll be very good in it. For Lady Macbeth, I have had engaged the only artist in France, perhaps, who can worthily interpret that great role. It is Mme. Rey-Balla, who has sung in all your operas with great success and whom the Paris Opera had the stupidity to let go five years ago. Carvalho plans a splendid production for *Macbeth*. Let me remind you, dear master, that, as a result of the promise you were good enough to make me,[2] I, in turn, have promised three *airs de ballet* to Carvalho. Now the time has come for you to fulfill it. Will you be so kind as to send them to me, since they should already be composed. So all goes well at this end. You will find your

dis pas de gloire, vous en avez assez, mais de billets de banque dans le succès, et j'en serai fort heureux, croyez-le bien ...

Sant'Agata

account replenished with, I won't say glory, for you have enough of that, but with bank notes from your success, and I will be very happy about that, believe me! ...

1. It was; see letter of 2 November 1864.
2. In late June, when Escudier visited the Verdis in Genoa

VERDI TO ESCUDIER

Busseto, 22 October 1864

... Ho scorso il Macbet coll'intenzione di fare le arie di ballo, ma ohimè! alla lettura di questa musica sono stato colpito da cose che non avrei voluto trovare. Per dire tutto in una parola vi sono diversi pezzi che sono o deboli, o mancanti di carattere che è ancor peggio...

1.º Un'aria di Lady Macbet nell'Atto II
2.º Diversi squarci a rifare nella Visione Atto III
3.º Rifare completamente Aria Macbet Atto III
4. Rittoccare le prime scene dell'Atto IV
5. Far di nuovo l'ultimo Finale togliendo la morte in scena di Macbet.

Per far questo lavoro, oltre il balletto,[1] ci vuol tempo, e converrebbe che Carvalho abbandonasse il pensiero di dare il Macbet in quest'inverno.
Parlatene e rispondete subito...

Paris: Bibliothèque de l'Opéra;
Rivista Musicale Italiana 35 (1928), 181

... I have looked through *Macbeth* with the aim of writing the ballet music, but alas!, on reading through this music I was struck by things that I would not have wished to find. To say it all in a word, there are certain numbers that are either weak or lacking in character, which is worse still...

1) An aria for Lady Macbeth in Act II
2) Various passages to rewrite in the hallucination scene of Act III
3) Rewrite completely Macbeth's aria in Act III
4) Retouch the opening scenes of Act IV
5) Recompose the last finale, doing away with the death of Macbeth on stage.

In order to do this work, besides the ballet,[1] time is needed, and Carvalho had better give up the idea of presenting *Macbeth* this winter.
Speak to him about this and answer me immediately...

1. In the event Verdi was to make even more extensive revisions. The extent of these is shown in tabular form at 465–68. According to Verdi's letter of 15 February 1865 to Tito Ricordi, Carvalho had already asked for not only a few dances but also a new choral finale in place of Macbeth's onstage death.

ESCUDIER TO VERDI

Paris, 28 October 1864

... Maintenant venons au Macbeth. Carvalho a engagé tout exprès Mme Rey-Balla pour chanter cet opéra. Il la paie 3500 par mois à partir du mois de novembre; il compte sur cette partition pour la fin de la saison et si bien que les chœurs sont déjà à l'étude. Il a été très sensible aux changements importants que vous jugez à propos de faire et qui donneraient à l'opéra et à son théâtre un grand éclat. Il voulait partir aujourd'hui même pour Turin avec moi, mais j'ai préféré avant vous écrire.

Tenez pour certain que Macbeth, qui sera mise en scène au lyrique comme c'est Robert à l'opéra[1] sera un succès colossal, surtout si vous

... Now let's turn to *Macbeth*. Carvalho has engaged Mme. Rey-Balla to sing this opera. He is paying her 3,500 francs a month, beginning in November; he is counting so much on having this score for the end of the season that the chorus is already at work. He has been very sympathetic to the important changes that you think necessary to make, which will lend brilliance to the opera and to his theatre. He wanted to leave for Turin with me this very day, but I preferred to write to you in advance.

You can be sure that *Macbeth*, which will be staged at the Lyrique as *Robert [le diable]* is at the Opéra,[1] will be an enormous success, espe-

faites les additions et changements dont vous me parlez. Voici cher maître ce que je vous offre avec la netteté et la franchise que vous me connaissez. Si d'ici à la fin de décembre votre temps vous permet de faire ces modifications, je vous offre la somme de dix mille francs (10.000) fr. pour la propriété des nouveaux morceaux france et Etranger et je vous laisse la propriété pour toute l'italie. Vous ferez ces changements sur des paroles italiennes; je n'aurai qu'à les faire traduire en français pour les intercaler dans la partition. Piave ou tout autre pourront vous écrire les scènes ou airs changés en italien; je me charge du reste. La scène finale du dernier acte est bien importante à modifier. Carvalho m'en avait déjà parlé. En sus des dix mille francs vous aurez tous les droits du musicien que Carvalho établira pour vous au taux des pièces nouvelles composées expressément pour son théâtre. C'est une affaire considérable, je crois; et je serai heureux personnellement si vous acceptez. On continuerait à répéter ce qui n'exige pas des changements, et pourvu que votre travail fut livré avant le 10 janvier prochain ce serait suffisant. Acceptez, cher maître, je vous en supplie, et ayez la bonté de me faire un prompte réponse . . .

Sant'Agata

cially if you make the additions and changes you mentioned to me. Here is what I can offer you, dear master, with the directness and sincerity you have come to expect of me. If, between now and the end of December, you have time to make these modifications, I offer you the sum of ten thousand francs (10,000 Fr.) for the French and foreign rights to these new pieces, and I leave you the rights for all of Italy. You will make these changes to Italian words; I will only have to have them translated into French to insert them into the score. Piave or anyone else could write the changed scenes or arias for you in Italian; I undertake to do the rest. It is important to alter the final scene of the last act. Carvalho has already spoken to me about it. In addition to the ten thousand francs, you will have all royalties for the music, which Carvalho will fix for you at the same rate as for new works composed expressly for his theatre. This will amount to a considerable sum, I think, and personally, I will be happy if you accept. We shall continue to rehearse everything that does not require changes, and, provided that your work is delivered before January 10, this should be sufficient. Accept, dear master, I beg you, and have the goodness to reply to me promptly . . .

1. See note 1 to Escudier's first letter of 2 February 1865.

VERDI TO ESCUDIER[1] *Turin, 2 November 1864*

Me voilà de retour depuis ce matin à Turin,[2] où j'ai trouvé et votre Dépêche et votre lettre qui m'annonce le succès de *Traviata*.[3] Comme vous pouvez imaginer, je n'ai pas pleuré, au contraire j'en suis fort content. Aussi je vous prie, cher ami, d'être mon intreprete pour remercier vivement en mon nom le perspicace et courageux Carvalho, les habiles artistes, les choeurs, et Monsieur Deloffre[4] qui, d'après ce que l'on me dit, a fait merveille avec son orchestre.

Venons au *Macbet*. Je suis desolé que Mr. Carvalho ne puisse pas me donner un temps plus large pour les changements et modifications que je voudrais apporter à la musique. De toute manière, je tâcherai de faire le travail que je m'étais proposé, et si je pourrai reussir à la finir pour l'époque demandée, c'est à dire pour le 10 Janvier, vous me payérez fr. 10,000 dix mille pour tous pays, excepté l'Italie, et j'aurai pour cet opera les droits d'auteur entiers pour tout l'Empire Français. Est-ce clair et bien entendu

Here I am back in Turin,[2] since this morning, where I found your telegram and your letter telling me of the success of *Traviata*.[3] As you can imagine, I didn't mourn; on the contrary, I'm delighted about it. So I beg you, dear friend, to be my intermediary and to thank heartily, in my name, the perspicacious and bold Carvalho, the accomplished artists, the choristers, and M. Deloffre[4] who, according to what I hear, did marvels with his orchestra.

Let's turn to *Macbeth*. I am very sorry that M. Carvalho cannot give me more time for the changes and modifications I would like to make in the music. In any case, I will try to do the job that I set for myself, and if I am able to finish by the required date—that is, by January 10—you will pay me ten thousand francs for rights in all countries except Italy; and I shall have all the author's rights for all of the French Empire. Is that clear and understood between us? If so, so be it . . .

entre nous? Alors, ainsi soit-il ...

... *Je vous embrasse vous, votre famille, et Paris* avec, avec *toute l'effusion de mon âme.—Dieu quels bras de Gargantua! Tâchez de persuader Verdi à venir à Paris, sans me laisser à S*ᵗ *Agata où je m'ennuis dans cette saison* très royalement! *Adieu adieu.*

J. Verdi[5]

Paris: Bibliothèque de l'Opéra;
Rivista Musicale Italiana 35 (1928), 181–82

... *I embrace you, your family, and Paris* with—with *all my soul. God, what Gargantuan arms. Try to persuade Verdi to come to Paris without leaving me behind at St. Agata where I shall die of boredom* very royally *this season. Farewell, farewell.*

J[oséphine] Verdi.[5]

1. Verdi's Italian draft of this letter is preserved at Sant'Agata, as is Giuseppina's French translation (in her hand), probably prepared so that Escudier could share the letter with Carvalho. Verdi's Italian draft, which contains a few small differences (the second paragraph is translated above) reads:

*Sono ritornato questa mattina da S*ᵗ *Agata e qui ho trovato la vostra lettera che mi annuncia il successo della Traviata. Ne godo assaissimo come potete immaginare e ne faccio i miei più vivi ringraziamenti al valente Carvalho, ai bravi interpreti cantanti, ai Cori, ed al sign[or] Delovre [i.e., Deloffre] il quale mi dicon ha fatto meraviglie con sua orchestra.*

Veniamo al Macbet. Mi spiace che Carvalho non possa aspettare tempo maggiore per i cambiamenti che vorrei fare in ogni modo—io cercherò di fare il lavoro che mi era proposto, e se potrò riescire a finirlo resta fissato che mi pagherete le 10,000 franchi per la proprietà della musica per ogni paese eccettuata l'Italia, ed avrò per quell'opera i diritti intieri d'autore per tutto l'impero francese—

2. Turin was then the capital, and Verdi was attending sessions of Parliament.

3. *La Traviata* was given by the Théâtre-Lyrique on 27 October; Christine Nilsson made her debut in the title role.

4. Deloffre had also conducted the Lyrique's *Rigoletto* (1863), and was to conduct *Macbeth*.

5. Giuseppina sent her greetings to Escudier and his family on a separate slip of paper. We give her final sentences; the full text appears in *Rivista Musicale Italiana* 35 (1928), 182.

VERDI TO TITO RICORDI

Turin, 2 November 1864

... Al Teatro Lirico di Parigi vogliono ora fare il *Macbet* tradotto in francese, e mi domandano di comporre le arie di ballo, e fare alcune modificazioni che io amerei estendere a diversi pezzi per dare maggior carattere a quell'opera. Ti prego però a volermi mandare uno spartito a orchestra per vedere cosa vi è da fare. Partirò da Torino Sabato sera a sarò Domenica a Borgo S. Don[n]ino ad un'ora pomeri...Se tu potessi farmi trovare colà lo spartito per quel giorno, lo porterei a casa meco ...

Milan: Archivio Ricordi (219)

... They now want to perform *Macbeth* translated into French at the Théâtre-Lyrique in Paris, and they've asked me to write the ballet music and to make some modifications which I would like to extend to various numbers so as to give greater character to that opera. So I'm asking you to send me an orchestral score, so that I can see what needs to be done. I'll leave from Turin Saturday evening [5 November] and will be in Borgo San Donnino [now Fidenza] on Sunday afternoon at 1. If you could arrange for me to find the score there on that day, I'd take it home with me ...

TORNAGHI[1] TO VERDI

Milan, 3 November 1864

In assenza del Sʳ. Ricordi è mio l'onore di accusarle la ricevuta del preg di lei foglio d'jeri e darle avviso che oggi stesso ho fatto spedire al di lei addresso *fermo in stazione* a Borgo Sᵗ. Donnino una copia della partitura d'orchestra del *Macbeth* a norma delle di lei disposizioni ...

Sant'Agata

In the absence of Mr. Ricordi I have the honor of acknowledging the receipt of your esteemed letter of yesterday and of advising you that this very day I have had a copy of the orchestral score of *Macbeth* sent to you care of the Borgo San Donnino station, as per your instructions ...

1. Eugenio Tornaghi (1844?-1915), *procuratore* of Casa Ricordi, Tito Ricordi's chief man-of-business. Verdi's letters to Ricordi, particularly those dealing with practical matters, were often answered by Tornaghi, sometimes directly, sometimes in letters written by Tornaghi and signed by Tito.

ESCUDIER TO VERDI   *Paris, 7 November 1864*

... Carvalho est enchanté de l'arrangement du Macbeth et moi aussi. A ce sujet, je ne voudrais pas qu'il put y avoir de malentendu sur les droits d'auteur. Vous me dites dans votre lettre que vous aurez les droits entier pour tout l'Empire français. Je vous ai dit que vous auriez tous les droits du musicien comme si Macbeth était une partition nouvelle écrite expressément pour le théâtre lyrique. Ces droits sont plus forts qu'à l'opéra puisque en prenant une recette moyenne de 5000 fr. ils représentent pour vous 900 fr. par soirée. Ceux de Rigoletto représentaient 150 fr. et ceux de Traviata sont de 200 fr. Il y a donc une notable différence pour Macbeth et ces droits vous les avez non seulement pour la france mais aussi pour toute la belgique. J'ai fait, croyez-le tout qui était possible, et demander davantage serait vouloir se butter contre une impossibilité. Par ses traités, Carvalho ne peut pas faire mieux, et le voudrait-il qu'il serait arreté par la société des auteurs. Je m'explique, n'est pas, très nettement et très sincèrement. J'ai bien mon amour propre à vous faire restituer vos droits d'auteur qui à mes yeux sont des droits sûres; et je ne désespère pas d'arriver à mon but même au théâtre italien.

J'ai vu tout à l'heure Alexandre Dumas fils qui est émerveillé de la musique de Violetta et qui m'a chargé de vous faire milles compliments.

Demain Violetta; tout est loué et samedi également ...

                                                     Sant'Agata

... Carvalho is delighted with the arrangement about *Macbeth,* and I am too. On this subject, I want to avoid any misunderstandings about the author's rights. You said to me in your letter that you are to retain all rights for the entire French Empire. I had told you that you are to have all composer's royalties, just as if *Macbeth* were a new score written expressly for the Théâtre-Lyrique. These royalties are considerably higher than at the Opéra since, assuming an average box office return of 5,000 francs, it means 900 francs per night for you. Your royalty for *Rigoletto* was 150 francs, and for *Traviata* 200. There is therefore a substantial difference for *Macbeth* and you will receive royalties not only for France but for all of Belgium as well. Believe me, I have done all that was possible, and to ask for more would be to aim at an impossibility. Because of his agreements, Carvalho cannot do better, and even if he wanted to, he would be stopped by the Society of Authors. I've explained it very clearly and very sincerely, haven't I? My self-esteem requires me to render to you your author's rights, which are in my opinion your certain due; and I do not despair of arriving at my goal, even at the Théâtre-Italien.

I just saw Alexandre Dumas fils, who was enchanted by the music of *Violetta* [*La Traviata*], and asked me to give you a thousand compliments.

Tomorrow, *Violetta;* it's sold out, and so is Saturday's performance ...

ESCUDIER TO VERDI   *Paris, 25 November 1864*

... Nous avons commencé les répétitions des choeurs de Macbeth. Vous n'avez pas indiqué des changements dans le premier acte; nous avons donc pensé que pour activer les études de l'opéra qui exigera de longues répétitions on pouvait se mettre à l'oeuvre et c'est ce que l'on fait. Je crois et vous êtes sans doute de mon avis que la mort de Macbeth doit être modifiée, vous me le dites du reste vous même. Carvalho désirerait que l'opéra finit d'une manière éclatante et sur un grand effet d'ensemble. C'est à vous à piger cela. On compte faire représenter l'*Africaine* au mois de février;[1] Carvalho, et il est dans le vrai veut opposer Macbeth à l'opéra comme musique comme décors et comme

... We have begun the chorus rehearsals for *Macbeth.* You haven't indicated any changes in the first act; therefore, so as to get on with our preparations for the opera, which will call for long rehearsals, we thought we could get started with it, and that's what we've done. I think—and you undoubtedly agree with me—that the death of Macbeth needs to be changed; in any case, you told me so yourself. Carvalho would like the opera to end on a brilliant note and with a great ensemble effect. It's up to you to manage that. They are planning to present *L'Africaine* [at the Opéra] in February;[1] Carvalho—and he's right in this—wants to set up *Macbeth* in rivalry to the Opéra, in music, in

exécution. Je suis sûr à l'avance qu'il n'aura pas le dessous.

Sant'Agata

decor, in execution. I'm sure in advance that it won't come off second-best ...

1. *L'Africaine* had its first performance on 28 April 1865, a week after *Macbeth*. By September it had had fifty performances; by March 1866 a hundred. *Macbeth* received fourteen performances in all.

VERDI TO ESCUDIER

Busseto, 2 December 1864

Sono da pochi giorni ritornato da Torino, ed ora sono alle prese con Macbet. Ah voi credete che travaglierò soltanto all'ultim'ora? No: travaglio anche adesso come un negro; non dirò che faccia molto, ma travaglio, travaglio, travaglio.—Nel primo Atto non cambierò che in parte l'ultimo tempo del Duetto; quindi i Cori resteranno intatti, e possono studiarli.—Son io pure di parere di cambiare la morte di Macbet, ma non vi potrà fare altro che un *Inno di vittoria*: Macbet, e Lady non sono più in scena, e, mancando questi, poco si potrà fare con parti secondarie.—Quello che m'imbarazza assai, si è il balletto. Non si può farlo che al principio, dopo il Coro, dell'Atto terzo: non vi sono in scena che Streghe, e far ballare per un quarto d'ora o venti minuti queste amabili creature, faranno un *divertissement* rabbioso. Non si potrebbe nemmeno far comparire Silfi, spiriti, ed altro perchè li abbiamo dopo, quando Macbet è svenuto. Se avete qualcosa di buono a suggerirme, scrivetemi subito.

Vi lascio perchè Macbet mi chiama...

Paris: Bibliothèque de l'Opéra;
Rivista Musicale Italiana 35 (1928), 183

I returned from Turin a few days ago and am now struggling with *Macbeth*. Ah, so you think that I am going to get down to work only at the last minute? No, I'm working like a slave even now; I won't say I'm doing much, but I am working, working, working. In the first act I will change, in part, only the final movement of the duet; therefore, the choruses will remain intact, and they can start learning them. I too am of the view that Macbeth's death should be changed, but the only thing that can be done is a Victory Hymn. Macbeth and Lady are no longer on stage and, without them, little can be done with the minor characters. What really perplexes me is the ballet. It can only take place at the beginning of Act III, after the chorus; only the witches are on stage, and to have these charming creatures dance for fifteen or twenty minutes would give us an insanely furious divertissement. Nor could sylphs, spirits, or others be brought on, because we have them later, when Macbeth has fainted. If you have any good suggestions, write to me immediately.

I leave you now because *Macbeth* is calling me...

TITO RICORDI TO VERDI

Milan, 3 December 1864

... scrivimi qualche cosa anche a proposito delle varianti che fai nel *Macbeth* e se dovranno servire anche pei Teatri d'Italia ...

Sant'Agata

... also let me know something about the changes you're making in *Macbeth* and whether they should be used for the Italian stage ...

VERDI TO TITO RICORDI

Sant'Agata December 1864

... Stò lavorando al Macbet pel Teatro Lirico ed è affare molto più importante di quello che credevo. Quando sarà finito nel [*sic*] parleremo pei Teatri Italiani. Intanto di mano in mano che sarà pronto qualche Atto te lo manderò onde farne una copia e potersene all'uopo servire per l'Italia.

Milan: Archivio Ricordi (220);
Abbiati 2, 803

... I am working on *Macbeth* for the Théâtre-Lyrique and it's a much more important affair than I thought. When it's finished, we'll talk about it for the Italian stage. In the meantime, as soon as each act is ready I'll send it to you, to take a copy from, which can be used in Italy if needed.

ESCUDIER TO VERDI

Paris, 9 December 1864

J'ai reçu aujourd'hui seulement votre lettre datée de Busseto du 2 X^bre. Les facteurs qui devraient savoir mon domicile ont mal lu *Rue Choiseul* que vous avez fort mal écrit et ils ont promené votre lettre pendant trois jours dans Paris. Décidemment il faudra que *nous* prenions un maître d'écriture.

Je suis très content d'apprendre que vous êtes à l'oeuvre, et Carvalho que j'ai vu tout à l'heure est très content aussi. Ce n'est pas un ballet complet que je vous ai demandé, mais bien deux ou trois morceaux de danse que nous intercalerons dans l'ouvrage.[1] Deux même suffiront aussi, nous voudrions une ronde très chaude des sorcières au premier acte et au troisième acte à la scène de l'enchantement une valse que nous appelerions la *Valse des Esprits*. Ces deux morceaux d'orchestre seraient dansés par le corps de ballet. Si vous trouvez une meilleure place pour les introduire ayez la bonté de le me dire.

Vous avez raison pour la fin de l'opéra. C'est bien un Hymne de victoire qui convient. Est-ce que vous ne pourrez pas ajouter quelque chose pour le ténor. Si ce n'est pas possible, n'en parlons plus.[2]

Macbeth sera monté d'une manière éclatante et je crois pouvoir vous assurer que ce sera un évènement à Paris. Je suis bien certain à l'avance que ce que vous y changerez ou y ajouterez ne déparera pas la partition; tout au contraire . . .

Lorsque vous aurez complété le deuxième acte, vous aurez la bonté de me faire connaître les changements afin qu'on ne répète pas des morceaux qui ne se chanteraient pas. Ne craignez pas d'allonger un peu plus la duré de la pièce . . .

[P.S.] Est-ce dans le premier duo du 1er acte, ou dans le grand duo de Macbeth et de Lady Macbeth que vous faites un changement?

Sant'Agata

Only today I received your letter dated from Busseto on December 2. The postmen, who should have known my address, misread "Rue Choiseul," which you wrote very badly, and they carted your letter around Paris for three days. Evidently we shall have to engage a writing master.

I am very pleased to learn that you are at work and Carvalho, whom I just saw, is also pleased. It's not a complete ballet that I've asked you for but, rather, two or three dance pieces that we will interpolate into the work.[1] Even two will suffice; we'd like a fiery round-dance for the witches in the first act and, in the sorcery scene of the third act, a waltz, which we would call "The Waltz of the Spirits." These two orchestral pieces will be danced by the corps de ballet. If you find a better place to introduce them, please let me know.

You are right about the end of the opera. A Victory Hymn is just what's needed. Couldn't you add something for the tenor? If that's not possible, let's say no more about it.[2]

Macbeth will be staged in a brilliant manner, and I think I can assure you that it will be a great Parisian event. I'm quite sure in advance that nothing you change or add will spoil the beauty of the score; quite the contrary . . .

When you have finished the second act, please let me know what changes you have made so that we don't rehearse pieces which will not be sung. Don't be afraid to increase the length of the work a bit . . .

[P.S.] Is it in the first duet of Act I or in the big duet between Macbeth and Lady Macbeth that you have made a change?

1. Verdi nonetheless provided a complete ballet, which he regarded as "important" (see letters to Ricordi of 23 September 1865 and 15 December 1870). The view that Verdi supplied ballets for his French operas merely because he was "compelled" to is untenable.

2. Verdi said nothing about it in his reply; but subsequently a great deal more was said, in letters of January to March 1865; see also GÜNTHER at 179–80.

VERDI TO ESCUDIER

Busseto, 13 December 1864

Vedo che anche a Parigi dei *facteurs* sono molti gli imbecilli (fra noi si direbbe *coglioni*)...amen.

I see that in Paris, too, among the postmen there are plenty of imbeciles (in our country they would be called *coglioni*). Amen.

Non dubitate che io scrivo, e m'occupo seriamente, e vorrei e spero mandarvi presto i tre primi atti completamente finiti.

Nel Atto primo come vi dissi vi sarà qualche ritocco nel Duetto tra *Lady-Macbet*, e *Macbet*. I ritocchi cadranno nel Adagio, e nel ultimo tempo. Tutto il resto stà bene; ed io non vorrei che si mettessero ballabili in quest'atto. Bisogna lasciarlo com'è: l'azione è rapida e calda. Vi è una piccola ronda alla fine del primo Coro che possono, e devono fare le Coriste come fanno in tutti i teatri d'Italia. È brevissima e non dura che poche battute; e per questo fà effetto purchè sia fatta bene.

Nel second'Atto cambierò la prima aria di Lady Macbet. La scena della Visione è cambiata e fatta.

Il Terzo Atto è quasi tutto nuovo e non mancano che i ballabili. Fatti questi ballabili e l'Aria di Lady nel second'Atto vi manderò i tre primi atti completamente istromentati ...

Paris: Bibliothèque de l'Opéra;
Rivista Musicale Italiana 35 (1928), 183–84

Do not doubt that I am writing, and that I am hard at work; I want and hope to send you soon the first three acts completely finished.

In Act I, as I told you, there will be some retouching in the duet between Lady Macbeth and Macbeth. The revisions occur in the *adagio* and in the final movement. All the rest is fine, and I do not want to have dances inserted into this act. It must be left as it is: the action is quick and fiery. There is a small round dance at the end of the first chorus which the choristers can and must do, as they do in all Italian theatres. It is very short, lasting only a few measures; and so it makes an effect, provided it is done well.

In Act II, I will change Lady Macbeth's first aria. The hallucination scene is changed and completed.

The third act is almost entirely new; the only thing missing is the ballet. Once this ballet and Lady's aria in Act II are done, I will send you the first three acts fully scored ...

VERDI TO PIAVE

Sant'Agata, [*c. 14 December 1864*]

Eccoti quanto si dovrebbe dire (secondo me) da Lady nell'aria dell'atto secondo:

Pallida divien la luce, il gran faro
che eterno viaggia per l'universo si
spegne; il corvo dirigge il volo
all'antica foresta, e gli agenti
d'atre tenebre si svegliano per
sorprendere le loro vittime.[1]   } 1ª quartina

Nuovo delitto!!...è necessario.
L'opera nefanda dev'esser compita. I morti regnar non possono.
Un Pater un Requiem e tutto è
finito.   } 2ª quartina

O voluttà del trono! O corona più
non vacillerai sul capo mio!   } due versi

Se tu trovi meglio tanto meglio; se no, acco-
modami subito questi versi; se nella prima
quartina v'è troppo a dire leva quello che credi.
Per togliere il troppo di terribile che vi è in
quest'aria vorrei che i due ultimi versi fossero di
slancio, e però vorrei che restasse la parola *voluttà*: se nel ritmo *Doppio Quinario* non può
stare, cambia metro e fa un distico d'endeca-

Here is what I think Lady should be made to say in the second-act aria:

Pale grows the light, the great
beacon that eternally roves the
universe is being extinguished;
the raven takes flight for the
ancient forest, and the agents of
dreadful darkness rouse them-
selves to surprise their victims.[1]   } 1st quatrain

New crime!! ... it is needed. The
execrable enterprise must be
completed. Dead men cannot
reign. A Paternoster, a Re-
quiem, and all is over.   } 2nd quatrain

O rapture of the throne! O
crown, no longer wilt thou totter upon my head!   } two lines

If you can find something better, so much the
better; if not, arrange these lines for me immediately. If there's too much to say in the first
quatrain, take out what you think. In order to
reduce the excessively "terrible" quality of this
aria, I'd like the last two lines to be impetuous,
and so I'd like the word "voluttà" to remain; if
it won't fit in the rhythm of a *doppio quinario*,

Piave's letter (left) and verses (right) of 18 December 1864, with (center) Giuseppina's and Verdi's later drafting. (See page 79, note 1.)

sillabi; oppure quattro versi settenari e sarà meglio. Il ritmo delle due prime quartine puoi farlo come: 'Oh i mondi tutti crollino pria[2]. Addio. Fà presto ...

Abbiati 2, 804–5

change the meter and write a couplet of *endecasillabi*, or, better yet, four *settenario* lines. You can make the rhythm of the first two quatrains like "Ŏh i mòndĭ tùttĭ cròllĭnŏ prìa[2] [accents added]." Farewell. Be quick about it ...

1. These lines are adapted from a speech of Macbeth in III.2: "Scarf up the tender eye of pitiful day...Light thickens, and the crow / Makes wing to the rooky wood;" as translated by Rusconi: "spegni il gran faro dell'universo...La luce si fa pallida, e già il corvo dirige il volo verso l'antica foresta...i neri agenti delle tenebre si svegliano per sorprendere le loro vittime." Although Abbiati reads "d'altre," "d'atre"—agents of black dreadful darkness—would be closer to Rusconi's "neri" and Shakespeare's "night's black agents."

2. This is a versification of Shakespeare's III.ii.16 (Macbeth's "But let the frame of things disjoint, both the worlds suffer, Ere...") as rendered by Rusconi: "Ma crollino prima entrambi i mondi."

VERDI TO TITO RICORDI

Busseto *18 December 1864*
Sant'Agata

... P.S. Fammi il piacere di mandarmi circa 24 fogli di carta da musica da 20 righe. Carta, come al solito, fina. Per la Ferrovia a Borgo S Donino con grande velocità.

Milan: Archivio Ricordi (223)

... P.S. Do me the favor of sending me about twenty-four sheets of twenty-stave music paper. Fine quality paper, as usual. By train to Borgo San Donnino, in great haste.

VERDI TO PIAVE

Milan, [c. 18 December 1864][1]

Per non perder tempo ho fatto la musica dell'Aria sui seguenti versi. Trovane tu dei migliori ma che abbiano l'istesso senso, l'istesse desinenze, e l'istesso ritmo.[2]

So as not to lose time, I've set the aria to the following lines. Find better ones, but be sure that they have the same sense, the same endings, the same rhythm.[2]

LADY

La luce è pallida—Il faro spegnesi
Ch'eterno scorre—Per gli ampj cieli
Notte tremenda—Eppur desiata[3]
La man colpevole—Provvida veli.
Nuovo delitto?...—È necessario!
Compier si debbe—L'opra fatale:
 Ai trapassati—Regnar non cale
A loro un requie—L'Eternità
  O voluttà del trono![4]
  O scettro[5] alfin sei mio!
  Ogni mortal desio
  Tace e s'acqueta in te.[6]

LADY

Daylight is paling now—See how the beacon fails
Which ever wanders —Through heaven's vastness.
Night of disaster—Night that I long for[3]
Shroud up the guilty hand—Hide it in darkness.
Further destruction?...—Yes, it is needed!
The fatal action—Must be completed.
Once in the graveyard—None think of ruling:
For them a Requiem—peace evermore.
  O joy to rule securely![4]
  O scepter,[5] you are mine now!
  Every desire and longing
  Finds its repose in thee.[6]

So bene che ci sono delle rime isolate come Desiata, Trono, Eternità...ma fa tu...Soltanto fa presto.

Abiati 1, 676

I'm well aware that there are some words that don't rhyme, such as "desiata," "trono," "eternità"...but you take care of it...just be quick about it.

1. The autograph is not available, and Abbiati's impossible claim that it is dated "Milano, 1847" is no help. The following scenario seems likely: Not receiving Piave's lines, Verdi grew impatient, worked up this text with Giuseppina's help, sketched the aria, and wrote this letter to Piave.

When Piave's letter of December 18 arrived, Verdi sent—or at any rate drafted—his first, scornful reply of December 20. Then, or meanwhile, Giuseppina transcribed the aria text beside Piave's lines to provide a basis for further revision. In doing so, she introduced several variants (assuming that Abbiati's reading of the letter is correct): incorporating Piave's "serto" in place of the "scettro" found in the letter, and substituting "Regno" for "regnar" and "requiem" for "requie." Giuseppina and Verdi then introduced further corrections into this intermediate text transcribed into the Piave letter (see reproduction at p. 78); these are shown in notes 3, 4, and 6, and as a result of them Verdi's second letter of December 20 was written. We are grateful to Francesco Degrada for transcribing the annotations on the Piave letter at Sant'Agata, before the films of the material were made available to us.

2. The English translation is rhythmic, not literal.

3. Verdi: Notte tremenda—provvida veli
                La man colpevole—
  Giuseppina: Notte desiata—provvida veli
                La man colpevole—che ferirà.

Giuseppina cancelled the second half of the two lines, but not the phrase "Notte tremenda," left as an alternative eventually to be resolved by Piave.

4. Giuseppina (borrowing from Piave?): soglio ("trono" is not crossed out)

5. As mentioned earlier, the version transcribed on Piave's letter has "serto."

6. As the reproduction indicates, before revising lines 3–4, Verdi added two final lines:
    Sarà fra poco esanime
    Chi vacillar la fè.

PIAVE TO VERDI

Milan, 18 December 1864

Eccoti i versi che spero ti serviranno. Il concetto che hai trovato era bellissimo opportunissimo, ma non ho potuto meglio esprimerlo in circa 100 sillabe ... se non ti servissero i versi abbi pazienza, scrivimelo, e te ne farò degli altri...

Infosca il giorno, l'immenso faro
Che l'universo, eterno, viaggia
Or di tua luce più non l'irraggia...
A neri agguati va l'assassin.

Nuovo delitto!!! È necessario!...
D'uopo è sia l'opra truce compita;
Regnar non puote chi uscì di vita...
Requiem..., un *Pater*...e tutto ha fin.

    Oh voluttà d'un soglio!!!
    Oh serto seduttor,
    Dal capo mio non voglio
    Che più vacilli ancor.

(oppure)

Oh voluttà del trono...oh serto! omai
Più sul mio capo non vacillerai.

                Sant'Agata

Here are the lines for you—I hope you can use them. The image you found was most beautiful and appropriate, but I wasn't able to express it any better in about a hundred syllables ... if the lines won't do, be patient, write to me about it, and I'll do some others for you ...

Darkling the daylight, the immense beacon
That, eternal, roams the universe
Now with thy light no longer irradiate it...
To dark ambushes comes the assassin.

New crime!!! It is necessary!...
Needed it is, if the grim work is to be completed;
He cannot reign who departs this life...
Requiem...an *Our Father*...and all's at an end.

    O delight of a throne!!!
    O seductive crown,
    On my head I do not want
    That you totter anymore.

(or)

Oh delight of the throne...o crown! nevermore
Will you totter on my head.

VERDI TO PIAVE

Sant'Agata, 20 December 1864

Ho ricevuto i versi, e, se me lo permetti, ti dirò che non mi piacciono. Tu mi parli di *100* sillabe!! È ben naturale che *100* sillabe non bastino, quando tu ne spendi 25 per dire che il *sole tramonta!!!* Ben duro è il verso:

Duopo è sia l'opra truce compita,

I've received the lines, and, if you permit me, I'll tell you that they don't please me. You talk of a *hundred* syllables!! Naturally a hundred syllables aren't enough when you spend twenty-five of them to say that the *sun sets.*

Needed it is if the grim work is to be completed

e. peggio: *un Requiem, un Pater...e tutto ha fin.* Prima di tutto quel *"tutto ha fin"* fa rima con: *Eh via prendila Morolin.*[1] Poi è senza suono, e non si capisce. Perchè questo *Requiem?...*Infine il *Pater* non si dice ai morti. Tu dirai che l'ho messo nel mio schizzo, ma tu sai che quelli schizzi non servono che per una traccia.

I settenarj poi!!! Per l'amor di Dio non farmi versi con dei *che,* dei *più...ancor.*

Ebbene, non vi sarebbe mezzo d'accomodarsi tenendo in gran parte quelli che t'ho mandato, e salvando anche le convenienze della rima?

Copialettere, 614

is a hard line, and still worse *"a Requiem, an Our Father...and all's at an end."* First of all, that "all's at an end" ["tutto ha fin"] makes a rhyme with "Well, take her then, Morolin."[1] Next, it lacks sonority, and is incomprehensible. Why that *Requiem?...*Finally, one doesn't say the *Our Father* to the dead. You'll say that I put it in my draft, but you know that those drafts serve only to provide an idea.

Then the *settenari!!!* For the love of God don't make lines for me with *thats,* with *anymores.*

Well, wouldn't there be some way of fixing it, keeping for the most part what I sent you, and also preserving the metrical scheme?

1. This is perhaps the refrain of some popular Venetian jingle in which *Morolin* and *provolin* (see next letter, and Piave's reply of December 22) are rhyme words.

VERDI TO PIAVE

No no, mio caro Piave: no, non va!...[1]

> Tutto ha fin...
> Eh via prendila provolin!

Scherzi a parte; non vi sarebbe mezzo d'accomodarsi tenendo in gran parte quei versi che t'ho mandato, salvando anche le convenienze della rima? Per esempio:[2]

La luce è pallida...(langue) Il faro spegnesi
Ch'eterno scorre per gli ampi cieli.
Notte tremenda (desiata) provvida veli[3]
La man colpevole che ferirà.
        Nuovo delitto?!! È necessario!...
Compier si debbe l'opra fatale.
Ai trapassati Regno non cale
A Loro un Requiem, l'Eternità.
        O voluttà del soglio
        O serto alfin sei mio
        Ogni mortal desio
        Tace e s'acqueta in te
        Sarà fra poco esanime
        Chi fu predetto Re.

Rispondimi subito. Addio.

Abbiati 2, 806–7

No, no, my dearest Piave; it won't do![1]

> Tutto ha fin...
> Eh via prendila provolin!

Joking aside, isn't there some way to fix this, keeping to a great extent the lines I sent you, while also respecting the metrical scheme? For example:[2]

[see opposite for Verdi's versified text].

Answer me immediately. Farewell.

1. Verdi is poking fun at awkward *endecasillabi.*

2. This version of the aria text incorporates all the corrections that Verdi and Giuseppina wrote into their original versified text (i.e., the text that Giuseppina copied into Piave's 18 December letter)—see the notes to Verdi's letter to Piave of c. 18 December 1864—and also supplies a more comprehensible final line. Apart from reversions to "regnar" and "scettro," the substitution of "cadrà" for "sarà" in the penultimate line, and a few minor differences of orthography and punctuation, and with Piave's choice of the bracketed alternatives in lines 1 and 3 (see his reply of December 22), it represents the text that Verdi copied into a first-version Ricordi libretto (see pp. 339–41) and set to music.

3. Abbiati reads "voli" here, but it appears in none of the drafts.

TITO RICORDI TO VERDI   *Milan, 21 December 1864*

... Jeri stesso ti ho mandato a mezzo ferrata a Bº St Donnino 25 fogli della solita carta da musica a 20 righe ...

Sant'Agata

... Just yesterday I sent you twenty-five sheets of the usual twenty-stave music paper by train to Borgo San Donnino ...

PIAVE TO VERDI   *Milan, 22 December 1864*

Che devo dirti?...Va troppo bene quanto ricevo in questo punto! E ti assicuro che quel *Morolin* così bello come un boccolo mi ha confortato della specie di fiasco a cui di buon grado mi sottopongo —Mi piacerebbe meglio

La luce langue / invece di è *pallida*

per evitare lo sdrucciolo.

Notte desiata / invece di *tremenda*

perchè già l'idea del tremendo è destata [?] da tutto l'insieme dell'aria, e dalla situazione.[1]—e Bravo il mio Vecchio!!!...

Sant'Agata

What can I answer? What I've just received goes all too well! And I assure you that that "Morolin"—beautiful as a little flower bud—comforted me for the sort of fiasco that I willingly let myself in for.

I'd prefer "La luce langue" instead of "è pallida" to avoid the *sdrucciolo*. "Notte desiata" instead of "tremenda," because the idea of the dreadful is already expressed by the aria as a whole and by the situation[1]—and Bravo, old-timer!!! ...

1. Piave's suggestions were accepted.

ESCUDIER TO VERDI   *Paris, 28 December 1864*

... J'ai entendu ces jours derniers Mme Rey-Balla dans l'air du premier acte et dans celui du Somnambulisme. C'est la femme du rôle; sa voix est puissante et dramatique; elle joue avec chaleur et intelligence; et elle est douée d'un physique très sympathique. Je suis convaincu qu'elle aura un énorme succès dans Macbeth. Elle fera son entrée au Théâtre-Lyrique dans votre opéra. On s'est mis au premier acte, qui est superbe. Nous attendons avec vive impatience la Suite. J'espère que vous ne tarderez pas à m'envoyer les trois actes instrumentés que vous m'avez annoncés, sans cela nous nous trouverons arrêtés. J'ai remarqué dans le quatrième acte que la scène d'orchestre de la bataille est loin d'être à la hauteur du reste; si vous aviez fait là un beau morceau symphonique, l'orchestre du Lyrique qui est excellent, l'aurait parfaitement exécuté. Mais vous savez mieux que moi ce qu'il y a à faire. Il me faudra encore faire traduire les nouveaux morceaux ce qui prendra un grand temps. Si j'insiste pour vous presser, c'est que je voudrais que l'ouvrage put être représenté vers la fin de février pour une

... In the past few days, I have heard Mme. Rey-Balla sing the first-act aria and the sleep-walking aria. This is the woman for the role; her voice is powerful and dramatic; she acts with passion and intelligence; and she is endowed with an attractive appearance. I am convinced that she will have an enormous success in *Macbeth*. She will be making her Théâtre-Lyrique debut in your opera. They've begun to stage the first act, which is superb. We await the rest with impatience. I hope you won't delay in sending me the three acts orchestrated, as you promised; without them, we will be held up. I've noticed that the orchestral interlude for the battle in the fourth act is far from being on the high level of the rest. If you had written a beautiful symphonic piece there, the Lyrique orchestra, which is excellent, would have been able to play it perfectly. But you know better than I what has to be done. I still have to have the new pieces translated, which will take a long time. If I am insistent in pressing you, it is because I would like the production to go on toward the end of February, for a

foule de raisons que je vous dirai une autre fois.

Vers le 10 ou le 12 janvier j'irai demander à Guyot votre note de droits d'auteurs; vous aurez la bonté de m'en envoyer le reçu et je vous expédierai la somme qui vous reviendra comme d'habitude et si vous le voulez, j'y joindrai une lettre de change payable à Turin de *dix mille* francs pour l'affaire de Macbeth ...

Sant'Agata

host of reasons I'll tell you some other time.

Toward January 10 or 12, I'm going to ask [the theatrical agent Jean Noël] Guyot for your royalty statements. Please send me the receipt and I will forward the amount due, as usual and, if you wish, I'll add a letter of credit for ten thousand francs payable in Turin for the *Macbeth* matter ...

VERDI TO ESCUDIER

Busseto, 31 December 1864

Mille, mille, mille, due milla, tre milla auguri per parte nostra a voi ed ai vostri, con cent'anni di vita, la borsa piena, ed una lingua lunga cento miglia per dire male di tutto e di tutti. Amen.

In quanto al Macbet io mi occupo e scrivo; vi raccomando un po' di pazienza e presto avrete quello che desiderate e tutto arriverà in tempo. Non potete immaginarvi come sia nojoso e difficile di rimmontarsi per una cosa fatta altra volta, e trovare un filo rotto da tant'anni. Si fà presto a fare; ma io detesto in musica i *Mosaici* ...

Vi manderò presto la ricevuta per esigere i miei *Droits d'auteurs:* come voi offrite, approfitterò delli altri 10 milla franchi perchè a dirvi il vero la mia povera cassa è completamente al verde ...

Paris: Bibliothèque de l'Opéra;
Rivista Musicale Italiana 35 (1928), 184

A thousand, thousand, thousand, two thousand, three thousand good wishes from us to you and yours: for a hundred years of life, a full purse, and a tongue a hundred miles long to malign everything and everyone. Amen.

As for *Macbeth*, I am busy and writing; please be a bit patient and soon you will have what you want and everything will arrive in time. You cannot imagine how boring and difficult it is to work oneself up for something all over again, and to find a thread that has been broken for so many years. Doing it doesn't take long—but I detest *mosaics* in music....

I will send you soon the receipt to claim my author's rights; since you offer, I'll take advantage of the other ten thousand francs, because, to tell you the truth, my poor old strongbox is completely in the red ...

1865

VERDI TO [TITO RICORDI]

[*Busseto, 4 January 1865*]

Domani ti spedirò due atti del *Macbet.* Farai copiare subito gli accomoda[menti] che vi ho fatti. Ti prego di far prestissimo per poter mandare subito lo spartito a L. Escudier perchè le prove a Parigi son già cominciate[.] Manderai questo spartito in cui fò gli accomodamenti. Quando avrò finito, combineremo cosa si dovrà fare.

Milan: Archivio Ricordi (1413)

Tomorrow I'll send you two acts of *Macbeth*. Have the changes I've made there copied immediately. Please do this very quickly so that the score can be sent immediately to L. Escudier, because the rehearsals in Paris have already begun. Send this score in which I'm making the changes. When I've finished, we'll work out what to do.

VERDI TO TITO RICORDI

Busseto, 6 January 1865

Avrai oggi ricevuto due atti del Macbet che t'ho spedito jeri dalla stazione d'Alseno.[1] Ti prego di far copiare ben esattamente tutti i cambiamenti fatti e mandare lo spartito mio (cio[è] quello che è in parte copia, ed in parte originale) a Leon Escudier. Ciò farai in mio nome e ti prego della massima massimissima sollecitudine. Fra pochi giorni ti manderò il Terz'atto, e farai come pei primi. Mi dirai se desideri e se ti conviene far rappresentare in Italia questo Macbet rifatto dopo che sarà stato dato a Parigi.

Raccomando di nuovo tutta la sollecitudine per l'invio ...

Milan: Archivio Ricordi (226)

1. Alseno lies four miles southeast of Fiorenzuola.

Today you will have received the two acts of *Macbeth* that I sent you yesterday from the Alseno station.[1] Please have all of the changes copied *exactly* and send my score (that is, the one which is partly a copy and partly in my hand) to Léon Escudier. Do this in my name and—*please*—with great, with the greatest possible haste. In a few days I'll send you the third act, and you'll proceed as you did with the first two. Tell me if you want, and if it suits you, to have this revised *Macbeth* performed in Italy after it has been given in Paris.

Again, I ask you for the greatest promptness in dispatching it ...

VERDI TO ESCUDIER [1]

Busseto, 6 January 1865

Ho spedito oggi due atti del Macbet totalmente finiti a Ricordi perchè ne faccia una copia e poi ve li mando subito, così potrete farli studiare e non perderete tempo. Lavoro al Terzo Atto e ci vorrà qualche giorno a finirlo perchè è quasi tutto nuovo—Nei due atti che v'ho spedito vi sono le annotazioni ben esatte, e basta farvi ben attenzione per interpretarle bene. Nell'aria di Lady al principio del second'atto nell'Allegro si trova un'annotazione che dice *"con voce pianissima ed un poco oscillante"* io voglio una mezza voce ed il più piano possibile, ma che sia voce con timbro e non ventriloca. *Oscillante* per esprimere la gioia, ma non che sia troppo tremola che allora esprimerrebbe la febbre. Insomma l'espressione della parola, e *voilà tout*.

in fretta

Today I sent two acts of *Macbeth*, completely finished, to Ricordi, so that he can make a copy, and then I will send them to you at once; that way, you'll be able to have them studied [put into rehearsal] and won't lose time. I am working on Act III, and it will take a few days to finish it because it's almost entirely new. In the two acts that I have sent you there are very precise directions, and it needs only careful attention to them to have them interpreted properly. In the Lady's aria at the start of Act II in the Allegro there is a direction saying, *"con voce pianissima ed un poco oscillante."* I want a *mezza voce* and as soft as possible, but it should be one with tone in it, not "ventriloqual." *"Oscillante"* to express joy, but it should be not too tremulous which then would express fever. In short, express the words, and *voilà tout*.

In haste

1. We are grateful to Dr. Philip B. Clements, Vancouver, British Columbia for supplying us with a photograph of this previously unknown letter, now in his collection.

TITO RICORDI TO VERDI

Milan, 7 January 1865

Ti avviso che ho ricevuto i primi due Atti del *Macbeth* e che si sta copiandone gli accomodi che vi hai fatti. Lunedi prossimo manderò ad Escudier lo spartito che mi spedisti unendovi copia degli accomodamenti fedelmente conformi al tuo originale e seguendo le tue istruzioni.

Pagherò a Piave i fr. 22.75 per tuo conto ...

Sant'Agata

I notify you that I have received the first two acts of *Macbeth* and that the changes that you have made are being copied. Next Monday [9 January] I will send Escudier the score that you sent me, enclosing a copy of the changes faithfully conforming to your original and following your instructions.

I will pay 22.75 francs to Piave out of your account ...

TITO RICORDI TO VERDI

Faccio seguito alla mia d'jeri per rispondere alla cara tua del 6 corr[ente] ed avvertirti che domani manderò ad Escudier lo spartito dei due primi Atti del *Macbeth* che mi hai spedito tu stesso, cioè quello che è in parte copia e in parte originale. Non aveva capito bene l'antecedente tua lettera e credeva che bastasse mandare ad Escudier una copia delle varianti che vi hai fatte. Io intanto ne ho fatto fare una copia esatta per me.—Gradirò moltissimo di potere fare rappresentare in Italia questo *Macbeth* rifatto come sarà stato dato a Parigi, e perciò ti prego di farmi conoscere le tue condizioni, non dubitando punto che vorrai trattarmi ancora con quell'amicizia di cui mi desti tante prove.— Sai verso quale epoca potrai andare in scena a Parigi? vi sarai tu stesso?

Sant'Agata

I continue my letter of yesterday to respond to yours of the sixth and to advise you that tomorrow I'll send Escudier the score of the first two acts of *Macbeth* that you yourself sent me, that is, the one that's partly a copy and partly in your hand. I didn't understand your previous letter correctly and thought that it would be sufficient to send Escudier a copy of the changes you made. In the meantime I had an exact copy made for myself. It would give me great pleasure to be able to have this revised *Macbeth* produced in Italy in the way it will be given in Paris, so please let me know your terms. I have no doubt that you will still want to treat me with that friendship of which you have given me so many proofs. Do you know when you go on in Paris? Will you be there yourself?

VERDI TO TITO RICORDI

Credo siavi un malinteso per lo spartito da mandare a Parigi. Tu mi scrivi che manderai quello che ti ho spedito *unendovi copia degli accomodamenti fedelmente conformi al originale* et... Non è la copia che devi mandare a Parigi, bensì l'originale: insomma bisogna spedire quello spartito tale e quale che io t'ho mandato per la Ferrovia d'Alseno. L'ultima mia lettera sarà stata più chiara e spero che avrai fatto come ti dissi.

Milan: Archivio Ricordi (227)

I believe there's a misunderstanding about the score that is to be sent to Paris. You write me that you'll send the one that I sent you, "enclosing a copy of the changes faithfully conforming to the original, etc." It's not the copy that you must send to Paris, but the original. In short, you must send on that score just as I sent it to you by the Alseno train. My last letter was probably clearer, and I hope you did what I said.

ESCUDIER TO VERDI

... Vous m'annoncez que vous avez envoyé les deux premiers actes de Macbeth à Ricordi pour qu'il m'en expédie une copie. Pourvu que Ricordi ne me fasse pas attendre tout ira bien. Vous pouvez être tranquille sur toutes les recommandations que vous indiquerez relatives à l'exécution. Je m'en charge. Je ne manquerai pas une répétition et vous tiendrai au courant de tout ce qui ce fera. J'espère que les autres actes arriveront à temps ...

Sant'Agata

... You tell me that you have sent the first two acts of *Macbeth* to Ricordi so that he can send me a copy. Provided that Ricordi does not make me wait, all will be well. You can feel easy about all the recommendations that you'll make for the performance. I'll see to them. I will not miss one rehearsal and will keep you informed about everything that goes on. I hope the other acts arrive on time ...

VERDI TO PIAVE

Nelle strofe del Duetto finale Macbet non sono ben chiari i due ultimi versi della prima quartina *Tremenda al pari / del tuo pensiero... chi tuo?* Mi pare che servendosi del pensiero e delle stesse

In the stanzas of the Duet finale of *Macbeth* [Act III], the last two lines of the first quatrain aren't very clear: "Equally dreadful / as your own thought..."—who is "*your*"? It seems to me

parole di Shakespeare sia più chiaro. Così:

> Ora di morte—e di vendetta
> Tuona rimbomba—per l'orbe intero
> Come assordante—l'aspro pensiero
> Del cor le fibbre—tutte intronò

> Ora di morte—ormai t'affretta...
> Incancellabile il fato ha scritto:
> L'impresa compiere deve il delitto
> Se dal delitto s'inaugurò.[2]

Rispondi se così va e se no correggi. 'Ora di morte' è meglio per musica . . .[3]

Abbiati 1, 675–76

that using Shakespeare's thought and even his very words would make it clearer. Thus:

> Hour of death and of vengeance,
> Thunder, redound, through all the world,
> As, deafeningly, the violent thought
> Dins through all the fibers of my heart.

> Hour of death, now hasten.
> Indelibly, fate has written:
> Crime must complete the enterprise,
> If in crime it had its inception.[2]

Tell me if this is all right, and if it isn't, correct it. "Ora di morte" is better in terms of the musical setting . . .[3]

1. The dating of this letter is based on the conjecture that Verdi had already set lines supplied by Piave and merely wanted to touch up the text before sending the act to Ricordi, which he did on 21 January. The text for the entire scene, including the recitative and two alternative versions of the "strofe" (one setting in *ottonari* as well as the one in *doppi quinari* that Verdi adopted in part), is transcribed in Piave's hand into a printed Ricordi first-version libretto (see pp. 339–41). Piave's *doppi quinari* are as follows (text in italics is the same as in Verdi's letter):

> Terribil ora — della *vendetta*
> Suona *rimbomba — per l'orbe intero,*
> Tremenda al pari — del tuo pensiero
> Che assiduo l'anima — ne conturbò.

> Terribil ora—*ormai t'affretta!...*
> *Incancellabile il fato ha scritto:*
> *L'impresa* compiersi—dee dal *delitto*
> Poiché *dal* sangue l'*inaugurò.*

Also in the libretto is the first quatrain of the version in Verdi's letter, transcribed in Verdi's hand.

2. The first four lines are based closely on Macbeth's speech at the end of IV.1 in the Rusconi version: "Ora della vendetta, rimbomba per l'universo, come assordante m'introni ogni fibra del core." But, so far from being "le stesse parole di Shakespeare," they replace Shakespeare's "No boasting like a fool; / This deed I'll do before my purpose cool," and thus provide convincing evidence of Verdi's having used Rusconi in 1864–65, as he did in 1846–47. The last two lines are a version of "Things bad begun make strong themselves by ill," from III.2—later in the speech from which the start of "La luce langue" had been extracted some weeks earlier. Rusconi expands the line into "le imprese incominciate col delitto, mestieri è pur che coi delitti si compiano," giving precedent for Piave's "impresa" and "compiersi," as well as Verdi's repeated "delitto." In the 1847 *Macbeth*, this idea had found its expression in Lady Macbeth's "Trionfai," as "Tra misfatti l'opra ha fine / Se un misfatto le fu culla" ("Through misdeeds an enterprise is brought to conclusion if a misdeed cradled it.") In the final setting of the duet, "l'aspro" becomes "l'atro," Verdi reverts to Piave's last line ("Poichè dal sangue l'inaugurò"), and the rest remains.

3. I.e., better than Piave's "Tĕrrìbìl òrä . . ." for the rhythm that Verdi had chosen for the musical setting.

GILBERT DUPREZ TO VERDI   *Paris, 19 January 1865*

Une petite infamie, comme on en sait faire au théâtre, se commet en ce moment au détriment de mon frère Edouard Duprez, qui a traduit une partie de vos Oeuvres.[1]—Voici le fait.—Il y a quelques mois mon frère vint me trouver en son nom comme en celui de Léon Escudier, à fin de me prier de revoir une traduction de votre *Macbeth,* qui n'avait pas entièrement eu votre approbation.[2] J'examinai cette traduction et je ne la trouvai point en effet ce qu'elle devait être. C'était la première fois que je la voyais. Je priai mon frère de recommencer certains fragments beaucoup plus en harmonie avec l'esprit

A small act of infamy, of the kind one finds in the theatre, is being committed at this moment against my brother, Edouard Duprez, who has translated some of your operas.[1] Here are the facts. A few months ago, my brother approached me, on behalf of Léon Escudier as well as himself, to look through a translation of your *Macbeth* which had not entirely met with your approval.[2] I examined this translation and, indeed, found that it was not all it should be. That was the first time I had seen it. I asked my brother to redo certain sections to render them more in harmony with the spirit of your

de votre musique, et je replaçai les paroles françaises sous votre musique avec le respect qu'on doit à un auteur de votre ordre.

Aujourd'hui voilà ce qui arrive au théâtre de Mr. Carvalho: à fin de satisfaire quelques faiseurs de l'endroit, Mr. Carvalho a donné à faire une autre traduction de *Macbeth*[3] ... Jusqu'à là, tout m'est profondément égal; mais il m'a été rapporté que quelques cuistres en musique, s'étaient permis d'alléguer pour raison que, moi Duprez, *j'avais dénaturé* votre musique; or, pour couvrir la petite infamie qu'on fait à mon frère, on se croit en droit d'en commettre une à mon endroit. Je proteste donc devant vous, mon cher grand Maître, et quelle que soit la traduction qu'on exécutera de votre *Macbeth*, lorsque j'aurais l'occasion de vous voir à Paris je vous montrerai mon travail: Vous jugerez vous même ...

Veuillez m'excuser si je viens vous déranger au milieu de vos loisirs, mais je tiens essentiellement à prévenir auprès de vous la mauvaise impression que mes chers ennemis cherchent à répandre sur mon travail.

Copialettere, 454–55

music, and I replaced the French words under your music with the respect due to an author of your calibre.

Today, this is what happened at M. Carvalho's theatre: to placate some poetasters about the place, M. Carvalho commissioned another translation of *Macbeth*[3]... So far, it's all the same to me; but I was told that several musical prigs had alleged that I, Duprez, had perverted your music; thus, to cover up the act of infamy against my brother, another was committed against me. So I make my protest to you, my dear great master, and—whatever translation of your *Macbeth* gets performed—when I have the chance of seeing you in Paris, I will show you my work. You will judge for yourself ...

Please forgive me for disturbing you in your leisure hours, but I feel it essential to forestall the bad impression that my dear enemies seek to cast on my work.

1. Edouard Duprez's translations of *Rigoletto* and of *Traviata* had been used by the Théâtre-Lyrique. For his work on *Macbeth*, see GÜNTHER at pp. 177–78. Gilbert Duprez had created the tenor role in *Jérusalem*.

2. Either an earlier attempt by Edouard Duprez or the translation by L. Danglas, published (according to Loewenberg's *Annals of Opera*) in 1853. Verdi's opinion of it is not elsewhere recorded; he may have given it to Escudier verbally, or Escudier may have invented the composer's disapproval.

3. From Nuitter and Beaumont, whose translation of *Die Zauberflöte* was in rehearsal at the Théâtre-Lyrique. Verdi evidently decided to take no part in the controversy and delayed replying to Duprez (see his letter of mid-February, placed after the February 12 letter).

ESCUDIER TO VERDI   *Paris, 21 January 1865*

Que se passe-t-il donc à Busseto? Seriez-vous malade? J'ai répondu le 10 de ce mois à votre lettre du 9; je comptais recevoir votre réponse le 16 ou le 17; nous voici au 21 et j'attends toujours. Dans ma lettre je vous priais de m'envoyer pour Guyot agent des auteurs un reçu de 9160 fr et je vous disais qu'aussitôt votre réponse, je vous enverrais en un billet sur Turin la somme de 19160 francs y compris les dix mille francs de Macbeth. J'avais tout préparé, et voilà que vous me laissez avec un pied en l'air, ne sachant, c'est le cas de le dire, sur quel pied danser. Je vous prie cher Maître de me tirer d'embarras en me donnant de vos nouvelles par retour du courrier. Si j'avais su par quel télégraphe je pouvais communiquer avec vous, je n'aurais pas attendu jusqu'à aujourd'hui pour savoir ce qui se passe à Busseto. Je vous serai obligé au cas où je pourrais avoir quelque

Whatever is happening at Busseto? Could you be ill? I replied on the tenth of this month to your letter of the ninth; I counted on receiving your reply on the sixteenth or the seventeenth; here we are at the twenty-first, and I am still waiting. In my letter, I asked you to send me for Guyot, the authors' agent, a receipt for 19160 francs and said that as soon as I had your reply I would send you a bill on Turin for the sum of 19,160 francs, including the ten thousand francs for Macbeth. I had everything prepared, and now you leave me with one foot in the air, not knowing, I can't help saying, which foot to dance on. I beg you, cher maître, to save me from embarrassment by giving me your news by return mail. If I had known by which telegraph I could communicate with you, I would not have waited until today to learn what is happening at Busseto. I would be

communication importante à vous faire à quelle station télégraphique et à quelle adresse je dois mettre mon télégramme.

Ouf! J'ai été fort ennuyé depuis un mois par les frères Duprez. Lorsque nous avons voulu répéter rien n'allait et Duprez *le grand* s'était permis de telles licences dans la musique que j'ai dû renoncer à sa traduction. Comme la question d'argent n'est que secondaire en tout ceci, j'ai largement indemnisé M. Duprez; j'ai mis son travail dans mon secrétaire, et d'accord avec Carvalho, nous avons pris les deux poètes les plus expérimentés, MM Nuitter et Beaumont, les traducteurs de Tannauser et de la flute enchanté de *Mozart,* etc.

Vous pouvez donc être parfaitement tranquille; je tiens trop à Macbeth pour qu'il soit représenté dans des conditions douteuses. On repète les deux premiers actes et on attend avec impatience le troisième. Tout marche admirablement; je vous réponds du succès et d'un énorme succès.

J'ai été souffrant pendant quatre ou cinq jours; je vais mieux aujourd'hui. Mercredi prochain on donne au Lyrique la 1ere représentation de *l'aventurier* un ouvrage en 4 actes de M. Saint-Georges, musique de Poniatowski. C'est bien flasque et peu original. Je crains que Carvalho n'y sort pour les frais de costumes et de décors . . .[1]

P.S. Si vous jugez à propos de répondre à Duprez qui a dû vous écrire dites-lui simplement que cette affaire me regarde entièrement.

Sant'Agata

1. *L'Aventurier* calls for spectacular Mexican decor.

grateful, in case I have some important communication to make to you, to know to what telegraph office and to what address I should send my telegram.

Ouf! I have had such troubles for a month now with the Duprez brothers. When we wanted to rehearse, nothing worked, and Duprez *le grand* had allowed himself such liberties with the music that I had to reject his translation. As the matter of money is secondary in all this, I paid off M. Duprez handsomely; I put his work in my desk, and, in agreement with Carvalho, we engaged the two most experienced poets, Mm. Nuitter and Beaumont, the translators of *Tannhäuser,* of Mozart's *Magic Flute,* etc.

So you can be perfectly at ease. I care too much about *Macbeth* to let it be performed in doubtful conditions. The first two acts are in rehearsal, and we await the third with impatience. All goes admirably; I promise you a success, and an enormous one.

I have been ill for four or five days; today I'm better. Next Wednesday [January 26] the Lyrique gives the first performance of *L'Aventurier,* a work in four acts by M. [Vernoy de] Saint-Georges, music by Poniatowski. It's flaccid and unoriginal. I fear that Carvalho will not recoup the costs of the costumes and decors . . .[1]

P.S. If you think fit to reply to Duprez, who must have written to you, tell him simply that this affair is my concern entirely.

VERDI TO TITO RICORDI   *Sant'Agata   21 January 1865*

Oggi t'ho spedito colla Ferrovia d'Alseno il terzo atto del Macbet. Ho tardato molto; ma vi è stato lavoro maggiore di quello ch'io credeva. Fà che tuoi copisti guadagnino il tempo ch'io v'ho perduto, e manda lo spartito (s'intende sempre lo spartito originale) a Leon Escudier il più presto possibile. Raccomanda al Capo della tua Copisteria di copiare ben esattamente, e di non ommettere [*sic*] nissuna delle annotazioni indicate nello spartito. Non dimentichi d'includere nello spartito tutti i fogli volanti, il Programma del Balletto i versi o accomódati od aggiunti et. et.

Milan: Archivio Ricordi (228)

Today I sent you Act III of *Macbeth* via the Alseno train. I've been slow about it, but it was more work than I thought. Let your copyists make up the time that I've lost, and send the score (meaning, as always, the original) to Léon Escudier as soon as possible. Urge the head of your copying office to copy it *exactly* and not to omit any of the annotations shown in the score. Don't let him forget to include in the score all of the loose sheets, the scenario for the ballet, and the added or revised lines, etc. etc.

TITO RICORDI TO VERDI

Ti accuso la ricevuta della partitura del 3° Atto *Macbeth* che faccio subito copiare per spedire il tuo originale a L. Escudier a Parigi fra un pajo di giorni. Ritengo che avrai ricevuto i 20 fogli di carta a 24 che ti mandai a B.° S. Donnino appena ricevuto la tua ordinazione.

Ti accludo un foglietto con de' versi trovato nella partitura del 1° Atto del *Macbeth* e che penso bene rimandarti pel caso che ti possa occorrere.

Quando poi avrai tempo mi scriverai in risposta alla mia dell'8 corr[ente].

Sant'Agata

I acknowledge the receipt of the orchestral score of Act III of *Macbeth*; I'll have it copied immediately so as to send your original to L. Escudier in Paris within a couple of days. I imagine you've received the twenty sheets of twenty-four-stave paper that I sent to you at Borgo San Donnino as soon as I received your order for them.

I enclose a slip of paper with some lines of text—it was found in the score of Act I of *Macbeth,* and I thought it as well to send it back to you in case you might need it.

When you have time, write me a reply to my letter of the eighth.

VERDI TO TITO RICORDI

Se Colui che presiede alla tua copisteria avesse dato un'occhiata *même en passant* allo spartito che t'ho mandato, si sarebbe accorto che il foglieto di poesia incluso nella tua di jeri non era altro che l'aria cambiata del principio del second'atto. L'aveva unito allo spartito per servirsene caso mai si dovessero rendere di pubblica ragione quei cambiamenti, (cosa che non so se converrà a te si [*sic*] a me) e perchè voleva anche che quel foglietto restasse nello spartito, onde riuscisse a quei di Parigi più chiara la poesia, e più facile la traduzione. Nel Terzo atto vi sono altri versi ed il Programma del Balletto. Desidero restino nello spartito che andrà a Parigi.

Ho ricevuto la carta da 24. Se fosse stata di Francia avrei impiegato qualche ora di meno per istromentare. In ogni modo te ne ringrazio.

Milan: Archivio Ricordi (229)

If the head of your *copisteria* had given even a passing glance at the score I sent you, he would have noticed that the little sheet of poetry included in your letter of yesterday was nothing other than the revised aria from the beginning of Act II. I enclosed it in the score to be used just in case these changes had to be made public (something which I'm not sure would suit either you or me), and because I also wanted that sheet to remain in the score so that the poetry would be clearer to the people in Paris and make the translation easier. In Act III there are other lines and the scenario of the ballet. I want them to remain in the score that's going to Paris.

I received the twenty-four-stave paper. If it had been the French sort I would have taken a few hours less for the orchestration. At any rate I thank you.

VERDI TO ESCUDIER

Voi avrete ricevuto da qualche tempo i due primi Atti del Macbet. L'altro giorno spedii il terzo a Ricordi per cui lo avrete forse contemporaneamente con questa lettera. Questo Terzo Atto ad eccezione d'una parte del 1° Coro, e d'una parte del ballabile delle Silfidi quando Macbet è svenuto, tutto il resto è nuovo. L'Atto finisce con un *Duo* fra *Lady,* e *Macbet.* Non mi pare illogico che Lady, intenta sempre a sorvegliare il marito, abbia scoperto ove sia. L'Atto finisce meglio.[1] Si fà apparire la Donna, e solleva un po' Macbet dalla molto fatica.—Voi vedrete che nel Balletto (*Divertissements*) vi è

You should have received the first two acts of *Macbeth* some time ago. The other day I sent the third to Ricordi so perhaps you will receive it at the same time as this letter. This third act, except for a part of the first chorus and a part of the sylphs' ballet, when Macbeth has fainted, is all new. The act ends with a duet between Lady and Macbeth. It doesn't seem illogical to me that Lady, always intent on watching over her husband, should have discovered where he is. The act ends better.[1] We have the Lady appear, and she takes some of the burden off Macbeth. You will see that in the ballet (di-

una piccola azione che lega benissimo col Dramma. Tutto è segnato nello spartito e troverete anche il Programma del *Divertissements*. L'apparizione d'*Ecate* la Dea della notte stà bene perchè interompe tutti quei ballabili diabolici, e dà luogo ad un adagio calmo e severo. Inutile che vi dica che *Ecate* non dovrebbe mai ballare ma soltanto fare delle pose. Inutile anche che io avverta che quell'adagio deve essere suonato dal *Clarone* e *Clarinetto-basso*[2] (come è indicato) onde all'unisono col violoncello e col Fagotto formare un suono cupo e severo come esige la situazione. Pregate anche il Direttore d'orchestra di sorvegliare di tratto in tratto lo studio delle danze onde indicare i tempi che io ho segnati.[3] I Ballerini alterano sempre tutti i movimenti, e così facendo questo baletto perderebbe ogni carattere, è non produrebbe quell'effetto, che mi pare, vi sia.—Altra cosa raccomando,[4] cioè di conservare rigorosamente gli istromenti che formano l'orchestrina sotto il palco scenico al momento dell'apparizione delli otto Re. Quella piccola Orchestra di due *Oboi*, sei *Clarinetti in la*, *Due Fagotti* e un *Contra-Fagotto* formano una sonorità strana, misteriosa, e nello stesso tempo calma e quieta che altri stromenti non potrebbero dare. Dovranno essere posti sotto il palco scenico vicini ad una *trappe* aperta ed abbastanza larga onde il suono possa partire, e spandersi per il teatro ma in modo misterioso, e come in lontananza.—

Altra osservazione per la scena del Convito Macbet nell'Atto secondo. Ho visto recitare più volte questo dramma in Francia, in Inghilterra, in Italia, dappertutto si fà apparire Banco da una *coulisse* che gira, si dimena, inveisce contro Macbet poi se ne va tranquillamente dentro un'altra *coulisse*. Ciò, secondo me, non ha illusione,[5] non fà alcuna sensazione, e non si capisce bene se sia ombra o uomo. Quando io posi in scena il Macbet a Firenze feci apparire Banco (con una larga ferita in fronte) da una *trappe* sottoterra precisamente nel posto di Macbet. Non si moveva; sollevava soltanto a suo tempo il capo. Faceva terrore.

La scena era distribuita così.

vertissement) there is a little plot which ties in very well with the drama. Everything is marked in the score and you will also find the scenario of the divertissement. The appearance of Hecate, goddess of night, is good because it interrupts all those devilish dances and gives way to a calm and severe *adagio*. I don't need to tell you that Hecate should never dance, but only assume poses. Nor do I need to advise you that that *adagio* must be played by the clarinet and bass clarinet[2] (as indicated), which, in unison with the cello and bassoon, will result in a hollow and severe sound, as the situation demands. Also, ask the conductor to supervise the ballet rehearsals from time to time, so that he can indicate the tempos I have marked.[3] Dancers always alter all the tempos, and, if that were done with this ballet, it would lose all its character and would not produce the effect that, it seems to me, it should have.

Another recommendation:[4] keep strictly to the instruments that form the small orchestra under the stage at the moment of the apparition of the eight kings. That small orchestra of two oboes, six clarinets in A, two bassoons, and a contrabassoon creates a strange, mysterious, and, at the same time, calm and quiet sonority that other instruments could not produce. They will have to be placed under the stage, close to an open trapdoor, large enough to permit the sound to come out and spread throughout the theater—but in a mysterious way and as if from a distance.

Another observation, on Macbeth's banquet scene in Act II. I have seen this play performed several times in France, England, and Italy. Everywhere they have Banquo appear from a revolving *wing*; he gesticulates, inveighs against Macbeth, and then goes off calmly behind another *wing*. In my opinion, that creates no illusion[5] or effect, and it is not clear whether he is a ghost or a man. When I staged *Macbeth* in Florence, I had Banquo appear (with a large wound on his forehead) through a trapdoor from underground, precisely in Macbeth's place. He did not move, but only raised his head at the proper moment. It was terrifying. The set was arranged as follows:

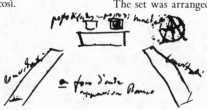

Questa distribuzione dà campo a *Macbet* di muoversi, e *Lady* le può stare sempre al fianco per dirle sotto voce[6] le parole che la situazione esige.[7] Trovando meglio, fate; ma badate che il pubblico capisca bene l'ombra di Banco.

Ultima osservazione—Nel Duetto del 1º Atto fra *Macbet*, e *Lady* c'è il primo tempo che fà sempre molto effetto, e vi è una frase ove le parole dicono...

> *Follie follie che sperdono*
> *I primi rai del dì.*

Bisogna che il traduttore francese conservi le parole *"follie follie["]* perchè forse in queste parole ed in questa derisione infernale di Lady stà tutto il segreto dell'effetto di questo pezzo.[8]—

Vi mando la lettera per Guyot. Voi avrete la conpiacenza d'esigere quei denari, e, come voi lo esibite, unirvi i vostri dieci mila franchi, e mandarmi di tutta la somma una cambiale *pagabile a vista* a Torino. La cambiale mandatela qui, che io andrò ad esigerla a Torino.

Questa lunga epistola era già scritta quando mi è arrivata l'ultima vostra del 21.—Voi già sapete che il terzo Atto è già spedito. Stò lavorando al Quarto. Credevo che non vi fosse che l'ultimo Coro da farsi ma vi sarebbe qualche cosa ancora da ritoccare e da rifare, se vi è un po' di tempo. Mi pare che con quei tre atti Voi potreste occuparvi un po' anche della *mise en scene* così avrei un po' di tempo per rifare il Quarto. Ditemi dunque quanto tempo mi lasciate, e quando volete (giorno fisso) che il Quarto Atto sia a Parigi. Scrivetemi subito.

Paris: Bibliothèque de l'Opéra;
Copialettere, 452–54 (draft)

This arrangement gives Macbeth room to move, and Lady can always be at his side to tell him, sotto voce,[6] whatever the situation requires.[7] If you find something better, do it, but see that the audience properly understands Banquo's ghost.

A final observation. In the duet between Macbeth and Lady in Act I, there is the *primo tempo*, which always makes a big effect, and there is a passage on the words:

> Follie follie che sperdono
> I primi rai del dì.

The French translator must retain the words *"Follie follie,"* because the whole secret of the effect of this number may well lie in these words and in the Lady's infernal derision.[8]

I am sending you the letter for Guyot. Be so kind as to collect that money, and, since you offer, add to it your 10,000 francs and send me a check for the entire amount, *payable on sight* in Turin. Send me the check here, and I shall go to collect it in Turin.

This long epistle was already written when I received your letter of the twenty-first. You should know by now that the third act has already been sent. I am working on the fourth. I thought there was only the final chorus to write, but there are some other things to revise and rewrite, if there is still a little time left. It seems to me that, having those three acts, you could set to work a bit on the mise-en-scène, so then I would have a bit of time to rewrite Act IV. Tell me, then, how much time you will allow me and when (the exact day) you want Act IV to be in Paris. Write to me immediately.

N.B. Verdi's draft of this letter, preserved at S. Agata, is published in the *Copialettere*; we give the most interesting variants below. Verdi drafted the letter after having received Duprez's January 19 letter, and put in a good word about him to Escudier. But, before recopying and sending the letter, Verdi received Escudier's January 21 letter, with its complaint about the Duprez brothers, and, not wanting to intervene in the dispute, he omitted all reference to Duprez when he recopied the letter. Verdi's belated reply to Duprez (mid-February, placed after the letter of February 12) is polite and highly complimentary, but it also makes it perfectly clear that Verdi had no intention of interceding on his behalf.

1. meglio ... Voi vedrete] meglio. Il macchinista ed il Régisseur hanno a divertirsi in questo atto. Voi vedrete ... better ... You will see] better. The machinist and the director will have a chance to enjoy themselves in this act. You will see ...

2. The draft reads clarone o clarinetto-basso, and a single instrument on the part is surely intended. The autograph calls it *Clarone basso.*

3. segnati ... perderebbe ogni] segnati. Voi sapete che i ballabili [?*recte* ballerini] alterano sempre i tempi. (All'*Opéra*, per esempio, dicono che non si può ballare la Tarantella come la voglio io. Un *gamin* di Sorrento o di Capua la ballerebbe benissimo col mio tempo.) Se si alterassero i tempi, questo Balletto di streghe perderebbe ogni

marked ... would lose all] marked. You know that the dancers always alter the tempos. (At the Opéra, for instance, they say that the Tarantella cannot be danced in the way I want. An urchin from Sorrento or Capua would dance it admirably at my tempo.) If one were to alter the tempos, this ballet of witches would lose all ...

4. raccomando, ... di conservare rigorosamente] raccomando poi al Sig. Deloffre: di tenere rigorosamente ...

recommendation, ... to keep strictly] recommendation for M. Deloffre now: to keep strictly ...

5. illusione, ... non si capisce] illusione nissuna, non ispira nessun terrore e non si capisce ...

illusion, ... it is not clear] illusion, does not inspire any terror, and it is not clear ...

6. sotto voce] *a parte* ...

sotto voce] *aside* ...

7. esige ... c'è il primo] esige. È egli vero che *Duprez* non fa più la traduzione del *Macbeth*? Me ne dispiace perchè difficilmente si potrà trovare chi sia maestro, chi sappia cantare e chi conosca l'italiano come lui. A proposito. Nel Duetto del 1º atto, fra Lady Macbeth e Macbeth, c'è il primo ...

requires ... there is the *primo*] requires. Is it true that Duprez will not be doing the translation of *Macbeth* after all? I regret that, because it will be difficult to find someone who is a musician, who knows singing, and who knows Italian as he does. By the way, in the Act I Duet, between Lady Macbeth and Macbeth, there is the *primo* ...

8. The *Copialettere* draft ends here.

ESCUDIER TO VERDI
Paris, 26 January 1865

C'est avec un extrême plaisir que j'ai reçu votre lettre ce matin. Votre silence me laissait croire qu'il vous été survenu à vous ou à Mme Verdi quelque chose de fâcheux. J'étais inquiet; me voilà rassuré.

Je vous envoie dans cette lettre une lettre de change payable à Turin de 19178.15^c. Dans cette somme se trouvent compris les droits de Guyot et les dix mille francs pour Macbeth. En même temps que cette lettre, et par craint qu'elle s'égare je vous en écris une autre aujourd'hui même dans laquel vous trouverez le traité relatif à la cession des morceaux de Macbeth que je vous prie de me retourner signé et approuvé par vous ...

Je n'ai pas encore reçu le 3me acte; mais d'avance, je suis ravi de ce que vous m'annoncez. Je suis sûr que ce que vous avez écrit est digne de votre grand génie. C'est assez dire. Tout ce que vous me dites sera rigeureusement observé, et s'il y avait des détails qu'on ne comprit pas bien, je ne manquerai pas de vous consulter. Quant au 4me acte, je crois qu'en me l'envoyant vers le 10 février, ce serait suffisant. Il m'a semblé que l'Introduction d'orchestre n'était pas à la hauteur du reste, je parle de l'Introduction qui précède le choeur au 4me acte. Peut être je ne suis qu'un imbécille [*sic*] mais je hazarde cette opinion. Si vous pouviez ajouter quelque chose pour le ténor, j'obtiendrai que Montjauze chantait le rôle et ce serait d'un bon effet pour l'ouvrage. A cet égard, vous seul êtes juge de ce qu'il y a ou il n'y a pas à faire ...

It was with great pleasure that I received your letter this morning. Your silence was making me think that something had happened to you or to Mme. Verdi. I was worried; now I am reassured.

In this letter I enclose a letter of credit, payable in Turin, for 19,178.15 francs. This amount includes the Guyot royalties and the ten thousand francs for *Macbeth*. At the same time as this letter, and lest it go astray, I am writing you another letter, today, in which you will find the contract about assigning the *Macbeth* numbers; please return it to me signed and approved ...

I have not yet received Act III, but I'm delighted in advance with what you tell me about it. I'm sure that what you have written is worthy of your great genius. No more need be said. Everything you tell me will be strictly observed, and if there are any details hard to understand I'll not fail to consult you. As for Act IV, I think that sending it to me about February 10 would give time enough. It struck me that the orchestral introduction—I mean the introduction to the Act IV chorus—was not on the level of the rest. Perhaps I'm just being stupid, but I venture this opinion. If you could add something for the tenor, I could arrange that Montjauze sings the role, and that would be a gain for the production. In this matter, you are the only judge of what should or should not be done ...

Sant'Agata

VERDI TO PIAVE

Sto per fare l'ultimo Coro, me è una delle mille e mille cose che son dappertutto e che non fanno né caldo né freddo.[1] Io ne ho immaginato uno che può avere qualche cosa di piccante e che sottometto alla tua approvazione.

Dopo la battaglia faccio venire dei *Bardi* che cantano l'Inno di vittoria. I Bardi (tu lo sai) seguivano in quei tempi le armate. I versi i primi tre tronchi, e l'ultimo sdrucciolo. Ciò dà un'aria secca e fiera che sta bene ed ha carattere.

Siccome poi non bisognerà privarsi del sussidio delle donne così ho trovato il modo di farle entrare in scena.

Volta pagine e troverai tutto per disteso. I versi hanno bisogno della lima e tu l'userai ma farai presto. Ho dovuto accorciare qualche cosa come vedrai.[2]

SCENA IX

Macbet incalzato da Macduff

MACD.
Carnefice de' figli miei t'ho giunto!
MAC.
Fuggi!...Nato di donna
Uccidermi non può.
MACD.
Nato non sono!
Strappato fui dal sen materno.
MAC. (*spaventato*)
Cielo!

(*brandisce la spada e disperatamente battendosi con Macduff escono di vista*)

SCENA X

Entrano donne scozzesi come nel principio dell'atto.
La battaglia continua

DONNE
Infausto giorno!...ovunque strage e morte!
Preghiam pe' figli nostri!...
Cessa il fragor!...
VOCI (*dentro*)
Vittoria!
DONNE (*con gioia*)
Vittoria?...

SCENA ULTIMA

Malcolmo seguito dai soldati inglesi i quali trascinano prigionieri quelli di Macbet—Macduff con altri—Bardi e popolo

I'm about to do the final chorus, but it's one of the thousands and thousands of things you find everywhere that leave you neither hot nor cold.[1] I have dreamed up one that may have a little zest to it, and I submit it for your approval.

After the battle, I have some Bards come on singing the victory hymn. The Bards, as you know, followed the armies in those days. The first three lines are *tronchi*, and the last, *sdrucciolo*. That gives it a dry and bold feeling that is appropriate and has character.

And then, since we mustn't deprive ourselves of help from the women, I've found the way to bring them on stage.

Turn the pages and you'll find everything laid out in full. The lines need polishing, and you'll do it, but do it quickly. I needed to shorten some things, as you'll see.[2]

SCENE IX

Macbeth hotly pursued by Macduff

MACDUFF
Murderer of my children, I have reached you!
MACBETH
Fly!!...None born of woman
Can kill me.
MACDUFF
I was not born!
I was ripped from the maternal womb.
MACBETH (*frightened*)
Heaven!

(*He brandishes his sword and fighting desperately with Macduff they leave the stage.*)

SCENE X

The Scottish women enter, as at the beginning of the act.
The battle continues.

WOMEN
Ill-fated day!...carnage and death all around!
Let us pray for our sons!...
The tumult ceases!...
VOICES (*offstage*)
Victory!
WOMEN (*joyfully*)
Victory?...

FINAL SCENE

Malcolm followed by English soldiers, who lead on Macbeth's men as prisoners—Macduff with others—Bards and people

MALCOLMO	MALCOLM
Ove s'è fitto	Where lurks
L'usurpatòr	The usurper?
MACD.	MACDUFF
Colà...da me trafitto!	There!...run through by me!
TUTTI	ALL
Salve o Re!	Hail, o King!...
(I Bardi s'avanzano ed intuonano l'Inno)	*(The Bards advance and intone the Hymn)*
BARDI	BARDS
(con entusiasmo)	*(enthusiastically)*
Macbet, Macbet ov'è?...	Macbeth, Macbeth, where is he?...
Sparì[3] l'usurpator...	The usurper has vanished.
Lo spense[4] il fulminò	The God of victory
Il Dio della vittoria	Destroyed him, struck him with lightning.
(volgendosi a Macduff)	*(turning to Macduff)*
L'Eroe, l'Eroe[5] egli è,	He, he is the hero
Che spense il traditor.	Who destroyed the traitor.
La Patria il Re salvò:	Country and king he saved.
a Lui onore e gloria.	To him, honor and glory.
SOLDATI	SOLDIERS
Ah sì; l'Eroe egli è	Ah yes: he is the hero
Che spense il traditor!	Who destroyed the traitor!
La Patria il Re salvò:	Country and king he saved.
a Lui onore e gloria.	To him, honor and glory.
DONNE	WOMEN
Salgan mie grazie a te	May my thanks rise to thee,
Gran Dio vendicator.	Great avenging God.
A chi ci[6] liberò	To him who freed us,
Inni cantiam di gloria.	Let us sing hymns of glory.
MALCOL.	MALCOLM
Fidate tutti[7] in me!	All, trust in me!
È[8] spento l'oppressor.	The oppressor is destroyed.
A Lui che ci salvò	To him who saved us
Inni cantiam di gloria.[9]	Let us sing hymns of glory.
MACDUFF	MACDUFF
Ciascun si fidi[10] al Re	Let everyone trust in the king
Che il Ciel ci rende ancor[11]	Whom God returns to us again,
L'aurora che spuntò	The dawn that has risen
Vi darà pace e gloria.	Will give you peace and glory.
Aggiusta e manda tutto al più presto.	Fix this up and send everything as soon as
Abbiati 2, 812–14	possible.

1. On or before January 24, Piave had supplied three quatrains of *decasillabi*, the preferred meter for patriotic choruses, and one which Verdi specifically asked Piave to avoid at the beginning of Act IV (22 December 1846 letter). For Piave's text for the chorus and preceding recitative, transcribed in his hand in a Ricordi libretto of the 1847 *Macbeth*, see p. 341.

2. Verdi has abbreviated the text of the exchange between Macbeth and Macduff (cf. the 1847 libretto at 478) and a few of the new lines Piave supplied after the cry "Vittoria!" Verdi set the recitative to music without further changes from the version found both in this letter and transcribed in his hand into the Ricordi printed libretto (except that the phrase "ovunque strage e morte" was not set).

Verdi and Giuseppina sketched most of the stanzas (see pp. 342–45) on a loose sheet and then Verdi transcribed them into the printed Ricordi libretto and into this letter. A few days later, presumably after Piave sent his corrections, Verdi added further changes in the stanzas transcribed in the printed libretto. These changes are shown in the following notes. (V[1], V[2], and V[3] indicate successive layers of revision.) The final layer of text corresponds closely to what Verdi actually set to music.

3. V¹: Dov'è

4. Abbiati reads "sperse" here and in the next two stanzas.
   V¹: D'un soffio

5. V¹: Il prode Eroe

6. V¹: ne

7. V¹: Confida o Scozia

8. V¹: Fu

9. V¹: A Lui che ne salvò
   Inni cantiam di gloria.
   V²: Chi Patria e Re salvò
   Inni cantiam di gloria.
   V³: La gioja eternerò
   Per noi di tal vittoria.

10. V¹: S'affidi ognun

11. V¹: Ridato al nostro amor.

VERDI TO ESCUDIER

[Sant'Agata,] 31 January 1865

Ricevo in questo momento le vostre lettere colle cambiali ed il contratto. Domani rispondero a tutto ed in regola. Spero avrete ricevuto il terzo Atto.

Paris: Bibliothèque de l'Opéra

I have just received your letters with the checks and the contract. Tomorrow I shall reply to everything in good order. I hope you have received Act III.

VERDI TO PIAVE

Sant'Agata, 1 February 1865

... Ho ricevuto i versi accomodati, e scusami, alcuni riescono più deboli e meno sonori. Per esempio il primo verso quando tu hai detto *Sparì Macbet*...non si può andar più avanti. Mi pare molto meglio, ed ha maggior enfasi

... I received the adjusted lines and, excuse me, but some have come out weaker and less sonorous. For example, the first line in which you wrote "*Sparì Macbeth*"..., one can't go on from there. What seems much better to me, and has more emphasis, is

> Macbet Macbet ov'è?
> Dov'è l'usurpator...
> Il prode eroe tu se'
> Che spense¹ il traditor
> Che etc....

> Macbeth Macbeth ov'è?
> Dov'è l'usurpator...
> Il prode eroe tu se'
> Che spense¹ il traditor
> Che etc....

quei due *Che* stan male assai.

Non mi par buono il primo verso dei soldati "*Ah sì Macduffo Egli è!*" Non importa che sia *Macduffo* o *Paolo* o *Ignazio*—è meglio "*Ah sì l'eroe egli è.*" Non mi piace pure la strofa delle donne, come anche l'ultimo verso "*Nunzio è di pace e gloria...*" È duro questo verso. ...

Abbiati 3, 815

those two *Che*'s go together badly.

The first line of the soldiers' "Ah sì Macduffo Egli è!" doesn't seem good to me. It doesn't matter whether it is *Macduff* or *Paolo* or *Ignazio*—it is better as "Ah sì l'eroe egli è." Nor do I like the women's strophe, nor its last line, "Nunzio è di pace e di gloria..." That line is hard. ...

1. Abbiati reads "spenge."

VERDI TO ARRIVABENE

Cremona, 1 February 1865

... Indovina: ho scritto in questo tempo...musica!! Sì signore: proprio della musica o almeno delle note. Tu dirai ch'io sono diventato pazzo; hai ragione. Ma ora sono in perfetta guarigione: ho finito. ...

Alberti, 44

... Guess what—recently I've written...music!! Yes sir, music, of all things—or at least notes. You'll say that I've gone mad. You're right. But now I'm completely cured: I've finished. ...

ESCUDIER TO VERDI

Paris, 2 February 1865

J'ai reçu le troisième acte qui est simplement un chef-d'oeuvre. A lui seul ce serait un énorme

I have received Act III, which is, quite simply, a masterpiece. It's enough in itself to be an enor-

succès. Carvalho et ses artistes sont dans l'enthousiasme. Carvalho fait pour ce troisième acte un décor et une mise en scène aussi beaux que ceux du tableau des Noces dans Robert.[1]

Hier nous avons fait une trouvaille, un ténor d'une voix admirable, 23 ans, très intelligent, beau garçon. C'est Villaret[2] avec une voix plus complète et plus fraîche. Il nous a chanté l'air du Trouvère; dans l'allegro il lance le fameux *ut* de Tamberlik avec une facilité, un charme, un éclat extraordinaire.[3] Je suis sûr que ce sera une bonne fortune pour le rôle de Ma[c]duff dans Macbeth. Carvalho va le styler et lui règler personnellement tout son rôle. Quoiqu'il *ait* peu de chose à chanter, il étonnera le public. Je réponds d'un grand succès pour la belle romance du 4ᵐᵉ acte. Il y a après la romance un cri aux armes; s'il était possible de le lui faire chanter seul en le modifiant et y ajoutant un passage pour son *ut* qui est splendide, nous aurions, j'en réponds un immense effet. C'est à vous à en juger.[4]

Je me suis trompé dans ma dernière lettre en vous parlant de l'introduction d'orchestre du 4ᵐᵉ acte; c'est de la scène d'orchestre de la bataille qui précède celle de la forêt qui marche dont j'ai voulu parler. C'est dans le récit qui précède le choeur que vous pourriez peut-être placer un phrase à effet pour le ténor.

L'air que vous avez composé au second acte est admirable. Mᵐᵉ Rey-Balla le chante avec un talent bien remarquable. Vous auriez pris mesure de sa voix que vous n'auriez pas mieux réussis. Vous avez eu une très bonne idée en faisant finir le 3ᵐᵉ acte par un duo très chaud et entraînant.

Si l'Hymne qui doit clore l'opéra a de l'importance. Carvalho voudrait le faire chanter par Cent choristes. Ce serait une belle clôture. . . .

Sant'Agata

mous success. Carvalho and his artists are ecstatic. For this third act, Carvalho is preparing decor and staging as fine as those of the wedding scene in *Robert le diable.*[1]

Yesterday we made a find, a tenor with an admirable voice, twenty-three years old, very intelligent, good-looking. He's Villaret[2] with a more complete and fresher voice. He sang the *Trovatore* aria for us; in the allegro, he launched the famous Tamberlik C with ease, with charm, with extraordinary brilliance.[3] I'm sure that this would enhance the role of Macduff in *Macbeth.* Carvalho is going to coach him and direct him personally in the entire role. Although he does have little to sing, he will astonish the public. I promise a big success for the fine *romance* of Act IV. After the *romance,* there's a cry to arms; if it were possible to have him sing this as a solo, modifying it and adding to it a passage for his splendid high C, we would have an immense effect from it, I promise you. It's up to you to decide.[4]

I made a mistake in my last letter when I referred to the orchestral introduction to Act IV; I meant the orchestral battle passage before the forest on the march. It's in the recitative before the chorus that you could perhaps place an effective phrase for the tenor.

The aria that you have composed in Act II is admirable. Mme. Rey-Balla sings it with a most remarkable talent. If you had written it especially for her voice, you couldn't have done it better. You had a very good idea, making Act III end with a fiery, exciting duet.

Yes, the Hymn that must close the opera is important. Carvalho wants to have it sung by a *hundred* choristers. That would be a fine ending . . .

---

1. Meyerbeer's *Robert le diable* (1831), with its spectacular decor by Ciceri, was a popular Opéra attraction; it reached its 500th performance there in 1867.

2. Verdi had written a new aria for Villaret for the Opéra's *Vêpres* revival in 1863. Villaret made his Opéra debut as Arnold in *Tell* in 1863; that year, he sang Eléazar in *La Juive;* in 1865, Masaniello in *La muette de Portici* and Raoul in *Les Huguenots.* The new tenor did not live up to his promise (see Escudier's letter of 7 March); Monjauze was engaged.

3. Enrico Tamberlik prided himself on the high C he introduced into "Di quella pira." He was the first Alvaro of *La forza del destino,* and Verdi employed this specialty of his to close Act III of that opera.

4. Verdi left the military music and recitative (ending with Malcolm's cry to arms) unaltered, but in recasting the coda of "La patria tradita," he did give Macduff at least a sustained high B flat, which was not there before. In the Escudier score and the Nuitter and Beaumont libretto, however, the "cry to arms" ("Si l'Écosse vous est chère,/ Combattez vaillants héros!") is reassigned from Malcolm to Macduff, and "De la patrie en larmes" (the principal tune of the *cabaletta*) is given out by Macduff alone, not by the two tenors in unison.

ESCUDIER TO VERDI

Je sors de la répétition de Macbeth; une lettre que vous recevrez en même temps que celle-ci était déjà jetée à la poste, et je n'ai pu y ajouter en quelques mots.

On a répété deux actes; magnifique! magnifique! il n'y a eu qu'un cri. Carvalho me disait en sortant que s'il ne ferait pas assurer sa salle, elle pourrait crouler sous ces applaudissements. Mme Rey-Balla et Ismaël sont très beaux et ont admirablement saisi le caractère de leur personnage. Banco est excellent. Enfin tout va pour le mieux.

Mais voici l'idée qui m'a passé par la tête. Il est très probable qu'elle soit absurde; dans ce cas vous la mettrez à néant comme toutes les idées absurdes.

Le Brindisi qui est chanté par le soprano sera bissé à coup sûr la première fois. Le public ignore s'il revient une seconde fois. Eh bien si Ma[c]duff le ténor entamerait la seconde strophe au lieu du soprano à la seconde reprise, l'effet en serait peut-être aussi grand que la 1ère fois et le rôle du ténor prendrait de l'importance. Encore une fois je hazarde peut-être une hérésie ou une bêtise, mais néanmoins permettez-moi de vous la soumettre. Le ténor en question a la voix qu'il conviendrait pour ce morceau et je crois pouvoir vous répondre qu'il n'y sera pas inférieur à Mme Rey-Balla.

Vous m'excusez n'est-ce pas cher maître de vous communiquer mes pensées; bonnes ou mauvaises, elles ne me sont inspirées vous n'en doutez pas que par les meilleurs sentiments.

Sant'Agata

I come from the *Macbeth* rehearsal; a letter you'll receive at the same time as this one had already been put in the mail, and I wasn't able to add a few words to it.

Two acts were rehearsed: Magnificent! magnificent! was the unanimous cry. On coming out, Carvalho said to me that he wouldn't be able to have his theatre insured, it would collapse in this storm of applause. Mme. Rey-Balla and Ismaël are very fine and have grasped the character of their parts admirably. Banquo is excellent. In short, everything is going for the best.

But here's the idea that came to mind. Quite probably it's absurd; in that case you'll consign it to oblivion, like all absurd ideas.

The *brindisi* that the soprano sings is certain to be encored the first time. The public doesn't know whether it returns a second time. Well, if Macduff, the tenor, were to take over the second strophe, instead of the soprano, the second time around the effect of it would perhaps be as great as the first time, and the tenor role would take on importance. Once again, I am perhaps suggesting a heresy or a foolishness, but nevertheless let me submit it to you. The tenor in question has the voice this number requires, and I think I can promise you that he won't be inferior to Mme. Rey-Balla.

You'll excuse me, cher maître, for passing on my thoughts to you; good or bad, they are inspired, as you know, by the best of feelings.

VERDI TO ESCUDIER[1]

Oggi ho spedito a Ricordi l'ultimo Atto del Macbeth completamente finito. Ho fatto di nuovo tutto il Coro che apre il 4.° Atto. Ho ritoccata ed istromentata l'aria del Tenore[.][2] Poi dopo la Romanza del Baritono fino alla fine tutto è nuovo; e vi è la descrizione della Battaglia e l'Inno finale. Voi riderete quando sentirete che per la Battaglia ho fatto una *Fuga!!!!* Una *Fuga?*...Io che detesto tutto quello che puzza di scuola[3] ed eran quasi trent'anni che non ne faceva!!! Ma vi dirò che in questo caso può andar bene quella forma musicale. Il corrersi dietro che fanno i soggetti e controsoggetti; l'urto delle dissonanze, il frastuono etc. etc. possono esprimere abbastanza bene una

Today I sent Ricordi the last act of *Macbeth* completely finished. I rewrote all of the chorus that opens Act IV. I retouched up and [re]orchestrated the tenor aria.[2] Then, after the baritone aria everything is new up to the end; and there is the description of the battle and the final Hymn. You will laugh when you hear that I wrote a *Fugue* for the battle!!!! A *Fugue?*...I, who detest everything that smells of school,[3] and it has been nearly thirty years since) wrote one!!! But I can tell you that in this case that musical form can fit very well. The subjects and countersubjects that follow each other, the dissonant clashes, the uproar, etc., etc., can express a battle quite well.[4] I only wish that the

battaglia.[4] Vorrei soltanto che l'attacco fosse fatto dalle *Trombe a macchina*, come abbiamo noi, che sono tanto squillanti e sonore. Le vostre *Trompettes a pistons* sono per questo caso fiacche e snervate. Del resto l'orchestra avrà a divertirsi.[5] Con comodo vi manderò tutte le osservazioni su questo Quarto Atto. Avete ricevuto il Terzo?

Parto Domenica per Torino e Genova ove mi fermerò per tutto il resto dell'inverno. Da Genova vi scriverò a lungo e voi mi risponderete allora.

Vedo che i giornali cominciano già a parlare di questo Macbet. Per l'amor di Dio, *ne blaguez pas trop*.[6] È perfettamente inutile.

Paris: Bibliothèque de l'Opéra;
Rivista Musicale Italiana 35 (1928), 186;
Copialettere (draft), 456

beginning could be played on *trombe a macchina*, such as we have, which are so penetrating and sonorous. Your *trompettes à pistons* are sluggish and weak for this passage. Anyway, the orchestra will have a chance to amuse itself.[5] When it's convenient, I will send you all my remarks on Act IV. Have you received Act III?

Sunday [February 5] I leave for Turin and Genoa, where I will stay for the rest of the winter. I will write you at length from Genoa, and you can answer me then.

I see that the newspapers are already beginning to talk about this *Macbeth*. For heaven's sake, *ne blaguez pas trop* [don't puff it up too much].[6] It is perfectly useless.

1. Verdi's draft of this letter, preserved at Sant'Agata, is published in *Copialettere;* we give the most interesting variants below.

2. Verdi refers to the *cabaletta* ("La patria tradita") of the aria; the rest (except for adjustments in the first five measures of the opening recitative, necessitated by the changed key of the preceding chorus) is unchanged.

3. di scuola ... Ma vi dirò] di scuola! Ma vi dirò

of school ... But I can tell you] of school! But I can tell you

4. battaglia.... Del resto] battaglia. Ah se vi fossero le nostre trombe, così sonore, squillanti!! Quelle vostre trompettes à pistons non sono nè carne nè pesce. Del resto

quite well ... Anyway] quite well. Oh, if only you had *our* trumpets—so sonorous and penetrating. Those piston-valve trumpets of yours are neither fish nor fowl. Anyway

Verdi's preference is for trumpets with rotary valves rather than (upright) piston valves.

5. In his 28 December 1864 letter, Escudier had criticized the 1847 version of the battle, noting that the Théâtre-Lyrique orchestra was excellent and capable of performing a "beau morceau symphonique" perfectly, if Verdi would provide one.

6. The *Copialettere* draft ends here.

VERDI TO TITO RICORDI

Sant'Agata, 3 February 1865

T'ho spedito stamattina colla Ferrovia d'Alseno l'ultimo Atto del Macbet che farai il piacere di far copiare, e manderai l'originale a Parigi a Leon Escudier come al solito. Non so ancora se tu hai spedito il Terzo atto a Parigi e desidererei saperne qualche cosa.—Domenica sera sarò a Torino, ma non mi rifermerò che 24 ore....

Milan: Archivio Ricordi (230)

This morning I sent you by the Alseno train the last act of *Macbeth*. Do me the favor of having it copied, and send the original to Escudier in Paris as usual. I still don't know if you've sent Act III to Paris and would like to know something about it.—On Sunday evening [February 5], I'll be in Turin, but will only stop there twenty-four hours....

VERDI TO TITO RICORDI

[4 February 1865]

Jeri ti spedii il quart'atto del Macbet. M'accorgo che ho dimenticato qualche cosa nell'ultimo squarcio con cui finisce l'opera. Mandami ti prego l'ultimo fascicolo dello spartito originale a Genova per Lunedi diriggendolo alla Croce di Malta.

Milan: Archivio Ricordi (231)

Yesterday I sent you Act IV of *Macbeth*. It occurs to me that I forgot something in the last passage that ends the opera. Please send the final fascicle of the original score to me in Genoa, in time to arrive by Monday [February 6], addressing it to the Croce di Malta.

VERDI TO ESCUDIER   *Genoa, 8 February 1865*

Ne cherchons pas midi à quatre heures! Non cerchiamo effetti o sopra un *ut* di petto, o sopra una voce fresca, o sopra una parte secondaria, ma cerchiamo un'effetto solido, e durabile su quello che vi può essere veramente di buono in questo Macbet. Abbiate per massima che i *roles* di quest'opera sono tre, e non possono essere che tre: *Lady Macbet, Macbet—il Coro delle Streghe*. Le Streghe dominano il dramma; tutto deriva da loro; sguajate e pettegole nel primo atto; sublimi e profetiche nel Terzo. Sono veramente un personaggio ed un personaggio della più alta importanza.[1] La parte di *Macduff* per quanto facciate non la ridurrete mai a grande interesse. Anzi più lo si metterà in vista più dimostrerà la sua nullità. Egli non diventa un'Eroe che quando finisce l'opera. Egli ha però abbastanza musica per distinguersi se ha bella voce,[2] ma non bisogna dargli una nota di più. Il fargli dire una parte del Brindisi nell'atto secondo sarebbe un errore ed un contro-senso drammatico. *Macduff* non è in questa scena che un cortigiano come tutti gli altri. Il personaggio importante, il Demonio dominatore di questa scena è *Lady Macbet;* e quantumque Macbet abbia a distinguersi grandemente come attore, pure, ripeto, *Lady Macbet* domina tutto, sorveglia *a tutto*, rimprovera a Macbet di non essere *nemmeno un'uomo*, e dice ai cortigiani di non badare ai deliri di suo marito "*è un affar nervoso*" e per assicurarli meglio ripete colla più alta indifferenza il Brindisi. Ciò è bello, ed in bocca sua ha un'alto significato; in bocca a *Macduff* non significa nulla, ed è un contro senso. È vero, o non è vero?...Convenite che ho ragione.

Voi riceverete fra un pajo di giorni il Quart'atto. Domani o dopo vi scriverò tutte le mie intenzioni su quest'atto.

Se il Sig.^r Carvalho vuol mettere nell'ultimo Coro cento coristi tanto meglio, ma io preferirei che Egli rinforzasse in generale il Coro delle Streghe specialmente dal lato dei contralti che sono sempre deboli. Vi ripeto che il Coro delle Streghe ha una grandissima importanza: *è un personaggio*. Non bisogna dimenticare che tanto nell'esecuzione musicale, come nell'azione devono nel principio essere brutali e sguajate fino al momento del Terz'Atto in cui si trovano in faccia a Macbet. Da questo punto sono sublimi e profetiche.—

Ne cherchons pas midi à quatre heures! [i.e., let's do the best with what we've got] Let us not look for effects from a high C *di petto* [from the chest] or a fresh voice, or a secondary role, but rather let us look for a solid and lasting effect with whatever is really good in this *Macbeth*. Above all, bear in mind that there are three roles in this opera and three is all there can be: *Lady Macbeth, Macbeth,* and the *chorus of witches*.—The witches dominate the drama; everything derives from them—coarse and gossipy in the first act, sublime and prophetic in the third. They are truly a character, and a character of the utmost importance.[1] So far as Macduff's part is concerned, no matter what you do, you will never succeed in making it very important. On the contrary, the more prominence you give it, the more it will show its insignificance. He does not become a hero until the end of the opera. He has, however, enough music to distinguish himself, if he has a good voice;[2] but there is no need to give him a single note more. To have him sing a part of the *brindisi* in Act II would be a mistake and a dramatic contradiction. In this scene, Macduff is just a courtier, like everyone else. The important character, the dominating demon of this scene, is *Lady Macbeth;* and however much *Macbeth* can distinguish himself as an actor, *Lady Macbeth,* I repeat, dominates and controls everything. She scolds Macbeth for being *not even a man* and tells the courtiers to pay no attention to her husband's delirium—"it is a nervous affliction"—and to better reassure them she repeats the *brindisi* with the utmost nonchalance. In this way it is beautiful, and coming from her lips it has great meaning; from Macduff, it means nothing and is a contradiction. True, or no?...Admit that I am right.

You will receive Act IV within a few days. Tomorrow or the day after I will send you all my ideas about this act.

If M. Carvalho wants to use a hundred voices in the final chorus, so much the better, but I would prefer that he reinforced the chorus of witches in general, especially *di* altos, who are always weak. Let me repeat that the chorus of witches is of the greatest importance; *it is a character*. It must not be forgotten that in both their singing and their acting, they must be brutal and coarse from the beginning up to the moment in Act III where they are confronted with Macbeth. From this point on, they are sublime and prophetic.

Una volta mi scriveste di far danzare nel Coro delle Streghe dell'1º Atto. Non lo fare; è un errore. Toglie l'effetto al Ballabile del Terzo Atto; e poi quel Coro sta bene così. *Ne cherchons pas midi à quatre heures.* Talvolta per voler moltiplicare troppo gli effetti si finisce con distruggerli l'un contro l'altro.

Godo che troviate bene quello che v'ho mandato; soltanto non scaldatevi troppo la testa, onde non abbiate a restarne deluso alla fine....

Ho esatto le cambiali a Torino: domanderò presto la scrittura segnata....

You once wrote to me about having some dancing in the witches' chorus in Act I. Don't do it—it is a mistake. It spoils the effect of the ballet in Act III, and, besides, that chorus is fine as it is. *Ne cherchons pas midi à quatre heures.* Sometimes, trying to increase the number of effects too much results in their canceling each other out.

I am glad you are pleased with what I have sent you; just don't become too worked up, so that you won't be disappointed in the end....

... I cashed the checks in Turin. Soon I shall ask for the signed contract....

Buenos Aires: Museo del Teatro Colón;
Rassegna Musicale 21 (1951), 260–61

1. Cf. Schlegel's "Note on Shakespeare's *Macbeth*," at 346–48.
2. On this point, see also Verdi's 24 January 1847 letter to Lanari.

TITO RICORDI TO VERDI

Milan, 8 February 1865

Sono in possesso della cara tua d'jeri e dell'ultimo pezzo del *Macbeth* corretto. Mi sembra però che manchi qualche battuta di cadenza del Coro di cui qui ti accludo una copia. Appena che mi avrai risposto su questo punto, manderò l'intero Atto quarto a Parigi.

Ho sentito da Tornaghi[1] che non hai difficoltà a lasciar produrre questo *Macbeth* nuovo anche in Italia e ne ho piacere. Accetto le tue condizioni, cioè Ottomila franchi e l'interessenza come per gli altri nostri contratti. Tornaghi mi dice che hai ceduto ad Escudier anche la proprietà per l'Inghilterra, ma ritengo che non l'avrai ceduta anche per la Spagna e la Germania e in questo caso dovresti comprenderla nel nostro contratto....

I have received your letter of yesterday and the corrected final number of *Macbeth*. However, it seems to me that some cadential measures in the chorus are missing—I enclose a copy for you. As soon as you've answered me on this point, I'll send the entire fourth act to Paris.

I heard from Tornaghi[1] that you have no objections to having this new *Macbeth* produced in Italy as well, and I'm glad. I accept your conditions, that is, eight thousand francs and profit sharing as in our other contracts. Tornaghi tells me that you ceded to Escudier the rights for England, too, but I assume you didn't cede them also for Spain and Germany, and if that's so, you ought to include them in our contract....

Sant'Agata

1. Verdi had seen Tornaghi in Turin a few days earlier (as Verdi's 29 August 1865 letter to Tito Ricordi establishes).

VERDI TO TITO RICORDI

8 February 1865

Ti rimando il foglio di musica corretto....

Credo veramente d'aver ceduta la proprietà dei cambiamenti ad Escudier per tutti i paesi salvo l'Italia.[1] Dico, *credo*, perchè non ne sono ben certo. È cosa che rettificherò e te ne scriverò quanto prima. Intanto tutto resti per ora in sospeso. Ti prevengo che questo *Macbet* nuovo non può prodursi in Italia prima d'esser stato rappresentato in Francia che sarà ai primi di Marzo.

I return to you the corrected sheet of music....

I really think that I've yielded the rights in the changed passages to Escudier for all countries except Italy.[1] I say, I *think* so, because I'm not really sure. This is something I'll put right, and I'll let you know about it as soon as possible. In the meanwhile, leave things in the air. Let me advise you that this new *Macbeth* cannot be [done] in Italy before it is performed in France, which will be at the beginning of March.

Milan: Archivio Ricordi (232)

1. He had indeed—see Escudier's letter of 28 October 1864 and Verdi's reply of 2 November 1864.

VERDI TO ESCUDIER

Genoa, 8 February 1865

Finalmente ho avuto questa mattina un rittaglio di tempo per esaminare un po' la scrittura che m'avete mandato, e trovo che ha delle braccia e delle ali che si allargano troppo, ed abbracciano quasi tutto. Non ho qui sott'occhio il nostro carteggio ed è possibile che questa scrittura sia conforme a quello; ma permettetemi un'osservazione. Cosa volete fare di questi cambiamenti in paesi dove voi non avete la proprietà del resto? Che voi ne abbiate la proprietà per la Francia, per il Belgio, e per l'Inghilterra, è giustissimo; ma che voi l'abbiate per la Spagna, Germania, ed altri paesi ove la proprietà di quasi due terzi dell'opera (i pezzi vecchi del Macbet) appartiene a Ricordi, non è giusto. È possibile, ripeto, che qualche parola a cui io non abbia fatta grande attenzione, vi dia diritto di proprietà generale sui nuovi pezzi, e qualora voi siate tanto fiero, e terribile da reclamare tutti i diritti che potete avere, non dubitate che vi saranno scrupolosamente conservati; ma io mi appello alla vostra giustizia ed al vostro buon senso, e son sicuro che voi troverete giusto di avere soltanto la proprietà per la Francia, Belgio, ed Inghilterra.—Del resto poi se l'opera piace voi avrete sempre fatto un buon affare; se non piace poco guadagnerete con queste proprietà. E permettetemi altresì d'aggiungere che io ho fatto molto più lavoro di quello che volevo, e che voi stesso volevate: vi sono stato trascinato, e ne sono contentissimo. Ma se voi in principio m'aveste detto: *"Fatemi tutti quei pezzi e vi dò 10m franchi,"* Io v'avrei risposto con un saluto graziosissimo ed avrei rifiutato. Rispondetemi · in proposito al più presto. . . .

Paris: Bibliothèque de l'Opéra;
Rassegna Musicale 21 (1951), 260–61

I finally had some spare time this morning to study a bit the contract that you sent me, and I find that it has arms and wings that spread out too far and envelop almost everything. I don't have before me our correspondence, and it is possible that this contract agrees with it, but allow me to make an observation: what do you want to do with these changes in countries where you do not have the rights for the rest? It is perfectly fair that you should have the rights for France, Belgium, and England; but that you should have them for Spain, Germany, and other countries where the rights to almost two-thirds of the opera (the old numbers of *Macbeth*) belong to Ricordi, is not fair. It is possible, I repeat, that some words to which I paid little attention give you complete rights to the new numbers, and if you are so cruel and terrible as to claim as many rights as you can have, do not doubt that they will be scrupulously observed. But I appeal to your justice and to your good sense, and am sure you will find it fair to have the rights for only France, Belgium, and England. Moreover, if the opera is successful, you will still have made a good deal; if it is not, you will earn little with these rights. And allow me to add also that I have worked much harder than I wanted to, and than you yourself wanted me to; I was dragged into it, and am very glad. But if in the beginning you had told me, "Write me all of those numbers and I'll give you 10,000 francs," I would have smiled sweetly and refused. Answer me about this as soon as possible. . . .

PIAVE TO VERDI

Milan, 9 February 1865

. . . Il *Macbetto* è dunque finito!. . .Non vedo l'ora di sentirne i nuovi pezzi. . . .

Sant'Agata; *Abbiati* 2, 816

. . . So *Macbeth* is finished!. . .I can't wait to hear the new numbers. . . .

ESCUDIER TO VERDI

Paris, 10 February 1865

Vous avez mille fois raison. Ma[c]duff ne peut pas chanter le Brindisi. J'ai relu la pièce de Schacspeare le soir même où je vous ai écrite; et j'ai vite compris que j'avais fait une bêtise et que je n'étais qu'un imbécile [*sic*]. Ne le répétez

You are right a thousand times over. Macduff cannot sing the *brindisi*. I reread Shakespeare's play the very evening I wrote to you, and soon understood that I had suggested something foolish and that I was simply an imbecile. Don't

pas, on le croirait. Tous les jours de midi à trois heures je suis au théâtre lyrique; on répète activement. Les artistes savent par cœur les deux premiers actes. Mme Rey-Balla et Ismaël sont vraiment superbes. Aujourd'hui nous avons commencé le troisième acte, qui est bien une des pages les plus grandioses et les plus originales que vous ayez composé. Tout cet acte sera d'un effet immense. J'attends maintenant le quatrième acte.

Je n'avais pas attendu votre avis sur les chœurs des femmes; j'ai fait engager dix choristes supplémentaires, dont huit Contr'alti. Vous pouvez donc être tranquille sur les effets des chœurs. Carvalho pour la scène des apparitions fait faire un petit orchestre sous le théâtre ainsi que vous l'avez indiqué. Demain j'ai rendez-vous avec Sax[1] pour la marche du premier acte; je crois que là encore nous aurons un grand effet. Dans la scène des apparitions, les chœurs chantent toujours ensemble, n'est-ce pas; il n'y a pas de groupes qui se détachent pour annoncer les apparitions. Vous avez toujours indiqué le chœur sur votre partition; c'est bien le chœur entier?

On ne mettra pas pas de ballet au 1er acte. Vous avez encore raison; c'est embêtant! Vous avez toujours raison. Le divertissement du 3me acte a une couleur infernale; c'est fort beau. Aussitôt que la *flûte enchantée* de Mozart sera représentée et Carvalho compte donner la première représentation de demain en huit, nous descendrons sur la scène. Les chœurs marcheront bien. Quant à la mise en scène et aux décors, ce sera féerique.

Il surgit tous les jours des difficultés pour cette malheureuse Africaine . . .

Sant'Agata

repeat that—people would believe it. Everyday from noon until three I am at the Théâtre-Lyrique. They are rehearsing busily. The artists know the first two acts by heart. Mme. Rey-Balla and Ismaël are truly superb. Today we began Act III, which is really one of the grandest and most original passages you have composed. The whole act will make a great effect. Now I am waiting for Act IV.

I didn't wait for your advice about the women's chorus; I had ten extra choristers engaged, eight of them contraltos. So you can rest assured about the effectiveness of the choruses. For the apparitions scene, Carvalho is having a little under-stage orchestra assembled, as you indicated. Tomorrow I have a meeting with Sax[1] about the Act I march: I believe that there, too, we'll have a great effect. Throughout the apparitions scene, the chorus sings together, doesn't it, not dividing into groups to announce the apparitions? In your score, you have always indicated "chorus": you do mean the whole chorus?

There'll be no ballet added to Act I. Again you are right; it's maddening! You are always right. The Act III divertissement has an infernal coloring; that's very fine. As soon as Mozart's *Magic Flute* has been performed—and Carvalho counts on giving the first performance a week from tomorrow—we move down onto the stage. The choruses will go well. As for the staging and the decors, all will be magical.

Difficulties are cropping up every day around that unhappy *Africaine*. . . .

1. Adolphe Sax (1814–1894), manufacturer and inventor of musical instruments (including the saxhorn and the saxophone), and regularly concerned with the provision of stage bands.

TITO RICORDI TO VERDI   *Milan, 11 February 1865*

In possesso della cara tua d'jeri. . . .

Jeri ho mandato a Escudier a Parigi il 4.º Atto del tuo *Macbeth*. A giorni poi ti manderò la mia copia dell'intero spartito che gentilmente offristi di rivedere.—È cosa intesa che non sarebbe a prodursi in Italia fin dopo che non sia andato in scena a Parigi. . . .

Sant'Agata

I have received yours of yesterday. . . .

Yesterday I sent Act IV of your *Macbeth* to Escudier in Paris. Then, in a few days I'll send you my copy of the entire score, which you kindly offered to correct.—It's understood that it is not to be produced in Italy until after it has been staged in Paris. . . .

ESCUDIER TO VERDI   *Paris, 12 February 1865*

J'ai reçu ce matin votre lettre et je m'empresse d'y répondre.

C'est bien vrai; vous avez fait un beau travail et un travail plus important que je n'aurais osé l'espérer! et ce n'est pas moi qui voudrais en abuser. J'avais entendu vous acheter toute la propriété de vos nouveaux morceaux, mais lorsque j'ai vu les manuscrits, je me suis rendu compte de l'importance que va acquérir le nouveau Macbeth; et à vous parler franchement, j'attendais le traité que je vous ai envoyé signé par vous pour vous offrir spontanément la moitié de toutes les cessions que j'aurais pu faire aux théâtres étrangers en prenant pour moi seul tous les frais de copie.

Je comprends que Ricordi veuille profiter aujourd'hui du nouveau Macbeth; je n'ai qu'à me louer de mes relations avec lui et je désire que la chose puisse s'arranger dans nos intérêts communs. Lorsque Ricordi m'a vendu Macbeth, il n'y avait aucune propriété garantie dans les pays étrangers. On pouvait faire entrer en Espagne, en Écossé partout des contrefaçons de Macbeth, et cela a lieu encore aujourd'hui pour l'ancien Macbeth sans que Ricordi puisse s'y opposer. On a représenté l'ancien Macbeth sur toutes les scènes d'Espagne, du Portugal, de Russie etc.[1] Il est évident qu'en acquérant la propriété des nouveaux morceaux, je n'entendais céder que les mêmes morceaux aux scènes étrangères. C'eut été parfaitement mon droit et en cela je ne causais aucun préjudice à Ricordi, puisque toutes ces scènes ont déjà l'ancien Macbeth. Quant à l'Édition du nouveau Macbeth, voici pourquoi je tiens à en avoir la propriété à l'Étranger. Je vends à mes correspondants la musique française et si je ne puis leur fournir ce que j'édit à Paris, on s'adresse à Ricordi ou à Lucca et je perds mes correspondants. Et Macbeth a une grande importance pour mon commerce surtout lorsqu'il doit être joué pour la 1ère fois à Paris. Ce n'est point pour céder la propriété à d'autres Éditeurs que je désire conserver le droit de faire entrer l'Édition de Macbeth en Espagne, en Russie etc. mais bien pour pouvoir soutenir la concurrence de Ricordi et de Lucca.[2] Voici cher maître ce que je propose, et je pense que vous l'approuvez:

1.° J'aurai la propriété entière pour la France, la Belgique et l'Angleterre.

2.° J'aurai en même temps que Ricordi le droit d'envoyer et vendre mes Éditions dans les autres pays étrangers excepté en italie.

I received your letter this morning, and hasten to answer it.

It's indeed true: you have done a big piece of work and one more important than I would have dared to hope for! And I am not one to want to take advantage of you on that account. I agreed to buy from you all rights in the new pieces, but when I saw the manuscripts, I realized how important the new Macbeth was going to be; and, to speak freely, I was waiting to receive the contract I sent you, signed by you, to offer you, of my own accord, half of all the fees I could have received from foreign theatres, taking on all copying expenses myself.

I understand that Ricordi now wants to profit from the new Macbeth; I have nothing to reproach myself with in my dealings with him, and I'd like the matter to be arranged in our common interest. When Ricordi sold me Macbeth [I], he had no guaranteed rights to it for foreign countries. Pirate editions of Macbeth could be distributed in Spain, in Scotland, everywhere, and that still happens today with the original Macbeth without Ricordi's being able to prevent it. The original Macbeth was performed in all the theatres of Spain, Portugal, Russia, etc.[1] It is evident that, in acquiring the ownership of the new pieces, I would expect to grant performing rights in only those pieces to foreign theatres. That was absolutely my right, and in it I did nothing against Ricordi's interests, since all those theatres already have the original Macbeth. As for the published edition of the new Macbeth, this is why I am anxious to have the foreign rights: I sell my agents French music, and if I cannot provide them with what I have published in Paris, they apply to Ricordi or Lucca,[2] and I lose my agents. And Macbeth is very important for my business, especially since it will be played for the first time in Paris. I wish to keep the right to distribute the published Macbeth in Spain, Russia, etc., not in order to grant it to other publishers but in order to be able to compete with Ricordi and Lucca. Here, *cher maître,* is what I propose, and I think you will approve of it:

1. I shall have complete rights for France, Belgium, and England.

2. I together with Ricordi will have the right to distribute and sell my publications in other foreign countries, Italy excepted.

3.º Vous conserverez le droit de vendre ou céder aux théâtres êtrangers à l'exception de la France et de l'Angleterre votre nouvelle oeuvre, m'interdisant de la vendre moi-même ailleurs que dans les trois pays stipulés, la France, la Belgique et l'Angleterre.

Cela vous parait-il juste? Ou si mieux vous préférez, je vous offre la moitié de toutes les ventes que je pourrai faire aux scènes étrangères sans distinction, en prenant les frais de copie et tous autres à ma charge. Dans ce cas le traité restera tel qu'il est; il n'y aura qu'à y ajouter cette nouvelle condition.

Voilà bien des explications, mais je les ai crues nécessaires; excusez-moi si elles vous ont ennuyé.

Tenez pour certain que je sais les devoirs que j'ai à remplir envers vous à qui je dois la petite position toute entière que j'ai aujourd'hui et qu'en ce qui touche vos intérêts dans Macbeth, vous n'aurez point à me reprocher dans l'avenir d'en avoir abusé. Ayez confiance en ma loyauté et en mon honneur, comme j'ai entière confiance en votre bonne amitié.

Ayez la bonté cher Maître et ami de me dire votre avis sur ces diverses propositions, et croyez bien en tout cas que quoique vous puissiez demander je me mets à votre disposition.

Sant'Agata

3. You will keep the right to sell or grant your new work to foreign theatres, except those of France and England, prohibiting me from selling it, except in the three countries mentioned above: France, Belgium, and England.

Does that seem fair to you? Or, if you prefer, I offer you half of all the sales I can make to foreign theatres, wheresoever, taking on myself the copying and all other expenses. In that case, the contract will stay as it is; one will just have to add that new condition.

What a lot of explanations! But I thought them necessary; forgive me if they have bored you.

Rest assured that I know my obligations toward you—you to whom I owe entirely the little position I have today; and that, as regards your interests in Macbeth, you will have no cause in the future to reproach me for having taken advantage of you. Trust in my loyalty and my honor, as I trust in your good friendship.

Be so good, *cher maître et ami*, to tell me your opinion about these various proposals, and in any case believe that, whatsoever you should ask, I place myself at your disposition.

1. See "A Hundred Years of *Macbeth*".
2. For Lucca, see note 2 to letter of 26 September 1846.

VERDI TO G. DUPREZ[1]   [*Genoa, mid-February 1865*]

Sono stato in questi ultimi giorni talmente occupato che mi perdonerete, spero, il lungo ritardo a rispondere alla vostra amabilissima del 19 passato.

Conosco il mondo in generale ed il teatro in particolare: motivo per cui non mi sorprendo nè delle piccole nè delle grandi perfidie che vi si possono commettere. Sono certissimo che vostro fratello, come ha fatto le altre, avrà fatto benissimo questa traduzione del *Macbeth,* e se voi l'avete approvata e ve ne siete occupato per aggiustarla alle note, voi che siete un *grand musicien,* un grand'artista ed un uomo di coscienza avrete fatto questo lavoro eccellentemente, nè vi è bisogno che io esamini questa traduzione per averne la più *certa* certezza. Io non posso in

I have been so busy these last few days that I hope you will forgive my long delay in answering your very kind letter of the 19th of last month.

I am acquainted with the world in general and with the theater in particular; for this reason I am surprised by neither the small nor the large acts of treachery that can be committed there. I am absolutely sure that your brother has done very well in this translation of *Macbeth*, as in others, and if you have approved it and taken on the responsibility of adjusting it to the music—you who are a *grand musicien*, a great artist, and a man of conscience—you have done this work excellently, nor is there need for me to examine this translation in order to have

quest'affare che dolermi che si faccia a voi ed a vostro fratello questo torto, ma tutti i vostri nemici (ammettendo che ne abbiate molti) non varrebbero ad alterare di un filo la profonda stima che io sento per voi sotto ogni rapporto.

Copialettere, 455

the *certain* certainty. I cannot but regret this affair in which this wrong has been committed against you and your brother, but all of your enemies (supposing that you have many) would not serve to alter in the slightest the profound esteem which I feel for you from every point of view.

1. Ursula Günther informs us that this letter is partly Giuseppina's work; in her *Copialettere* there is this draft: "Edouard Duprez è un distinto poeta e se voi avete approvato le modificazioni ch'erano necessarie alla traduzione del Macbeth, vuol dire che vanno benissimo.... Dunque, caro Duprez, non vi è bisogno ch'io veda il lavoro del Macbeth per essere persuaso che sia ben fatto.... "

See, besides Duprez's 19 January 1865 letter, Escudier's 21 January 1865 letter, the notes to Verdi's 23 January reply, and GÜNTHER at pp. 177–78.

VERDI TO TITO RICORDI   *Genoa, 15 February 1865*

... Parliamo intanto un po' del *Macbet* sul quale è necessario ti faccia un po' di storia. Quando Leon Escudier fù l'anno scorso in Italia mi disse che Carvalho voleva far tradurre e rappresentare il Macbet, e mi pregava di fare i balletti e sostituire un Coro alla morte di Macbet. Dissi che l'avrei fatto. Più tardi esaminai lo spartito, e scrissi a Leon che qualora Carvalho m'avesse lasciato un po' di tempo avrei anche desiderato rifare alcune scene del Terzo atto, e la scena dell'apparizione al secondo et et...Egli mi rispose che se avessi fatto quel lavoro mi offriva la somma di...più i diritti d'autore intieri per Francia tutta. L'esibizione era generossisima e dissi *"accetto le vostre condizioni"*[.] Mi misi al lavoro, ed una volta incominciato sono stato trascinato a fare molto di più di quello che volevo e di quello che aveva promesso. Di fatti io avevo promesso un lavoro di poca importanza, ed ora si vede che questo Macbet se non è nuovo per metà, lo è per un buon terzo almeno. Ma io ho creduto di non rinvenire [*sic*] su quello che era stato fatto; soltanto dopo la tua lettera ho scritto a Leon cercando di conciliare il tuo col suo interesse. Egli mi propone quest' accomodamento: [Here Verdi quotes the three numbered points in Escudier's previous letter.]

È certo che io, non credendo di fare il lavoro che ho fatto nè prevedendo che potesse avere interesse per altri paesi eccettuata la Francia, ho lasciato colle mie parole *"accetto le vostre condizioni"* la proprietà dei pezzi nuovi a Leon Escudier. Pensa ora tu se ti possono convenire le condizioni che t'offre Escudier e scrivimi subito a Torino Albergo Trombetta ...

Milan: Archivio Ricordi (234)

... For now let's talk a bit about *Macbeth;* I'll have to go into the history of it a bit. When Léon Escudier was in Italy last year he told me that Carvalho wanted to have Macbeth translated and performed, and he asked me to do the ballets and to substitute a chorus for the death of Macbeth. I said that I'd do it. Later I examined the score and wrote to Léon that if Carvalho would allow me some time, I'd also like to rewrite some scenes in the third act, the apparition scene in the second, etc., etc...He answered me that if I were to do that work he would offer me the sum of...plus complete author's rights for all of France. The offer was most generous and I said "I accept your conditions." I set to work, and, once begun, I felt impelled to do much more than I wanted and had promised to do. In fact, I had promised a job of little importance, but now it turns out that this *Macbeth*, if not half new, is at least a good third new. But I thought I shouldn't go back on what had already been settled; only after your letter did I write to Léon, attempting to reconcile your interests with his. He proposes the following arrangement to me: [Verdi quotes the three numbered points in Escudier's previous letter].

It *is* certain that, not thinking of doing all the work that I actually did, and not foreseeing that it might gain some currency in countries other than France, with my words *"I accept your conditions,"* I ceded the rights in the new numbers to Léon Escudier. Now you decide whether you can agree to the terms that Escudier offers you, and write to me immediately at the Hotel Trombetta in Turin....

TITO RICORDI TO VERDI
Milan, 16 February 1865

In possesso della cara tua d'jeri da Genova, mentre ti ringrazio per la tua premura a favorirmi schiarimento circa l'estensione del contratto che facesti pel *Macbeth* con Escudier, mi dichiaro dispostissimo a ritenere per fermo le tue condizioni che aveva già accettate prima di conoscere il contratto stesso. La mia proprietà si estenderebbe quindi a tutti i paesi eccetto Francia, Spagna ed Inghilterra; concesso però ad Escudier di mandare e vendere le sue edizioni in tutti i paesi eccetto l'Italia.—Ti confesso che questa concessione mi fa temere una forte concorrenza nello smercio delle mie edizioni, principalmente in Spagna ed in Germania, dove le edizioni francesi sono quasi preferite alle mie. Se tu puoi in vista di ciò usarmi qualche facilitazione te ne sarò obbligatissimo, se no, sai che con te non voglio mercanteggiare e restano egualmente accettate per parte mia le tue condizioni e con esse quelle di Escudier. Lo ritengo adunque affar fatto e ne sono contento, perchè si ha proprio bisogno di musica nuova e buona. . . .
Sant'Agata

I've received yours of yesterday from Genoa. While thanking you for your speed in clarifying for me the full extent of the contract you made with Escudier for *Macbeth,* I declare myself most willing to regard as settled your terms, which I had already accepted before coming to know the contract itself. My rights would thus extend to all nations except France, Spain, and England; Escudier, however, is conceded the right to send his editions to, and sell them in, all nations except Italy.—I confess that this concession makes me fear strong competition in marketing my editions, especially in Spain and Germany, where the French editions are almost preferred to mine. In view of that, if you could pull some strings for me I'd be very grateful to you. If not, you know that with you I don't want to haggle, and I continue to accept your terms, along with Escudier's. I therefore regard the business as settled, and I'm glad, because good new music is really needed. . . .

VERDI TO TITO RICORDI
Genoa, 18 February 1865

. . . Bisogna che resti il contratto del Macbet come te l'ho proposto perchè Escudier non concederà dippiù. Nella tua lettera dici, Francia, Spagna ed Inghilterra: No; deve dire Francia, Belgio, Inghilter[r]a che appartengono ad Escudier.
Milan: Gallini collection; Abbiati 2, 822

. . . The contract for *Macbeth* must remain as I set it out to you, because Escudier won't concede anything more. In your letter you write: France, Spain, and England. No; it should specify France, Belgium, and England as belonging to Escudier.

TITO RICORDI TO VERDI
Milan, 20 February 1865

In possesso della cara tua del 18 . . .
Del tuo *Macbeth* nuovo lasciamo adunque il contratto come stabilito. Fu un errore di penna mettere nella mia ultima lettera Francia, *Spagna* e *Inghilterra,* e deve dire *Francia, Belgio* e *Inghilterra.*
Sant'Agata

Received, yours of the 18th . . .
Let's therefore leave the contract of your new *Macbeth* as agreed upon. Putting "France, *Spain,* and *England*" in my last letter was a slip of the pen. It should say *"France, Belgium, and England."*

VERDI TO ESCUDIER
Genoa, 20 February 1865

Mandatemi scrittura pel Macbet conforme agli articoli della vostra 12 Feb:—e sia così finita la faccenda.
Avete ricevuto il 4.º atto del Macbet? Con

Send me a contract for *Macbeth* conforming to the terms of your letter of February 12—and thus let the matter be settled.
Have you received Act IV of *Macbeth?* In

altra mia manderò le osservazioni su quest'atto.[1]

Scrivetemi a che punto sono le prove e come vanno.

Paris: Bibliothèque de l'Opéra

another letter I will send my observations on this act.[1]

Write and tell me at what point the rehearsals are and how they are going.

1. See his first letter of 11 March 1865.

VERDI TO TITO RICORDI

Genoa, 20 February 1865

... Mandami intanto che ho un po' di tempo, lo spartito del Macbet nuovo onde lo corregga, in modo che ti possa servire come originale.[1]

Milan: Archivio Ricordi (235)

... While I have some time, send me the score of the new *Macbeth* so that I can correct it and you can then use it as the master copy.[1]

1. This score would have consisted of a manuscript copy of the 1847 *Macbeth,* with the addition or substitution of a copy of the new music. (Ricordi had sent the autograph scores of the new music to Escudier after having copies made.) Verdi corrected this score and returned it to Ricordi on 12 March 1865; perhaps destroyed during the last war, it is no longer to be found in the Ricordi Archives.

In correcting the score, Verdi probably paid little attention to the 1847 music (see his comment in the March 12 letter), and, without access to the autograph, could not check every detail of the new music either, even if he had been inclined to do so. If Ricordi used this manuscript copy as the basis for their printed orchestral scores and material, it might explain the variants between these and the autograph scores noted by Budden (*The Operas of Verdi* 1, 280n).

ESCUDIER TO VERDI

Paris, 22 February 1865

En sortant de la répétition de Macbeth je prends la plume pour vous écrire ces quelques lignes: J'ai reçu le quatrième acte qui couronne de la façon la plus majesteuse votre grande et admirable partition. Il n'y a au théâtre qu'un cri d'admiration. Tout ce quatrième acte est maintenant d'un effet électrique. Les savants vont être bien surpris en entendant votre fugue qui n'est rien moins qu'un chef-d'oeuvre et qui a le rare de mérite pour ce genre de morceaux de ne pas être ennuyeuse. Les répétitions marchent bien; les artistes savent par coeur les trois premiers actes; les poètes s'occupent du dernier acte. Les choeurs travaillent. Jusqu'à présent rien ne nous a embarrassé.

Demain (jeudi) on joue la Flûte Enchantée;[1] le théâtre sera débarrassé; nous descendrons vendredi sur la scène.

J'ai écrit à Ricordi de m'envoyer un *Contrafagotto;* nous n'avons pas cet instrument à Paris. Meyerbeer l'a introduit à ce qu'il paraît dans son *Africaine.* Vous verrez à ce sujet ce que je dis dans mon numéro de demain.[2]

Je vous envoie le traité relatif à Macbeth; je pense qu'il est bien ainsi. Vous n'aurez qu'à mettre au bas *vu lu et approuvé, G. Verdi* et vous aurez la bonté de me le retourner ...

Sant'Agata

On leaving the *Macbeth* rehearsal, I take up my pen to write these few lines to you: I have received the fourth act, which crowns your large, admirable work in the most majestic way. In the theatre there was simply one cry of admiration. The whole of the fourth act is now electric in effect. The savants are going to be surprised when they hear your fugue, which is nothing less than a masterpiece and which has the rare merit, for this genre of piece, of not being boring. The rehearsals go well; the performers know the first three acts by heart; the poets are busy with [translating] the last act. The chorus is working. So far, there has been no hitch.

Tomorrow (Thursday) *The Magic Flute* goes on;[1] the theater will be freed, and on Friday we can get down onto the stage.

I wrote to Ricordi to ask him to send me a contrabassoon; we don't have this instrument in Paris. Meyerbeer introduced it, it seems, in his *Africaine.* You'll see what I said on the subject in my issue of tomorrow.[2]

I send you the contract relating to *Macbeth;* I think everything is in order. You have only to put at the bottom "Seen, read, and approved, G. Verdi," and have the goodness to return it to me ...

1. Translated by Nuitter and Beaumont; Christine Nilsson as the Queen of the Night

2. From the 23 February 1865 issue of *L'Art Musical:* " ... Verdi too has made use of the contrabassoon (*contrafagotto*), in the *grande scène fantastique* in Act III of his *Macbeth,* and if we speak about this today, it is so that no one will later take it into his head to accuse the illustrious Italian master of having borrowed this effect from the author of *L'Africaine.*" Berlioz in a short section on the contrabassoon in his *Grand Traité d'instrumentation et d'orchestration modernes* (1843), cites just two works that use the instrument, Beethoven's Fifth and Ninth Symphonies (both of which had been heard in Paris , as had *Fidelio*) and deplores the use of an ophicleide in its stead.

VERDI TO ESCUDIER

Genoa, 28 February 1865

Sono ritornato jeri sera da St Agata[1] ed ho trovato la vostra car^{ma} del 22 con entro la scrittura che vi rimando segnata.

Non ho tempo scrivervi a lungo e mi riservo a farlo ben tosto. Datemi notizie frequenti delle prove del Macbet, e ditemi se per l'*attacco delle trombe* nella Fuga del 4.º Atto si serviranno delle *Cornettes a pistons* ...

Paris: Bibliothèque de l'Opéra

I returned yesterday evening from Sant'Agata[1] and found your letter of the twenty-second along with the contract, which I am returning signed.

I have no time to write you at length, but am planning to do so very soon. Send me frequent news of the rehearsals for *Macbeth,* and tell me if they will use *cornettes à pistons* for the trumpet entry in the fugue of Act IV ...

1. Verdi had returned to Sant'Agata to visit his father, who was ill.

VERDI TO RICORDI

Genoa, 28 February 1865

Sono di ritorno da St Agata. Credevo di trovar qui lo spartito del *Macbet* per rivedere e correggere. Se non lo mandi ora che ho un po' di tempo sarebbe inutile mandarlo più tardi. Una volta in campagna non ho più tempo a correggere musica. Resterò qui tutta la settimana. Lunedì andrò a Torino, poi subito a casa.

Milan: Archivio Ricordi (236)

I've just returned from Sant'Agata. I thought I'd find the *Macbeth* score here to check and correct. If you don't sent it now, when I have a bit of time, it would be useless to send it later. Once I'm in the country I don't have time anymore to correct music. I'll remain here all week. On Monday I'll go to Turin, and then straight back home.

TORNAGHI TO VERDI

Milan, 2 March 1865

... Jeri le ho spedito a mezzo ferrata franco di spese la partitura del *Macbeth* che Ella tanto gentilmente si propone di rivedere perchè possa servirmi per originale. Ho tardato qualche giorno a mandargliela avendomi pregato il Capo-copista di lasciargliela ripassare per diminuire a Lei, se possibile, la noja delle più facili correzioni ...

Sant'Agata

... Yesterday I sent you by rail prepaid the *Macbeth* score that you so kindly offered to check so that it could serve me as a master-copy. I delayed sending it to you for a few days because I had asked the head copyist to check through it, to save you the trouble, if possible, of the more obvious corrections ...

VERDI TO RICORDI

Genoa, 4 March 1865

Ho ricevuto il Macbet che rimanderò ben presto ...[1]

Milan: Archivio Ricordi (236 bis)

I've received *Macbeth,* which I'll return very soon ...[1]

1. He returned it on March 12.

VERDI TO ARRIVABENE

... Nel Macbeth vi è un controfagotto ed è vero che hanno mandato a prenderne uno a Milano.[1] Se quei dell'*Africaine* ne fanno soggetto di *réclame* hanno torto perchè quest'istromento è conosciuto persino a Busseto, ov'io ho scritto (per quell'istromento) delle marcie trent'anni fa.

Alberti, 47

1. See Escudier's 22 February 1865 letter to Verdi.

... There is a contrabassoon in *Macbeth,* and it's true that they've sent for one from Milan.[1] If the *Africaine* people make a lot of publicity about it, they're wrong, because this instrument is known even in Busseto, where I wrote some marches thirty years ago (for this instrument).

ESCUDIER TO VERDI

J'ai reçu hier votre lettre[1] renfermant diverses erreurs que vous croyez exister dans votre oeuvre. En effet il y en avait quelques uns mais d'autres n'existaient pas. J'ai fait tout rectifier. Le copiste fait en ce moment l'extrait des parties. Je sors de la répétition de Macbeth; tout jusqu'à présent marche à merveille et tout le monde est dans l'admiration. Les artistes seuls répètent en scène.

Carvalho qui tient à ce que rien ne cloche mal dans l'ouvrage a demandé à M. Montjauze de chanter le rôle de Ma[c]duff au lieu du ténor que nous avions engagé qui a une fort belle voix, mais qui est trop inexpérimenté comme acteur. M. Montjauze a accepté et il répète. D'ici à huit ou dix jours les choeurs répéteront en scène. Je voudrais bien avoir les indications que vous m'avez annoncées pour le 4me acte.

Je vous dirai que Perrin[2] est aux cent coups depuis qu'il a appris l'importance qu'avait acquis le nouveau Macbeth. Il regrette dit-il qu'on donne cet opéra au lyrique en même temps que l'Africaine à l'Opéra, moi j'en suis au contraire très content.

Carvalho fait faire des décors et des costumes splendides. Tout donc jusqu'à présent se présente on ne peut mieux. J'espère que les premières répétitions d'orchestre pourront commencer vers le 20 mars. Deloffre le chef d'orchestre assiste à toutes les répétitions de piano. Moi, je ne quitte plus le théâtre lyrique, et c'est sur le bureau de Carvalho que je vous écris à la hâte ces lignes après la répétition du 3me acte qui a fini à cinq heures. Excusez-moi donc si je ne vous en dis pas plus long aujourd'hui.

Sant'Agata

1. This letter has not been found.

Yesterday I received your letter[1] enclosing several mistakes that you thought your work contained. In fact, there were some, but not others. I've had everything put right. At the moment the copyist is making the individual parts. I've just come out of the *Macbeth* rehearsal; so far, all goes marvelously, and everyone admires it. The soloists are rehearsing on the stage.

Carvalho, who insists that there should be no weak point in the production, has asked M. Monjauze to sing the role of Macduff in place of the tenor we had engaged, who had a splendid voice but was too inexperienced as an actor. M. Monjauze accepted, and he is rehearsing. In eight or ten days' time, the chorus will rehearse on stage. I should very much like to have the directions for the fourth act that you said would be coming.

I can tell you that Perrin[2] is distraught, now that he has learned what an important piece the new *Macbeth* has become. He regrets, he says, that this opera is being played at the Lyrique at the same time as *L'Africaine* at the Opéra; I, on the other hand, am very pleased.

Carvalho is having splendid scenery and costumes made. So far, then, nothing could be better. I hope the first orchestral rehearsals can begin about March 20. Deloffre, the conductor, is present at all the piano rehearsals. As for me, I don't leave the Théâtre-Lyrique anymore, and it's at Carvalho's desk that I'm writing you these lines, after the third-act rehearsal, which ended at five o'clock. So forgive me if I don't go on any longer about things today.

2. Director of the Opéra

VERDI TO ESCUDIER
Genoa, 11 March 1865

Bisogna correggere nell'Adagio del Balletto dell'atto 3° diversi bequadri ♮ che mancano

In the *Adagio* of the Act III ballet, several natural signs, ♮, that are missing need putting right:

Battuta 18

Measure 18

così anche alla seconda volta
Nello stesso Adagio dopo il *solo* dei tre stromenti *clarone, fagotto, violoncello solo* bisogna aggiungere la parola *tutti* perchè entrino a suonare tutti i violoncelli

and likewise the second time.
In the same *Adagio*, after the solo passage of the three instruments, bass clarinet, bassoon, and solo cello, the word *tutti* must be added so that all the cellos come in to play

All'atto quarto nella Battaglia bisogna correggere la seconda tromba alla Battuta 70[1]

In the Act IV Battle, the second trumpet at measure seventy needs to be corrected[1]

Ora eccovi alcune osservazioni sull'atto quarto. Il primo coro deve essere *triste, desolato* come indicano la parola e la scena. Così *l'adagio* dell'aria del Tenore: L'Allegro vivo e col massimo entusiasmo.—Eccoci al *Sonnambulismo* che è sempre la Scena capitale dell'opera. Chi ha visto la Ristori sa che non si devono fare che pochissimi gesti, anzi tutto si limita quasi ad un gesto solo, cioè cancellare una macchia di sangue che crede aver sulla mano. I movimenti devono esser lenti, e non bisogna vedere fare i passi; i piedi devono strisciare sul terreno come se fosse una statua, od un'ombra che cammini. Gli occhi fissi, la figura cadaverica; è in agonia e muore subito dopo. La Ristori faceva un rantolo; il rantolo della morte.[2] In musica non si deve, nè si può fare; come non si deve tossire nell'ultim'atto della *Traviata;* nè ridere nello *scherzo od è follia* del *Ballo in Maschera.*[3] Qui vi è un lamento del corno inglese che supplisce benissimo al rantolo, e più poeticamente. Bisogna cantarlo colla massima semplicità e colla *voce cupa* (è una morente) senza però mai che la voce sia ventriloca. Vi è qualche momento in cui la voce può spiegarsi, ma devono essere lampi brevissimi che sono indicati nello spartito. Infine per l'effetto, e pel terrore che deve incutere questo pezzo abbisogna, *figura cadaverica, pochi gesti,* movimenti lenti, voce cupa, espres.,

Now here are some remarks for you about Act IV. The first chorus must be *sad, desolate,* as the words and the scene suggest. The *Adagio* of the tenor's aria likewise: the Allegro lively and with the utmost enthusiasm.—And so we reach the sleepwalking scene, which is always the high point of the opera. Anyone who has seen Ristori knows that it should be done with only the most sparing gestures, even being limited to just about a single gesture, that of wiping out a bloodstain that she thinks she has on her hand. The movements should be slow, and one should not see her taking steps; her feet should drag over the ground as if she were a statue, or ghost, walking. The eyes fixed, the appearance corpse-like; she is in agony, and dies soon after. Ristori employed a rattle in her throat—the death-rattle.[2] In music, that must not and cannot be done; just as one shouldn't cough in the last act of *La traviata;* or laugh in the "scherzo od è follia" of *Ballo in maschera.*[3] Here there is an English-horn lament that takes the place of the death-rattle perfectly well, and more poetically. The piece should be sung with the utmost simplicity and in *voce cupa* [a hollow voice] (she is a dying woman) but without ever letting the voice become ventriloquial. There are some moments in which the voice can open up, but they must be brief flashes, as

et. etc...Notate poi che tanto qui, come nel Duetto del prim'atto, se i cantanti non cantano *sotto voce* l'effetto ne riuscirà disgustoso perchè vi è troppa sproporzione e troppo squilibrio fra cantanti ed orchestra (l'orchestra non ha che pochi istromenti e violini con sordine).–Le scene che succedono al *Sonnambulismo* non han bisogno di commenti. A voi che siete maestri di *mise en scene* non abbisognano suggerimenti, nonostante permettete che vi dica che si ottiene un effetto magnifico nella *Foresta di Birna* con pochissimi mezzi, e colla semplice velocità dei movimenti. Intanto che *Macbet* (con una scena corta) canta la Romanza *"pieta rispetto onore [sic]"* etc...bisogna preparare una scena lunga e vasta a tutto teatro, e con una semplice tela dipinta nel fondo senza ingombri di machinismo. In fondo 3 o 4 file di comparse (soldati di Macduff); ognuna di queste con un gran ramo d'albero che copra tutta la persona; alcuni di questi rami dovranno essere alti perchè figurino alberi. Quando la scena si scopre dovrà essere in movimento tutta questa massa di uomini e fronde, e più sarà lontano meglio sarà.[4] Il movimento sarà lento ed eguale. A questo aggiungete l'altro che vien dopo quando gettano a terra i rami all'ordine di Macduff *"via le fronde"* ed il subito sparire di tutta l'armata, e tutti questi effetti di sorpresa formano un'insieme e teatrale purchè tutti i movimenti sieno fatti esattamente e rapidamente. La scena *a vista* che scopre la vasta scena della foresta non dòvrebbe sparire che sul gran forte della musica = *Battaglia* alla battuta 21

indicated in the score. In sum, for the effect and the terror that this number should inspire, one needs a *corpse-like appearance, few gestures*, slow movements, *voce cupa, espressivo*, etc., etc...Note too that here, just as much as in the Act I duet, if the singers do not sing sotto voce the result will be disagreeable, because there is too much disproportion, too much imbalance between the singers and the orchestra (the orchestra has only a few instruments and the violins are muted). The scenes after the sleepwalking need no comment. You who are past masters of mise-en-scène need no suggestions, but nevertheless let me say to you that with the Forest of Birnham, a magnificent effect can be obtained with a minimum of means and with simple speed of movement. While Macbeth (in a scene set shallow) sings the *romanza* "Pietà, rispetto, onore," etc., there should be prepared a deep, vast scene using all the stage, with a simple painted backdrop, uncluttered by machinery. At the back, three or four rows of supers (Macduff's soldiers); each of them with a huge branch totally concealing him; some of these branches should be tall, since they represent trees. When the scene is revealed, this whole mass of men and branches should be in motion, and the further away the better.[4] The movement will be slow and regular. Add to this what happens later when they throw the branches to the ground at Macduff's order "Away with the branches," and [later] the sudden disappearance of the entire army, and all these effects of surprise create a theatrical whole, provided the movements are precisely and rapidly executed. The open-stage scene change that reveals the vast forest scene should not happen until the big forte in the music, measure 21 of the Battle:

Sul resto di quest'atto non v'è da dire che di dar molto carattere al costume dei *Bardi* e di servirsi per questi delle migliori voci del Coro.

For the rest of this act, one need only remark that the costuming of the Bards should have plenty of character, and that they should be cast from the best voices in the chorus.

Qui a Genova si fà ora il *Macbet* (vecchio) e per l'apparizione dei Re nel Terz'atto si fà un machinismo che mi par buono e che vi voglio indicare.–Ciò consiste in una gran ruota, che non si vede, su cui sono posti i Re; e questo circolo in moto che alza ed avvanza, abbassa e fà sparire la figura di questi Re produce un'ec-

Here in Genoa they are now doing the (old) *Macbeth,* and for the apparition of the Kings in Act III they are constructing a mechanism which seems to me good and which I want to describe to you. It consists of a large wheel, not visible, on which the Kings are placed; and this circle in motion, which elevates and advances

cellente effetto. I Re sono sopra un[a] piccola base appoggiati per stare in piedi ed in equilibrio ad una forte spranga di ferro; la base si piega in modo che la persona sia sempre diritta, e ciò si ottiene con dei contrapesi. La ruota è tutta sotto terra, e soltanto la sua estremità è al livello del palco scenico.

these royal figures and then lowers them and makes them vanish, produces an excellent effect. The Kings are on a little base, leaning on a strong iron crossbar to keep them on their feet and in balance; the base is hinged in such a way that the person is always upright, and this is effected by counterweights. The whole wheel is underground, and only its extremity reaches the stage level.

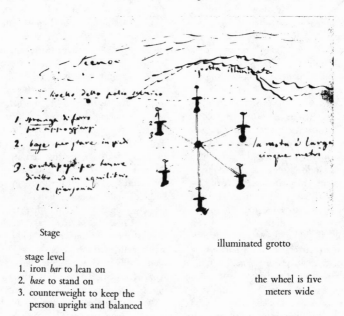

Stage

stage level
1. iron *bar* to lean on
2. *base* to stand on
3. counterweight to keep the
   person upright and balanced

illuminated grotto

the wheel is five
meters wide

La scena è oscura; soltanto vi è la luce elletrica [sic] che batte sulla figura dei Re.—

The stage is dark except for electric light playing on the figures of the Kings.

La Ruota non ha che sei raggi, mentre i *Re* sono otto, ma è facile vedere che i due ultimi Re si possono mettere nel posto dei primi. La Ruota gira per conseguenza vi sono sempre posti vuoti.—

The wheel has only six spokes, while there are eight Kings, but it is easy to see that the last two Kings can take the place of the first two. The wheel rotates, so there are always empty places.

Io trovo buonissimo questo machinismo perchè toglie la monotonia dei *Re* in processione a linea diritta, e perchè fà muovere questi *Re* senza che sieno obbligati a camminare. Ciò è più fantastico. Se voi trovate *meglio,* tanto meglio. Dall'ultima vostra lettera, parmi che potreste portare il vostro letto *chez Monsieur Macbet*...Buon divertimento ed addio. Parto stassera per St. Agata a piantar cavoli. Scrivetemi dunque a Busseto.

I find this mechanism admirable, since it avoids the monotony of the Kings in a straight-line procession, and because it sets those Kings in motion without their having to walk. This is more fantastical. If you find something *better,* so much the better. From your last letter, it seems to me you might as well have your bed brought round *chez Monsieur Macbet*...Have fun, and farewell. This evening I leave for Sant'Agata to plant cabbages. So write to me at Busseto.

Washington: Folger Shakespeare Library

1. All three corrections are incorporated into the Paris autograph score, in a hand other than Verdi's (at least in the two cases where a judgment about the handwriting can safely be made).

2. Ristori's analysis of her performance of the scene (see pp. 362-63) shows that she meant the "rantolo" to represent the difficult breathing and signs of a diseased person in troubled sleep. Verdi's interpretation of the "rantolo" as a death-rattle, together with his comment that Lady dies soon afterward, suggests that he did not credit Shakespeare's pointedly inconclusive report: "his fiend-like queen, /Who (as 'tis thought) by self and violent hands / Took off her life." (V.8.69-71). A third interpretation of the significance of the "rantolo" was offered by Eleonora Duse, who recalled that Ristori performed the scene with "classic dignity," mixed with a "curious verismo: between one phrase and the next, a light *rantolo* of a sleeping person: She was snoring! A display of regal solemnity!" (Leonardo Bragaglia, *Shakespeare in Italia: personaggi ed interpreti: vita scenica del teatro di Guglielmo Shakespeare in Italia [1792-1973]* [Rome: Trevi, 1973], p. 55)

3. A letter dated 21 May 1898, Milan, purporting to be from Verdi to the tenor Alessandro Bonci (published in Giacomo Lauri-Volpi: *Voci parallele* [Milan, 1955], p. 132; now in the possession of Olga Bonci, Bologna), expresses the composer's delighted approval of Bonci's interpolation of bursts of naturalistic but rhythmical laughter into the rests of Riccardo's "È scherzo." Bonci's "aggiunta," preserved on a famous record, has become traditional; there is even, it seems, a pirated tape of a rehearsal in which Toscanini demonstrates to Jan Peerce how it should be done. But Arnaldo Marchetti has—on grounds of date, content (the letter goes on to discuss the absurdities of Somma's verse and contrasts the writer's own carefree approach to words with the scrupulousness of Boito, Leoncavallo, and "il mio rivale Wagner"), diction, and general tone—argued convincingly that the document is a forgery ("La famosa lettera di Verdi a Bonci," *Rassegna Musicale Curci,* 26, no. 3, December 1973, 23-24). And a facsimile of it in Peter Southwell-Sander's *Verdi: his Life and Times* (London: Midas, 1978; p. 154) shows it to be even a poor imitation of the composer's hand.

4. Cancelled: Macduff solo nel davanti sarà senza fronde ed [Only Macduff, in the foreground, should be without a branch and]

VERDI TO ESCUDIER

[*11 March 1865
(added in another hand, possibly Escudier's)*]

V'ho scritto stamattina una lunga lettera, ed ora prima di partire vi scrivo queste poche righe perchè m'ha sorpreso il vostro foglio che annuncia *Macbet opera en cinq actes!!!* En cinq actes?—da quando in quà? Se voi l'avete ridotto in cinque atti avete torto, grandissimo torto perchè invece di averne completi di giusta misura, ne avrete cinque che saranno smozzicati, miseri!. E d'altronde quale degli atti ridureste [*sic*]? Il Primo?...dove lo finireste? Dopo il Duetto?...ma allora varebbe [*sic*] un'atto meschinissimo; ed il secondo non sarebbe che d'un solo finale che sarebbe peggio. È un errore grande grande assai assai...Cosa ci guadagnate? Volete allungare lo spettacolo? ma tenete gli *Entre'actes* un po' più lunghi!...Per l'amor di Dio non cerchiamo *Midi à quatre heures!*[1]

Paris: Bibliothèque de l'Opéra

This morning I wrote you a long letter, and now before leaving I am sending you this short note because your sheet announcing *Macbeth* as an *opera in five acts* surprised me!!! In five acts? Since when? If you have turned it into five acts, you are wrong, very wrong, because instead of having acts that are complete and well-proportioned, you will have five wretched little stumps! And, besides, which of the acts would you alter? Act I?...Where would you end it? After the duet? But then it would be a miserable little act; and the second [act] would be nothing more than a finale, which would be even worse. It is a *very, very,* grave error...What would you gain? Do you want to lengthen the performance? Make the intermissions a little longer?...For God's sake, let's not look for *midi à quatre heures!*[1]

1. The opera *was* given in five acts. See GÜNTHER at 180, and the review in *L'Art Musical,* 27 April 1865, at 405-06.

VERDI TO TITO RICORDI

Genoa, 12 March 1865

Ti rimando il *Macbet* di cui ho corretto diversi sbagli; ma altri ne resteranno ancora sui pezzi vecchi ...

Milan: Archivio Ricordi (238)

I'm sending *Macbeth* back to you. I've corrected various mistakes, but there are probably still others in the old numbers ...

113

TITO RICORDI TO VERDI

Milan, 15 March 1865

Ti accuso ricevuta della cara tua lettera 12 corr[ente] da Genova, nonchè della partitura *Macbeth* e della bontà che avesti rivedendola ti sono davvero obbligatissimo . . .

Sant'Agata

I acknowledge receipt of your letter of the twelfth as well as the *Macbeth* score. I'm very grateful to you for your kindness in correcting it . . .

ESCUDIER TO VERDI

Paris, 25 March 1865

Voici quelques jours que je n'ai pas eu le plaisir de causer avec vous . . .

Les répétitions de Macbeth vont très bien. Tous les jours je suis là avec Carvalho qui soigne tout particulièrement l'exécution et la mise en scène. Décidemment Carvalho est le seul directeur intelligent et actif qu'il y est à Paris. Hier il m'a menagé une surprise. Je vous ai écrit dans le temps pour vous demander s'il n'y aurait pas inconvénient à faire dire la seconde partie du Brindisi par le ténor. Vous m'avez répondu que la logique s'y opposait et vous aviez raison. Eh bien il a essayé hier une mise en scène à lui dans laquelle il donne à Macduff un caractère soupçonneux et indiquant légèrement qu'il se méfie de Macbeth; dans cette situation, et pendant que Lady Macbeth va d'un invité à l'autre pour les tranquiliser et puis arrive en souriant à son époux, Macduff chante la seconde strophe du Brindisi et je dois l'avouer avec un très grand effet au quel nous ne nous attendions pas. Par la manière dont Macduff est présenté, il n'y a pas de contresens et tout y gagne. J'étais opposé à cette modification mais j'ai dû me rendre à l'évidence. Je vous soumet mon impression; Carvalho du reste me charge de vous dire que s'il n'était pas assuré d'un plus grand effet il n'insisterait pas. Donc si vous voulez nous laisser opérer cette petite modification qui ne nuit pas à la marche du drame, et qui jette de la variété dans tout le final, nous la ferons. Au cas contraire nous resterons dans vos idées. Tout du reste marche à merveille; les choeurs sont superbes; vous avez fait au quatrième acte un choeur d'hommes, la Patria[,][1] qui est un chef-d'oeuvre. C'est beau, comme ce que peut exister de plus beau; quant à l'Hymne final; c'est tout bonnement sublime! Lundi nous répétons les deux premiers actes à l'orchestre, mais sans les chanteurs, j'ai jugé à propos de faire avant tout des répétitions d'orchestre de toute la musique pour bien initier les musiciens à son caractère et en second lieu pour arriver aux grandes répétitions d'ensemble avec c

For some days now I've not had the pleasure of chatting with you . . .

The *Macbeth* rehearsals are going well. I'm there every day with Carvalho, who is taking particular care about the execution and the staging. There's no doubt that Carvalho is the only intelligent and energetic director we have in Paris. Yesterday he prepared a surprise for me. I wrote to you some time ago to ask if there would be anything against having the second part of the *brindisi* assigned to the tenor. You replied that logic was against it, and you were right. Well, yesterday Carvalho tried a staging of his own in which he gave Macduff a suspicious character, lightly suggesting that he distrusted Macbeth. In this situation, and while Lady Macbeth goes from one guest to another to calm them down and then arrives, smiling, at her husband, Macduff sings the second verse of the *brindisi*—with, I must confess, an effect that we did not expect. Because of the way Macduff is presented, it does not contradict the sense, and everything gains by it. I was opposed to this modification, but I had to yield to the evidence. I submit my impression to you; however, Carvalho charges me to tell you that were he not convinced of a greater effect he would not insist. So, if you let us put into practice this little modification, which does not harm the progress of the drama and which throws some variety into the whole finale, we will do so. If not, we'll stick to your ideas. All the rest goes wonderfully. The choruses are superb; in Act IV you have composed a male chorus, "La Patria,"[1] which is a masterpiece. It's fine, as fine as anything could be. As for the final Hymn, it's simply sublime. On Monday we rehearse the first two acts with the orchestra, but without the singers. I thought it wise to give priority to orchestral rehearsals of all the music, to initiate the players into its character, and to reach the big ensemble rehearsals with very correct parts. For the choruses, I have had eight extra women engaged, six of them con-

parties très corre[c]tes. Pour les choeurs j'ai fait engager en plus huit femmes dont six contr'alti et six hommes dont quatre basses. Je crois que toute l'exécution sera admirable. La mise en scène du troisième et du quatrième n'est pas facile. Les décors tous neuf seront superbes et dignes de l'oeuvre et les costumes aussi. Carvalho voudrait donner Macbeth le 7 avril afin d'avoir deux représentations avant pâques, et puis faire la réouverture le lundi de Pâques avec cet opéra, mais je doute qu'il puisse être just[e]. Ce diable d'homme a de la poudre fulminante dans les veines; nous allons bien ensemble. Madame Rey-Balla a été vraiment admirable aujourd'hui dans la scène du somnambulisme. Elle la joue et la chante en grande artiste. Quelle page merveilleuse! Enfin, cher maître, n'ayez aucune inquiétude sur l'interprétation. Rien n'y manquéra.

Dès que les grandes répétitions d'orchestre commenceront je vous écrirai tous les jours. D'ici-là donnez-moi de vos nouvelles ...

Sant'Agata

traltos, and eight extra men, four of them basses. I believe the whole execution will be admirable. The staging of Acts III and IV is not easy. The decor, all new, will be superb and worthy of the work; the costumes, too. Carvalho would like to give *Macbeth* on April 7, so as to have two performances before Easter, and then reopen on Easter Monday with this opera, but I doubt whether he'll make it. He's a devil of a fellow, with gunpowder in his veins; we get on well together. Mme Rey-Balla was truly admirable today in the sleepwalking scene. She acts and sings it as a great artist. What a marvellous passage! Finally, *cher maître*, have no worries about the interpretation. Nothing will be lacking.

Once the big orchestral rehearsals begin, I'll write to you every day. Give me your news from time to time ...

1. In fact, neither the newly composed "La patria oppressa" nor "La patria tradita," which was newly worked, is for male chorus.

VERDI TO ESCUDIER

Busseto, 28 March 1865

È certamente ingegnoso il trovato di M.ʳ Carvalho per far cantare il Brindisi al Tenore, ma per me son sempre d'avviso che questo nuoccia all'effetto complessivo del Finale. Mi pare molto più bello e più teatrale che *Lady*, cedendo all'invito dello stesso Macbet *"il brindisi lieto di nuovo s'intuoni"* ripigli il Brindisi, e lo finisca. Poi se Macduff dice parole di sospetto; queste parole staranno male colle note brillanti del Brindisi. Ed intanto cosa farà Lady? Il pertichino?[1] Ciò non può essere: Lady in questa scena è, e deve essere il personaggio dominante tanto drammaticamente, quanto musicalmente. Aggiungete che in questo modo si pregiudicherebbe anche il pezzo concertato *Finale* che chiude l'Atto. Soltanto in questo punto e non prima Macduff deve sospettare e decidersi ad emigrare. Non abbiate paura per la *varietà* in queste scene, e riservate il colmo dell'effetto pel Finale. Un po' di tregua, dopo tutto il trambusto precedente, non farà male. Sia bene in scena, ben concertato ed unito, e con tutti i coloriti indicati, e voi vedrete che l'atto finirà bene.—Capisco benissimo che lo scopo di tutto ciò è per far dire qualcosa a Monjauze; ma

M. Carvalho's idea of having the tenor sing the *brindisi* is certainly ingenious, but I am still of the opinion that this detracts from the overall effect of the *finale*. It seems far more beautiful and theatrical to me that Lady, yielding to Macbeth's own invitation ("the cheerful brindisi let sound anew"), should take up the *brindisi* again and finish it. Moreover, if Macduff expresses suspicions, these words of his would be ill-suited to the brilliant music of the *brindisi*. And in the meantime, what would Lady do? Be a *pertichino*?[1] That cannot be: in this scene Lady is, and must be, the dominant character dramatically as well as musically. In addition, doing this would also compromise the ensemble *finale* closing the act. Only then, and no sooner, should Macduff become suspicious and decide to leave the country. Have no fear for *variety* in these scenes, and reserve the climactic effect for the *finale*. A short respite after all the preceding turmoil will do no harm. If it is well staged, with good ensemble, and with all the indicated shadings, then you'll see that the act will end well. I understand perfectly that the purpose of all this is to give Monjauze something to sing,

queste sono considerazioni personali che non hanno nulla a fare col Dramma, e che io sono convinto sono di danno al Dramma stesso.[2]

Scrivetemi pure sovente, e datemi notizie del modo in cui sono stati fatti i *machinismi* del 3.º e 4.º Atto.

Paris: Bibliothèque de l'Opéra;
Rivista Musicale Italiana 35 (1928), 188–89
(misdated May 28)

but these are personal considerations which have nothing to do with the drama and which, I am convinced, are damaging to the drama itself.[2]

Write to me often, and tell me what sort of *stage effects* have been devised for Acts III and IV.

1. In the operatic parlance of the time, *pertichini* (lit., little posts) were those onstage listening and occasionally adding comments while someone else sang a solo.

2. Macduff *did* sing the reprise of the *brindisi*: see GÜNTHER at 179–80 and the reviews of the performance at 406–08.

ESCUDIER TO VERDI

Paris, 31 March 1865

J'ai reçu ce matin votre amicale lettre ainsi que les lignes beaucoup trop courtes de notre excellente Mme Verdi. J'ai fait ce qu'elle désire relativement au journal de modes. J'ai fait part à Carvalho de ce qui concerne le Brindisi; je trouve que vous avez raison; et par la manière dont il a mis le morceau en scène, je dois dire aussi qu'il n'a pas tout à fait tort. Du reste demain, nous allons reprendre votre version! Ne croyez pas que le final souffrît en rien du changement. Ce final est d'un effet colossal. Hier, avant-hier et aujourd'hui on a répété trois actes à l'orchestre et je ne saurais vous dire quel est le morceau qui a produit le plus d'effet. Ils ont tous enthousiasmé les artistes de l'orchestre. Cet ouvrage est d'une beauté complète. Je dois vous dire néanmoins qu'on a particulièrement admiré vos airs de ballet. Il y a là un *andante* qui est tout bonnement sublime. Mme Rey-Balla a produit la plus grande sensation. Après son air du premier acte qu'elle chante magistralement, l'orchestre tout entier ne se lassait pas d'applaudir. Je suis persuadé qu'elle aura un immense succès. Ismaël ne lui cède en rien. Macbeth le posera très haut dans l'estime du public. Tous les chœurs sont d'une exquise originalité; celui des Sicaires et celui des esprits aériens au 3ème acte ont produit le plus grand effet. Demain on fera une répétition complète des trois premiers actes et lundi on répétera le 4ème. La musique militaire qui doit jouer la marche et le petit orchestre souterrain n'ont pas encore répété; je pense qu'ils seront prêts aussi lundi. Enfin tout va bien. Comme on s'est jusqu'à présent plus occupé de la musique que de la mise en scène, je ne puis vous dire rien de précis sur les machinations du 3me et 4me actes;

I received your friendly letter this morning, together with the all-too-brief lines from our excellent Mme. Verdi. I have done what she asked for about the fashion magazine. I have informed Carvalho about the matter of the *brindisi;* I find that you are right; and that, because of the way he staged the number, I must say that he was not completely wrong. In any case, tomorrow we are going to resume your version! Do not fear that the *finale* will suffer by being changed. This *finale* is of colossal effect. Yesterday, the day before, and today the orchestra rehearsed three acts, and I couldn't tell you which piece produced the greatest effect. The players were enthusiastic about all of them. This work is beautiful through and through. Nevertheless I must tell you that they particularly admired the ballet pieces. There's an andante there that is quite simply sublime. Mme. Rey-Balla caused a great sensation. After her first-act aria, which she sings with mastery, the whole orchestra wouldn't stop applauding. I am convinced that she will have a tremendous success. Ismaël is equally good; Macbeth will place him high in the public esteem. All the choruses are exquisitely original; the one for the assassins and the one for the aerial spirits in Act III produced the greatest effect. Tomorrow there'll be a complete rehearsal of the first three acts, and on Monday a rehearsal of Act IV. The military band that should play the march and the little understage orchestra have not yet rehearsed; I think they will also be ready on Monday. In sum, all goes well. As we have been more concerned so far with the music than with the staging, I can tell you nothing precise about the stage machinery for Acts III and IV;

mais tout cela est réglé et marchera à merveille, j'en suis sûr. Les costumes sont de toute beauté! Voilà cher maître ce qui s'est passé jusqu'à ce moment; je ne manquerai pas de vous tenir au courant de tout ce qui va se faire. Carvalho veut faire passer Macbeth le 10 avril si les décorateurs ne le retardent pas. Arrivera-t-il? J'en doute. Toujours est-il que d'ici là on répétera tous les jours, et que l'ouvrage ne sera donné que lorsque l'exécution en sera parfaite.

Sant'Agata

but all that has been arranged and will work marvelously, I'm sure. The costumes are completely beautiful! That's what has happened so far, *cher maître;* I shan't fail to keep you up-to-date with what is going to happen. Carvalho wants to put on *Macbeth* on April 10 if the designers don't hold him up. Will he make it? I doubt it. As things stand, from now till then there'll be daily rehearsals, and the work will be given only when its execution is perfect.

VERDI TO ARRIVABENE

Sant'Agata, 5 April 1865

... P.S. Mi scrivono che il *Macbeth* a Parigi si prova mattina e sera per andare in scena il 10 ma temono potervi riescire. Se sarà fiasco te ne darò io la notizia.

Alberti, 50

... P.S. They write me that *Macbeth* is being rehearsed day and night in Paris for performance on the tenth, but fear they can't make it. If it is a fiasco I'll let you know myself.

ESCUDIER TO VERDI

Paris, 6 April 1865

Je sors du théâtre lyrique et n'ai que le temps d'écrire quelques lignes à la hâte. Hier on a répété l'ouvrage en entier avec l'orchestre, les choeurs et les artistes. L'effet a été colossal. Tout a posté à la scène du somnambulisme. Les musiciens de l'orchestre étaient si fortement impressionnés qu'ils se sont arrêtés pour écouter; M. Deloffre s'est écrié: Messieurs, arrêtons-nous tout à fait; applaudissez à votre aise puis recommençons. Les applaudissements ont duré cinq minutes. Mme Rey-Balla est admirable dans cette scène comme dans le reste de l'ouvrage. Les musiciens ne tarissent pas d'éloges sur la fugue!!

Carvalho voulait jouer Macbeth lundi, mais il a reconnu hier que l'ouvrage n'était pas assez mûr. Hier on a fait relâche; on fera encore relâche demain. Et l'on profitera de la semaine sainte pour arriver le plus possible à la perfection dans l'ensemble. La première représentation n'aura lieu que le 19 de ce mois ...

P.S. Dites-moi je vous prie où je dois envoyer mon télégraphe pour que je puisse vous donner promptement des nouvelles?

Sant'Agata

I come from the Théâtre-Lyrique and have time only to write a few lines in haste. Yesterday we rehearsed the whole work with orchestra, chorus, and singers. The effect was colossal. Everything came to a halt at the sleepwalking scene. The orchestral players were so powerfully impressed by it that they stopped to listen; M. Deloffre called out, "Gentlemen, let us stop altogether; applaud your fill, and then we'll begin again." The applause lasted five minutes. Mme. Rey-Balla is admirable in this scene as in the rest of the work. The players couldn't stop praising the fugue!!

Carvalho wanted to play *Macbeth* on Monday, but yesterday he realized that the work was not yet ripe enough. Yesterday they gave no performance at the theatre, and they'll give none tomorrow. And they'll take advantage of Holy Week to arrive at the most perfect ensemble possible. The first performance will not take place until the nineteenth of this month ...

P.S. Please tell me where I should send my telegram to give you news as promptly as possible.

VERDI TO ESCUDIER

Turin, 15 April 1865

Sono a Torino; parto stassera per St Agata, ma sarò qui di ritorno mercoledì mattina. Se il

I'm in Turin; I leave tonight for Sant'Agata, but I'll be back here Wednesday morning

Macbet và in scena lunedì scrivetemi a Torino e dirigete la vostra lettera

Hôtel Trombetta
Torino
Paris: Bibliothèque de l'Opéra

[April 19]. If *Macbeth* goes on on Monday, write to me in Turin, addressing your letter

Hotel Trombetta
Turin

VERDI TO ESCUDIER

Turin, 19 April 1865[1]

V'ho spedito or ora un dispaccio per pregarvi a darmi con un telegramma notizie del *Macbet* se va in scena questa sera. Io resto qui fino a sabato sera per cui desponete in modo di scrivermi e darmi dettagliate notizie per lettera. Dite pure francamente la verità perchè io sono anche disposto ad un *fiasco;* e ciò si avvera facilmente quando le prove van molto bene. Addio dunque. Scrivetemi per lungo e per largo la verità.

Paris: Bibliothèque de l'Opéra;
Rivista Musicale Italiana 35 (1928), 187

I have just sent you a telegram to beg you to wire me news about whether *Macbeth* is to be performed tonight. I'll remain here till Saturday night [April 22], so take care to write and give me detailed news in a letter. Go ahead and tell me the truth frankly, because I am even prepared for a fiasco; and that can easily happen when the rehearsals go very well. Farewell then. Write me the truth at length and in breadth.

1. Written on parliamentary writing paper, headed "Camera dei Deputati"

TORNAGHI TO VERDI

Milan, 22 April 1865

Ricevo un telegrafo di stamane da Escudier: Macbeth enthousiasme immense—trois morceaux bissés—succès colossal—execution superbe—mise en scène merveilleuse. . . .

Sant'Agata

I have just received a telegram Escudier sent this morning: "*Macbeth* immense enthusiasm—three numbers encored—colossal success—superb execution—marvelous staging." . . .

VERDI TO ARRIVABENE

Sant'Agata   25 April 1865

Ritorno ora da Torino e sono seguito da due dispacci sul *Macbeth* diretti a Torino a l'Hôtel Gambetto!!![1] Uno è del Direttore del Teatro, l'altro dell'editore.

I've just returned from Turin and have been followed by two telegrams about *Macbeth*, sent to Turin to the Hotel Gambetto!!![1] One is from the director of the theater, the other from the publisher.

Maître, je vous écris sous l'effet d'une de mes plus grandes emotions musicales. *Macbeth* vient d'obtenir au Théâtre-Lirique un immense succes. Merci, maître, de la confiance que vous avez eu en moi. Dès que je serai libre j'irai vous remercier d'avoir donné un troisième chef d'oeuvre au théâtre lirique.[2]

Carvalho

Maestro, I am writing to you under the influence of one of my greatest musical emotions. *Macbeth* has just had an immense success at the Théâtre-Lyrique. Thank you, Maestro, for the confidence you have had in me. As soon as I am free, I am going to thank you for having given a third masterpiece to the Théâtre-Lyrique.[2] Thank you again.

Carvalho

Macbeth succès immense. "Final" premier acte, "Brindisi" bissés. Execution admirable. Mise en scène merveilleuse, enthousiasme général. J'écris par poste a Busseto.

Escudier

Macbeth immense success. Finale of first act and *brindisi* encored. Wonderful execution. Marvelous mise-en-scène, general enthusiasm. I'm sending a letter to Busseto.

Escudier

Ecco tutto. Vedremo dalle lettere e dai giornali cosa ne sarà....

Alberti, 51

There it all is. We'll see from letters and newspapers what will come of it....

1. The point is that Verdi was staying at the Albergo *Trombetta*.

2. After *Rigoletto* (1863) and *La traviata* (1864)

VERDI TO CARVALHO   *[Sant'Agata,] 26 April 1865*

Merci, mille fois merci, de la dépêche télégra-phique que vous avez eu l'obligeance de m'en-voyer à peine fini la première représentation du Macbeth. Cette amabilité est d'autant plus ex-quise/aimable[1] de votre part, que je n'ai pas l'honneur d'être connu personnellement. C'est donc tout naturel que je vous en sois double-ment reconnaissant. Quant au Macbeth, per-mettez-moi de vous dire que ce n'est pas vous mais moi qui dois vous remercier pour l'avoir donné au Théâtre Lyrique. Vous avez eu foi dans cette partition, vous l'avez jugée digne de vos soins...elle a réussi.

Thanks, a thousand thanks, for the telegram that you had the thoughtfulness to send me almost as soon as the first performance of *Mac-beth* was over. This kindness of yours is all the keener/kinder[1] in that I do not have the honor of knowing you personally. So it is natural that I should be doubly grateful to you. As for *Macbeth,* let me say to you that it is not you who should thank me, but I you, for having given it at the Théâtre-Lyrique. You believed in this score, you judged it worthy of your pains...it succeeded.

Sant'Agata (draft in Giuseppina's hand)

1. Giuseppina drafted the alternatives one above the other.

VERDI TO ESCUDIER   *Busseto, 28 April 1865*

Ho ricevuto anche la vostra lettera dopo la 1ª rappresentazione che mi da i dettagli della prima sera, ed avrei desiderato ricevere altra lettera sulla seconda recita per sentirne l'esito o confermato o diminuito tanto più che qualche vostro giornale e qualche notizia particolare danno un'esito un po' dubbio. Diffatti ho os-servato in alcuni giornali francesi alcune frasi che ammetterebbero questa dubbiezza. Chi ri-marca una cosa e chi l'altra. Chi trova il sog-getto sublime, e chi non musicabile. Chi trova che io non conoscevo Shaspeare quando scrissi il Macbeth.[1] Oh in questo hanno un gran torto! Può darsi che io non abbia reso ben il Mac-beth, ma che io non conosca, che non capisca e non senta Shaspeare no, per Dio, nò. È un poeta di mia predilezione che ho avuto fra le mani dalla mia prima gioventù, e che leggo e rileggo continuamente. Tutto ciò non importa. Desi-dero sapere cosa n'è avvenuto in seguito e vi sarò obbligatissimo se vorrete dirmelo sincera-mente e francamente, e mi farete il piacere di mandarmi anche (dicono quel che vogliono) i Débats, Siècle, e tutti i grandi giornali.

I have also received your letter after the first performance, which gives me details about the first evening, and I should have liked to receive another letter about the second performance to hear whether the favorable reception was con-firmed or diminished, especially since some of your newspapers and some other comments re-ported a somewhat dubious outcome. In fact, I have seen a few sentences in some French papers which would admit some doubt. One says one thing; another, something else. One finds the subject sublime, another, that it cannot be set to music. One states that I didn't know Shake-speare when I wrote *Macbeth.* Oh, in this they are very wrong. It may be that I have not ren-dered *Macbeth* well, but that I don't know, don't understand, and don't feel Shakespeare—no, by God, no. He is a favorite poet of mine, whom I have had in my hands from earliest youth, and whom I read and reread constantly. All this doesn't matter. I want to know what happened subsequently, and I would be very grateful if you would tell me sincerely and frankly, and do me the favor of sending me also the *Débats*, the *Siècle*, and all the big newspapers (no matter what they say).

Paris: Bibliothèque de l'Opéra;
Rivista Musicale Italiana 35 (1928), 187–88

VERDI TO ARRIVABENE
Busseto, 28 April 1865

... ho ricevuto sul *Macbeth* di Parigi diversi giornali ed una lettera lunga e dettagliata. La lettera era dell'Editore ed i giornali, mandati dallo stesso, saranno stati scelti tra quelli che parlavano bene, così si può supporre.

Del resto la vera verità starà negli introiti, ed il successo sarà vero e reale, se, nello spazio di un anno circa, verrà annunciata la centesima rappresentazione del *Macbeth*,[1] come è avvenuto del *Rigoletto* ...

Alberti, 52

... About the Paris *Macbeth* I've received various newspapers and a long, detailed letter. The letter was from the publisher, and the reviews, sent by him, were probably chosen from among the favorable ones, or so one supposes.

Anyway, the real truth will be found in the box office receipts, and the success will be real and true if, in about a year's time, the hundredth performance of *Macbeth* is announced,[1] as happened with *Rigoletto* ...

1. In fact, *Macbeth* was performed only fourteen times during the season and not revived in Paris during Verdi's lifetime. Furthermore, box office receipts were poor, as COHEN points out (at 182–83).

VERDI TO TITO RICORDI
Sant'Agata, 3 May 1865

È vero che alla Cannobiana in una stagione non musicale, fra commedia e ballo si voglia dare il *Macbet* di Parigi?[1] Oh se si trattasse d'un'opera francese, russa, turca, chinese [*sic*] si sceglierebbero i momenti solenni; ma per un'opera italiana qualunque posto è buono!!!! Tu ti lagni dei nuvoloni che ci vengono dal Nord?!! Hai torto: per me gli faccio tanto di capello, e sieno i benvenuti dal momento che sono sì bene accetti. Ho sempre amato e desiderato il progresso, e se la cotteria (permettimi quest'espressione che dico nel senso il più benevolo) creatosi in Milano di cui il tuo Giulio fà parte, e di cui tu stesso, (forse senza volerlo) sei complice potrà riuscire a rialzare la nostra musica io griderò *Hosanna!* Anch'io voglio la musica dell'avvenire, vale a dire che credo ad una musica a venire, e se non l'ho saputa, come volevo, fare, la colpa non è mia. Se anch'io ho sporcato l'altare,[2] come dice Boito, Egli lo netti, ed io saro il primo a venire accendergli un mocolo. Evviva dunque la cotteria; evviva il Nord se ci reca la luce, ed il sole.[3]

Milan: Archivio Ricordi (240 bis)

Is it true that they want to put on the Paris *Macbeth* at the Canobbiana, in the midst of a season not devoted to music, in between plays and ballet?[1] Oh, if it were a matter of a French, Russian, Turkish, or Chinese opera, a solemn time would be chosen; but for an Italian opera any spot is good enough!!!! You complain about the clouds approaching from the North?!!! You're wrong; so far as I'm concerned, I take off my hat to them, and may they be welcome from the moment that they are so well accepted. I've always loved and wanted progress, and if the coterie (allow me this expression, which I employ in the most benevolent sense) created in Milan, of which your Giulio is part and of which you yourself (perhaps without knowing it) are an accomplice, could succeed in elevating our music, I'll cry *Hosanna!* I too want the music of the future; that is, I believe in a music to come, and if I didn't know how to write it, as I wanted to, it's not my fault. If I too sullied the altar, as Boito says,[2] let Him cleanse it and I'll be the first to come light a candle to him. So hurrah for the coterie; hurrah for the North if it brings us light and sun.[3]

1. It was true, as Tornaghi confirmed in his reply.

2. An allusion to Boito's ode *All'arte italiana* (1863), in which he deplored the debased state of Italian music since "the holy harmonies of Pergolesi and Marcello." Referring to Franco Faccio, he said, "Perhaps the man is already born who will restore art in purity, on the altar now defiled like the wall of a brothel." Verdi took the ode as a personal insult, and it rankled for many years; cf. his letters to Clarina Maffei of 13 December 1863 (Alessandro Luzio, *Profili biografici bozzetti storici* [Milan: Cogliati, 1906] p. 522), to Piave on 21 May 1865 (*Carteggi* 2, 355), and to Giulio Ricordi in April 1875 (Walker, *The Man Verdi*, 469–70), all of which contain further allusions to Boito's ode. Moreover, at the time of the letter above Boito had embarked on a series of articles in the *Giornale della Società del Quartetto* enthusiastically lauding the sublimity of German music, and Faccio's *Amleto* was in rehearsal at La Scala.

3. Giulio Ricordi, champion and friend of Faccio and Boito, evidently considered writing to Verdi to counter the charges that the composer had made in this letter. Tornaghi asked Giuseppina to intercept any letter of Giulio's lest it offend the composer. See Walker, *The Man Verdi*, 456–57.

VERDI TO ESCUDIER   *Busseto, 4 May 1865*

Sono furente con Voi! Come? Dopo un dispaccio, una lettera, ed alcuni giornali non mi scrivete più, e non mi dite più nulla delle successive rappresentazioni del Macbet. Vi hanno forse ammazzati tutti di fischi?...In secondo luogo l'*Affricana* va in scena,[1] e voi non mi scrivete una parola? Non mi date notizia di questo grande avvenimento che avrà messo in convulsione tutta Parigi, e scosso il mondo musicale?. Non so spiegarmi questo vostro silenzio! Sareste ammalato?. Io spero di nò. In ogni modo avreste potuto almeno farmi scrivere una parola. Rimediate dunque alla mancanza e scrivetemi

1.º Intorno all'Affricana
2.º Sulle successive recite del Macbet
3.º⁻ Mandatemi gli articoli sul *Macbet* del *Figaro* e dei *Debats*. Non abbiate paura mi venga uno svenimento per quanto sia il male che potranno dire.

Avete ricevuta la mia lettera? Carvalho ne avrà pure ricevuta un'altra.

Paris: Bibliothèque de l'Opéra;
Rivista Musicale Italiana 35 (1928), 188

I am furious with you! What, after a telegram, a letter, and some newspapers, you don't write to me anymore, you tell me nothing more about the subsequent performances of *Macbeth*? Have they perhaps killed you all with their hisses?...In the second place, L'*Africaine* is being performed[1] and you don't write me one word about it? You do not send me news about this great event, which must have convulsed all of Paris and shaken the musical world? I don't know how to explain this silence of yours! Are you ill? I hope not. At any rate, you could at least have had a word sent to me. Make up for this lack, then, and write to me:

1. About *L'Africaine*;
2. About the subsequent performances of *Macbeth*;
3. Send me the reviews of *Macbeth* from the *Figaro* and the *Débats*. Have no fear that I shall faint, no matter how bad the reviews are.

Did you receive my letter? Carvalho should also have received another.

1. First performance, Opéra, 28 April 1865, exactly a week after *Macbeth*

VERDI TO ESCUDIER   *Busseto, 3 June 1865*

Tutto ben calcolato, pesato, e sommato il *Macbet* risulta *Fiasco*. Amen. Confesso però che non me l'aspettava. Mi pareva di non aver fatto troppo male, ma pare che io abbia avuto torto. Permettetemi per altro che io pure faccia alcune osservazione [*sic*]. Il *Duetto* del 1.º Atto, il *Finale* del Secondo, ed il *Sonnambulismo* non hanno avuto l'effetto che dovevano avere. Ebbene! ci deve essere qualche guasto nell'esecuzione. Non parlo del resto ma tante volte per voler *far troppo* non si *fà nulla*. È il difetto dell'*Opèra* [*sic*] temo diverrà lo stesso al *Teatro Lirico*. Le opere non sono che un pretesto al machinismo.[1]—Ricordi non m'ha scritto nulla sul progetto del *Macbet* alla Scala. Sarebbe un'altro errore. La Scala è il teatro ove non si sanno più interpretare le opere. Sarebbe un'altro Fiasco. . .

Paris: Bibliothèque de l'Opéra;
Rivista Musicale Italiana 35 (1928), 189–90

When all is considered, weighed, and summed up, *Macbeth* is a *fiasco*. Amen. I confess, however, that I did not expect it. I thought I had not done too badly, but it seems I was mistaken. Allow me, however, to make a few observations too. The *duet* in the first act, the *finale* of the second, and the *sleepwalking scene* did not make the impression they should have. Well! there must be something wrong in the performance. As for the rest, I won't say anything, but often by trying to do too much, one achieves nothing. It is the defect of the Opéra; I fear it will become the same at the Théâtre-Lyrique. The operas are nothing but a pretext for the machinery.[1]—Ricordi has not written to me about the plan for *Macbeth* at La Scala. It would be another mistake. La Scala is the theater where they no longer know how to interpret operas. It would be another fiasco. . .

1. "Carvalho wanted me to make the tempo of certain numbers slower or faster, to add sixteen bars, eight bars, four bars here, and remove two or three bars there, in order to suit some stage business of his own devising. In his eyes the production is not made for the music but the music for the production ... " Berlioz on Carvalho's production of *Les Troyens*. See David Cairns, ed., *The Memoirs of Hector Berlioz* (New York: Norton, 1975), p. 488.

VERDI TO TITO RICORDI

Turin, 8 August 1865

... Sarebbe bene ora di regolare le cose intorno il *Macbet*. Prepara addunque una piccola scritturina conforme le condizioni già stabilite, e dimmi quando potrai mandarmene la somma convenuta ...

Milan: Archivio Ricordi (247)

... It would be good now to straighten things out with regard to *Macbeth*. So prepare a little contract, incorporating the terms already settled, and tell me when you can send me the sum agreed on ...

TITO RICORDI TO VERDI

Milan, 12 August 1865

... Quanto all'affare del *Macbeth*, eccoti accluso una scritturina conforme alle condizioni stabilite e che, se non hai correzioni a farvi, potrai rimandarmi onorata della tua firma ...

Mi permisi mandarti un esemplare del *Macbeth* nuova edizione. Ora tengo in lavoro quella a grande formato che è ancora preferito fra noi. Spero che sarai soddisfatto della riduzione, se no, dimmelo sinceramente che provvederò altrimenti.—[1]

Sant'Agata

... As for the business of *Macbeth*, here's your little contract conforming to the terms agreed upon, which, if you have no corrections to make, you can return to me honored with your signature ...

I've taken the liberty of sending you a copy of the new edition of *Macbeth*. I'm now having prepared the one in large format, which is still preferred in this country. I hope that you'll be satisfied with the orchestral reduction. If not, tell me so frankly, so that I can make other provisions.—[1]

1. The score Ricordi sent was the octavo edition of the piano-vocal score (plate numbers 38841-65), which had been published about two weeks earlier. Verdi does not seem to have commented on the score.

VERDI TO TITO RICORDI

Busseto, 29 August 1865

... Prima di tutto spiacemi doverti dire che non possa aspettare il pagamento delli *8 mila* franchi fino al gennaio venturo. Prenditi dunque una dilazione più breve ma molto più breve, e dimmi quando.—

Manca qualche cosa nella scrittura *del Macbet* nuovo. Come dissi al Sign. Tornaghi a Torino, io aveva venduto la proprietà al Escudier per tutti i paesi tranne l'Italia. Dietro tue dimostrazioni accomodai la cosa, come ti scrissi, con Escudier il quale mi faceva queste concessioni...[Here Verdi transcribes the three numbered points of Escudier's 12 February 1865 letter[1]] ...

Bisogna addunque aggiungere queste condizioni nel contratto che dovrei firmare, e sarà bene farne un doppio.

Milan: Archivio Ricordi (248)

... First of all, I'm sorry to have to tell you that I can't wait until next January for the payment of the eight thousand francs. So allow yourself a shorter delay—*much* shorter—and tell me when.

Some things are missing in the contract for the new *Macbeth*. As I said to Mr. Tornaghi in Turin, I sold Escudier the rights for all countries except Italy. As a result of your objections, I adjusted things with Escudier, who, as I wrote you, made the following concessions: [Here Verdi transcribes the three numbered points of Escudier's 12 February 1865 letter[1]] ...

So these terms need to be added to the contract I am to sign, and it would be well to make a copy.

1. Verdi omits only the final phrase of point 3, beginning with "m'interdisant."

VERDI TO TORNAGHI

Sant'Agata, 12 September 1865

Sia pure il pagamento del Macbet metà a Novembre, metà a Gennajo, quantunque questa

Agreed, let the payment for *Macbeth* be half in November and half in January, although this

dilazione sconcerti alquanto i miei affari pecuniarj!– ...

Milan: Archivio Ricordi 249

delay upsets my financial affairs somewhat!– ...

TITO RICORDI TO VERDI

Lago di Como, 21 September 1865

Mi si domanda con *insistenza* il *Macbeth* nuovo per la Scala, stagione corrente. Sono la *Stolz* e *De Bassini* che fanno il diavolo per fare quest'opera—[1]

Tornaghi mi chiede consiglio, ed io sono più titubante di lui—

La Stolz *si* potrebbe prima sentire nella *Gio. d'Arco* e poi decidere, ma De Bassini, sarà ancora capace di una parte sì importante?

Nella mia incertezza ho scritto a Tornaghi di tenere a bada per alcuni giorni l'Impresa e frattanto ho pensato di domandare a te un parere decisivo, proprio in tutta confidenza ed amicizia—

Ti do la mia parola che nessuno saprà cosa tu mi risporderai—Abbi pazienza. Scrivimi subito a Milano, mi basta una riga, o sì o nò—

Sant'Agata

They're asking me *insistently* for the new *Macbeth* for La Scala, the current season. It's Stolz and De Bassini who are making a devil of a fuss to do this opera.[1]

Tornaghi asked my advice, and I'm more uncertain than he. One could first hear Stolz in *Giovanna d'Arco* and then decide, but as for De Bassini, will he still be capable of doing such an important part?

In my uncertainty, I wrote to Tornaghi to keep the Direction waiting for a few days, and meanwhile I thought to ask you for a deciding opinion, in all confidence and friendship.

I give you my word that no one will know anything that you reply to me. Please. Write to me at once in Milan, a line will do, either yes or no.

1. Stolz had sung *Macbeth* I at the Teatro Bellini, Palermo, in March 1865; De Bassini had been singing it since June 1847. As Giovanna, Stolz made her Scala debut two days after this letter.

VERDI TO TITO RICORDI

Sant'Agata, 23 September 1865

Intorno al *Macbet* fà quello che vuoi. Tu a Milano saprai meglio di me a St Agata se de Bassini potrà reggere.

Tu saprai se la Stolz è artista tragica, e tragica in sommo grado per fare Lady (l'esempio di Giovanna non varrebbe).

Tu saprai se l'impresa ha coraggio per spendere per la *mise en scene,* intelligenza per spender bene, ed impegno per un'opera italiana...Fi!!! che avrebbe, per esempio, per un'opera straniera.[1]

Bisognerebbe eseguire l'opera come stà senza tagliare nè aggiungere una nota, e montare bene il balletto che è importante.

Resta la parte musicale...Ahimè!...anche jeri ho ricevuto lettera da Milano che dice: Lo spettacolo alla Scala è, come sempre, impossibile.

Addunque osserva, giudica, e decidi.

Milan: Archivio Ricordi (250)

So far as *Macbeth* is concerned, do what you want. You in Milan will know better than I at Sant'Agata if De Bassini will hold up.

You'll know if Stolz is a tragic artist, and tragic in the highest degree, for doing the Lady (the example of Giovanna wouldn't count).

You'll know if the management has the courage to spend money on the mise-en-scène, the intelligence to spend well, and the sense of commitment to an Italian opera...Fie!!! that they would have, for example, to a foreign opera.[1]

The opera would have to be performed just as it is without cutting or adding a note. The ballet, which is important, would have to be put on well.

Then there's the musical side. Alas!...just yesterday I received a letter from Milan which says: the performances at La Scala are, as always, impossible.

Therefore observe, judge, and decide.

1. That season, Halévy's *La Juive* had its first La Scala performance; Gounod's *Faust* and Flotow's *Martha* were revived.

TITO RICORDI TO VERDI

Avendo fatto una corsa a Milano per alcuni affari d'importanza trovo la lettera che tu avesti la bontà di indirizzarmi a proposito del *Macbeth*. Alle tue giustissime riflessioni s'aggiunga che De Bassini va perdendo di voce di giorno in giorno e che chi sa come potrà arrivare alla fine della stagione, poi l'Impresa ha idee di troppa economia ... , l'ho indotta a mettere questo progetto da una parte per tempi migliori ...[1]

Sant'Agata

1. *Macbeth* II was not done at La Scala until 1874.

Having made a quick trip to Milan for some important matters, I find the letter which you kindly sent me about *Macbeth*. To your very just observations let it be added that De Bassini loses his voice day after day and who knows how he'll manage to reach the end of the season. And then the management has ideas about over-economizing ... , I persuaded it to put this project aside until better times ...[1]

VERDI TO TITO RICORDI

Ho ricevuto ed esatti li 4 mila franchi che mi hai mandato a conto del pagamento *Macbet* nuovo...

Milan: Archivio Ricordi; *Abbiati* 3, 62

I've received and collected the four thousand francs which you sent me as payment for the new *Macbeth*...

1870–1875

VERDI TO GIULIO RICORDI

... In quanto al *Boccanegra* o *Macbet,* io sarei pel Macbet nuovo perchè non credo avreste un buon attore pel Boccanegra; la parte della figlia non sarebbe adattata alla *Fricci,* nè quella del tenore a *Tiberini.*[2] Nel Macbet di due parti ne avreste una buonissima la Fricci; ma bisognerebbe trovare un Macbet. Non credo in Colini per quella parte. Il *Macbet* si presta poi ad una *mise en scene* e ad uno spettacolo superiore a tutte le opere che si conoscono. L'avete eseguito più volte a Milano, e, non so musicalmente, ma scenicamente sempre malissimo.—Nel *Macbet* nuovo credo sia tolta o cangiata un'aria pessima della Donna, credo sia migliorato di molto il terz'atto, e credo vi sia un balletto di grande

As for *Boccanegra* or *Macbeth,* I'd be for the new *Macbeth,* because I don't believe you have a good actor for Boccanegra; the role of the daughter isn't well suited to Fricci, nor that of the tenor to Tiberini.[2] Of the two roles in *Macbeth* you'd have one of them excellently cast with Fricci, but a Macbeth would have to be found. I don't believe in Collini for that role. And then *Macbeth* calls for a better staging and spectacle than all operas that are known. You've performed it several times in Milan, and, while I don't know about the musical side, scenically it was always done wretchedly.—In the new *Macbeth* I believe that an awful aria of the prima donna was cut out or changed, I

importanza. Non ho qui lo spartito del nuovo Macbet, mandatemelo, e ve ne darò un giudizio schietto schietto come si trattasse d'un'opera d'un altro.—Ma non fatevi illusioni: non avete alla Scala nè Direttori di musica nè di scena, e senza una buona direzione non è possibile un successo al Macbet. Io non sono abbastanza ciarlatano per correre dietro a tutte le mie opere, e non è possibile che io venga a Milano.—Dunque? O non dar l'opera; o rimettersi nelle mani della Provvidenza! . . .

Milan: Archivio Ricordi (437); *Abbiati* 3, 411–12

believe that Act III was improved a lot, and I believe that there's a very important ballet. I don't have the score of the new *Macbeth* here. Send me one, and I'll give you my opinion pure and simple, just as if it were someone else's opera.—But don't delude yourselves; at La Scala you have neither musical directors nor stage directors, and without good direction a successful *Macbeth* is impossible. I'm not enough of a charlatan to go running after all my operas, and it's not possible for me to come to Milan.—So? Either don't give the opera, or put one's self in the hands of Providence! . . .

1. After Abbiati

2. Antonietta Fricci (1840–1912) was a celebrated Lady Macbeth; Mario Tiberini (1826–1880) was the Alvaro of the revised *Forza*; Virginio Collini (d. 1893)—not to be confused with Filippo Colini, who had died in 1863—sang Don Giovanni and Valentine in the 1870–71 season, which had opened with all three singers in *L'Africaine*.

VERDI TO GIULIO RICORDI

Sant'Agata, 28 December 1873

. . . Sono dolente di non aver un momento di tempo da dar un'occhiata alla *mise en scene* del Macbeth. Noi partiremo per Genova Martedi verso mezzogiorno per essere a Genova la sera dopo le 8. per cui voi potete immaginarvi quanto ho da fare. Vi rimando questo Macbet e state pure tranquillo che andrà benissimo. Io non vi ho nissuna fede: questo vi deve rassicurare, e spero potervi dire ancora la prima frase *"son felice d'essermi ingannato"*!¹ . . .

Milan: Archivio Ricordi (633); *Abbiati* 3, 658

. . . I am sorry that I've not had a moment's time to glance at the mise-en-scène of *Macbeth*. We leave for Genoa on Tuesday at about midday, to be in Genoa that evening after eight. So you can imagine how much I have to do. I'm sending this *Macbeth* back to you. Go ahead and feel confident that it will go very well. I have no faith in it at all—that must reassure you, and I hope to be able to repeat to you my first sentence, *"I am happy to have been mistaken."*[1] . . .

1. Verdi opened the letter with a similar phrase, referring to his incorrect prediction that the Scala production of *Aida* would be poorly received. Earlier he had written, " . . . note well that I'm rarely wrong in such matters. Remember the fiascoes that many of my operas made in Milan in the past, fiascoes that I had predicted: *Vespri*, *Macbeth*, *Boccanegra*, *Ballo*, etc. etc. (I'm speaking of their first performances)" [(June 1872 letter to Giulio Ricordi, in *Abbiati* 3, 570–71). Apparently Verdi was later convinced that the Scala production of *Macbeth* had, after all, been successful (see letters of 28 February 1874 to L. Escudier and 1 July 1874 to Giulio Ricordi, in *Abbiati* 3, 676 and 703).

INTERVIEW WITH VERDI, *NEUE FREIE PRESSE* (VIENNA), JUNE 1875

When we came to talk about Wagner, Verdi remarked that that great genius had rendered incalculable services to melodramatic art because he had had the courage to rid himself of the traditional decadent ("baroque") forms. "I, too, have attempted the fusion of music and drama," he said, "and that in *Macbeth;* but I could not write my own librettos, as Wagner does."

From Frank Walker, "Verdi and Vienna, With Some Unpublished Letters," *The Musical Times* 92 (1951), 404

THE
DANVILLE
PAPERS

Florence, 1847

JOSÉ VERDI, HERCULES CAVALLI, AND THE FLORENCE *MACBETH*

Mary Jane Phillips Matz

On 18 April 1977, a stack-runner in the Trieste City Library brought up from the archive storerooms a loosely-bound volume that, according to the library records, no one had ever asked to see. It was a miscellany, and between its covers lay a book which may be the earliest published Verdi biography. Its title is *José Verdi*. One of two *Biografias artisticas contemporaneas* by Hercules Cavalli, it is the only Verdi biography published by a native of Busseto and close friend of the composer.[1] Cavalli was the brother-in-law of Giovannino Barezzi, who, in turn, was Verdi's brother-in-law, and the most intimate companion of the composer from 1823 until about 1847.[2] *José Verdi*, written in Spanish and published in Madrid in 1867, by the Imprenta de J. M. Ducazal, was dedicated to the celebrated tenor Gaetano Fraschini.[3]

This unexpected discovery of an unexplored 110-year-old Verdi biography was cele-brated that April evening by another composer, Gian Carlo Menotti, who was in Trieste to direct *Aida* for the first time in his life. Studying the Spanish text of *José Verdi* with friends and colleagues from the Teatro Verdi, Menotti speculated on Hercules Cavalli's relationship to Verdi and to music, and reminded everyone at supper that he owns two portraits, supposedly of Verdi and Giuseppina Strepponi, painted in Florence in 1847. Menotti asked for clues to the identity of the unknown artist of the portraits. These show an elegant, haughty maestro holding one music score rolled up in his hand, with another score on the piano behind him, and a pensive, diffident woman, caught in the act of sketching a boy's head on an artist's pad. Both portraits were bought in Lyon in the mid-1960s.

Astonishingly, the research trail for both *José Verdi* and the two portraits led to the same source: the Cavalli-Piatti family, whose members have lived in Parma, Siena, Busseto,

---

1. The earliest biography is by Giuseppe Demaldè, treasurer of the Monte di Pietà of Busseto, great-grandfather of the present Verdi heirs, the Carrara-Verdi family. Demaldè's manuscript was unpublished until 1976–77, when it appeared in Italian and English in the *Verdi Newsletter* of the American Institute for Verdi Studies (Nos. 1, 2, 3).

2. The Barezzis and Verdi's mother's family, the Uttinis, knew each other well at least eight years before the composer's birth, and we may assume that the Verdis and Barezzis were intimates at least from 1805–6. In 1807, Antonio Barezzi's aunt and godmother, Donna Margherita Carrara, became the godmother of Verdi's first cousin, Margherita Uttini. Donna Margherita was also the godmother of Verdi's wife, Margherita Barezzi. Baptismal records, Church of San Bartolomeo, Busseto.

3. See PERSONALIA.

Piacenza, Florence and Milan, and have been directly involved in various ways with Verdi, his teachers and his education, his career, his music, and his private life from the 1790s until the present. Today we know a great deal about Hercules Cavalli, the book's author, and about Giulio Piatti, the artist of the portraits. And both were directly involved with Verdi's visit to Florence for the premiere of *Macbeth*.

Hercules Cavalli was a businessman, a dilettante journalist, and a historian of music and art. The other of his *Biografias artisticas* is a study of the sculptor Antonio Canova, whose disciple Lorenzo Bartolini became, in 1849, the mentor of Giuseppina Strepponi's son Camillo Luigi Antonio Strepponi.[4] Cavalli lived and worked everyday within the intimate circle of the Barezzi-Verdi clan. Present at Verdi's engagement and wedding banquets (1836), he also knew Verdi's mother, whom he alone among Verdi biographers interviewed and described. Working back in history from Hercules Cavalli and his mother's family, the Piattis, and working forward into the twentieth century, one can reconstruct a whole dynasty of this influential family, from Antonio Cavalli and Hercules Piatti, the patriarchs, to Carlo Maria Giulini, the Milanese conductor, their descendant. Tracing the artist Giulio Piatti in Florence, one is led to the Bonapartes, the sister, brothers, niece, and nephews of Napoleon I, and to Giuseppina Strepponi. From this reconstruction emerges a wholly unknown Verdi iconography centered on Florence and *Macbeth*, on Verdi, Piatti, the sculptor Giovanni Dupré (another Bartolini pupil), Emanuele Muzio, Antonio and Giovannino Barezzi, and the Strepponi sisters Giuseppina, soprano and singing teacher, and Barberina, tutor and art teacher, who attended the premiere of the opera.

The Cavalli family originated in the small city of Sissa, near Parma, where they were the most important and richest landowners of the region.[5] In the late 1790s they became the patrons of Ferdinando Provesi, the organist of their parish, who was later Verdi's first teacher of composition and music theory. Sometime after 1795, the Cavalli family emigrated to Busseto, where they bought the mansion of the mayor, Count Annibale Dordoni, a liberal, Bonapartist nobleman.[6] The Palazzo Cavalli, as it then was called, was remodeled at the beginning of the nineteenth century by Giuseppe Cavalli, another member of the family, and the only major architect ever to work in Busseto.[7] From his restoration emerged the stately neo-classical house where Hercules Cavalli was born in 1824.[8]

Ferdinando Provesi, who had remained behind in Sissa, committed a grave crime in 1799: he stole from the Church of Santa Maria Assunta, where he was organist.[9] Arrested and dragged in chains to prison, he languished for nearly two years, untried. Because he was a poet and librettist of no mean skill, Provesi sent all his appeals to the Duke of Parma in verse, but to no avail. No response came to his pleas for clemency. Finally he took another tack, and asked to be tried. Convicted, he was condemned to lifelong exile and to forced domicile in a village in the Appenines. For a man dedicated to music, theatre, and writing, this was rather like being sent to hell, and Provesi soon fled to Busseto, where the police traced him in 1801. In normal circumstances, he would have been seized and dragged back

4. Camillo Luigi Antonio Strepponi was born in Turin on 14 January 1838.

5. Sissa, Church of Santa Maria Assunta, archive

6. Emilio Seletti, *La Città di Busseto* 2 (Milan: Bortolotti, 1883), 223

7. Ibid. See also Vol. 3, 133–34.

8. Busseto, Church of San Bartolomeo, baptismal registers.

9. Ascanio Alessandri, "Un gravissimo fallo di Ferdinando Provesi," in *Parma per Arte*, Nos. 7, 9, 10, 11 (1957–61)

to Sissa, but in Busseto he enjoyed the patronage of the Cavallis, and thus he was saved. Given an apartment for his wife and child, he was also made director of the Busseto drama academy and music school, and of the organ and orchestra of the Church of San Bartolomeo in Busseto.[10] The importance of the Cavallis can be gauged from the fact that they could oust a rich, church-sponsored organist from his post to make way for a fugitive and ex-convict whose name was never legally cleared in the Duchy of Parma.[11]

Hercules Cavalli grew up in this arena of power; his father, Contardo Cavalli, became the mayor of Busseto. His mother, Donna Alba Piatti of Piacenza, was the daughter of one of the richest industrialists of northern Italy, another Hercules Piatti, who revolutionized silk manufacture and fathered a generation of jurists, bankers, and statesmen.[12] One of the Piatti sons, Camillo, was the pro-French, liberal president of the National Bank who became an active patriot in 1848, financed the revolutionary government, and served in Parliament with Verdi.[13]

After Hercules Cavalli's sister Adele married Verdi's brother-in-law, Giovannino Barezzi, his bonds with the Barezzis, the Uttinis, and the Verdis were strengthened. The Cavallis helped to fund Verdi's education through the Monte di Pietà in Busseto, where Contardo Cavalli was chief council member, and helped young Verdi with moral support as well.[14] Together with Verdi and Margherita Barezzi, their children studied music under Provesi. Emanuele Muzio later became the pupil first of Provesi, then of Margherita, then of Verdi.[15] Some of the Cavallis and Piattis went on to study in Milan when Verdi did. When Verdi decided in 1838 to leave Busseto and try his luck as an opera composer in Milan, it was to Contardo Cavalli that he wrote, resigning his post as municipal music master.[16]

Returning triumphant to Busseto after the success of *Nabucco, I lombardi,* and *Giovanna d'Arco,* Verdi bought the Palazzo Cavalli from Contardo Cavalli.[17] As we know from a letter to Ricordi, Verdi intended to live in it for the rest of his life, "col desiderio di abitarla e finirvi forse i miei giorni."[18] By May 1846, the house was completely paid for. An imposing mansion on the main street of Busseto, it boasts seven rent-yielding shops opening onto the nine-arched arcade of its facade. Inside are a spacious courtyard, stables, storerooms, apartments for rental, and thirty-odd rooms for the owner's use. Verdi moved his parents here from Roncole, and here he composed all or much of *Luisa Miller, Rigoletto, Stiffelio, Il trovatore,* and perhaps *La traviata* and the later operas as well. Officially, he never moved from Palazzo Cavalli.[19]

After selling to Verdi, the Cavallis moved to another of their properties in Busseto, but Hercules Cavalli continued his close relationship with Verdi and the Barezzis, becoming

---

10. F. T. Garibaldi, *Giuseppe Verdi* (Florence: Bemporad, 1904), pp. 8ff.

11. Busseto, Church of San Bartolomeo, Transactions File (1802) gives rank and titles of *Dominus Capitanus Aloysius Soncini* organist, who was first dismissed to make way for Provesi, and then later was "sick" and could not play at the concert in the Church of Sant'Ignazio which was Verdi's official debut in Busseto.

12. Piacenza, Cathedral archive and baptismal and death registers. Archivio di Stato, Piacenza, Registri della Popolazione. Municipal archive, Piacenza, Ufficio Anagrafe.

13. Schedario Rapetti, *voce* "Piatti," in Biblioteca Passerini-Landi, Piacenza

14. Busseto, Archive of the Monte di Pietà in Biblioteca Civica

15. F. T. Garibaldi, *Giuseppe Verdi*

16. The original of this letter is in Museo Civico Villa Pallavicino, Busseto.

17. Research by Gabriella Carrara-Verdi on the Palazzo Cavalli is reproduced in Walker, *The Man Verdi,* p. 195n.

18. Carlo Gatti, *Verdi* (Milan: Mondadori, 1951), p. 515

19. Busseto, Municipal archive, Ufficio Anagrafe: Registri per Cambiamento di Domicilio

their trusted courier in Piacenza, Genoa, Nice, and Madrid.[20] Deputy and jurist Camillo Piatti saw Verdi in Piacenza and Turin.[21]

When Verdi went to Florence in 1847, he was at the apex of his career as a young composer. "More and more, Verdi seconds the work of the eminent patriots who announce the imminent revolution and wish to translate their proposals into action. The Milanese populace, fired by them to faith in the just cause, prepare the new crusade against the foreigner. Verdi chooses to be an interpreter of popular feelings."[22] In a widely read yearbook, *Strenna Europea Teatrale*, the poet-librettist Andrea Maffei had just published a long poem hailing Verdi's apotheosis: "A Giuseppe Verdi, Gloria d'Italia," which ended with the line "Verdi e Vittoria." "You live and reign in every heart," wrote Maffei, expressing what had by then become a common sentiment.[23]

With Verdi in Florence were Maffei, Muzio, and Antonio Barezzi and his son Giovannino, lodged at the Hôtel Suisse. Verdi had left Milan with a letter of introduction from Alessandro Manzoni to Giuseppe Giusti, the most celebrated Tuscan nationalist literary figure. "Caro Geppino," Manzoni wrote, in a note which he correctly supposed Verdi did not need.[24] Rehearsals began at the Pergola, with Pietro Romani's orchestra and the crew and cast assembled by Alessandro Lanari, "The Napoleon of Impresarios." Verdi was the the cynosure of every eye, the center of a group of liberal and revolutionary intellectuals headed by the Florentines Giovanni Dupré, sculptor, and Giulio Piatti, artist.[25] They matched sentiments with the fiery warrior-patriot young Luciano Manara, who was also in Verdi's entourage, as he had been in Venice when *Attila* had its premiere.[26] These were intoxicating weeks indeed. Piatti was one of the most courageous Tuscan patriots of the day, brother of a publisher who used his printing house and bookshop as an outlet for revolutionaries—among them several members of the Bonaparte family.[27] Guglielmo Piatti frequented the future Napoleon III, his father and uncles, and Giuseppina Strepponi's lover Count Filippo Camerata dei Passionei, the son-in-law of Elisa Bonaparte, the Emperor's sister.[28] The Piattis also backed the women's movement in Tuscany, where their sister became the first woman to win a major prize for literature.[29] Giulio Piatti had already painted the huge canvas *The Sicilian Vespers*, where Barbarina Strepponi may appear as one of the protagonists of revolution, and he punctuated his letters with phrases like "Death to the Germans" (with a skull and crossbones in the margin) and "Viva l'Indipendenza d'Italia."[30]

For Verdi, who had lived long as the target of harassment by the Austrian police in Milan, Florence meant freedom, where he could express himself without fear of censors and

20. Letter of Antonio Barezzi to Verdi, 1848, Sant'Agata archive

21. Schedario Rapetti, Piacenza; see Note 13.

22. Gatti, *Verdi*, p. 167

23. *Strenna Europea Teatrale* (Milan: Carpano, 1846), pp. 55ff.

24. The letter is reproduced on pp. 45–46.

25. Giovanni Dupré, *Ricordi Autobiografici* (Florence: Successori La Monnier, 1898), pp. 163, 168ff.; and see Muzio's letter of 25 February 1847, and the excerpt from Dupré's memoirs that follows it, in "Letters".

26. Letter of Giovannino Barezzi to his father in Garibaldi, *Giuseppe Verdi*, p. 261

27. G. Corsini, *I Bonaparte a Firenze* (Florence: Olschki, 1961), pp. 148ff., 164, 180–81, 333–34

28. Florence, Biblioteca Nazionale, Carteggi Vari, Box 411, Strepponi letters of 1841–42; also Camerata, Box 351

29. Spoleto, Biblioteca Carducci, archive; Rosalia Piatti, *Racconti di una Donna*, 2d ed. (Florence: Barbera, 1872)

30. Pistoia, Biblioteca Forteguerriana, manuscript collection, letters of Giulio Piatti to Niccolò Puccini; also Pistoia, Museo Civico, archive and library. "Morte ai Tedeschi" is a prominent cry in *La forza del destino*, II.1.

theatre closings, without fear of having the police chief Baron Luigi Torresani-Lanzenfeld impound his passport, as he had the passport of Verdi's baritone Giorgio Ronconi.[31] Living in Tuscany, Verdi became the idol of the duchy. Emanuele Muzio's letter of 9 March 1847 to the Barezzi family describes the furore Verdi's presence provoked.

If this was a moment of great joy and of triumph for Verdi and his cronies, it was a time of confusion for Giuseppina Strepponi and her sister. In Florence, the soprano had known moments of professional success like those Verdi enjoyed in 1847, but she had also known anguish, horror, and shame. Here, eight years before, Peppina Strepponi had been an accomplice to a felony, that of concealing the birth of her second child, who was born dead, before dawn on 9 February 1839.[32] The night before, Peppina had sung *Il giuramento*, under Pietro Romani's direction, after having caused an uproar backstage because of her ill-fitting costumes and boots. Before five o'clock the next morning, labor began, and a six- or seventh-month baby was born. No civil record of this event exists, but in police reports there are references to "La Strepponi's accident" and her "misfortune" which wrought havoc with Lanari's season.[33] After this incident, Strepponi only appeared in one complete Lanari Florence season. After the birth of her third child, Adelina, in 1841, she began to make plans to leave Italy.[34] By 1845, she had decided to settle in France, which she did the following year, almost certainly leaving her son Camillo in Florence, in boarding school.[35] Thus her return to Florence was prompted not only by a desire to see Verdi again but also by the need to set family matters in order. In Florence, she found "her Verdi" (to use Donizetti's sarcastic appellation) the lion of the year. Not only was Verdi free to make all the political and artistic statements he wished; *he was himself a political statement*, a rallying point, the national hero of a nation laboring to be free.

From Hercules Cavalli and from Giuseppe Demaldè, another early Verdi biographer, we have two descriptions of the Florence *Macbeth*. Cavalli writes:

The most famous city of Italy, the modern Athens, mother of painting, she who brought forth the most eminent artistic geniuses such as Dante, Leonardo Da Vinci, Michelangelo Buonarroti, and Macchiavelli, most excellent city, wise and cultured, knew the Maestro's operas but had never had the pleasure of seeing their premieres, not having taken advantage of the first blooming of the New Orpheus; but if the Florentines wanted some souvenir from Verdi, he, for his part, wanted to bear witness to his goodwill and respect toward the worthy metropolis of the fine arts. A tragedy by Shakespeare, adapted by F. M. Piave as a musical drama, inspired him, and during Carnival of 1846–47 he gave the Florentines an original, bizarre work, completely different from its predecessors; full of beauty and new harmonies, in which Maestro tried to move away from the method he had used up to that time, and to bind his genius into the imaginative genre; the ballets, the choruses of the witches, the apparitions, the drinking songs, and everything else new and surprising in music of this

31. Florence, Biblioteca Nazionale, Florence, Carteggi Vari, Box 398, Giovannina Ronconi to Alessandro Lanari.

32. Florence, Biblioteca Nazionale, Florence, Carteggi Vari, Boxes 364–65. Antonio Gazzuoli to Alessandro Lanari.

33. Florence, Archivio di Stato. Police report on 1839 season, manuscript collection, special section. Research on this subject has been done by Dottoressa Manno-Tolù.

34. Trieste, Church of Santa Maria Maggiore, baptismal records, November 1841. Adelina Rosa Maria Strepponi was born on November 4 and baptized the next day. Her godmother was Teresa Paradisi, theatrical actress and singer, and wife of the great comic *ballerino* and mime Salvatore Paradisi, whose long collaboration with the choreographer Antonio Monticini at Florence, Turin, and Milan established a standard for the mime and ballet theatres for decades to come.

35. Walker, *The Man Verdi*, pp. 200–1. Letters to, from, and about Livia Zanobini and her brother-in-law Filippo Pagliai are also at Sant'Agata and in the Biblioteca Nazionale in Florence (General manuscript card catalogue). Verdi tried to persuade Senator Piroli to find work for Pagliai.

kind—all can be found in *Macbeth*. The Florentine intellectuals showered the composer with praise and demonstrations of their esteem: the nobility, artists and literary figures fought with each other to pay honour to him.[36]

From Verdi's intimate friend and supporter Giuseppe Demaldè, of Busseto, we have a more succinct account of the Florence *Macbeth*, which can only have come from Verdi himself:

March, 1847

Macbet fantastic drama in 4 acts

Librettist: Piave, Francesco M[a], Venetian

Surname and christian name of the person for whom he wrote the opera: Lanari, Alessandro, Impresario

Theatre in which it was sung for the first time: Florence, La Pergola

Artists: Barbieri Nini, Marianna; Brunacci, Angelo, Varesi, Felice

Outcome: Absolutely stupendous

Given to Verdi: A gold crown with a legend of all Verdi's operas; a silver vessel and green velvet cushion with gold edging; engraved, written montage with biography of Maestro

Reviews: An infernal criticism by the journalists

Given to the artists: Crowns and flowers to Barbieri and Varesi

Fee: 19,800

Rights: Both the Music and the Poetry are property of the Publisher Gi[o] Ricordi, assigned by the said Lanari

[Other]:   The [illegible] was accompanied from the Theatre to his house by the Flower of the Youth [of Florence] and at the third (performance) Verdi was drawn home in his carriage [without horses][37]

In sum, a triumph with the public, especially with the young people of Florence, accompanied by "infernal" reviews from uncomprehending critics.

After the first performances, Verdi returned to Milan with his entourage, while the Barezzis made for Busseto, and the Strepponi sisters for Paris, where Verdi visited them four months later and Barezzi visited them at the end of the year.[38] From Milan, on 25 March 1847, Verdi wrote to Barezzi that *Macbeth* was dedicated to him.[39] This letter was first published in Spanish, in *José Verdi*. Cavalli was in the room with Antonio Barezzi when it was delivered:

Few men will ever have the occasion to feel the pleasure of gratitude in such an intimate way as did the good, old Barezzi when he read such sweet words; and shedding copious tears, profoundly moved, he exclaimed: "I recognized his goodness and talent when he was a boy, and I protected him as best I could, and he has not let me down."[40]

Cavalli goes on to observe that Verdi was notably loyal to his early friends and to those who contributed to his artistic development. Here Cavalli was speaking from his own experience.

36. Hercules Cavalli, *José Verdi*, p. 29

37. Giuseppe Demaldè, *Schèda delle opere di Giuseppe Verdi* in the archive of the Monte di Pietà, Busseto, now in the Biblioteca Civica

38. Barezzi to Verdi, Sant'Agata; Demaldè to Verdi, Sant'Agata

39. For a reproduction of this letter, see p. ii.

40. Cavalli, *José Verdi*, p. 31.

Miniatures of Verdi and Giuseppina Strepponi, possibly by Barberina Strepponi (Gallini Collection)

In 1851, Verdi sent Cavalli to Genoa armed with a letter of introduction to the leading tenor of the Carlo Felice, Settimio Malvezzi.[41] Later in the decade (1854) he provided a home at Sant'Agata for Pietro Cavalli, a cousin of Hercules.[42] In the early 1860s, the composer solicited Senator Giuseppe Piroli, his lifelong friend, to find work for Hercules Cavalli's youngest brother, Camillo, described as "a spy, deserter and former soldier" but "a good boy" all the same.[43] In parliament Verdi sat with Hercules Cavalli's millionaire uncle Camillo Piatti, who, in 1913, was chosen to give the commemorative address honoring "the life and the triumphs of the Great Man" and recalled Verdi's generosity to the nursery schools and day-care centers established by his first cousin, Monsignor Carlo Uttini, pioneer in the early education movement.[44] It is worth noting that many of these nursery schools are still functioning, more than a century after their founding, and that among their supporters are the Piattis, one of whom, a grandnephew of Hercules Cavalli, is Giulio Piatti, the President of the Supreme Court of Piacenza. The nephew of the attorney Camillo Piatti is Carlo Maria Giulini.

As for the documentation and iconography of the Florentine *Macbeth*, we have, besides all the letters and other documents presented in this volume, more of Dupré's and Giusti's and Manara's correspondence with Verdi. Dupré's sculptured hand of Verdi, done in the artist's studio, remains on Verdi's writing desk at Sant'Agata. There stand statuettes of Manara and Manzoni. Also surviving are three extraordinary miniatures by an unknown artist, perhaps Barberina Strepponi herself, which were used by Giulio Piatti while he worked on the portraits now owned by Menotti.[45] The miniature of Verdi shows him with

41. Verdi to Settimio Malvezzi, 14 February 1851, Sant'Agata
42. Busseto, Municipal archive, Ufficio Anagrafe, Registri della Popolazione
43. *Carteggi* 3, 9–11.
44. *Bolletino Storico Piacentino* (1914), 31
45. Milan, Gallini collection. Private archive of Dr. Annarita Caputo-Calloud, Florence. (Dr. Caputo-Calloud is the authority on Giulio Piatti.)

a *Nabucco* score on the piano and a rolled-up score of *Macbeth* in his hand. Barberina is sketching the head of a boy, while Peppina stands by a piano with a roll of music in her hand. The Piatti portrait of Barberina Strepponi is virtually the same in every detail as the miniature. A portrait of Giuseppina that Piatti probably executed at the same time has not yet been found.[46]

From this disparate collection of documents, from these scraps of memorabilia scattered across two continents, we look back across a hundred and thirty years and reconstruct the scene—the stage, the offstage, and the backstage—of the premiere of *Macbeth,* the first of Verdi's creations to come to life in an atmosphere of true artistic freedom.

46. Letters of Romani to Lanari, Biblioteca Nazionale Centrale, Florence, Carteggi Vari, Boxes 405–6. Camillo Cirelli to Lanari, Box 419 (note that these are catalogued separately from the mass of the Fondo Lanari). Letters of Giuseppina Strepponi to Lanari are not only in the Carteggi Vari (see Note 28) but also in the archive of the Teatro La Fenice, Venice (manuscripts: Artiste di canto). The earliest Strepponi letters are not cataloged anywhere, but are in the Cirelli file, Box 419, inserted in Cirelli's letters.

VERDI'S *MACBETH* AND
THE FLORENTINE CRITICS

Leonardo Pinzauti

The important role played by Florence in nineteenth-century Italian culture, especially with regard to musical life, still awaits a thorough study, one that will neither rely upon facile generalizations nor, worse yet, fall under the influence of *campanilismo*—parochial pride. These two failings are present throughout the sparse literature of the past century and a half concerning the literary, artistic and musical life of Florence. I, Florentine by birth and education, would not want to add a contribution that could in any way be faulted for excessive enthusiasm about the extraordinary events of which my city has been witness and protagonist for so many centuries. Nevertheless, even with the most scrupulous historical objectivity, one must recognize that Florence really is not—at least in the past it was not—an ordinary city. Its unique "personality" is easily recognized in the great epochs of Dante and Boccaccio, Donatello and Brunelleschi, Leonardo and Michelangelo. It may seem much more difficult to discern when one considers instead the social and political life of the Grand Duchy of Tuscany of Leopold II, who, despite all his civic achievements, was certainly not on the same level as Lorenzo de' Medici. Nevertheless, in Florence during the first half of the nineteenth century were intellectual currents which reach almost to the present day; for example, we could easily show the connection between certain ideals of the proud and cultivated bourgeoisie of the Grand Duchy epoch and those leading to the birth of the *Società del Quartetto* in 1861, the *Stabile Orchestrale Fiorentina* in 1928, and, a few years later, of the *Maggio musicale*. Even in the Grand Duchy period, then, certain emblematic dates come forward in justification of the epithet applied to Florence: "The Athens of Italy."

In 1812, Ugo Foscolo established his third sojourn in Florence. Rossini's *Barbiere di Siviglia* came to the Teatro della Pergola in 1816, the year of its premiere in Rome.[1] In 1818 Niccolò Paganini gave his first concert in Florence at the Pergola, where in 1822 he was to make two more of his rare appearances. In 1821, Gian Pietro Vieusseux founded the important periodical *L'Antologia, Giornale di Scienze, Lettere e Arti*, and in 1824 Meyerbeer's opera *Il crociato in Egitto*, directed by its thirty-three-year-old composer, came to the Pergola and enjoyed a great success—a notable event in the history of the Florentine cultural elite and its early acceptance and welcoming of the music of *maestri oltremontani* (composers from beyond the Alps). Giacomo Leopardi visited Florence in 1827, the same year that Alessandro Manzoni went there to revise *I promessi sposi*, and to adapt it to the Italian language as spoken in Florence—an event of the greatest importance for the development of a modernized version of the literary language. In 1828, the year the Grand Duke ordered the draining of the Maremma swamp, a private entrepreneur, Angiolo Lucherini, founded a

---

1. Further information about many of the musical events mentioned here can be found in Marcello de Angelis, *La musica del Granduca: vita musicale e correnti critiche a Firenze 1800–1855* (Florence: Vallechi, 1978).

piano factory in Florence, with technicians and workmen brought in from Vienna. Amidst this fervor of cultural and social initiative, it is not surprising that in 1830 the "virtuosi di Camera e Cappella" of the Grand Duke, together with numerous Florentine artists and amateurs, presented in the Salone dei Cinquecento of the Palazzo Vecchio a performance of Haydn's *Creation*.[2] In 1831, Berlioz visited Florence and "was carried away in spite of [himself]"[3] during a performance of Bellini's *I Capuleti e i Montecchi* at the Pergola. In the same year another Frenchman, Felice Le Monnier, settled in Florence and in a short time launched one of the most celebrated publishing houses in Europe. In 1833 Donizetti presented *La Parisina* at the Pergola, a work expressly commissioned by the impresario, Alessandro Lanari. Particularly important events in the next decade include: the birth, in 1834, of the Società Filarmonica, dedicated to the dissemination of the so-called "musica classica," namely, symphonic and chamber music, especially of ultramontane composers; the publication in 1836 of *I canti popolari toscani* of Luigi Gordigiani (pianist and composer known as "the Italian Schubert" for his cultivation of a field virtually forgotten in Italy—though not in Florence—vocal chamber music); and the founding of the *Rivista Musicale di Firenze* in 1840, to be followed around 1844 by other musical publications edited by Gian Gualberto Guidi, a contrabassist at the Pergola. In these years Florence had also witnessed the Italian premieres of Meyerbeer's *Robert le diable* (1840) and Weber's *Der Freischütz* (1843). Between 1843 and 1846, the Pergola had produced six of Verdi's nine operas, all, with one exception (*Nabucco*), within nine months of their world premieres.[4] We must also cite the presence in Florence of many writers (from Gian Pietro Vieusseux to Giuseppe Giusti), a sculptor of the stature of Giovanni Dupré, and, about to burst forth in 1848, the avant-garde painters who would be known as the *"macchiaoli"* (named after *"macchia,"* patch or spot).

I have lingered over the varied panorama of this half century of Florentine culture to provide a context for the reactions that Verdi and his music aroused in musical circles before his arrival in Florence for *Macbeth* and to help to clarify the responses of the Florentine critics, both in their immediate reactions and in their more studied reflections, such as those of Basevi. I would include among the constants of the Florentine cultural tradition a horror of rhetoric, a resistance to letting oneself be carried away by enthusiasm, distrust of innovations arising from mere fashion rather than artistic necessity, an attraction to rationalism—but a rationalism capable of accommodating even the dramatic absurdities, the "lack of realism," inherent in opera.[5] These attitudes and the fact that Florence has always been—even in its less celebrated epochs—the most European of Italian cities, allow one to understand the kind of love-hate relationship that was established between Florentine culture and Verdi from the very first appearances of his works. To be sure, there were errors of perspective, but these too can be understood as part of the intellectual and artistic tradition that made Florence at the same time the city for which Verdi chose to create his

---

2. Though performances were rare, they were not unknown: Rossini had directed the work at the San Carlo Theatre (Naples) in April 1821 (Weinstock, *Rossini*, p. 109), and the young Verdi was to direct a performance in Milan in 1834 (Walker, *The Man Verdi*, pp. 16–17).

3. David Cairns, ed., *The Memoirs of Hector Berlioz* (New York: Norton, 1975), pp. 160–62.

4. As might be expected, the three works still awaiting their Florence premiere were *Oberto*, *Un giorno di regno*, and *Alzira*; *Nabucco* (1842) had not been performed there until January 1844.

5. One sees this from Bardi's Camerata to the success of the "classic" Rossini among the nineteenth-century Florentine elite. See Adelmo Damerini, *Il R. Conservatorio di musica "Luigi Cherubini" di Firenze* (Florence: Le Monnier, 1941), p. 14; Leonardo Pinzauti, "Prospettive per uno studio sulla musica a Firenze nell'Ottocento," *Nuova Rivista Musicale Italiana* 2 (1968), 255–73.

Macbeth in 1847, a city not easily swept away by unthinking enthusiasm for him, and the city where the first brilliant monograph about his works, Abramo Basevi's *Studio sulle opere di Giuseppe Verdi,* would appear in 1859.[6]

It is in this climate, summarized so briefly here, that we must place the reviews of *Macbeth* in the Florentine press of 1847.[7] Understandably enough, the Florentine critics, both in praising and in censuring Verdi, wished to project the image of intellectual objectivity, without partisanship either for or against this new star of Italian opera. Nevertheless, in the subconscious of this elite, Verdi bore the "guilt" of being a phenomenon sufficiently vigorous to retard or compromise the efforts to revive the so-called "musica classica," and, in particular, the performance of instrumental music. For example, Luigi Ferdinando Casamorata, in the first dispatch about *Macbeth* that he sent to the *Gazzetta Musicale di Milano,* makes a brief report about the performance of the opera, then proceeds to discuss a recital of the French pianist Émile Prudent in the hall of the Albergo d'Italia. Casamorata notes:

The intellectuals were pleased by his composition entitled *Souvenir de Beethoven,* in a style at once broad, severe, and elegant; the others, as was natural, preferred the new fantasy entitled *Souvenir d'Hernani.* . . Present at the recital was the celebrated Golinelli,[8] who had come to Florence from Bologna to hear it. Prudent announced that he wished to give another recital in a public theater; in the meantime he was invited by the court to play a private recital next Saturday evening in the Ducal Palace.[9]

The composition evoking Beethoven pleased the knowledgeable, but the work based on the themes of Verdi's *Ernani* was better received "as was natural"—"natural" because *Ernani,* being an opera, was therefore intended for an audience much larger than the number of cognoscenti.

In the very first days of *Macbeth*'s run, the violinist Antonio Bazzini gave a number of recitals in the Imperiale e Regio Teatro del Cocomero that served as a point of comparison with the opera. Emphasizing the "brillantissimo" reception of the recital, Casamorata wrote, "In addition to the applause he earned for himself as a performer, he won applause also as a composer, especially for that precious fantasia on Neapolitan popular melodies, a piece in which grace competes with skillful technique."

The Florentine musicians and critics of this period considered themselves to be an elite, an inner circle of specialists with more refined perceptions. We find this attitude in the introduction to Antonio Calvi's article, "The First Performance of M. Verdi's *Macbeth,*" (*Il Ricoglitore,* 20 March 1847). Having referred to the existence of two "opposing factions" of *verdiani* and *antiverdiani*—shades of the Guelphs and Ghibellines—Calvi emphasizes that the first group is much larger than the second, but he goes on to note:

Between them stand a scanty number of those who, considering the issues more tranquilly, while they recognize in *Verdi* an unusual capacity and proclaim him one of the best of our living writers of music, yet do not consider it blasphemous if they dare aver that not everything that emerges from his

6. For Basevi's chapter on *Macbeth,* see "Reviews" at 421–25.

7. A further, larger selection of these appears at 370–96.

8. Stefano Golinelli (1818–91), Bolognese pianist and composer, began his concert career in 1842; Florence was among the first cities in which he performed. See Sergio Martinotti, "Poetiche e presenze nel pianismo italiano dell'Ottocento," *Quaderni della Rassegna Musicale 3* (1965), 181–94.

9. *GMM,* 24 March 1847. All reviews quoted in this article appear in chronological order in the "Reviews" section.

pen is pure gold. And it is these, I think, whose suffrage must be the most welcome and most advantageous to the Lombard Maestro; for those who are not obfuscated with blind passion, be it enthusiasm or envy, are better able, in their judgments, to hold to the path of reason and of the eternal laws of the beautiful. To this not very numerous band we glory in belonging.

This detached attitude is found also in several articles from Enrico Montazio's *Rivista:* C. Mellini's discussion, "Concerning the Musical Style of Maestro Giuseppe Verdi," and a number of pieces signed by Montazio himself.[10] In the first of his own articles, Montazio states: "The public gave vent neither to fanaticism nor to enthusiasm: it judged fairly," even though he later reports the fact that after the performance of his new opera, Verdi was escorted to his hotel by "a cheering swarm of Florence's finest youth." Montazio's "finest youth," it is easy to see, is not to be confused with the "vulgar herd" of "fanatic admirers."

And if this reserved, impartial attitude is shared by all the Florentine commentators, who often reached different conclusions about the music of *Macbeth*, it is symptomatic that they agreed in their negative judgment of the opera's libretto and its author, Francesco Maria Piave. Antonio Calvi in *Ricoglitore*, the caustic Montazio, and the haughty Casamorata—all mercilessly attached the unfortunate poet, who, however, has only recently gained so many influential advocates among the ranks of literary scholars (though less so from musicians). But in the rarefied cultural climate of Gian Pietro Vieusseux, of Gino Capponi, and of Giuseppe Giusti, the gawky verses of Piave could not possibly win favor and were inevitably viewed as another typically shoddy example of the "World of Opera"—an example against which one had to take a firm stand. This attitude can perhaps be viewed as the reemergence, from underground channels, of that feeling for the dignity of the word, that attraction to "rationalism," which, two and a half centuries earlier, had given birth in Florence to the *"opera in musica"* in reaction to music's excessive power over poetry. In their discussions of *Macbeth*, Calvi and Montazio pay much more attention to the libretto than to the music; even Casamorata's long, serialized article, while concerned primarily with the music, dedicates no little space to an analysis of the libretto. If these writers chose to mask their criticism of Maestro Verdi behind a show of formal respect, poor Piave bore the brunt of all their ill-temper. Calvi, for example, refused to believe that Maffei had collaborated in the libretto, and considered it an outright slander about this "noted professor, the elegant translator of many fine works of foreign literature,"

for verses of the kind of those which I shall have the displeasure of citing to you—and you the displeasure of hearing—could not possibly have escaped from his pen, not even while asleep . . . There are others who say that all he did was to correct the stupidities of Piave—Herculean task!—but not even this do we believe, for if that were the case, he would not have left the infinite number of them still to be found in the libretto.[11]

In short, Piave is mercilessly scrutinized down to the smallest detail, even to the selection of individual words, as when Calvi, summarizing the plot, writes *"Poscia spariscono* (Thereupon they disappear), or, as Piave would say, *'vaniscono'* (they evanesce)."

Montazio first deals with *Macbeth* in a brief note in the March 17 issue of his *Rivista,* in

10. Montazio was "direttore responsabile" of the *Rivista* (or, as it was known from March 1847, *La Rivista di Firenze*), which was published from March 1843 to June 1848. The dates of the articles are 27 February 1847 (Mellini), 17 March, and 27 March.

11. As Verdi pointed out ten years later, the two numbers written by Maffei were precisely those criticized the most by the Florentine critics (11 April 1857 letter to Tito Ricordi).

which he refers to this new "imposing work," which for its "musical philosophy and its instrumental richness and beauty [seems to be] one of the best and perhaps the most beautiful and perfect of Verdi's operas." Here there is no mention of Piave, but the issue of March 27, entirely dedicated to *Macbeth*, contains Montazio's lengthy essay entitled "*Macbeth*: Profanation in Four Acts by F. M. Piave." Starting from the premise that the "fantastic" and the "supernatural" should be banished from the theatre, Montazio accuses the librettist of rendering every situation "ridiculous." The tone of the article is polemic, facetious, and willfully ironic. For example, when commenting on the phrase Macbeth addresses to his servant—"Tu di sangue hai brutto il volto" (Your face is soiled with blood)—he jokingly maintains that from this phrase one understands how attentive were Macbeth's servants in the execution of his commands, "not losing time in such a superfluous task as washing their faces when they had good news to bring." And so on, on to the conclusion in which Verdi himself is indirectly criticized for having chosen a "trivialissimo" librettist. The young maestro, Montazio writes, should convince himself that "if there are 22,000,000 bipeds in Italy, 21,999,999 would consider themselves covered with indelible disgrace if they were regarded as the father of such an abominable profanation."[12]

The basic criticisms of the Florentine critics, then, depend upon dramatic and literary considerations, and these in turn strongly influence their judgment of the music as well—an unusual criterion in the cultural life of Italy, which had difficulty for so long even in digesting the reforms of Gluck. By reading the Florentine critics, I believe one can understand the thirty-four-year-old composer's ambition to test himself in this fascinatingly ambivalent milieu—a milieu in which battles against the innovations of *Macbeth* might eagerly be undertaken, but one which served as a brake to the further spreading of operas of the older style. In choosing Florence as the proving ground of his *Macbeth*, the young Verdi was probably also attracted by the renown of its intellectuals, and especially by their patriotic commitment to the Risorgimento. But probably what carried the most weight was his realization that he was about to undertake an "experimental" work,[13] a work that would therefore require an especially sharp-witted and sensitive audience.

And indeed, browsing through the 1847 Florentine reviews, whether in their praise or their criticism, one notices that none of the opera's innovations or principal episodes went unnoticed. Thus, while Montazio dwelled upon the "ridiculous pasticcio" of the libretto, it is significant that he asserts that the sleepwalking scene ("the fundamental pivot, the characteristic piece for the opera") and the "marvelous duet" in Act I—precisely the two numbers that Verdi himself considered the "pezzi principali" of the opera[14]—would be sufficient to distinguish *Macbeth* as one of the most original and beautiful of Verdi's works. But he also observes that Verdi is neither Weber, Mozart, Beethoven, nor Meyerbeer, and therefore failed in the "genere fantastico." Because of this, and because of certain pages written "commercialmente," Act III seemed to be a real "aborto"—a miscarriage—in that it tried to wed fantastic music and text without turning to the indeterminate language of orchestral music, that is, without following the path of Weber and Meyerbeer. (Once more one sees how certain characteristics of ultramontane music are used as a touchstone.) Verdi,

12. For further examples see the ironic side comments within Casamorata's plot summary and Basevi's well-known criticism of the choice of a drama "where love plays no part." For a discussion of the critics' objections to Verdi's treatment of the "genere fantastico," see CONATI at 231–34.

13. As Mila terms it in *La giovinezza di Verdi*, p. 272

14. Letter to Cammarano, 23 November 1848

Montazio seems to say, precisely because he is a composer of unusual strength—so much so as to upset the plans of those who, especially in Florence, looked to a restoration of the "Italian classical tradition" and of instrumental music—should no longer be content with retracing the road of *I lombardi*,[15] for example; if, on the other hand, he wishes to follow the road of the "fantastico" he must employ more suitable means, mastering the lessons of the

great German musicians who in their creations reached the heights in this genre, a peak beyond which opens a frightening precipice at the bottom of which there is no longer harmony, but rather a "meccanismo da idioti;" no longer knowledge and skill, but rather the quintessence of pedantry. And at the bottom of this chasm . . . having immersed themselves up to their necks, are the two professed maestri of this genre, the two champions of "musica grottesca" in the 19th century: Hector Berlioz and Félicien David.

Judgments such as these explain a great deal about what the Florentines meant by "classicismo" in their battles on behalf of Beethoven, Mozart, Weber, and Meyerbeer. It was for good reason that they provoked in Verdi and his entourage a rather violent aversion to poor Montazio, regarded by posterity—unjustly, I believe—as a savage critic ("stroncatore") of Verdi,[16] even though his article actually concludes with a veritable shower of praise on the young maestro, singling him out as the most gifted and powerful musician of the day.

Moreover, one finds on careful examination that Montazio's objections are almost identical with those in Casamorata's long article and in the well-known and widely quoted chapter on *Macbeth* in Basevi's study. It is to the credit of these distinguished Florentine critics that many of their opinions are still accepted today. Casamorata considered the procession of Duncan and his followers as "bizarre," noting that it appeared so "ridiculous that the audience would have burst into laughter had it not been for the freshness and charm of that graceful music that the libretto styles rustic ('villereccia'), but which has few rustic characteristics besides the 6/8 meter." He calls the dagger monologue "one of the finest examples of dramatic musical declamation to have come from Verdi's pen," regretting that this most beautiful episode passed unnoticed, even by Verdi's admirers. Nor does he fail to observe the woodwind accompaniment, the dark color of the bass clarinet, and so on. And again it is Casamorata who emphasizes the "tragically sombre coloring" of the sleep-walking scene. He regrets, however, that Verdi, so powerful in the "non-fantastic" parts of the opera, had not abandoned in this ambitious work a certain careless workmanship, almost like one who knows how to write but does not bother about punctuation. He is also perhaps one of the first nineteenth-century Italian critics to complain of the "arpeggios and repeated chords . . . almost always" present in the accompaniments. "And I wrote 'almost'," he added, "because on the other hand a few of them are well worked out, so much so that they show that the maestro, when he wishes, does not lack the ability [for this]." Casamorata advises the young Verdi to learn from Mozart, particularly *Don Giovanni*, recognizing, however, that in the instrumentation of *Macbeth*, Verdi "has come even closer to perfection" than in his earlier works.

15. In fact, Montazio remarks that the chorus of the Scottish refugees would have been beautiful were it not reminiscent of a chorus in *I lombardi*.

16. Montazio has usually been identified as the "Fiorentino" who spoke badly of *Macbeth* in the pages of the Paris *Gazette des Théâtres* (but see note 1 to Muzio's 12 April 1847 letter to Barezzi. Eds.).

Although Basevi was present at the premiere of *Macbeth*,[17] he had much more time than Montazio and Casamorata to reflect upon the *novità* put forward by Verdi at the Pergola, for his *Studio sulle opere di Giuseppe Verdi* appeared only in 1859. Nonetheless, even today his work startles the reader for the acuteness of many of its observations—observations that take one back to the cultural climate of an intellectually daring and skeptical city where, even in a moment of nationalistic fervor, one could affirm without creating a scandal a judgment such as, "the much vaunted simplicity [*facilità*] of many Italian arias is in large part the result of their old-fashioned rhythms." Basevi was not enthusiastic about the sleepwalking scene, but he found the Macbeth-Banquo duet "extremely well conceived" and the duet of Macbeth and Lady Macbeth (Act I), the "crowning piece of the opera." But also in his negative comments, in his horror of Verdi's "shrieking" (*urli*), in his feeling that the apparition scene was "unworthy of carrying Verdi's name," and, in short, in his timely and comprehensive analysis of the phenomenon of Verdi's place in the musical panorama of Italy in the first half of the nineteenth century, it is as though Basevi spoke not in his own right, but as the interpreter and spokesman of a culture that first posed—and posed with a clear and original point of view—the problem of Italian music and its relationship to Western culture as a whole.

17. At this time Basevi had not yet given up his composing career; 1847 is, in fact, the date of the second and last of his operas, *Enrico Howard*.

Verdi, Shakespeare,
and the Libretto

THE SHAKESPEARE VERDI KNEW[1]
William Weaver

Any discussion of Verdi and Shakespeare should begin with the famous letter Verdi wrote to Escudier on 28 April 1865: "He is a favorite poet of mine, whom I have had in my hands from earliest youth, and whom I read and reread constantly." As has been noted elsewhere,[2] this letter clearly indicates that in his young manhood Verdi's knowledge of the poet came exclusively from books; he had seen no Shakespeare performed. In fact, it is likely that the first Shakespeare play he ever saw acted on a stage was *Macbeth*, in London, where he had come in June 1847 (only a short time after the premiere of his own *Macbeth*), to supervise the first production of *I masnadieri*. William Macready was acting at the Princess's Theatre in Oxford Street, giving *Macbeth* in an authentic text. In his diary for 14 June, Macready wrote: "Acted Macbeth in the very ablest manner—quite myself in the character: the audience were greatly excited. Called for and very warmly welcomed."[3]

But if it is evident that the young Verdi knew Shakespeare only from printed texts, we may well ask: Which ones? Verdi was born in 1813. His "early youth" can thus be considered the 1820s or early 30s. Well, it so happens that in those years there was precious little Shakespeare available in Italian, and no complete edition at all.

Apparently the first Shakespeare play to be translated into Italian was *Julius Caesar* in 1756. The translator was Domenico Valentini, and the work was published in Siena. More than forty years later, in 1798, three tragedies were published in Venice, under the title *Opere drammatiche di Shakespeare volgarizzate da una dama veneta*. The Venetian lady's name was Giustina Renier Michiel, and the plays she chose to render in the vulgar tongue were *Othello*, *Macbeth*, and *Coriolanus*.[4] In the years 1814–22, a more serious and methodical translator devoted himself to the English poet, translating a generous selection of the tragedies in several volumes. This man of letters was Michele Leoni, and it is quite possible that Verdi knew him. Leoni was born in 1776 in the town of Borgo San Donnino (now

---

1. See also DEGRADA and PORTER.

2. William Weaver, "Verdi the Playgoer," *Musical Newsletter* 6 (1976), 3–8

3. *The Diaries of William Charles Macready: 1813–1851*; ed. William Toynbee (London: Chapman and Hall, 1912), 2:368

4. Alessandro De Stefani, *Shakespeare: La Tragedia di Macbeth* (Turin: Bocca, 1922)

Fidenza), only a few miles from Busseto; and he died in Parma, where he had spent the last thirty-five years of his life, in 1858. As Secretary of the Accademia delle Belle Arti there, appointed by Marie-Louise, he was a prominent public figure, and by 1858 so was Verdi.

Leoni's translations belong to his young manhood, when he was in exile from Parma for political reasons. He wandered about northern Italy, forming many literary friendships—with Ugo Foscolo in Milan, with Byron, Gino Capponi, G. B. Niccolini in Florence—and he wrote various tragedies and volumes of verse, and he translated a wide variety of works, ranging from Homer and Virgil to Milton, Goldsmith, and Sheridan. His Shakespeare was published in Pisa, that most anglicized of Italian cities at the time, and the translation is of considerable interest, not least because Verdi—or Piave or Maffei—surely had a copy of Leoni's *Macbeth* at hand while the first libretto was being drafted. A modern critic—Alessandro De Stefani, in 1922—has said of Leoni's Shakespeare: "In *Macbeth* he poured the baroque treasure of his arabesques until the tragedy was totally suffocated.... Worse than the many, serious mistakes, it is the error of tone that is dire.[5]

In a preface to his Shakespeare versions, Leoni indicates that his three masters were Vincenzo Monti, Melchiorre Cesarotti, and Vittorio Alfieri—three writers whose concept of poetry and theater was quite far from Shakespeare's. Leoni's preface also tells us a great deal about the attitude of Italian culture toward Shakespeare in the early years of the nineteenth century. Leoni narrates his experience as a Shakespeare translator: he began with *Julius Caesar*, but was shocked that such a lofty subject should begin with a dialogue between a carpenter and a cobbler. He almost gave up the enterprise right there. When he did persevere and came to *Macbeth*, he was equally shocked, and he actually eliminated part of the scene between Lady Macduff and her child, since he considered it too vulgar. For that matter, he was not unwilling to improve Shakespeare. Noting that the English author had neglected to give Christian names to Ladies Macbeth and Macduff, Leoni corrected the omission: the former is named Margherita, the latter Emilia.[6]

Still, in its way, on its own terms, and in the context of the literary taste of the time, Leoni's Shakespeare is no mean achievement. It is, admittedly, surpassed by the translation of Verdi's friend Giulio Carcano, which was published between 1843 and 1852 (including a *Macbeth* in 1848)—some time after Verdi's "early youth." Like Leoni, Carcano translated into verse, and again the influence of Alfieri can be detected; but Carcano has a greater feeling for style and, one suspects, a better knowledge of English. Leoni, in his preface, confesses that he began translating Shakespeare from the French translation of Le Tourneur; but then he took two years off to study English, in order to work directly from the original. At times one feels that those two years were not enough.

Between the Leoni translations of 1814–22 and the Carcano of 1843–52 came those of Carlo Rusconi, in 1838, in prose. Rusconi's versions were reprinted many times and remained widely used even into this century, doing considerable harm to the cause of Shakespeare in Italy. They are, quite simply, execrable. The prose is heavy, flat, cluttered. Often the translator omits expressions that he finds difficult ("rump-fed ronyon," for example, in *Macbeth*) or that he deems improper (again the Lady Macduff scene is abbreviated). Worse still, he adds words—or even sentences—when the fancy moves him. A

5. De Stefani, *Shakespeare* (but Leoni's revised, less baroque, 1820 translation was used for the opera; see PORTER at 351–52.)

6. In the 1820 revision, these Christian names were dropped.

typical Rusconi offense occurs in the sleepwalking scene. In Lady Macbeth's line "Yet who would have thought the old man to have had so much blood in him?," Rusconi adds the modifier "dannato" to "vecchio," altering and cheapening the nightmarishly casual tone of Lady Macbeth's question and thus draining it of its horror.

Rusconi's translation would not be worth much discussion if we did not know that it was his version that Verdi kept at his elbow while working on his opera, in the last months of 1846.[7] In the long letter dated December 10, Verdi gives Piave his own suggested text for the sleepwalking scene. It is clearly drawn from Rusconi. One example. Shakespeare says: "Here's the smell of blood still: all the perfumes of Arabia will not sweeten this little hand." Rusconi goes: "Quest'odore di sangue per tutto mi seque...I più eletti profumi d'Arabia non varranno a rendere tersa questa piccola mano." Verdi to Piave (in the letter just mentioned): "Quest'odore di sangue dappertutto mi segue...Tutti i profumi dell'Arabia non varrebbero a lenire l'odore di questa piccola mano." The first sentence is almost identical, and the use of the verb "valere" is significant (future tense in Rusconi, conditional in Verdi). But there is also the curious word "lenire" to complicate matters. It is used not by Rusconi but by Carcano, whose translation reads: "Qui sempre odor di sangue!/Lassa! tutti i profumi dell'Arabia/Giammai lenir questa picciola mano/Non potran. Lassa me!.."[8]

Elsewhere in the libretto, the presence of some other unusual words indicates that the collaborators also had Leoni's *Macbeth* somewhere around. For example: in Shakespeare [I.7], Macbeth says of Duncan: "His virtues will plead like angels, trumpet-tongued." Rusconi's translation is pedestrian as usual: "Ah! le sue virtù, come altrettanto angeli dalla voce di bronzo, grideranno eternamente vendetta." Leoni interpolates a significant adjective: "sue virtuti, al par d'angioli *irati*/Dalla voce di bronzo..." And, oddly, that adjective—changed into a genitive phrase—appears in the libretto: "Vendetta! tuonarmi, com'angeli d'ira,/Udrò di Duncano le sante virtù" [I, 13].[9] Elsewhere, an even more eccentric expression of Leoni's is taken over into the libretto. Translating "make assurance double sure" [IV, 1], Leoni uses the image of a double hauberk—"doppio usbergo"—an image we find in the libretto but in no other Italian translation of Shakespeare. (There was also an 1830 translation of *Macbeth* by Giuseppe Nicolini—not to be confused with the much-admired Florentine dramatist G. B. Niccolini, Leoni's friend, whom Verdi knew at the time of *Macbeth*. Back in 1975 Francesco Degrada suggested its link with the opera, and clinching evidence has since come to light.[10])

Naturally, in saying these things I am indulging in some guesswork. There are expressions which will be translated by everyone in more or less the same fashion: "good evening" is likely to be "buona sera" no matter who does the translating. So, inevitably, many phrases are similar, if not identical, in Leoni, Rusconi, Carcano, and Verdi. Still, while we guess what versions the composer, Piave, and Maffei had on hand in 1847, we can also guess what ones they did *not*. Frits Noske, is convinced that yet another version of *Macbeth* played a

---

7. On this point, see DEGRADA and PORTER, and especially pp. 351-52. Verdi used Rusconi again for the revised version; see, e.g. the note to his letter of ca. 15 December 1864.

8. Carcano's translation was not published until 1848. It is possible that Verdi saw a manuscript version, but also possible that the 1847 libretto influenced the Carcano translation; see PORTER at 352.

9. In the musical setting, Verdi reversed the opening phrases ("Com'angeli d'ira, vendetta tuonarmi")—and incidentally obscured the rhyme with Lady Macbeth's "Quell'animo trema, combatte, delira."

10. Francesco Degrada, program notes for *Macbeth*, La Scala, Milan, 1975; see also pp. 156n and 456.

significant role in the genesis of Verdi's opera.[11] This *Macbeth* is not exactly Shakespeare's: it is a version of the tragedy that Friedrich Schiller made in 1800 for the Court Theatre in Weimar. Schiller's adaptation is very free. The witches, for example, like true daughters of the Enlightenment, insist that Macbeth is the captain of his own fate, and thus free not to kill Duncan. Schiller also changes radically the scene of the drunken Porter, making his comic speech into a poetic flight, a cross between matins and an aubade. Needless to say, the Porter is cold sober. However, Andrea Maffei, who—as we know—collaborated extensively with Verdi on the libretto, published a translation of the Schiller *Macbeth* in 1863, long after the first version of the opera; but in 1846 he was presumably already familiar with the original German. Noske bases his argument partly on an ingenious, beguiling, but not entirely persuasive examination of some "ritual" scenes in the score, and particularly on the Shew of Kings [IV, 1]. However, I think that on the question of a possible Schiller influence in the *Macbeth* libretto, the verdict must be: unproven.[12]

As I said, much of this discussion is conjecture. We can feel sure that Verdi knew and used the Rusconi translation. I personally believe—and I hope I have shown why—that he also had Leoni and Carcano at hand. But the significant thing about Verdi's *Macbeth*, really, is his choice of the subject in the first place. This was not the first Italian opera with a Shakespearean subject—Rossini's *Otello* was a well-known precedent, though it does not follow the play at all closely. But Verdi's *Macbeth* was the first Italian opera to make a real attempt to be Shakespearean, as we know from the composer's many insistent, angry letters to Piave. Verdi's recourse to Maffei for help is indicative. The composer wanted the moral support of a recognized man-of-letters. And though Maffei has been derided by some modern critics, he was valuable to Verdi, confirming the composer's faith in a drama for which its own translators sometimes felt required to make apologies.

In the very year of Verdi's *Macbeth*—1847—the great Neapolitan critic Francesco De Sanctis, then thirty years old and at the outset of his brilliant career, gave a course on Shakespeare, a bold venture at the time. At one point, the scholar said: "Shakespeare is now much admired...but there are those who continue to reprove him, judging him outside the context of his times, or reproaching him precisely for what there is in him of his times." And further: "Shakespeare has been the banner of the romantic movement...And as there are mixtures and contradictions in real life, so in Shakespeare we find jumbled together the most varied actions, both comic and tragic, juxtaposed."[13] Comic: the Drunken Porter. Verdi, in 1847, did not yet have the courage to include such a bizarre character in a tragic opera. He was to do this only many years later, with Fra Melitone, a different kind of porter, in *La forza del destino,* perhaps the Verdi opera that most nearly creates a Shakespearean world. But even in the early *Macbeth,* Verdi can be said to have achieved what De Sanctis said of Shakespeare: "He joins, to an immense reality, an immense truth and poetry."[14] Even though he omitted the porter—and much else—Verdi showed courage. It was not until he had successfully brought his *Macbeth* to the opera stage that a leading

11. Frits Noske, "Ritual Scenes," 415–39, and "Schiller e la genesi," 196–203

12. Wolfgang Osthoff, in "Die beiden Fassungen," indicates some similarities between the *Macbeth* libretto and Maffei's Schiller translation, but it may well be that the former influenced the latter. See also pp. 156–58 and 353–55.

13. Agostino Lombardo, *Shakespeare e De Sanctis,* (Florence: Le Monnier, 1963), pp. 6, 8

14. Lombardo, *Shakespeare,* p. 9

Italian actor, Alemanno Morelli, dared present the Shakespeare tragedy. In 1849 Verdi's opera came to La Scala for the first time; a few months after it opened, Morelli appeared in Milan in *Macbeth*, in the Carcano translation, the Italian premiere of Shakespeare's tragedy.[15]

I have been unable to find out much about Morelli's production, but I suspect that the play was severely cut. Certainly, a generation later, the *Macbeth* of Ernesto Rossi—also using the Carcano translation—could more aptly have been called "scenes from *Macbeth*." This acting version was printed[16], and it makes illuminating reading. The porter is, expectedly, cut entirely. So is Lady Macduff. Even the scene of Banquo's murder is missing. The long speeches are severely reduced. And there is a further curiosity: Carcano or Rossi apparently altered the original Carcano translation on the basis of the Verdi libretto. In his first translation, Lady Macbeth's opening words were: "Esse mi rincontrâr nel giorno stesso/ Della vittoria..."; Rossi's Lady, like Verdi's, said: "Nel dì della vittoria io le incontrai..."

To conclude my little investigation of Verdi's Shakespeare, I paid a visit to the Villa Sant'Agata. The library there dates almost entirely from the period after 1847. Verdi can have taken few books with him to the villa. But there is the 1838 edition of Rusconi's Shakespeare, as well as the first complete Carcano. Neither, alas, has any autograph annotations or even underlinings. Verdi treated his books with a respect that scholars now can only deplore. There was the French translation by François-Victor Hugo (Victor Hugo's younger son), and a handsome, one-volume illustrated Shakespeare in English, edited by Charles Knight and published in 1852.

In an article written in 1912[17], Michele Scherillo said: "Verdi, who did not know English, preferred to hear his [Shakespeare's] voice in the literal, even if dim versions of Rusconi. Arrigo Boito assures me that, latterly, Verdi had a special liking for the literal and at once literary version of François-Victor Hugo. And, for some passages, it seems that he at times sought an even more faithful interpretation from his wife, since, on the shelf still in the room she occupied, there stands, beside Byron, a handsome edition of the works of Shakespeare in the English text." Actually, the set of François-Victor Hugo's Shakespeare at Sant'Agata has many uncut pages (even in *Macbeth* and *Othello*), while Knight's English edition looks well-thumbed. So I choose to believe that—beyond Rusconi, Leoni, Maffei, beyond even his friend Carcano—Verdi's favorite translator of Shakespeare was that wise and witty observer of men and letters, Giuseppina Strepponi.

15. Hilary Gatti, *Shakespeare nei teatri milanesi dell'ottocento* (Bari: Adriata editrice, 1968). I am grateful to Francesco Degrada for drawing my attention to this volume. A useful appendix lists early performances of ballets entitled *Macbet* (1802) and *Macbetto* (1830); see pp. 454–58. Also in the 1830s a play called *La caduta di Macbet* was performed several times; no information beyond the title has survived.

16. *Macbet*, Carcano translation ("avec le français en regard"), "Répertoire dramatique de M. Ernesto Rossi," (Milano, n.d.; also Paris: Calmann Levy, 1876). An Italian/English translation was published for the Drury Lane performances of 1876.

17. Michele Scherillo, "Verdi, Shakespeare, Manzoni," *Nuova Antologia* 16 (July, 1912)

MADNESS, HALLUCINATION, AND SLEEPWALKING

Jonas Barish

Verdi's *Macbeth,* it has often enough been observed, is an "operatic," as distinct from Shakespeare's "dramatic" *Macbeth.* It treats its original with unceremonious freedom, condensing, expanding, reordering, and embellishing, so as to produce a very different and much more flamboyant-looking work. But it has not quite so often been remarked, and certainly not emphatically enough, that this "operatic" treatment of the story—using the term "operatic" partly in its loose pejorative sense—is by no means an innovation of Verdi's, but stems from a long stage tradition, beginning in Shakespeare's own lifetime, which stressed the spectacular and supernatural elements of the play, promoting Hecate and the witches to the rank of main characters and lavishing attention on such things as interpolated songs and dances, gorgeous costumes, and stage machinery, especially for the "flying" of the witches. Throughout the late seventeenth and eighteenth centuries, and well into the nineteenth, *Macbeth* was played in England in debased versions, first that of William Davenant, then that of David Garrick. The former, especially, made the play over into a kind of operatic extravaganza, punctuated by what Pepys referred to as "divertissements." In short, in the years before Verdi's opera there was no tradition, either in England or on the Continent, of authenticity of performance to which an audience could have appealed or by which it could have judged a new version; and on the other hand, there was a long tradition of *in*authenticity, of deliberate playing-up of the sensational features of the text, which had routinely turned the play into something sometimes actually spoken of as an opera.[1] Verdi's version, then, far from being bizarrely or outrageously theatrical, seems in many respects a heroic effort to *recover* in music something of the spirit of Shakespeare's tragedy.

One obvious way in which Verdi conforms to custom is in greatly expanding the role alloted to the witches. Another is giving such prominence to Lady Macbeth that she becomes a much more potent and commanding figure than her husband. This has consequences for the sleepwalking scene which I should like to comment on. First, Verdi confers exceptional weight and importance on this scene. He makes it the musical high point of the opera. A glance at some statistics may help to clarify the point. Act III of the opera is devoted entirely to Macbeth's second meeting with the witches, his questioning of them, the

---

1. Godefroy, *The Dramatic Genius of Verdi* 1:103–4, has commented on the staging of the play before Verdi. For the stage history, see Hazelton Spencer, *Shakespeare Improved* (Cambridge, Mass., 1927), 152–74; Christopher Spencer, ed. *Five Restoration Adaptations of Shakespeare* (Urbana, 1965); the essay on stage history by C. B. Young in John Dover Wilson, ed. *Macbeth,* 1947 (Cambridge, 1968), lxix–lxxxii; and Bartholomeusz, *Macbeth and the Players,* 1–179 passim. *Macbeth* was translated into Italian a number of times before 1847 (see p. 351), and it was one or more of these versions that Verdi studied. He did not, apparently, see the play in the theatre until after he had composed his own opera. There had been one earlier lyric version, that of Hippolyte Chélard, to a libretto by Rouget de Lisle, done at the Paris Opéra in 1827, so wildly and shamelessly divergent from Shakespeare as to make Verdi and Piave look pedantically faithful by comparison (see p. 457).

apparitions they summon to answer his questions, and the ensuing ballet of undines and sylphs. If we go back to Shakespeare, we find that from this point on—that is, from near the end of Act IV—the play contains about ten scenes, including the incident with Lady Macduff and her child, the English scene in which Malcolm tests Macduff and they plan for the invasion of Scotland, the sleepwalking scene, and a number of shorter scenes that alternate between the advancing army in the field and Macbeth besieged in his castle. All this comes to about 680 lines of text, of which roughly 85, or 1/8 of the total, occur in the sleepwalking scene. In Verdi, the same stretch of action occupies Act IV and consists of three episodes: first, the English scene, where the Scottish exiles mourn their oppressed country and Malcolm arrives to take charge of the campaign; then, the sleepwalking scene; finally, a rapid sequence of vignettes of battle, death, and (in 1865) victory. The act runs (in either version) approximately thirty-five minutes, of which fully a third are devoted to the sleepwalking scene. We know from his letters that Verdi regarded this as one of the two most significant numbers in the opera,[2] but we would know it in any case because of its central position in the act, its length, and the amount of material that has been sacrificed in order to place it in such high relief.

But this is only the beginning. In its own right the scene is an altogether grander and more towering affair than the Shakespearean original. Shakespeare's characters at this point speak prose, as does the Porter when he answers the knocking at the gate, and Lady Macbeth when she reads the letter. The letter obeys a familiar convention of Elizabethan drama; so does the Porter's speech, which is a drunk speech. Verdi, of course, omits the Porter, and he has Lady Macbeth read her letter as melodrama, in a speaking voice through a sustained chord in the strings. A third staple use for prose in the Elizabethan theatre was for madness. (Marlowe had helped to bring this about when he made the Persian queen Zenocrate, in *Tamburlaine the Great,* discover her husband's mutilated body and run lunatic, babbling hysterically.) Prose is used presumably because, lacking a regular metrical basis, it can better express, or better imitate, the disintegration of the mind. It can convey exaggerated and unnatural states of feeling through dislocations of rhythm and syntax that would go more against the grain of verse, by straining metrical regularity. Now drunk scenes, mad scenes, and sleepwalking scenes have at least one thing in common: they all represent a mind in an abnormal condition, one which has thrown off its usual restraints. This is very much the case with Ophelia, of whom one could say, as of Lady Macbeth, that her eyes are open but their sense is shut. Ophelia is unable to recognize the people around her, though her unconscious might. And as Lady Macbeth's repressed guilt comes out in her clutching of the candle, her handwashing, and her compulsive reenactment of the events she has been through, so Ophelia's repressed sensuality comes out in her bawdy jingles and ballads, and her bewildered grief for her father in the addled prose she is given to speak. In both cases, buried feelings swirl to the surface in a seeming disorder. Speech breaks down into disconnected fragments that nevertheless observe a rigorous psychological coherence, as in free association. An analogous moment would be the hero's epileptic breakdown in Act IV of *Othello,* where loss of rational control is mimed by a frantic, ejaculatory prose. Still another such moment would be the heath scenes in *King Lear,* where Lear's ravings, along with the chatter of Edgar disguised as Poor Tom, are cast in a jumbled, headlong prose that reflects Lear's disastrously disintegrated sense of his own identity.

2. See, for example, his 23 November 1848 letter to Cammarano.

A further link between madness and the somnambulism of Lady Macbeth would seem to be suggested in the eighteenth century by the fact that Mrs. Siddons, the most celebrated Lady Macbeth of the day, performed the sleepwalking scene in white satin. This, to at least one observer, indicated lunacy.[3] A convention is evidently at work, one referred to by Mr. Puff, the fatuous playwright of Sheridan's burlesque *The Critic*. His heroine, Tilburina, enters at one point "stark mad in white satin. . . . Yes," he declares, consulting his book, the script of his play, "Here it is. 'Enter Tilburina stark mad in white satin, and her confidant stark mad in white linen.'" White designates the mental disequilibrium of the wearer; while the stuff of which the gown is made designates her social standing.

Finally, we may notice that the sleepwalking scenes in Bellini's *La sonnambula* share resemblances to the mad scenes from other operas of the early nineteenth century—with mad Imogen's in *Il pirata*, Elvira's in *I puritani*, Lucy's in *Lucia di Lammermoor*, Linda's in *Linda di Chamounix*, and Anna's in *Anna Bolena*, not to mention the operatic Ophelia's in Ambroise Thomas's *Hamlet* some years later. What these scenes have in common is an attempt, sometimes primitive, to register madness, or enact it, by emphasizing recitative; by breaking up the vocal line with alternations of feverish agitation and unearthly calm; by sudden changes of tempo (skittish speedings up and slowings down, the appearance from nowhere of rhythmic figures which may as quickly disappear back into nowhere, as thoughts gather, crystallize, and dissolve in the mind); by unforeseen changes of key and mode; by unaccompanied singing, with the orchestra serving merely as intermittent punctuation; and by a good deal of fioritura, especially the running up and down of chromatic scales. These are all ways in which the composers in question try to simulate effects of distraction, though some scenes use them more than others, and the most beautiful of all, that in *I puritani*, uses them very little. Sometimes, too, the cantabile will consist of a kind of pastoral revery, in which the betrayed maiden—for they are nearly all betrayed maidens— dreams of the innocence and idyllic happiness she once possessed, or hoped to possess. One also finds frequent recourse to flowers, dishevelled hair, and other symptoms of the Ophelia syndrome. Some of the scenes, such as that of the mad Lucy, could just as well be termed sleepwalking as mad scenes. The eyes of the protagonists are open, but their sense is shut. They fail to take in their surroundings or the identity of the bystanders, who crowd around them with expressions of horror and sympathy.

Verdi turns his back on all this. He makes no attempt to equate somnambulism with madness. He shuns the devices of musical discontinuity that correspond to the discontinuities of Shakespeare's prose. He had Lady Macbeth's nocturnal mutterings set by his friend and backup librettist Maffei not in prose, as Julian Budden has unaccountably claimed,[5] but in rhymed stanzaic verse: three double quatrains of *versi ottonari*, in which the first and third lines of each quatrain rhyme ("codardo, vegliardo;" "il Sire, pulire;" etc.), as well as the fourth and eighth lines of each brace of quatrains ("entrar, immaginar;" "saprò, non può", etc.), and in which even the fragmentary utterances of the doctor and waiting gentlewoman are fitted carefully into the metrical scheme. Alongside Shakespeare's prose, this makes

3. Bartholomeusz, *Macbeth,* p. 118. Mrs. Siddons appears also to have "based her interpretation partly on the observation of the real behavior of somnambulists" (p. 119). It was in large measure the impact of her performance, which dominated the stage for a generation, which upset the balance of the play in production, tilting it away from Macbeth himself and toward his consort.

4. Richard Brinsley Sheridan, *The Critic: or a Tragedy Rehearsed* (1777), in *Dramatic Works,* ed. Joseph Knight (Oxford, 1944), 332

5. *Operas* 1: 308, but corrected in 3:ix

for a decidedly intricate arrangement. In spite of an occasional rough spot, the verbal medium is highly formalized, highly symmetrized, and on that account alone makes a different impact from its Shakespearean counterpart:

MED.	Vegliammo invan due notti.	
DAMA	In questa apparirà.	
MED.	Di che parlava	
	Nel sonno suo?	
DAMA	Ridirlo	
	Non debbo ad uom che viva...Eccola!...	
MED.	Un lume	
	Recasi in man?	
DAMA	La lampada che sempre	
	Si tiene a canto al letto.	
MED.	Oh come gli occhi	
	Spalanca!	
DAMA	E pur non vede.	
MED.	Perchè sfrega la man?	
DAMA	Lavarsi crede!	

LADY	Una macchia è qui tuttora...	a
	Via, ti dico, o maledetta!...	b
	Una...due...gli è questa l'ora!	a
	Tremi tu?...non osi entrar?	c
	Un guerrier cosi codardo?	d
	Oh vergogna!...orsù t'affretta!...	b
	Chi poteva in quel vegliardo	d
	Tanto sangue immaginar?	c

MED.	Che parlò?...	

LADY	Di Fiffe il Sire	e
	Sposo e padre or or non era?...	f
	Che n'avvenne?...e mai pulire	e
	Queste mani io non saprò?...	g

DAMA E MED.	Oh terror!...	

LADY	Di sangue umano	h
	Sa qui sempre...Arabia intera	f
	Rimonda si piccol mano	h
	Co'suoi balsami non può.	g

	Oimè!...	
MED.	Geme?	
MED.	I panni indossa	i
	Della notte...Or via ti sbratta!...	j
	Banco è spento, e dalla fossa	i
	Chi morì non surse ancor.	k

MED.	Questo a presso?...	

LADY	A letto, a letto...	l
	Sfar non puoi la cosa fatta...	j
	Batte alcuno!...andiam, Macbetto,	l
	Non t'accusi il tuo pallor.	k
DAMA E MED.		
	Ah di lei, pietà, Signor!	k

But this greater verbal intricacy is not all. Verdi respects the integrity of the strophic form and reflects it in the music. The musical phrases correspond closely to the verbal phrases. The treatment is by and large syllabic; except in the cadenzas, there is little melisma. Pauses tend to occur at the same points. The rhymes are heard clearly, and the stanzas (with one exception) are marked off from each other by orchestral bridge passages. Moreover, after the second stanza the character of the orchestral accompaniment changes sharply with each successive stanza, further reinforcing the separate identity of each. The scene starts, we must note too, with its own extensive and solemn prelude, which serves as a formal introduction to the dialogue of the Doctor and the Gentlewoman, which itself provides a suspenseful prelude to Lady Macbeth's aria. All this makes for a far more elaborate preamble than in Shakespeare. Then comes the high formalism of the aria itself, with its complex orchestral obbligato punctuated by the recurrent wail of the English horn on a minor second, and with separate climaxes for each stanza—separate cadenzas, indeed, for three of them. Each of these principal climaxes, in the second, fourth, and sixth stanzas, reaches a higher point of tension than those before it, until, after the final climactic climax, a coda follows in which, first vocally and then instrumentally, the throbbing intensity dies away and loses itself in silence.

We have then a highly organized framework into which is inscribed a series of highly organized inner parts. As a result, and as a result also of the arching and luscious character of the melody, Verdi's sleepwalker makes an impression of power and grandeur, very different from that of the pitiable wreck who murmurs her broken phrases in the original tragedy. Clearly, Verdi is not trying to simulate the effects of madness or distraction found in comparable scenes by his predecessors. And this, interestingly, directly reverses his procedure earlier in the opera, in the dagger soliloquy, where he not only adopts all the conventions for rendering madness, but extends and intensifies them. Macbeth's blank verse is turned into *versi sciolti* by the librettist, and then set as an irregular, jagged recitative, parlando throughout, with frequent breakings off, abrupt changes of tempo, and sudden shifts of key. Though more powerful and expressive, the technique is reminiscent of that in Bellini's and Donizetti's mad scenes, and for good reason: Macbeth is hallucinating at this point, and is in fact on the verge of what we would call madness if it went any further or persisted for very long. Verdi instructs his baritone to sing *sotto voce e cupo* for most of the scene, and he eschews all melodic sumptuousness, the better to counterfeit the agitated, discontinuous motions of a deranged spirit. At a given moment, Macbeth is pulled back from the brink by the sound of the bell, which tolls him back to his true self, or at least to a semblance of lucidity. "È deciso," he announces, "quel bronzo ecco m'invita." Now at last he is permitted full-throated utterance, *a voce spiegata:* "Non udirlo Duncano! È squillo eterno / Che nel cielo ti chiama, o nell'inferno." In this sequence, then, hallucination is treated musically as a species of madness, while in Act IV the sleepwalking is treated more as a kind of meditation, in which the serenity and splendor of the vocal line work in some degree against the disruptions indicated in the words.

Another capital difference may be remarked between Shakespeare's scene of sleepwalking and Verdi's. The scene in Shakespeare, like Ophelia's mad scene in *Hamlet*, is a scene of *recollection*. The sleeper replays in her imagination all the crucial moments of the action. The dispute over Macbeth's valor, the sound of the bell, the sight of the murdered Duncan weltering in his blood, the washing of the blood from their hands, the hasty donning of night clothes, the marching off to bed, the dreadful appearance of Banquo at the feast, and the terrible fate of Lady Macduff and her children—all these horrifying moments from the ordeal she and her husband have inflicted on themselves (as well as on others) come surging pell-mell into Lady Macbeth's mind as she stalks about the stage in her trance. They form the substance and also the texture of Shakespeare's scene, a mosaic or crazy-quilt of appalling memories, which she would strip from her brain as she would rinse the blood from her hands. Most of it, to be sure, can still be heard in the language of the scene, but in an opera it is the music that counts, and here the music does not remember very much. Verdi deliberately passes up the opportunities for motivic recall offered by the text, which would have been an obvious and natural way to preserve Shakespeare's recapitulatory effect. He would certainly not have lacked precedent had he followed such a course. During the mad scene in *Lucia di Lammermoor*, the orchestra plays a fragment from Lucy's earlier love duet with Edgar, in a new key, to suggest the memory flitting through Lucy's disordered mind, while in Linda di Chamounix's delirium scene not only does the orchestra recall the tune Linda sang in her Act I duet, when she and Carlo prayed for the happy accomplishment of their love, but Linda herself remembers it, and in the same key, and with the same words. Bellini's *sonnambula*, walking in her sleep for the second time, revisits, through orchestral fragments, the wedding scene she dreamed of when she walked in her sleep the first time. Verdi himself had experimented with the device in *Nabucco*, where the monologue of the demented king Nebuchadnezzar "involves several past themes as well as a future funeral march."[6] He would hardly, then, have been setting out to create any new custom had he resorted to some such procedure to render Lady Macbeth's flood of memory. He may have felt, indeed, that such treatment would be too banal, too literary, or he may have felt that to invoke it on anything like the grandiose scale needed to convey the swollen tangle of memories in Lady Macbeth would stretch the convention to the breaking point. In any case, he almost ostentatiously refrains from adopting anything like it.[7] Lady Macbeth's outpouring consists of entirely new material. It carries us not back into the subterranean chambers of her soul but forward into an unexplored realm of tormented sensibility.

Verdi thus confers on the whole scene the character of a splendid set piece, which crowns all that has preceded it but does not, as in Shakespeare, convey the same sense of a crumpled, defeated, decomposed personality. If anything, the sleepwalking aria forms a last gorgeous act of assertion, with only the slight jumpiness of the orchestral figure to remind us of the undercurrent of derangement. Despite Verdi's insistence that his heroine not sing at all in

6. Joseph Kerman, "Verdi's Use of Recurring Themes," in H. Powers, ed., *Studies in Music History, Essays for Oliver Strunk* (Princeton, 1968), p. 499

7. The fact that in preparing the libretto for this scene Verdi at one point wrote in, then later scratched out, a direct quotation from a phrase spoken earlier by Lady Macbeth (see DEGRADA, at 170–71), makes it plain that at least in the case of the text he made a conscious decision *not* to use elements of direct recall. From which one may reasonably infer that he made a similar decision for the musical setting.

this scene, or sing only in a raw, choked, hollow voice, despite his objection to Tadolini on the ground that she was too beautiful, too perfect,[8] it is hard to imagine the Lady Macbeth of this scene as other than beautiful, and hard, above all, to imagine this extraordinarily sumptuous music being sung other than beautifully. To put it another way, Verdi apparently thought he had written music which for greatest effectiveness should be sung *un*beautifully, whereas, in fact, the natural character of the music is such that it must almost of necessity be sung "beautifully." My guess is that Verdi was trying to make the soprano do with a deformed appearance and a distorted voice what the score was reluctant to do for her.

His instructions remind us, however, that he is not so much interested in making Lady Macbeth psychologically convincing as in making her vivid and terrifying. For not only does he drastically abbreviate and so seriously dilute the impact of the scene immediately following the murder, in which Shakespeare shows her to be already possessed by the blankness and futility that reach their inevitable climax in the sleepwalking scene, but he inserts outbreaks of open triumph and gloating from her, which forbid any hint of the coming collapse that Shakespeare charts so carefully.[9] Verdi never quite allows her the psychological veracity that marks her Shakespearean model. What he provides, in truth, is something closer to the "fiend-like queen" of Malcolm's final description, just as he provides a Macbeth closer to the "dead butcher" of the same speech. What he also provides, however, as he does always, is the depiction of a state of blazing passion, here one of burning anguish and remorse, with a purity that has rarely been equalled either in literature or in music.

8. Verdi's letter of 23 November 1848 to Cammarano.

9. Schmidgall, *Literature As Opera,* 207, accounts for Verdi's making Lady Macbeth's "insanity" (*sic*) so abrupt, on the ground that "it is equally abrupt in Shakespeare." But in fact, Shakespeare prepares us for it well in advance. Verdi does the reverse. He sets all the signals going in the opposite direction, so that when the breakdown comes we have had no forewarning, no prior inkling at all of what the character has been going through inside.

OBSERVATIONS
ON THE GENESIS
OF VERDI'S *MACBETH*[1]

Francesco Degrada

Verdi's correspondence has allowed us to define in detail Francesco Maria Piave's contribution to the libretto of *Macbeth,* but until now Andrea Maffei's contribution has remained enigmatic. In this, Verdi's first encounter with Shakespeare, Piave's task was purely technical: the composer's dramatic conception was fully and clearly defined, and Piave was required merely to clothe it in poetically appropriate language. Verdi provided detailed suggestions and advice, and even versified whole sections himself, but that did not help Piave out of his difficulties. The history of relations between Verdi and Piave, at least as regards *Macbeth,* is that of a failure, as is documented by Verdi's letter to Piave of 21 January 1847:

Oh no indeed, you're not at fault at all—except for having taken so incredibly little trouble with these last two acts of mine. But never mind! St. Andrew [Andrea Maffei] came to your aid and to mine. Especially to mine, because—if I must be frank with you—I couldn't have put them to music, and you can see what a mess I'd have found myself in. Now everything is fixed up, but just about everything had to be changed.[2]

Verdi later summarized Maffei's contribution thus:

Ten years ago I got it into my head to write *Macbeth;* I wrote the scenario [*selva*] myself and, indeed, more than the scenario; I wrote out the whole drama in prose, with divisions into acts, scenes, numbers, etc., etc...then I gave it to Piave to put into verse. Since I found things to criticize in the versification, I asked Maffei, with the consent of Piave himself, to go over those lines, and rewrite entirely the *witches' chorus* from Act III, as well as the *sleepwalking scene.* (11 April 1857 letter to Tito Ricordi)

---

1. For a comprehensive critical evaluation of *Macbeth* see my "Lettura del *Macbeth*" and my *"Macbeth: Commentaire littéraire et musical,"* in *L'Avant-Scène,* March–April 1982, pp. 26–77.

2. Piave's reaction to this letter was to emphasize his role as author of the *Macbeth* libretto. On 23 January 1847 he asked whether Ricordi had received from Verdi a preface to the libretto; if not, Piave would send him a copy because "it is absolutely my intention that your publication should be preceded by this note *of mine."* [Italics here and in the following quotation are mine]. Five days later he sent Ricordi the preface, defining it in his covering letter as "indispensable for a full understanding of *our* [Piave's and Verdi's] treatment of Shakespeare's play." Piave's preface (placed with his 28 January 1847 letter) is a summary (including verbatim quotations) of the *Notizia ai lettori* that Giuseppe Nicolini placed at the head of his translation of *Macbeth* (see p. 38). Piave's preface, hitherto unknown, is interesting for several reasons. It demonstrates that Piave knew Nicolini's translation; it furnishes a key to Piave's interpretation of the drama; and it shows that Piave was not aware of the precise changes made by Maffei (for example, Piave still uses the Shakespearian term "thane," which Verdi and Maffei had replaced with "sire").

Not only was Piave's preface not incorporated into the Florentine and Ricordi editions of the libretto, but the poet did not even receive a copy of the libretto, as his 27 April 1847 letter indicates.

According to this account, Maffei was brought in only after the libretto—or at least its structural framework—had come into being. Maffei's task was to versify two particularly problematical sections (one of which, however—the sleepwalking scene—had already been sketched to Verdi's satisfaction)[3] and to look over the whole to bring it more closely into line with the composer's conception. As we shall see presently, Maffei probably also wrote the whole of II.4 (Banquo's scena), a late addition, probably made during the Florence rehearsals.

On the basis of this, it is clear that Verdi turned to Maffei only because Piave had fallen short of even the most pessimistic predictions, and that Maffei's contribution was to be of a subordinate nature with respect to the overall conception. This in itself should be enough to lay to rest the notion that Maffei exerted a determining influence on the form of the libretto or on the "ideological" interpretation of Shakespeare's tragedy. But certain issues external to the opera itself have led some critics to attribute to Maffei virtues that he did not possess and work that had, in fact, never been asked of him. These issues include: his long association with Verdi during the preparation of *I masnadieri;* the position Maffei, because of his work as a translator, assumed in nineteenth-century Italy (and not only in his dealings with Verdi) as a cultural middleman; and finally the fact that Maffei published (if only in 1863 and through the intermediary step of Schiller's adaptation) a translation of *Macbeth* in which there are, in fact, certain parallels with the Verdian libretto, although it seems to me that they are of small importance.[4] The real source of such notions, however, is the hidden conviction that Verdi on his own could not have stood up to the awesome confrontation with Shakespeare, that he lacked the cultural equipment to condense into an opera one of Shakespeare's most problematic and complex tragedies without falsifying its meaning. And, as though Maffei were not enough, frequent reference is made to unspecified contributions of another able translator and friend of Verdi's, Giulio Carcano, because it is known that at the end of 1846 he and Verdi spent some time together at Clarina Maffei's villa in Clusone.[5] Rumors to this effect began to circulate before the first performance, and on 27 February 1847 Carcano hastened to inform Maffei that he had had to "protest that there wasn't one syllable of mine, and that I didn't do anything besides discuss this tragedy with our friend Verdi." It is not even certain that Verdi had Carcano's translation in hand—it was not published until 1848—although according to one (late and unverified) account, Verdi had *heard* Carcano himself read his translation aloud in Clusone.[6] But Verdi in his long, solitary meditations on Shakespeare[7] had been able to find solid support in a critical mind far deeper and sharper than that of a Maffei, a Carcano, or a Piave.

This was August Wilhelm Schlegel. Verdi was clearly suspicious of the accuracy of the verse translations current in Italy in the first half of the nineteenth century (those of Leoni, Nicolini, and others), and read Shakespeare in Carlo Rusconi's prose translation; this is borne out by an examination of the "selva" of *Macbeth,* which displays frequent parallels with that translation. As an appendix to his *Macbeth,* Rusconi had published some illu-

---

3. See Verdi's 10 December 1846 letter to Piave.

4. Cf. Noske, "Schiller e la genesi," 196–203. See also WEAVER at 146–47 and PORTER at 353–55.

5. *Abbiati* 1, 637, 639, 666–67

6. See Giulio Carcano's 27 February letter, note.

7. "He is one of my favorite poets, whom I have had in my hands since early youth, and whom I read and reread continually" (28 April 1865 letter to Escudier).

minating pages from Schlegel's celebrated *Course of Lectures on Dramatic Art and Literature*.[8] Their influence on Verdi's interpretation of *Macbeth* is clear: not only did the composer follow Schlegel in his delineation of the opera's formal and expressive structure, but he paraphrased his key concepts and even quoted him in his letters to Piave and others.

Among these concepts are: the idea that Shakespeare expressed through the witches—a projection of popular traditions deeply engrained in the hearts of men—"that dread of the unknown, that presage of a dark side of nature and of a world of spirits"; that he created for them "a language of their own" which evokes "the hollow music of the nocturnal dances of these tenebrous beings"; that "with one another the witches discourse like women of the very lowest class" but that "when," however, "they address Macbeth they assume a loftier tone"; that "their predictions ... have all the obscure brevity, the majestic solemnity of oracles"; that Macbeth is a "noble but ambitious hero ... all [of whose] crimes ... cannot altogether eradicate the stamp of native heroism"; that "truly frightful is it to behold that same Macbeth, who once as a warrior could spurn at death, ... clinging with growing anxiety to his earthly existence ... and pitilessly removing out of the way whatever to his dark and suspicious mind seems to threaten danger"; and that "we cannot refuse to compassionate the state of his mind"; or, further, the idea that Lady Macbeth is "the most guilty of all the participators in the king's murder" while Macbeth himself "is still found worthy to die the death of a hero on the field of battle." All of this coincides perfectly with Verdi's interpretation. And which scenes of the play, according to Schlegel, are the most striking for the terror they evoke? "The murder of Duncan, the phantom dagger that hovers before the eyes of Macbeth, the vision of Banquo at the feast, the nocturnal entry of Lady Macbeth, walking in her sleep"—a choice which sounds like a list of the high points of Verdi's *Macbeth*.

Surely it is not by chance that, after the classicistic criticism with which the opera was greeted in Florence, a preface summarizing Schlegel's ideas should have been added (certainly at Verdi's wishes) to the "standard" Ricordi libretto as early as spring 1848 (see pp. 349-50).

It is noteworthy that in those very pages Schlegel should have deplored the distortion of Shakespeare's play perpetrated by Schiller in *his* version of *Macbeth* (the very version that Maffei later used for his Italian translation). It is questionable to credit Maffei with having involved Verdi with the new twist introduced by Schiller, the conflict between free will and determinism, for Verdi's *Macbeth* is anything but a tragedy of fate. It is, rather, a moral drama in which the lacerating conflict of the protagonists with their own conscience is always in the forefront, a drama of souls realistically enmeshed in history, in the web of their conditioning and their contradictions, in the ruthless struggle between holders of power, in the tragic link between the destiny of individuals and the collective destiny of a people.[9]

8. See pp. 346–48. For Rusconi's translation, see WEAVER at 145–46 and PORTER at 351–52; a copy of this translation is still at Verdi's bedside at Sant'Agata. The libretto's dependence upon Rusconi's translation was demonstrated in 1968 by Gerhartz (*Die Auseinandersetzungen*, pp. 377, n.182, and 382, n.216).

Recognition of Verdi's awareness of Schlegel can be traced back to Monaldi's *Verdi, 1839–1898* (Turin: 1899, pp. 250–51), as I noted in my essay "*Otello*, da Boito a Verdi" (first printed in a program booklet for the Teatro alla Scala, 1976, and now reprinted in *Il palazzo incantato* 2, 166, n.13).

9. The classicistic misinterpretation of Schlegel's ideas is quite clear in the preface that Maffei wrote in 1863 for his translation of Schiller's *Macbeth* adaptation: he still regards the work as a "tragedy of fate."

For a comparison of Verdi's and Maffei's interpretation of the play see my "*Macbeth*, un'opera sperimentale"

Having stressed the subordinate role played by Maffei in the overall conception of the opera, I would now emphasize his function as a capable reviser of the libretto sketched by Piave and as the intelligent implementor of Verdi's conceptions. My starting point is a valuable document never before studied: a manuscript copy of the *Macbeth* libretto in Verdi's own hand, strewn with Maffei's corrections.[10] This is in Milan in the Museo Teatrale alla Scala (C.A. 6415). Together with other documents, this libretto, of which I have prepared an edition (see pp. 306-08), sheds new light on Verdi's creative process and the formation of the dramatic structure of his *Macbeth*.

The manuscript, as far as is known, was once the property of the Casa di Riposo per i Musicisti of Milan and therefore can be supposed to have come directly from Verdi. That it is autograph is not in doubt: see the reproductions of the pages containing the first two scenes (Illus. 1-2). Corrections in a second hand are apparent—the obvious candidates for their authorship are Piave and Maffei. The hand is not Piave's (see Illus. 3); that it is Maffei's is borne out by comparison with his letter to Verdi of 11 April 1847 (Illus. 4).

How did this manuscript version of the libretto come about? As Piave versified and reversified Verdi's draft text—with less than satisfactory results, to judge from Verdi's comments—the composer must have felt the need to make a fair copy of a version doubtless covered with additions and corrections. He wished—or was compelled—to consider this, at least provisionally, as the version needed to begin composition. But he remained dissatisfied with certain lines and even whole scenes, and his attempts to get Piave to set these right met with scant success.

The existence of a version of at least some versified scenes predating the manuscript libretto is proved by numerous indications in the letters. Verdi's 22 September 1846 letter to Piave shows that the first four scenes had been differently conceived and versified by the librettist. The same is true of Lady Macbeth's *cavatina*, from which several lines are quoted that are no longer present in our source, and the 22 December 1846 letter provides similar information about the last act. Other scenes are discussed in detail below. Furthermore, in the autograph score I.11 originally closed with "È suono eterno / che nel cielo ti chiama o nell'inferno," but "suono" was later amended to "squillo," in conformity with the only reading of the manuscript libretto. Verdi apparently composed this scene at least from a version of the text predating the compilation of the autograph libretto.

When, toward the end of 1846, it became clear that Piave would not be up to satisfying Verdi's demands, the composer turned to Maffei. For the first two acts, Maffei's task was only to make additions and corrections to a text already substantially settled and even, as we shall see, set to music in part. While many alterations were made, they were not so radical as to require recopying of these acts: thus the abundance of alterations recorded in the first half of the manuscript. For the third and fourth acts, which we know to have been

(program booklet for the Teatro alla Scala, 1975, pp. 7-29) and "Lettura del *Macbeth*." Already in the first of these two essays, I demonstrated Verdi's complete independence from Maffei in the dramatic conception of *Macbeth* (see especially pp. 8-10). Shakespearean influences on the libretto are also discussed in Gerhartz, *Die Auseinandersetzungen*, pp. 82ff., and Schmidgall, *Literature as Opera*, pp. 181-215.

10. That these corrections are in Maffei's hand was demonstrated—on the basis of documents supplied by the present writer—by Daniela Goldin in a paper read at the international meeting "Il melodramma romantico in Italia ..." (Venice, Fondazione Giorgio Cini, 15-17 September 1977). For the published version of this paper, "Il *Macbeth* verdiano ...," see the *Bibliography*.

the most "carelessly handled" by Piave, Verdi probably recopied the libretto *after* Maffei had himself rewritten the most problematical scenes. This explains why the witches' chorus that opens Act III and the sleepwalking scene have few corrections, even though Verdi tells us that these two numbers were entirely rewritten by Maffei.

If this theory is correct, the further corrections in Acts I and II of this manuscript are yet later thoughts, part of the process of revision that continued to within a few days of the Florence premiere. Differences in ink and a comparison with the readings of the autograph score seem to confirm that the text underwent further changes by Maffei and by Verdi himself after the first revision of Piave's work.

The date of Maffei's first and presumably most substantial revision may be placed between the end of December 1846 (on December 22 Verdi again asked Piave to send him the last act) and 21 January 1847 when Verdi brusquely advised his collaborator of the decisive intervention of "Sant'Andrea." This is supported by Verdi's 7 January 1847 letter to Varesi, in which the creator of the role of Macbeth was asked to make certain changes in the text of the banquet scene (which he had received from Verdi *before* 19 December 1846),[11] corresponding to the new version prepared by Maffei, with one further correction made to that by Verdi himself. Thus, 7 January 1847 must be considered—at least as regards that scene—as the *terminus post quem non* for Maffei's intervention.

Let us now examine this new source, treating it as evidence for a survey of the genesis of *Macbeth*,[12] rather than as a literary document. (We will not deal with various basic, "canonical" topics such as the relationship of the libretto to the Shakespeare play—topics which can now be approached with new and significant data.) As mentioned above, Acts I and II show the largest number of corrections and additions by Maffei; they also shed light on previous stages of the making of the libretto. In other words, they show us passages from Piave's original version, rejected and changed by Verdi himself even before Maffei's intervention.

The most significant case is found in II.1, one of the most troublesome passages in the whole of the preparation of the libretto. On 25 October 1846, Verdi wrote to Piave:

At the beginning of the second act of *Macbeth*, don't have the Lady, in her soliloquy, write the letter to Macbeth about the murder of Banquo. I don't like having her write a letter in that hall; instead, it can be done just as well in a few words, without having her write the letter.

"Banquo and his son live...but Nature did not create them immortal...Oh Macbeth...a new crime...Enterprises begun, etc..."

Four days later, he suggested, "In the Lady's first scene in Act II have her say just one simple sentence alluding to the murder of Banquo...'Oh Macbeth, another crime is needed!'" Nothing remains of the very first draft of this scene, but the autograph libretto does preserve the version that immediately followed it. Here is the new scene written by Piave, perfectly parallel to I.5 (even after the inessential motif of the letter was removed): again there is a soliloquy for Lady Macbeth that, after a quick summary of events, ends in a *cabaletta* in dark nocturnal colors (of clear Shakespearean parentage) in which Lady Macbeth turns her thoughts toward a murder she intends her husband to commit:

---

11. In a letter written on that date, Muzio reported that Varesi had already left for Rome, carrying with him, and praising highly, the *Convito* and *Visione*.

12. Further discussion of the libretto will appear in the introduction and apparatus of the critical edition of *Macbeth* that I am preparing.

Illus. 1 and 2: the opening scenes of Macbeth *in the "Scala" libretto.*

Illus. 3: An 1847 Piave letter (and see page 78)

Illus. 4: Maffei's letter to Verdi of 11 April 1847 (transcribed on page 59)

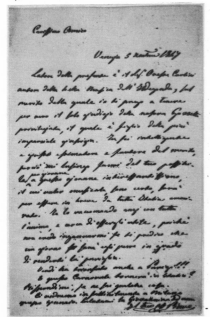

The witches spoke true, and thou art king,
Macbeth! The son of Duncan, fleeing
From Scotland into Britain
Was declared a parricide, and left the throne
Empty for you: but the daemonic women
Predicted Banquo the sire of kings...
So will his children reign?...Will it be for him
That Duncan was slain?...He and his son
Live, 'tis true, but life
Of immortal mettle was not allotted them.

Before the dark nocturnal angel
  Flees the morning ray,
  The assassin's dagger
  Has new blood to shed.

An enterprise is brought to conclusion by misdeeds
  If in a misdeed it was cradled,
  O Macbeth, the crown is nothing
  If on the brow it is insecure.

   (*For the Italian text, see pp. 321.*)

Apparently satisfied with this, Verdi transcribed it into the evolving manuscript libretto. But subsequently—perhaps as he began to compose the music of this scene—he had second thoughts. On 3 December 1846 he sent Piave another version, together with instructions and exhortations to be concise (see this letter below). This new version, which transforms the soliloquy into a dramatic confrontation between Lady Macbeth and her husband, regains all the body and complexity of the original Shakespeare, while adopting a significantly different interpretation of the two characters. Here Lady Macbeth is depicted as the real instigator of the crime and Macbeth as her pawn.

Here is Piave's new version, based closely on Verdi's draft:

LADY   Why do you flee me, and why do I
            Ever see you rapt in deep thought?
            The deed is irreparable. The sorceresses
            Spoke true, and you are king.
            The son of Duncan by reason of his sudden
            Flight into England
            Was declared a parricide, and left the throne
            Vacant for you.
MACBETH   But the daemonic women
            Predicted Banquo the sire of kings.
            So will his children reign?...Will it be for them
            That Duncan was slain?
LADY   He and his son
            Live, 'tis true, but do not have
            Life immortal.
MACBETH   That comforts me.
LADY   Another lifeblood must flow...
MACBETH   Another lifeblood?
LADY   You have no choice!

MACBETH	And when?
LADY	When night falls.
MACBETH	Alas, it is necessary!
LADY	Now what do you intend?
MACBETH	Banquo! Eternity opens its realms to you.

(*For the Italian text, see pp. 321–22*)

Two further changes were to be made even after Verdi copied this text into the manuscript libretto. In the first of these, Maffei reverses the roles: it is Lady Macbeth who is carried along by the homicidal fury of her husband:

LADY	He and his son.
	Live, 'tis true...
MACBETH	but do not have
	Life immortal...It is necessary, oh woman,
	That another lifeblood flow.
LADY	Another lifeblood?
MACBETH	It is necessary!
LADY	And when?
MACBETH	When night falls.
LADY	Will you be immovable in your plan?
MACBETH	Banquo! Eternity opens its realm to you.

But Verdi has the last word. By means of an insistent series of insinuating calls to action and pressing questions, he restores the active role of Lady Macbeth in the decision to commit further crimes.

LADY	He and his son
	Live, 'tis true...
MACBETH	but do not have
	Life immortal.
LADY	Ah yes, they do not have that.
MACBETH	It is necessary that another lifeblood flow, oh woman!
LADY	Where? And when?
MACBETH	When night falls.

The progressive transformations of this passage are essential for an understanding of Verdi's relationship with his collaborators, in which Verdi always played a sharply defined and active role, based as it was on a dramatic conception already fully defined in its essentials, susceptible of modification in specifics but not in substance.

The scene here analyzed displays an ever-present characteristic of the genesis of the *Macbeth* libretto: the search for an ever more energetic dramatic dialectic, the abandonment of relatively static in favor of more dramatic, dynamic situations. It also shows a progression from delineating the basic shape of the opera (which underwent no substantial alterations) to polishing and highlighting details barely sketched in the initial writing.

We find this tendency in at least two other numbers, one being the duet "Fatal mia donna." In the first version, Lady Macbeth is savage and inhuman, but—in part for that very reason—monochromatic in the long run, for she acts without hesitation or second thoughts, and therefore without truth.

(The lines subsequently changed are shown in italics.)

MACBETH   Then in my breast I seemed to hear sounding:
        "Thou shalt have only thorns for thy pillow, O Macbeth;
        Glamis, *thou hast driven a stake into sleep;*
        Perpetual wakefulness awaits thee, O Cawdor."
LADY   But, tell me, did you not seem to hear another voice?
        "You are proud, O Macbeth, *but weak and base;*
        Glamis, halfway through the enterprise *courage fails thee;*
        Cawdor, *thou hast the heart of a* windy babe!"
        Take the dagger back there,
        Smear his guards with blood
        That the accusation may fall on them.
MACBETH   I return there? I cannot enter.

(*For the Italian text, see pp. 317–18.*)

The insertion of two more lines for Macbeth:

    I shall hear Duncan's holy virtues
    Thunder revenge at me, like angels of wrath

and of the scornful but secretly terrified aside of Lady Macbeth:

    (That spirit trembles, struggles, raves;
    Who would now call him the invincible hero he once was?)

introduces a play of light and dark that achieves a far greater subtlety and depth of meaning. This becomes even clearer when the music is considered. The four added lines are set to the superb episode in B♭ major that Budden has rightly compared to the B♭ "transfiguring melody" in the quartet of *Don Carlos*.[13] In fact, the reason for the insertion, in this as in other cases, is probably related to musical considerations.

    Something similar is found in the banquet scene. At an early stage, Verdi had considered a festive chorus of guests:

Viva il felice Macbet   Long live fortunate Macbeth
Viva l'amato rè   Long live the beloved king!
A lui onore e gloria   To him honor and glory,
A lui coraggio e fe'!   To him courage and faith!

Apart from the banality of the text, it would have presented a dramatically inert situation. The new version, with its lively give and take between Macbeth, Lady Macbeth and the guests,[14] immediately imparts dramatic movement to the scene by means of effective contrast between the principals and the crowd of guests who will later be alarmed by Macbeth's recurrent fits of terror. A similar need is filled by the choral interjection immediately preceding the *brindisi,* a later addition.

    A few significant examples can help to define other trends in the shaping of the libretto.

13. Comment made in round-table discussion on "Problèmes de Création Musicale au XIXᵉ siecle," *Acta Musicologica* 3–4 (1971), 189

14. See KNOWLES at 285–88 on the use of parlante here.

At an early stage, Verdi had decided on the need for brevity and conciseness in the scenic structure; in his correspondence with Piave "Concise style! Few words!" became a motto. The result was an extremely compressed dramatic scheme, marked by uninterrupted forward motion, even excessively hasty and precipitous in some respects. He may well have been influenced by Schlegel's observation, "it is as if the drags were taken from the wheels of time, and they rolled along without interruption in their descent." Our libretto shows that Verdi continued to follow this line, removing the final obstacles from the swift unfolding of the action.

Here, in III.2, an unnecessarily roundabout phrase is replaced, with the conciseness of an Alfieri, by a single word:[15]

MACBETH *alle streghe*	MACBETH (*to the witches*)
Vivran costor? Voi ditelo	Will these live? Tell me that!
LE STREGHE	WITCHES
Sarà come hai veduto!...	It will be as you have seen!

become the far more effective

MACBETH		MACBETH	
Vivran costor?		Will these live?	
WITCHES	Vivranno!	WITCHES	They will!
MACBETH	Oh me perduto!	MACBETH	Oh, I am lost!

From the touching introduction to Macduff's aria,

O figli, o figli miei! Da quel tiranno	Oh, my children, my children! By that tyrant
Tutti uccisi voi foste e insiem con voi	You all were killed, and together with
La madre *ahi* sventurata! *e quanti accolse*	Your mother, *alas,* unfortunate! *and all who*
L'infelice mia rocca ...	*were assembled*
	In my unhappy castle ...

the allusion to the other victims of Macbeth's ferocity (the italicized text) was removed in order to concentrate attention on the children and their mother mourned in the succeeding *adagio.*

Far more frequent, however, are the opposite sort of changes, aimed at expanding the excessively compressed rhythm that resulted from Verdi's preoccupation with a rapid and concise form. Thus Macduff's *adagio,* originally planned in "two affecting" quatrains, gained a third, concluding quatrain.[16] Macbeth's death scene, originally expressed in six exclamatory *ottonari,* grew to eight broader, more solemn lines set out in two quatrains.

In Act I.3 the last lines for the messengers,

Perchè sì freddo n'udì Macbetto	Why does Macbeth receive the news so coldly?
Perchè l'aspetto non serenò?	Why does his glance not become calm?

---

15. This is not to say that Verdi decided upon the change entirely—or even primarily—for the sake of concision; the change is surely a consequence of the necessity to switch from *versi lirici* to recitative at this point. In the first version the lines quoted are the beginning of the final quatrain of a series of five quatrains in *settenario* meter. Verdi set the first four as a monologue (the first two declamatory, the last two cantabile); after this cantabile a change to recitative (and hence *recitative verse*) was appropriate. Nonetheless, once the decision to revert to recitative was reached, Verdi could have chosen a recitative couplet with the prolixity of the original, but he chose instead to use a single taut *endecasillabo.*

16. See TOMLINSON at 272–73 on the musical implications of this change.

were clearly added at a later time. Initially there were lacking both a component indispensable to the structure of the *concertato* (the presence of a chorus) and an important dramatic element (the troubled query of the unsuspecting messengers, which subtly points towards Macbeth's anguished lust for power).

In the opera's penultimate scene, at the point of Macduff's revelation that he was not of woman born, Macbeth was unable to respond with anything more than a conventional "Che ascolto!" (What do I hear!). This was expanded into a desperate and titanic appeal to the force of arms:[17]

Tutto m'inganna! oh stolto!	Everything deceives me! Oh fool!
(*brandendo la spada*)	(*brandishing his sword*)
Tu non tradirmi almeno!	May at least you remain faithful to me!

Proceeding in this way, Verdi actually inserted whole scenes: I.9 (to which we shall return) and, even later (perhaps in Florence)—for the scene is absent from this manuscript libretto—all of II.4 (Banquo's scena "Come dal ciel precipita"). This may have been to take better advantage of the abilities of the bass, once Verdi had had the opportunity to hear him (Benedetti had been engaged later than the other singers),[18] but it was also manifestly intended to increase the brief time between the chorus of murderers and the banquet scene, a need that Verdi had already obscurely expressed to Piave: "Then follows the assassins' chorus, and here the scene goes on a good bit in order to set up the banquet scene" (letter of 3 December 1846).

Naturally not all of Verdi's changes resulted in condensation or expansion of the original lines; often Verdi was able to heighten the dramatic effect by the simple substitution of a phrase or the rearrangement of a line. A significant example, in IV.8, is the alteration of the two lines

MACBETH	MACBETH
Prodi all'armi! altro scampo non v'è!	Bravely to arms! There is no other escape!
CORO	CHORUS
Dunque all'armi! altro scampo non v'è!	To arms, then! There is no other escape!

to a new version which, besides eliminating a tedious repetition, clinched the heroic tone of Macbeth's final battle:

MACBETH	MACBETH
Prodi all'armi! la morte, o la gloria!	Bravely to arms! Death or glory!
CORO	CHORUS
Dunque all'armi! sì, morte, o vittoria!	To arms, then! Yes, death or victory!

One of the most celebrated and intense moments in the opera, Macbeth's exclamation when he learns of his wife's death, originally read as follows:

DAMA		GENTLEWOMAN	
	Finita		The Queen
La Regina ha la vita!		Has completed her life!	

17. In the 1865 revision, curiously enough, Verdi reduced Macbeth's couplet to the exclamation "Cielo!" (see his 28 January 1865 letter to Piave).

18. See the discussion of the Ricordi *libroni*, pp. 302–03 below.

MACBETH	MACBETH
La vita!	Life!
È il racconto d'un povero idiota	'Tis the tale of a poor idiot,
Vento e suono che nulla dinota.	Wind and sound, signifying nothing.

Verdi altered the opening to

DAMA	GENTLEWOMAN
È morta	The Queen
La Regina!	Is dead!
MACBETH	MACBETH
La vita! che importa!...	Life...What does it matter!...

which not only removes the awkward periphrasis of the Gentlewoman's announcement, but provides that "che importa" absent in the Shakespearean model—the crucial phrase of the whole passage.

Thus far we have focused on modifications of the libretto definitely ascribable to Verdi himself. We come now to Maffei's changes. First of all, we note that these were specifically requested by Verdi himself, who noted in various ways the places he regarded as unsatisfactory.

A single example: in Lady Macbeth's Act I *cavatina,* at the lines

D'Averno a te promettono	The messengers of Hell
Le Messaggere un trono	Promise you a throne

Verdi felt the need for an expression corresponding to the translation of Rusconi—"messaggieri d'un'altra natura"—as he noted beside the lines provided by Piave. Maffei satisfied him only after several attempts. After

Di Scozia a te promettono	The mysterious women promise you
Le arcane donne il trono	The throne of Scotland

"arcane donne" became "strane donne" (strange women) and, finally, "profetesse" (prophetesses).

In some instances, in fact, Verdi's impatience was probably aroused by Maffei's uncertainty. Shakespeare's "Go bid thy mistress, when my drink is ready,/She strike upon the bell . . . " was originally rendered as

Lady s'avverta che [appr]estata appena
La mia notturna tazza
Un rintocco di squilla a me lo avvisi.
(Il servo parte)

After trying the simple substitution of "la notturna bevanda," Maffei offered

Sappia la sposa mia che la notturna
Mia tazza apparecchiato [sic]
Vo' che un tocco di squilla a me lo avvisi.

and, finally,

Sappia la sposa mia che pronta appena
La mia tazza notturna ...

Other passages, such as I.6, the beginning of I.13, II.1, II.5, and IV.8 show a similar laborious evolution. Sometimes a single word, clearly considered as critical for the dramatic definition of a scene, became the object of Verdi and Maffei's search. This is the case in I.8: to hit upon "Oh donna mia!" Verdi passed through the stages of "Oh Ledy mia" and "Oh moglie mia"; he had noted that all the tension of the infernal prophecy and the imminent arrival of Duncan was condensed into Macbeth's exclamation. And in II.7, where Macbeth is thrown into confusion at the apparition of Banquo, Lady's Macbeth's "Inver folle siete" (You are truly mad) was restored after a number of variants were proposed and rejected: Verdi's "Sei forse demente?" and "Sei fatto demente?," and Maffei's "Sei tu forsennato?"

In general, Maffei was skillful at improving Piave's text with more pertinent and precise locutions: the witches' "barba deforme" (misshapen beard) was rightly amended to "sordida barba" (filthy beard); the "gemito" (moan) of the owl was substituted for an absurd "ululo" (hoot); the fuzzy "presenti" (presents) in "Fuggi regal fantasima/che Banco a me presenti" (Flee, royal phantom that presents Banquo to me) was changed to the more precise "rammenti" (recalls). Still, it must be recognized that Verdi's language has an evocative power absent from Maffei's more accurate writing. This is evident especially in the stage directions, which in Verdi's versions always stem from a datum perceived by the senses, from a sharp image of what is going on onstage, while in Maffei's they have an objective, purely functional tone. For example, Verdi's "Odesi un gran colpo alla porta del castello" (A great blow is heard at the door of the castle) is entirely different from Maffei's "bussano forte alla porta del castello" (they knock loudly at the door of the castle). "Macbet fa per sedersi e vede l'ombra di Banco al suo posto...visto soltanto da Macbet" (Macbeth goes to sit down and sees the shade of Banquo in his seat...seen only by Macbeth) has quite another significance compared with "Macbeth fa per sedere. Lo spettro di Banco veduto solo da lui ne occupa il posto" (Macbeth makes as if to sit. Banquo's ghost, seen only by him, is occupying his seat). The same could be said of "Con un colpo di tuono apparisce un fanciullo insanguinato" (With a clap of thunder, a bloody child appears) versus "Tuona: appare un fanciullo insanguinato" (It thunders ...).

But in particular Maffei satisfied another requirement, expressed emphatically—although to no avail—by Verdi to Piave: the need for a "sublime" poetic style. The libretto's literary finish, clearly based on the tone of the most illustrious traditions of Italian poetry, is due specifically to Maffei. Here are a few examples of this ascent from an unpretentious and colloquial level to a more elevated vocabulary:[19] Maffei changed "accorgersi" to "avvedersi"; "accendere" to "avvampare"; "avvicinarsi" to "accostarsi"; "rivolgere altrove [il ciglio]" to "stornare [il ciglio]"; "ondeggiare" to "vacillare"; "qui con voi" to "insiem con voi"; "sparita" to "scomparsa"; "spiriti" to "spirti"; "leon" to "lion" and "castello" to "alta rocca".

The search for literary decorum is evident in other, more involved corrections:

Ma la parola indocile	But the recalcitrant word
Gelò sui labri miei	Froze upon my lips.

19. Unfortunately, these stylistic distinctions are too delicate to survive translation, and none will be attempted. Eds.

was substituted for

Ma ciò non fu possibile,
Gelaro i labri miei. [I.13]

But that was not possible;
My lips froze up.

Or

Non t'accusi il tuo pallor

May your pallor not accuse you.

replaced the laughable

Così smorto non ti vuò. [IV.4]

I do not want you so pallid.

In certain cases, knowledge of Piave's first version permits us on one hand to justify Verdi's violent reactions and on the other to appreciate Maffei's literary expertise. Compare, for example, these two versions of the murderers' chorus:

Piave	Maffei
The sun vanishes and night comes;	The sun vanishes!...Let the night now reign,
Blind, wicked night,	Wicked—bloody
By your veil may	O blind night, hasten to extinguish
The light of such a day be obscured.	Every light on earth and in the heavens.
The time is near!...Now let us hide;	The time is near!...Now let us hide,
Let us await him in silence.	Let us await him in silence.
Descend O night, descend O night:	Tremble, o Banco! In your side
He must die here.	Is the point of a knife!

(*For the Italian texts, see p. 323*)

Similar considerations hold for the first quatrain of Macbeth's "Pietà, rispetto, amore."

Original version	Maffei's final version
Love, the pious respect	Piety, respect, love,
That consoles our last years:	The comfort of our dying days,
Do not expect it, Macbeth	Will not cast a flower
In your old age.	On your hoary age.

(*For the Italian, see p. 335*)

These examples reveal both Maffei's undeniable literary expertise and the strictly functional nature of his changes. It is no accident that Maffei's verses for *Macbeth* do not display the pompous, neo-baroque rhetorical solemnity for which he was chided in the nineteenth century, even by the least hostile of his critics.[20] Nothing of the large-scale conception of Verdi's *Macbeth* is to be attributed to Maffei; for the most part, Verdi merely adopted suggestions he had himself solicited and on occasion did not hesitate to reject even those.

20. Vittorio Imbriani—in a violent essay significantly entitled "Traduttore-traditore (Andrea Maffei)" (*Fame usurpate*, 2nd ed. [Naples 1888], pp. 257–302)—denounced "that noisy versifying which wearies the eardrums just like a frequent nearby cannonade: the school of Vincenzo Monti" (p. 260). He supported this judgment also by quoting Giuseppe Mazzini, who, as early as 1837, writing of translations of foreign authors, said that "in Maffei's translations the sense and spirit of the originals are sacrificed to artifice and convention" (Ibid., p. 259). Even Enrico Nencioni, who appreciated Maffei's literary talent and skill—indeed, he called him "the greatest virtuoso of *endecasillabi* . . . since the death of Monti" (*Saggi critici di letteratura italiana* [Florence, 1911], p. 243)—admitted the monotony and essentially "oratorical" nature of his poetry, as well as its "solemnly rhythmical" and "floridly rhetorical" character.

Our libretto shows this beyond any doubt. See, for example, I.9, which at first was not present at all, the arrival of Duncan being inferred. At a later stage the composer felt the need for a moment's pause in the turbulent piling up and speeding forward of events. He limited himself to noting, "Mime scene. Arrival of Duncan." In his revision of the stage directions, Maffei generally concerned himself only with their wording, but in this case he did more, suggesting a scene change: "Exterior of Macbeth's castle, with its drawbridge lowered. Mime scene in which, to the sound of a warlike [later altered to 'triumphal'] march, King Duncan is seen passing with magnificent retinue (*seguito pomposo*)." Verdi eliminated the scene change, and instead expanded the existing scene—not with a banal "warlike" or "triumphal" march, but with that graceful "*musica villereccia,* which signals the arrival of the King as it gradually approaches." The King "passes through," not only with the conventional *seguito pomposo,* but with the disturbing presence of Banquo, Macduff, Malcolm, Macbeth, and Lady Macbeth as well. Gabriele Baldini rightly considered this section "one of the gems of the opera."[21]

One final, conclusive illustration of this idea: the sleepwalking scene, set in verse by Maffei on the framework of a detailed sketch by Verdi, shows toward the end a series of corrections by Verdi and by Maffei himself. If we examine the genesis of this scene, we come to realize that these textual modifications are motivated—at least in their substance—by factors not purely literary. At an early stage, Verdi must have planned to link the sleep-walking scene to the *grande duetto* "Fatal mia donna" (which he considered the two expressive pivot points of the opera) by means of thematic repetitions. Indeed, he wrote to Piave on 10 December 1846, "It will be best if you cast this entire scene in *ottonari,*[22] because, as the Lady repeats in her dream themes already stated in the drama, that way I wouldn't have to add notes." Since Piave's versification of the sleepwalking scene has not survived—even the earliest version in the manuscript libretto is presumably Maffei's—we do not know whether he had included textual reprises of earlier scenes. But if we read the first extant version of the sleepwalking scene, we find that in the process of revising and expanding the *stretta* of the Act I duet from four lines to eight, he worked in a pair of lines (printed in italics here) from the sleepwalking scene:

Batte alcuno! a letto, a letto,	Someone is knocking! To bed, to bed,
Sfar non puoi la cosa fatta,	You cannot undo what has been done,
Vieni meco, *ogni sospetto*	*Come* with me, *let us remove*
Rimoviam dall'uccisor.	*Every suspicion from the murderer.*

Later, probably during the actual composition, Verdi became aware of the unsuitability or impossibility of linking the two sections by means of textual and musical parallels. At this point he decided to make changes in the text of the sleepwalking scene, even writing the lines himself.

MEDICO	DOCTOR
Questo ancora?...	This too?...
LADY	LADY
A letto, a letto,	To bed, to bed,
Sfar non puoi la cosa fatta,	You cannot undo what has been done

---

21. *Abitare la battaglia,* p. 127

22. For a list of the passages in *ottonario* meter that Verdi may have wanted to recall, see the notes to this letter below.

Batte alcuno! oh vien Macbetto
Così smorto non ti vuò.

Someone knocks! Oh come, Macbeth
I do not want you so pallid.

Maffei's final version, which corresponds to the version of the printed libretto, once again added only a patina of literary dignity. Verdi's integrity and consistency led him also to change a detail in the duet: the cadential phrase of the *adagio* which, with its long chromatic ascent in the voice in a progressive, almost exhausted, *smorzando*, too obviously foreshadowed the hallucinatory, desperate, and visionary atmosphere of the sleepwalking scene (see the music example below.) [23]

Let us now deal with a final question about the genesis of *Macbeth:* in what order were the numbers composed and upon which version of the text? [24]

The 1847 autograph score, in the Ricordi archives, shows beyond doubt that a good part of Acts I and II, along with some scenes of Acts III and IV, was set to music by Verdi before Maffei's revision of the libretto and then corrected in accordance with the new version. Signs of correction appear in I.2, 3, 5, 6, 8, 13, 15, 17, and 18; II.1, 3, 4, and 6; III.2; and in IV.8 and 9. At times, the original version has left traces on the music. One might say that the Act II chorus of murderers is even more in keeping with the cruder, original version of the text. And the sinister sound, drawn out in the oboes and clarinets like a lament, at Banquo's words "Gemea cupo l'augel dei tristi auguri" (the bird of ill omen gloomily groans) in the definitive version (I.17) was doubtless inspired by the original reading "gemea *lungo*" (long). Moreover, at the beginning of the *adagio* of Lady Macbeth's *cavatina*, the questionable caesura between "accendere" and "ti vo' quel freddo core" seems to be the result of the replacement of the original incipit, better suited to the melodic line if less effective poetically: "Sorgi, a me vieni, affrettati/Rinfranca il dubbio core." [25]

Further evidence about the genesis of *Macbeth* is found in the Casa Ricordi registers, the so-called *libroni* (see pp. 302–03). These establish the dates that the individual numbers, in Muzio's piano-vocal arrangement, were received by the engravers (see Table 1). [26]

23. For a different explanation of this change, based upon Verdi's 31 January 1847 letter to Barbieri-Nini, see LAWTON at 223–25. However, whatever Verdi's reasons for making the change—whether connected with compositional problems or with the vocal prowess of Barbieri-Nini—the elimination of the thematic recollection was surely a dramatic improvement.

24. See also LAWTON at 211–15.

25. See GOSSETT at 206–07.

26. This table adopts Ricordi's numeration and titles; for a complementary scheme, using Verdi's own numeration and titles and arranged in order of the pieces' appearances in the opera, see p. 215.

The *libroni* also note that the opera (presumably meaning the libretto) was approved by the Censor on 24 February 1847, and that the individual numbers were to be published in three groups: on March 20 (nine numbers), April 8 (nine numbers), and April 17 (the remaining six numbers). While publication dates are in part determined by business factors and are thus not absolutely decisive for the chronology of composition, it is reasonable to suppose that the individual numbers of the opera were sent to the publisher in their order of composition or orchestration, even if it is not definitely known whether Muzio worked from the orchestrated score, as seems likely, or from a sketch still lacking the orchestration (or at any rate the final orchestration). In any event, between 5 and 15 February 1847 (the date of Verdi's departure for Florence) nearly the whole of the opera was sent to the printer, roughly in the order of the scenes in the libretto, but with a few exceptions which need to be noted.

The "Gran Scena del Sonnambulismo" turns up in the first group of numbers sent to the publisher; may we hazard the guess that it was the first or among the first to be completed by Verdi? Between February 13 and 15, three numbers that for various reasons are problematical were sent: the Act I duet, "Fatal mia donna," for which Verdi had had to rewrite, along with the text, also the music of the *cabaletta;* the *scena* and *cavatina* "Vieni t'affretta" (still listed with the original incipit, "Sorgi a me vieni affrettati"); and finally, the chorus of murderers.

Only after a month were the remaining four numbers consigned to the engravers. All four were evidently completed in Florence: Duncan's march, for which Verdi found the happy solution of the *musica villereccia*, possibly only with the premiere close at hand; Lady Macbeth's Scena ed Aria "Trionfai!," which Verdi postponed writing until he could work together with Barbieri-Nini;[27] Banquo's scena "Come dal ciel precipita," a very late addition to the plan, as it is missing from the manuscript libretto and was inserted into the *libroni* only at a later stage; the prelude, which was the last to go to the publisher, as was the usual practice.

All the evidence we have examined testifies to Verdi's intelligence, sureness, and authority in this first encounter with Shakespeare, which was among the most difficult and complex challenges he had faced thus far. His absolutely principal role vis-à-vis his own collaborators and the decision-making autonomy he reserved for himself are confirmed by a comparison between the text of this manuscript libretto and that of the printed version: a comparison which shows—as has been indicated—how the process of rethinking and emendation continued up to the opera's production. Even for Banquo's scena (II.5)—a late addition written in Florence—the printed libretto displays a small but significant variant from the autograph score, probably reflecting Verdi's final thoughts:

Autograph score	*Libretto*
Come dal ciel precipita	Come dal ciel precipita
La notte ognor più scura	L'ombra più sempre oscura

As Verdi so aptly observed to Piave, "In this *Macbeth*, the more one thinks about it, the more one finds ways to improve it." (3 December 1846 letter). And it is truly striking to

27. On 31 January 1847 Verdi wrote to Barbieri-Nini that he would write this *cabaletta* for her in Florence "so that it will suit your voice perfectly and be sure to make an effect."

find confirmation of this search for an ever more suitable and well-defined dramaturgical image in the sketches for the 1865 revision of *Macbeth* (see pp. 339-45).

After reconsideration of the problems connected with the genesis of *Macbeth*, the conviction of the absolutely exceptional position occupied by Giuseppe Verdi not only within the framework of music but, more generally, in nineteenth-century Italian culture emerges ever more clearly. Of this, his encounter with Shakespeare—when set against the way esteemed men of letters understood Shakespeare's art—is the most outstanding and convincing touchstone.

TABLE 1

Consignment Date	Number and Act	Title Given by Ricordi	Projected Publication Date
February 5	2/I	Introduzione—*Che faceste? dite su!*	April 17
February 5	3/I	Scena e Duetto—*Due vaticinii compiuti or sono*	March 20
February 5	4/I	Coro di streghe—Stretta dell'Introduzione—*S'allontanarono*	April 8
February 5	20/IV	Gran scena del sonnambulismo—*Una macchia è qui tuttora*	March 20
February 6	8/I	Scena e sestetto—Finale I—*Schiudi inferno la bocca*	April 17
February 7	11/II	Convito e Brindisi nel Finale II—*Si colmi il calice*	March 20
February 7	13/II	Quartetto—Finale II—*Sangue a me quell'ombra chiede*	April 8
February 9	12/II	Apparizione e replica del Brindisi—*Che ti scosta o re mio sposo*	April 8
February 9	14/III	Introduzione—Incantesimo—*Tre volte miagola la gatta in fregola*	April 8
February 10	15/III	Gran scena delle apparizioni—*Fuggi o regal fantasima*	March 20
February 10	16/III	Coro e Ballabile—*Ondine e silfidi*	April 8
February 10	17/III	Gran scena—Finale III—*Vada in fiamme e in polve cada*	March 20
February 10	18/IV	Introduzione—Coro di profughi scozzesi—*Patria oppressa*	April 8
February 12	19/IV	Scena ed aria—*Ah, la paterna mano*	March 20
February 12	21/IV	Scena ed aria—*Pietà, rispetto, amore*	March 20
February 12	22/IV	Scena e Battaglia—*Prodi all'armi!*	April 8
February 12	23/IV	Scena e morte di Macbeth—*Mal per me che m'affidai*	April 8
February 13	7/I	Gran scena e duetto—*Fatal mia donna, un murmure*	March 20
February 15	5/I	Scena e Cavatina—*Vieni, t'affretta*	March 20
February 15	10/II	Coro di sicari—*Chi v'impose unirvi a noi?*	April 9
March 13	6/I	Scena e Marcia—*Oh donna mia!*	April 17
March 13	9/II	Scena ed Maria—*Trionfai! Securi alfine*	April 17
March 15	10½/II	Gran Scena—*Come dal ciel precipita*	April 17
March 15	1/I	Preludio	April 17

Paris, 1865

THE VERDI-ESCUDIER
CORRESPONDENCE
ABOUT *MACBETH*

Ursula Günther

Léon Escudier, Verdi's French publisher, kept the bulk of his correspondence with the composer; 217 of these letters, written between 1847 and 1877, are preserved in the Paris Bibliothèque de l'Opéra.[1] In the 1920s, J. G. Prod'homme published a large selection of them.[2] The peak of the correspondence, with twenty-eight letters from Verdi, occurred between March 1864 and June 1865, when the Théâtre-Lyrique under the direction of Léon Carvalho produced French versions of *Rigoletto* and *Traviata* and, finally, the *Macbeth* revised especially for Paris. Prod'homme's publications, together with some letters in the *Copialettere* and the *Carteggi* and an important letter discovered by Hans Busch in the Teatro Colón, Buenos Aires, provide a fairly complete picture of Verdi's side of the correspondence concerning the *Macbeth* revision.[3] But eight letters in the Opéra remained unpublished; further, Prod'homme misreads some key words and dates. This becomes clear when one examines the other side of the correspondence, Escudier's letters at Sant'Agata. The Carrara Verdi family holds 110 of his replies, dating from 1857 to 1876.[4] Although twenty-four letters belong to 1864–65, only short quotations from them have hitherto been used in Verdi research. [Dr. Günther has generously let us transfer her transcriptions of the unpublished letters, and her new transcriptions of those imperfectly published, to the Letters section. Eds.]

1. In the collection, filed as "Verdi lettres à Escudier," there are also eight letters from Giuseppina Verdi.

2. "Verdi's Letters to Léon Escudier," *Music and Letters* 4 (1923), 62–70, 184–96, 375–77; "Lettres inédites de G. Verdi à Léon Escudier," *Bulletin de la Société Union Musicologique* 5 (1925), 7–28. *Rivista Musicale Italiana* 35 (1928), 1–28, 171–97, 519–52.

3. All the letters relevant to *Macbeth* are reproduced in the "Letters" section. During the preparation of this volume, two more important letters to Escudier, of 6 January and 11 March 1865, came to light. Eds.

4. I am indebted to the Carrara Verdi family for permission to copy these letters and for other assistance. Thanks to Francesco Degrada and to the staff of Casa Ricordi, I can provide some additional information about Ricordi's interest in the affair. Franca Cella-Arruga, whose edition of the Verdi-Ricordi correspondence awaits publication, provided copies of various Ricordi letters at Sant'Agata, and indicated to me the location of an Escudier letter filed apart from the others. H. Robert Cohen sent me some reviews of the 1865 *Macbeth*. I thank Martine Kahane and Nicole Wild of the Bibliothèque Musée de l'Opéra for help in the preparation of this paper.

Escudier's letters make it clear that the story of the Macbeth revision begins earlier than one would suppose: with the great financial success of the Lyrique's *Rigoletto* in 1864, a success from which Verdi benefitted, thanks to the good will of Carvalho, acting under the influence of Escudier. Both men decided to pay author's rights to Verdi, although French law did not require this in the case of operas performed in Italy before the contract with France was signed. Therefore Carvalho declared this money to be a *prime personnelle* (a personal compensation), which at the same time prevented Ricordi from sharing in the profits.

In March 1864, Verdi received a large sum, his author's rights for five months, obtained by Escudier from the French agent Guyot.[5] According to Escudier's 29 February 1864 letter, the 11,288 francs and 85 centimes included royalties from the performances of *Rigoletto* at the Lyrique, including 2523 francs for January and about 2200 for February. On March 11, Verdi thanked his publisher; a day later he asked precisely why the money had been given him. Escudier's prompt response of March 13, designed to allay Verdi's misgivings about the payment, also stated that for *Macbeth*, the opera Carvalho wanted to perform the following winter, he would demand an even higher rate of compensation: "I don't want it said that in France you are deprived of the fruits of your genius through any fault of mine."

Verdi and Escudier met in late June in Genoa, where Giuseppina had fallen ill.[6] They discussed producing *Macbeth* at the Lyrique, and, as is clear from the next reference to the opera in the correspondence (Escudier's letter of 27 September 1864), Verdi had agreed to write some new ballet music. Escudier's request for ballet music prompted Verdi's well-known criticism of five numbers "which are either weak or lacking in character, which is worse still." Verdi realized that he needed time to rework the numbers, and asked Carvalho to give up the idea of producing *Macbeth* during the winter (letter of 22 October 1864). Escudier's reply of 28 October opens with an enthusiastic report on the premiere of *Traviata* at the Lyrique. In the continuation, he urged Verdi to revise *Macbeth* as quickly as possible. Verdi's affirmative response of November 2, written in a marvellously fluent and elegant French, is in part Giuseppina's work. I found Verdi's incomplete Italian draft and her complete French model, virtually identical to the final version, in the pile of Escudier letters at Sant'Agata. The passage concerning *Macbeth* (as Verdi originally drafted it) reads

> Let's turn to *Macbeth*. I am very sorry that Carvalho cannot give me more time for the changes I would like to make in the music in any case. I will try to do the job that was proposed to me, and if I can succeed in finishing it, it is agreed that you will pay me ten thousand francs for the ownership [*proprietà*] of the music for all countries except Italy, and for this opera I shall have the complete author's rights [*diritti ... d'autore*] for all the French Empire.[7]

In his reply of November 7, Escudier explained that the value of author's rights at the Lyrique was high, considerably higher than at the Opéra: 900 francs a night, assuming an

5. Since Guyot was expected to die in the near future, Escudier offered to help in his financial affairs.

6. A series of unpublished letters from 31 May to 22 June 1864 discusses plans for this meeting; that it actually took place is shown by two comments in Verdi's July 6 letter. Verdi asks Escudier to buy him a stove "of which I spoke to you in Genoa" (di cui vi parlai a Genova), and Giuseppina speaks of "the annoyance of seeing you in Italy and not being able to spend a few peaceful days in a good mood at Sant'Agata" (la bile de vous voir en Italie et ne pouvoir pas passer à St Agata quelques jours tranquilles et en belle humeur!). These letters, not being directly relevant to *Macbeth*, are not reproduced in this volume.

7. Note that Verdi is asking for more than Escudier had offered—see Escudier's letters of October 28 and November 7. Eds.

average box-office return of 5000 francs. And again Escudier underlined his good will and Carvalho's best intentions.

It was not until three months later, after Verdi had finished his work, that he signed the contract with Escudier. But before doing so he tried to arrange for Ricordi to regain some rights. The Verdi-Ricordi correspondence shows that Tito Ricordi was in fact the first person to see the new music for *Macbeth*. On 6 January 1865 Verdi wrote to Tito:

Today you will have received the two acts of *Macbeth* that I sent you yesterday from the Alseno station. Please have all the changes copied *exactly* and send my score (that is, the one which is partly a copy and partly in my hand) to Léon Escudier ... Tell me if you want, and if it suits you, to have this revised *Macbeth* performed in Italy after it has been given in Paris.

But Ricordi must have misunderstood or simply neglected the composer's instructions sent two days earlier, for on January 7 he promised to send Escudier a *copy* of the revised passages (rather than the autograph pages). In his letter of January 9 Verdi specified, "It's not the copy that you must send to Paris, but the original. In short, you must send on that score just as I sent it to you by the Alseno train."

Verdi informed his French publisher of the copying in what must have been a long letter. (This seems to have gone astray; because it contained information about the mise-en-scène it possibly ended up on Carvalho's desk.) Escudier, though obviously worried about the loss of time, did not dare to upset the composer. His answer (10 January 1865) brought Verdi good news about the author's rights received in December: 9160 francs for Paris alone. But Escudier announced he would send at once 19,160 francs, including the 10,000 francs agreed upon for *Macbeth*. About the score of *Macbeth*, Escudier added:

Provided that Ricordi does not make me wait, all will be well. You can feel easy about all the recommendations that you'll make for the performance. I'll see to them. I will not miss one rehearsal and will keep you informed about everything that goes on. I hope the other acts arrive on time.

Verdi sent Act III on January 21—Ricordi acknowledged its receipt the same day—and Act IV on 3 February; however, because of some omissions in the score,[8] Ricordi did not have the complete Act IV in his hands until February 8. Only after having been copied for use in Italy did the partially-autograph full score, now at the Bibliothèque Nationale,[9] come to Escudier. He acknowledged the receipt of Act III on February 2 and of Act IV on February 22.

On February 8, Ricordi accepted Verdi's conditions for the new *Macbeth*: "8000 francs and profit-sharing as in our other contracts." Knowing that Verdi had ceded the property rights for England to Escudier, he asked to have those for Spain and Germany. Verdi received Ricordi's offer the day it was sent; it prompted a hitherto unpublished letter to Escudier, the second Verdi wrote to him on 8 February 1865. In his reply of February 12, Escudier tried to reconcile his interests with Ricordi's, also offering Verdi the option of a separate arrangement between the two of them, one that would leave Ricordi no better off than before. On February 15, Verdi informed Ricordi of the compromise offered by Escudier—but not of his proposal of a separate arrangement, of which no further mention is made. The next day, Ricordi accepted Escudier's and Verdi's conditions, nevertheless com-

8. See Verdi's February 4 letter to Ricordi and the letters Ricordi and Verdi exchanged on February 8.
9. For a description of this source, see CHUSID at 299-301.

plaining that he feared Escudier's strong competition in Spain and Germany, where French editions were often preferred to Italian ones.

Verdi's next letter to Escudier, dated 20 February 1865 and hitherto unpublished, begins: "Send me a contract for *Macbeth* conforming to the terms of your letter of February 12—and thus let the matter be settled." The matter was settled on February 28, when Verdi returned the signed contract to Escudier.

The correspondence for 1864–65 demonstrates clearly that Escudier's concern for Verdi's success in Paris was not limited to financial affairs but extended to artistic matters. A good instance is this passage, written on 25 November 1864:

I think—and you undoubtedly agree with me—that the death of Macbeth needs to be changed; in any case, you told me so yourself. Carvalho would like the opera to end on a brilliant note and with a great ensemble effect. It's up to you to manage that.

Another example comes from Escudier's December 9 letter, in which he informed Verdi that not a complete ballet was required, but only

two or three dance pieces that we will interpolate into the work. Even two will suffice: we'd like a fiery round-dance for the witches in the first act and, in the sorcery scene of the third act, a waltz, which we would call "The Waltz of the Spirits." These two orchestral pieces will be danced by the corps de ballet. If you find a better place to introduce them, please let me know.

You are right about the end of the opera. A Victory Hymn is just what's needed. Couldn't you add something for the tenor? If that's not possible, let's say no more about it.

In the letter conveying Escudier's New Year's greetings and wishing Verdi a huge financial success in France amounting to forty-or fifty-thousand-francs profit, we find:

I've noticed that the orchestral interlude for the battle in the fourth act is far from being on the high level of the rest. If you had written a beautiful symphonic piece there, the Lyrique orchestra, which is excellent, would have been able to play it perfectly. But you know better than I what has to be done. I still have to have the new pieces translated, which will take a long time. (28 December 1864)

As is well known, Verdi replaced the original battle scene with a fugue. "The orchestra will have a chance to amuse itself," he told Escudier on 3 February 1865.

As for the French translation: Escudier's previously unpublished January 21 letter shows that he himself—not Carvalho, as Gilbert Duprez's 19 January 1865 letter had suggested— was primarily responsible for dismissing Edouard Duprez, the translator originally engaged for *Macbeth*. We can appreciate the validity of Escudier's decision to change translators by comparing the French libretti of *Macbeth* preserved in the Archives Nationales.[10] Three of the four libretti are virtually identical to the one published under the names of Nuitter and Beaumont, showing only minor alterations made in the course of the revision. The fourth libretto differs completely. Stamps and handwritten annotations on the first page show that it was the version submitted to the Paris censors, the *Commission d'examen des Ouvrages dramatiques,* on 15 March 1865, and approved on April 18. The text is neatly copied and bound in one volume.

Two brief examples can show the enormous differences between the translation of the

10. AJ^{XIII} 1157 (quatre livrets manuscrits de *Macbeth*)

libretto in question and the definitive French text.[11] Piave's libretto begins:

Che faceste? Dite su!
Ho sgozzato un verro! E tu?

The censor's version reads:

Quelle est l'œuvre!. Que fait-on?
J'égorgeais un mouton.
Et vous?

While this version disregarded Piave's original rhyme scheme, Nuitter and Beaumont respected it:

Que fais-tu là? dis le moi!
J'ai tué la chèvre. Et toi?

And in I.2, as the witches greet Macbeth, Piave writes:

Salve, o Macbetto, di Glamis sire!
Salve, o Macbetto, di Caudor sire!
Salve, o Macbetto, di Scozia re!

The censor's version has:

Salut à toi, Macbeth, de Cawdor' sire!
Salut à toi, Macbeth, de Glamis sire!
Roi d'Ecosse, salut à toi!..

While this would have meant minor changes in the rhythm of every line, Nuitter and Beaumont respected not only the music but also the identical start of the three lines:

Salut Macbeth! thane de Glamis!
Salut Macbeth! thane de Caudore!
Salut Macbeth! à toi Roi d'Ecosse!

It seems likely that Escudier gave a fair copy of Duprez's translation to the censor because Nuitter and Beaumont, working independently of Duprez, had not yet finished their translation. Nuitter copied the definitive version into Acts I and II of Escudier's partially-autograph full score,[12] but there was not time enough to complete the job. On many pages of the last two acts the French text is completely missing, while other pages show only some key words. The Italian text is present throughout.

How deeply Escudier was involved in the choice of translators, singers, and even in the details of the staging we can learn from reading the whole correspondence in the Letters section. Two further issues about the Lyrique's production remain to be discussed here:

11. During the entire first scene, for example, there is but one rhymed couplet in which the pair of final rhyming words is the same in both versions: "vagabondes" and "ondes," obviously prompted by the "vagabonde" and "onde."

12. In order not to deface the autograph parts of the score, Nuitter there copied the text on small strips of paper which were then attached to the pages, rather than writing directly on the score, as he did with the non-autograph parts.

Escudier's efforts to expand the tenor's part and the reshuffling of *Macbeth*'s four acts into a five-act version.

On 9 December 1864, Escudier had asked Verdi, "Couldn't you add something for the tenor? If that's not possible, let's say no more about it." Verdi did not say anything about it, but Escudier returned to the point on 26 January 1865: "If you could add something for the tenor, I could arrange that Monjauze sings the role, and that would be a gain for the production. In this matter you are the only judge of what should or should not be done." Again Verdi ignored the issue, and Escudier tried once again, in the first of two letters of 2 February 1865. By this time he seems to have renounced any hopes he may have had for obtaining a completely new solo number from Verdi and limits himself to suggesting expansions of the existing music:

After singing the praises of a new tenor they had discovered, Escudier suggests:

After the [Act IV tenor] romance, there's a cry to arms; if it were possible to have him sing this as a solo, modifying it and adding to it a passage for his splendid high C, we would have an immense effect from it, I promise you. It's up to you to decide. . . . It's in the recitative before the chorus that you could perhaps place an effective phrase for the tenor.

Verdi rejected this idea in a letter of February 8—"there is no need to give Macduff a single note more"—but some of Escudier's suggestions were nonetheless followed in the production. As both the partially-autograph full score and Escudier's French piano-vocal score [13] show, the structure of the *cabaletta* was altered to allow Macduff to begin it with a twenty-one-measure solo. While no one dared to compose a "phrase à effet" for him, most of Malcolm's lines in the recitative were turned over to Macduff.

In the second of his February 2 letters, written after a rehearsal of Acts I and II, Escudier proposed another idea (see the fourth paragraph of his letter). Verdi's reply (the first of his February 8 letters to Escudier) should be read in its entirety. Escudier groveled. He wrote on February 10:

You are right a thousand times over. Macduff cannot sing the *brindisi*. I reread Shakespeare's play the very evening I wrote to you, and soon understood that I had suggested something foolish and that I was simply an imbecile.

Nevertheless, the subject was not closed. In Escudier's March 25 letter we find another attempt to convince Verdi.

Yesterday Carvalho tried a staging of his own in which he gave Macduff a suspicious character, lightly suggesting that he distrusted Macbeth. In this situation, and while Lady Macbeth goes from one guest to another to calm them down and then arrives, smiling, at her husband, Macduff sings the second strophe of the *brindisi* . . . Because of the way Macduff is presented, it does not contradict the sense, and everything gains by it . . . If you let us put into practice this little modification, which does not harm the progress of the drama and which throws some variety into the whole finale, we will do so. If not we'll stick to your ideas.

In his March 28 reply, Verdi expressed strong opposition to Carvalho's "ingenious" idea for the staging of the *brindisi,* stressing that "in this scene Lady is, and must be, the dominant character dramatically as well as musically." His various objections were so

13. For a description of this source (L.E. 2442) see CHUSID at 301.

clearly and forcefully expressed that Escudier did not dare to confess the truth. In his March 31 reply, he reported only, "I have informed Carvalho about the matter of the *brindisi*; I find that you are right; and that, because of the way he staged the number, I must say that he was not completely wrong. In any case, tomorrow we are going to resume your version!"

What actually was done? We can learn this from the detailed review of *Macbeth* published in Escudier's *L'Art Musical* of 27 April 1865 and signed "Ralph":

... On the subject of changes, we must mention that which consists in having the tenor repeat the *brindisi* ... which in the Italian version is sung twice by Lady Macbeth...

In Italy, the role of Macduff not being important enough, or rather, not flattering enough for a worthy tenor to *deign* to play it, it was entrusted to a second tenor.... In France, that same tenor role ... could be entrusted to an artist of talent. It is therefore not surprising that, for the sake of variety, he should be given the repetition of the *brindisi* sung the first time by the soprano. Possibly the dramatic logic suffers somewhat in consequence, but that logic so often yields to musical requirements that it would be really childish to quibble with the composer over a change whose effect is so captivating. [Fuller text at 406.]

This description, as well as Escudier's French language piano-vocal score[14] and the four manuscript librettos mentioned earlier, prove beyond a doubt that Escudier and Carvalho did not respect Verdi's wishes. Claiming that the opera had been and continued to be successful, Escudier wrote in *L'Art Musical* of 4 May 1865, after the sixth performance: "Every evening the audience asks that the Act II *brindisi* should be repeated." Were the passages cited here intended to be read by the composer?

There is another instance of Escudier's and Carvalho's failure to heed Verdi's wishes. In a hitherto unpublished letter, Verdi protested against their decision to divide his opera into five acts (see Verdi's second letter of 11 March 1865). We do not have Escudier's answer, and he does not return to the matter. However, in discussing the forthcoming production, in the 16 March 1865 number of *L'Art Musical*, the publisher stated, "It is in error that some papers have ascribed five acts to Verdi's work: *Macbeth* has only four acts."

Nonetheless, the work was performed in five acts. The Théâtre-Lyrique playbill advertised it as an opera in five acts, and in Escudier's French language piano-vocal score, Act IV consists of only three numbers (20–22 in Escudier's numbering): the opening chorus, Macduff's aria, and the sleepwalking scene. Act V (23–25) opens with Macbeth's scena and continues with the battle and concluding Victory Hymn. The 1865 Ricordi piano-vocal score, which presumably corresponded to Verdi's intentions, presents the work in four acts.

Escudier offered a justification for the modification in the extended review already quoted:

The fourth act, which in the Italian version was the last, had nothing truly remarkable to offer but the sublime sleepwalking monologue of Lady Macbeth. It was a great deal, regarded as a dramatic situation and as a piece of music, but it was not enough to constitute an act of an opera, especially not a final act...

In the French score, this act, which by itself was not self-sufficient, has been so much amplified, enriched, strengthened, that it was necessary to divide it and cut it in two. The result has been an opera in five acts with excellent proportions.

---

14. Martin Chusid informs me that not all impressions of this edition incorporate the unauthorized modification.

When Verdi received an enthusiastic telegram from Carvalho after the première,[15] he had the best of feelings about his revised *Macbeth*. In Giuseppina's *copialettere* there is a draft of a letter to Carvalho, dated 26 April 1865:

Thanks, a thousand thanks, for the telegram that you had the thoughtfulness to send me almost as soon as the first performance of *Macbeth* was over. This kindness of yours is all the keener/kinder in that I do not have the honor of knowing you personally. So it is natural that I should be doubly grateful to you. As for *Macbeth,* let me say to you that it is not you who should thank me, but I you, for having given it at the Théâtre-Lyrique. You believed in this score, you judged it worthy of your pains...it succeeded.

But very soon the composer began to suspect that Escudier was not telling him the truth. In his letter of April 28, Verdi complained, "I should have liked to receive another letter about the second performance to hear whether the favorable reception was confirmed or diminished." And on May 4: "I am furious with you! What, after a telegram, a letter, and some newspapers, you don't write to me anymore, you tell me nothing more about the subsequent performances of *Macbeth*? Have they perhaps killed you all with their hisses?"

And finally he came to the conclusion that "When all is considered, weighed, and summed up, Macbeth is a *fiasco*" (3 June 1865). This must have been partly due to the performance, he continued, for even the Act I duet, the Act II finale, and the sleepwalking scene "did not make the impression they should have . . . often by trying to do too much, one achieves nothing. It is the defect of the Opéra; I fear it will become the same at the Théâtre-Lyrique. The operas are nothing but a pretext for the machinery."

---

15. For the text of the telegram, see Verdi's letter to Arrivabene, 25 April 1865.

MACBETH IN PARIS:
NEW ICONOGRAPHICAL DOCUMENTS[1]

H. Robert Cohen

Iconographical documents dealing with operas performed in Paris during the nineteenth century may, for the most part, be divided into two categories:[2] production materials required for the performance of a work, and illustrations in contemporary publications. Production materials include costume sketches, set designs, and the highly accurate three-dimensional representations of scenery, known as *maquettes à monter,* which served as models for the construction of the sets. Documents in contemporary publications include engravings and lithographs in illustrated newspapers and the satirical press, and colored lithographs in volumes that specialized in reproducing costumes seen on the stages of important Parisian theatres.

This division helps one to understand why numerous iconographical documents may exist for one opera, and few for another. The number and present location of extant production materials depend on several factors, including the life span of a particular administration, the number of different theatres occupied by the same company, contracts dealing with property rights for scenery and costume designs,[3] an administration's interest in conserving documents, and, of course, the ever-present threat to all theatre archives, fire. The amount of published materials depends largely upon the public's immediate reaction to a work. This becomes apparent when one compares surviving iconographical production materials and illustrations in the contemporary press for two works first performed, in Paris, in April, 1865: Meyerbeer's *L'Africaine,* an extraordinarily popular work done at the Opéra many times during its first season, and Verdi's *Macbeth,* an unpopular work which appeared only fourteen times at the Théâtre-Lyrique.

The procedure for tracing contemporary engravings and lithographs is identical for both works. One compiles a list of illustrated publications noted for their interest in the theatre, identifies the Parisian libraries possessing this material, and examines the relevant volumes. For a work such as *L'Africaine* there is a wealth of material: reproductions of performers in costume, set designs, representations of mises-en-scène, and numerous caricatures. In fact, almost every illustrated newspaper with even the slightest interest in the arts dealt with Meyerbeer's work. What one can expect to discover for a work such as *Macbeth,* however,

1. Research for this study and the bibliography of reviews dealing with the Paris premiere (see p. 198) was supported by grants from the Social Sciences and Humanities Research Council of Canada and the American Council of Learned Societies.

2. For a survey of the types of archival documents that permit us to explore the mise-en-scène of the works performed at the Paris Opéra during the 1830s and 1840s, see my "On the Reconstruction of the Visual Elements of French Grand Opera: Unexplored Sources in Parisian Collections," *Report* of the XIIth Congress of the International Musicological Society, Berkeley, 1977 (Cassel: Bärenreiter, 1981), pp. 463–80.

3. Nicole Wild's, "Un demi-siècle de décors à l'Opéra de Paris," *Regards sur l'Opéra* (Paris: Presses Universitaires de France, 1976, pp. 11–22), examines these with regard to the *décorateurs* of the Opéra.

is, understandably, quite little. Nevertheless, published documents for *Macbeth* do exist, but their number reflects the work's relative failure. Recent research on the nineteenth-century French illustrated press has demonstrated the importance of this neglected corpus of iconography and directed attention to those journals of particular interest to the music historian,[4] but little has been done to trace the movement of theatre archives from the original theatre to their present locations in public libraries or private collections. This, as we shall see, is a major problem when dealing with works performed in the lesser-known Parisian theatres such as the Théâtre-Lyrique.

Obviously, someone seeking original iconographical documents for *L'Africaine* would begin in the Bibliothèque et Musée de l'Opéra, for it is likely that the administration responsible for producing this work would have conserved the production materials. Here, simply by examining the card catalog, one would discover a large number of iconographical materials, including original costume designs, set designs, and *maquettes à monter*. Next, one would work at the Archives Nationales; important materials, although little of an iconographical nature, were transferred there from the Opéra in 1932 and again in 1961. Finally, one would examine the Collection Théâtrale Rondel at the Département des Arts du Spectacle of the Bibliothèque Nationale. In each collection there are materials of interest, but most of the original iconographical documents are still to be found in the archives of the Opéra. But what of *Macbeth* and the other works performed at the Théâtre-Lyrique? This is a far more complicated problem, for neither previous research nor catalogs of Parisian collections account for iconographical production materials for the works performed at this theatre. Where are, in fact, the archives of the Théâtre-Lyrique?

The administration known as the Théâtre-Lyrique functioned continuously for approximately twenty years, from 1851 to 1870. For a relatively short period (September 1854 to October 1855) the theatre was directed by Émile Perrin, and—for reasons explained by Brigitte Labat-Poussin in her catalog of the Archives du Théâtre National de l'Opéra (AJ[XIII])[5]—the Archives Nationales possess contracts, correspondence, and accountants' reports dating from Perrin's fourteen-month tenure. The Archives also preserve a collection of libretti in manuscript for operas performed at the theatre, including three for *Macbeth*,[6] and certified box-office receipts from April 1862 to May 1870.[7] The receipts (Illus. 1) permit us to establish the exact dates of the fourteen performances of *Macbeth* and to ascertain precisely the poor financial returns.[8] For example, between 21 April 1865 and 31 May 1865—the dates of the first and last performances of *Macbeth*—Mozart's *La Flûte enchantée* was presented at the same theatre twenty times. The average evening's receipts for *Macbeth*, 1.677 francs; for *La Flûte*, 5,753 francs. Unfortunately, the series AJ[XIII] at the Archives Nationales preserves neither iconographical documents nor any other material dating from Léon Carvalho's directorship of the Théâtre-Lyrique (1856–60, 1862–68), the period en-

---

4. See my "Les Gravures musicales dans L'Illustration de 1843 à 1899," *Revue de Musicologie* 62 (1976), 125–31 and "Musical Iconography in the Nineteenth-Century French Illustrated Press: A Method for Cataloguing and Indexing," *Report* of the XIIth Congress of the International Musicological Society, pp. 838–42.

5. *Archives du Théâtre National de l'Opéra AJ*[13] *1 à 1466* (Paris: Archives Nationales, 1977), p. 392n.

6. Archives Nationales AJ[XIII], 1157. These libretti are discussed in GÜNTHER at 177–78.

7. Archives Nationales AJ[XIII], 459

8. 1865: 21 April (733.81 francs); 24 April (3,098.39 francs); 26 April (2,687.27 francs); 28 April (2,096.31 francs); 1 May (2,178.81 francs); 3 May (1,979.31 francs); 5 May (1,431.89 francs); 10 May (1,804.35 francs); 17 May (975.31 francs); 19 May (1,693.35 francs); 24 May (1,900.81 francs); 26 May (1,062.31 francs); 28 May (934.31 francs); 31 May (896.81 francs)

compassing the performances of *Macbeth*. Furthermore, the catalog of the Bibliothèque de l'Opéra reveals only one document of interest for *Macbeth*—an illustrated poster—and there is no catalog accounting for the holdings of the Bibliothèque Nationale's Département des Arts du Spectacle.

Because at first glance so few archival documents appear to exist, one might assume that at least some of the Théâtre-Lyrique archives were destroyed in 1871 by what Soubies refers to as an *"incendie partiel."*[9] However, Albert de Lasalle in his *Mémorial du Théâtre-Lyrique* (1877) assures us that "the fire did not spread into the part of the attic ... which housed, along with the storage area for the costumes, all of the archives, scores, brochures, registers and administrative papers."[10] While it is not yet possible to trace completely the dispersed archives, the search for *Macbeth* materials did prove fruitful.

From 30 October 1862 until the fire of 24 May 1871, the Théâtre-Lyrique was housed in a newly constructed theatre that bore its name (Illus. 2). The building still stands; situated on the east side of La Place du Châtelet, it is known today as the Théâtre de la Ville. Secondary sources offer little information about the visual elements of the works performed there. In fact, not a single study appears to have been devoted to the subject, and volumes such as Germain Bapst's *Essai sur l'histoire du théâtre,* ... [11] while dealing extensively with the Opéra, barely mention the works performed at the Théâtre-Lyrique. Even tracing the names of the *décorateurs* responsible for the scenery of a given work—a relatively simple task for the Opéra [12]—poses problems for the Théâtre-Lyrique. Contemporary criticism, a traditional source for such information, [13] reveals, at least for *Macbeth*, very little. In some twenty-five reviews of the Parisian premiere of *Macbeth*, [14] not one critic names a *décorateur*.

9. Albert Soubies, *Histoire du Théâtre-Lyrique 1851–1870* (Paris: Fischbauer, 1899), p. 35

10. Albert de Lasalle, *Mémorial du Théâtre-Lyrique* (Paris: Librairie Moderne, J. Lecuir et Cie, 1877), p. 99

11. Germain Bapst, *Essai sur l'histoire du théâtre, la mise en scène, le décor, le costume, l'architecture, l'éclairage, l'hygiène* (Paris: Librairie Hachette, 1893)

12. See, for example, "Les Décorateurs de l'Opéra au XIXe siècle (1809–1981), Ibid., 633–40.

13. Berlioz's *Journal des Débats* feuilletons often list the *décorateurs* in the captions of articles about first performances at the Opéra.

14. See my "Bibliography of Reviews and Articles Dealing with the Paris Premiere of *Macbeth*," p. 198.

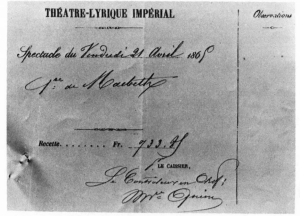

Illus. 1: Box office receipt for the first performance of Macbeth *in Paris, Archives Nationales, AJ XIII,459*

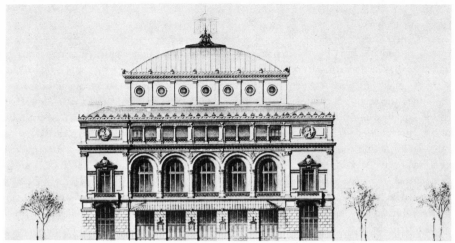

Illus. 2: "Théâtre-Lyrique Impériale. Façade principale," known today as the Théâtre de la Ville, C. Daly and G. Davioud, Les Théâtres de la Place du Châtelet (*Paris: Librairie Générale de l'Architecture, n.d.*)

However, while criticism offers little specific information, it clearly suggests that the Théâtre-Lyrique productions in the 1860s were among the most impressive in Paris. Joseph d'Ortigue, for example, Berlioz's successor at the prestigious *Journal des Débats*,[15] often describes them as "beautiful," "stunning," "magnificent" and "splendid," while frequently noting that they display "care," "taste," and "skill." Perhaps d'Ortigue's respect for the staging at this theatre may be best appreciated in his review of 16 January 1864 in which he compares two Parisian productions of *Rigoletto*. D'Ortigue writes: "with respect to the sumptuousness of the mise-en-scène, scenery and even the costumes, la salle Ventadour [the home of the Théâtre-Italien] does not pretend to challenge the production at the Théâtre-Lyrique." His opinion may well be justified, for it is supported both in secondary sources such as César Daly and Gabriel Daviour's *Les Théâtres de la Place du Châtelet*—in which the authors maintain that the Théâtre-Lyrique "under the direction of M. Carvalho produced operas with a mise-en-scène just as luxurious as those at the Opéra"[16]—and indeed in reviews of the first performance of *Macbeth* (see pp. 402–12). *L'Art Musical* states: "nothing has been neglected in the mise-en-scène which is superb. The scenery is splendid." *La France Musicale* also refers to the mise-en-scène as "splendid," adding "varied" and "intelligent" to its praise; *Les Modes Parisiennes* extols the "ten tableaux painted by skillful *décorateurs* [and an] irreproachable mise-en-scène." Paul Smith, in the *Revue et Gazette Musicale de Paris*, is even more elaborate in his praise. Only Jules Ruelle in *Le Guide Musical* is generally critical of the mise-en-scène, claiming that "the public was tired and irritated by the lack of scenic variety."[17]

What remains today of this production? To what extent can we reconstruct the scenery,

15. For a study and complete bibliography of d'Ortigue's feuilletons for the *Journal des Débats*, see Sylvia L'Ecuyer-Lacroix, "Les Feuilletons de Joseph d'Ortigue au *Journal des Débats* (1852–1866)," Master's thesis, Université Laval (Québec), 1978.

16. César Daly and Gabriel Daviour, *Les Théâtre de la Place du Châtelet*, Paris, Librairie générale de l'architecture, n.d., 7. Théophile Gautier, in his review of the first performance of *Macbeth* (*Le Moniteur Universel*, 24 April 1864) expresses a similar opinion: "La mise en scène est riche et soignée, comme c'est l'usage au Théâtre-Lyrique ... "

17. Ruelle, in another review of Macbeth published four days earlier (*Messager des Théâtres*, 23 April 1865) appears to contradict himself: "les décors et la mise en scène, depuis les costumes jusqu'aux moindres accessoires, méritent tous les éloges."

costumes, and blocking of the French *Macbeth?* One important element has not come to light: a *livret de mise en scène,* or staging manual. Prepared by *régisseurs généraux,* such *livrets* were originally intended to permit stage managers in the French provinces and abroad to reproduce the scenic elements of celebrated Parisian productions.[18] For this reason, they contain detailed information about all aspects of the mise-en-scène. At the foot of the table of contents for Escudier's piano-vocal score (French-language edition) there is the following note: "Information concerning the mise-en-scène, scenery, costumes and properties, may be obtained from M. Arsène, *Régisseur général* of the Théâtre-Lyrique Impérial."[19] Given the fact that M. Arsène prepared and distributed a number of *livrets de mise en scène* for works performed at the Théâtre-Lyrique, including *Rigoletto* and *Violetta (La Traviata),*[20] this notice implies that a similar volume was planned for *Macbeth.* It is likely, however, that the project to distribute, or perhaps even to complete, a staging manual for *Macbeth* was abandoned with the failure of the opera. Works unsuccessful in Paris were rarely produced in the provinces, and so there was no need for it.

In one area, however, the search for original material was particularly worthwhile, namely, scenery designs and *maquettes à monter.* Because the box-office receipts and three libretti survive in the Archives Nationales, after having been transferred there from the Bibliothèque de l'Opéra, it was reasonable to assume that iconographical material might have survived as well—perhaps in the attic of the Théâtre de la Ville, perhaps in private collections or in uncatalogued *fonds* of the Bibliothèque de l'Opéra. A meeting with the administrator of the Théâtre de la Ville established that nothing has remained in the theatre. The search for uncatalogued material, however, proved successful. File cards of *maquettes à monter* presently being prepared at the Bibliothèque de l'Opéra by Nicole Wild[21] and of the uncatalogued *Fonds Cambon* in the same library revealed a number of previously unexplored items. Why this material should be at the Opéra, while most of the archival documents from Carvalho's direction of the Théâtre-Lyrique have not come to light, remains a question.

The Bibliothèque de l'Opéra possesses: three set designs by Charles Antoine Cambon, a disciple of Ciceri and one of the most important *décorateurs* of the period; two designs for parts of one or perhaps two *maquettes à monter* by Edouard-Désiré-Joseph Despléchin, another of Ciceri's well-known disciples; two studies and several parts of two other incomplete *maquettes* attributed to Despléchin; and five studies (four architectural studies for the construction of scenery and one preliminary set design) attributed to Robecchi, an Italian *décorateur,* active in Paris in the 1860's, but less well-known than his distinguished French collaborators. There is also an engraving from *L'Univers Illustré,* the only one of the three important French illustrated newspapers (the others being *L'Illustration* and *Le Monde Illustré*) to have published a scene from the opera.

---

18. See my "La Conservation de la tradition scénique sur la scène lyrique en France au dix-neuvième siècle: les livrets de mise en scène et la Bibliothèque de l'Association de la Régie Théâtrale," *Revue de Musicologie,* 64 (1978), 253-67.

19. For additional information about this edition, see "Some Early Piano-Vocal Scores . . . ," first item, p. 301. A similar note is found in the *Macbeth* libretto published by Michel Lévy, frères (Paris 1865). At the foot of the page containing the "distribution de la pièce" one reads: "S'adresser pour la mise en scène exacte, à M. Arsène, régisseur du Théâtre-Lyrique Impérial."

20. Bibliothèque de l'Opéra, C.4910(5) and C.4911(3), respectively

21. Nicole Wild made her notes available to me and on many occasions, offered valuable suggestions and assistance.

It is possible to identify original production material for five of *Macbeth's* ten designs (tableaux) and to suggest where some of the additional material may have appeared. Let us consider the scenes as they appear in the opera. For tableaux I, III, VII, IX, and X, no clearly identifiable sources have come to light.

Tableau II (Act I) is described in the libretto as "Macbeth's castle, in the background a vast arcade (*galerie*), to the right, Macbeth's apartment." The inscription on the envelope containing Despléchin's two studies and *maquette* parts reads simply "The Palace. Interiors and Exteriors." The artist's preliminary design (Illus. 3) and more advanced drawing (Illus. 4)—note here the figures representing Duncan and his entourage entering through the gates on the left and moving across the courtyard—depict only the exterior of the castle. The extant *maquette* parts, however, are clearly divisible into two sections: the first (Illus. 5), based on the drawings, represents the exterior of the castle; the second (Illus. 6) represents a room within the castle. Because the drawings depict only the castle's exterior and because the action in tableau II does not require a visible interior, it is likely that the *maquette* parts represent two different scenes, namely, one of the opera's interior scenes (tableaux III, V or

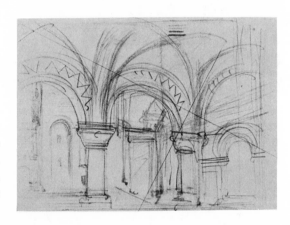

Illus. 3: Preliminary drawing by Despléchin for a maquette à monter, *exterior of Macbeth's castle, tableau II, Act I, Bibliothèque de l'Opera (F:Po) MAQ. A153*

Illus. 4: Drawing by Desplé-chin for a maquette à monter, *exterior of Macbeth's castle, tableau II, Act I, F:Po, MAQ. A153*

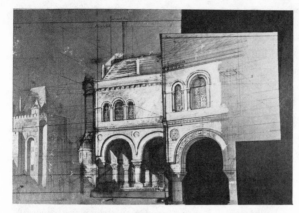

Illus. 5: Part of incomplete ma-quette à monter by Despléchin, interior of Macbeth's castle, tab-leau II, Act I, F:Po, MAQ. A153

Illus. 6 Part of incomplete ma-quette à monter by Despléchin, interior of Macbeth's castle, tab-leau II, Act I, F:Po, MAQ. A153

Illus. 7: Study by Despléchin for part of a maquette à monter, "site pittoresque," tableau IV, Act II or tableau I, Act I, F:Po, MAQ. A151

Illus. 8: Study by Despléchin for part of a maquette à monter, "site pittoresque," tableau IV, Act II or tableau I, Act I, F:Po, MAQ. A151

Illus. 9: Engraving, banquet scene, tableau V, Act II, L'Univers Illustré, 29 April 1865, p. 265

Illus. 10: Set design by Cambon, banquet scene, tableau V, Act II, charcoal drawing, F:Po, Fonds Cambon 73

Illus. 11: Alternate set design by Cambon for banquet scene, tableau V, Act II, charcoal drawing, F:Po, Fonds Cambon 72

Illus. 12: Set design by Cambon, ruins of castle, tableau VI, Act III, charcoal drawing, F:Po, Fonds Cambon 74

IX) and tableau II, the exterior view. In his review,[22] Arthur Pougin is highly critical of the latter decor, which he calls "perfectly ridiculous", pointing out that Macbeth's castle is represented in Moorish style although located in Scotland.

Tableau IV—the "deserted, narrow path not far from Macbeth's castle" in which Banquo is assassinated—is described in the Escudier piano-vocal score as "site pittoresque." This phrase appears on the folder containing Illus. 7 and 8. Attributed to Despléchin, these designs are studies for parts of one or perhaps two *maquettes*. While both may depict elements of tableau IV, Andrew Porter has pointed out that the two designs depict foliage seen at different times of the year and that the two parts do not fit properly together. If this is the case, then only one of the designs belongs to tableau IV (perhaps Illus. 7); the other may depict elements of tableau I, "the edge of a woods".

There are three sources for the banquet scene (tableau V, Act II), two charcoal drawings by Cambon and the *Univers Illustré* engraving which appeared eight days after the Parisian premiere. The engraving[23] (Illus. 9) depicts Macbeth recoiling at the appearance of Banquo's ghost before the throne. Cambon's drawing (Illus. 10) for the scene published in the journal includes, set off to the right, a single banquet table and the King's throne. A second drawing by Cambon, perhaps an alternative (and rejected) design for the banquet scene (Illus. 11), is somewhat more grandiose. Note that the table, as described in the libretto, is prepared for the banquet. Curiously, neither of Cambon's conceptions conforms to the staging indications set forth by Verdi in his letter of 23 January 1865. The final design by Cambon (Illus. 12) is his setting for tableau VI, Act III, the "ruins of the castle devastated by war ... In the middle of the ruins is a vast cauldron under which crackles a sinister fire."[24]

The inscription on the envelope containing the five drawings attributed to Robecchi identifies them as studies for "Act IV [tableau VIII, the sleepwalking scene]: Galerie du

22. Arthur Pougin, in *Le Théâtre*, 22 April 1865

23. The engraving of the banquet scene (tableau V) is incorrectly identified in *Le Monde Illustré* as depicting tableau II, Act I. Moreover, this error and the existence of a second banquet scene by Cambon, attributed at the Bibliothèque de l'Opéra to *Macbeth*, led to the reproduction of the second design in the AIVS *Verdi Newsletter* No. 4 (Jan. 1978), 18.

24. A published catalogue of works by Cambon sold at auction on 17 May 1877 at the Hôtel Drouot includes the following entry number 55: "Intérieur de cloître, palais en ruine, pour *Macbeth*. Trois dessins, estompe, encre de Chine et crayon noir." [*Dessins et aquarelles pour décors de théâtres par feu Cambon*, (Paris, 1877), p. 12]

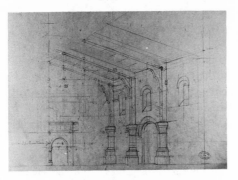

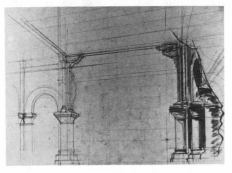
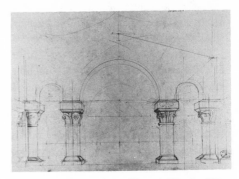

Illus. 13–16: Four architectural studies for scenery by Robecchi, attributed to tableau VIII, Act IV, F:Po, MAQ. A152

château de Macbeth." Four of these drawings, which cannot conclusively be attributed to tableau VIII, appear to be architectural studies for the construction of scenery (Illus. 13–16). The fifth sketch (Illus. 17), however, clearly resembles Despléchin's two drawings (Illus. 3 and 4) representing the exterior of Macbeth's castle.

We turn now to the costumes, and particularly to a manuscript brochure of Italian origin located in the Département des Arts du Spectacle [Collection Rondel] of the Bibliothèque Nationale, which contains on fourteen pages, designs for twenty-three *Macbeth* costumes (Illus. 18–31).[25] The brochure also contains a list of performers[26] who partici-

25. Marie-Francoise Christout, *Conservateur* at the Département des Arts du Spectacle, searched for *Macbeth* materials on my behalf in the uncatalogued archives of this collection and brought these *figurini* to my attention.

26. See "A Hundred Years of Macbeth" at 429.

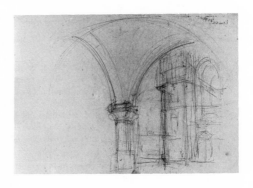

Illus. 17: Study by Robecchi attributed to tableau VIII, Act IV, but which may have served as a study for Despléchin's maquette à monter for exterior of Macbeth's castle, tableau II, Act I (see Illus. 3-4), F:Po, MAQ, A152

pated in a production of this work at the Teatro Regio of Parma on 26 December 1849—a production in which, no doubt, at least some of these costumes were employed.

Five of the fourteen pages of this brochure contain carefully drawn and vividly colored *figurini* (Illus. 18–22) representing Macbeth as Warrior, Macbeth as King, Lady Macbeth as Queen, the witches, and Lady Macbeth during the sleepwalking scene. The remaining designs, which are presented successively as they appear in the folder, may be divided as follows: a pen design with some shadings of wash for Macbeth, three pencil designs retraced in ink for Macbeth as General, Lady Macbeth as Queen (Illus. 23–25), and the soldiers (Illus. 31); and five line drawings for a maidservant (?), the witches, sorceresses and nuns, Macbeth (Illus. 26–28), Macbeth when he encounters the witches (?), and the assassins (Illus. 29–30).

Between 3 November and 22 December 1847 five lithographs of costumes for *Macbeth* designed by Roberto Focosi were published by the *Gazzetta Musicale di Milano* [see pp. 413–20]. Part of the general romantic tendency towards historical accuracy in costume and set design, the lithographs were intended "to remedy possible errors in costume, for new operas of our musical theater . . . " A comparison of the five published lithographs [see pp. 415–19] with the five fully colored designs at the Bibliothèque Nationale (Illus. 18–22) reveals that both sources depict the same costumes. Because the lithographs were published only seven to eight months after the first performance of *Macbeth* by the house organ of Ricordi, one wonders if they represent costumes employed for the world premiere of the work. Moreover, because the Bibliothèque Nationale dossier also contains different representations of the same costumes for Macbeth, Lady Macbeth and the witches (as well as additional designs), one wonders when this second series might have been first employed. And, finally, one wonders why these Italian *figurini* are located in Paris.

The existence of a large collection of costume designs for predominantly nineteenth-century Italian operas was recently brought to light. Located at the Bibliothèque de l'Opéra, the collection consists exclusively of *figurini* sent by an unidentified Italian theatrical agency to the Théâtre-Italien in Paris, presumably to serve as production materials. [27] The style of these designs as well as the folders in which they are enclosed allow us to identify the *Macbeth* material as emanating from the same source. Given the fact that the Théâtre-Italien planned to produce *Macbeth* around the end of 1858, [28] it is possible that *Macbeth figurini* were sent to Paris as part of the established Italy-Théâtre-Italien circuit. However, it is also possible that the designs were sent to Paris to assist the *costumier* at the Théâtre-Lyrique, for the *Macbeth figurini* are the only such designs thus far located in Paris that are not part of the Théâtre-Italien collection.

Unlike the *Macbeth* dossier, however, *figurini* distributed by theatrical agencies generally contain a single set of costume designs for each opera. Moreover, the dual nature of the.

---

27. The collection consists of ten volumes [D130] entitled simply "costumes italiens." See Cohen and Conati's "Un élément inexploré de la mise en scène du XIXe siècle: les *figurini* italiens des opéras de Verdi," a paper presented at the Convegno internazionale di studio (Venice, Fondazione Cini, September 1979). This study discusses and demonstrates the relationship between a large number of previously unexplored manuscript and published costume designs for Verdi's operas in Italian and French collections. It will be published in the Congress Report entitled *Drammaturgia musicale e disposizioni sceniche di Giuseppe Verdi*. An abridged version of this paper has been published in Italian in *Da Rossini a Verdi, immagini del teatro romantico* . . . (Turin: Biblioteca Musicale Andrea Della Corte), pp. 7–15.

28. Plans for the production were canceled in November 1858. (See p. 402)

Illus. 18–26: Nine costume designs for Macbeth. *Illus. 19–23 are copies of the Focosi figurini (see 413–19). Bibliothèque Nationale, Département des arts du spectacle (Collection Rondel)*

Illus. 27–31: Five more costume designs for Macbeth; *see caption to Illus. 18–26*

Macbeth dossier is particularly perplexing because published designs, considered authoritative, were regularly copied and integrated into Italian theatrical archives as production materials.[29] In fact, copies of the five lithographs, prepared by the same agency, exist on tracing paper in the archives of the Teatro Regio of Parma, and a second manuscript copy of the same lithographs has been located in the Cellini Collection in Turin. Furthermore, the importance of the *Macbeth* lithographs can be demonstrated by the fact that they were copied, re-engraved and published by a second journal, *Il Cosmorama Pittorico*.[30]

Given the practice of distributing a single series of designs, how can one explain the existence of this alternate set? Does the Bibliothèque Nationale dossier consist of *figurini*-

29. For a discussion of this practice see, Cohen and Conati, "Un élément . . . ." op. cit.

30. Previously in private hands, the Cellini Collection was purchased in 1980 by the Biblioteca Musicale Andrea Della Corte, Turin. The Bertarelli Collection (Milan) possesses copies of the *Cosmorama* lithographs.

gathered together at different dates, both before and after the 1849 Parma performances, as the somewhat varying stylistic nature of the second series might suggest; or, were the copies of the Focosi lithographs added before the 1849 Parma performances to a preexistent dossier? Certainly there would be no reason for an agency to create new designs after the publication of the *figurini,* but there would be every reason to add copies of published designs to a preexistent dossier, especially since the *Macbeth* lithographs represent the first efforts in Italy to reflect historical accuracy in costume design. Moreover, as Verdi was actively involved in the preparation of the *figurini* employed at the first performance of *Macbeth,*[31] and as agencies distributed designs from early performances, it is likely that the agency would have distributed the original designs.

Two documents of a different nature remain to be added: an illustrated poster by A. Barbizet (Illus. 32) located at the Bibliothèque de l'Opéra, and a series of caricatures accompanying an amusing two-page satire of the production which appeared in Marcelin's *La Vie parisienne*[32] on 13 May 1865 (Illus. 33–34). The text[33] introduces us to Macbeths who are surprisingly up and singing in their castle at barely the break of dawn; a Macduff, transformed into a Mac-Muff; and a conductor who, with arms outstretched, seems to float blissfully in the air in the middle of an orchestral uproar. Accompanying the text are tiny caricatures of Macbeth, Lady Macbeth, Banquo, the witches, Macduff, Banquo's son, the guards, a confidante, a druid, a battle scene between Macbeth and Macduff, and a Lady of the Court.

31. See Verdi's letter of 21 January 1847 to Alesandro Lanari and his letter of late January or early February 1847 to Tito Ricordi.

32. For a study and catalogue of caricatures dealing with music in this periodical see, Jacques Léveillé, "Les Caricatures musicales dans *La Vie Parisienne* de 1863 à 1880," Master's thesis, Université Laval (Québec), 1982.

33. The text is a parody of the "Entry of the Kings" ensemble in Offenbach's *La Belle Hélène* (1864).

Illus. 32: Illustrated poster by A. Barbizet, F:Po, Af. Tit. II

We have, to use a French expression, *fait le tour de la question*. While there exist fewer iconographical documents for *Macbeth* than for the more popular Verdi operas performed in Paris, there are more than might have been expected. And, by bringing these previously unexplored documents to light we not only gain a more accurate picture of this production and a greater understanding of its reception in the press, but also learn that two of the most important nineteenth-century French *décorateurs*—Cambon and Despléchin—created sets for

Illus. 33–34: Two-page illustrated satire entitled "Macbeth *au Théâtre-Lyrique,*" La Vie Parisienne, *13 May 1865, pp. 262–63*

the Paris *Macbeth*. Moreover, in the process of tracing archival material for the Théâtre-Lyrique, we have demonstrated the extent to which the administration responsible for a production as well as the public's reaction clearly influence the number of iconographical documents one can hope to locate for a work performed in Paris during the second half of the nineteenth century.

REVIEWS AND ARTICLES DEALING WITH THE PARIS PREMIERE OF *MACBETH*

*When a feuilleton or article begins on the first page of a newspaper, no page reference is given. An * indicates that portions of the review appear in the "Reviews" section of this volume.*

* Anon. "Chronique Théâtrale. Théâtre-Lyrique: *Macbeth* . . . ." *Les Modes Parisiennes*, 6 May 1865, 214–16.

———. "[*Macbeth* . . .]." *Le Hanneton*, 30 April 1865, 3.

———. "*Macbeth* au Théâtre-Lyrique." *La Vie Parisienne*, III (13 May 1865), 262–65. Illustrated satire, eleven caricatures.

Bernard, Paul. "Les Deux *Macbeth* de Verdi." *Le Ménestrel*, XXXII, 34 (7 May 1865), 179–80.

Chadeuil, Gustave. "Revue Musicale. Théâtre-Lyrique: *Macbeth* . . . ." *Le Siècle*, 25 April 1865.

* Escudier, M. "*Macbeth*." *La France Musicale*, XXX, 18 (30 April 1865), 134–35.

———. "*Macbeth*." *La France Musicale*, XXIX, 17 (23 April 1865), 125.

* Ferry, Paul. "G. Verdi. Le nouveau *Macbeth* . . . ." *La Comedia*, 23 April 1865.

Fournier, Edouard. "Théâtres. Théâtre-Lyrique: *Macbeth* . . . ." *La Patrie*, 1 May 1865.

Gautier, Théophile. "Revue des théâtres. Théâtre-Lyrique.—*Macbeth* . . . ." *Le Moniteur universel, Journal Officiel de l'Empire Français*, 24 April 1865.

Gérome. "Chronique . . . Théâtre-Lyrique: *Macbeth* . . . ." *L'Univers Illustré*, VII, 428 (29 April 1865), 265–66.

* Hennette, A. "*Macbeth* . . . ." *Revue et Gazette des Théâtres*, 23 April 1865, 2.

Héquet, G. "Chronique musicale [*Macbeth*]." *L'Illustration*, XLV, 1157 (29 April 1865), 270–71.

Hyenne, Robert. "Théâtres [*Macbeth*]," *Le Moniteur de la Mode*, 1865, 156.

* L——, M——. "Revue Musicale, *Macbeth*." *Journal des Demoiselles*, July, 1865, 217–18 [article signed "M.L."].

* Lasalle, Albert de. "Théâtre-Lyrique: *Macbeth* . . . ." *Le Monde Illustré*, IX, 420 (29 April 1865), 270.

Pougin, Arthur. "*Macbeth* . . . ." *Le Théâtre*, 23 April 1865.

* Ortigue, Joseph d'. "Première représentation de *Macbeth* . . . ." *Journal des Débats*, 29 April 1865.

Ottens, Alfred d'. "Théâtre Lyrique Impérial. *Macbeth* . . . ." *La Semaine Musicale*, Nº 17, 27 April 1865.

Ralph. "*Macbeth* . . . ." *L'Art Musical*, V, 22 (27 April 1865), 169–73.

Roqueplan, Nestor. "Théâtres. Théâtre-Lyrique: *Macbeth* . . . ." *Le Constitutionnel*, 24 April 1865.

* Ruelle, Jules. "Correspondance particulière [*Macbeth*]," *Le Guide Musical* [Brussels], XI, 17 (27 April 1865), 2–3.

———. "Premières Représentations. Théâtre-Lyrique Impérial. *Macbeth* . . . ." *Messager des Théâtres et des Arts*, 23 April 1865.

Saint-Victor, Paul de. "La Semaine Théâtrale. Théâtre-Lyrique: *Macbeth* . . . ." *La Presse*, 24 April 1865.

* Smith, Paul. "*Macbeth* . . . ." *Revue et Gazette Musicale de Paris*, XXXII, 17 (23 April 1865), 129–30.

Trianon, Henry. "Chronique Musicale, [*Macbeth*]," *Revue Française*, V, tome 11 (May-August 1865), 139–46 and 611–17.

* Villars, F. de. "Shakespeare et Verdi. A propos de *Macbeth* et de quelques critiques." *L'Art Musical*, V, 24 (11 May 1865), 185–90.

Composition and Performance

TOWARD A CRITICAL
EDITION OF *MACBETH*
Philip Gossett

Critical editions, facsimile editions, diplomatic editions, practical editions, performing editions. ... With the linguistic and conceptual confusion engendered by these various terms, it is not surprising that members of the operatic community show a certain resistance to replacing the Verdi scores they know and love with new editions. In the best of all possible worlds, of course, we could produce the best of all possible editions, celestial harmony (from which all wrong notes are banned) would reign, and a triumphant finale bring down the curtain to shouts of "Vittoria, vittoria!" Since such an ideal can be realized only "lassù in cielo," if at all, we must face the sad reality that a musical edition of whatever kind is a series of compromises, compromises forced on an editor by limitations in the sources for an opera, by the requirements of performance, by the very process of printing music, and by human fallibility. And we must face the even more bitter realization that our particular vision of the ideal edition may not be shared by our neighbors.

The critical edition of the works of Verdi to be published by The University of Chicago Press and Casa Ricordi will be consulted both by those who want to know precisely what is in the Verdi sources and nothing else, and by those who want to perform the opera by dropping parts in front of the orchestra and beating time. There is no way a single musical edition can satisfy both, nor should it try. These extremes are in their respective ways mindless. A critical edition, on the other hand, is a product of reflection and analysis by those who have prepared it and requires reflection and analysis from those who would use it. It does not pretend to be a bearer of absolute truth, nor does it profess indifference to the truth. It seeks to be scientific yet knows that a performing art must be practical. Despite the paradoxes in which it must ever be enmeshed, a critical edition remains our best hope for bringing the operas of Verdi (not to mention Rossini, Bellini, and Donizetti) before ourselves and the wider public in as accurate and sensitive a manner as possible within the limitations of our imperfect world.

The criteria established by the editorial board of the Verdi edition, criteria open to modification, are intended to guide individual editors in applying a theoretical stance toward editing Verdi's music to the music itself. Faced with actual problems in an opera such as *Macbeth,* where the slurring in the very first three measures alone is of frightening complexity, one quickly comes to appreciate the difficulties which confronted the anonymous editors of Casa Ricordi who prepared the Verdi orchestral scores for publication as rental editions at the end of the nineteenth century. It is one thing to say we must be faithful to authentic sources, in this case primarily the 1847 autograph, and quite another to translate the prescription into reality. It is one thing to go through the operas of Verdi and select examples of possibly meaningful conflicting articulation or diverse dynamic levels and another to face every problem arising in each measure of an opera. There are problems whose solutions we can all agree upon; there are also depressingly many where we cannot be certain of a uniquely correct solution. And with enough examples of unquestionable omissions or particularly unlikely combinations of articulation in the autographs, even our selected examples begin to be called into question.

Where do we strike a balance? Users of the Verdi edition must always know what is Verdi's and what has been added or altered: about this there is widespread agreement. But how far should an editor go toward completing or modifying the readings of the autograph? And how firmly must an editorial board impose general standards on each individual volume so that users of the entire edition may reasonably expect that certain levels of consistency have been maintained?

Let us bring these abstractions into focus by examining the editorial problems found in a single passage from *Macbeth.* Practically any section of the opera might be chosen, but the *primo tempo* of Lady's *cavatina,* "Vieni! t'affretta! accendere," serves the function admirably. To anyone who would claim that Verdi writes precisely what he means and means precisely what he writes, a sufficient rebuttal would be the notation of the string accompaniment which underlies the opening vocal period, an antecedent-consequent phrase of four plus six measures, the latter half firmly modulating to the dominant. (See pp. 202–5) The slur for the triplet and staccati for the repeated sixteenth notes are precisely notated at the start, but already in measure 3 Verdi becomes careless. A slur is lacking in the second violins, and staccati are absent in the violas. Similar omissions continue. Staccati, for example, are lacking in the second violins and violas in the first half of measure 5, in the first violins in the second half of measure 5, and in the second violins throughout measure 6. It would be preposterous to assert that Verdi meant these omissions. The upper strings are playing chords together, but in measures 3, 4, and 6, two parts are marked with staccati while in the third the staccati are lacking. Surely in a D♭ major chord, given this musical context, no reasonable man would accept that the F played by the first violins should be staccato, the D♭ a third below played by the second violins not staccato, and the A♭ in the violas below staccato with the first violins. Not even an argument on grounds of scale degrees is possible, since the identical chord is found in measures 1, 2, and 4 with all notes bearing staccati. I emphasize the absurdity of the situation far beyond necessity to insist that there are indeed examples in which Verdi clearly did not mean literally what he wrote. A casual glance at Verdi autographs will turn up innumerable such places. A critical edition which preserved such absurdities would itself be absurd, and we could not expect any serious musician to bother with it.

But how far does the agreement of our mythical "reasonable man" extend? Before long these missing staccati become pesky indeed. The rhythmic accompanimental pattern comes in two forms, laid out with great care during the course of the phrase:

The second rhythm is found first in measure 3, where staccati are present in both violin parts, but not in the violas. We seem to have no choice but to add them. In measure 5 the figuration returns. Now only the first violins have staccati. Somewhat disgruntled, we nonetheless trot out our square brackets and complete the articulation in the second violins and violas. In measure 7 the figure returns once again. Although the orchestral parts in this measure are identical to those of measure 3, here none of the parts have staccati on the pair of sixteenth notes. Truly puzzled, we start to wonder whether Verdi might not be telling us something. As the consequent phrase expands in measures 8 and 9, the figuration appears three times in succession. Would there had been no staccati whatsoever here, for it might convince us that Verdi's notation should be taken seriously. Unfortunately, the violas have clear staccati in the first half of measure 8. Feeling positively betrayed, we extend them throughout. The extent to which slurs are also lacking for the opening triplets in measures 8 and 9 help convince us that carelessness is at the root of these omissions.

And yet we must remain cautious. Remember the cadence, in which the first violins ascend with the voice to the high B♭ (measures 9–10). The violins have a series of staccati during their ascent but descend from this peak without them. The ascent is accompanied by the opening rhythmic figure, with four sixteenth notes. Staccati are present in the violas, from which they must be extended to the second violins, which lack them. The melodic descent is also accompanied by second violins and violas, but here there are no staccati notated and, furthermore, the repeated sixteenths continue into the fourth beat of the 6/8 measure. The autograph shows unmistakably that this continuation was an afterthought of Verdi's, the second violins and violas having originally closed with an eighth note on the fourth beat as in all the other instruments. Are we justified in extending the staccati here? To only the second and third beats, or to the fourth as well? Suddenly arguments fly from every direction. There are good musical reasons for adding all of them, some of them, or none of them. And, although the question is phrased as in a multiple-choice test, the result is by no means trivial, since the accompaniment figure will sound very different depending on our choice. Given the clear pattern of increasing carelessness on Verdi's part as the phrase continues, we may feel it appropriate to extend the staccati, but there are excellent musical reasons for not doing so. Doubt gnaws at us, and no unequivocal answer is to be found. In such a situation it would probably be wisest to leave the autograph reading untouched.

Staccati in the accompaniment become even more uncertain in the following cadential phrases. Verdi constructs the end of the *primo tempo* with two similar passages, each leading to a tremendous tonic cadence. He gives the impression of parallelism between them, but while in part the second passage is practically a variation of the first, in part it is entirely new. The melodic line opening the first passage:

Act 1, No. 3: Cavatina Lady Macbeth measures 1–14

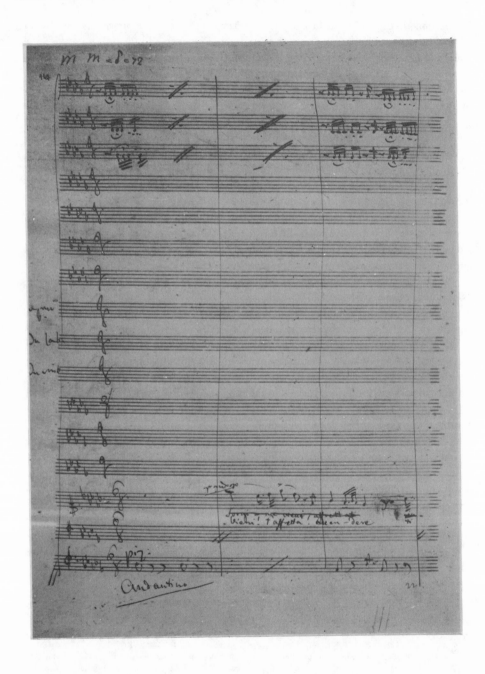

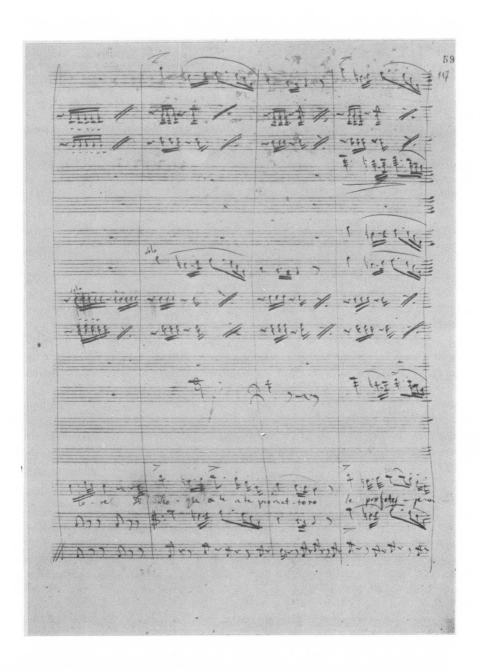

has a different harmonic basis from that of the second, but the intervals of the latter practically duplicate those of the former:

The similarities extend to the accompaniment, but whereas the pattern in the first passage (measures 12*ff.*) is:| ⸴ ♫ ⸴ ♪⸴ ♫ ⸴ ♪| in the second (measures 21*ff.*) Verdi reverses it, thus:| ⸴ ♪⸴ ♫ ⸴ ♪⸴ ♫ |Both times, however, these repeated chords are played by second violins, violas, and horns.

For the first passage there are no staccati whatsoever in this accompaniment. However, in the preceding measure, an introductory vamp setting up the characteristic accompaniment combination of second violins, violas, and horns, all notes in these instruments have explicit staccati. For the second passage there is no measure of vamp. The accompaniment is written only once (at measure 21), and the following three measures have repeat signs. In the one notated measure, violas have explicit staccati on the repeated sixteenths in both halves of the measure, but second violins and horns have no staccati whatsoever. It would be absurd to accept the staccati in the violas here and not extend them to the second violins and, given the context, to the horns. But should we also extend them back to the first passage? Or is Verdi using this too as an element of variation? Again we are talking about a point of interpretation which has a fundamental effect upon the sound of the music. We know that we cannot trust the composer to put everything in. Can we trust him when he leaves everything out? There are arguments to be made on both sides, and we cannot look for certainty. I personally would leave them out in the first passage, but I can easily understand the appeal of the opposite solution.

After all this, it is a relief to leave the accompaniment and examine the vocal line. Although there are problems here too, they are largely individual ones, whose implications do not keep growing. As soon as the voice enters, for example, the autograph has an unmistakable but puzzling articulation:

Why would Verdi adopt an articulation which so patently goes against the division of the text? The autograph reveals that the slurring may refer to a primitive version of the words, "Sorgi a me vieni, affrettati," which has been crossed out and replaced with the definitive text by Verdi:

The articulation is not much better in this original version, since "a me" clearly goes with "vieni" and not with "Sorgi," but the phrase cannot conclude on the second note, since the elision of "Sorgi" and "a" demands that "me" not be separated from its preposition. Though the accent on "vieni" helps justify the division of the phrase after "me," the text remains awkwardly treated. This may have motivated Verdi to abandon the original words.

We are left with an articulation whose appropriate text has been abandoned. Altering the words, however, Verdi seems to have neglected to bother with the slurs. Is one really justified in maintaining them under these circumstances? Might it not be preferable to consign the first slur to a note, explain its history, and suggest a slur covering only the first two notes, "Vieni!," as in the modern Ricordi edition? We must resist presuming that those who prepared these editions were ignorant. Some of their musical judgments stem from real dilemmas in the autograph, dilemmas we do Verdi and ourselves injustice to ignore.

In measure 7 there is a note in the vocal line in the autograph which is changed in every printed source of the opera. The phrase concludes on an F, instead of the expected E♭, which would parallel the antecedent phrase. Given the harmony here, the F, an added sixth to the A♭ major chord in the orchestra, is impossible:

In their rush to alter the vocal line, however, printed sources may have falsified the passage. Is it altogether sure that the vocal line is incorrect? Might it not be the orchestral part that Verdi has confused? The legendary sketches might help clarify just such a passage, although Gatti implies that complete sketches do not exist for *Macbeth*.[1] But were we actually to find this pitch in a sketch too, we might be justified in imagining that Verdi had actually planned the passage to proceed basically as in the following version:

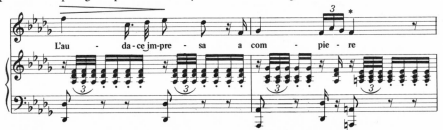

1. Carlo Gatti, *L'Abozzo del* Rigoletto *di Giuseppe Verdi* ([Rome], 1941), Introduction

io   ti   da-rò   va - lo - re

I needn't emphasize what a difference this interpretation might make in the passage. The problem may not be soluble, but it is certainly the function of a critical edition to raise such issues and offer alternative solutions.

Despite these examples the melodic line poses far fewer significant problems than the instrumental parts. Even when small contradictions exist, as in measures 16 and 17, where a short phrase appears three times in succession with three different markings, we can resist the temptation to make alterations or additions. The vocal line is independent and there is no reason to modify it unless the readings are truly problematical. Singers will adjust these markings to their own requirements in any case.

When we turn to melodic lines in the orchestral parts the most distressing problems arise. Not all passages are equally difficult to resolve. The four measures which open the second cadence (measures 21–24), whose accompaniment we examined before, present a coherent picture. In the first two measures the vocal melody is doubled by oboe and first violins. These instruments are slurred in the same way, although they lack the accents of the vocal part, presumably a purposeful omission. The last slur in the second measure is carried over into the third measure in the first violins, but not in the oboe. This makes sense, for the oboe is joined here by flute and clarinet. Its explicit rearticulation parallels the entrance of the other winds, while the strings alone are allowed to carry the phrase to its conclusion over the bar line. In the next two measures, all the articulation present in the autograph is consistently handled in the instruments, but some signs are lacking: a slur in the clarinet on the second half of the third measure; all articulation in the oboe (and the clarinet, which is in unison with the oboe) throughout the fourth measure. The models present, however, are unequivocal, and there is absolutely no reason to presume that Verdi, in a page in which all the instruments are playing the same line, wants flute, piccolo, oboe, trumpet, and violins, but not clarinet, slurred in the third measure, and flute, piccolo, trumpets, and violins, but not oboe or clarinet, slurred in the fourth. Extending these unequivocal models vertically seems self-evident.

The picture is quite different in the four measures which open the first cadence (measures 12–15). There are nine separate appearances of the following melodic phrase in the orchestra:

The autograph shows eight distinct articulations of this phrase, none of which agrees with the vocal articulation.

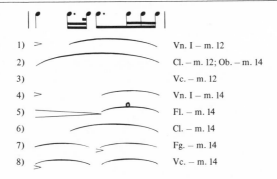

The diversity is staggering. How, faced with this, should a critical edition operate? How, indeed, should any edition operate? Do we find a common denominator? Do we throw up our hands in despair? Do we leave the passage strictly alone? I have been asking many rhetorical questions. In practically every case I have at least a personal answer to them. Here I have no clear answer, although there are certainly better and worse possibilities. In such cases the editor's responsibility is particularly difficult. Similar occasions will arise in every opera.

I could go on and detail many other problems, some of them quite serious, in this *primo tempo*. There are problems surrounding the use of dynamics, problems of conflicting dynamics (which on one occasion can clearly be justified but in the very next measure make no sense whatsoever), problems concerning the advisability and means of extending crescendo signs, problems which arise because of page turns, and so on. But my primary concern has been simply to demonstrate the processes of thought which seem to me must underlie every page of a critical edition of the works of Verdi. Verdi's autographs pose enormously difficult problems of interpretation, and a critical edition cannot shrink before them. We cannot use the difficulty of finding solutions as an excuse for not seeking them; nor can we use the apparent inconsistencies of the autographs as an excuse for ignoring what we find there. We must cope with those who will persist in believing every sign and with those who believe none of them. A critical edition presents and interprets the evidence. It can do neither less nor more.

OBSERVATIONS ON THE
AUTOGRAPH OF *MACBETH I*

David Lawton

The discovery of the autograph libretto of the first version of *Macbeth* has cleared up many of the mysteries that surrounded the fashioning of the text, particularly with respect to the roles played by Piave, Maffei, and Verdi himself. Working from this important new source—published for the first time in this volume—Francesco Degrada has traced the evolution of the libretto from Verdi's earliest prose drafts, from Piave's unsuccessful efforts to find verses that would satisfy the composer to the book in its final form, incorporating Maffei's changes and corrections.[1] It is not possible to trace the compositional history of the music to any comparable extent, for no sketches or drafts are known to exist for *Macbeth*. Nevertheless, careful study of the autograph full score can provide insights into Verdi's compositional process during its final stages. The aim of this essay is twofold: 1) to postulate approximate composition and orchestration dates for the opera; and 2) to examine some of the more significant revisions in the autograph.

Verdi's autographs are composing scores—not sketches, but records of at least two complete stages of notation, frequently with signs of revision at an intermediate stage. Such revisions show that he generally notated his manuscripts in two separate steps. Time and time again, one finds passages he crossed out in which only the voice part(s) with or without bass line had been written, with enough blank staves—with bar lines drawn through them—for the rest of the orchestra. A striking example can be found in the autograph of *Luisa Miller*, Act II, fol. 165v–170v. There Verdi first wrote out the entire soprano part for Luisa's "Tu puniscimi, o Signore" in B♭ major. Then, before even notating the bass line, he changed his mind, crossed out what he had written, and rewrote the whole line a half step lower, in A major.

The autograph in its earliest stage—the "skeleton score"—represents the completion of what Verdi considered the principal act of composing, *la parte creativa*. There is abundant evidence in his correspondence that he thought of orchestration as a separate, later process, and that once he had composed the principal vocal parts and the bass line the main job was done. Consider, for example, the letter that he sent to Piave with nine numbers of *Rigoletto*:

I could go into production in a few days from now, because just today I finished the opera. All that remains for me is to copy out [*mettere in netto*] the second act and the last piece. Meanwhile, in order not to lose any time, I'm sending you all the rest of the opera [i.e., Numbers 2, 3, 4, 5, 6, 7–11, 12,

---

1. See pp. 156–73 for the edition of the libretto see pp. 306–38.

13]. Take these nine pieces of music to Gallo in my name. Tell Gallo to have the vocal parts copied out, and then you distribute them ... I'll bring the rest of the opera with me, and while we're rehearsing I'll do the orchestration.[2]

This tends to confirm the hypothesis developed above:

1. Although Verdi had not yet orchestrated any of the opera, and would not do so until the rehearsals, he considered the opera finished.
2. What he sent Piave was probably a skeleton score. That would be adequate for the copying and distribution of the vocal parts, work that had to be completed as soon as possible so that the singers could begin learning their roles. Later, Verdi would use the same manuscript to complete the orchestration.

A similar picture emerges from Emanuele Muzio's account of the composition of *Macbeth*, the main topic of our investigation.

1. Muzio to Barezzi, 14 December 1846: Today I'll take almost a whole act to the *copisteria*.
2. Muzio to Barezzi, 19 December 1846: The first two acts are almost finished and, except for the arias, the rest is already at the *copisteria* and will be sent next week to the respective performers.
3. Muzio to Barezzi, 18 January 1847: The Maestro is working hard at Macbeth; today and tomorrow he'll finish Act III. All that's left for him to do is Act IV, and so maybe by the end of the month he'll have finished everything.
4. Muzio to Barezzi, 28 January 1847: By Sunday [January 31] the Maestro will have finished the entire opera, and Monday he'll begin the orchestration, and once the orchestration is finished, he'll go to Florence.[3]

Muzio's distinction between composition and orchestration is the same one made in Verdi's letter about *Rigoletto*. The opera was considered finished, and was sent to the *copisteria*, even though the orchestration remained to be done. In the case of *Macbeth*, however, Verdi completed most of the orchestration well before the rehearsals began, as we shall see.

Muzio's letters clearly establish two major stages in the gestation of the *Macbeth* score: composition and orchestration. On the basis of evidence drawn from the correspondence of the period, the autograph full score, and Verdi's autograph libretto with Maffei's revisions, we can postulate approximate dates by which the composition of each number must have been completed; from information in the so-called *libroni* (those invaluable publication records in the Ricordi archives) we can offer corresponding dates by which the orchestra-

2. Verdi to Piave, 5 February 1851, in *Abbiati* 2, 105. Martin Chusid has pointed out to me that the hypothesis developed here is something of an oversimplification in the case of *Rigoletto*, for which a continuity draft exists. For *Rigoletto*, the process of composition actually involves two separate stages: 1) the completion of the continuity draft; and 2) the preparation of the skeleton score. Thus when Verdi writes in this letter that he has "finished the opera," he must be referring to the continuity draft, for he goes on to say that he still has to "copy out [i.e. prepare in skeleton-score form] the second act and the last piece." Nevertheless, the general distinction between composition and orchestration is well documented in Verdi's correspondence, where it is found as early as the letters he wrote to Nani Mocenigo on 9 April and 25 May 1843. See Andrew Porter, "Verdi, Giuseppe," in *The New Grove Dictionary of Music and Musicians* 19, 643–44. [For locations and facsimiles of Verdi skeleton scores in public collections, see BUDDEN at 227, notes 1–3.]

3. The announcement that Verdi was to have "finished the entire opera" by January 31 is not quite accurate. We know from other sources—to be discussed below—that he composed four of the numbers only after his arrival in Florence: the Prelude, Duncan's march in Act I, Lady Macbeth's Act II *cabaletta*, and Banquo's scena in Act II.

tion must have been finished.[4] These sources require examination and interpretation before they can be used to support the information presented in tabular form on p. 215.

Muzio's letters provide only rough dates for the completion of each Act: I—14 December 1846; II—19 December 1846; III—19 January 1847; and IV—31 January 1847. These dates can be refined somewhat by information from other sources. Thus for Act I Muzio says "quasi un atto." Which pieces did he *not* bring to the *copisteria* that day? The next letter (December 19) offers a clue: Acts I and II are in the *copisteria*, except for the arias. There is only one aria in Act I, Lady Macbeth's *cavatina*; this was probably not among the Act I numbers that Muzio delivered to the *copisteria* on December 14. Neither was Duncan's march, one of the four pieces composed later in Florence, as will be shown below. The numbers that Muzio brought to the copyists on December 14, then, were probably Nos. 2 (*Introduzione*), 5 (*Scena e Duetto*), and 6 (*Finale* I). In any event, these three numbers must have been finished by January 7, the date that Verdi sent them to Varesi.

In Act II there are two pieces that could be called arias: Lady Macbeth's *cabaletta* ("Trionfai!") and Banquo's scena. We know from Verdi's letter to Barbieri-Nini of January 31 that he had decided not to compose her *cabaletta* until he had worked with her in Florence, so that it would be perfectly suited to her voice and of "sicuro effetto." Banquo's scena, No. "8½," is surely a later addition to the score. Verdi probably decided to compose the piece only after hearing Benedetti in rehearsal. The peculiar numbering of the piece in the autograph (8½—and not in Verdi's hand) suggests that it was indeed an afterthought. No text is provided for it in the manuscript libretto, and its entry in the *libroni* (see facsimile on p. 302) as No. 10½, is squeezed in between the entries for Nos. 10 and 11, in a different hand.[5] It seems likely, then, that by December 19 Nos. 8 (*Coro di Sicari*) and 9 (*Convito Visione, e Finale* II) were in the *copisteria*. We can be certain about No. 9, for Muzio reports in his letter of December 19 that Varesi had already picked up the music for the *Convito* and *Visione* and taken it with him to Rome, shouting its praises everywhere he stopped.

For Act III, we have only Muzio's letter of 18 January 1847 and Verdi's second letter to Varesi, in which he sends the baritone his music for Act III. Although the letter is unfortunately undated, it was probably written during the period 23-30 January 1847. For Act IV, aside from the completion date of January 31 given by Muzio, we know that Verdi sent Barbieri-Nini No. 14 (the sleepwalking scene) on January 31, and that he sent Varesi No. 15 (the final scene and death of Macbeth) on February 4.

We must mention one further source of information for composition dates before we address the question of orchestration. In the autograph full score, Nos. 2, 3, 5, 6, 8, 9, 11, and 15 all show corrections of an earlier text layer (for Verdi's titles of the individual numbers, see pp. 295-97). In his contribution to this volume, Francesco Degrada calls attention to the relationship of those text changes to Maffei's changes and corrections in Verdi's autograph libretto. According to Degrada, most (if not all) of these date before 21 January 1847, the date of Verdi's famous "S. Andrea" letter to Piave.[6] Clearly, all the numbers

---

4. Though similar in approach, Francesco Degrada's account of the chronology of composition differs in some respects—see pp. 171-73. For the *libroni*, see pp. 302-03. Eds.

5. I am indebted to David Rosen for this information. The discrepancy between the numbering in Verdi's autographs and that in Ricordi scores is attributable to Ricordi's practice of subdividing longer pieces into separate numbers for convenience of publication. Unless otherwise specified, the numbers in this article are those of Verdi's autograph.

6. See p. 160.

mentioned above must have been entered into the skeleton score before then. For No. 9—the finale that Varesi had taken to Rome—we can establish even an earlier date for Maffei's revisions. In his letter of 7 January 1847 Verdi asked Varesi to incorporate some text changes into his copy of that number.

There is no direct proof in Verdi's correspondence or elsewhere that could assist us in determining completion dates for the orchestration of the opera. But we can provide indirect proof, because there is a way of dating the earliest piano-vocal score, prepared by Verdi's pupil Muzio. The reader may wonder what the piano-vocal score has to do with orchestration; the answer is that the preparation and publication of the piano reduction presupposes the completion of the orchestration. It is inconceivable that Muzio could have prepared his reductions from anything but Verdi's autograph in its final stages, with the orchestration finished. The skeleton score would have been far too sketchy for this purpose. Even if one were to posit an intermediate orchestral draft that was sufficiently detailed—and there is no evidence for such a stage in Verdi's compositional procedure—a reduction prepared from it could not possibly reflect any changes that Verdi made in the accompaniment while putting his autograph into its final form. Almost any non-trivial change in the orchestration would have necessitated redoing the plates of the piano-vocal reduction. While Verdi doubtless did, on occasion, make changes in rehearsal that necessitated reengraving the plates, this was obviously a situation to be avoided where possible. And so Muzio (and his counterparts for the reductions of other operas) would have been set to work on the piano-vocal reduction of a number only after Verdi had completed what he expected would be its definitive orchestration.

So it is clear that establishing dates for the completion of the piano-vocal reduction of a number will give at least a *terminus post quem non* for its orchestration. The *libroni* in the Ricordi archives provide just this information. Volume 10, fol. 83v–84r gives the corresponding *data di consegna* (consignment date) for each number in the earliest piano-vocal score of *Macbeth*. There are two rival interpretations of the *data di consegna*: (1) the date Muzio handed over his manuscript reduction to the publisher; (2) the date a particular engraver (usually specified by name in the *libroni*) was given the (presumably) edited reduction and set to work. (These two dates may of course be very close—or even identical.) Whichever interpretation is correct, the *data di consegna* represents a *terminus post quem non* for the completion of the reduction, and therefore for the completion of Verdi's orchestration as well.

There is a pattern in the *date di consegna* that corresponds closely to what we know about the opera's chronology. Muzio's letter of 28 January 1847 states that Verdi intended to begin orchestrating on February 1, and that he would go to Florence only after the orchestration was finished. He left for Florence on February 15.[7] Had he actually finished orchestrating by then? There is no way to be certain, but it is significant that the *date di consegna* for all of the pieces except the four he composed in Florence are entered in the *libroni* during the period of February 5–15. The remaining four are entered a full month later, around the time of the premiere. With a few notable exceptions, the dates for the first group of pieces reflect the order in which they appear in the score, and in which their composition was completed:

7. According to Verdi's 14 February 1847 letter to Piave

February 5: Nos. 2 and 14
February 6: No. 6
February 7: part of No. 9
February 9: rest of No. 9, No. 10
February 10: Nos. 11 and 12
February 12: Nos. 13 and 15
February 13: No. 5
February 15: No. 3

The early date for No. 14, and the late dates for Nos. 3 and 5 are puzzling. The available evidence does not suggest a satisfactory explanation for the very early date for the *sonnambulismo* (No. 14), although it is tempting to think that the special sonority of this dramatically central piece may have been clear in Verdi's mind from the earliest stages of composition. As for No. 3, Lady Macbeth's *cavatina*, it is clear from Verdi's letter to Barbieri-Nini of 31 January 1847 that the soprano had raised some objections about the piece. However, since Verdi countered these objections and defended his original conception in his letter, her reservations cannot have been the reason for the delay. And while there are two revisions in the autograph of No. 3, as we shall see, they were almost certainly made during the rehearsals, i.e., after the *data di consegna*. In the case of No. 5, the duet of Macbeth and Lady Macbeth, it is possible that the late *data di consegna* was caused by a delay in hearing from one or both of the principals. Verdi had written to both Varesi and Barbieri-Nini with specific questions about the piece, and as of February 4 he had not yet heard from the baritone.

With the exception of these three pieces, then, the *date di consegna* provide a reliable chronology of the orchestration of *Macbeth*. Table 1 summarizes the chronology of composition and orchestration.

The distinction between composition and orchestration drawn earlier in this essay is central to the question of revisions in the autograph. Depending on what Verdi changed, and how he did so, we can usually determine whether revisions were made during the early (skeleton score) or late (full score) stages of notation. Generally speaking, revisions that reveal an earlier, discarded layer in skeleton score form, but show no corresponding erasures or cancellations in the orchestral accompaniment, are among the earliest changes in the manuscript. But revisions that alter orchestral parts other than the bass line of the skeleton score reflect a later stage in the evolution of Verdi's thoughts. The examples chosen illustrate both stages: changes made in the skeleton score, and in the full score. But first we must consider the ways in which Verdi made changes and corrections in his manuscripts.

1. In the case of trivial, localized corrections—for example, of a wrong horn note resulting from a transposition error—Verdi generally acted quickly enough to smear the wet ink and enter the correction on top of the original layer. There are countless instances of this in the *Macbeth* autograph, and all are easily deciphered. Since few of them involve compositional decisions, they will not be examined here.
2. In the case of actual compositional revisions, he made changes in the following ways:
   a. for a single line: he crossed out the original reading and wrote the revision on an adjacent staff.
   b. for all the staves: he crossed out the earlier reading. There is rarely any difficulty in reading cancellations of this sort.

TABLE 1

MACBETH I: CHRONOLOGY OF COMPOSITION AND ORCHESTRATION

Numbers	Composition completed no later than:	Orchestration completed no later than:
ACT I:		
1. Preludio	14 March 1847 (P)[1]	14 March 1847 (P); 15 March 1847 (L)
2.[2] Introduzione	14 December 1846 (M-B1)– 7 January 1847 (V-V1)	5 February 1847 (L)
3. Cavatina Lady Macbeth	31 January 1847 (V-BN)	15 February 1847 (L)
4. Recitativo e marcia	13 March 1847 (L)	13 March 1847 (L)
5. Scena e Duetto	14 December 1986 (M-B1)– 7 January 1847 (V-V1)	13 February 1847 (L)
6. Finale I°.	14 December 1846 (M-B1); 7 January 1847 (V-V1)	6 February 1847 (L)
ACT II:		
7. Scena ed Aria Lady	13 March 1847 (L)	13 March 1847 (L)
8. Coro di Sicarj	19 December 1846 (M-B2)– 21 January 1847 (V-P)[8]	15 February 1847 (L)
8½. Scena Banco	14 March 1847 (P)	14 March 1847 (P); 15 March 1847 (L)
9. Convito Visione, e Finale II	19 December 1846 (M-B2)	7 and 9 February 1847 (L)
ACT III		
10. Coro	19 January 1847 (M-B3)	9 February 1847 (L)
11. Recitativo Apparizioni, Ballabile ed Aria Macbeth	19 January 1847 (M-B3)– 4 February 1847 (V-V2; V-V3)	10 February 1847 (L)
ACT IV		
12. Coro	31 January 1847 (M-B4)	10 February 1847 (L)
13. Scena ed Aria con Cori Macduff	31 January 1847 (M-B4)	12 February 1847 (L)
14. Sonnambulismo di Lady Macbeth	31 January 1847 (M-B4; V-BN)	5 February 1847 (L)
15. Scena, Battaglia, Morte di Macbeth	31 January 1847 (M-B4)– 4 February 1847 (V-V3)	12 February 1847 (L)

1. Sources used to substantiate the dating of each number are abbreviated as follows:

L = *libroni*, vol. 10, fol 83v–84r
M-B1 = Muzio to Barezzi, 14 December 1846
M-B2 = Muzio to Barezzi, 19 December 1846
M-B3 = Muzio to Barezzi, 18 January 1847
M-B4 = Muzio to Barezzi, 28 January 1847
V-P = Verdi to Piave, 21 January 1847

V-BN = Verdi to Barbieri–Nini, 31 January 1847
V-V1 = Verdi to Varesi, 7 January 1847
V-V2 = Verdi to Varesi [23–30 January?] 1847
V-V3 = Verdi to Varesi, 4 February 1847
P = premiere, 14 March 1847

2. Boldface numbers indicate the presence, in Verdi's autograph, of text layers preceding Maffei's corrections.

8. Since the autograph of No. 8 preserves an earlier, canceled layer with Piave's original text, it is clear that the skeleton score must have been completed before 21 January 1847, the date that Verdi informed Piave of Maffei's revisions.

c. Often he erased an earlier reading with a sharp blade and entered the revision on the same staff. This method makes transcription from microfilms or xerox copies difficult at best; in some cases it is practically impossible to decipher the original layer even from the manuscript. Perhaps some of the special techniques used by art historians, such as infrared light, could reveal earlier readings in these passages.

d. Occasionally (rarely in *Macbeth*) he wrote the new version on a strip of paper and glued it over the old one. By holding the page up to a very strong light, one can usually read what is on the original surface.

e. There are also more radical revisions involving the removal of old pages or their replacement with new ones glued to the remaining stubs; here one can only speculate about the content of the excised passages.

The examples that follow have been arranged in chronological order: not in the sequence in which they appear in the opera, but in relation to an early or a late stage of the manuscript. In the case of revisions affecting passages not further revised in 1865, page references are to the Ricordi piano-vocal score No. 42311 (also available in a Kalmus reprint). In other cases, we refer the reader to the Bureau Central piano-vocal score of *Macbeth I* or to pages from that edition reproduced at pp. 480ff.

REVISIONS MADE AT AN EARLY STAGE

The first three examples illustrate changes that Verdi apparently made on the spot, while writing out the skeleton score.

Example 1
Act I, No. 3: Cavatina, measures 38ff.
(Ricordi, p. 37; Autograph, vol. 1, fol. 55r)

Only Lady Macbeth's part shows any signs of revision. Verdi erased the original layer in measures 38–39 and wrote the new version directly over it. That the first reading breaks off abruptly indicates that Verdi made this change while writing out the skeleton score. The revision is simple, and primarily rhythmic in nature: the original pitches are unchanged, but the phrase begins two beats later and takes exactly twice as long to cover the same melodic ground. The change sets the voice off from the orchestra more effectively, and the longer rhythmic values give a stronger emphasis to the text.

Example 2
Act I, No. 2: Introduzione, measures 386ff.
(Ricordi, p. 29; Autograph, vol. 1, fol. 44v)

Verdi had notated only the voice part before he removed measure 387 from the score. The absence of a text underlay for the C of measure 387 and the presence of an accent at the beginning of measure 388 (which makes little sense under a tie) suggest the following chronology: Verdi wrote the melodic line first. Then, while putting in the text, he decided that the C was too long, crossed out measure 387, resumed with the text in the next measure, and added an accent to retain something of the emphasis that the long duration had provided. The same correction is found in the analogous measure in the following phrase ("E il nostro oracolo").

Example 3
Act I, No. 2: Introduzione, passage replaced by present measure 324
(Ricordi, p. 25; Autograph, vol. 1, fol. 39v)

The three measures transcribed here are the total content of one canceled page: fol. 39v. This page is marked off into three measures, but of its twenty staves only the sixteenth from the top, Macbeth's part, is notated. The canceled passage does not connect well textually or musically with its immediate surroundings. Closer inspection shows, in fact, that there are revisions both immediately before and immediately after the canceled passage. Verdi erased and rewrote the voice parts and the bass line in measure 323, the last measure on fol. 39r. The first three measures on fol. 40r show changes in Macbeth's part, and the second of these also has a revision in the bass line. Unfortunately the original layers underneath all these erasures on fol. 39r and 40r are illegible. In any case, it seems certain that the three-measure cut is part of a larger, seven-measure revision including the last measure on fol. 39r, the canceled fol. 39v, and the first three measures on fol. 40r. Since the erasures and revisions around the cut are only in the voice parts and the bass line, it is certain that the revision was made at a very early date. The nature and location of the changes suggests the following order:

While writing out the skeleton score, Verdi had completed all three voice parts (Macbeth, Banquo, and the messengers) through the last measure on fol. 39r. He continued with Macbeth's part—the leading voice in the passage—at least as far as the third measure on fol. 40r. Perhaps he next resumed notation of the bass line on fol. 40r. He then decided to rewrite the whole seven-measure passage, cutting fol. 39v, and to revise the parts already written before and after the cut.

Example 4
Act IV, No. 12: Coro; rejected reading corresponding to measure 44 of 1847 version.
(See p. 515; Autograph, vol. 4, fol. 284v)

Here again, Verdi had notated only the vocal parts and the bass line before crossing out this measure, the last on the page. The canceled measure is only the beginning of what must have been an earlier form of the coda for this chorus, for a whole folio was removed between the present fols. 284v and 285r. Since the continuation is lacking, little can be said about the substance of the musical changes. The harmonic progression in the canceled measure implies a move in the following measures towards the submediant, a degree not used earlier in the piece. Verdi may have felt that the freshness of its appearance would be out of place in a coda. The revised coda, with its emphasis on the subdominant minor—a degree borrowed from the parallel minor mode—serves as a unifying, associative link with the first part of the piece.

Example 5
Act II, No. 8: Coro di Sicari, measures 19ff.
(Ricordi, pp. 117–18; Autograph, vol. 1, fols. 151v–152v)

This interesting change, although limited to the orchestra, must date from the early stage of the manuscript, because it involves only the bass line. The musical design involves an orchestral introduction (measures 1–17) that is repeated in measures 19–34 as a backdrop for the exchanges between the tenors and basses of the chorus. The original layer, which Verdi replaced with the simple instruction "come sopra" (i.e., repeat the first seventeen measures), indicates that his first idea was to vary the orchestral repeat of measures 1–17, preserving the essential harmonic structure while changing rhythmic and melodic details. This example shows more clearly than any so far presented that the bass line was the first orchestral part to be notated in the score.

Example 6
Act IV, No. 15: Scena, Battaglia, Morte di Macbeth,
measures 279ff.
(Bureau Central piano-vocal score, p. 235; Autograph, fol. 341v)

Verdi had written only the bass line of this purely orchestral passage before he decided to cancel measures 280–81 and 285–86 (the phrase is repeated). The original sequence, indicated by brackets on the example, expanded the four-measure metric module to six measures, creating the effect of a composed *ritardando* appropriate to a closing section. What the revised version loses in time, it gains in directness of harmonic movement from the tonic to the dominant in the cadential progression.

REVISIONS MADE AT A LATE STAGE

Example 7
Act I, No. 4: Reci.v e Marcia, measures 64–67 and 72–75.
(Ricordi, p. 51; Autograph, vol. 1, fol. 78v–79v.)

Verdi never orchestrated offstage *banda* music himself; he simply wrote it out in a short score of two staves. Thus the distinction between skeleton score and full score that has helped us to determine whether changes are early or late does not apply to this example. The revisions certainly represent a late stage in the manuscript as a whole, however, for Verdi did not even compose the march until he had arrived in Florence.

Verdi left the accompaniment unchanged, and revised only the principal melodic part. Let us examine measures 64–67 as representative of the kind of improvements that he made in this piece. Ex. 8 presents harmonic-metric reductions of both versions:

Example 8

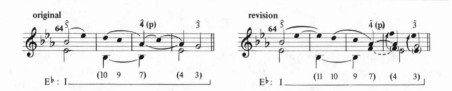

The reductions show that both versions have the same basic structure: a motion from B♭, the fifth, through A♭, a harmonized passing tone, to G, the third of the tonic (E♭) triad. In each case, the B♭ is followed by a prolonging, ascending leap of a perfect fourth to E♭, and the A♭ is delayed by an answering, descending leap—embellished by a passing C—of an augmented fourth from D:

Verdi's revisions therefore affect primarily the foreground, and in my opinion they are a distinct improvement. By spinning out the rhythmic motive ♪ ⁊ ♪ | ♪ until the cadence in measure 67, he eliminated the two-bar rhythmic parallelism that had split the four-bar phrase into halves. The original dissonance treatment contributed further to the squareness of the passage. In both measures 65 and 67, appoggiaturas on the first beat delay the arrival of the chord tones (though measure 65, strictly speaking, contains a consonant appoggiatura followed by a dissonant resolution!). The dissonance treatment of the final version, on the other hand, creates a sense of continuous motion towards the cadence by shifting the same prolonging tones (E♭, D, and C) to new positions in the metric framework. The E♭ from the second beat of measure 64 is carried over as a suspension to the downbeat of measure 65. The delay in the appearance of the D displaces the C in turn to the downbeat of measure 66. The final suspension from A♭ to G in measures 66–67 (present also in the first draft) is overlayed in the revision by the projection of an inner voice, F-E♭) to the upper octave.

Example 9
Act I, No. 3: Cavatina Lady Macbeth,
a. measure 90 (Ricordi, p. 40: Autograph, vol. 1, fol. 61v);
b. rejected reading, condensed into measure 151 of 1847 version (Ricordi, p. 44;
Autograph, vol. 1, fol. 67v).

These two revisions of Lady Macbeth's *cavatina* are difficult to date, even approximately. On the basis of internal evidence alone, the first could have been made at any time. The change, though restricted to the voice part, would not have affected the orchestral accompaniment, because the passage is a solo cadenza. The second is evidently late, because it involves the whole score. Indeed, its existence in another source—a manuscript score in the Bologna conservatory library—points to a very late date, possibly sometime during the rehearsals for the premiere.

Both changes are the kind that a composer might make for a particular singer. Without altering the function or the character of the original, Verdi extended the range of his cadenza and made its melodic shape more florid. The *cabaletta* revision does have more far-reaching compositional ramifications. Verdi has compressed his original two-measure chromatic ascent, building in intensity over a prolonged dominant of the full orchestra, to a single, unaccompanied measure in which the voice, after coming to rest on low B, sweeps up rapidly to the climactic *con slancio* phrase. And yet the revision undoubtedly solved a practical problem as well, for the first version required the singer to compete, in an unfavorable register, with the full orchestra.

The transcription of measures 151ff is a composite reading from two different sources. The first measure was illegible in the autograph, because Verdi erased it so thoroughly but fortunately it was legible in the Bologna manuscript (RR 180). The second measure, which had been crossed out rather than erased, was easily deciphered from the autograph.

Example 10
Act II, No. 9: Convito Visione, e Finale II, measures 94ff. (Brindisi)
(Ricordi, p. 133; Autograph, vol. 2, fol. 178r)

This is certainly the "passage in two ways" to which Verdi refers in his letter of January 31 to Barbieri-Nini. He asked her to inform him which version she preferred before he orchestrated it. She chose the alternate of the two *brindisi* readings, for the original is crossed out in the autograph. He must have known her preference before he orchestrated, because the orchestral parts doubling the voice show no trace of revision. The reprise of the *brindisi* is written out in abbreviated form—only the voice part appears. The analogous passage—measures 300–1—is found there only in its original form, without the "oppure." Verdi clearly forgot to make the corresponding adjustment there.

Example 11
Act I, No. 5: Scena e duetto (1847 version),
a. measures 210ff. (see pp. 482–83; Autograph, vol. 1, fol. 104 v);
b. original ending of cantabile (see p. 483; Autograph, vol. 1, fol. 106r);
c. rejected reading immediately preceding measure 302 in 1847 version (see p.
487; Autograph, vol. 1, fol. 113r)

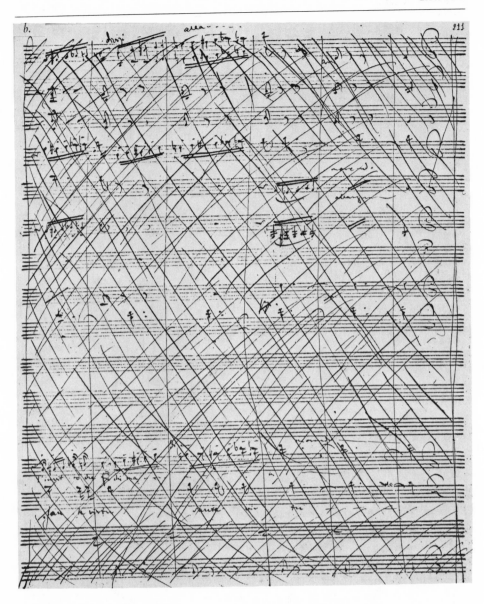

Example 11a: The layered transcription of fol. 104v. shows that three parts have been revised: the voice part in measures 215–16 (crossed out and rewritten on an adjacent staff), and the violin I and clarinet parts in measure 215 only (erased and rewritten on the same staff). The violin and clarinet parts, which double the voice, show signs of an earlier layer only in measure 215, suggesting that Verdi decided to revise the passage while working on the orchestration. Apparently he had fully scored the piece up through measure 215. At that point, he rewrote Lady Macbeth's part in measures 215–16. This meant that he had to change the clarinet and violin parts in measure 215 as well, for they reflected the earlier version of the vocal line. There was no need to emend those parts in measure 216, for he

had not yet written anything in that measure. When he resumed orchestration, he simply took up where he left off.

Example 11b: Of all the revisions within the *Macbeth* autograph, fol 106r, which has been crossed out but is still perfectly legible, offers the most exciting picture of Verdi's musical ideas in a finished but ultimately rejected form. Verdi's letter to Barbieri-Nini of 31 January 1847 refers explicitly to the ending of this *adagio:*

In the 3/8 *adagio* of this duet there is a chromatic scale at the end: [for the musical example, see the letters section] it must be sung rallentando and end in a pianissimo; if this proves difficult for you, let me know.

This letter raises the possibility that vocal difficulties were the primary reason for Verdi's revision, even though he did orchestrate his original ending before deciding that it should be changed. Perhaps, he never received a reply from Barbieri-Nini, and assuming that the chromatic scale would be no problem for her, orchestrated the passage as he had first conceived it. Or maybe the singer did approve the chromatic scale, but it proved to be problematic after all. In any case, it is a late revision, most likely made during the rehearsals. Verdi must have preferred the final version from a musical and dramatic standpoint as well, for he retained it, and not the original ending, as the basis for his 1865 revision.

As with some of the other examples, the canceled passage does not tell the whole story about the revision. Fol. 105 is not the original folio; it is pasted onto the stub of an earlier, excised folio. The last three measures on fol. 105v, the sheet facing the canceled fol. 106r, now contain the definitive 1847 ending for the duet. But at some point these three measures were crossed out with a single, large X; this X was later erased, and there are no traces of an earlier layer underneath the revised ending. So it would seem that the canceled passage is part of a larger, more extensive revision.

Example 11c (fol. 113r.): This is a very late revision, made after the original layer had been fully orchestrated. The two canceled measures do not constitute a logical musical continuation of the measure immediately preceding them (i.e., what is now measure 300). Fol. 112 was pasted into the autograph, replacing another page which had been cut out; therefore the original form of the passage cannot be reconstructed in its entirety.

Example 12
Act III, No. 11: Rec.v ed Apparizioni,
Ballabile ed Aria Macbet, measures 107ff.
(Ricordi, p. 218;[9] Autograph, vol. 3, fols. 242v–243r)

Shown above is the passage as it is found on page 301 of the manuscript in the Milan Conservatory, Noseda I 195. In the apparition scene, after the disappearance of the cauldron, a small group of wind instruments beneath the stage plays a brief fanfare anticipating the music that will accompany the Shew of Kings. In the autograph this "suono sotteraneo di cornamusa" is scored for two oboes in unison, doubled one octave lower by four clarinets in A, but this passage is written over an illegible earlier layer. Fortunately, four other manuscript full scores of the period preserve the original scoring of the passage: trumpets and horns in D, a rather surprising combination when one remembers Verdi's insistence, in his 23 November 1848 letter to Cammarano, that there should be "neither trumpets nor

9. The revisions made in 1865 do not affect the point under discussion, so the later score may be cited here.

trombones." But Verdi probably had made the revision even before the piano-vocal reduction of the number was issued, for the reduction, like the definitive reading in the autograph, gives an octave a-a′ in measure 110, a reading shared by none of the four contemporary manuscript copies. [10] The definitive scoring has the important advantage of using instruments already in place beneath the stage.

I have attempted to show, from the autograph full score, that the compositional history of *Macbeth I* is every bit as complex as the evolution of its libretto. The numerous revisions in it reveal that Verdi continued to refine his ideas right up to the last moment. In his desire to do full justice to Shakespeare's great tragedy, Verdi applied the same uncompromising artistic ideals to the criticism of his own notes that had compelled him to reject as unsatisfactory draft after draft of Piave's verses, until he was driven to seek Maffei's assistance. And the long, difficult gestation of this, his first Shakespeare opera, left him with more profound dramatic insights, increased powers of musical characterization, and a surer grasp of large-scale structure.

APPENDIX

In the Library of Congress, there is a copyist's full score of *Macbeth I* (M 1500 V48 M12) in four volumes. Marked "Per Originale," the manuscript bears the label of the Regio stabilimento nazionale TITO DI GIO. RICORDI. [11] This score has some changes in the second-act *finale*, in Verdi's hand. The original version of the two measures Verdi revised is in all full scores and piano-vocal reductions of *Macbeth I* that I have consulted. Even the partially-autograph score in the Bibliothèque Nationale, the principal source for *Macbeth II*, presents these two measures in their original form. For the final version the reader may consult pp. 167–68 of the Ricordi edition of *Macbeth II* (plate number 42311). Indeed, all printed scores of

Macbeth II examined have the revised form of these two measures. Verdi may have made the revision for the performances that he directed in Bologna, in autumn 1850. At a first glance, the reason for the change would appear to be the difficulty of the soprano's unprepared entrance on a high B. Verdi also retouched Macbeth's part, however, and in so doing he not only improved the declamation but also differentiated it more effectively from Dama's part in the ensemble. Also, by removing the high B here, he was able to save it for the climax of the *finale* in measure 435. The use of the new version in the vocal scores of *Macbeth II* indicates that Verdi considered the revision to be definitive.

10. Two manuscripts in the Milan Conservatory Library—Partitura manoscritta no. 441 (marked "per originale") and Noseda I 195—give both trumpets and horns a concert D at the end. The Bologna manuscript previously cited (RR 180) and the Library of Congress manuscript described in the Appendix give the horns a concert D and the trumpets a B (!), probably a transposition error for an intended concert A.

11. While the label "Tito di Gio. Ricordi" clearly dates from after Giovanni Ricordi's death in 1853, the label may have been pasted to the cover of the score long after the manuscript was copied.

MACBETH:
NOTES ON THE INSTRUMENTATION
OF THE TWO VERSIONS
Julian Budden

In his contracts with theatrical managements Verdi would usually stipulate that he should not be required to score a new opera until the piano rehearsals had begun. From this one might conclude that, like most composers of today, he would first of all write his operas for voice and piano before making out an orchestral score. Not at all. Having made any preliminary sketches that might be necessary he set out the music as a skeleton full score with voice parts, bass and such instrumental cues as might have occurred to him. Drafts of this kind exist for the scena ultima of *I due Foscari*,[1] the first scene of *Attila*[2] and the discarded recitative and aria for Procida, "O Sicile, ma patrie," from *Les Vêpres siciliennes*.[3] At some stage they would be put into short score and dispatched to the singers concerned, either piecemeal (i.e. number by number) or else in the form of rehearsal books. Where these last survive, as at the Paris Opéra and in the Library of the Imperial Theatres in Leningrad[4] they, no less than the drafts, often reveal notable divergences from the definitive scores. Clearly, then, the process of composition continued even during rehearsals; as well as that, the harmonization and the scoring were virtually inseparable in the composer's mind. So it is no surprise to find that in those works which he revised, no matter how long after their first performance, the original music that remains is scored as before. There are exceptions, notably where an opera was revised for Paris whose public, reared on the music of Meyerbeer and the concerts of Habeneck, expected a more sophisticated manner. The baptism scene in *Jérusalem* is shorn of the naïf concertante violin that had adorned it in *I lombardi*. For *Le Trouvère* Verdi rescored several passages of *Il trovatore* without in any way affecting their musical substance[5]—though even here it is rare to find a case in which the harmony has not been slightly elaborated as well. Likewise in the French version of *La forza del destino* which Verdi made in 1881 the vocal score published by Choudens indicates that certain parts have been rescored, though until the matching full score comes to light we can never be certain of the extent of the changes. In the revised *Macbeth*, written for the Théâtre-Lyrique, such examples of window dressing are rare—the reallocation of a few chords in the apparition scene, a contrapuntal enlivening of the texture of the *tempo di mezzo*

---

1. On display in the Museo Comunale, Busseto. See P. Petrobelli, "Osservazioni sul processo compositivo in Verdi," *Acta Musicologica* 43 (Basel, 1972) 125–42; facsimile in William Weaver, *Verdi: a Documentary Study* (London: Thames & Hudson, no date), plates 76–79

2. Bibliothèque Nationale, Paris MS 2208; facsimile page in Weaver, *op. cit.*, plate 88

3. Bibliothèque de l'Opéra, Paris MS A 593a. [MS A 619 Supplément I contains the skeleton score of a monologue for Carlos at the start of *Don Carlos*, Act V; transcription in Andrew Porter, "A Sketch for *Don Carlos*," *Musical Times*, 111 (1970), 882–85; facsimile page in *The New Grove*, 19, 656.]

4. See G. Barblan, "Un po' di luce sulla prima rappresentazione della Forza del Destino a Pietroburgo," *Bollettino dell'Istituto di Studi Verdiani* 5 (Parma, 1962) 832–79.

5. See D. Rosen, "Le Trouvère," *Opera News* 41 (April 9, 1977) 16–17.

of the grand duet in Act I, and a more elaborate accompaniment for "La patria tradita," the cabaletta of the tenor aria. The harp part that embellishes both the prelude and sleepwalking scene in the printed edition of the revised version is an editorial interpolation. In general the rule stands: same harmony, same scoring.

Given the steady enrichment of Verdi's style over the years, it might be thought that this threatened to make a patchwork of operas revised a long time after their birth. If it does not, the reason lies partly in that continuity of vision which enabled Verdi even in his later works to draw upon some of the procedures of his youth, and partly in the skill with which the transition between old and new is effected. The revised versions of *Simon Boccanegra*, *Don Carlos* and *La forza del destino* show no trace of stylistic incongruity. In the revised *Macbeth* this fusion was much more difficult to achieve, not so much because of the length of time that separates the two versions of the opera, but rather because it spanned a watershed not only in Verdi's own style of scoring but also in the development of the Italian stage orchestra.

In 1847 the musical direction of an opera was still divided between the *maestro al cembalo*, who taught the singers their notes and took charge of the piano rehearsals, and the leader of the first violins who conducted the music intermittently with his bow, using not a full score but his own violin part fitted out with vocal cues. Hence the value of those self-perpetuating accompanimental patterns in which the operas of the *Primo Ottocento* abound; hence, too, the sparing use of first violins during an aria so as to leave the leader's bow arm free to accommodate the tempo to the singer. By 1865 the authority of the conductor had been established, if precariously, throughout Italy and France; therefore such expedients were no longer necessary. In 1847 sopranos were still accustomed to use coloratura as a vehicle for dramatic expression; by 1865 coloratura had become relegated to the decorative showpiece. No purpose, therefore, was served by brilliant *cabalettas* such as "Trionfai, sicuri alfine" in which the projection of a roulade is aided by various combinations of woodwinds; for that reason if for no other it had to be replaced. Finally, beginning with *La battaglia di Legnano* Verdi had begun to score his more monumental scenes in a new way. Previously he had grouped his instruments by register; now he tended to group them in "families," thus producing a far richer effect. (The scene of Arrigo's consecration to the Company of Death is a landmark here.) In the first *Macbeth*, Banquo's "Come dal ciel precipita" with its unison strings above thudding trombones, bassoons and cimbasso comes near to the new manner—if only Verdi had not added oboes and clarinets to the melody, omitted violas, and kept the basses on the accompaniment! By the ninth bar the scoring has reverted entirely to the old "risorgimentale" manner with all strings except first violins forming the accompaniment. This is the style in which all the arias (excepting the sleepwalking scene, if that can properly be termed an aria) and most of the ensembles of the 1847 Macbeth are scored. Lady Macbeth's *cavatina* is conceived in much the same orchestral terms as Odabella's in *Attila*. The orchestral melody which takes over toward the end of Macbeth's "Pietà, rispetto, amore" is for violins, flute, oboe and clarinet with an accompaniment of cellos and popping bassoons. Even the cello and clarinet embellishment of Macduff's cantabile, though novel in its effect, does little more than vary a traditional obbligato procedure. From here it is a far cry to numbers such as Lady Macbeth's "La luce langue" of 1865. Verdi bridges the gap by beginning the new aria with a self-perpetuating orchestral pattern for strings alone without first violins, then after eight bars easing into a different style of accompaniment in which every phrase is colored by an appropriate instrumental combination. Particularly effective use is made of strings on their own. So skillfully is it all managed that the listener is unaware of the transition. In the new hallucination scenes the conventional conglomerations of instruments are unpicked so as to yield greater strength and variety of color. Trombones are no longer indissolubly wedded to bassoons and the brass bass. The telling use of low flute in the new exiles' chorus is a legacy from the Paris Opera, whose influence pervades the ballet music and the final chorus that replaced the death scene.

Together with these two styles of scoring there exists yet a third which is peculiar to *Macbeth*—that is, the deliberately strange manner reserved for the more gruesome scenes of the opera. This remains constant in both versions except where the music itself has been changed. Examples include the weird combination of oboe, trumpet, clarinets, bassoons and trombone which accompanies the witches' first salutation ("Salve o Macbetto, di Glamis sire!"), the curiously "voiced" brass and bassoon chords to which the apparitions speak their prophecies, the underground woodwind band that plays during the "Shew of Kings"; and most notable of all, the selective scoring of the grand duet in Act I and the sleepwalking scene. Not that there was anything new in the principle of selective scoring as far as Verdi was concerned. All his early operas contain at least one number in which the voice is accompanied by a mere handful of instruments—the six cellos of Zaccaria's *preghiera;* the cor anglais, clarinet, bassoon, harp, cello and double bass of Abigaille's death scene, the eight violins, two violas, bass, flute and clarinet of Giselda's "Ave Maria" are all instances of this. Sometimes the effect is all too consciously decorative, a "purple patch" extraneous to the drama, as in Carlo's "Quale al più fido amico" from *Giovanna d'Arco* and Odabella's "Oh nel fuggente nuvolo." Not so in the above-mentioned scenes from *Macbeth.* Here all traces of the "concertante" element have gone. In his letter of 7 January 1847 to Varesi, Verdi mentions that the duet is scored for "two horns, two bassoons, muted strings and a kettledrum." In the event he added flute, cor anglais and clarinets; he even briefly introduced trombones and bass drum where Macbeth describes the voice that haunted him at the moment of Duncan's murder. Rarely do any of these instruments play on their own; but certain combinations, such as cor anglais and low clarinet or cor anglais and bassoon give the illusion of a new instrument altogether, not unlike the blend of cor anglais and horn that opens Rimsky-Korsakov's version of Mussorgsky's *Boris Godunov.* Throughout Macbeth's dagger speech the dark, shifting colors evoke a world of insubstantial shapes. In the sleepwalking scene, the same selection of instruments is handled differently but with no less resource. Here the cor anglais is used in certain passages like a spotlight, keeping the eye focused on the central figure. In both these scenes the instrumental palette is an integral part of the dramatic concept to a far greater extent than in the examples cited earlier. What is more, if we except the "prison prelude" in Act III of *Il corsaro,* which we know to have been drafted in the late spring of 1846, probably before *Macbeth* was even thought of, there are no further examples of selective scoring in Verdi's operas until much later, and those that come to mind carry still further the principle first exemplified by the grand duet of *Macbeth,* whereby a certain basic color is established by a particular instrumental "mix" which is then appropriately varied, or variously "shaded," even to the extent of drawing upon other instruments where required. Thus to express the unique mood of Leonora's *melodia* in *La forza del destino,* in which nostalgic dreams are joined with a sense of foreboding, Verdi uses a basic palette of strings, harp and solo woodwind, with occasional interventions from second oboe and second clarinet. At the words "Fatalità! Fatalità!" the two trumpets put in a brief appearance. For once all four horns are silent throughout, or at least until the final few bars of orchestral pandemonium. A case of what might be called "submerged" selective scoring is the love duet from *Otello* where, from "Quando narravi l'esule tua vita" onward, cor anglais, bass clarinet and harp, mostly low in its register, provide the foundation for the unusually mellow coloring of the music. Never, as in the early operas are we given the impression of an instrumental stunt, only of a state of mind or an atmosphere depicted with rare precision. It is for such feats as these that *Macbeth* paves the way—another instance of the opera's importance as a pioneering work in the Verdian canon.

ASPECTS OF THE PRODUCTION
OF *MACBETH*
Marcello Conati

"In short, the things that need special care in this work are: *Chorus and Machinery.*" Thus Verdi wrote to the impresario Lanari, in his 15 October 1846 letter accompanying the outline of *Macbeth*. Five months later, after the opera's first performance, the composer's words were echoed by the baritone Felice Varesi: "This opera calls for an elaborate mise-en-scène and twice the usual number of choristers ..."[1] In this same letter, Varesi also observed that: "In *Macbeth* Verdi has adopted a new style suited to the fantastical nature [*genere fantastico*] of Shakespeare's tragedy."

The impression that Verdi had purposefully ventured upon a new genre (new not only for him but for the whole practice of Italian melodrama of the period)—i.e., the *genere fantastico*—was, moreover, rather widespread among contemporary Italian critics. In this they were unaware, or had forgotten, that this genre had ancient roots in the Italian theatrical tradition—roots that, as far as musical theatre was concerned, could be traced back almost to the very origins of opera in the seventeenth century. At that time appeared also the incorporation into Italian scenic design of "machines" and the taste for effects a sorpresa, for scene changes *a vista* (in plain view), for apparition scenes, and so on.

Equally widespread was the impression that in such experiments Verdi had been influenced by musical theatre from beyond the Alps—not only Meyerbeerian *grand opéra* (which, in the high Romantic era, preserved certain aspects of the baroque theatre's machinery a sorpresa) but also the operas of Weber and Mozart. Reviewing the opera after the premiere, Antonio Calvi wrote in his *Ricoglitore*:

All those pieces in which the supernatural powers intervene, ... though in themselves beautiful and charming, yet lack that mysterious, *fantastic* character that the situation calls for, of which Weber, Mozart, Meyerbeer, and a few others have shown us such splendid examples. And I should be almost inclined to say that Italian talents, born under a warmer sun and a more splendid sky, lack in their palettes (if I may so express it) colors suitable for representing supernatural objects in the manner that Northerners can.[2]

At this point we must recall that precisely here, at the Pergola in Florence, the very first performances in Italy of Meyerbeer's *Robert le diable* (26 December 1840) and Weber's *Der Freischütz* (2 February 1843) had taken place, and that in December 1846 the Società filarmonica had presented a revival of Mozart's *Don Giovanni*. Thus the frequent references of the Florentine critics to these masterpieces when evaluating the supernatural elements in *Macbeth* are not surprising. Particularly insistent is the mention of *Robert*. According to

1. Varesi to Ranzanici, 17 March 1847

2. *Ricoglitore*, 20 March 1847. For substantial excerpts from the contemporary criticism cited in this article, see the Reviews section, where the items are arranged in chronological order.

Alessandro Gagliardi, for example, the scene in which the sylphs revive Macbeth "is an imitation of one in *Robert le diable,* and the music in it is a rather pronounced reminiscence of that employed by Meyerbeer on that occasion."[3] Just as frequently, the episode of Banquo's ghost was compared with that of the ghost of Nino in Rossini's *Semiramide*—the comparison usually so framed as to underline the inferiority of the dramatic result achieved by Verdi. This was suggested, for example, by Vincenzo Meini (an ex-singer, who subsequently turned to a career as a writer, for whom Donizetti had written a role in *Maria di Rudenz*):

Nor do I understand how the sublime *terribilità* of Shakespeare in this supremely dramatic moment failed to inspire in Verdi something comparable to the finale of *Semiramide*.[4]

But above all it is on the "fantastic" element per se that the critics focus. Montazio wrote:

As for the fantastic element—let us be quite honest—Verdi is still far from reaching that high point of idealism attained by Weber, Mozart, Beethoven, and the still-living Meyerbeer. Perhaps he was afraid that he would end up involuntarily plagiarizing one of these sublime masters; perhaps he wished to place himself at the opposite pole from that which these fantastic composers have provided as models of the *genere fantastico;* perhaps he did not have enough time to work out his conceptions—in a word, whatever the excuses that may be offered on Verdi's behalf, the one thing that cannot be said is that in the specifically "fantastic" part of the Shakespearean poem he has set to music there exists any example of fantastic grandeur, of a musical setting that characterizes the mood.[5]

A critic of the *Ricoglitore* has this to say about the results achieved by Verdi in the "fantastic" part of the opera:

Were it permissible to offer advice when not bidden to do so, I should tell the fortunate maestro not to pick any more fantastic subjects, for in such demanding works it is not enough to wish to succeed and to set to with a will, but there is need, more than ever, of a versatile and imaginative talent, whose effects must be all-encompassing yet unlike any others, precisely the requirement for pristine creations of genius: that is, having no type to follow or models to imitate; of these we have incontrovertible specimens in Meyerbeer, Rossini, and a very few others.[6]

Similar advice to abandon the *genere fantastico,* along with an exhortation not to let himself be seduced "by the fair siren songs of foreign liaisons," was offered by Giuseppe Giusti in his 19 March 1847 letter to Verdi. This letter, often glossed by scholars and now celebrated to the point of tedium, bears witness to the narrow-mindedness of so many elements in mid-nineteenth-century Italian culture toward the daring Verdian experiments[7] (even though, as Baldini observed,[8] in defense of the letter's idealistic content can be

---

3. *Revue et Gazette Musicale de Paris,* 28 March 1847. Another reference to *Robert* is found in G. Stefani's review in *Caffè Pedrocchi,* 1 August 1847.

4. *La Moda,* 20 March 1847. See also Enrico Montazio's "Il Macbeth e la musica fantastica," in the *Rivista di Firenze,* 27 March 1847. This number of Montazio's periodical, dedicated entirely to Verdi, is printed on green paper!

5. Montazio, op. cit.

6. The article, signed D. J., is cited here from *Bazar di novità artistiche, letterarie e teatrali* (Milan), 24 March 1847.

7. See Mila's severe comment on the letter in his *La giovinezza di Verdi,* pp. 273–75.

8. *Abitare la battaglia,* pp. 138–40

cited that warm exhortation to political *engagement* that was the principal concern of the Tuscan poet).

The confusion of the critics mirrors that of the first-night audience. The accounts of the evening are in substantial agreement: much applause for Acts I and II (particularly for the first chorus of the witches, Lady Macbeth's *cavatina*, the *primo tempo* of the soprano-baritone duet, and the chorus of murderers), a frigid reception for Act III (the act with the "fantastic" goings-on and the apparitions), and scanty applause for Act IV (only for the sleepwalking scene and Macbeth's aria). Those numbers which Verdi considered "the principal pieces of the opera"—the soprano-baritone duet in Act I and the sleepwalking scene[9]—had practically assured the success of the premiere (and seems to have done so still more vigorously in the eight successive performances). But there remained the cold reception of Act III.

In the third act, a very long one, even his admirers failed to applaud, and there was only silence, interrupted occasionally by some hissing; and if the impatience was mitigated and not followed by worse, that must be ascribed to the favor the maestro enjoys in Florence.[10]

And Meini, in the previously-cited dispatches to the *Moda* of Milan:

The third act is wholly given over to fantasy, apparitions, and witches who engage in soup-making with rather odd ingredients, such as, for example, toads, monkeys, bat-skins, and other such dainties (literally), and while those spiritual sorceresses stir the *infernal broth*, Macbeth forces them to utter certain auguries which at the drama's conclusion are realized with his ruin. This act, which I shall not dissect, was either not appreciated or not understood; the fact is, it was not favorably received. And who knows but that the apparitions, the eight kings filing past like huge, wobbly marionettes, swaying behind a black scrim meant to represent the mist, who knows, I say, but that these did not contribute to the cold reception? The fact remains that neither the *Ondine*, nor the sylphs, who descended from the clouds in a boat to weave *harmonious* carols[11] meant to revive poor Macbeth, who had fallen to the ground like a rag, I know not whether out of musical exhaustion or from fear induced by so many visions, kings, witches, etc., etc., could secure for the third act the success of the other two. We must confess the public was not able to devote its attention to the music, being exhilarated or distracted by so many things and visions of a rather too fantastic quality.[12]

In his long review previously cited, Calvi wrote:

Where, however, it seems to us that the music has remained inferior to the dramatic situation is in the second act when Banquo's ghost appears and also in the third, and in general in all those pieces in which supernatural powers intervene.[13]

And Montazio found that:

9. Verdi's letter to Cammarano, 23 November 1848
10. D. J., in the *Ricoglitore;* see note 6.
11. Many of the critics poked fun at Piave's opaque couplet "Tessete in vortice/Carole armoniche."
12. *La Moda*, 20 March 1847
13. *Ricoglitore*, 20 March 1847

The third act, entirely devoted to displaying the witches and their incantations, is likewise the one in which the fantastic element is meant to predominate.... But we are forced to admit that, except for the witches' first chorus and perhaps the *Allegro ballabile* that they sing during the descent and pantomime of the ondines and sylphs (which, moreover, recalls a chorus from *Attila*), we can find nothing characteristic or the least bit fantastic in this third act.[14]

From these impressions, and from others to be cited later, we can deduce that the public was distracted during the third act by the spectacular aspect of the "fantastic" element, and more specifically by the machinery that gave it material support. Not to be excluded is the possibility that something went wrong in the production, even though it was personally supervised by Verdi and even though he had taken steps early on to ensure as careful a mise-en-scène as possible.[15] It is nonetheless certain that the public found itself suddenly face-to-face with unexpected scenic and technical novelties, apparently exceeding the limits to which it was accustomed and such as to divert its attention—at least, let us repeat, at the premiere—from listening to the music.

The principal occasions during the production of *Macbeth* in which the "machines" take part are five in number,[16] four of them in Act III alone; their appearance is always at the service of the drama's "fantastic" element:

Act II: Banquo's ghost (two appearances)
Act III: The three apparitions
The disappearance of the cauldron
The procession of the eight kings
The ballet of the aerial spirits

How did Verdi intend these to be realized? Although no *disposizione scenica* (production book)[17] for either the Florence or Paris *Macbeth* is known, the manner of realization of four of the five above-mentioned scenic effects is documented by Verdi's letters, the unusually ample directions in the autograph orchestral scores, and in the printed librettos and piano-vocal scores, and by certain contemporary accounts.

BANQUO'S GHOST

Concerning the technically very difficult and delicate realization of Banquo's ghost in the banquet scene, Verdi had scrupulously requested information direct from London, and on 22 December 1846 he transmitted it to the impresario Lanari:

Note that Banquo's ghost must make his entrance from underground; it must be the same actor that played Banquo in Act I. He must be wearing an ashen veil, but quite thin and fine, and just barely visible; and Banquo must have ruffled hair and various wounds visible on his neck.

14. "Il Macbeth e la musica fantastica," *Rivista di Firenze*, 27 March 1847. See also the final paragraph of Gagliardi's review in *Revue et Gazette Musicale de Paris*, 28 March 1847.

15. See Verdi's letter to Piave, 25 October 1846.

16. Not included in this count are the scene changes "a vista," including the one which transforms the hall in the castle into a spacious plain with Birnam Wood in the background, an "effetto di scena" suggested by Verdi in his 22 December 1846 letter to Piave.

17. Doug Coe's "The Original Production Book for *Otello*: An Introduction" (*19th Century Music* 2: 148–58) is a useful and easily available introduction to the *disposizioni sceniche* in general.

A few months after the Florentine premiere, Verdi went to London to present *I masnadieri;* while there, he naturally took advantage of the occasion to attend a performance in English of Shakespeare's *Macbeth,*[18] as is confirmed by his letter to Cammarano of 23 November 1848. This experience, however, did not lead him to modify the solution he had adopted from the Florence premiere on, a solution that sought to obtain the maximum scenic illusion possible consistent with the exigencies of the musical action. The technical means which Verdi used to realize this solution we learn, not from contemporary theatrical reports, but from his 23 January 1865 letter to Escudier.

With that acute sense of theatrical practicality that always sustained him in the production of his operas, Verdi did not a priori exclude other solutions, provided they yielded the scenic effect he had imagined. It is, however, interesting to note that, at a distance of almost twenty years, he considered the solution adopted for the Florence premiere still valid, and in any case more convincing than any offered by the practice of the spoken theatre, including the English tradition.

THE THREE APPARITIONS

Verdi's reference, in his 21 January 1847 letter to Lanari, to the *fantasmagoria,* apropos the scene of the apparitions, is well known. The *fantasmagoria* was, in essence, an apparatus based on the principle of the magic lantern, still employed today for the projection of slides and as an aid in scenography. The name *fantasmagoria* derives from the spectacles presented, beginning in the early years of the nineteenth century and soon extremely popular, by the Belgian physicist Ètienne-Gaspard Robert (better known under his pseudonym Robertson), using a machine he had patented and christened the "Fantascope." Robertson was quickly imitated in all parts of Europe.[19] As one critic rightly observed in connection with Verdi's advice to Lanari on the use of the *fantasmagoria:*

Though it would doubtless be too much to assert that Verdi anticipated motion pictures, he can certainly be considered a pioneer of the most modern systems of moving projections that today, more than a century later, are used in the better-equipped theatres.[20]

From the aforementioned letter to Lanari, it seems evident that Verdi intended to use the *fantasmagoria* for the three apparitions—but not for the procession of the kings, for which, as we shall see, Verdi wanted "men of flesh and blood."

In the Verdi correspondence, no further references are found to either the *fantasmagoria* or the mechanism actually adopted for the realization of the three apparitions. However, an article by Montazio in the *Rivista* of Florence, four days before the premiere, gives us some clues. According to Montazio, the machine for the *fantasmagoria* was indeed—as Verdi had proposed and Lanari agreed—built in Milan (in spite of Canovetti, the machinist at the Pergola, who, Montazio implies, would have been perfectly capable of building such a machine himself), and then shipped to Florence. After having arrived safely in Florence, it

18. Verdi would have had no opportunity to have seen a production of the play earlier; it was not produced in Italy until two years after the premiere of the opera (see WEAVER at 148).

19. *Enciclopedia dello spettacolo,* s.v. "lanterna magica"

20. *Verdi e Firenze* (Florence: Maggio Musicale Fiorentino, 1951), p. 15

was not used at all, as we learn from the postscript to Montazio's article:

Alas! The last and the greatest of the adventures of the phantasmagoric machine was, in fact, destined to occur in Florence! Absolute darkness not being considered decent in a first-class theater, the chandelier was forbidden to indulge a capricious taste for a game of *cache-cache* (hide-and-seek). This prohibition to the chandelier, as anyone may see, dealt the coup de grace to the phantasmagoria, for which the most profound darkness is a sine qua non, an obbligato accompaniment, a necessary condition. Hence it is that at this very moment Canovetti is busy interring the machine, which is to be unceremoniously entombed in the cellar, there to wait in blessed patience for some future antiquarian to disinter it and palm it off as some masterpiece of more or less Etruscan origin.[21]

Reading between the lines of Montazio's contorted prose, we can deduce that a prohibition was issued by the authorities, in the interests of "decency," against the total darkness in the auditorium that was an indispensable condition for the *fantasmagoria* to produce all the illusion demanded by the scenic effect. Deprived of his magic lantern, Verdi probably used the *rete nera* (black scrim) already arranged for the procession of the kings for the three apparitions as well.[22]

That is all we now know about the "machinery" adopted for the three apparitions at the Florence premiere, and Verdi did not return to the subject, not even in the aforementioned letters to Escudier about the Paris production almost twenty years later.

THE PROCESSION OF THE EIGHT KINGS

Meini's reference to "the eight kings filing past like huge, wobbly marionettes, swaying behind a black scrim meant to represent the mist" is the only one so far located describing the expedient Verdi adopted for this procession in the Florentine production. In addition, from an indication in the manuscript-copy orchestral score preserved in the Florence Conservatory, we learn that the *trappa* (trap door) from which was to emanate the sound of the subterranean orchestra (the *cornamusa*) was also used for the entrance of the eight kings: "These instruments must be placed under the stage, near the trapdoor from which will appear the shades of the kings."[23] Although the corresponding indication in the 1847 autograph does not mention the entrance of the Kings, the instruction just quoted reappears verbatim, in Verdi's hand, in the 1865 Paris score.

More precise details are found in Verdi's 23 November 1848 letter to Cammarano, filled with valuable suggestions for the production of the opera at San Carlo in Naples (perhaps embodying certain modifications of the Florentine mise-en-scène suggested by the performances of the Shakespeare tragedy Verdi had meanwhile attended in London), and in his recently discovered important 11 March 1865 letter to Escudier.

---

21. *La Rivista*, 10 March 1847. (This is the same periodical as that cited in notes 4, 5, and 15; it was during March 1847 that Montazio changed the title to *La Rivista di Firenze*. Eds.) While Montazio admits that much of his feuilleton is fantasy, he implies that the beginning and end are true.

22. See also Meini's comment quoted above.

23. "Questi Istromenti dovranno essere sotto il palco scenico, vicini alla Trappa da cui sortiranno le ombre dei Re." Verdi discusses the *cornamusa* in his 23 November 1848 letter to Cammarano and his 23 January 1865 letter to Escudier. While contrabassoons are mentioned in both, they appear in an autograph portion of the 1865 Paris orchestral score, but not in the 1847 autograph. The bass clarinets mentioned in the 1848 letter appear in neither score.

THE BALLET OF THE AERIAL SPIRITS

On 23 November 1846 Lanari notified Piave that dances were prohibited during Lent, so that the aerial spirits would not be allowed to dance as had been planned. But on 10 December Verdi replied to Piave, who had evidently passed on Lanari's remarks, "What's all this trouble you're giving me about the aerial spirits who aren't supposed to dance? ... Do them as indicated. The poem and the music must be that way, and in that way they must be done."

"Dancing of any kind is forbidden during Lent," Lanari had written. But the kind of dance Verdi had in mind was not to encounter obstacles from the Grand Ducal censors. In fact, as realized scenically, the ballet of the aerial spirits consisted of aerial maneuvers of sylphs and ondines suspended by winches and pulleys, perhaps followed by a short panto-mime. That is all we learn from contemporary reports. Montazio refers to "the *allegro ballabile* that [the witches] sing during the descent and the pantomime of the ondines and sylphs,"[24] while Antonio Calvi remarks that:

the ondines and sylphs appear descending from certain scaffolds, and set about stimulating the bewildered senses of Macbeth; but as for the *carole armoniche* (harmonious dance-songs) they take care not to listen to the witches—first because it is Lent, second because it is not easy to know just what *carole armoniche* are.[25]

Finally, Stefani, writing after the July 1847 production in Padua, the first production outside of Florence:

The first witches' chorus [in Act III] ... and the *allegro ballabile* sung by them while the ondines and sylphs take on the task of using their petticoats to cool off poor Macbeth, fallen to the ground like a rotten pear, are two most excellent fantastic inspirations.[26]

Reading between the lines of these excerpts from contemporary reports, one may easily imagine that the "machinery" required by the ballet of the aerial spirits was employed in a manner so ponderous and obvious (not to say clumsy) as to destroy the scenic illusion that the composer intended (similar to that later intended by Wagner in *Das Rheingold*).

I have limited myself to summarizing the historical documentation concerned with the "fantastic" scenes of the opera, those in which the principal machinery played a part, insofar as it can be deduced from Verdi's correspondence and from contemporary journalistic accounts. These scenes constitute the crucial—and thus the trickiest—points in the staging of the opera, not so much from the merely technical viewpoint as from that of the general interpretative conception; the latter must take account of the "fantastic" element not for its own sake (as a mere game of "machines" working to capture the spectators' fancy) but rather in relation to the "human drama." To illuminate the relation that runs through the drama between the "human" and the "fantastic" is the major problem in the production of

24. "Il Macbeth e la musica fantastica," *La Rivista di Firenze*, 27 March 1847. See also Montazio's "Macbeth: Profanazione in quattro atti di F.M. Piave" in the same issue.
25. *Ricoglitore*, 20 March 1847
26. *Caffè Pedrocchi*, 1 August 1847. See also Meini's remarks quoted above.

Macbeth, the key to realizing the composer's intentions. These intentions, it is important to note, are inspired by a musico-dramatic conception that was to remain in essence unchanged even by the revision made, nearly twenty years after the Florence premiere, for the Théâtre-Lyrique. On 22 October 1864, Verdi wrote to Escudier:

I have looked through *Macbeth* with the aim of writing the ballet music, but alas!, on reading through this music I was struck by things that I would not have wished to find. To say it all in a word, there are certain numbers that are either weak or lacking in character, which is worse still.

The letter continues with a list of pieces to be rewritten and retouched;[27] of these five, only one—"various passages to rewrite in the hallucination scene of Act III"—involves the *genere fantastico* or *machinismo,* and not only do the text and dramatic structure remain unchanged, but the musical changes affect primarily the part of Macbeth rather than the supernatural elements. The only changes projected in the text—or, for that matter, actually made—occur in "natural" scenes: Lady Macbeth's aria (Act II), the replacement of Macbeth's *cabaletta* (end of Act III) by a duet, and the substitution of the "Inno finale" for his death scene. Changes were effected in the music of some of the other supernatural scenes, but they do not reveal any substantial dissatisfaction with the treatment of the *genere fantastico* as conceived in 1847. The changes in the *brillante* of the opening witches' music in Act III are slight, as are those in the *ballabile* of the aerial spirits. While the changes in the two appearances of Banquo's ghost in the Act II *finale* are musically significant, they do not alter the dramatic structure. Despite the adverse critical reception of Verdi's treatment of the *genere fantastico,* then, he kept these scenes in 1865. Furthermore, as we have seen, there is no evidence that he had any second thoughts about the manner in which these scenes were staged two decades earlier in Florence.

N.B. It was unfortunately necessary to abbreviate Professor Conati's article, keeping only the section dealing directly with the staging of *Macbeth;* the complete article, "Aspetti della messinscena del *Macbeth* di Verdi," appears in *Nuova Rivista Musicale Italiana,* 15 (1981), 374–404. Eds.

27. I should like to call attention to the fact that, from the things that Verdi in 1864 "would not have wished to find" in this opera of his so-called "youthful" period, he excluded precisely those pages that critical opinion, both then and especially now, has often considered trivial or inferior: the scene of the witches in Act I; the little march for the arrival of Duncan; the introductory scene of the witches in Act III; and others that for the very same reasons are customarily omitted in modern performances: the *stretta* of the introduction to Act I ("S'allontarono") and the ballet of the aerial spirits—while on the other hand it has become a senseless custom to interpolate in the opera's *finale* the single scenic idea that Verdi had decided to suppress: the death of Macbeth on stage.

VOCAL GESTURE IN *MACBETH*

Marilyn Feller Somville

Macbeth is Shakespeare's best acting play, the one in which he shows most understanding with respect to the stage ... [Shakespeare] regarded his plays as a lively and moving scene, that would pass rapidly before the eyes and ears upon the stage, not as one that was to be held firmly, and carped at in detail. Hence, his only point was to be effective and significant for the moment. [1]

GOETHE

Having invoked the genius whose critical commentaries on Shakespeare sparked the movement toward dramatic realism throughout the nineteenth century, I propose that Verdi also understood *Macbeth* as an acting play. Although he had not seen a production of it before writing his opera, he grasped the significance of its lively, moving "scene" for both eye and ear and was challenged by the work to take a new direction in his musical theatre.

If Verdi's first consideration of Shakespeare's *Macbeth* as a possible libretto seems to focus on the supernatural and phantasmagorical elements, it is because the composer had decided a priori that the work for the Pergola would be in the *genere fantastico*. The decision may have been partly politic, a move to satisfy the Florentines with a *gran spettacolo* of *coro* and *macchinismo*, but it was ultimately an aesthetic commitment to explore a new and more complete vocal theatre than he had achieved. Whatever the preliminary motives and deliberations, a crucial factor in Verdi's decision was finding singers who could handle the principal roles.

It is often said that Verdi wrote his operas for certain singers. This is not true if we imply by it that he continued the practice of his predecessors who wrote expressly to show off the virtuosity of star singers; it is true in the sense that his *Macbeth* was conceived with two particular singers in mind. He demanded from Lanari, impresario of the Teatro della Pergola in Florence, Sophia Loewe, who created roles in *Atilla* and *Ernani,* and the baritone, Felice Varesi. They were not the finest singers of the day, as we learn from Verdi's letter to Lanari of 19 August 1846, but they had certain expressive powers which were essentially linked in Verdi's mind with his aspirations for the new opera:

In this case I would absolutely need the following two artists: Loewe and Varesi. Varesi is the only artist in Italy today who is able to do the part I have in mind, both because of his style of singing and feeling—and even because of his appearance. All other artists, even those better than he, couldn't do that part for me as I'd like—not to detract from the merits of Ferri, who is better looking, has a more beautiful voice, and if you like, is even a better singer, but in that role certainly couldn't give me the effect that Varesi would.

As it happened, Sophia Loewe had strained her voice; the role of Lady Macbeth was

1. *Conversations of Goethe with Eckermann and Soret,* John Oxenford tr. (London, 1882), pp. 164 and 250 (conversations of 25 December 1825 and 18 April 1827).

given to Marianna Barbieri-Nini, a younger singer who had a powerful voice and a persuasive stage personality but was notoriously ugly.

That Verdi was not looking for the *buon* or *bel cantante* for the parts of the monstrous Macbeths is further borne out in his famous letter to Cammarano of 23 November 1848 about Tadolini.

Though Verdi wanted the singers to look their parts and to move intelligently, it should not be construed from these letters that he hoped to compensate for bad or faulty singing with fine and subtle acting. What he required from singers was an ability to *act out* the secret stirrings of the soul.

I maintain that this "acting out" was essentially vocal. It was not histrionic; nor was it equivalent to speaking the lines of a play, for we are no longer dealing with the poetic language of Shakespeare. I therefore suggest the term "vocal gesture" to describe both Verdi's use of the voice to create the audible part of his lively and moving "scene" on the stage and the specific physical efforts made by the singer in the areas of respiration, phonation, articulation and resonation, to accomplish the composer's musico-dramatic purposes.

Before pursuing the idea of vocal gesture, I should like to look beyond Verdi's statements about what he wanted from his singers and point out certain features which were most likely characteristic of the voices he chose to interpret the principal roles in this new opera. First, these singers had tremendous power in the upper range. I am speaking not about a special natural endowment of robust lungs and iron vocal cords but of an acquired technique of carrying a large component of chest-register quality (maintaining chest-register, vocal-cord action) into the acute range with concomitant tensing of extra-laryngeal muscles to hold the larynx in place against enormous breath pressures. In fact, Verdi did not invent this "yelling" technique, though his critics, mostly bel canto partisans, claimed that he had. (Rossini himself, deplored the results of the technique and referred to it as "l'urlo d'un cappone sgozzato," the scream of a slaughtered capon.) But Verdi did require tense, cutting, and violent sounds in the upper register with as much insistence as Rossini had exploited limpid and smooth agility throughout the upper range.[2]

These sounds were the gestures by which Verdi's characters expressed extreme states of passion: for example, the high B double-flat (*voce piena*) in the cadenza of Macduff's aria "La paterna mano," in Act IV, or Macbeth's long E at end of "Vada in fiamme," the violent *cabaletta* of Act III, which gives heroic, though villainous, dimensions to Macbeth's character in the original version. Such sounds were necessary to establish characters firm in resolve or ferocious in their struggle against each other, and also when voices were concerted against doubled orchestral parts and full chorus; as, for example, the Lady's high C which she screams (*tutta forza*) over full chorus and full orchestra (*ff*) in the finale of Act I.

In the long run, this loud singing resulted in the extension of range in all voices of about a major third beyond the tessitura of Rossini's singers and contributed to the process of mutating voices higher: basses to baritones, baritones to tenors, etc. But a more important repercussion of loud singing was on registration. The secret of bel canto lay in smooth, gradual change from the heavier vocal-cord action of chest range to the lighter and more taut action of upper range. This change was supported by steadily increasing breath pressures of medium intensity and resulted in a light, finely graded, and extremely agile

---

2. See Rodolfo Celletti: "Caratteri della vocalità di Verdi," in *Atti del III° congresso internazionale di studi verdiani* (Parma, 1974), pp. 81–88.

emission of voice throughout the entire range.

Verdi's singers were required to use what might be called "optional registration"—that is, to sing notes in the middle range with either pure chest register or mixed register depending upon the nature of figuration given them and the dynamic level at which this figuration had to be projected. A good case in point is Lady Macbeth's *cavatina*, "Vieni! t'affretta." Here Verdi has written tight little turns with added trills which are not so much ornamental or pretty as a strong gesturing of the lust for power that drives the Lady. These figures require the pithy, harsh quality of pure chest register even up to A flat. The challenge for the singer is that Verdi makes the voice soar up and out of this figuration for even more florid singing in the upper register. Few sopranos, even today, can grab with pure chest register, and leave gracefully, any note in the middle range. However, failure to produce these raucous and vicious gestures in the *cavatina* will destroy the character Verdi wished for.

The loud singing and optional registration also had repercussions on agility. Verdi's voices had to be agile. But the "beefing up" of the acute register and the changes in registration pattern brought about a different kind of agility from that of pure bel canto. Moreover, we do not find in Verdi's scores the long winding points that display the voice in smooth, continuous flow with subtly modulated gradations of color from one extreme of the range to another. Instead, when Verdi uses *canto figurato*, it is usually in short spurts. The voice must move fast between fixed points of take-off and fixed points of arrival and repose. These runs have the emotional nature of outbursts or tirades and often the singer can prepare the registration for the whole run in advance or can, if need be, cheat a little by adjusting the registration through special articulation of various notes in the phrase. Verdi's soprano would probably have to do this on the extended runs of "Trionfai." But here, she is aided by the fact that the runs are made up of triplet figures and every note gets a staccato, if not portato, articulation, which might facilitate sudden adjustments of registration. A problem for the singer occurs in the last, legato roulade up to high C. There, I would say, the diva had better not take Verdi at his word and be content merely to look *brutta e cattiva*! She will need the old bel canto agility, even if it requires some compromise of dynamic intensity. It is significant that Verdi cut this aria in the revised version, because he found it banal and characterless, and replaced it with the vastly more subtle "La luce langue." The gaudy agility of "Trionfai" is replaced with more deliberate gestures, such as the *sprezzatura* or parlante statements of "nuovo delitto!," which allow us to see, early in the drama, the incipient weakness of the Lady, anticipating her behavior in the sleepwalking scene. The repeated descending-octave passages on "è necessario compiersi debbe l'opra fatale" are also strong gestures indicating in what way the Lady has screwed her courage to the sticking point.

With the same insistence and care Verdi had shown trying to convince Piave, his librettist, that the kingdom of heaven lay in "poche parole," he later instructed his singers in the manner of singing or declaiming the few, well-chosen words of the libretto. In the letter to Cammarano of 23 November 1848, he wrote:

Note that there are two principal numbers in the opera: the duet between the Lady and her husband and the sleepwalking scene. If these numbers fail, then the opera is ruined. And these pieces absolutely must not be sung. They must be acted out and declaimed with a very hollow and veiled voice; otherwise, they won't be able to make any effect.

Barbieri-Nini wrote in her memoirs that for three months she was required to imitate the "deadpan" and vague gestures of those who walk and speak in their sleep. She added that the duet "Fatal mia donna" was rehearsed more than 150 times to make it, as Verdi insisted "closer to *speech* than *singing*" (see p. 51).

Still, we should not assume that it was solely the use of *voce parlata* or *voce declamata* that caused Piave to write to Lanari on 28 October 1846:

Loewe's part in particular will be the most loftily conceived that has ever appeared on the Italian operatic stage; the baritone's likewise. I believe that this opera, if it is well received, will give new directions to our music and open new paths to present and future composers.

Certainly, the *voce parlata* or *voce declamata* were not new to the Italian stage. The idea that the spoken word was closer to dramatic truth than florid singing had been around since the days of Giulio Caccini and the Florentine Camerata. We find the very effective use of *canto sillabico* for realistic effects in the works of Rossini, Bellini, Donizetti and Mercadante.

What is new and vocally innovative in *Macbeth* is Verdi's attempt to control *all* the elements of the vocal gesture so as to imitate speaking and "act out" the full dramatic and emotional meaning of the words. The process is no better described than in Verdi's performance instructions to Varesi set out in his letters of 7 January, c. 23–30 January, and 4 February 1847. By means of his directions, and the suggestive verbal cues in the score, Verdi urged his singers (almost as if he were instructing them to grasp and use drawing pen and chisel) to realize vocally by means of the right breath impulse, the right accent, rhythm, color and intonation, the substance and meaning of particular words and phrases. This is what Verdi intended by *cavare un effetto*, and he judged singers by their ability to do it. Of all singers, he particularly admired Adelina Patti for the effect she created on the three-note phrase "Io l'amo" at the beginning of Act III of *Rigoletto*.[3] It appears from his letters to Varesi that he had much confidence in the baritone's ability to carve or draw out an effect.

But just what does it mean to bring off these words with the right breath impulse, the right accent, color and intonation? What is being asked of the singer in terms of respiration, phonation, articulation and resonation? Let me suggest some possible explanations and illustrations:

The indication *pensieroso* over Macbeth's line "saranno i figli tuoi sovrani!," I.2, means that the singer should observe the dotted rhythms of the words but suggests a possible treatment of the long notes with some form of *messa di voce* such as *esclamazione languida* (cresc.–dim.–cresc.) to indicate the gradual formation of thought.

The indication *con orrore* over Banco's line "È morto assassinato," I.19, means: observe the dotted rhythms, but halt on each long note (and perhaps add an *esclamazione viva* [dim., or dim.–cresc.]) as if no other thoughts could follow.

The indication *soffocata*[4] *e lento* in Macbeth's "Tutto è finito" just before the duet "Fatal mia donna" requires, in addition to covering the voice, the sobbing affect (accomplished by

---

3. *Copialettere*, 625

4. The terms *voce cupa, voce velata, voce muta* and *soffocata* refer to various techniques of covering or damping vocal tone, accomplished by tensing and shaping the pharyngeal wall and/or coupling small amounts of nasal resonance. In addition, *cupo* and *soffocato* refer to shaping the mouth, jaw and tongue to achieve articulations that are imploded rather than exploded.

quick *coups de glotte*)[5]—strong gestures conveying to us Macbeth's recoil from so much bloodshed and his ineptness as a murderer.

The indication *con trasporto* for Lady's "O voluttà del soglio! o scettro" (the final section of her aria in Act II of the revised opera) requires some of those "yells" (maximum chest quality, *voce piena*) which quickly calm down to *pp* and a wavering tone (*oscillante*)[6]—crucial gestures by which Verdi delineates in the revision a more subtle Lady, one whose excessive and glutted ambition render her vulnerable to self-doubt long before the sleep-walking scene.

These few examples—plus, of course, the explicit and obvious directions given the singer in the sleepwalking scene—illustrate that in general Verdi's vocal gestures express the inner feelings and secret motivations of characters in a situation. The composer's myriad other indications of *sotto voce, fra sè, voce spiegato, tutta forza* create important spatial effects and relationships in the audible scene on the stage. For example, the indications *con esclamazione* and *cupo* for Macbeth's line "ma perchè sento rizzar il crine," with its strong accents (*exclamazioni vive*) followed by slurs, have the effect of drawing us into Macbeth's body space, into his interior world. We know that Macbeth is so moved by the prophecies that, he feels his hair standing on end, but that is not something we can see; we must infer the terror accompanying these private thoughts from the respiratory pattern, the rhythm, color and intonation of the vocal gesture.

Often indications such as *cambiando istantaneamente* show us a character coming out of a private meditation, ready to engage in action or a relationship.

The *voce ripresa* quality of both voices in the duet "Ora di morte" provides an audible transparency through which we hear the conniving interaction and fatal complicity Verdi intends for the couple in the revised Act III.

Articulation marks such as staccato, portato, and even the ornaments are important features of the vocal gesture as it establishes the internal life of the character and delineates relationships of characters in the moving scene: one has only to think of the *acciaccature* sung by Lady Macbeth in the *brindisi*. With these brittle, hysterical strokes of the throat the Lady tells us that her gaiety is intended to conceal worrisome things.

The most obvious and straightforward gesturing is done by the chorus. This is accomplished, for the most part, by an exaggerated musical accent (which may or may not coincide with verbal accent) that shapes the vocal lines and allows the chorus to point its finger at various characters and to distinguish various relationships in the larger perspective of the dramatic situation. Verdi provides the chorus with such gestures as:

Mac-bet - to   rie - de - re   ve - drem   ve-drem   co - là

Here the accent on the weak part of the 6/8 measure acts with whiplash energy to shake the rest of the notes into place (or so the chorus director hopes!).

Does this rhythmic simplification and unison accent make the choral gestures in *Macbeth* trivial and weaken the dreadful, supernatural effects of the deeper prophecies and incantations? The question poses perplexing and interesting aesthetic problems. Perhaps such ges-

---

5. Successive, sharp strokes, that is, attacks and releases of the vocal cords
6. Wavering pitch produced by rapid but controlled variations of breath pressure

tures allow the chorus to fulfill its traditional function in the drama, which is, as Goethe elegantly pointed out, to provide the "required change" in tragedy. Goethe proposed that behind all tragic action, there exists, as a backdrop or ground, a kind of "cheerful reality" that will reinstate and reinsert itself at every crack, chink and turning point in the dramatic action.

Certainly Verdi's rhythmically simple but extremely vital choral gestures are a recognition of that "cheerful reality." By using them, the composer assures us that even while the Macbeths are deep in bloody thoughts and actions, elsewhere in the castle, servants go unconcernedly about their daily rounds, messengers come running in breathless and joyous with good news, witches cook up a stew with all kinds of delectable ingredients, and murderers go about their work with the bonhomie of a bowling team. Perhaps this "cheerful reality" is after all the ultimate and universal *verismo* of Verdi's *work*.

It should be clear that Verdi's vocal gestures in *Macbeth* contributed to a realism which was in all ways closer to the humanistic and romantic realism of Shakespeare's theatre than to the truly ugly realism of modern times with its photographically accurate and therefore boring account of superficial minutiae. Verdi's gestures established characters in the fullness and depth of being and gave voice to the dark, phantasmagorical and evil sides of human nature as well as to a more cheerful reality presiding over the tragic action. Nevertheless, his vocal gesture was meant to "pass rapidly before the eyes and ears upon the stage, not to be held too firmly in the mind." Perhaps it should not too long be "carped at in detail!"

TRANSLATING *MACBETH*

Andrew Porter

There has been perhaps but one successful Shakespeare opera—Britten's *A Midsummer Night's Dream* (1960)—set to Shakespeare's own words (in a skillful arrangement and abridgment of the play). And there has been one admirable opera—Ernest Bloch's *Macbeth* (1910)—set to Shakespeare in translation. Otherwise, the very free handling of the Bard shown in the librettos for Verdi's *Macbeth*, *Otello*, and *Falstaff*—the three great operatic tragedies after Shakespeare—points to the same moral as, from the opposite point of view, do the "straight" settings of Mario Zafred's *Hamlet* (1961) and Humphrey Searle's *Hamlet* (1968). For, as Winton Dean wrote in a review of Lawrance Collingwood's *Macbeth* (1927; revived in 1970), another "straight" setting: "Unless the composer imposes his own personality on a great play, it is apt to reduce the music to a pale commentary. Instead of taking Shakespeare by the scruff of the neck, Collingwood treats him with such respect that we are tempted to concentrate on the words and wish the music would not keep 'interfering.'"

Bloch composed his *Macbeth* in French—a clear French naturally declaimed and easily followed on the contours and rhythmic stresses of his vocal lines. On those lines, for an English version he and Alex Cohen then sought to reimpose Shakespeare. Reviewing the Juilliard's 1973 production of Bloch's *Macbeth*, I wrote of what resulted. First, misaccentuation: the Third Witch's "Un jour tu seras ROI!" (my capitals indicate emphasis), for which fitting English would be "One day thou shalt be KING!," became "Thou shalt be King hereAFTER!" Second, lines hard to follow: the phrase to which Lady Macbeth sang "les deux chambellans qui veillent auprès de lui" now carried the words "[so convince] his two chamberlains, that the receipt of reason shall BE a limbeck only"—a difficult line at the best of times, doubly so as here set. Third, jarring little repetitions, such as Banquo's "And yet are on't, *and yet are on't*" (Et qui pourtant foulent la terre), or Macbeth's "Out, out, *out, out,* brief candle!" And so, I concluded, one should "do *Macbeth* in the original or else boldly translate the libretto into an unaffected English that sings naturally." A few years later, when I came to translate Verdi's *Macbeth*, I felt I might have to eat some of that crow making wing to the rooky wood.

Verdi, Piave, and Maffei, the authors of the libretto, versified the Rusconi translation pretty freely but included an awkwardly large number of "well-known quotations" that have to be dealt with. How, for example, is one going to handle the famous phantom dagger of "Mi si affaccia un pugnal"? Walter Ducloux, the translator of the version hitherto standard in America (in the G. Schirmer score), has: "'Tis a dagger I see, hilt turned upon me! Unless you are a vision, here, let me wield you!" I felt that the lines were too well known to be thus paraphrased, if not so well known that the omission of just a "which" would disturb many people. With a freedom perhaps justifiable only in recitative, I removed the first two of the four A-naturals with which the phrase begins, divided the quarter-note of "-gnal" into two eighths, and found that "Is this a dagger I see before me, The handle toward my hand? Come, let me clutch thee" sang easily and naturally.

Each passage in each translation is a separate puzzle, and the rules for solving the different puzzles keep changing. Usually something must be sacrificed. It may be the exact sense. It may be the best sounds, in a passage where precise sense does matter more than anything else. It may be the rhyme. What I found myself least willing to sacrifice was singable sounds and accurate musical articulation. Two little examples from *Macbeth* can illustrate the last point. On the surface, the witches' *coro ballabile* from Act III seems to scan:

rum tum ti-tum, tiddlety um tum rum ti-tum,

which Ducloux represents as:

Elves of the night, fly to the ground and bring to him.

But Verdi's scansion is subtler. His comma is differently placed: "Ondine e silfidi, dall'ali candide." The English just quoted corresponds not to that but to "Ondine e sil, Fidi dall'ali candide." I settled for "Elves of the green forest, and nymphs of water-brook." Similarly in the cutthroats' chorus of Act II, whose tune—the point has not escaped psycho-dramatic commentary—is a variant of the witches'. Scansion at first glance is:

dum dum diddle-diddle dum dum dum.

Ducloux has: "Day is dying and the night will fall." But Verdi, breaking the obvious scansion by his comma, set: "Sparve il sol, la notte or regni" (Day is die, ing and the nightwill fall). I made it: "Day is done, the evening shades fall." Notice that the Italian does not allow "night will fall" or, as I carelessly wrote at first, "shadows fall." The word *regni* is actually *re-e-gni*, two syllables over three detached notes. I think Verdi was more deliberate in such details than some of his translators have allowed.[1] In the bonfire chorus of *Otello* there is a staccato ascent in triplets, "*fuga* la *notte col* suo splen*dor*," which is not syllable-to-a-note, but, as it were, "*fuga* la *no-*otte *col* suo splen*dor*," and that pattern—only one syllable across the fourth and fifth notes—persists throughout the chorus. Ducloux uses two syllables: "turning the night into radiance of day." I wrote "turning the night to fiery day," and made rather a fuss when a chorus master at the theatre where this *Othello* was first done expanded "to" into "into" so as to get a regular run of syllables, not Verdi's more interesting pattern.

In Lady Macbeth's sleepwalking scene, there are a few phrases of Shakespeare that fit Verdi's music easily: " 'Tis time to do 't"; "Fie, my lord!"; "All the perfumes of Arabia"; "What's done cannot be undone." I used them, but with qualms, since they were exact quotations dropped into a context of, so-to-speak, misquotation. Verdi's music had to be paramount. *Macchia* has two syllables, so it had to be a "bloodstain," not a "spot." With a slight adjustment of underlay, Shakespeare's "will not sweeten" can be fitted to Verdi's notes, but the phrase where it falls is attacked on a *c*, "*co*' suoi balsami," and so I changed it to "*ca*nnot sweeten."

Alliteration is forcefully employed in *Macbeth*, more so, I think, than in any other Verdi opera: "Si *c*olmi il *c*alice"; "In*ghi*otti nel tuo *gr*embo"; "*cr*eato ... ese*cr*ato." (Translating *The Ring* had been good practice for me in dealing with this device, and for finding crunchy attack-consonants for "*schi*ude," "*squ*arciar," etc.) In Lady Macbeth's "Trionfai," an aria replaced in the 1865 revision, she triumphs in the first line and defies in the third. I reversed

1. Or some of his critics! See Casamorata's review (p. 389), which deals with this passage and derides what I respected.

them so that "trion*fai*" could be "I de*fy*"—but again with qualms, since I believe that the closer a translator can stick to the exact sense, phrase by phrase, word by word where possible, the better. Rhyme schemes were preserved where rhymes came naturally, and sometimes where they did not but the pattern of the music seemed to demand a rhyme. But not rhyme at *any* cost. I had never much liked the way the Ducloux Macbeths welcome their guests:

> My thanes and nobles, hail and welcome on your entry!
>
> Hail and welcome to you, Sirs, and Ladies of the gentry.
>
> Now if it please you gentlemen, let us begin the party!
> Never before I've hosted here a crowd so proud and hearty.
> My Lady will not think it wrong that, ere she start the dinner,
> She offer us a drinking-song, raising our spirits high!
>
> My royal husband never fails to be the winner:
> I gladly shall comply.

And there are moments when a translator is tempted to "edit." In the Act I quartet of *Falstaff*, each woman introduces her individual stanza separately before all four sing together. Quickly embarks on "Quell'uom è un cannone," and Meg on "Un flutto in tempesta," but they switch words when the ensemble begins. Verdi's evident slip continues to be reproduced in every edition. As a "translator-editor" of *Falstaff*, I straightened the lines out, and I imagine that the editor of the new critical edition will do the same—adding a note, of course, to explain what he has done. Similar decisions had to be made in *Macbeth* when the same words to the same notes were distributed slightly differently. I acted empirically and tried to decide, case by case, whether there was any significance in the change, worth reproducing in English, or whether it was simply a slip and I might as well save the singers trouble by regularizing the two phrases. When repeating words in codas, and in the subsidiary parts of ensembles, Verdi sometimes slammed the syllables in any way.[2] In that *coro ballabile*, "anima" is sometimes "aniMA" and sometimes "aNIma", so it had to be translated in two different ways. Just before the *brindisi*, Lady Macbeth seems unsure how to stress "regale"; she tries it two ways, singing "Al tuo reGAle, REgale invito."

And then there is the composer's disconcerting habit, familiar to anyone who has analyzed the structure of a Verdi aria, of, when setting a double or triple quatrain, repeating the final words over and over again until they seem to carry the whole weight of the aria. This happens in Banquo's aria, "Come dal ciel." The piece is twenty-eight measures long and has eight lines. In twelve measures, Verdi gets through the first six lines, and then for sixteen measures he repeats the final couplet. As the lines are "and oppress my thought with phantoms and terror," the sense of the whole is not harmed. But in Macduff's aria, twelve lines long, Verdi gets through the first ten lines in twenty measures, and continues for ten measures with: "Thou mayst open to him the arms of Thy forgiveness, Thou mayst open to him the arms, Thou mayst open to him the arms of Thy forgiveness, O Lord, Thou mayst open to him the arms of Thy forgiveness." "Le braccia del tuo perdona aprir" is the dominant phrase; the unwary listener is left with the sense that Macduff, so far from thirsting for vengeance, is imploring God to have mercy on and pardon Macbeth. So here I

---

2. Again, see Casamorata at 391.

took a liberty and, instead of repeating just the final couplet, repeated the whole quatrain with its conditional clause: "Bring me to face that tyrant, and *if* he should escape me, then Thou mayst ... " etc.

In the 1847 banquet scene, the passage that begins "Diventa pur tigre, leon minaccioso" contains much repetition of "conoscer potrai s'io provi timor"—too much, Verdi himself seems to have thought, for in 1865 after a single repetition of "conoscer" the phrase is sung only once. Instead of repeating it, I was tempted to bring on the full Shakespearean menagerie: the rugged Russian bear, the arm'd rhinoceros, the Hyrcan tiger. But here I resisted. Verdi's verbal repetitions often make musical and dramatic points, and I dislike the translations that abjure them.

But each passage is a special case. I translated the 1847 score first; when, later, I tackled 1865 and "La luce langue" I felt I had exhausted the vocabulary for darkness, shadows, nightfall, sun sinking, and the rest of it—in Macbeth's monologue, the cutthroats' chorus, and Banquo's aria. "La luce langue" begins, literally, "Light wanes, the beacon that eternally courses the ample heavens goes out! Longed-for night, providently veil the guilty hand that strikes." It is a free paraphrase of Macbeth's speech in III.2: "Light thickens, and the crow makes wing to the rooky wood; good things of day begin to droop and drowse" and then (jumping back to an earlier part of the speech) "Come, seeling night, scarf up the tender eye of pitiful day." I tried a different paraphrase that fitted the music: "Daylight is dying, dark fills the firmament, good things of daytime droop to their slumber! See where the raven flies t'ward the forest; come, seeling darkness, to shroud deeds of death." (And offered "gloomy" as a simpler alternative to "seeling.") Originally I wrote "See where the crow makes wing t'ward the forest" but then realized that on Verdi's phrasing it would come out as "See where the crowmakes/Wing t'ward the forest." My qualms about introducing that gratuitous crow or raven were somewhat allayed when a few months later I came across Verdi's letter to Piave (ca. 13 December 1864) in which he says: "Here is what I think the Lady should be made to say in the second-act aria, Stanza 1: Pale grows the light ... the raven takes flight for the ancient forest."

Essays in Analysis

EVIL, GUILT, AND THE SUPERNATURAL IN VERDI'S *MACBETH*: TOWARD AN UNDERSTANDING OF THE TONAL STRUCTURE AND KEY SYMBOLISM[1]

Martin Chusid

Above all, bear in mind that there are three roles in this opera ... Lady Macbeth, Macbeth, and the chorus of witches. The witches dominate the drama; everything derives from them ... They are truly a character, and a character of the utmost importance.[2]

Although a larger portion of the opera than the play is devoted to scenes of the supernatural, both Shakespeare and Verdi draw essentially the same moral from *Macbeth*. As Banquo points out:

1. The study of precisely how tonality and drama may be correlated has been under way for some time with the operas of German and Austrian composers. See for example Werner Lüthy, *Mozart und die Tonartencharakteristik* (Strassburg, 1931) and M. Chusid "The Significance of D Minor in Mozart's Dramatic Music," *Mozart Jahrbuch* 1965/66. But only recently has the subject begun to interest Verdi scholars. See David Lawton: "Tonality and Drama," and Daniel Sabbeth: "Principles of Tonal and Dramatic Organization in *Falstaff*" (City University of New York Ph.D. dissertation, 1976). Also M. Chusid, "Rigoletto and Monterone: A Study in Musical Dramaturgy," Papers for the Eleventh Congress of the International Musicological Society (Copenhagen, 1974) and "Drama and the Key of F Major in *La Traviata*," Atti di III° congresso internazionale di studi verdiani (Parma, 1974). I should also like to mention an unpublished paper on tonality in *Macbeth* by Steven Billington written for a seminar on "Verdi and Shakespeare" (New York University, Spring 1977), and the paper for this congress by Daniel Sabbeth, with whom I had many fruitful conversations.

2. Verdi's first letter of 8 February 1865 to Escudier. Verdi's choice of a supernatural topic was decided upon even before the specific subject was chosen. See his letter to Alessandro Lanari of 17 November 1846. The other subject under consideration was Franz Grillparzer's *Die Ahnfrau* (*L'Avola* or *The Ancestress*), a gothic ghost story set in the German forest. In this regard it is noteworthy that three supernatural operas by *oltremontani* were performed with some success in Italy during the 1830s and 1840s. These were the years of Verdi's compositional studies (mid-1830s) and his early career. Performance locations and dates are cited only for Milan and Florence: Mozart's *Don Giovanni* (Milan, 1836; Florence, 1837 and 1846); Hérold's *Zampa*, plot heavily indebted to *Don Giovanni* (Milan, 1835; Florence, 1834–35 and two different seasons in 1845); and Meyerbeer's *Robert le Diable* (Florence 1840–41, 1841–42 and 1843; Milan, 1846). Tom Kaufman drew my attention to *Zampa* and allowed me to consult his unpublished research on nineteenth-century operatic performances.

... spesso l'empio spirto d'averno	... oftentimes to win us to our harm
Parla, e c'inganna, veraci detti	The instruments of darkness tell us truths;
E ne abbandona poi maledetti	Win us with honest trifles, to betray's
Su quell'abisso che ci scavò.	In deepest consequence.
(*Act I*, introduzione)	(I, 3)

With the expression "instruments of darkness" Shakespeare employs a metaphor for evil common to our culture. And he does this so frequently that Shakespearean scholars often refer to *Macbeth* as the dramatist's dark play. Perhaps the most effective use occurs after Duncan's death. Ross comments to the old man:

> ...Ah, good father,
> Thou seest, the heavens, as troubled with man's act
> Threaten his bloody stage: by the clock, 'tis day,
> And yet dark night strangles the travelling lamp;
> Is't night's predominance, or the day's shame,
> That darkness does the face of earth entomb,
> When living light should kiss it?   (III.2)

Verdi too uses darkness as a metaphor for evil. But it is the thesis of this paper that the composer conceives evil as only one side of the dramatic coin. For him the supernatural exists on two planes, and he differentiates them by using a particular tonal region for each.

Before pursuing this point further, it might prove instructive to glance at Table 1, Principal Keys in *Macbeth* I and II. The diagram suggests that for Paris Verdi made the overall tonal plan of the opera more symmetrical. At the beginning of Act II, the new aria for Lady Macbeth "La luce langue" in *E*, following the prelude in *F*, provides a sequence of keys (*F-E*) paralleling the same keys at the beginning and end of the second *finale*, the banquet scene. [In the text of this article, italic capitals refer to tonalities independent of mode, lowercase letters to pitches; brief episodes are enclosed in brackets.] Furthermore, as a result of the new duet-finale "Ora di morte e di vendetta," in *F*, these same keys frame the revised version of Act III, although now in reversed order (i.e., *E* at the beginning and *F* at the end). For Paris Verdi also added the obligatory ballet, in which these keys are presented

TABLE 1
PRINCIPAL KEYS IN *MACBETH* I AND II

		Keys[1]		
Nos.	*Titles*	*1847*	*Both*	*1865*
	ACT I			
1.	**Preludio**[2]		f	
2.	**Introduzione:**			
	Chorus		a/A	
	Duet		(C)[3]...F	
	Chorus		d/D	
3.	**Cavatina Lady Macbet**			
	Reading of Letter & Rec.		(e)...	
	Andantino		D♭	
	Tempo di mezzo		(A)...	
	Cabaletta		E	

4.	Rec.vo 4 e Marcia		(G)...Eb	
5.	**Scena e Duetto**		(Eb)... f/Bb/f	
6.	Finale 1°		(c)... bb/Db	
	ACT II			
7.	**Scena ed Aria Lady**			
	Prelude & Rec.		f/(f)...	
	Aria5	Bb		e/E
8.	**Coro di Sicarj**		C	
8½.	**Scena Banco**		e/E	
9.	**Convito Visione, e Finale6**		F/Bb6... F/Bb6... E	
	ACT III			
10.	**Coro**		e/E	
	Ballet			
	No. 1			e/E
	No. 2			(F)/Bb/(F)
	No. 3			e/E
11.	**Rec.° Apparizione,**		(e)...(bb)... (B...Db...eb...)7 (D/d)...F...8	
	Ballabile ed		G	
	Aria Macbet (1847); Duetto5			
	(1865)	(G)...a/A		(G)...f
	ACT IV			
12.	**Coro Int[roduzione]**	g/G		a
13.	**Sc.9 ed Aria con Coro Macduff**			
	Rec.	(c)...		(a)...
	Aria		Db	
	Tempo di mezzo		(Bb)...	
	Cabaletta		Ab	
14.	**Sonnambulismo di Lady Macbeth**		f/Db	
15.	**Scena ed Aria,**		(e)...Db	
	Battaglia,	...(e)...D		...(c)...C
	Morte d[i] Macbeth	f (end first version)		
	Inno di Vittoria5			(C)...a/A

1. Keys:
   Upper case = Major key.
   Lower case = Minor key.
   (C)... = Modulatory passage beginning in C major (N.B. Modulations are not indicated within tonally-rounded numbers: Arias, Cabalettas, Duets, etc.).

2. Titles set in bold type are taken from the autograph score of *Macbeth I.*

3. Predictions by witches

4. Rec.vo (Rec.) = Recitativo (Recitative).

5. New text as well as music in 1865

6. Brindisi (drinking song) in two strophes

7. Predictions by apparitions. Much harmonic revision in 1865

8. Apparitions of the Kings and Banco

9. Sc. = Scena.

in mirror fashion at beginning and end: E [F] $B\flat$ [F] E). In Act IV new music for the introductory chorus, "Patria oppressa," in A, is balanced by the new *finale* in the same key. Both, I believe, refer back to the opera's opening chorus, "Che faceste? Dite su!," which is also in A. The revised battle scene, near the end of Act IV, is now in C and moves easily into the opening of the new *finale*, in the key of its relative, A minor. On a tonal level this reflects well the inexorable dramatic progression of battle, death of Macbeth and Victory Hymn. Furthermore, the progression from $D\flat$ in the three successive fourth act arias to the C of the battle scene, mirrors the progression from C to $D\flat$ framing the huge and extremely effective *finale* of Act I.

It is frequently observed that the revised opera focuses less on Macbeth himself than did the original. His death occurs now offstage, and his moving scena in F minor, "Mal per me," is replaced by the Victory Hymn in A minor-major. Since, as Julian Budden has indicated, F major-minor is associated with Macbeth,[3] and since A major-minor is associated with Scotland, its throne, king or people,[4] the new overall tonal plan of the opera reflects the increased importance of the nation at the expense of Macbeth. In addition to the heavy emphasis still given to F (in the preludes to Act I and II, the *finales* to Acts II and III, and the duets in the first act, "Due vaticini" and "Fatal mia donna"), there is in the revised opera a new area of tonal emphasis, A (in the opening choruses for Acts I and IV and the *finale* to Act IV). Preparing the listener aurally for the new emphasis on A in Act IV, there is more stress on its dominant, E, in Acts II and III.

Table 2 indicates the principal keys and compares Budden's and my interpretations of their possible dramatic associations.

The five keys listed first are those most frequently used. The remaining two, C and D, are more complex for several reasons. First, they are used infrequently for tonally-rounded selections or for sizable sections of other numbers, and this is precisely the level on which key symbolism is most consistent. Second, on the level of local events (e.g., phrases or other short passages of recitative, or contrasting sections of the tonally-rounded numbers), purely musical factors often take precedence. Such a passage may form part of a modulating sequence or it may help provide either an harmonic contrast or a tonal link with an already

---

3. "One curious feature of *Macbeth* ... is the use of key, not architectonically, but for purposes of dramatic definition. Perhaps one should speak of 'areas of pitch' rather than keys, since both the modes are included, while the relation of one 'area' to another is not exploited. Three are of special importance: F major/minor which belongs to Macbeth himself; A major/minor which denotes the outside world, including the witches; $D\flat$ major which is associated with the idea of murder. There are two subsidiary areas: E connoting power and $B\flat$, escape. Against this more or less constant background, the dramatic events spring all the more vividly into relief. Note how the idea of murder first insinuates itself into Macbeth's mind in the form of $D\flat$ major against the prevailing F major of the duettino in Act I; how Lady Macbeth's *cavatina* proceeds from an andante in $D\flat$ to a *cabaletta* in E major—i.e., from the idea of murder to that of power; how the unequivocal E major of the Act II *finale* is shaken by jagged rhythms as though Macbeth's newly-acquired power were already tottering. Whether such a scheme was adopted by Verdi consciously we cannot be sure. But it is significant that the 1847 ending in which Macbeth dies on stage is in F minor, while the new *finale* of 1865 is in A major." *Operas of Verdi* 1, 312n.

4. See the opening chorus, especially the text "Le sorelle vagabonde ... sanno un circolo intrecciare che comprende e terra e mar;" the chorus "Patria oppressa" (revised version, Act IV); the revised *finale* for the opera, especially Macduff's "Ognun s'affidi al re", Malcolm's "Scozia, t'affidi in me", and the chorus "La patria il re salvò"; and the finale to Act III, first version, "Vada in fiamme," especially the text to which most of the music is set, "L'ira mia, la mia vendetta per la Scozia si diffonda." See also the following short passages in A: Act I, the witches, "Salve, o Macbetto di Scozia re"; Act I, Macbeth, "Si promette dal terzo un trono" (sonority of A as dominant of VI in F); Act I, Lady Macbeth, "Che tardi? Accetta il dono, ascendivi a regnar"; Act I, Lady Macbeth to a servant, "Trovi accoglienza quale un re si merta"; Act II, Lady Macbeth: "Veraci parlar le maliarde, e re tu sei! Il figlio di Duncan, per l'improvvisa sua fuga in Inghilterra, parricida fu detto, e vuoto il soglio a te lasciò."

TABLE 2

Budden[1]	Key	Chusid
Outside world, including the witches	A	Scotland, its King or people.
Macbeth	F	Macbeth (minor is usually used when Macbeth is tormented or suffering)
Power	E	Evil, darkness (often in minor),[2] the witches.
Escape	B♭	Other supernatural forces or manifestations (e.g., the goddess Hecate and Banquo's ghost); the ultimate powers punishing those who give in to evil
Idea of murder	D♭	Guilt, guilty thoughts
	C	Murder, death; Macbeth's destiny
	D	Reality or truth; prophecy fulfilled

1. Budden seems to be restricting his ideas on *E, B♭* and *D♭* to the major mode. In general I find that Verdi equates major and minor, although minor may suggest more strongly some particular aspect of the dramatic association (e.g. *F* minor and *E* minor as indicated above).

2. There are three noteworthy instances. During Lady Macbeth's *cabaletta* "Or tutti sorgete" at the text "Tu notte ne avvolgi di tenebra immota (Act I)," the first sections of Lady Macbeth's aria "La luce langue," and Banquo's scene "Come dal ciel precipita / L'ombra" (both Act II).

established or forthcoming tonality. It is surprising to me that in *Macbeth* so many of these local events do in fact seem to reflect the associations suggested. At this level, however, it is often more appropriate to speak of a sonority, namely, an emphasis on a chord sometimes reinforced by other chords (tonicization), or even of a strikingly identified or isolated motive or pitch, rather than a key. Sometimes these chords or pitches are found in the context of another key.

As mentioned earlier, two keys represent the supernatural and are of particular importance for this paper, *E* and *B♭*. Their associations and their relationship one to another are made particularly clear in the ballet Verdi wrote for Paris, to which he attached considerable importance.[5] The scenario and music of this ballet suggests three major divisions. The first and last stress the key of *E* and the central portion is in *B♭*. Two almost identical short passages in *F* precede and follow the middle section. In Table 3, keys, numbers of measures involved, tempo markings, and meter signatures are given on the left, and the scenario as written in the score is presented on the right.

The hierarchy suggested by the ballet seems to me both clear and important. Hecate, who is presented in *B♭*, clearly belongs to a more powerful realm of the supernatural than the witches and other demons, presented in *E*.

A notable aspect of both play and opera is the trust—in retrospect unwarranted—that both Macbeth and his Lady place in the witches. Lady Macbeth, in her *cabaletta* "Or tutti sorgete" (Act I), and the aria "La luce langue" (revised version, Act II), actually calls on the demons, the dark forces, and on darkness itself to assist them in their evil designs. Both pieces are in *E*. At the conclusion of the second-act *finale,* Macbeth swears to visit the witches and compel them to reveal his destiny. This entire section, the extended Largo

5. See letters to Escudier of 23 January 1865, to Tito Ricordi of 23 September 1865 and to Giulio Ricordi of 15 December 1870.

TABLE 3

[SECTION I]	
E minor, 76 measures Allegro vivacissimo (2/4).	The stage is filled with spirits, devils and witches who dance around the cauldron.
E major, 33 measures Un poco ritenuto; I° tempo	They stop dancing and conjure up Hecate.

[SECTION II]	
Modulatory transition, 10 measures Allegro (C)	Hecate, the Goddess of Night and of Sorcery, appears.
F major, 12 measures Andante (2/4)	All [present] have assumed a devout pose and, almost trembling, contemplate the Goddess.
B♭ major, 52 measures Andante (2/4)	Hecate tells the witches that she understands their task and the purpose for which she was invoked.
	Hecate examines everything carefully.
	Hecate announces that King Macbeth will come to consult them about his destiny and they will have to satisfy [his request].
	If the visions [they have conjured up] should overly depress his senses [i.e. overcome him], they are to invoke the aerial spirits in order to reawaken him and renew his vigor.
	But the ruin that awaits him must be postponed no longer.
F, 12 measures Andante (2/4)	While receiving the decrees of the Goddess, all [present] assume a respectful pose.
Modulation and transition, 11 measures Allegro (C)	Hecate disappears amidst thunder and lightning.

[SECTION III]	
E minor, 164 measures Allegro vivacissimo (3/4)	Waltz
E major, 56 measures Poco più mosso (3/4)	All [the witches, spirits, and devils] encircle the cauldron and, taking each other by the hand, form a circle while dancing.

closing the *finale*, is in E. Later he arrives at their cave, again in E (Act III). But significantly enough, when the witches speak of "incognite posse ... cui ministri obbediam" (unknown powers ... whose ministers we obey) the music is in B♭.

Let us return for a moment to the banquet scene closing Act II. Three keys are of approximately equal importance, F, B♭, and E. The festive music heard at the opening and again between the strophes of the *brindisi* is in F major. The Macbeths are celebrating his ascent to the throne with a great feast in their castle. As a result of the first appearance of Banquo's ghost, the new king is terrified. The music turns to F minor to help mirror his suffering, and Lady Macbeth tries to rally him and keep the party from disintegrating while still in F.

The $B\flat$ sections seem to be primarily associated with the murdered Banquo, and particularly with his appearances as a ghost. Both times the ghost appears, it is to the accompaniment of a $B\flat$ minor sonority. Furthermore, the reprise of the $B\flat$ brindisi is a toast to the absent Banquo. By this time Lady Macbeth knows full well he is dead, and the toast is a cynical and thoroughly gratuitous insult to the murdered nobleman. Finally, the continuation and repetition of the music of the first strophe, also in $B\flat$, is the musical setting for the report to Macbeth of Banquo's demise by one of the murderers who is still covered with the dead man's blood. Lady Macbeth's arrogance in this scene, her implicit defiance of the gods who presumably control man's fate and punish his transgressions, is also made clear in the aria "Trionfai" (original version, Act II). It too is an aria in $B\flat$. I think Verdi chose this key because an exultant Lady Macbeth challenges the gods with the line "Or ti sfido il lampo il tuono" (Now I defy your lightning, your thunder).

At other crucial points in the opera the key or the sonority of $B\flat$ is associated with the supernatural or its manifestations. During the dagger soliloquy (Act I), when Macbeth hears the bell toll, he says, in F minor, "È deciso, quel bronzo m'invita! Non udirlo Duncano!" (It has been decided, that bronze [bell] summons me! Hear it not, Duncan!), and continues, in $B\flat$ minor, "È squillo eterno che nel cielo ti chiama o nell'inferno" (It is the eternal blast that calls you to heaven or to hell). Only moments later, Lady Macbeth is on stage alone. She is frightened by what she takes to be a sign from the supernatural, the eerie lament of an owl. The lament is heard twice and the passage is in $B\flat$ minor.

Macbeth then returns from Duncan's quarters, and husband and wife sing the extended duet "Fatal mia donna." The key is F minor, and appropriately so since the principal subject is Macbeth and his tortured conscience. However, the *adagio* is in $B\flat$, and it begins with Macbeth terrified because he had heard a (supernatural) voice say:

Avrai per guanciali sol vepri, o Macbetto!	For pillows, you will have only brambles, oh Macbeth!
[Il sonno per sempre, Glamis, uccidesti!]	[Glamis, you murdered sleep forever!]
Non v'è che vigilia, Caudore, per te!	Cawdor, there will only be wakefulness for you!

And he continues to sing repeatedly, still in $B\flat$:

Com'angeli d'ira, vendetta tuonarmi	Like angels of wrath, I shall hear vengeance
Udrò di Duncano le sante virtù	Thunder [within] me of Duncan's holy virtues

During the Act I *finale* which follows, the hastily assembled crowd hears of Duncan's murder and it sings in $B\flat$ minor one of the most impressive phrases of the entire opera:

Schiudi, inferno, la bocca ed inghiotti	Hell, open your mouth and swallow
Nel tuo grembo l'intero creato;	All of creation into your womb.

The continuation begins in the same key, but the text points toward Macbeth and there is a momentary tonicization of F minor:

Sull'ignoto assassino esecrato	May your flames descend, oh heaven,
Le tue fiamme discendano, o ciel.	Upon the unknown, accursed murderer.

In Act IV, during the $A\flat$ cabaletta "La patria tradita," there is a turn to $B\flat$ minor for the text "Già l'ira divina sull'empio ruïna" (Already divine wrath crushes the wicked one).

Later in the act, the first version of the excited report to Macbeth that "La foresta di Birnamo si muove" (The forest of Birnam is moving) is set in the key of the witches, *E*. On revision, however, Verdi set the passage in *B♭*. Macbeth sees the movement of the forest to be a stratagem of the supernatural, as his very next words attest: "M'hai deluso, infernale presagio" (You have deceived me, hellish foreboding). In this instance the key of the revision, *B♭* minor, is better suited than *E* minor on two counts. It was the forces more powerful than the witches that had made the prophecy, and the previous reference to Birnam Wood in Act IV (during the *tempo di mezzo* preceding the *cabaletta* "La patria tradita") was in *B♭*. The key, then, provides a tonal reference point for the second mention of the forest as well.

The key or sonority of *C* major-minor seems to be associated with two not unrelated phenomena, murder and Macbeth's destiny. During the duet "Fatal mia donna" (Act I), Macbeth recounts the statements by the supernatural voice. The passage, as we saw, was basically in *B♭*. The words "Il sonno per sempre, Glamis uccidesti" (Glamis, you murdered sleep forever), however, are set in *C* minor.

The *finale* of Act I begins with a section stressing *C* during which Macduff and Banquo come to Duncan's chambers to waken him. While Macduff enters, Banquo sings in *C* minor. There is constant tonicization of IV and VI but the sonority of *C* is prominent, especially in the setting of the word "morte."

In the recitative to the first scene of Act II, Macbeth tells his wife "Forza è che scorra un altro sangue, o donna!" (More blood must flow, oh woman). She asks, "Where? when?"; he replies, "At the coming of night." Except for the first word, the entire passage is in *C* major. When Lady Macbeth questions Macbeth's steadfastness, his will to *evil*, in the next phrase of the revised version, there is, appropriately enough, an emphasis on the sonority of *E*: "Immoto sarai tu nel tuo disegno?" (Will you remain steadfast in your design?).

The second scene of Act II shows the rather large group of murderers lying in wait for Banquo and Fleance. They sing in *C* major:

Sparve il sol, la notte or regni	The sun is gone,
Scellerata, insanguinata;	Let wicked, bloody night reign;
Cieca notte, affretta e spegni	Hurry blind night, and extinguish
Ogni lume in terra, in ciel. . . .	Every light on earth and in the sky.

Since the key or sonority of *E* is so closely associated with darkness and evil, it is noteworthy that Verdi should stress prominently the note *e* in the main melodic idea of the chorus, an idea that recurs often in the composition.

During the coda to Banquo's aria in the next scene, "Come dal ciel precipita," the murderers attack. On his last word, "tradimento" (treachery), there is a deceptive cadence in *E* minor. The submediant, a sonority of *C*, is prolonged for twelve beats with *C* in the bass for sixteen beats. It seems reasonable to assume that Banquo receives his mortal wounds to the accompaniment of that sonority, the most sustained harmony in the passage.

In the course of the revised *finale* to Act III, there is a modulation to *C* major at the point where the bracketed words end:

LADY MACBETH:
 [Di Banco il figlio] si rinvenga, e muoia!
MACBETH:
 Tutto il sangue si sperda a noi nemico!

LADY MACBETH:
 [Banquo's son] must be sought out and murdered!
MACBETH:
 The blood of everyone who is our enemy must be spilled.

In the 1847 version of Macduff's recitative to his aria "Ah, la paterna mano," he refers to the murder of his children in C minor: "O figli, o figli miei! Da quel tiranno tutti uccisi voi foste (Oh sons, oh my sons! You were all murdered by that tyrant).

In both versions of the scene preceding the battle, Macbeth hears from a Lady-in-waiting that "È morta la regina" (The Queen is dead). Originally the passage stressed C major; on revision it was set in C minor). In the revised version, the battle itself, murder on the grandest scale possible, is in C major. After the battle, Malcolm asks, "Where is the usurper?" Appropriately there is in both versions an F sonority for the accented syllable of the word "l'usurpator." Macduff replies "trafitto" (run through) in the first version and "Colà da me trafitto" (Over there, run through by me) in the revision. Both settings provide a melodic line on c and a C-major harmony in the orchestra.

Another dramatic association with the key or sonority of C seems to be Macbeth's destiny. Toward the end of the scene in which Macbeth and Banquo meet the witches, the latter, knowing full well their future, sardonically sing to them in C major: "Macbeth e Banco vivano" (Long live Macbeth and Banquo).

Finally, during both versions of the apparitions scene Macbeth demands that the witches reveal to him his destiny. On the accented syllable of the word "destin," the orchestra enters with a sonority of c (first version), key of C minor (revised version).

D major is used less than any of the other keys discussed. If there is a tonal-dramatic association, it would appear to be truth, or prophecy fulfilled. After their first meeting with the witches, Macbeth and Banquo are approached by Duncan's messengers. Macbeth is addressed as Thane of Cawdor (C major, tonicizing A minor at the cadence). He responds: "But that lord still rules" and, as the music modulates to D minor, the messengers reply: "No! percosso dalla legge sotto il ceppo egli spirò" (No! he died on the block, struck down by the law) and Banquo says: "Ah! l'inferno il ver parlò" (Ah! Hell spoke the truth) in D minor. Macbeth and Banquo then sing their duet "Due vaticini compiuti" and leave. The witches return for their second chorus "S'allontanarono! n'accozzeremo" set in D minor-major, and the words defining the tonality are:

... s'attenda	Let us await the Witches' Sabbath
Le sorti a compiere nella tregenda.	To see his destiny fulfilled.
Macbetto riedere vedrem colà,	There we shall see Macbeth return
E il nostro oracolo gli parlerà.	And our oracle will speak to him.

Another section of the introduction deserves discussion. When Macbeth and Banquo meet the witches the key is C. There is a temporary emphasis on the dominant minor with Macbeth's reaction and Banquo's "Who are you? Of this world or of the other region?" As Banquo continues, his statement focuses on the contradictory quality of their appearance, and the passage is in D minor: "Dirvi donne vorrei, ma lo mi vieta quella sordida barba" (I should like to call you women, but your sordid beards forbid me [to do so]). They respond with their first prediction, actually a statement of fact, still in D minor: "Salve, o Macbetto, di Glamis sire" (Hail, oh Macbeth, Thane of Glamis).

The apparitions scene (Act III), the longest section with a relatively fixed key, is in D and accompanies the vision of the kings and Banquo. Both of the kings visible to Macbeth and the reflections he sees in the mirror resemble Banquo; this suggests the future fulfillment of the prophecy "Non re, ma di monarchi genitore!" (Not King, but father of Kings!).

During Act IV Malcolm and his men are in the vicinity of Birnam Wood and the key is $B\flat$. As he tells them "Svelga ognuno e porti un ramo, che lo asconda, innanzi a se" (Let everyone tear off a branch and carry it in front of him, so that it may hide him), there is a modulation to D minor. The passage explains how the last prophecy is to be fulfilled. Similarly, the music stresses D minor during both versions of the battle scene as Macduff explains that "he was not born but torn from his mother's womb." Once again the reality behind the fulfillment of a seemingly impossible prophecy is explained in the key of D.

Several commentators have noted Verdi's use of chromaticism or the interval of a half step in *Macbeth*.[6] I find that not only the interval, but two sets of keys or sonorities a half step apart, C-$D\flat$ and F-E, have dramatic significance. At the beginning of the *finale* to Act I, Duncan's murder is discovered by Malcolm and an alarm raised in C minor. A crowd assembles, expresses horror, and in effect asks: "Who is the guilty one?" The key for this section is $D\flat$. In the course of Act IV there are three confessions of guilt, all arias, and all in $D\flat$. The first "Ah, la paterna mano" is by Macduff who castigates himself for having left his family unprotected while he sought aid in England for the overthrow of Macbeth. But his guilt is unpremeditated and serves to activate his anger against the real culprit. Both the recitative "O figli" and the second part of his aria, "Ah, trammi al tiranno in faccia," fasten the guilt on Macbeth. Lady Macbeth's overwhelming confession, "Una macchia," is also in $D\flat$. As Verdi himself pointed out, "the Sleepwalking Scene...is always the high point of the opera" (11 March 1865 letter to Escudier).

Another $D\flat$ aria, "Pietà, rispetto, amore," is sung by Macbeth. Here Macbeth recognizes for the first time the full consequences of his behavior: "Sol la bestemmia, ahi lasso! la nenia tua sarà" (Alas, curses alone will be your funeral lament). Three $D\flat$ arias in sequence; this is an extraordinary structural emphasis on a single key, and each aria is concerned with guilt. Further, the principal key of contrast within each aria is $F\flat$ ($=E$) the key of evil, and each aria is preceded by a passage in F minor. In symbolic fashion Verdi inextricably links the Macbeths, evil and guilt.

Here then is the answer, in tonal as well as dramatic terms, to the question posed in $D\flat$ during the Act I *finale*. The Macbeths are guilty, and guilt must be punished. The three $D\flat$ arias are followed immediately by the report of Lady Macbeth's death in C, and shortly thereafter by the battle and the report of Macbeth's death in the same key. The tonal and dramatic progression in the central portion of the last act is, then, a thrice reiterated statement of guilt in $D\flat$, followed by the violent deaths of the Macbeths in C.

On local levels the juxtaposition of $d\flat$ and c, usually as tones or sonorities on the lowered submediant and dominant of F, appears frequently in the opera. Perhaps the first time is the most revealing. Macbeth is contemplating the witches' predictions ("Due vaticini com-

6. See, for example, Francis Toye's *Verdi: His Life and Works*, paper ed. (New York, 1959), 266–68, Alpert, "Verdi's Use of the Minor Second," *The Opera Journal* (Fall, 1971), 11–14 and Francesco Degrada, "Lettura del *Macbeth*."

piuti," Act I); his words "Pensier di sangue" are set to repeated db's falling to a c. An even more emphatic use of these two pitches is the setting for "Tutto è finito," Macbeth's first words after having murdered Duncan. Verdi indicates the importance of this particular figure in the prelude to Act II, where it is played by trumpets and trombones in octaves as it was in Act I. The figure is then followed by the music of the duet "Fatal mia donna," again as in Act I.

Before leaving the matter of guilt, I should like to discuss two other passages. The first is from "Trionfai," sung by Lady Macbeth in the first version of the opera (Act II). The text "Tra misfatti l'opra ha fine se un misfatto [le fu culla]" (The affair will end with misdeeds, if a misdeed was its cradle) is set in Db, although the key of the aria is Bb. Again Lady Macbeth accepts with equanimity the guilt for additional misdeeds, in this case the projected murder of Banquo and his son, Fleance. With respect to the plot, perhaps the most important statement is by the second of the three apparitions (Act III):

O Macbetto, Macbetto, Macbetto!   O Macbeth, Macbeth, Macbeth
Esser puoi sanguinario, feroce: You can be bloodthirsty, cruel:
Nessun nato di donna ti nuoce.   No one born of woman will harm you.

Macbeth, falling further into the trap set for him, takes the pronouncement as his license to murder with impunity, to be as guilty as he pleases, and the key is Db in both versions of the opera.

From the very beginning Lady Macbeth accepts guilt and embraces evil more easily than her husband. Her opening scene consists of the aria "Vieni! t'affretta!" in Db, framed by the key of E. Recall that E is the chord accompanying her letter, the tonality in which her recitative begins, and the key of the *cabaletta* "Or tutti sorgete." In effect, her guilty thoughts (i.e., the anticipated murder of Duncan) are tonally imbedded in evil. Again, at the beginning of Act II,[7] revised version, it is Lady Macbeth who calls on the forces of darkness to aid in their plan to murder Banquo in "La luce langue," also in E. Macbeth, on the other hand, doesn't completely overcome his conscience until the end of Act II when, in the last section of the *finale*, he vows, in E:

Sangue a me quell'ombra chiede   That shade [Banquo's ghost] asks me for blood
E l'avrà, l'avrà, lo giuro!   And he will have it, he will have it, I swear it.

Verdi suggests then, as did Shakespeare, that it was Lady Macbeth who first completely and unequivocally embraces evil. And the musician does so with the most powerful tool at the disposal of a composer in the eighteenth or nineteenth century—the dramatic use of tonality. In the opera it is only during the *finale* of Act II and in Acts III and IV that Macbeth takes full responsibility for his actions. This new dramatic orientation is reflected by the closer juxtaposition of the keys of F and E, as in the recitative to Macbeth's aria in Act IV. (Ricordi, pp. 275–76. See also Table 1 above.)

As with db and c, the notes f and e or the harmonies F and E are often joined in the

7. The opening words of the recitative following the prelude explain the choice of thematic materials. Lady Macbeth says to her husband: "Perchè mi sfuggi, e fiso ognor ti veggo in un pensier profondo?" Macbeth is still troubled by his conscience, and the key is F minor until the last syllable of the phrase. Then there is a modulation to Db for her continuation "The deed is irreparable!" She is, in effect, saying you must learn to live with your guilt. As in the duet "Due vaticini compiuti" (Act I) and the three Act IV arias, here is another juxtaposition of F and Db, Macbeth and guilt.

opera. The first part of the opening chorus of the witches refers to their wicked deeds.[8] The initial line of text, "Che faceste? Dite su!," is set melodically to the pitches f and e (Ricordi, p. 6, measures 1–4). Throughout the chorus, the two pitches or chords recur juxtaposed (Ricordi, p. 5, measures 13–23; p. 6, measures 12, 18; p. 7, measures 5–6, 10; p. 8, measures 1–3, 5–7; p. 9, measures 1, 3). At the midpoint of the chorus Macbeth's drum is heard and the reaction of the witches is harmonized by the sonority of F. This is followed immediately by a cadential progression on E (Ricordi, p. 9, measures 10ff). In the very next scene when the witches encounter Macbeth and Banquo, the first harmonized measures have as their most important sonorities those of E and F (Ricordi p. 16, measures 4–5). Finally, in the revised version of the *finale* to Act IV, Malcolm asks "Where is the usurper?" to the harmonic progression E-F, evil and Macbeth linked for the last time (Ricordi, p. 290, measures 16–17).

In summary, *Macbeth II* reveals a more mature Verdi displaying a greater interest in the architectural aspects of tonal organization. At the same time there are also more sharply focused tonal-dramatic associations. But it should be emphasized that in the vast majority of cases both versions show the same associations, even when the exact words of the text have been reset musically. Where there are tonal differences (e.g., "Patria oppressa," Act IV), the new version is usually more consistent with the tonal-dramatic associations found in the opera as a whole.[9]

Several letters suggest that *Macbeth* marked a new stage in Verdi's compositional career, one in which there was an increased concern for tonal planning and key symbolism. With one isolated exception, Verdi stopped writing substitute arias when he came to *Macbeth*.[10] Furthermore, on at least three occasions during his earliest years Verdi himself suggested the possibility of transposing his music.[11] In 1847, however, the composer proposed a contract to Ricordi which, in Verdi's words, prohibited "any insertions, any mutilations, any lowering or raising of keys."[12] Additional proof of how strongly he had begun to feel with regard to transpositions exists in a letter dated 1 December 1851 to the Roman sculptor, Vincenzo Luccardi:

These impresarios have not yet understood that when operas cannot be presented in their totality, as they were conceived by the author, it is better not to present them; they do not realize that the transposition of a piece, of a scene, is almost always the cause of the opera's lack of success.[13]

8. Although in this chorus the witches are singing of an area which is Scotland and the key is A minor-major (see note 4 above), in effect it is the sonority of E, their evil, which predominates. See, for example, the orchestral introduction where the opening measures of A are not confirmed. Instead there is a modulation, first to B (dominant of E), then to E, and finally to E as a lengthy dominant of A.

9. Without the explanation offered by key symbolism, it is difficult to understand why Verdi would choose to write three duets for Macbeth in the same key, F (i.e. with Banquo, Act I, and with Lady Macbeth, Act I and revised Act III); two extended numbers in E to begin Act III of the revised version (i.e. witches chorus, and the ballet for Paris); and especially the three arias in $D\flat$ in successive scenes of Act IV.

10. Lawton and Rosen, "Verdi's Non-Definitive Revisions," p. 224

11. For the soprano Almerinda Granchi and a performance of *Nabucco* (Venice, 1842–43); for the soprano Erminia Frezzolini Poggi in *I lombardi* (Senigallia, 1843); and for the tenor Mario in *I due Foscari* (Paris, 1846). See Lawton's "Tonality and Drama," 360–61, 364.

12. See Lawton and Rosen, "Verdi's Non-Definitive Revisions," p. 224 and *Copialettere*, 39.

13. *Copialettere*, 496. I take it that Verdi is here referring to transposition (*trasposizione*) of keys, a practice common at the time, and not to the repositioning of individual numbers elsewhere in an opera, which was not common.

ON THE TONAL ORGANIZATION
OF *MACBETH II*
Daniel Sabbeth

"Bloody instructions ... being taught, return to plague th'inventor," says Shakespeare's Macbeth (I.7.8–10), before he finally decides to kill Duncan, the father-king. With unclear vision and only a partial understanding of the supernatural prophecies upon which he relies, Macbeth is both tempted and betrayed by the witches, as he is by his wife, who, spurring him on, leaves him to die alone in the end after the deed is done. Shakespeare's drunken porter expresses well the antitheses with which Macbeth must deal:

It makes him, and it mars him; it sets him on, and it takes him off; it persuades him, and disheartens him; makes him stand to, and not stand to; in conclusion, equivocates him in a sleep, and, giving him the lie, leaves him. (*II,3,29–32*)

Throughout his opera, Verdi also shows that the forces that encourage Macbeth and give him hope are the very ones that prove to be the agents of his destruction. More specifically, it is the tonal progressions initiated by the witches and the Lady that eventually destroy the usurper king. These tonal gestures permeate the opera as a musical counterpart to Shakespeare's concise opposition: "Fair is foul, and foul is fair" (I.1.10).

The repetition of a limited number of tonal procedures generates organic cohesion. These appear at various levels of structure: on the surface as motives, and in the remote background as tonal motions organizing entire acts, or even spanning several acts. One such procedure is the mode mixture so pervasive in *Macbeth*. Its use goes far beyond the norms of Verdi's musical language, as it generates both surface- and remote-level phenomena. As much of the tone of Shakespeare's play derives from night and the supernatural, much of the *tinta* of Verdi's opera results from mixture. Most obvious is the mixture affecting the third degree of the scale. This creates the motion from the minor to the major mode characteristic of many of the numbers. Usually there are lengthy passages within each mode, but the move to major may be delayed until the very end—with highly poignant effect—as in the final measures of the refugees' chorus in Act IV, "Patria oppressa."

Verdi uses mode mixture to create different versions of the same harmonic progression, thus providing both variety—through surface-level change—and unity—through the recurrence of the basic progression. Example 1 illustrates two frequently-used modal variants of the progression I–III–V–I. In Ex. 1a the progression is I–bIII–V–I, using the form of III that would be expected if the passage were in the minor mode. In the progression in Ex. 1b (I–III♯–V–I), F is the root of III as expected, but with a major triad instead of the more usual minor.

At the beginning of the opera, I–III–V is used prominently by the witches; later, by Banquo's murderers, by Banquo himself as he is about to die, and by the people of Scotland

Example 1a   Act I, Finale (reduction of pp. 86–88)

Example 1b   Act I, Cavatina Lady Macbeth (p. 39)

in their Hymn of Victory.[1] In Act IV, I–bIII–V of Db is used consecutively by Macduff (Ricordi, pp. 250–51), Lady Macbeth (pp. 268–72), and Macbeth (pp. 277–78). This is one of the means by which Verdi establishes a similarity among these three agents of a supernatural order, a similarity that is otherwise much more clearly stated in Shakespeare.[2]

Also subject to tonal variation is the lowered second degree, derived from the Phrygian mode. I believe that in *Macbeth* it is associated with horror and terrible deeds. This can be seen in the mourning of Scotland (final cadence of "Patria oppressa") and in the first appearance of the Phrygian II, Banquo's cry "Inferno" when told that the witches spoke the truth (*Introduzione*, p. 20).

More than any other modal alteration, however, the lowered sixth—both as a motivic and an harmonic gesture—dominates the opera. It is used specifically as an upper neighbor,

1. These progressions may be found in the Ricordi piano-vocal score as follows: witches, 17.1–3 (D minor); murderers, 119.4–120.1 (C major with mixture); Banquo, 124.2–4 (E minor); the people of Scotland, 295.2–296.2 (A major with mixture).

2. In Shakespeare's play, the Macbeths receive supernatural auguries, and, as the reader will recall, Macduff is not of woman born.

drawn to or proceeding from the dominant. If a motive is to generate organic cohesion and provide a *tinta*, it should begin at the beginning. And indeed the frozen combination Db-C appears as early as the sixth measure of the Preludio. Moreover, Verdi's setting of the opening text "Che faceste? Dite su!" states b6-5 in A minor.

The most concise statement of 5-b6-5 is Macbeth's exclamation "Tutto è finito" (p. 59). But even before these words are sung, the b6-5 neighbor alternation invades the vocal and orchestral parts, appearing on three local tonics—Eb, Bb, and F—as the music drives on towards Macbeth's anguished affirmation.[3] Multiple statements of 5-b6-5 are reserved for particularly horrific moments, such as this one and that in which Macduff realizes that his family has been destroyed (p. 249). There the motive appears four times—as a neighbor gesture to triads on A, F, Bb, and F once again.

Frequently the neighbor gesture 5-6-5 appears in an upper or middle voice while a local tonic or structural bass is retained or embellished below. This is seen in Lady's first suggestion to Macbeth that Duncan be murdered (Ex. 2a) and in Macbeth's horrified reaction to the vision of Banquo's royal descendants (Ex. 2b). By linking these two passages through the use of 6-5 in Eb major, perhaps Verdi suggests that "Bloody instructions ... being taught, return to plague th'inventor."

Example 2a   Rec.v e Marcia (p. 49)   *Example 2b   Act III, Scena e Duetto (p. 234)*

When the neighbor relationship between the lowered sixth and the dominant appears in the bass, it may support a chordal sequence in which the semitonal pull of V on its upper neighbor is so great that the latter lacks independence. Examples can be found at both immediate and remote levels of structure. On the surface, the attraction exerted by V upon its upper neighbor is particularly evident in E major; this relationship first appears in Act I during Lady Macbeth's *cabaletta* (48.3.2); it is also associated with the witches (192.3.1-4). In Ex. 3, as Macbeth sings of his resolve to learn the future, the neighbor gesture B-C-B is prolonged through four measures. The final appearance of the bass gesture C-B punctuates Macduff's announcement that he has slain Macbeth (the preparation for the final chorus, 291.1-2, Ex. 4). In this example, the lowered sixth supports an harmonically-independent triad to produce the progression I-bVI-V-I on E (here acting as the dominant of A). Because the C-B gesture—so often used by the Macbeths and the witches they follow—is now used to announce the destruction of the tyrant, I believe that we have once again "Bloody instructions ... being taught [have returned] to plague th'inventor."

So far we have examined elements of the E-major progression I-bVI-V-I that appear as colorful details at immediate levels of structure. It is a mark of Verdi's genius to use such microcosmic statements to parallel broad underlying progressions. This technique insures that the large is reflected in the small and that no irrelevant, coloristic "effects" detract from the unity of the opera. In Act II, I-bVI-V-I in E major organizes several levels of time, as it

3. Cb-Bb (57.3.2-4.1), Gb-F (58.4) and Db-C (59.1.2-3, etc.)

Example 3   Act II, Finale (p. 155)

Example 4   Act IV, transition to Inno di vittoria, graph (see pp. 290–91)

both prepares and depicts Banquo's murder (Ex. 5). First, in the scena preceding the aria "La luce langue," Macbeth, encouraged by his wife, expresses his resolve to kill Banquo and Fleance. Here the E major that will be prolonged in Lady Macbeth's exultant aria is first achieved (110.1.4). After the C-major murderers' chorus, Banquo enters on B, the dominant (p. 123). The return to E, the completion of the prolonged I–bVI–V–I progression, occurs as Banquo sings "Come dal ciel precipita" (p. 124). At a more immediate structural level, within the death scene itself, the I–bVI–V–I progression depicts Banquo's fears (p. 125/3–4) before it underlines his death (p. 127/1–4).

Within Lady Macbeth's opening scena with its descent from F to E, C (the bVI of E major), is so strongly felt as a neighbor—so totally dependent on V—that the surface V–bVI–I motion does not destroy the integrity of the underlying V–I harmonic progression (Ex. 6 and 107–110.1). This striking use of the incomplete neighbor chord is one of Verdi's favorite devices, found as late as *Falstaff*. It permits surprising digression and tonal explora-

Example 5   Act II, tonal outline of the first three numbers

Example 6   Act II, graph of scena preceding "La luce langue"

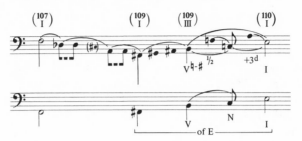

tion at an immediate tonal level while a cadential harmonic progression organizes the structure from below.[4]

There is another semitonal pull of great importance: that of E on F, and it too is both motivic and harmonic. The motive usually appears in A minor, as, for example, at the first four words of the opera. The first and last numbers of Act IV present E–F as an incomplete neighbor gesture in A (Ex. 4 and 7). Thus, when F is used as an upper neighbor to the V of A its presence does not affect the broad tonal motions surrounding it: it lacks structural independence.

Example 7   Act IV, graph of final cadence of chorus "Patria oppressa" (see p. 248)

By understanding the function of F as an incomplete neighbor, we can grasp the tonal coherence of large segments of the opera. We have seen that the dependence of C on B yields cohesion at both immediate and remote structural levels; the neighbor gesture F–E, as ♭VI–V of A, has an even greater unifying force.

Act II may be divided into two waves of activity, both of which begin on F and end on E (Ex. 8). The first of these motions deals with Macbeth's destruction of Banquo. In the second, through an identical semitonal descent, Macbeth, besieged by the vision of Banquo's ghost, begins in turn to be destroyed by his own guilt.[5] Again, Verdi has used a tonal gesture to demonstrate that "Bloody instructions . . . being taught, return to plague th'inventor."

In Act III, the dependence of F on E continues. Now at his wit's end, Macbeth is totally

4. For an example in the major mode, see the passage leading to "Due vaticini" (*Introduzione*, pp. 20–21), where the progression is V–VI–I of F major.

5. The motion is by the descending (perfect and diminished) fifths: F–B♭–E.

Example 8   Acts II-III, graph

at the mercy of the witches, whose E major-minor governs the chorus "Tre volte miagola la gatta," the ballet sequence, the apparitions, and the remainder of the act. Yet once more, Lady Macbeth incites her husband to carnage; this time the half-crazed tyrant lashes out blindly at Macduff's family, the final and least appropriate victims of his sword. At this point the music turns toward F for "Ora di morte," the last show of strength of the now weakened usurpers.

Example 9   Acts II-IV, graph

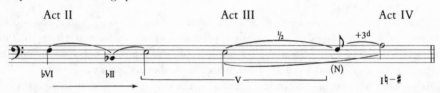

Ex. 9 shows the underlying tonal structure of Acts II-IV.[6] We now see that F, the key that Budden has quite properly associated with Macbeth,[7] has never had an independent existence after Act I. It has been drawn to E, just as Macbeth has been lured by the powers of the witches and the Lady. In the final act, the drama shifts from the Macbeths and the witches to the people of Scotland and the proper continuity of the Scottish throne. Now there is no further alternation of F and E; the barren, wintry forces of destruction have lost their strength. Birnam wood will soon come to Dunsinane, and the green rebirth of Scotland is close at hand. Here, Verdi demonstrates by tonal means that the Macbeths and the witches cannot keep Scotland from its lawful king; they have only been able to delay his entrance. This being so, E—the long, long dominant of Acts II and III—eventually must yield to A, the tonic of Act IV, and the key related to Scotland and its throne (see below). The enclosure of this final act in A is well prepared by the enormous expansion of the preceding dominant. Indeed the motion to A has been a series of descending fifths utilizing the Phrygian II: ♭VI-♭II-V-I. Few stronger progressions are available.

Ex. 10 presents the tonal structure of the final act. Two choruses surround broad expressions of grief and loneliness by Macduff, the Lady, and Macbeth. They also enclose the following battle in which Macduff kills Macbeth. Verdi has clearly gone to extraordinary

6. The F of "Ora di morte" now reveals itself as an incomplete neighbor, similar to the C major chord in Ex. 6. I believe that Act I contains organized motion between the tonic and submediant of F major-minor; however, the issues and tonal gestures involved are complex and cannot be discussed within the framework of this study.

7. Budden, *Operas* 1, 198

Example 10   Act IV, graph

Coro   Scena ed Aria   Sonnambulismo   Scena,   Battaglia e Inno di vittoria
        Macduff   di Lady Macbeth

lengths to link these three characters—a single hero among two murderers. In each of the three numbers, a slow movement in D♭ major is preceded by an introductory recitative, partially in F minor.[8] Moreover, in each recitative, the motion B♭–C acts as IV–V of F (Macduff, 249.3.3–5; Lady, 266.2.2–3; Macbeth, 276.4.3–5.2), and, coincident with the arrival on C, the "Tutto è finito" motive is stated at its original pitch level and followed by a pause.

Even more striking, each D♭ section contains the motion I–♭III–V, providing a reference to F♭ or E major, the key that Verdi has associated with the power of those who would destroy nature's order. Furthermore, in each of the E-major segments—as in the numbers as a whole—the inability to undo past offenses is accepted:

MACDUFF
E me fuggiasco, occulto,
Voi chiamavate invano
Coll'ultimo singulto . . .
(*pp. 250–51*)

LADY MACBETH
Di sangue umano
Sa qui sempre. Arabia intera
Rimondar sì piccol mano
Co' suoi balsami non può
(*pp. 270–71*)

MACBETH
Sol la bestemmia, ahi lasso!
La nenia tua sarà!
(*p. 278*)

Thus does the power associated with E bring grief to those guilty mortals who have sought it.

Why has Verdi so closely associated the hero with the murderers? Psychoanalytic critics who have looked at the archetypal family situations underlying Shakespeare's *Macbeth* suggest some intriguing hypotheses.[9]

A "son," prompted by half-masculine "mothers" [the witches and the Lady], kills a father (Duncan) and becomes a father (king) himself. Then sons . . . "none of woman born," kill that bad son-become-father.[10]

8. David Lawton has noted this similarity in his doctoral dissertation ("Tonality and Drama,") 89. He also notes the F♭ segments within the key of D♭ that I discuss below.

9. For a fine synthesis of the psychoanalytic writings on Shakespeare, see Norman N. Holland, *Psychoanalysis and Shakespeare* (New York: McGraw-Hill, 1966). An excellent collection of essays on the subject is M.D. Faber, ed. *The Design Within: Psychoanalytic Approaches to Shakespeare* (New York: Science House, 1970).

10. Holland, *Psychoanalysis,* p. 287

In other words, Macbeth acts first as a bad son: by criminal action, he replaces Duncan, his father-king. Then he "takes over the part of the father-king, but unlike Duncan, he proves a bad father, killing one son (Banquo) and trying for the other (Macduff)."[11]

Macduff is also a bad son, especially in the Shakespearean original: he refuses to come to Macbeth's coronation, and he does not attend the banquet.[12] Then, as a bad father, Macduff leaves his family open to murder—unlike Duncan and Banquo who protect and nourish their children. Both Macduff and Macbeth, therefore, prove the adage: *a bad son will make a bad father.*[13] In one case, the bad son-become-bad-father is socially useful, a hero; in the other, he is a tyrant. Artistic unity consists in the welding of such unexpected, underlying similarities.[14]

These three D♭ sections of the final act are essentially variations of one another, just as are the three guilt-ridden, lonely parents who sacrifice their sons and in so doing, also forfeit the blessing of continuous descent.[15] Clearly, it is through tonality rather than text that Verdi points out the unconsciously-sensed parallels between the childless Macduff and the barren rulers of Scotland.

A musical relationship we have emphasized—that of mode mixture to musical structure—is well-demonstrated in the final act (Ex. 10). In the opening chorus the mode shifts from minor to major. The C♯, as raised third of the tonic triad, is an enharmonic anticipation of the prolonged D♭—the III of A major—that follows. Similarly, the Battaglia is presented in C major—the III of A minor—and thus prepares the return to the tonic minor. Even as late as the final chorus there is still an alternation between A minor and major— between C and C♯. Only at the end is an irrevocable decision made for the raised third.

Ex. 11 illustrates the neighbor motions from C to C♯ resulting from the A minor-major mixture. Furthermore, this graph demonstrates how F is generated as an upper neighbor to E when D♭ major (rather than C♯ minor) is chosen as the III of A. The neighbor alternations C–C♯ and E–F are two that also proved important in our motivic study.[16]

In closing, we note that the overall motion of Acts II–IV, F–B♭–E–A, is one in which each key serves a fairly consistent dramatic function. While certain of these associations are discussed more fully and from a different point of view in CHUSID (at 249–60), a brief discussion here will relate the dramatic functions of these four keys to the descending-fifth motion which serves to organize them. F is Macbeth's key. B♭, a fifth below, depicts him in his role as murderer as he enters Duncan's chamber to perform his first bloody deed. Haunted by his crime, Macbeth hears an internal voice in this key:

> Avrai per guanciali sol vepri, o Macbetto!
> Il sonno per sempre, Glamis, uccidesti!
> Non v'è che vigilia, Caudore, per te! (*p. 63*)

11. Ibid., p. 222

12. Ibid., p. 287

13. Ludwig Jekels, "The Riddle of Shakespeare's *Macbeth,*" *Psychoanalytic Review* 30 (1943), 361–85; reprinted in his *Selected Papers* (London: Imago, 1952), with the quotation appearing on p. 116 (underlined in original)

14. Holland, *Psychoanalysis*, p. 223

15. Jekels, *Papers*, p. 119

16. It is worth noting that earlier C♯ (D♭) acted as an upper neighbor to the structural tone C. Now the roles are reversed, and C appears as a lower neighbor to the structural C♯ (D♭). I believe that there is dramatic purpose to this reversal: The murders of Duncan and Banquo by the Macbeths have utilized C as a structural tone (in the "Tutto e finito" motive and the murderers' chorus), but the death of Macbeth returns order to Scotland—and so the C major of the battle moves to C♯ in the final A major of the opera.

Example 11   Act IV, neighbor motions from C to C♯ (D♭) and E to F

Banquo's ghost is the internalized visual counterpart to these words; and, as Exs. 8 and 9 indicate, the B♭ of the second vision is part of the motion that leads to the prolonged E of Acts II and III.

Other forces leading to Macbeth's downfall are also presented in B♭: his wife (in the *brindisi*), Hecate (in the central portion of the Act III ballet), and the motion of Birnam Wood (p. 253). When Macbeth realizes that doom may be close at hand, there is one last poignant turn from F to B♭ (p. 276), recalling his initial crime (p. 58) and providing a further demonstration that "Bloody instructions . . . return to plague th'inventor."

An E-major sonority accompanies the third prophecy "Salve o Macbetto, di Scozia re!" (17.3.7).[17] Hearing this, Macbeth trembles, although a man without guilty thoughts would have no reason to do so. E is the key in which Macbeth the hero yields, first to the influence of the witches, and then to the prodding of his wife. The key in which this once-brave soldier has succumbed returns to depict his decay in Act II and to announce his death in Act IV (Exs. 8 and 4).

The A major of the final act is well prepared as the key of Scotland and its crown. In an A major segment of the scena introducing "La luce langue," Lady Macbeth reminds her husband that he is king and commands the throne (108.3.2–4.2). But much earlier, at the very beginning of Act I, the Introduzione presents the initial statement of A. The major mode appears only after the weird sisters announce Macbeth's arrival. Here they sing of weaving a circle of lands and seas, and, presumably, of nations and peoples. Although the witches' prophecies lead Macbeth to destroy Duncan and disrupt the royal succession, they also lead him to destroy himself and return Scotland to its lawful king. Thus if fair is foul, foul may also prove fair. Whatever has been lost, the ambiguities and antitheses of Shakespeare seem well preserved in Verdi.

17. Here E is the dominant of A, but when used as a tonic later, its associations remain the same.

MACBETH, ATTILA,
AND VERDI'S SELF-MODELING

Gary Tomlinson

When, in his *Studio sulle opere di Giuseppe Verdi* of 1859, Abramo Basevi turned to a consideration of Verdi's *seconda maniera*, he singled out *Luisa Miller* as "the first opera worthy to figure at the head of the new manner."[1] That Basevi should have passed over *Macbeth* for this honor comes as little surprise. *Macbeth* occupies a somewhat unenviable position in Verdi's output—a not wholly refreshing oasis in the barren artistic landscape stretching from 1845 to 1849—whereas *Luisa Miller* gives us a clear vista to the panorama of the early 1850s. Moreover, Basevi castigated Verdi for his choice of an *argomento fantastico* in *Macbeth*, more suited to the "nordic spirit" than to the Italian.[2] The sharp distinction drawn here between Italian and northern musical styles developed into a full-fledged anti-Wagnerian tirade in Basevi's discussion of *Simon Boccanegra*.[3]

For a less emphatic rejection of the ultramontane elements supposedly creeping into Verdi's operas in the late 40s and mid-50s we must turn to another contemporary consideration of the Maestro's works: that of Antonio Ghislanzoni. In 1856 the future versifier of *Aida* published his novel *Gli artisti da teatro*. To the 1865 reprint of this work he appended a volume of "Note critico-biografiche" on the Italian theatre of his time, which includes a six-page disquisition on Verdi's operas, seemingly written in conscious response to Basevi's *Studio*.[4] Indeed, Ghislanzoni pointedly pronounces *Simon Boccanegra* a "magnificent work"[5]—a remarkable evaluation coming as it does after the opera's dismal premiere and long before its revision and revival. And he sees in *La traviata* the dramatic revolution to which Basevi, absorbed in stodgy moralizing on the subject matter, was blind:

> *La traviata* is true modern drama, intimate, sentimental, passionate, and heart-rending drama—in my view, the drama in which Verdi's originality stands out most clearly.[6]

In its broad outlines, Ghislanzoni's view of the various stylistic *maniere* of Verdi's early career owes much to Basevi's.[7] But in drawing the boundary between the first and second

---

1. Basevi, *Studio*, p. 159

2. Ibid., p. 99

3. Ibid., pp. 264–5

4. Milan: G. Daelli e C., Editori. The discussion of Verdi is on pp. 14–20 of vol. 6. William Weaver called attention to this work in his "A Librettist's Novel," *Opera News* (December 26, 1955), but did not have access to an edition that included the documentary appendix.

5. Ibid., p. 18

6. Ibid., p. 17. This judgment is all the more surprising as the novel it follows is a pointed moral condemnation of all those involved in the musical theatre.

7. Both see a first "stile grandioso" giving way in the late 1840s to a new style, "sopratutto, più dramatico" according to Ghislanzoni, allowing an optimum translation of drama into music: "*Rigoletto* is the genuine musical translation of *Le Roi s'amuse*, while *Ernani* was but an uncontrolled paraphrase of Victor Hugo's drama" (Ibid., p.

style periods Ghislanzoni shows an important, if small, revision of the earlier scheme. Basevi had been bound by his strong stance against the supernatural elements of *Macbeth* to look forward to *Luisa Miller* as the first opera of the new style, though he seems uneasy about writing off the best music of *Macbeth* and other early operas:

... in the operas of the first manner the germs of the second are seen, just as in [the operas of the second manner] the advances of the first are found; other operas can be considered to be transitional.[8]

Ghislanzoni, however, is straitjacketed by no such biases, and makes explicit the evaluation with which Basevi would probably have agreed:

In my view, the second manner of Verdi begins in some scenes from *Macbeth*, and is fully developed in all the operas that stand between *Luisa Miller* and *La Traviata*.[9]

What precisely is the nature of this transition in the style of Verdi's operas, a transition which led to a new, individualized portrayal of character, and to a generally more faithful translation of drama into opera? We are given a clue toward its understanding in the continuation of the above quotation from Basevi:

... other operas can be considered to be transitional. Moreover, all the works of Verdi show points of analogy, which constitute the essence of the Verdian *genre* and are the expression of his genius.[10]

Basevi himself does not follow up this suggestive aside; but the comparison of these *punti d'analogia* to which he refers offers a valuable critical tool. Nowhere in Verdi's output, I believe, can its use more clearly demonstrate a stylistic breakthrough than in a comparison of *Macbeth* with the operas before it.

The existence of numerous large-scale correspondences among Verdi's operas should not surprise us in a composer who also sought models for set pieces and scenes in the most successful works of his predecessors.[11] The fact that these "points of analogy" have not been widely recognized and utilized in Verdi criticism is, perhaps, an inevitable result of the opera-by-opera approach taken in most extensive treatments of his works. In the best such treatments—for example, in the two great Bs of Verdi studies, Basevi and Budden—the authors show some awareness of these correspondences, but do not fully integrate them into their critical systems. This limitation of approach is, unfortunately, encouraged by the format of recent Verdi congresses. Another time it would perhaps be fruitful to devote a meeting to particular aspects of Verdi's entire output—his recitative techniques, or the development of the Verdian duet, for example—rather than to *Macbeth*, to *Simon Boccanegra*, or to *Don Carlos*.[12]

---

17). And Basevi stresses a central feature of this *seconda maniera:* "... each person represents only himself. The emotion, because it is individualized, does not have need of ... exaggeration...." (*Studio*, p. 158).

8. Ibid.

9. Ghislanzoni, *Gli artisti* 6: 17.

10. *Studio*, pp. 158-59.

11. See, for example, the numerous relationships between the works of Donizetti and Verdi pointed out by Winton Dean in "Some Echoes of Donizetti in Verdi's Operas," *Atti del III° congresso internazionale di studi verdiani* (Parma, 1974), pp. 122-47. Dean emphasizes that these "echoes" arise mostly in parallel dramatic situations.

12. Absent from this essay is any consideration of the many small-scale musical relationships between the operas, which usually take the form of stylistic tics recurring with special frequency in a few nearly contemporaneous

The first and clearest sort of large-scale correspondence among Verdi's operas is the modeling of a conventional musico-dramatic structure on a similar structure from an earlier opera. That is, Verdi responds to a stock situation in the first libretto with a conventional musical formula, and, presented with a similar dramatic situation in another libretto, he reutrns to his first response as the specific musical model for his setting.

An example of such a correspondence in *Macbeth* is the adagio of Macduff's aria "Ah, la paterna mano," closely modeled on Foresto's *romanza* "Che non avrebbe il misero" from *Attila*—an opera which, as we shall see, shows many points of analogy with *Macbeth*. Here Verdi was presented with utterly conventional dramatic material—the tenor lament at the loss, one way or another, of loved ones. And, as is so often the case with Verdi, a conventional text inspired a conventional musical response. The similarities of these two slow movements are numerous (for Foresto's *romanza* see Ex. 1; for Macduff's *adagio* see *Macbeth*, Ricordi pp. 249-52). Their phrase structures, after an initial divergence, are almost identical. And their tonal plans parallel one another quite as closely, each piece moving to the relative major in the b phrase (in Macduff's aria, at "E me fuggiasco . . . "), to the dominant minor in the c phrase ("coll'ultimo singulto . . . "), and closing in the tonic major. Even the smaller musical gestures are analogous: the melodic outline of the opening phrase, and the tonic pedal under a V^7 chord in its second measure; the 2 + 2, tonic-dominant, tonic-dominant structure of the d phrase opening the *maggiore* section; and the prominent deceptive cadence introduced as a harmonic prolongation at the fourth measure of the e phrase (in Macduff's aria, at "perdono aprir").

Against these similarities the differences between the two works stand out all the more clearly. Whereas Foresto's aria sets the usual two quatrains, Macduff's is a setting of three. This one unconventional characteristic of the text played perfectly into Verdi's hand. In addition to allowing a more natural treatment of the text in the *maggiore* section, the third quatrain allowed him to expand the breathless tonal layout of the *Attila* piece, and thus to linger for a full five measures in the relative major. And this subtly sets the stage for the repetition of this D flat-F flat tonal framework in the following two scenes, the sleepwalking scene and Macbeth's "Pietà, rispetto, amore." It comes as little surprise, then, that the *Macbeth* libretto in Verdi's hand at the Museo teatrale della Scala reveals that the third quatrain of Macduff's text was an emendation of the composer himself.[13]

Another sort of large-scale correspondence among Verdi's operas takes us out of the realm of the most conventional dramatic structures in the Rossinian tradition, and leads us an important step forward toward a definition of the *genere Verdiano* to which Basevi refers. Here Verdi responds to a more or less exceptional dramatic situation with a musical solution of a strikingly original nature. Then, when presented with similar dramatic situa-

---

operas. One example of this is the repeated woodwind *acciaccatura* which occurs in *Un ballo in maschera, La forza del destino*, the 1865 revision of *Macbeth*, and *Don Carlos*. This sort of relationship remains distinct from the large-scale types discussed here in that it is not "text-bound"—that is, its recurrence is not inevitably linked with the appearance of similar dramatic gestures and situations in the text.

13. The recurrence of this D^b-F^b tonal plan in *Macbeth* is discussed by David Lawton, "Tonality and Drama" pp. 89-90. Note that Verdi underlines the structural connection of these three pieces by the similarity of their melodic material in the F^b sections: all three show a prominent I→V stepwise descent at this point, emphasizing a D^b appoggiatura over the tonic harmony. The manuscript *Macbeth* libretto at La Scala is discussed by DEGRADA at pp. 159-72.

Example 1

tions in other operas, he returns to that first unconventional solution as a model, thus establishing it as a distinctive element of his personal operatic idiom. With regard to this type of relationship we should not underestimate the importance of Verdi's ever-growing tendency (at least from the late 1840s to the outset of his collaboration with Boito) to control and even bully his librettists. In exercising this control Verdi could seek precisely those uncommon dramatic situations with which he had been successful in the past.

One example of this sort of correspondence is found in some of those scenes which Frits Noske has termed "ritual scenes."[14] Whether or not we agree with Noske's interpretation of the larger dramatic significance of these scenes, it is clear that those from *Giovanna d'Arco*, *Jérusalem*, the original *Don Carlos*, and *Aida*—all confrontation scenes involving a chorus and soloists, and built upon a large-scale chromatic ascent—show Verdi responding again and again to similar circumstances in the libretto with a characteristic musical solution. Another well-known example is the unison patriotic chorus that Verdi used in *Nabucco*, *I lombardi*, and the original *Macbeth*—one of those fortuitous strokes that most clearly define the early "Verdian genre," and which led Ghislanzoni to speak of Verdi's music as "un bisogno del tempo."[15]

Macbeth affords a more complex example of this second sort of structural analogy. To

14. See his "Ritual Scenes in Verdi's Operas."

15. Ghislanzoni, *Gli artisti*, 6: 16. A later example of this second sort of correspondence is the adaptation of musical techniques employed in the duet of Rigoletto and Sparafucile in the confrontation of Philip and the Grand Inquisitor in *Don Carlos*.

Example 2a

Example 2b

conclude the *finale* of the second part of *Nabucco*, Verdi had stunningly represented the contrasting sides of Nabucco's madness by alternating two enraged F minor episodes (allegro) with a confused and pathetic A♭ major arioso (adagio; see Ex. 2a). Basevi has no term for such a solo outburst at this point in the traditional *finale* structure, and refers to it loosely as an "aria del delirio"; but he recognizes in it a typically Verdian dramatic self-assurance.[16] Its effect, he says, arises from the contrapposto of its allegro episodes—"of a piece, without symmetry of phrase, without repetitions, and without imitations"—with the adagio material—"symmetrical, regular, and melodious."[17] To these contrasts we might add that of the forte syncopations and brusque orchestral flourishes at the end of the first F minor section with the parallel thirds in the woodwinds which characterize the A♭ major episodes.

Four years later, in the Act I finale of *Attila*, Verdi found a situation similar enough to allow him to adapt and reuse his original solution (see Ex. 2b). Here Attila has arrived at the gates of Rome, and is dumbfounded and horrified by the appearance there of Leo, whose apparition he had earlier seen in a dream. His horror is expressed in a broken *declamato*, in F minor as in *Nabucco*. As he rallies himself—only enough to capitulate to Leo's demand that he not pillage Rome—his music abruptly turns to A♭ major, where he sings a two-phrase arioso leading into the closing chorus of the finale. The emotions in play here are not those of the *Nabucco* passage, of course, so Verdi reshapes the musico-dramatic concept borrowed from the earlier opera to suit his new dramatic ends. Thus the chugging accompaniment and progressive breakdown of phrase structure in Nabucco's F-minor sections give way to the halting accompaniment and pointedly clear phrasing of Attila: Attila is horrified, but unlike Nabucco he is in control of his senses. And, in a development which was to be exploited to the fullest in *Macbeth*, the F minor and A♭ major sections in *Attila* bear contrasting instructions to the singer: *declamato sottovoce* vs. *canto spiegato*. Finally, Verdi shows a growing concern to integrate this sort of coup de théâtre into the framework of the *finale* around it: the harmonization and phrase structure of Attila's A♭ major material anticipate the A♭ choral melody which follows it and ends the act.

The dramatic concept first hit upon in Nabucco's mad scene undergoes an extraordinary further development in the banquet scene of the original *Macbeth*.[18] In both *Attila* and *Nabucco* Verdi had set off the emotions of his protagonist in music clearly demarcated from the responses of the chorus and other soloists onstage. In *Macbeth* the situation is more complex. Verdi must incorporate the responses of both the chorus and Lady Macbeth to Macbeth's terror; Macbeth himself does not react solely to the apparition, but also to Lady Macbeth's nervous admonitions. Finally, as Banquo appears twice, there must be two renderings of Macbeth's terror, not one. Verdi articulates these with the repetition of Lady Macbeth's *brindisi*.

The first apparition, in the 1847 version, is given on pp. 492–95 below. As in the earlier operas, the main tonal dichotomy in the first appearance of Banquo is F-minor-A♭ major, but the F minor sections are enhanced by a recurring melodic and harmonic emphasis on ♭VI, that is, D♭ major. This emphasis of ♭VI in F (major or minor) occurs again and again throughout the *Macbeth* score; here it becomes a part of the characterization of Macbeth's

---

16. Basevi, *Studio*, pp. 11–12

17. Ibid., p. 11

18. Budden, *Operas*, 1: 297, has noted the similarity of these two passages.

terror.[19] A♭ major is reserved for Macbeth's peremptory response to Lady Macbeth's "Are you a man?" (E un uomo voi siete?). Though different in emotional significance from the A♭ passages in *Nabucco* and *Attila*, it contrasts strongly with the other material in the first apparition in its melodically and tonally closed lyric form. But even this A♭ episode has a tinge of F♭—the same ♭VI relationship heard in the F minor sections—and, as Macbeth turns his attention back to the specter, so the music turns back to F minor. This first apparition ends with an F minor outburst marked *incalzando sempre*, and culminating in the frantic syncopations Verdi had used analogously in *Nabucco*.

The second apparition is, like the second F minor episode of Nabucco's madness, similar but not identical to the first (see p. 496 below). There is no second A♭ major episode, for Macbeth addresses only the ghost now. Its place as the central lyrical episode of the passage is assumed by new material in E major with more than a hint of minor. This new interpolation at once adds to the tonal confusion of Macbeth's fear—it is reached abruptly from an A♭ major chord, and is reinterpreted as a leading tone for another abrupt move, back to F minor—and anticipates the tonic of the following quartet "Sangue a me." Thus, in the course of the remarkable expansion of Nabucco's mad scene into the apparition scene of *Macbeth*, Verdi has begun to turn basic tonal dichotomies to the clarification of his dramatic ends. The tonal tension between D♭ major and F minor heightens the rendering of Macbeth's terror, as does the sudden move to E major; but both of these tonal areas also serve to better integrate this scene into the music around it. And the F minor-A♭ major polarity with which Verdi began in *Nabucco* here differentiates Macbeth's response to Lady Macbeth from his responses to the specter itself.[20]

A final sort of large-scale correspondence in Verdi's operas is perhaps the most interesting and revealing. Here Verdi first responds predictably to a conventional dramatic framework. In a later text he is confronted with a situation which he comes to view as a dramatic analogue of the earlier, though the resemblance may not at first seem obvious. He responds to the second situation with the patterns established in the first, transforming the once conventional musical material to support the new and original musico-dramatic whole.

Cases of this kind can afford valuable insight into Verdi's concept of drama—a concept dependent, as we would expect, on the narrow range of dramatic situations employed in the Italian opera of his formative years. Verdi approached the dramas that he knew in terms of these situations, seeking in the sources or prospective sources of his operas characters and actions which could be tailored to these relatively restricted operatic patterns. Such a capacity for generalization eased the strain of a well-nigh continuous demand on his creative powers in the mid-1840s, and led at times to a stereotyped musical treatment of

19. This ♭VI emphasis is an important element in the distinctive *colorito* of *Macbeth*, the compelling unification of which is surely one of the most striking advances in the score over Verdi's earlier works. It is not out of place to recall here Verdi's remarks of 4 September 1846 to Piave on *Macbeth*: "I have its general character and its *tinte* in mind as if the libretto were already finished."

20. Regarding "Sangue a me," Professor Oliver Strunk kindly called to my attention another correspondence between *Macbeth* and *Attila*: the E-minor interjections of the chorus at "Biechi arcani! sgomentato da fantasmi egli ha parlato" are clearly developed from the similar E-minor interjections of the chorus in the Act II *finale* of *Attila*, at the beginning of the andantino "Lo spirto de' monti ne rugge alle fronti." Indeed the similarities of "Sangue a me" with this andantino extend beyond these choral melodies to include other motives, details of harmonic structure, and even the E minor→E major tonal layout of both pieces. This is another example of the first sort of correspondence discussed above—the modeling of one conventional musico-dramatic structure (in this case a concerted *finale* movement) on another.

hackneyed characters and situations. But at other times it led Verdi to the exploration of new dramatic ground, not heretofore reduced to the means and gestures of the operatic stage; and in the process it gradually expanded the dramatic possibilities of Italian opera itself. Such was the case when Verdi modeled the duet "Fatal mia donna" of *Macbeth* on Attila's aria "Mentre gonfiarsi l'anima."

This latter scene is a traditional *racconto*: Attila recounts the dream he has just had to his slave Uldino.[21] The andante sets four quatrains of text (not an unusual textual expansion for such narrative pieces) in an expanded minor-to-major slow movement form, with a somewhat exceptional declamatory interpolation at the third quatrain, where Attila relates the words he heard in his dream. When Verdi came to set the dagger scene and duet of *Macbeth*, the visions of Macbeth's troubled conscience must have lodged themselves in the composer's imagination in the dramatic terms of a *sogno* scene, for Verdi returned to Attila's piece as his musical model.

The most striking correspondences between these pieces are aligned in Exs. 3-6 (they occur in the same order in both pieces). First—and this is the only significant musical correspondence between Attila's perfunctory *scena* and the great introductory scene of *Macbeth*—there is the descending chromatic bass line under a string tremolo at Attila's monotone declamation "sua voce parea vento in caverna!" (see Ex. 3a & b). This is developed into Macbeth's "Now o'er the one-half world / Nature seems dead ..." (Sulla metà del mondo, marked *misterioso*). The chromatic line is now in the upper strings, accompanied by eerie rustlings in the basses; Attila's one-note declamation is extended into Macbeth's slow chromatic ascent, while the orchestra's chromatic descent undergoes diminution, and culminates in one of those chromatic progressions which Verdi handled more and more skillfully as his career unfolded. In *Attila* this chromatic material is not heard again; in *Macbeth* it is developed into the fortissimo transition to Lady Macbeth's entrance.

The next example, Ex. 4a and b, takes us into the first movement of each of these set pieces. Both are in F minor and in 6/8 meter, and although Attila's sotto voce fear (*andante piuttosto mosso*) seems tame next to the whirlwind of Macbeth's terror (*allegro*), both pieces open with strikingly similar melodic ideas.[22] In *Attila* the opening melody comes to a well-rounded close and a sequential rise begins, leading to Attila's intonation of the words he heard in his dream. In *Macbeth* the melody receives no tonal closure, and the orchestra moves to new material under the hurried parlante exchanges of Macbeth and Lady Macbeth. After a contrasting episode in A♭ major at Macbeth's description of the courtiers' prayers—an episode recalling the E♭ courtiers' march preceding the dagger scene—Lady Macbeth admonishes her husband with an ornamental melody adapted for use also in the second movement of the duet (and in three of the four movements of the 1865 version). The flighty style of many a heroine in Verdi's early works is here put to use in the portrayal of Lady Macbeth's feigned ease in the attempt to reassure Macbeth.

21. An earlier example of this sort of scene in Verdi's operas in Alzira's "Da Gusman, su fragil barca." Other well-known predecessors of Attila's aria are Pollione's "Meco all'altar di Venere" from *Norma*, and Orsini's "Nella fatal di Rimini/e memorabil guerra" from *Lucrezia Borgia*. In the latter, Donizetti's use of a monotone declamation ascending slowly by half steps for Orsini's narration of the words spoken by the apparition is particularly significant for Verdi. For an example of his development of this technique, see the Act III finale of the revised *Macbeth*, where Macbeth relates the prophecies he has heard to Lady Macbeth.

22. This F-minor melodic germ seems to be used by Verdi in *Attila* as one of those vague and perhaps only half-conscious unifying device in which he so often indulges: see Attila's F-minor response to Ezio's proposition in the duet of the Prologue.

Example 3a

Example 3b

In the following andantino, at "Methought I heard a voice cry" (Allor questa voce m'intesi nel petto), Macbeth broods upon the warnings of his conscience—a point dramatically analogous, for Verdi, to Attila's recitation of his dream. And the composer once again patterns Macbeth's music on that of Attila (see Ex. 5). Both texts are set to three slow-moving sequential periods in ominous minor harmonies. But whereas Attila's music seeks its effect in the crude juxtaposition of D♭ minor, C minor, and B♭ minor, in *Macbeth* the passage moves from and returns to B♭ minor smoothly. The drama here is embodied in the slow rise of the sequence, and in the skillful reharmonization of its third member to bring it, at its melodic peak, powerfully back to the home key.

Both of these sequential passages are followed by analogous *maggiore* sections, Attila's in F major, Macbeth's in B♭. Here Macbeth's "Com'angeli d'ira" (... his virtues / Will plead like angels) again betrays its origin in *Attila,* at Attila's sweeping melody "in me tai detti suonano" (see Ex. 6). Attila's melody is worked out in the essentially decorative, four-bar

Example 4a

Example 4b

antecedent-consequent phrase pattern so typical of Verdi's early lyric forms. Macbeth's, on the other hand, is a single melodic arch, obsessed with the rhythmic motive ♩ ♪ ♪ as Macbeth is with his horror and guilt. Part of its power arises from its contrast with the ornamental flutters of Lady Macbeth (and of her orchestral accompaniment) before and after it. This contrast prolongs the dramatic tension introduced by Lady Macbeth's over-sweet entrance at "Ma dimmi, altra voce. . . ." At "Sei vano, o Macbetto" Verdi complicates this play of contrasting responses to the murder by giving Lady Macbeth a B♭ major echo of Macbeth's sequential passage in B♭ minor. But the most subtle stroke, at once maintaining

Example 5a

Attila
tuonante

Di fla-gel-lar l'in - car - co con-tro j mor-ta-li hai sol_____ T'ar-

ff

re-tra! or chiu-so è il var - co: que-sto de'Nu-mi è il suol_____

sotto voce   *morendo*

pp   etc.

Example 5b

Andantino
Macbeth
p

Al - lor que-sta vo - ce m'in-te-si nel pet - to. a - vrai per guan-cia - li sol

pp

pausa longa

ve - pri, o Mac-bet - - to! Il son - no per sem - pre, Gla-mis, uc - ci-

de - sti! Non v'è che vi - gi - lia, Cau - do - re, per te!

etc.

Example 6a

In me tai det - ti suo - na - no cu - pi fa-ta - li an-

cor,_____ e l'al - ma in pet - to_ad At - ti - la, in pet-to_ad

At - ti-la s'ag-ghiac - cia, s'ag-ghiac - cia, s'ag-ghiac - cia pel ter - ror

etc.

Example 6b

(la voce spiegata)

Macbeth

Com'an - ge-li d'i - ra, ven-det - ta tuo-nar - mi u - drò di Dun-

ca - no le san - te vir - tù.

etc.

this high level of tension and tying together the *minore* and *maggiore* sections of the andantino even further, was to harmonize Macbeth's melody "Com'angeli d'ira" (see Ex. 6b) with a major-mode analogue of the harmonization at the end of his sequential passage ("Non v'è che vigilia ...," see Ex. 5b). The 1865 revisions of this passage, especially the changes of Lady Macbeth's melody at "Sei vano, o Macbetto" and the over-enrichment of the harmonization of Macbeth's "Com'angeli d'ira," do much to blur the subtly drawn dramatic lines of Verdi's original.

In all of these advances in the reshaping and development of the *Attila* material, we see Verdi honing in on the essence of music-drama. Musical gestures that were used earlier simply in the hope of making a musical effect somewhat analogous to the dramatic situation are now profoundly bound up in the interpretation and expression of the drama. Precisely these kinds of advances in the best passages of *Macbeth* must have led Ghislanzoni to see beyond the inefficacy of its witches' music, and to recognize in this opera the beginning of Verdi's *seconda maniera*. Interestingly, Verdi returned to many of the techniques developed in these scenes from *Attila* and *Macbeth* in Francesco's *sogno* scene in *I masnadieri*. Here, however, Schiller's long text as adapted by Maffei strained the musical material: it had neither the conciseness of Attila's text nor the panic-ridden play of tensions of Macbeth's. Verdi responded indifferently—and so did Basevi, recognizing in the scene "some praiseworthy passages," but faulting it for its "heterogeneous sections, awkwardly connected to one another."[23]

A comparison of the refashioning of Attila's *sogno* aria into the *Macbeth* duet with our first example, the modeling of Macduff's "Ah, la paterna mano" on Foresto's *romanza*, points up an important distinction between the three sorts of correspondences we have discussed. In the first, the modeling of conventional forms on older conventional patterns, the advances made are advances of musical style alone. Macduff's aria shows an important breadth of musical expression not seen in Foresto's, and, on a larger scale, a fascinating effort to emphasize in it certain repeated tonal structures. But these advances do not affect in its essentials the characterization of Macduff—he remains the insipid tenor who appears in so many of Verdi's works, and the massacre of his family could as well be his disappointment in a failed love affair. In the other cases, where Verdi is at some point dealing with relatively unconventional dramatic material, his musical response can be framed in terms of music *and* drama, and his stylistic advances can be seen to lead him toward a deeper musico-dramatic expression. Verdi's " 'discovery' of the high baritone"—which Budden calls "his most striking single innovation"[24]—can be understood in the light of his ever-widening search for such unconventional material. That is, it was one response to the realization early in his career that the musical stereotypes controlling the soprano and tenor voices implied dramatic stereotypes just as rigid.

Verdi's fascination in the late 1840s with the particular character type of the "guilt-ridden baritone" can also be viewed in this light. Having succeeded with the representation of this type in *Nabucco*, Verdi turned after the composition of *Alzira* to subjects which afforded him the opportunity to reuse and develop the more salient features of Nabucco himself. Attila's most striking musical features—the representation of his dream, and the depiction of his fear in the Act I *finale*—have their counterparts in Nabucco (though Attila is nominally a high bass rather than a baritone role). They undergo an extraordinary

---

23. *Studio*, p. 119

24. Budden, *Operas*, 1:33

further transmutation in *Macbeth*, and the *sogno* theme even spills over into the careless composition of *I masnadieri*. And throughout these years, from as early as 1843, Verdi had been fascinated by the operatic potential of the epitome of this character type: Lear. To the librettist of this opera, Cammarano, he wrote in 1850:

You'll have realized that we can't make it a drama with the forms that have been more or less continually in use up to now. It must be treated in an entirely new way.[25]

Finally, the particular relationship between *Attila* and *Macbeth* bears a closer look, for the analogies we have discussed above are not the only ones between the two works. Also notable is the occurrence in the opening act of both operas of an F-major duet for bass and baritone. Though the seeds of the stunning "Due vaticini . . ." are almost unrecognizable in the unpretentious "Tardi per gli anni e tremulo," duets for two low voices are unusual enough in these years that we may speak with confidence of another *punto d'analogia*. More extensive are the similarities between the soprano *cavatine* of the two works, Odabella's "Allor che i forti corrono" and Lady Macbeth's "Vieni! t'affretta." These pieces show motivic and structural resemblances in both the *adagio* and *cabaletta* movements and the same tonal relationship between these movements (C major to E$\flat$ major in *Attila*, D$\flat$ major to E major in *Macbeth*). Finally there is the orchestral prelude to *Attila*. Like the *Macbeth* prelude, this piece is constructed around the contrast of thunderous tutti episodes with fragments of a hushed melody in the high strings, supported by soft arpeggios in the basses. Verdi had not written this sort of prelude before, and, although the haunting melodic fragments in the *Attila* prelude never find as satisfying a lyric closure as the sleepwalking scene melody in the *Macbeth* prelude, perhaps nowhere else in his earlier operas does Verdi so clearly anticipate the distinctive *colorito* of the *Macbeth* score. It is as if the *Attila* prelude were the first, hesitant expression of the musical stirrings which would find their finished statement in the prelude to *Macbeth*.

The relationship of the preludes to *Attila* and *Macbeth* can be seen to extend to the operas as a whole. Verdi's enthusiasm for Zacharias Werner's play had revitalized him after the darkest of his "anni di galera," 1845, which saw the problem-plagued production of *Giovanna d'Arco* and the uninspired composition of *Alzira*.[26] Only his problems with Solera and later with Piave in the preparation of the *Attila* libretto, perhaps, cooled this enthusiasm.[27] But it was soon rekindled, stronger than before, in the *Macbeth* project. Julian Budden focused attention on this phenomenon when he wrote:

. . . in 1847 the Shakespearian experience brought about what [Verdi] had hoped for, mistakenly, from *Attila*; over and over again it lifted him out of the rut of operatic cliché which ever since *Giovanna d'Arco* had been threatening to canalize his invention.[28]

Given this new lease on his creative life and the many correspondences between *Attila* and *Macbeth*, we may go a step farther to suggest that in 1847 Verdi may have consciously been composing the opera which he had begun to conceive in 1846. To see the "precomposition" of *Macbeth* in *Attila*, in any case, is to see *Macbeth* a little more clearly and a little more luminously.

25. *Copialettere*, 478. Translation from Budden, *Operas*, 1:449.

26. Cf. Budden, *Operas*, 1:206, 229–30. Verdi's letter of July 30, 1845, to Maffei on the composition of *Alzira* (Ibid., p. 230; *Copialettere*, 431) is especially telling.

27. For an account of these problems, see *Abbiati*, 1:586 ff.

28. Budden, *Operas*, 1:279

THE BANQUET SCENE
FROM VERDI'S *MACBETH*:
AN EXPERIMENT
IN LARGE-SCALE MUSICAL FORM
John Knowles

In 1846, as Verdi was beginning work on *Macbeth*, he wrote to his librettist, Francesco Maria Piave: "This tragedy is one of the greatest creations of man!... If we can't do something great with it, let us at least try to do something out of the ordinary..." (4 September 1846). One of the many extraordinary results of that determination was the second-act *finale*—the banquet scene, or "Convito"—in which Verdi created an extended musical and dramatic entity unprecedented in his earlier works.[1]

Verdi's internal *finales* (i.e., *finales* to acts other than the last) were generally much more extensive than other pieces such as the aria, *cavatina*, or *duetto*. One of the clearest examples is the Act I *finale* of *Alzira*, which at 476 measures is well over twice as long as the next largest musical number, the Act II duet (206 measures). In the operas before *Macbeth*, however, this greater length had not been matched by a higher level of structural complexity. The conventional internal *finale* had a four-part structure similar to that of the aria—two dramatically active "kinetic" movements, each leading up to a dramatic crisis and followed by a "static" movement in which the characters react to the immediately preceding events.[2] In the Act I *finale* of *Alzira*, for example, the first movement (kinetic) includes Gusmano's discovery of Alzira and Zamoro together and his condemnation of Zamoro; this is followed by an andante *concertato* sextet (static-slow) in which the characters express their various feelings about the situation. In the third movement (kinetic), the news of the approach of the Inca army persuades Gusmano to spare Zamoro's life, and in the fourth—the *stretta* (static-fast)—the two sing threats at one another while the other characters react appropriately.

The banquet scene of *Macbeth* includes some aspects of the conventional *finale* just described (see Table 1), in that it begins with a dramatically active (kinetic) scene leading eventually to a static *concertato* in which the characters give voice to their reactions to the preceding events; in this scene, however, there is no final *stretta*, and consequently no second kinetic movement. This is not unprecedented: in several earlier operas, Verdi had likewise truncated the "standard" form,[3] apparently feeling that a conventional *stretta* would have been inappropriate dramatically. Similarly, a *stretta* at the end of the banquet scene would

---

1. The question of possible models for this scene outside of Verdi's own works requires further investigation.

2. For general discussions of the *finale*, see Philip Gossett, "The 'Candeur virginale' of 'Tancredi'," *Musical Times* 112 (1971), 327–28, and Budden, *Operas* 1: 18–20.

3. See, for example, Act III of *Ernani* and Act II of *I due Foscari*.

have been anticlimactic after the two appearances of Banquo's ghost.

More significant than the omission of a *stretta*, however, are the unusual length and complexity of the part of this scene before the *concertato*. In earlier Verdi operas, the first kinetic movement had most typically consisted of a mixture of recitative, short cantabile phrases, and occasionally a somewhat longer cantabile melody or section; the Act I *finale* of *Alzira* is again a good example. There had also been finales in which the first kinetic movement began with a self-contained number: a chorus[4] or a solo piece, as in the Act I *finale* of *Ernani*, which begins with Silva's andante.[5] In the banquet scene, however, Verdi went far beyond his earlier efforts, organizing almost the entire first kinetic movement into a unified musical structure. In recognition of the importance of this part of the scene, he identified it separately in his autograph score: "Convito visione, e Finale II."[6] Moreover, as we shall see shortly, this two-part designation reflects a new kind of structure for the scene as a whole—a division into two parts, where the first part consists of a large self-contained unit and the second of elements related to the old conventional *finale* (see Table 1).[7]

One of the most striking formal innovations in the "Convito" appears at the very beginning. Before *Macbeth*, Verdi might have opened a festive scene such as this with a chorus (as in *Alzira*, Act II *finale*), and he had originally intended to do so in *Macbeth* as well: such a chorus appears in an early draft libretto in his own hand.[8] However, he later replaced the chorus text with a text to be set as *parlante*, a texture in which the orchestra provides the melody and musical structure, while the voices play only a subordinate role in the musical fabric.[9]

One motivation for this change may have been dramatic: by reducing the musical weight given to the formalities that open the scene, Verdi increased the emphasis on the more important events occurring later. (At the same time, this change brought the banquet scene more in line with its Shakespearean model, which similarly begins with fairly brief, almost perfunctory greetings.) The replacement of this projected chorus also marked Verdi's first use of *parlante* as a central element in constructing an extended scene: this new role included not only the use of *parlante* to begin the scene, but having it return later on to help shape the large-scale form.[10] Moreover, in the period of *Macbeth*, *parlante* was beginning to be used extensively for action that would earlier have been set as recitative (for example, the dialogue between Macbeth and the murderer near the beginning of this scene). *Parlante* provided a regular musical structure for such sections—most commonly through the use of clear-cut melodies—reducing the distinction between dramatically active music and set pieces and thus allowing the action to be incorporated more fluidly into a larger musical plan.

4. Instances in which Verdi's autograph score identifies an opening chorus as part of the *finale* include Act I of *Nabucco*, Act II of *I due Foscari*, and Acts I and III of *Giovanna d'Arco*. See Chusid, *A Catalog of Verdi's Operas* (Hackensack: J. Boonin, 1974).

5. The *cabaletta* that appears in the published score was not part of the basic formal plan of the scene, but a later addition; see Lawton and Rosen, "Non-definitive Revisions," pp. 198–200 and Budden, *Operas* 1; 167–69.

6. For the titles in Verdi's autograph scores of *Macbeth*, see pp. 295–97.

7. The conventional *finale* could also be considered a "two-part" form, each part consisting of a kinetic-static pair of movements; in the banquet scene, however, the division occurs within the first kinetic movement, not after the *concertato*.

8. See pp. 323–24.

9. Basevi, *Studio*, pp. 30–33

10. These uses of *parlante* were not original with Verdi, but had been common in earlier works of other composers, notably Rossini.

TABLE 1

	PART 1 — CONVENTIONAL FINALE (KINETIC)							PART 2		
								STATIC-SLOW	KINETIC	STATIC-FAST (*STRETTA*)
Macbeth II: 3 (1847)	OPENING PARLANTE — F¹	BRINDISI — B♭	PARLANTE (BRINDISI) — B♭		FIRST APPARITION — f	REPRISE OF BRINDISI — B♭	SECOND APPARITION — b♭ → E	CONCERTATO — c → E		
Rigoletto I: 1 (1851)	OPENING PARLANTE — A♭	BALLATA — A♭	PARLANTE (MINUET) — A♭	OPENING PARLANTE — E♭	PERIGORDINO — C	OPENING PARLANTE (+ ENSEMBLE) — A♭	MONTERONE'S CURSE — c → f → V/D♭			ENSEMBLE — d♭ → D♭
La Traviata I: 1 (1853)	OPENING PARLANTE — A	BRINDISI — B♭	PARLANTE (WALTZ) — E♭	DUET — F	RETURN OF PARLANTE (WALTZ) — E♭	STRETTA (OPENING PARLANTE) — A♭				
Les Vêpres Siciliennes III: 2 (1855)	OPENING CHORUS — A	PARLANTE — E	OPENING CHORUS — A	RETURN OF PARLANTE — D	OPENING CHORUS — A	RETURN OF PARLANTE ; ASSASSINATION ATTEMPT — d → a ; A♭ → V/g		CONCERTATO — g → D		ENSEMBLE — B♭
Aroldo I: 2 (1857)	INTRODUCTION (CHORUS 1) — E	PARLANTE — e	RECURRING CHORUSES 2–1 — E – A	RETURN OF PARLANTE — a	RECURRING CHORUSES 1–2 — A – E	AROLDO'S NARRATIVE — f → V/A♭; A♭ → V/g		CONCERTATO — g → G	RECIT. — F → V/a	ENSEMBLE — a → A
Un ballo in maschera III: 2 (1859)	OPENING CHORUS — B♭	PARLANTE — g; E♭	CANZONE — G	OPENING CHORUS — B♭	RETURN OF PARLANTE — g; E♭	OPENING CHORUS — g; E♭	MURDER — F → D♭; A → a	SLOW ENSEMBLE — b♭ G♭	SHORT RECIT.	FAST ENSEMBLE — b♭

Upper case = Major key; Lower case = Minor key

The opening *parlante* section is followed by Lady Macbeth's *brindisi*, which does not appear in Shakespeare's play, but which is suggested by Macbeth's line: "Be large in mirth; anon we'll drink a measure the table round" (III.4.11–12). After its first appearance, the *brindisi* music continues as background for a *parlante* dialogue between Macbeth and the murderer. The use of this tune *ppp* with a much-reduced orchestra and accompanied by sharp dissonances and minor-mode inflections emphasizes the dramatic distance between the banquet atmosphere and Banquo's murder,[11] and foreshadows the disintegration of Macbeth's world at the appearance of the ghost.

The opening *parlante* music returns after Macbeth's dialogue with the murderer, only to be interrupted by the first appearance of Banquo's ghost. After the ghost has vanished, Lady Macbeth attempts to get the party moving again by repeating her *brindisi*. This reprise corresponds to Macbeth's toast in the play following the first apparition,[12] and after Lady Macbeth has admonished him: "My worthy lord, your noble friends do lack you" (III.4.83–4). Since Lady Macbeth is the moving force at this point, trying to restore order after Macbeth's distraction, it is appropriate that she should have a prominent musical role as well,[13] and the return of her *brindisi* reflects her influence on the action.

The two appearances of the opening *parlante* and the return of the *brindisi* together constitute a rondo-like framework for the part of the scene preceding the second apparition (see Table 1). Although at its first appearance, surrounded by presentations of the opening *parlante* music, the *brindisi* acted as an episode, its reappearance following the first apparition marks a return—musical and dramatic—to a point of relative stability. This framework establishes a large, well-defined unit at the beginning of the scene; an important division is thus created within the first kinetic movement, with the passage containing the dramatic climax (the second apparition) differentiated from the preceding self-contained unit. This formal division also separates the scene as a whole into two large parts: the first part consists of the opening rondo-like structure and the second part contains the dramatic crisis and the reaction to it in the *concertato*.

This two-part division is marked off tonally as well. While not the same as the key of the opening (F), the key of the *brindisi* (B♭) is closely related to it, and both keys are distant from that of the concluding concertato (E). If the B♭ of the *brindisi* does not close off the first part of the scene as completely as F would have, it contrasts even more strongly with the following E, defining the first part as a tonal unit distinct from the second (the second appearance of the ghost and the *concertato*). This striking tonal shift underscores the fundamental change in the dramatic situation. After the first appearance of the ghost, Lady Macbeth was able to recall the festive atmosphere and, by implication, the world of power that she and Macbeth had sought;[14] but after the second appearance, such a return is no longer possible: Macbeth's doom has been sealed as he is drawn once more to the witches, and the finality of this event is mirrored in the move to the most distant possible key—from B♭ to E.

11. According to Basevi, "The instrumentation of . . . *parlante* sometimes depicts the spirit of the character who is singing, and the scene in general; at other times, it refers to some event without relation to that character" (*Studio*, pp. 31–32). For his specific comments on this passage see p. 424 below.

12. In Shakespeare's scene Macbeth ends by toasting Banquo; reflecting this, the final quatrain of Lady Macbeth's *brindisi* is replaced in the reprise by similar praise of the absent Banquo.

13. For Verdi's reaction to a proposal to have the tenor sing the reprise of the *brindisi*, see his letters to Escudier of 8 February 1865 and 28 March 1865, and GÜNTHER at 179–80.

14. Note that she is not able to return all the way to that situation: the key of her *brindisi* is not the initial tonic F, but only the closely related B♭.

The musical form of the banquet scene is thus remarkably faithful to the Shakespearean scene on which it is based. Even when an aspect of the musical structure is not directly implied by the model, it clarifies some dramatic point. To take only one example, though Shakespeare gave Lady Macbeth relatively few lines in this scene, she is nonetheless an important force here, and Verdi makes her importance clear not only by giving her a substantial solo—the *brindisi*—but by having it return at a critical dramatic juncture. (Since each appearance of the *brindisi* corresponds to a toast in the original version, Verdi respects both the spirit and the letter of his model.)

Although the banquet scene is related to the conventional finale, it also contains some radical innovations: especially notable are the increased use of *parlante* and the complex musical structure of the first part of the scene. Indeed, far from being forced into a preexisting mold, the drama has generated a musical form all its own. As we shall now see, this new structure had repercussions beyond *Macbeth* as well, directly influencing Verdi's attempts to construct extended scenes in a number of works composed during the following decade.

Four years after composing the banquet scene, Verdi built a strikingly similar musical structure in the opening scene (*introduzione*) of *Rigoletto* (see Table 1). In both scenes, one of the static movements of the conventional four-part *finale* has been eliminated, while the first kinetic movement has been greatly expanded. Although the first kinetic movement still leads up to a dramatic crisis that motivates elements of a traditional *finale*, that crisis is preceded by a highly organized musical structure unlike anything in Verdi's earlier operas.

Each of these scenes is in two large parts: the second part begins with a dramatic crisis; the first part, which encompasses everything up to that crisis, is tonally unified and framed by recurring music.[15] Both scenes begin with instrumental introductions, similar in character, that are immediately repeated as the basis for *parlante*. Each scene then has an episode that begins with a set piece in a more "popular" vein, and after which the opening music returns. Following a second contrasting section, a final return of previously heard music rounds off the first part. (The sense of musical identity and closure of the first part of the scene is sharper in *Rigoletto* than in *Macbeth*: the third appearance of the opening *parlante* music returns to the initial key and develops into a large ensemble, which heightens the contrast with the interruption by Monterone.)

The close musical parallels indicate that Verdi took the banquet scene as a model for the *Rigoletto introduzione*. It is clear, however, that he did not repeat the form of the earlier scene mechanically, but adapted the ideas that had been successful there to the new dramatic situation.

In *Macbeth*, the musical framework of the first part of the scene consisted of the two appearances of the opening *parlante* together with the return of the *brindisi*; in *Rigoletto*, the structure is less complex, with the opening music simply returning twice. While a simpler musical structure was itself perhaps one of Verdi's goals here, there are also important dramatic reasons for the divergence of the two scenes. First, the special circumstances that motivated a reprise of Lady Macbeth's *brindisi* are not present in *Rigoletto*, and a return of the Duke of Mantua's *ballata* within the *introduzione* would be redundant and obtrusive. Second, the recurring *parlante* performs different roles in the two operas: in *Macbeth* it was

15. In the scenes to be discussed, sections are normally modified upon their reappearance—shortened, extended, rearranged, or given new text—but are nonetheless perceived as reprises.

associated only with general, rather blandly festive sentiments, and a return of these be-tween the two apparitions would have destroyed the build-up of tension in the scene; in *Rigoletto*, on the other hand, the recurring *parlante* is used to set the conversations that carry much of the action, and its third appearance is prompted by an important element of the plot—the development of the plan to abduct Rigoletto's supposed mistress.

The second part of each of these scenes begins with a dramatic crisis that brings a point of tonal instability, and ends with an ensemble in a key different from that of the first part. In each scene, this second part is comparable to half of a conventional *finale*, with a kinetic movement (or at least its final portion) followed by a static one. In *Macbeth*, this static movement is the slow *concertato*; in *Rigoletto*, it is the final *stretta*, which is more suited than a concertato to the scornful outburst of the courtiers.

The formal ideas that Verdi had developed in the banquet scene of *Macbeth* and reused in the *introduzione* of *Rigoletto* also shaped a number of scenes written during the following decade (see Table 1 for a simplified synopsis): the *introduzione* of *La traviata*, the Act III *finale* of *Les Vêpres siciliennes*, the Act I *finale* of *Aroldo*, and the Act III *finale* of *Un ballo in maschera*. Although diverse dramatically, these six scenes have similar musical structures, which draw on a common body of formal techniques—the use of recurring material, the introduction of a strophic piece near the beginning, the extensive use of *parlante*, and the disposition of the scene as a whole according to a two-part plan.[16]

The large-scale plan of the scenes from *Macbeth* and *Rigoletto* reappears in all the others but one (the *introduzione* of *La traviata*). These scenes consist of an unusually long first part, tonally stable and framed by recurring music, and a second part including at least some elements of the conventional four-part *finale*. Near the beginning of the second part, there is a dramatic crisis and an accompanying area of tonal instability, corresponding to the end of the first kinetic movement of the standard four-part plan. (The sole exception, the *introduzione* of *La traviata*, has no dramatic crisis to motivate the traditional *finale* structure; as a result, its form corresponds to that of only the first part of the scenes from *Macbeth* and *Rigoletto*.)

While the two large parts of this scheme are distinct, in several cases there are strong musical links between them. For example, in *Vêpres* the second part begins with a section of *parlante* based on the same tune as that in the first part, and in the 1847 version of *Macbeth* (though not in that of 1865), the two appearances of Banquo's ghost are related by recurring music.[17]

16. Two other scenes, the Act II *finale* of *La traviata* and the inn scene of *La forza del destino* (II.1) also have some of the characteristics of this group. The scene from *La traviata* begins with a section of *parlante*, which is followed by two strophic choruses; the remainder of the first part of the scene is set in *parlante*. In the scene from *La forza*, the opening consists of dance music repeated as the basis for *parlante*, followed immediately by a quasi-strophic piece. (Preziosilla's solo is not strophic musically, but the text begins strophically, and there is a musical refrain through all four stanzas.) Moreover, there is an extended section of *parlante* (when the "Student" is trying to learn Leonora's identity) that is reminiscent of the *parlante* card game in the Act II *finale* of *La traviata*. As in the *introduzione* of *La traviata*, the opening music returns at the end.

17. There are actually two short passages, one leading to a cadence on the dominant of A♭, and one in F minor. They first appear with the text "Favella! il sepolcro può render gli uccisi?"; at their appearance in Part 2 ("Con-oscer potrai—s'io provi terror . . . Ma fuggi fantasma tremendo"), their order is reversed. This change in order helps effect the transition to the final ensemble: in its first appearance, the E flat of the cadential passage moves up to E♮, preparing the following F minor; the second time, the E♭ is prolonged, and reinterpreted as the leading-tone of E, the key in which the scene ends.

In the scenes from *Vêpres, Ballo,* and *Aroldo,* the framework of recurring music in the first part consists not of *parlante* as in *Macbeth* and *Rigoletto,* but of a returning chorus.[18] These later scenes contain recurring *parlante* as well, but its function is different from that in *Macbeth:* there it depicted the general festive atmosphere,[19] and the interspersed sections carried the dramatic action; on the other hand, in *Vêpres* the atmosphere is established by the recurring chorus, and the dramatic events within that setting take place in *parlante.*[20] The general character of the choruses in *Vêpres* and *Ballo* is, in fact, not very different from that of the corresponding *parlante* sections of *Macbeth* and *Rigoletto.* Furthermore, since the primary melodic content of the chorus from *Vêpres* ("O fête brillante") appears in the orchestra, this piece has a texture very like that of the *parlante* in the two earlier operas. Although this is not the case for the recurring chorus from *Ballo,* in which the vocal parts predominate, the melody of the chorus had been introduced earlier as the basis for *parlante*—in the short scena that follows Riccardo's romanza. Toward the end of that scena, which takes place in Riccardo's study, a *banda* tune is heard from off stage; after a passage of *parlante* based on this tune, the set opens to reveal a ballroom and the chorus takes up the tune to begin the scene discussed here.

In four of these six related scenes, a set piece, generally a strophic aria,[21] appears as part of the first episode.[22] Two of these pieces were already present in the source for Verdi's libretto: in the scene of Dumas's play corresponding to the *introduzione* of *La traviata,* a *brindisi* was sung by Gaston, and in the Scribe libretto on which that for *Ballo* was closely based, there was an aria analogous to Oscar's *canzone.* On the other hand, the pieces in the scenes from *Macbeth* and *Rigoletto* represent significant additions to the dramatic models, and it is likely that the idea for their insertion came from the composer, who was at that time especially concerned with doing "something out of the ordinary" in terms of large-scale musical form.

The inclusion of these set pieces was a corollary of the extensive use of *parlante* and its new structural function: in these particular scenes the set pieces provided clear, "singable" tunes to delight the audience, and this same tunefulness made them especially suitable for use in episodes contrasting with the *parlante* framework of these scenes.[23] Furthermore, although the extent to which these pieces are involved in the action around them varies from scene to scene, their mere presence helps to create the general lighthearted atmosphere against which the dramatic events that follow are to be highlighted.

The pervasive influence of the ideas discussed here in Verdi's thinking in the years following *Macbeth* and *Rigoletto* can be seen clearly from a comparison of the Act I *finale* of *Stiffelio* (1850) with Verdi's revision of it in *Aroldo* (1857). Although the scene in *Aroldo* still differs in some details from the others in the group described above, the revision has

---

18. For at least two of these scenes, this may have been suggested by preexisting material: there is a recurring chorus in the Scribe libretto on which *Ballo* was based, and the chorus that frames the *Aroldo* scene opened the scene in *Stiffelio* as well.

19. See Gerhartz, *Auseinandersetzungen,* pp. 152–56.

20. The recurring *parlante* in the *introduzione* of *Rigoletto* combines these two functions: it not only represents the festive atmosphere, as in *Macbeth,* but also carries the dramatic action, as in *Vêpres.*

21. Lady Macbeth's *brindisi* is not strictly strophic: although, as mentioned above (n. 12), its final quatrain is changed in the reprise into a toast to Banquo, most of the text remains unchanged.

22. This is also true of the Act II *finale* of *La traviata* and the inn scene of *Forza.*

23. In the scenes from *Vêpres* and *Aroldo,* such added set pieces would have been superfluous, since these functions were already being performed: in these scenes the recurring chorus music provides the tunes and the *parlante* supplies the contrasting episodes within the rondo framework.

strikingly increased the similarities (see Table 2). The Act I *finale* of *Stiffelio* consisted essentially of a conventional four-part structure. Three of the movements of that four-part structure are retained in *Aroldo*: the *concertato* and second kinetic movement have been taken over essentially unchanged, and the *strettas* of the two operas are similar in character, overall form, and key. In a major structural change, however, the relatively simple beginning of the scene in *Stiffelio* has been expanded to a musical complex much like those in the scenes previously discussed.

In *Stiffelio*, the *finale* was preceded by a short, isolated *parlante* scena in which Raffaele hid a letter to Lina in a copy of Klopstock's *Messias*.[24] The first kinetic movement of the *finale* began with a chorus of welcome for Stiffelio, which continued as the basis for a section of *parlante* in which Jorg told Stiffelio about the letter. Following this *parlante* passage, the coda of the chorus returned to round off the first part of the scene.

In *Aroldo*, the welcoming chorus appears three times, providing a choral framework like those in *Vêpres* and *Ballo*: in addition to the statement of the chorus in the middle of the scene, retained from *Stiffelio*, its music also appears without text at the beginning of the scene, and the entire chorus (not just the coda as in *Stiffelio*) returns to end the first part. The *parlante* scena in which Raffaele (now Godvino) hides the letter has been enclosed within this framework as part of the first episode; no longer isolated (as in *Stiffelio*), this action is now closely associated with the events that will soon develop from it. The Briano-Aroldo *parlante* dialogue is related not to the preceding chorus (as was the corresponding section in *Stiffelio*), but to Godvino's earlier *parlante* music, thus pointing up the close dramatic connection between the two sections.[25] Since this dialogue is now a clearly contrasting episode, the return of the chorus at the end produces a greater sense of formal closure than was present in the earlier opera. Closure is also increased by the new short chorus (No. 2) that replaces the introduction ("Plaudiam") of the chorus from *Stiffelio* and returns to end the first part of the scene firmly in the tonic. Taken together, these changes bring the scene much more in line with those discussed earlier, the parallels with the scene from *Vêpres* being especially clear.

In the scenes considered here, we see Verdi experimenting with the creation of musical complexes beyond the scope of the conventional four-part structure. In the banquet scene of *Macbeth*, he produced an extended musical structure unlike anything in his previous works. This original plan then served as the model for the form of the *introduzione* of *Rigoletto*, and continued to inform Verdi's thinking during the succeeding decade.

The reuse of these musical ideas might have led to a certain rigidity in dramatic expression, but in fact, the emphasis on musical organization brought with it a greater flexibility in representing the dramatic situation. This was already apparent in the comparison of the banquet scene and the *Rigoletto introduzione*: though the musical similarities there are striking, the changes are equally significant and reflect care in depicting the different dramatic circumstances. Furthermore, this care continued to govern the use of the formal ideas considered here as they reappeared in later scenes. No matter how innovative Verdi the composer may have been, he was always guided in his musical creation by Verdi the dramatist.

24. Although this scena is associated with the *finale* in Verdi's autograph title—"Scena, Coro e Finale I," the change of setting between the scena and the following chorus separates the scena from the *finale*.

25. In the first *parlante* episode Raffaele (Godvino) hides the letter to Lina (Mina) in the book, and in the second, Jorg (Briano) tells Stiffelio (Aroldo) about the letter.

TABLE 2

	PART 1					PART 2		
	CONVENTIONAL FINALE					STATIC-SLOW	KINETIC	STATIC-FAST (*STRETTA*)
	KINETIC							
Stiffelio (1850)	PARLANTE (RAFFAELE)	WELCOMING CHORUS INTRO.; 1	PARLANTE (CHORUS 1) (JORG-STIFFELIO)	CHORUS 1 (CODA ONLY)	STIFFELIO'S SERMON	CONCERTATO	RECIT.	ENSEMBLE
	a^1	A^1 — A →	A	A	$f \to d \to V/g$	$g \to G$ →	$F \to V/a$ →	$a \to A$ ---→
Aroldo (1857)	INTRODUCTION (CHORUS 1) / PARLANTE (GODVINO)	RECURRING CHORUSES 2 — 1	RETURN OF PARLANTE (BRIANO-AROLDO)	RECURRING CHORUSES 1 — 2	AROLDO NARRATIVE	CONCERTATO	RECIT.	ENSEMBLE
	E / e	E — A	a	A — E	$f \to A^b \to V/g$	$g \to G$	$F \to V/a$	$a \to A$

Upper Case = Major key; Lower case = Minor key

292

DOCUMENTS

LIBRARY SIGLA

Sigla	Place	Library
A-Wgm	Austria—Vienna	Gesellschaft der Musikfreunde
A-Wn	Austria—Vienna	Oesterreichische Nationalbibliothek, Musiksammlung
A-Woa	Austria—Vienna	Archiv der Staatsoper
B-Bc	Belgium—Brussels	Conservatoire Royale de Musique, Bibliothèque
Dddr-Bds	East Germany—Berlin	Deutsche Staatsbibliothek, Musiksammlung
F-Pn	France—Paris	Bibliothèque Nationale
F-Po	France—Paris	Bibliothèque, Musée de l'Opéra
GB-En	Great Britain—Edinburgh	National Library of Scotland
GB-Lam	Great Britain—London	Royal Academy of Music
GB-Lbl	Great Britain—London	British Library (formerly British Museum)
I-Bc	Italy—Bologna	Civico Museo Bibliografico-Musicale "G. B. Martini" (Liceo Musicale)
I-Fc	Italy—Florence	Biblioteca del Conservatorio di Musica "L. Cherubini"
I-Fn	Italy—Florence	Biblioteca Nazionale Centrale
I-Mc	Italy—Milan	Biblioteca del Conservatorio "Giuseppe Verdi"
I-Nc	Italy—Naples	Biblioteca del Conservatorio di Musica S. Pietro a Maiella
I-PAc	Italy—Parma	Sezione Musicale della Biblioteca presso il Conservatorio "Arrigo Boito"
I-PAvi	Italy—Parma	Istituto di Studi Verdiani
I-Rsc	Italy—Rome	Biblioteca Musicale Santa Cecilia (Conservatorio)
US-AA	Ann Arbor (MI)	University of Michigan, Music Library
US-Bp	Boston (MA)	Boston Public Library, Music Department
US-Bu	Boston (MA)	Boston University, Mugar Library
US-BE	Berkeley (CA)	University of California, Music Library
US-Cn	Chicago (IL)	Newberry Library
US-CA	Cambridge (MA)	Harvard University, Music Library
US-CHH	Chapel Hill (NC)	University of North Carolina, Music Library
US-MADrosen	Madison (WI)	David Rosen private collection
US-NYaivs	New York (NY)	Archive of the American Institute for Verdi Studies at New York University, Bobst Library, Music Division
US-NYfuld	New York (NY)	James J. Fuld private collection
US-NYj	New York (NY)	Juilliard School of Music Library
US-NYmartin	New York (NY)	George Martin private collection
US-NYp	New York (NY)	New York Public Library, the Research Libraries
US-NYmet	New York (NY)	Metropolitan Opera House, Library
US-NYporter	New York (NY)	Andrew Porter private collection
US-NYq	New York (NY)	Queens College of the City University, Paul Klapper Library, Music Library
US-PHf	Philadelphia (PE)	Free Library of Philadelphia, Music Department
US-PHu	Philadelphia (PE)	University of Pennsylvania, Music Library
US-R	Rochester (NY)	Sibley Music Library, Eastman School of Music, University of Rochester
US-Wc	Washington (DC)	Library of Congress, Music Division
US-WATcox	Watertown (NY)	Sidney T. Cox private collection

Publication History

THE AUTOGRAPH
AND THE EARLY EDITIONS
Martin Chusid

MACBETH I

Libretto by Francesco Maria Piave with changes by Andrea Maffei.
After the tragedy *Macbeth* by Shakespeare.
First performance: March 14, 1847, Teatro della Pergola, Florence.

LIBRETTO FOR THE FIRST PERFORMANCE

Title Page

MACBETH/Da rappresentarsi nell' I. e R. Teatro/IN VIA DELLA PERGOLA/LA QUARESIMA DELL'ANNO 1847/Sotto la Protezione di S. A. I. e R./LEOPOLDO II/GRANDUCA DI TOSCANA/ ec. ec. ec./FIRENZE/Tipografia di G. Galletti/in Via delle Terme. 30 p. US-BE.

AUTOGRAPH MANUSCRIPT

Orchestral score in 4 volumes, Milan: Ricordi.
Volume 1: Act I. Folios 1–134, 33 × 24 cm. Folio 134 contains additional percussion parts
for the *Adagio* of the "Finale 1°"
Volume 2: Act II. Folios 135–210, 33.5 × 24.5 cm.
Volume 3: Act III. Folios 211–77, 33.5 × 24 cm.
Volume 4: Act IV. Folios 278–346, 33 × 24 cm.

Atto 1°

1. Preludio

2. Introduzione
    Che faceste? Dite su [Coro]

3. Cavatina Lady Macbet [sic]
   Nel dì della vittoria [Lady Macbeth]
   Vieni t'affretta! [Lady Macbeth]

4. Rec.^{vo} e Marcia
   Oh donna mia [Macbeth]

5.[1] Scena e Duetto
   Sappia la sposa mia [Macbeth]
   fatal mia donna! [Macbeth]

6. Finale 1°
   Di destarlo per tempo [Macduff]
   Oh qual orrenda notte [Banco]

Atto 2do

7. Scena ed Aria Lady [Macbeth]
   perchè mi sfuggi [Lady Macbeth]
   Trionfai! securi alfine [Lady Macbeth]

8. Coro di Sicarj
   Chi v'impose unirvi a noi [Coro]

8½. Scena Banco
   Studia il passo [Banco]
   come dal ciel precipita [Banco]

9. Convito Visione, e Finale II
   Salve o Re! [Coro]
   Brindisi
   Si colmi il calice [Lady Macbeth]

Atto III

10. Coro
    Tre volte miagola la gatta [Coro]

11. Rec° Apparizione, Ballabile ed Aria Macbet[2]
    Che fatte voi misteriose donne? [Macbeth]
    fuggi regal fantasima [Macbeth]

Atto 4°

12. Coro Int[roduzione]
    Patria oppressa! [Coro]

13. Sc. ed Aria con Coro Macduff
    O figli o figli miei! [Macduff]
    Ah la paterna mano [Macduff]

---

1. Originally no. 4.
2. There is an "ed" crossed through between "Rec°" and "Apparizione."

14.[3] Sonnambulismo di Lady Macbeth
         Vegliammo invan due notti [Medico]
         una macchia è qui tutt'ora [Lady Macbeth]

15.   Scena, Battaglia, Morte d[i] Macbet
         Perfidi all'anglo [Macbeth]
         Ella è morta [Coro]

MANUSCRIPT COPIES

Orchestral scores
A-Wn (2, German text only), I-Bc (2), I-Fc,[4] I-Nc (2), I-Rsc, US-Bu, US-NYaivs,[5] US-Wc.

Orchestral score
"Scena e Morte di Macbeth" (Act IV, no. 15): US-NYmet.[6]

SELECTED EDITIONS

Some Early Piano-Vocal Scores from Milan and Paris (upright format unless otherwise specified)

Macbeth. Milan: I. R. Stabilmento Naz[e] ... Giovanni Ricordi [1847], 257 p. Plate nos. H19621H[7]-19643. Oblong. Dedicated by Verdi to his father-in-law, Antonio Barezzi.[8] A-Wn, GB-Lbl (2), I-Fc, I-Fn, I-Mc, I-PAvi[9], I-Rsc, US-NYfuld, US-NYp, US-NYporter[10], US-Wc. Illustrated cover reproduced in Carlo Gatti, *Verdi nelle immagini* (Milan: Garzanti, 1941), p. 58; Gustavo Marchesi, *Verdi* (Turin, 1970), p. 104; and *Abbiati* 1, 688 (a later printing).

Macbeth. Dramma lirico in quattro atti. Paris: Bureau Central de Musique [1847?], 238 p. Plate no. B.C. 1027. B-Bc, D-Ddr-Bds, F-Pn (2), F-Po, US-BE, US-Bp (2), US-CA, US-NYj, US-NYmartin, US-NYp, US-NYq, US-PHf, US-PHu, US-R, US-Wc. Reprint, as *Macbeth. Opera Seria in Quattre* [*sic*] *Atti:* Paris: Léon Escudier [1865?]. F-Pn (2), US-AA, US-Cn, US-WATcox.

---

3. Originally No. 13

4. Acts I and II with corrections in Verdi's hand; title page signed "Visto da me, G. Verdi"

5. Critical edition by David Lawton for performances by the Kentucky Opera Association in Louisville and at the Fifth International Verdi Congress, Danville, Kentucky, November 1977.

6. A MS copy of the scene bound into a printed edition of *Macbeth II*

7. Plate no. with letter H on first page of score—H or another letter with plate nos. in remainder of score

8. "Posto in musica da GIUSEPPE VERDI e per grata memoria dedicato al suo amatissimo suocero ANTONIO BAREZZI"

9. "Tito di Gio. Ricordi dallo Stabilmento Nazionale" pasted over original name of firm—Plate no. H19621F on first page

10. "Dallo Stabilmento Nazionale di Giovanni Ricordi," pp. 241–46 removed; other cuts and alterations indicated. Copy used for first performances in the British Isles (Dublin, 1859), marked to correspond with Pauline Viardot's requirements (see p. 364). Instrumental cues written in (e.g., "harmonium" for the subterranean music of III.1)

Macbeth. Milan: Johann Ricordi [ca. 1848], 271 p. Plate nos. 20571–20594. Oblong. German-Italian. German translation by K. A. Ritter. A-Wgm, A-Wn, D-Ddr-Bds, I-Mc.

Macbeth. Milan et al: Regio Stabilmento Ricordi, n.d. (but probably 1860–68). Plate nos. d19621d[11]–19643. Dedication to Barezzi. "Nuova edizione riveduta." US-Cn.

Macbeth. Milan: Ricordi. Plate nos. 31445–31467. Not printed.[12]

MACBETH II

Libretto revised by Piave, translated into French by Charles Louis Étienne Nuitter[13] and Alexandre Beaumont.[14]

First performance: April 21, 1865, Théâtre-Lyrique Impérial, Paris (in French).

First documented performance in Italy (or in Italian): 28 January 1874, Teatro alla Scala, Milan.

LIBRETTO FOR THE FIRST PERFORMANCE

Title Page

MACBETH/OPÉRA EN QUATRE ACTES/IMITÉ DE SHAKSPEARE [*sic*]/PAROLES DE MM. NUITTER & BEAUMONT/MUSIQUE DE/G. VERDI/Représenté pour la première fois, à Paris, sur le THÉÂTRE-LYRIQUE IMPÉRIAL, le 19 [*sic*] avril 1865./ML/PARIS/MICHEL LÉVY FRÈRES, LIBRAIRES ÉDITEURS/RUE VIVIENNE, 2 BIS, ET BOULEVARD DES ITALIENS, 15/A LA LIBRAIRIE NOUVELLE/ 1865/Tous droits réservés. 56 p. F-Pn, US-NYj, US-Wc.

Characters	Performers
MACBETH	ISMAËL [Baryton]
MACDUFF	MONJAUZE [Fort Ténor]
BANQUO.	[BILIS] PETIT [Basse][15]
MALCOLM	HUET [2.me Ténor]
UN MÉDECIN	GUYOT [2.me Basse]
UN SICAIRE	CAILLOT [2.me Baryton]
DUNCAN	N.N. [Mime]
FLEANCE	N.N. [Mime]
LADY MACBETH	REY-BALLA [Soprano dramatique]
LA COMTESSE	MAIROT [2.me Soprano]
HÉCATE	N.N. [Mime]
[OFFICIER DU PALAIS]	[TROY] [2.me Baryton]
[1.me FANTOME]	[PERONT] [Basse]
[2.me FANTOME]	[GILLAND] [Ténor]
[3.me FANTOME]	[RENAUDY] [Soprano]

Seigneurs, Dames, Officiers, Soldats, Sorcières, Fantomes.

11. Plate no. with letter d on first page of score; d or another letter with plate nos. of remainder

12. David Rosen informs me that the handwritten register of works published by Ricordi, the *libroni*, reports work begun on this edition in March 1864 as part of the series *Biblioteca scelta*. The additional annotation "non publicato" probably indicates suspension of work on the edition pending the appearance of the revised Paris version.

PARTIALLY AUTOGRAPH MANUSCRIPT

Orchestral score in 4 volumes, Paris: Bibliothèque Nationale. Based on a copy of the first version with Italian text throughout. For most of the manuscript French text is added on strips of white paper pasted above the voice parts. There are also many corrections and alternate versions written in pencil on the manuscript. The original (replaced) sections of music are bound into the manuscript together with Verdi's revisions in volumes 1 and 2 (Acts I and II). In addition to the revised (autograph) passages in the Paris MS, given below are the corresponding pages of the revised edition of the Ricordi piano-vocal score (plate number 42311) and the corresponding folios of the 1847 autograph (i.e., the original passages later revised).

Volume 1: Act I. Folios 1–183, 198–230, paper of varying size: 32–33.5 × 23.5–25 cm. In Verdi's hand: folios 184r–197v, 34.5 × 27 cm., from "parti d'udire. Sei vano o Macbetto" to end of "Duet" (Ricordi p-v score, 63–71; 1847A, 101v–114r.

Volume 2: Act II. Folios 1–9, 26–101, 108–29, 133–53, 33 × 24 cm. In Verdi's hand: folios 10r–22r (22v to 25v are blank), 35 × 27.5 cm., from "[al ve]nir di questa notte" to end of "Aria" (Ricordi p-v score, 110–15; 1847A, 140v–149v). Folios 102r–107v, 35 × 27.5 cm., from "[Di] voi chi ciò fece?" to "nè Banco obliate che lungi è tuttor" (Ricordi p-v score, 140–45; 1847A, 187r–193v). Folios 130r–132v, 34.5 × 27 cm., from "ossa quel sangue fumante" to "fuggi fantasma tre[mendo]" (Ricordi p-v score, 150–52; 1847A, 198v–201v).

Volume 3: Act III. Folios 1–27, 33 × 24.5 cm. Folios 94–120,[16] 32.5 × 23 cm. In Verdi's hand: folios 28r–93v,[17] 35 × 26 cm., from "[rime]scete rimescete voi che mescere ben sapete," including the "Ballet" and "Après le Ballet" (the apparition scene), to "al Re svenuto" (Ricordi p-v score, 190–225; 1847A, 227r–254r). Folios 121r–136v, 35.5 × 26 cm., from "[conforta]te e sensi ed anima" to the end of Act III (Ricordi p-v score, 232–41; 1847A, 266r–277v).

Volume 4: Act IV. Folios 11–24, 32.5 × 23 cm. Folios 25–26, 34.5 × 25.5 cm. Folios 34–71, 33 × 24.5 cm. In Verdi's hand: folios 1r–10v, 36.5 × 26 cm., from the beginning to "la madre sventu[rata]" (Ricordi p-v score, 242–49; 1847A, 278r–287v). Folios 27r–33v,[18] 34.5 × 26 cm., from "la patria tradita" to the end of the scene (Ricordi p-v score, 255–61; 1847A, 296v–302v). Folios 72r–97v, 35 × 26.5 cm., from "Ella è morta" to the end of the opera (Ricordi p-v score, 280–302; 1847A, 328r–346v).

---

13. Pseudonym for Truinet

14. Pseudonym for Beaume

15. For evidence that Petit performed the shade of Banquo as well, see Paul Smith's review in the 23 April 1865 number of *Revue et Gazette Musicale de Paris.*

16. Folios 107r.–108v. include additional parts for flute and clarinet in Verdi's hand (Ricordi p-v score, 229; 1847A 260v.–261r.); in folios 110r.–112r. Verdi writes Violin 1 part *divisi* and adds sustained wind chords (Ricordi p-v score, 229–30; 1847A, 261v.–262v.).

17. Portions of text from folio 75ff. are in Italian only. There is one unnumbered folio between 84 and 85; 93 verso should be bound in as 85 bis recto(!).

18. The structure of the *cabaletta* has been altered, without Verdi's knowledge, by non-autograph additions (folio 25r–26r) and cancellations (27v and 29r–v).

Atto 1°

1. (Preludio) [19]
2. (Introduzione)
   Che faceste? [Coro]
3. (Cav^na Lady Macbeth)
   Nel dì della vittoria [Lady Macbeth]
   Vieni t'affretta! [Lady Macbeth]
4. (Recit^vo e Marcia)
   Oh donna mia [Macbeth]
5. (Scena e Duetto) [Macbeth, Lady Macbeth]
   Sappia la sposa mia [Macbeth]
   fatal mia donna [Macbeth]
6. (Finale 1°)
   Di destarlo per tempo [Macduff]
   Oh qual orrenda notte [Banco]

Atto 2do

7. (Scena ed Aria Lady)
   Perchè mi sfugge [Lady Macbeth]
   La luce langue [Lady Macbeth]
8. (Coro di sicarj)
   Chi v'impose unirvi a noi [Coro]
8½. (Scena Banco)
   Studia il passo, o mio figlio [Banco]
   come dal ciel precipita [Banco]
9. (Convito, Visione, e Finale 2do)
   Salve, o Re [Coro]
   (Brindisi)
   Si colmi il calice [Lady Macbeth]

Atto 3°

10. (Coro)
    Tre volte miagola la gatta [Coro]
11. Ballet No. 1
    No. 2
    No. 3
    (Apres le Ballet)
    Finchè apelli silenti [Macbeth]

Atto Quarto

12. Coro
    Patria oppressa! [Coro]
[13] Scena ed Aria Macduff
    o figli! o figli miei [Macduff]
    Ah, la paterna mano [Macduff]

19. The titles in parentheses are in the copyist's hand and derive from the first version of the opera.

14. (Sonnambulismo di Lady Macbeth)
Vegliammo invan due notti [Medico]
Una macchia è qui tutt'ora [Lady Macbeth]

15. (Scena, Battaglia e Morte di Macbeth) [20]
Perfidi! All'onglo [*sic*] [Macbeth]
Battaglia
Via le fronde [Macduff]

MANUSCRIPT COPIES

Orchestral Scores   I-Bc

SELECTED EDITIONS

Orchestral Scores

Macbeth. Milan: G. Ricordi & C., n.d. 156 p., 108 p., 168 p., 113 p. Plate nos. 120820 P-I/P-IV. With ballet. Rental only. A-Woa, US-NYmet (2). Reprint: New York: Edwin F. Kalmus [ca. 1977].

Macbeth. Milan: G. Ricordi & C., n.d. 741 p. Plate nos. 120820-Atto I/Atto IV, 120820 P-IV (pp. 602–9).[21] With ballet. Rental only. GB-Lbl, US-NYmartin

Some Early Piano-Vocal Scores from Paris and Milan

Macbeth. Grand Opéra en Cinq Actes.[22] Paris: Léon Escudier [1865], 290 p. Plate no. L.E. 2442, L.E. 1027 and L.E. 2442 (Ballet). French translation by [Charles L. E.] Nuitter and [Alexandre] Beaumont. With ballet. B-Bc, F-Pn (2), GB-En, GB-Lbl, I-PAvi, US-CHH, US-MADrosen, US-NYfuld.

Macbeth. Dramma lirico in quattro atti.[23] Paris: Léon Escudier [1865], 290 p. Plate nos. L.E. 1027, L.E. 1027 and L.E. 2442 (Ballet). "Nuovo." F-Pn, GB-Lbl

Macbeth. Melodramma in quattro atti. Milan et al: Regio Stabilmento Tito di Gio. Ricordi [1865], 282 p. Plate nos. 38841–65. "Riformato pel Teatro Lirico di Parigi." I-Bc, I-PAc, US-NYmet.

Macbeth. Melodramma in quattro atti. Milan et al: Regio Stabilmento Tito di Gio. Ricordi [ca. 1865], 282 p. Plate nos. 38966–90. "Riformato pel Teatro Lirico di Parigi." GB-Lam, I-Fc (2), I-PAvi.

Macbeth. Melodramma in quattro atti. Milan et al: Edizioni Ricordi [ca. 1877], 302 p. Plate no. 42311. "Riformato . . . 1865." Numerous reprints to date.

20. Copyist's title does not reflect Verdi's substitution of the new *finale*, the Victory Hymn for "Mal per me," the onstage death of Macbeth in the original version.

21. Additional plate nos.: 126859 (pp. 110–44), 126482 (pp. 268–81), 125835 (pp. 422–94), 126412 (pp. 638–46, 651–73), 126605 (pp. 675–89)

22. Some title pages and first pages of score read "Quatre Actes," but table of contents and score are consistently divided into 5 acts. The number of acts and Macduff's singing the reprise of the *brindisi* (Act II, *finale*) disregard Verdi's intentions. See GÜNTHER, at 179–80.

23. The table of contents (though not the score itself) is divided into 5 acts.

THE *LIBRONI*, AND ADDITIONAL
NOTES ON RICORDI PUBLICATIONS
OF *MACBETH*

David Rosen

I. THE *LIBRONI*

Shown here is the entry for the piano-vocal score of *Macbeth I* in the so-called *libroni* (big books) in the Casa Ricordi archives. The firm began to keep these records in 1808 with its first publication, Nava's *Le 4 Stagioni* for guitar solo. Verdi's name first appears in volume 7 with an arrangement of *Oberto* (plate numbers 11336–47); fifteen volumes and about 87,000 plate numbers later his last compositions were registered in the *libroni*. These records extend beyond his death, and beyond Puccini's as well.

As works were ready for the engravers or typographers, the individual titles were entered into the pre-numbered pages of the *libroni*, thus determining the plate number assigned to each publication. Since individual pages—and sometimes even large blocks of pages—were allotted to a particular "class" of publication (for example, "Quarta categoria," shown above, includes piano-vocal scores; "quinta" indicates violin music), it would often be necessary to fill in remaining blank spaces on a page with plate numbers suggesting an unrealistically or even impossibly early date. Fortunately one need not rely on plate numbers *per se* as a guide to chronology, for the *libroni* provide more secure information.

The column of dates given after Verdi's name in the reproduction shows the date that the edited manuscript of each number of Muzio's piano-vocal arrangement was consigned to the engraver. (In another volume, the column is headed "data di consegna".) Since the piano arrangement of the orchestra presupposes the existence of an orchestrated score, each date constitutes a *terminus post quem non* for Verdi's orchestration of the number (see

302

LAWTON at 211–15 and DEGRADA at 171–73), valuable information for the compositional history of the work, as well as for its publication history.

In the case of *Macbeth* the projected publication dates ("da pubblicarsi") merely corroborate information that can be gleaned from advertisements in Ricordi's *Gazzetta Musicale di Milano*, but the *libroni* may sometimes be the only source of the actual or projected date of publication. The indications in the far right column assure us that the numbers actually were published (although they do not confirm that the original schedule was maintained). To the right of the projected publication date the number 733/24/2/47 205 tells us that the libretto was approved by (or, less likely, submitted to) the Censor on 24 February 1847.

We pass over the names of the thirteen engravers who worked on this score, the numbers indicating price, number of pages, and number of engraved plates and turn to a few points of interest in the *Macbeth* entry. The *libroni* originally recorded an early version of the opening phrase of Lady Macbeth's *cavatina* (No.5)—"Sorgi, a me vieni"—and, in No.21, the phrase "Pietà, rispetto, onore" (rather than " . . . amore"). More important, Banquo's scena ("10½") was not only composed late, but also conceived after the other numbers. Furthermore, this entry seems to be in the same hand as the name of the basso, "Benedetti", added in No.3. It seems then that Benedetti may have been signed on late, and this at least raises the possibility that Verdi may have decided to write the scena only after hearing him in Florence.

II. THE PIANO-VOCAL SCORE OF *MACBETH I*

As was the firm's practice until the mid-1860's, Ricordi issued the *Macbeth I* piano-vocal score first as individual pieces ("pezzi diversi") with separate plate numbers; when all the numbers had appeared in print they were gathered together with a title page and sold as the *Opera completa*.[1] The publication history of scores issued in this fashion is therefore the history of the publication of the constituent numbers. While this history is quite complicated for some of Verdi's operas,[2] it is simple in the case of *Macbeth I*. Even before the

1. See Hopkinson, *Bibliography of Giuseppe Verdi* 2, xi–xii. Ricordi does not seem to have issued a Verdi opera in a piano-vocal score with a single plate number until *Don Carlos* (1867), and the first opera issued *only* with a single plate number was *Simon Boccanegra II* (1881). Escudier and Lucca commonly issued single-plate number editions long before Ricordi.

2. Consider *La traviata*, for example. The engravers did not begin work on any number until two days after the unsuccessful premiere of 6 March 1853. The arias and duets were published within the next two months, but the less marketable choruses and finales had to wait until the successful revival of the work in May 1854. This explains why one of the five numbers revised for this revival—the *largo concertato* of the Act II *finale*—was never published in its original version.

premiere Ricordi had decided to publish the entire opera; his engravers had been set to work on all but two numbers, and work on these commenced the day after the premiere.[3] The numbers were published in three batches. Within five weeks of the premiere all had been published—they are all advertised in the 18 April 1847 issue of Ricordi's *Gazzetta musicale di Milano*, and the "opera completa" was announced in the May 2 issue.

III.   OTHER ARRANGEMENTS.

In addition to the piano-vocal reduction, Ricordi published the *opera completa* in various other arrangements as well. While the piano-vocal reduction would be of use to professional singers learning the opera for performance as well as to amateurs, these purely instrumental arrangements were intended only for informal music making. Within seven months of the premiere of *Macbeth I*, Ricordi published eight arrangements (in parentheses here are the dates the arrangement was first advertised in Ricordi's *Gazzetta*, followed by the plate number): Piano-vocal (May 2; 19621-43); Piano solo (May 2; 19621 and 19652-66); Piano duet (May 19; 19821-39); Simplified Piano solo (21 July; 19761-66); Violin and Piano (July 21; 19901-20); Flute and Piano (July 21; 19921-40); 2 Flutes (October 6; 19805-11), and Flute solo (October 6; 19813-9). In the following year there appeared a Cello and piano arrangement (19951-68)—and in 1849, both Angelo Mariani's arrangement for string quartet (20942) and an arrangement for Flute and string trio (20943).

IV.   PRINTED PERFORMANCE MATERIAL.

In order to reduce the time needed for copying and proofreading, Ricordi printed chorus and string parts (i.e., those requiring many duplicate copies) for a number of Verdi's operas, including *Macbeth II* (although apparently not for *Macbeth I*). These printed parts, together with the manuscript woodwind, brass, and percussion parts, were intended for rental only. The printed parts for *Macbeth II* are as follows: women's chorus, men's chorus, "violino principale," violin I, violin II, viola, and cello and contrabass (39262-8). The part for violino principale would have consisted of the Violin I part on one stave, with cues for the rest of the ensemble on two additional staves.[4] It seems then that even as late as 1865 some operatic performances were led by the first violinist.

IV.   FANTASIES.

In the wake of any successful opera—and despite the reservations of the Florentine critics, *Macbeth I* was a success—followed a raft of salon pieces based upon its themes: Souvenirs, *Fantaisies, Capricci*, and the like, all doubtless of commercial and sociological, rather than aesthetic, importance.[5] The following short-title list of all *Macbeth* fantasies advertised in Ricordi's *Gazzetta* through the end of 1847 will at least give an idea of this curious collision

3. This information comes from the *libroni*.

4. No Violino principale part for *Macbeth* is known to have survived, but one for *Un ballo in maschera* has—see James J. Fuld, "Nineteenth-century Operatic Violin Conductors' Scores," *Music Library Association Notes* 31 (1974), 278–80.

5. For a recording of several fantasies for flute and piano, see p. 458.

of *Trivialmusik* with high-minded *dramma per musica* (unless otherwise specified the works are for solo piano; dates refer to their advertisement in the *Gazzetta*): E. Golinelli, *Souvenir de Macbeth* ("drawn from the *famoso applauditissimo* murderers' chorus," this work was distributed gratis to the *Gazzetta*'s subscribers on May 26); Alex. Billet, *Fantaisie élégante,* op. 35 (June 9); Carlo Bosoni, *Fantasia,* op. 1 (June 30); Alex. Billet, *Caprice brillant,* op. 40 (July 21, but already advertised in the July 10 number of *Il Pirata*—one day after his op. 35 was announced!); Levy and Rudersdorff, *Fantaisie brillante* for piano and violin (July 28); Truzzi, *Gioja delle madri,* fascicles 41–47, from the "collection of sonatinas for piano, based upon themes from modern operas performed with brilliant success" (August 11); De-Pauli, *Capriccio* for flute with piano accompaniment (August 25); G. Tutsch, *Macbeth-Walzer* für das Pianoforte (August 25); C. A. Gambini, *Reminiscenze dell'Opera Macbeth* (August 25); Giulio Briccialdi, *Macbeth di Verdi: Fantasia* for flute with piano accompaniment (September 1; this may have been the Macbeth "divertissement" that Briccialdi performed on a newly-developed Boehm flute in his October 30 Munich concert—a Briccialdi duet performed with Boehm was also on the program);[6] C. A. M. Brini, *Fantasia,* op. 2 (September 29); S. Paraladoff, *Pièce fantasque et allégorique:* trio for violin (or flute), viola, and cello (October 20); G. Micheuz, *Fantaisie brillante* (November 3).

6. See *Gazzetta musicale di Milano,* 10 November 1847.

THE "SCALA" *MACBETH* LIBRETTO:
A GENETIC EDITION

Francesco Degrada

I have discussed the nature and importance of the "Scala" *Macbeth* libretto—the libretto in Verdi's hand with Maffei's interventions—elsewhere (see pp. 159–73), but a few more points about the physical state of the manuscript should be made.

The manuscript is unbound and consists of

1. the libretto proper, written on 16 unnumbered folios measuring 20.5 cm x 29 cm (8 nested bifolios of 41 cm x 29 cm).
2. a cover with title and *dramatis personae* (a smaller bifolio—36.5 cm x 27 cm—of a different paper).

Bifolio 7 is a later insertion, and fol. 7v was attached with sealing wax to fol. 8r, covering it completely. The structure of the manuscript at the time of its completion (before fols. 7 and 8 were separated) can be represented as follows:

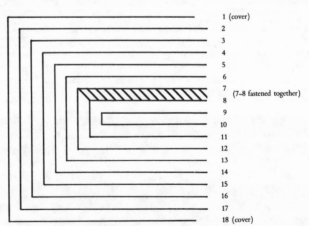

At one time, little strips of paper with corrections were stuck to the pages with sealing wax, but, to prevent their loss, these collettes, as we shall call them, have been collected on a separate sheet by the administration of the museum.

Fol. 7r contains an intermediate version of II.1. On 3 December 1847 Verdi had asked Piave for a new version of this scene (to replace the one on fol. 8); on December 10 Verdi complained that he still had not received Piave's lines. This tells us that by December 3 Verdi had transcribed at least as far as Act II.1 and that the new bifolio was not inserted before December 10. It is also clear that whenever Verdi did insert the new bifolio, he had copied no further than fol. 11v, which ends with III.2.9—i.e., directly before the witches' evocation "Dalle basse, e dall'alte . . . ," which begins fol. 12, part of the added bifolio. That is, fol. 13, whose text lacks significant corrections and follows directly from fol. 12, was obviously filled in after the addition of the new bifolio.

Another physical aspect of the manuscript, again with ramifications for any examination of the shaping of the libretto, is the color of the inks used by Maffei. Maffei's corrections were apparently made in at least three different stages, which can be tentatively described as follows:

1. A first series of interventions made in brown ink. These are found principally in Acts III and IV, presumably the first acts on which Maffei worked, and, to a lesser extent, in Acts I and II as well. In the edition these interventions are indicated by the symbol *M*.
2. A second series in blue ink, found throughout the libretto and indicated here by the symbol M.
3. A third series in which Maffei corrects in brown ink a previous intervention written in blue ink. These cases are very rare and will be cited in the notes.

This edition offers a reconstruction of the different layers or states of each passage. Obviously, the grouping of individual changes into a single state is a matter of interpretation, and other editors might offer different solutions. A diplomatic edition recording all variants as independent changes without attempting to group them into separate layers would not avoid the problems of interpretation, but merely shift them from the editor to the reader.

Other problems in editing the libretto are inherent in its origin and composite nature. As we have seen, Acts I and II provide a reading drawn up by Verdi and Piave before the involvement of Maffei, who made his own corrections on a text already completed, if still in need of final adjustments. Acts III and IV, on the other hand, were probably copied out by Verdi after a first revision by Maffei; this seems to be borne out by the lack of any alterations by Maffei in III.1 (the chorus of witches) or in the bulk of the sleepwalking scene, both of which were attributed to him by Verdi. On earlier drafts of this version, Maffei may well have made many successive corrections. So, on one hand, it is impossible to reconstruct precisely how much should be attributed to Piave and how much to Verdi (although I am inclined to believe that the composer played a principal role even in the versification of many passages), and, on the other hand, it is correct to suppose that not *all* changes and suggestions are actually documented by this source.

Thus it is impossible to supply a "base text" related to a single definite stage in the preparation of the opera. The method of transcription, chosen for simple reasons of convenience, is:

1. The "base text" consists of a strictly literal transcription of the version that represents (to the extent that the source can reveal it) what is presumably the earliest stage in the preparation of the text.

2. Notes, in chronological order, show the variations made by Verdi and Maffei, preceded by the letters V and M (or *M* if the intervention is in brown ink) plus a numerical superscript; thus, V, V[1], V[2] and M, M[1], M[2] indicate successive alterations by Verdi (or Verdi/Piave) and by Maffei. The notes normally consist of an attribution and colon (e.g., V[1]:), followed by the variant reading. The placing of the footnote number locates the end of the passage affected by the revision. Where the beginning of the revision might be unclear (e.g., where it might not be clear whether the newly-written words were intended as a replacement for, or as an addition to, the original text), the variant reading includes a word or two unaffected by the revision. For example, Maffei added "re di Scozia" after Verdi's "Duncano" in the list of *Personaggi*. The note (Personaggi, n. 2) reads "M: Duncano re di Scozia," clarifying that Maffei let Verdi's "Duncano" stand. It should be observed that the note does not indicate whether Maffei recopied Verdi's "Duncano"—the edition is not a diplomatic one—but since "M" is in roman rather than italic, it does show that whatever Maffei did write to effect the change, he wrote in blue ink.

3. In order to allow easier and quicker comparison between the various versions, variants not limited to one or a few words but involving whole scenes or sizable groups of lines are given in the main text rather than in the notes—also in chronological order preceded by the appropriate signs. An asterisk in the text signals that the passage beginning at that point has been revised and that the variant reading will appear in the main text.

4. The following have been regularized tacitly: stage directions are italicized and placed in parentheses; punctuation indicating abbreviation of proper names is given as a period (Verdi sometimes uses colons instead); parentheses left open have been closed.

5. All editorial additions are in square brackets.

1r

Macbeth
Melodramma[1]

1v

Personaggi

Duncano[2]
Macbet[3] ⎫
Banco ⎭ generali delle armate del Re Duncano
Lady Macbet moglie di Macbet[4]
Dama confidente di Ledy[5]
Macduff nobile scozzese Thane di Fife[6]
Malcolmo figlio di Duncano
Domestico di Macbet
Medico
Sicario
3 Apparizioni
L'ombra di Banco che non parla
Cori[7] di Streghe, Nunzi[8] del Re, Nobili Scozzesi, Profughi Scozzesi[9], Sicarj, Soldati inglesi, Spiriti aerei etc. etc...

La scena è in Iscozia e principalmente nel[10] Castello di Macbet: nel[11] principio dell'Atto 4° è sui confini tra Scozia ed Inghilterra.[12]

1. Both words written by M   2. M: Duncano re di Scozia

3. M: Macbeth [Throughout the libretto Maffei corrects the spelling of the protagonist's name, which Verdi usually writes without the final *h*. Further instances will not be noted.]

4. V wrote "moglie di Banc[o]" before noting his error.

5. M: Dama al servizio di Lady Macbeth [Maffei systematically corrects Verdi's "Ledy" to "Lady." Further instances will not be noted.]

6. M cancelled "Thane di Fife"

7. V¹: Cori e comparse ["e comparse" cancelled by M]

8. V¹: Messaggeri [the second *g* added by M]

9. M: Nobili e Profughi Scozzesi

10. M: al   11. M: sul

12. M: tra il confine di Scozia e d'Inghilterra.

2r

V

ATTO 1°

Bosco

Fra lampi e tuoni comparisce un drapello di streghe
poi un'altro, indi un terzo[1]

Scena I

1.	Che faceste? dite su!
2.	Ho sgozzato un verro. E tu?[2]
3.	M'ha frullato[3] nel pensier
	La mogliera d'un nocchier.
	Al dimòn la mi cacciò.[4]
	Ma lo sposo che salpò
	Col suo legno affogherò.
1.	Un rovajo io ti darò
2.	I marosi io leverò
3.	Per le secche io lo trarrò.

(Odesi un tamburro[5]*)*

Tutte[6]   Un tamburro! Che sarà?

Vien Macbetto. Eccolo quà!

(S'uniscono in giro facendo un
circolo e danzando)[7]

Le sorelle vagabonde

Van per l'aria van sull'onde

Sanno un circolo intrecciar

Che comprende e terra e mar.

1. M: *Tre crocchi di streghe appariscono l'un dopo l'altro fra lampi e tuoni*
2. V¹: 2.   Morto ho un verro.
   I.   E voi...Che fu?
   V² restores the first version.
3. M: M'è frullata   4. M: cacciò...
5. M: *tamburo* [This correction appears throughout the libretto, and, as with the similar examples noted above, further instances will not be noted.]
6. M: *Tutte in coro*
7. M: (*Si confondono insieme e intrecciano una ridda*)

2v

Scena II
Macbet e Banco. Dette[1]

Mac.	Giorno non vidi mai sì fiero e bello
Banc.	Nè tanto glorioso!
Mac. (*accorgendosi delle streghe*)	Oh chi saran[2]
	Costor?
Banc.[3]	Chi siete voi? Di questo mondo
	O d'altra regïone?[4]
	Dirvi donne vorrei, ma lo mi vieta
	Quella barba deforme.[5]
Macb.	Or via[6] parlate!
Streghe[7] 1°	Salve o Macbetto di Glamis thane.[8]
2°	Salve o Macbetto di Cawdor thane.[9]
3°	Salve o Macbetto di Scozia re.
(*Macbet trema*)	
Banc.[10]	Tremar vi fanno così lieti auguri?
	Favellate a me pur se non v'è scuro
	Creature fantastiche, il futuro.
1°	Salve!
2°	Salve!
3°	Salve!
1°	Men sarai di Macbetto e pur maggiore![11]
2°	Non quanto lui ma più di lui felice!
3°	Non re, ma di monarchi genitore!
Tutte	Macbetto e Banco vivano[12]
	Banco e Macbetto vivano!

(*spariscono*)

[3r]

Macb.	Vanir!...Saranno i figli tuoi sovrani
Banco[13]	E tu re pria di loro.
Banco e Mac.	Accenti arcani!

1. M: *Macbeth. Banco. Le Precedenti*

2. M: (*s'avvede delle streghe*) Oh chi saranno

3. M: Banc. (*alle streghe*)

4. The dieresis added by M

5. *M:* Quella sordida barba [Verdi's version may have originally read "Quelle barbe deformi" and Maffei seems to have first written "sordide".]

6. M: Or via,

7. added by M

8. *M:* di Glamis Sire! [In this line and the two following lines, M sets off "o Macbetto" with commas and changes the periods to exclamation points.]

9. *M:* di Caudor Sire!

10. M: Banc. (*alle streghe*)

11. In this and the following two lines M replaces the exclamation points with periods.

12. M: vivano!

13. V, apparently momentarily distracted as he recopied an earlier draft of the libretto, had originally switched the names of Banco and Macbeth in this exchange.

Scena III
Deputati[1] del Re e detti[2]

V *	Deput.	Del trionfo il re giulivo Ti fa thane di [Caudo]re
	Mac.	Che dì tu? Quel thane è vivo![3]
	Deput.	No non vive: il traditore Sul patibolo spirò.

M	* Messa.	Pago il re del tuo valore Sir t'elesse di Caudore
	Mac.	Ma quel rio non è già spento
	Messa.	Come reo di tradimento[4] Sul patibolo spirò.

M[1]	Messa.	Pro Macbetto! il tuo Signore Sir t'elesse di Caudore
	Mac.	Ma quel Sire ancor vi regge!
	Messa.	No! Percosso dalla legge Sotto il ceppo egli spirò.

V	Banc.	(Ah l'inferno il ver parlò!)
	Mac.	Due vaticini compiuti or sono: Mi si promette dal terzo un trono![5] Ma perchè sento rizzarsi il crine? Pensier di sangue d'onde se' nato?... Alla corona che m'offre il fato La man rapace non stenderò.[6]

V *	Banco	Oh come accend[e qu]el vano core L'ardita speme del regio onore.

M[1] *	Banco (*fra sè*)	Oh come avvampa [quel] vano core L'ardita speme d[el] regio onore[7]

M[2] *	Banco (*fra sè*)	Come in quel petto pieno d'orgoglio La speme esulta d'un regio soglio!

V[1]	Banco (*fra sè*)	Come si gonfia quel cor d'orgoglio Nella speranza d'un regio soglio!

V		Ma spesso l'empio spirto d'averno Parla, e c'inganna, veraci detti E ne abbandona poi maledetti Su quell'abisso che ci scavò!
	Dep.[8]	Perché sì freddo n'udì Macbetto Perché l'aspetto—non serenò?

(*Tutti partono*)

1. V[1]: Messaggeri   2. M: I Precedenti   3. V[1]: Che diceste? Il sire è vivo!

4. M[1]: Non è più, per tradimento   5. M: trono...   6. M: non alzerò.

7. An earlier attempt at correcting this couplet, in Maffei's hand, is almost impossible to reconstruct.

8. These two lines a later addition by V[1]
   V[2]: Messa: [i.e. replacing "Dep:"]

[3v]

Scena IV
Ritornano le streghe[1]
*S'allontanarono!—N'accozzeremo
Quando di fulmini—lo scroscio udremo[2]
. . . .
. . . .
. . . .
. . . .
Macbetto riedere—fra noi dovrà
E il nostro oracolo—gli parlerà!

V[1]   S'allontanarono!—N'accozzeremo
Quando di fulmini—Lo scroscio udremo
S'allontanarono!—Fuggiam!...s'attenda
Le sorti a compiere—Nella tregenda.
Chè dalle tenebre—d'un antro oscuro[3]
A noi risplendere—debbe il futuro.
Macbetto riedere—vedrem colà,
E il nostro oracolo—gli parlerà.[4]

1. M: Le streghe. (*Ritornano*)
2. The following four lines, which show traces of corrections, were later crossed out by Verdi and cannot be reconstructed.
3. This line and the next subsequently removed by V
4. M: (escono)

Scena V
Sala[1] *nel castello di Macbet che mette in altre stanze*
Ledy[2] *leggendo una lettera*

"Nel dì della vittoria le incontrai.[3]
Stupito io n'era per le udite cose[4]
Quando i nunzi del re mi salutaro
Thane[5] di Caudorre,[6] vaticinio uscito
Dalle veggenti stesse
Che predissero un serto al capo mio.
Racchiudi in cor questo segreto. Addio."
Ambïzoso spirto
Tu sei Macbetto....alla grandezza aneli....
Ma sarai tu malvagio?
Pien di misfatti è il calle
Della potenza, e mal per lui chi[7] il piede
Dubitoso vi pone, e retrocede!

[4r]

Sorgi, a me vieni, affrettati,[8]
Rinfranca il dubio[9] core.
L'audace impresa a compiere
Io ti darò valore.

        * D'averno a te promettono
         Le messaggere un trono....[10]

M   Di Scozia a te promettono
         Le arcane donne[11] il trono...

      Che tardi? Accetta il dono
      Ascendivi a regnar.

1. V[1]: Atrio
2. M: Lady Macbeth [Here, as in other cases that will not be noted, the *h* is in blue ink.]
3. V[1]: io le incontrai
  M: Scontrai
4. M: cose;
5. *M:* Sir
6. M: Caudore,
7. M: che
8. M: Sorgi! a me vieni, affrettati!...
9. M: dubbio
10. Near this couplet Verdi wrote "d'un'altra natura."
11. *M*[1]: Le strane donne
  M[2]: Le profetesse

        Scena VI
       Un servo, e detta[1]

V Servo   *Al cader della notte il re qui giunge.
   Ledy   Che dì? Con esso è Macbet?...
   Servo   Sì,
        Ne venne or or l'annunzio.
   Ledy   Trovi accoglienza che di lui sia degna..
              (*Il servo parte*)

Ṁ Servo   *Al cader della sera il re qui giunge.
   Ledy   E Macbetto è con esso?
   Servo   Ei l'accompagna.
        L'annunzio or or ne venne
   Ledy   Trovi accoglienza che di lui sia degna.
              (*Il servo parte*)

V[1] Servo   Al venir della sera il re qui giunge.
   Ledy   Che dì? Macbetto è seco?
   Servo   Ei l'accompagna!
        La nova o donna è certa.
   Ledy   Trovi accoglienza quale un re si merta.
              (*Il servo parte*)

1. M: Un servo. La Precedente [The collette containing the definitive version of the scene has been lost.]

Scena VII

V

Ledy[1] sola

Duncano sarà qui?...qui...qui la notte?
Or tutte sorgete—o furie infernali[2]
Che al sangue incorate—spingete i mortali.
Tu notte ne avvolgi—di tenebra immota.
Qual petto percota—non vegga il pugnal.

1. M: Lady Macbeth sola
2. M: Or tutti sorgete—Ministri infernali

Scena VIII
Macbet e detta[1]

Mac.	Oh Ledy[2] mia!
Ledy	Caudorre![3]
Mac.	Vedrai qui il re tra poco....[4]

[4v]

Ledy	E partirà?[5]
Mac.	Domani
Lady	Non mai splenderà il sol su tal domani.[6]
Mac.	Che parli?
Lady	Non intendi?.... (*sotto voce*)[7]
Mac.	Intendo, intendo!! (*con un grido*)
Lady	Ebbene?....[8]
Mac.	E se fallisse il colpo?
Lady	Non fallirà!..se non tremate[9]

(*odonsi lieti suoni che a poco a poco s'avvicinano*)[10]

Mac.	Il Re!..
Lady	Lo vieni or lieto[11] ad incontrar con me.

(*partono*)

1. M: Macbeth e la Precedente
2. V[1]: Oh moglie
   V[2]: Oh donna
3. M: Caudore
4. M: Fra poco il re vedrai...[originally these words were said by Lady Macbeth]
5. M: Ripartirà?
6. M: Non risplenda il mattin su tal domani
   M[1]: Mai non risplenda il sole a tal domani
   M[2]: Mai non ci rechi il sole un tal domani
7. M[1]: Lady (sommessa) Oh [M[2]: E] non intendi?
8. M: Orbene?....
9. *M*: Se tu non tremi
10. M: (*lieti suoni che a poco a poco si accostano*)
11. M: Lieto or lo vieni

314

Scena muta[1] [*Scena IX*]
Arrivo di Duncano

1. M: *Scena IX nella quale al suono d'una marcia guerresca* [M[1]: *trionfale*] [...] *vedesi passare il Re Duncano con seguito pomposo. Esterno: il castello di Macbeth col ponte levatoio calato.* [This entire scenic indication was later cancelled.]

Scena IX [*recte* X][1]
Notte
Macbet ed un servo

V	Mac.	* Lady s'avverta che [appr]estata appena
		La notturna tazza[2]
		Un rintocco di squilla a me lo avvisi.
		(*Il servo parte*)

M	Mac.	* Sappia la sposa mia che la notturna
		Mia tazza apparecchiato [*sic*]
		Vo' che un tocco di squilla a me lo avvisi.
		(*Il servo parte*)

M[1]	Mac.	Sappia la sposa mia che pronta appena
		La mia tazza notturna
		Vo' che un tocco di squilla a me lo avvisi.
		(*Il servo parte*)

1. From here to the end of the act Maffei has raised by one the number of each scene, to reflect the insertion of Scene IX. These corrected numbers are given in square brackets in the text, in order to facilitate comparison with the printed libretto.
2. V[1]: la mia notturna tazza
V[2]: la notturna bevanda

Scena X [*recte* XI]
Macbet solo[1]

V	Mi si affaccia un pugnal?!...l'elsa a me volta?!...
	Se larva non sei tu ch'io ti brandisca....
	* Mi sfuggi...eppur ti veggo!...Orrenda imago!...
	Solco sanguigno la tua lama irriga!...

M	Mi sfuggi, eppur ti veggo! A me precorri
	Sul confuso cammin che nella mente
	Di seguir designava. Orrenda imago!...
	Solco sanguigno la tua lama irriga!...

V	* Ma nulla esiste ancora...Il sol pensiero
	Che ravvolge il delitto è che m'affanna:
	Desso m'incalza, m'atterrisce, inganna!

M	Ma nulla esiste ancora...Il sol cruento
	Mio pensier le dà forma e come vera
	Mi presenta allo sguardo una chimera.

[5r]

V	Or su[2] metà del mondo

315

Morta par la natura:[3] or l'assassino
Come fantasma per l'ombre si striscia:
Or consuman le streghe i lor misteri.
Immobil terra! a' passi miei sii[4] muta...(*odesi un suono di campana*)[5]
È deciso...quel bronzo ecco m'invita!...
Non udirlo Duncano. È squillo eterno
Che nel cielo ti chiama, o nell'inferno![6]

1. "Macbet solo" is cancelled by M.
2. *M:* Sulla
3. *M:* Or morta è la natura
4. M: sta
5. M: (*Un tocco di campana*)
6. *M:* (*entra nella stanza del re*)

Scena XI [*recte* XII]

Ledy[1] *sola*

Regna il sonno su tutti.—Oh qual lamento!
Risponde il gufo al suo lùgubre addio!

(*Macbet*   Chi v'ha?...
  di dentro)
Ledy   Che[2] fosse di letargo uscito
          Pria del colpo mortal?...

1. *M: Lady Macbeth*
2. *M:* Ch'ei

* *Scena XII* [*recte* XIII]

Tutto è finito!

Macbet
  (*stravolto*)[1]   Donna fatale un murmure
          Pur or' non intend[esti]?
          Udii del gufo l'ululo....
          Ma tu che poi dicesti?

M

Scena XII [*recte* XIII]

* *La Precedente. Macbeth* (*stravolto*
esce d'una stanza attigua con un pugnale
insanguinato)

Macbet   Tutto è finito!
          Fatal mia donna! un murmure,
          Com'io non intend[esti]?
[Ledy]   Udii del gufo il gemito....
          Pur or, tu che dicesti?[2]

M[1]

La Precedente. Macbeth (*stravolto con un pugnale in mano*)

Macbet   Tutto è finito!
          Fatal mia donna! Un mormore,
          Com'io non intendesti?
Ledy   Del gufo udii lo stridere....
          Testé che mai dicesti?

V	Mac.	Io?.
	Lady	Dianzi udirti parvemi.
		Mentre io scendeva?
	Lady	Sì![3]

[5v]

	Mac.	Chi nella stanza attigua
		Dimmi, chi dorme?
	Lady	Il figlio!...
	Mac.	Vista fatal, terribile![4]
	(*guardandosi*	
	le mani)	
	Ledy	Rivolgi altrove[5] il ciglio....
	Mac.	Nel sonno udii che oravano
		I cortigiani, e: *Dio*
		Sempre ne assista, dissero.[6]
		Amen dir volli anch'io,
		* Ma ciò non fù possibile
		Gelaro i labri miei.

M		Ma la parola indocile
		Gelò sui labri miei.

V	Ledy	Follie!
	Mac.	Perchè ripetere
		Quell'*Amen* non potei?
	Ledy	Follie, follie che sperdono
		i primi rai del dì.
	Mac.	* Allora mi parve suonarmi nel petto,
		Avrai per guanciali sol vepri o Macbetto:
		Glamìs tu cacciasti nel sonno lo stile:
		Perpetua vigilia t'aspetta o Caudor.
	Lady	Ma dimmi altra voce non parti d'udire?
		Sei vano o Macbetto, ma debole e vile:
		Glamis a mezz'opra ti manca l'ardire
		D'un bimbo ventoso Caudorre è il tuo cor!

V[1]	Mac.	Allor questa voce m'intesi nel petto.
		Avrai per guanciali sol vepri o Macbetto:
		Il sonno per sempre Glamis uccidesti:
		Non v'è che vigilia Caudorre[7] per te!
	Lady	Ma dimmi altra voce non parti d'udire?
		Sei vano o Macbetto[8] ma privo d'ardire:
		Glamis a mezz'opra ondeggi,[9] t'arresti,
		Un bimbo ventoso Caudorre tu se'!
	Mac.	Vendetta tuonarmi, com'angeli d'ira
		Udrò di Duncano le sante virtù.
	Ledy	(Quell'animo trema, vacilla,[10] delira
		Chi mai lo direbbe l'invitto che fu!)

V	Il pugnal là riportate[11]	
	Le sue guardie insanguinate[12]	
	Che l'accusa in lor ricada.	
Mac.	Io colà?...non posso entrar!	

[6r]

| Lady | Dammi il ferro. | (*strappa dalle mani di Macbet il pugnale ed entra nella stanza del re*). |

1. Subsequently cancelled by M
2. V[1]: Pur or, tu che dicesti? [Maffei recopied this reading in two stages, using two different inks—brown ("Pur or, tu") and blue ("che dicesti").]
3. M: scendea? [Lady] Si! Si!
4. V[1]: Vista fatale orribile!

   M: O vista, o vista orribile!
5. M: Storna da questo [An earlier reading of Maffei, subsequently cancelled, is illegible.]
6. M: ei dissero.
7. M: Caudore
8. M: Sei vano, o Macbetto,
9. M: vacilli
10. M: combatte,
11. M: riportate,
12. M: insanguinate....

V	*Scena XIII* [*recte* XIV]	
	Macbet solo	
		(*odesi un gran colpo alla porta del castello.*)[1]
Mac.	Ogni romore	
	Mi spaventa!...Oh questa mano![2]	
		(*si guarda le mani*)
	Non potrebbe l'oceàno[3]	
	Queste mani a me lavar!	

1. M: (*bussano forte alla porta del Castello*)
2. M: mano...
3. M: l'Oceàno

	Scena XIIII [*recte* XV][1]	
Ledy	Vè?[2] le mani ho lorde anch'io.	
	Poco spruzzo e monde son.	
	L'opra anch'essa andrà in oblìo.	
Mac.	* Non ascolti? Addoppia il suon!	(*odesi di nuovo bussare alla porta*)[3]
Ledy	Vien: non prostri un'ombra, un vano	
	Vil terror la tua virtù!	
Mac.	Qual delitto!...O Re Duncano	
	Non ti svegli?...ah no mai [più]!!	
		(*Macbet è trascinato via da Ledy.*)

M	Mac.	Odi tu? Raddoppia il suon!
	Ledy	Vieni altrove! Ogni sospetto
		Rimoviam dall'uccisor.
		Torna in te! fa cor, Macbetto!
		Non ti vinca un vil timor.
	Mac.	* Ah potessi il mio delitto
		Cancellar dal mio pensier!
		Fosse almeno, o re trafitto
		Lo svegliarti in mio poter!

(*Macbeth è trascinato via da Ledy*)

M¹

Ah potessi il mio delitto
Dalla mente cancellar!
Deh sapessi, o re trafitto,
L'alto sonno a te spezzar!

(*Macbeth è trascinato via da Ledy*)

1. M: *Lady Macbeth* (*ritorna*). *il Precedente*
2. M: Vè!
3. M: (*battono di nuovo alla porta*)

V		*Scena XV* [*recte* XVI]
		Macduf¹ e Banco
	Mac.	Di destarlo per tempo il re m'impose²
		E di già tarda è l'ora
		Qui m'attendete o Banco³ (*entra nella stanza del re*).

1. M: Macduff
2. An earlier version of this line is undecipherable.
3. M: Qui m'attendete, o Banco...

[6v]

Scena XVI [*recte* XVII]
Banco solo

Oh qual orrenda notte!
Per l'aer¹ cieco lamentose voci,
Voci s'udian di morte...
Gemea lungo² l'augel de' tristi auguri,
E della terra si sentì il tremore.³

1. M: aëre
2. M: cupo
3. M: E si sentì della terra il tremore...

Scena XVII [recte XVIII]
Macduf e Banco

Mac.	Orrore! orrore! orrore!
Banc.	Che avvenne mai?
Mac.	Là dentro

Contemplate voi stesso...io dir nol posso

(*Banco entra nella stanza del re*)

Correte olà...tutti accorrete, tutti.[1]
Oh delitto! oh delitto! oh tradimento!

1. M: tutti accorrete! tutti!

Scena XVIII [recte XIX]
Ledy,[1] Macbeth, Macduf, Banco, Dama di Ledy, domestici[2]

Ledy e Mac.	Qual subito scompiglio!
Banco	Oh noi perduti!
Tutti, *tranne* Mac. e Banco	Che fu? parlate,[3] che seguì di strano?
Banco	È morto assassinato il re Duncano!!.[4]
Tutti	Schiudi, o inferno,[5] la bocca ed inghiotti
	Nel tuo grembo l'intero creato
	Questo covo di serpi esecrato
	Le tue fiamme distruggano, o ciel!

M   Macb. e Lady   Sull'ignoto assassinato esecrato
Le tue fiamme discendano o ciel.

V

O gran Dio che ne cuori discendi[6]
Tu ne assisti, in te solo fidiamo.
Da te lume e consiglio cerchiamo[7]
A squarciar delle tenebre il vel!
* Del castigo ora tutte ne appresta
Le tue folgori o Dio punitor!
La veggente giustizia ridesti,
Del delitto percoti l'autor!

M

L'ira tua formidabile e pronta
Colga l'empio o gran Dio[8] punitor,
E vi stampi sul capo[9] l'impronta
Che stampasti sul primo uccisor.

---

1. M: Lady Macbeth,   2. M: Servi   3. M: parlate!
4. M: (*stupore universale*)   5. M: Schiudi, inferno,
6. Two earlier, cancelled versions of this line are illegible. Later versions are as follows:
   M: che i misfatti palesi [subsequently cancelled]
   V[1]: penetri [replacing "discendi"]
7. V[1]: Da te lume, consiglio cerchiamo
8. *M[1]:* o fatal   9. *M[1]:* volto

V

[8r]

* ATTO SECONDO

Sala come nella scena V dell'Atto I°
Scena I
Lady sola

Fur le streghe veraci, e re tu sei
Macbetto! Il figlio di Duncan fuggendo
Dalla Scozia in Brettagna
Parricida fù detto, e vuoto il soglio
A te lasciò: ma le spirtali donne
Banco padre di regi han profetato...
Dunque i suoi figli regneran?..Duncano
Per costor sarà spento?...Egli e suo figlio
Vivono è ver, ma vita
Di tempera immortal non han sortita.
Pria che il tetro angel notturno
Fugga al raggio mattutino
Il pugnal dell'assassino
Novo sangue ha da versar.
Tra misfatti ha fin l'impresa
Se un misfatto a lei fù culla
O Macbetto il serto è nulla
Se può in capo vacillar.

V¹

[7r]

ATTO SECONDO
Scena I¹
Macbeth concentrato seguito da Ledy²

Ledy	Perchè mi sfuggi³ e fiso
	Ti veggo ognora in un pensier profondo?
	Il fatto è irreparabile!!. Veraci
	Parlar le maliarde,⁴ e re tu sei.
	Il figlio di Duncan⁵ per l'improvvisa
	Sua fuga in Inghilterra⁶
	Parricida fù detto, e vuoto il soglio
	a te lasciò.
Mac.	Ma le spirtali donne
	Banco padre di regi han profetato:
	Dunque i suoi figli regneran?..Duncano
	Per costor sarà spento?
Ledy	*Egli e suo figlio
	Vivono è ver. Ma vita
	Immortale non han.
Mac.	Ciò mi conforta.
Led.	Scorrere un' altro sangue...
Mac.	Un altro sangue?
Lad.	T'è forza!

Mac.	E quando?
Led.	Al venir della notte
M.	Necessario è pur troppo![7]
Led.	Or che disegni?
M.	Banco! L'eternità t'apre i suoi regni!

(Parte precipitoso)

M   Ledy

                                Egli e suo figlio
        Vivono, è ver...

   Mac.   Ma vita
        *Immortale non hanno....è d'uopo, o donna
        Che scorra un'altro sangue!

   Lady   Un altro sangue?

   Mac.   È forza!...

   Lady   E quando?

   Mac.   Al venir della notte.

   Lady   Immoto sarai tu nel tuo disegno?

   Mac.   Banco! L'eternità t'apre il suo regno.

(parte precipitoso)

V[2]

                 Immortale non hanno...

   Lady   Ah sì non l'hanno!...

   Mac.   Forza è che scorra un altro sangue o donna!

   Lady   Dove? E quando?

   Mac.   Al venir di questa notte.

   Lady   Immoto sarai tu nel tuo disegno?

   Mac.   Banco! L'eternità t'apre il suo regno.

(parte precipitoso)

---

1. M: stanza nel castello
2. M: *Macbeth* (*pensoso* seguito da Lady Macbeth)
3. M: sfuggi,
4. M: le malïarde,
5. M: Duncan,
6. M: Inghilterra,
7. *M:* Dunque un novo misfatto?

[*Scena II*]
Ledy sola

Trionfai! securi alfine
  Premerem di Scozia il trono
  Or disfido il lampo il tuono
  Le sue basi a rovesciar.
Tra misfatti ha l'opra il fine
  Se un misfatto le[1] fù culla
  La regal corona è nulla
  Se può in capo vacillar!

1. M: Se un misfatto a lei

[7v–blank]

[8v]

Scena II [*recte* III] [1]
Un parco che mostra in lontananza il castello di Macbet [2]
Coro di Sicarii

I.	Chi v'impose unirvi a noi?
II.	Fù Macbetto...
I.	Ed a che far?
II.	Dobbiam Banco trucidar.
I.	Quando?..dove?..
II.	Quì con voi. [3]
	Con suo figlio qui [4] verrà
I.	Rimanete...bene [5] stà.

Tutti	* Sparve il sole e vien la notte
	Cieca notte scellerata
	Del tuo velo ottenebrata
	Sia la luce di tal dì.
	L'ora è presso!...or n'ascondiamo
	Nel silenzio lo attendiamo
	Scendi o notte, scendi o notte
	Egli debbe morir qui.

M	Sparve il sol!...la notte or regni
	Scellerata—insanguinata
	Cieca notte affretta e spegni
	Ogni lume in terra e in ciel
	L'ora è presso!...or n'occultiamo,
	Nel silenzio lo aspettiamo
	Trema, o Banco!—nel tuo fianco
	Sta la punta del coltel!

1. From here to the end of the act Maffei has raised by one the number of each scene. Although he did not label it as such, he considered Lady Macbeth's aria "Trionfai!" to constitute a separate scene (II.2). Furthermore, since Banco's scena—II.5 in the printed libretto—is not present in the manuscript, after that point Verdi's numeration is two numbers lower than that of the printed libretto. As in Act I, the number corresponding to the final version of *Macbeth I* is given in square brackets.

2. M: Un parco. In lontananza il castello di Macbeth

3. M: Insiem con voi

4. M: ei qui

5. M: or bene

Scena III [*recte* V]
Magnifica sala nel regio palazzo. V'ha un banchetto imbandito. [1] *Guardie d'onore ne custodiscono gli additi.* [2] *Lady, Macbet, Macduff, Dame, Thani con seguito*

Coro	* Viva il felice Macbet
	Viva l'amato rè
	A lui sia onore [3] gloria!
	A lui coraggio e fe'! [4]

V[1]	Coro	Salve o Re!
	Mac.	Voi pur salvete
		Nobilissimi signori!
	Coro	Salve o Ledy[5]
	Ledy	Ricevete
		La mercé de vostri onori.

[9r]

	Mac.	* [Ora] ciascuno assidasi
		Ne' seggi destinati
		Ci sarà dolce scorrere
		Tra nostri convitati....
		La sposa mia si collochi
		Nel trono a lei sortito
		Ma prima un lieto brindisi
		Propizi a vostro onor.

(Tutti prend[ono] posto)

M	Mac.	Prenda ciascun l'orrevole
		Seggio al suo grado eletto!
		Lieto son io d'accogliere
		Tali ospiti[6] a banchetto.
		La mia consorte assidasi
		Nel trono a lei sortito
		Ma pria le piaccia un brindisi
		Sciogliere[7] a vostro onor.

| V | Ledy | * Siccome ne destini |
| | | Son pronta o mio Signor! |

V[1]	Ledy	Al tuo regale invito
		Son pronta o mio Signor!
	Coro	E tu n'udrai rispondere
		Come ci detta il cor![8]

V	Lady[9]	Si colmi il calice
		Di vino eletto
		Nasca il diletto
		Muoja il dolor.
		Da noi s'involino
		Gli odj e gli sdegni
		Folleggi e regni
		Solo l'amor[10]
		Gustiamo il balsamo
		D'ogni ferita
		Che nuova vita
		Ridona al cor.

Tutti	Cacciam le torbide
ripetono	Cure dal petto
	Nasca il diletto
	Muoja il dolor.
(2da volta)	Vuotiam per l'inclito
	Banco i bicchieri!
	Fior de' guerrieri
	Di Scozia onor![11]

1. M: palazzo. Mensa imbandita
2. M: Senti[nelle] d'onore ne custodiscono l'ingresso [the entire sentence subsequently cancelled]
3. V[1]: A lui trionfo
4. These four lines cancelled by Verdi
5. V[2]: o donna
6. "Tali ospiti" replaces an earlier version in Maffei's hand, possibly "Grand'ospiti."
7. "Sciogliere" replaces an earlier, undecipherable reading, possibly "le piaccia"
8. These two lines are later additions by V.
9. "Lady" in Maffei's hand.
10. V[1]: Qui solo Amor
11. This second strophe is probably a later addition by Verdi.

Scena IV [*recte* VI]
Detti, indi un sicario che si affaccia ad una porta. Macbet se gli appressa[1]

Mac.	Tu di sangue hai brutto il volto
Sica.	È di Banco.
Mac.	Il vero ascolto?

[9v]

Sic.	Sì	
Mac.	Ma il figlio?	
Sic.		Ne sfuggì!
Mac.	Cielo!.... e Banco?...	
Sic.		Egli morì.[2]

(*Macbet fà un cenno*[3] *al
sicario che parte*)

1. M: *I Precedenti. Un sicario che si affaccia ad un uscio laterale. Macbeth gli si fa presso.*
2. M: Morì!
3. M: *fa cenno*

Scena V [*recte* VII]
Detti,[1] *meno il Sicario*

Ledy	Che ti scosta, o re mio sposo[2]
	Dalla gioja del banchetto?...
Mac.	Banco falla! il valoroso
	Chiuderebbe il serto eletto
	A quant'avvi di più degno
	Nell'intero nostro regno.
Ledy	Venir disse e ci mancò

Mac.	In sua vece io sederò	
		(Macbet va per sedersi e vede l'ombra di Banco al suo posto...vista soltanto da desso)[3]
Macbet *(spaventato)*[4]	Di voi chi ciò fece?!!	
Tutti	Che parli?	
Mac. *(all' ombra)*	* Non dirmi Ch'io fossi...quel crine cruento, scomposto Non scuotermi incontro....	
Tutti	Il sire è indisposto Partiamo...	
Lady	Restate...—È morbo fugace	

M *(allo spettro)*	* Non dirmi ch'io fossi....quel crine scomposto	
Mac.	Non scuotermi incontro....	
Tutti	Il sire è indisposto Partiamo...	
Lady	Restate! Gli è morbo fugace...	

M[1] Mac. *(allo spettro)*	Non dirmi ch'io fossi! le ciocche cruente Non scuotermi incontro....	
Tutti *(sorgono)*	* Partiamo! soffrente È il re.	
	No! restate! Gli è morbo fugace...	

V[1] Tutti	* Macbetto è soffrente Partiam.	
Lady	Rimanete! Gli è morbo fugace...	

V[2] Tutti	Macbetto è soffrente Partiamo...	
Lady	Restate! Gli è morbo fugace...	

V Lady *(piano a Macbet)*	E un uomo voi siete?...	
Mac.	Lo sono ed audace	

[10r]

S'io guardo tal cosa che al demone stesso
Porrebbe spavento...Là...là...nol ravvisi...?
Oh[5] poi che le chiome crollar[6] t'è concesso
Favella! il sepolcro può render gli uccisi?...

(l'ombra sparisce)

Ledy *(piano a Macbet)*	Inver folle siete![7]	
Mac.	Quest'occhi l'han visto...	
Ledy *(forte)*	Sedete o mio sposo!...Ogni ospite è tristo[8] Svegliate la gioja!...	
Mac.	Ciascun mi perdoni... Il brindisi lieto[9] di nuovo risoni,	

Nè Banco obbliamo[10] che lungi è tuttor.

(Lady fa per ricominciare il brindisi e l'ombra di Banco appare di nuovo)[11]

Mac. *(spaventato)*	Và...spirto d'abisso!...dischiudi[12] una fossa O terra e l'ingoia[13]...Fiammeggian quell'ossa!! Quel sangue fumante mi balza[14] nel volto!! Quel guardo a me volto—traffiggemi il cor!!	
Tutti	Sventura! terror!—	
Mac.	Quant'altri, io pur oso... Diventa pur tigre, leon[15] minaccioso... M'abbranca...Macbetto tremar non vedrai[16] Conoscer potrai, s'io provi timor... Ma fuggi deh fuggi fantasma tremendo!!... La vita riprendo!!...	*(l'ombra sparisce)*
Ledy *(piano a Macbet)*	(Vergogna Signor.)	

[10v]

Mac.	Sangue a me quell'ombra chiede E l'avrà, l'avrà, lo giuro! Il sigillo[17] del futuro Alle streghe io frangerò.[18]
Ledy *(a Macbet)*	Spirto imbelle! il tuo spavento Vane larve t'ha creato Il delitto è consumato[19] Chi morì tornar non può.
Macduf[20] *(fra sé)*	Biechi arcani!...s'abbandoni Questa terra or ch'ella è retta Da una mano maledetta,[21] Viver solo il reo vi può.
Tutti	Biechi arcani! sgomentato Da fantasmi egli ha parlato! Uno speco di ladroni Questa terrà diventò.

---

1. M: *I precedenti* 2. M: *sposo,*

3. M: *(Macbeth fa per sedere. Lo spettro di Banco veduto solo da lui ne occupa il posto.)*
   M[1]: *(Macbeth fa per sedersi e trova al suo posto lo spettro di Banco veduto soltanto da lui.)*

4. M: *(atterrito)* 5. M: *(allo spettro)* Oh 6. M: scrollar

7. V[1]: *Sei forse demente?* 8. M: *Ciascuno è qui tristo* 9. V[1]: alfine 10. M: obbliate
   V[2]: *Sei fatto demente?* V[2]: lieto
   M: *Sei tu forsennato?*
   V[3]: *Inver folle siete!?*

11. V: *Lady ricomincia il brindisi sul finire del quale l'ombra di Banco appare di nuovo.*
    M: *Lady Macbeth ridice il brindisi, sostituendo all'ultima strofa che vien ripetuta dal coro quest'altra: Vuotiam etc. Sulla fine riappare lo spettro.* [The entire stage direction, except for the words "riappare lo spettro," has been cancelled.]

12. M: spalanca 13. M: lo ingoia 14. *M*: sblaza 15. M: lion

16. M: farai 17. V[1]: velame 18. V[1]: squarcierò 19. M: consumato;

20. M: Macduff 21. M: maledetta:

[11r]

V   ATTO TERZO
Un'oscura caverna: nel mezzo una caldaja che bolle. Tuoni e lampi

Scena I
Entrano le Streghe[1]

I.   Tre volte miagola la gatta in fregola
II.   Tre volte l'ùpupa lamenta ed ulula
III.   Tre volte l'istrice guaisce al vento
                      Questo è il momento.
Tutte   Su via sollecite giriam la pentola
                  Mesciamvi in circolo gli arcani[2] intingoli
                  Sirocchie all'opra! l'acqua già fuma
                      Crepita e spuma.
I.   Tu rospo venefico
                  che suggi l'aconito
                  Tu vepre, tu radica
                  sbarbata al crepuscolo
                  Va cuoci e gorgoglia
                  Nel vaso infernal.
II.   Tu lingua di vipera[3]
                  Tu pelo di nottola
                  Tu sangue di scimia
                  Tu dente di bottolo
                  Và, bolli e t'avvoltola
                  Nel brodo infernal.

[11v]

III.   Tu dito d'un pargolo
                  Strozzato nel nascere
                  Tu labbro d'un tartaro
                  Tu cor d'un'adultera
                  Va dentro e consolida
                  La polta infernal.
Tutte (*danzando* E voi spiriti
intorno)   Negri e candidi
                  Rossi e ceruli
                  Voi che mescere
                  Ben sapete
                  Rimescete!
                  Rimescete!
                  Rimescete![4]

1. V[1] removed first two words
2. *M:* circolo possenti
3. M: vipera,
4. *M* cancelled the final "Rimescete!" and inserted it after line 3.

Scena II
Macbet e dette[1]

Mac.	Che fate or voi,[2] misteriose donne?
Streghe	Un'opra senza nome.
Mac.	Per quest'arte[3] infernale io vi scongiuro[4]
	Ch'io sappia il mio destin, se cielo e terra
	Dovessero innovar l'antica guerra.
Streghe	Dalle incognite posse udir lo vuoi
	Cui ministre obbediam, o pur da noi?
Mac.	Evocatele pur, se del futuro
	Mi possono chiarir l'enigma oscuro

[12r]

Streghe	Dalle basse, e dall'alte dimore
	Spirti erranti, salite, scendete!

(scoppia un fulmine e sorge da terra un capo coperto d'elmo)

Mac.	Dimmi o spirto...
Streghe	T'ha letto nel core
	Taci e n'odi le voci segrete.
Apparizione	O Macbetto! Macbetto! Macbetto!
	Da Macduffo ti guarda prudente

(sparisce)

Mac.	Ah[5] m'afforzi l'interno sospetto!...
	Solo un motto...
Streghe	Richieste non vuole.
	Ecco un altro di lui più possente!

(Con un colpo di tuono apparisce[6] un fanciullo insanguinato)

	Taci e n'odi le arcane[7] parole.
Apparizione	O Macbetto! Macbetto! Macbetto!
	Esser puoi sanguinario, feroce
	Nessun nato di donna ti nuoce.

(sparisce)

Macbet	La tua vita, Macduffo, perdono...
	No!.. morrai!.. Sul regale mio petto
	Doppio usbergo sarà la tua morte.

(Tuoni e lampi: sorge un fanciullo coronato che porta un arbuscello)

	Ma che annuncia quel subito tuono?[8]
	Un fanciullo col serto dei re?

12v

Streghe	Taci ed odi...
Apparizione	Stà d'animo forte
	Gloryoso, invincibil sarai
	Finchè[9] il bosco di Birnam[10] vedrai
	Ravviarsi e venir contro te.

(sparisce)

Mac. (*con gioia*) Lieto augurio! Per magica possa
Selva alcuna fin or non fu mossa.

(*alle streghe*) Or mi dite! Salire al mio soglio
La progenie di Banco dovrà?

Streghe Non cercarlo!

Mac.   Lo voglio! lo voglio
O sù voi la mia spada cadrà. [11]

(*la caldaja magica* [12] *cala sotterra*)

La caldaja è sparita? [13]...perchè?...

(*odesi un suono di cornamuse sotto terra*) [14]

Qual concento! Parlate? [15]...che v'è?

Streghe I. Apparite!

II.   Apparite!

III.   Apparite!

Tutte Poi qual nebbia di nuovo sparite

(*Otto re passano l'uno dopo l'altro: l'ultimo è Banco che ha uno specchio* [16] *in mano*)

Mac. Fuggi o regal fantasima

(*al primo*) Che Banco a me presenti! [17]
La tua corona è folgore
Gli occhi mi fai roventi...

13r

(*al secondo*) Via spaventosa immagine
Che il crin di bende hai cinto

(*alli altri*) Ed altri ancor ne sorgono?
Un terzo.... un quarto .... un quinto.... [18]
O mio terror!...dell'ultimo
Splende uno speglio in mano
E nuovi re s'attergano
Dentro al cristallo arcano.
E Banco?.. [19] ahi vista orribile
Ridendo a me gli addita?
Muori fatal progenie!
Ah! che non hai tu vita!

(*traendo la spada e avventandosi alli spettri poi s'arresta*)

*(*alle streghe*) Vivran costor? Voi ditelo

Le streghe Sarà come hai veduto!...

(*Macbetto sviene a tale annunzio*)

Streghe Rendete aerei spiriti
La mente al re svenuto

V[1] (*alle streghe*) Vivran costor?

Le Streghe   Vivranno.

Macbet   Oh me perduto!... (*Macbetto sviene a tale annunzio*)

Streghe   Ei svenne!..Aerei spiriti[20]
               Ridonate la mente al re svenuto!

(scendono li spiriti e mentre danzano intorno a Macbet le Streghe cant[an]o il seguente

1. M: *Macbeth. le precedenti*	11. An earlier, cancelled version may read "l'ira mia scenderà."
2. M[1]: Che fate qui M[2]: Che fate voi	12. M: *la caldaja*
3. M: opra	13. *M:* scomparsa
4. M: scongiuro!	14. M: (suono sotterraneo di cornamuse)
5. *M:* Tu	15. M: Parlate!
6. *M:* (*Tuona: appare*	16. M: *da ultimo vien Banco con uno specchio*
7. *M:* occulte	17. V[1]: rammenti.
8. V[1]: Ma che avvisa quel lampo, quel tuono?	18. M: Un terzo?...un quarto?...un quinto?
9. M: Sin che	19. M: E Banco!...
10. M: Birna	20. M: spirti

V

Scena III
Coro

Ondine e silfidi
 Dall'ali candide
Su quella pallida
Fronte spirate.

Tessete in vortice
 Carole armoniche
E sensi ed anima
Gli confortate.

(*Li Spiriti e le Streghe spariscono*).[1]

1. M: (*Spiriti e Streghe spariscono*).

13v

Scena IV
(*Macbet rinviene*)

Spariro![1]...Oh sia nei secoli
Maledetta quest'ora in sempiterno!
Fugge[2] il tempo, o Macbetto, e il tuo potere
Dei per opre affermare[3] non per chimere.
* Il Castello di Macduffo
      Vada in fiamme e in polve cada;

M: Vada in fiamme e in polve cada
              L'alta rocca[4] di Macduffo!

Figli, sposa a fil di spada:
Scorra il sangue a me fatal.
L'ira mia, la mia vendetta
Pel creato si diffonda
Come fiera il cor m'innonda
Come l'anima m'assal.

1. V[1]: Ove son io?...Spariro [M: Fuggiro]!...[The order of V's and M's interventions here is not certain.]
2. M: Vola
3. M: affermar
4. M recopied "Il Castello di M[acduffo]" before altering this line.

14r

ATTO IV

Luogo deserto sui confini tra Scozia ed Inghilterra.
vedrassi in distanza[1] la foresta di Birnam
Profughi Scozzesi. Uomini, donne, fanciulli
Macduff in disparte addolorato
Coro
Scena I

Patria oppressa! il dolce nome
Nò di madre aver non puoi!
Or che tutta a figli tuoi
Sei conversa in un avel.
D'orfanelli e di piangenti
Chi lo sposo e chi la prole
Al venir del novo sole
S'alza un grido e fere il ciel,
A quel grido il ciel risponde
Quasi voglia impietosito
Propagar per l'infinito
Patria oppressa, il tuo dolor.
Suona a morte ognor la squilla
Ma nessuno è audace tanto
Che pur doni un vano pianto
A chi soffre od a chi muor.

[14v]

Macduffo   O figli, o figli miei! Da quel tiranno
Tutti uccisi voi foste, e insiem con voi
* La madre ahi sventurata!... e quanti accolse
L'infelice mia rocca...E[2] fra gli artigli
Di quel tigre io lasciai la madre e i figli?...

V[1]   La madre sventurata!...Ah fra gli artigli
Di quel tigre io lasciai la madre e i figli?....

Oh la paterna mano
Non vi fù scudo, o cari,

Dai perfidi sicari
Che a morte vi ferir!
E me fuggiasco occulto
Voi chiamavate invano
Coll'ultimo singulto
Coll'ultimo respir.
Trammi al tiranno in faccia
Signore! e s'ei mi sfugge
Possa a colui le braccia
Del tuo perdono aprir.[3]

1. M: *Luogo deserto ai confini dalla Scozia e dall'Inghilterra. In distanza*
2. V[1]: Ah
3. These four lines were added later by V.

Scena II
A suon di tamburro entra Malcolmo conducendo molti soldati inglesi

Malcol.	Dove siam? che bosco è quello?
Coro	La foresta di Birnamo
Malcol.	Porti ognuno un verde ramo,[1]
	Che lo asconda, innanzi a se.
(*a Macduf*)	Ti conforti la vendetta
Macduff	Non l'avrò....di figli è privo!
Malcol. (*al popolo*)	Chi non odia il suol nativo
	Prenda l'armi e segua me.

*(Malcolmo e Macduffo
impugnano le spade)*

[15r]

V   *Tutti*

La patria tradita
Piangendo ne invita
Fratelli! gli oppressi
Corriamo a salvar!
Già l'ira divina
Sull'empio ruïna:
Gli orribili eccessi
L'Eterno stancâr.

1. V[1]: Ognun svelga e porti un ramo
   V[2]: Svelga ognuno e porti un ramo

Scena III
*Sala nel castello di Macbet come nell'Atto 1°
Un Medico e Dama di Lady[1]*

Medi.	Vegliammo invan due notti
Dama	In questa apparirà.
Medi.	Di che parlava
	Nel sonno suo?

333

Dama	Ridirlo
	Non debbo ad uom che viva...[2]

1. M: *Medico e Dama di Lady Macbeth* [*Un* cancelled]
2. M: che viva...Eccola!...

Scena IV
Lady e detti[1]

Medi.	Un lume
	Recasi in man?
Dama	La lampada che sempre
	Tiensi a canto del letto.
Medi.	Oh come gli occhi

[15v]

	Spalanca!
Dama	E pur non vede
Medi.	Perchè sfrega la man?
Dama	Lavarsi crede!
Lady	Una macchia è qui tuttora....
	Via, ti dico, o maledetta!...
	Una...due...gli è questa l'ora!....
	Tremi tu?...non osi entrar?
	Un guerrier così codardo?
	Oh vergogna!...or sù t'affretta!...
	Chi poteva in quel vegliardo
	Tanto sangue immaginar?
Medico	Che parlò?...
Lady	Di Fife il sire
	Sposo e padre or or non era?...
	Che n'avvenne?...e mai pulire
	Queste mani io non saprò?....
Dama e Medi.	Oh terror!...
Lady	Di sangue umano
	Sa qui sempre...Arabia intera
	Rimondar sì piccol mano

[16r]

Lady	Ohimè!...
Medi.	Geme?
Lady	I panni indossa
	Della notte...oh pria ti sbratta...
	* Banco è spento, e dalla fossa
	Più risorger non può!...
Medico	Questo ancora?
Lady	Batte alcuno!... a letto a letto...[2]
	Sfar non puoi la cosa fatta
	Vieni meco!..ogni sospetto
	Rimoviam dall'uccisor.
Dama e Medico	Signor pietà di lei...[3]

V[1]		* Banco è spento, e dalla fossa
		Più risorgere non può!...
	Medico	Questo ancora?
	Lady	a letto a letto...
		Sfar non puoi la cosa fatta...
		Batte alcuno! oh vien Macbetto...
		Così smorto io non ti vuò.
	Dama e Medico	Ah soccorso a questa misera
		Dia la man che tutto può!

M		Banco è spento, e dalla fossa
		Chi morì non surse ancor
	Med.	Questo a giunta?[4]
	Led.	a letto a letto....
		Sfar non puoi la cosa fatta...
		Batte alcuno! andiam Macbetto
		Non t'accusi il tuo pallor.
	Dama e Med.	Ah di lei, pietà, Signor.

1. M: *Ledy Macbeth e precedenti*

2. "Questo ancora?" and "Batte alcuno!" seem to be alternative versions of the first part of this line.

3. This unmetrical line may be an early version from the prose *selva*. Apparently it was within this layer that Verdi first replaced it with "Ah di lei pietà Signor!."

4. M[1]: Questo a presso?

V	*Scena IV* [*recte* V]
	Sala nel castello
	Macbet
	Perfidi! all'anglo contro me v'unite!
	Le potenze presaghe han profetato
	"Esser puoi sanguinario feroce
	Nessun nato di donna ti nuoce".
	No! non temo di voi, nè del fanciullo
	Che vi conduce!...Raffermar sul trono
	Questo assalto mi debbe,
	O sbalzarmi per sempre...E pur la vita
	Sento nelle mie fibre inaridita!....

[16v]

V	L'amore, il pio rispetto
	Che i tardi anni consola
	Non aspettar, Macbetto
	Nella tua grave età.

M	Pietà, rispetto amore
	Gioja degl'ultim'anni[1]
	Non spargeran d'un fiore
	La tua canuta età.

V   Nè sul tuo regio sasso
                  Sperar mite parola.[2]
                  Sol la bestemmia, ahi lasso!
                  La nenia tua sarà.

* (*grida di dentro*) La Regina!...
Macb.   Qual grido?

1. M^1: Conforto agl'ultim'anni
M^2: Conforto ai dì cadenti [At the same time M^2 changed the corresponding line in the second quatrain to "Sperar soavi accenti."]

2. See preceding note.

Scena V [*recte* VI]
Dama della Regina e detto

Dama   Finita
          La Regina ha la vita!
Macbet   La vita!

V^1 (*grida*[1] *di dentro*) La Regina!...[2]
Macb.   Qual gemito?

Scena V [*recte* VI]
Dama della Regina e detto[3]

Dama   È morta
          La Regina!
Macbet[4]   La vita! che importa!....

V   È il racconto d'un povero idiota
            Vento e suono che nulla dinota.

1. *M: grida interne* [The changes described in notes 1–4 may possibly precede Verdi's revision.]
2. *M:* Ella è morta   3. *M: e Macbeth*   4. *M:* (*pensoso*)

Scena VI [*recte* VII]
Coro di guerrieri. Macbet

Coro   Sire! ah Sire!
Mac.   Che fù?...quali nove?...
Coro   La foresta di Birna si muove!
Mac. (*attonito*) M'hai deluso presagio infernale!..

[17r]

          Qui l'usbergo, la spada, il pugnale.
     * Prodi all'armi! altro scampo non v'è!
Coro   Dumque all'armi!..altro scampo non v'è!

V^1 Prodi all'armi! la morte, o la gloria.
            Dumque all'armi! sì morte o vittoria.

V   (*odesi suono di*[1] *trombe e tamburri. Intanto la scena si muta e presenta una vasta pianura. Il fondo è occupato da soldati inglesi i quali lentamente si avvanzano portando ciascheduno una fronda innanzi a sé*)
          Malcolmo, e Macduff e Soldati

1. M: (*Suono di*
   V¹: (*Suono interno di* [The order of these interventions may be reversed.]

Scena VII [*recte* VIII] ¹

Malc.   Via le fronde e mano all'armi!
        Mi seguite!...

(*Malcolmo e Macduff e Soldati
partono lasciando vuota la
scena*)²

Grida interne   All'armi! all'armi!...

(*di dentro odesi il fragore della
battaglia*)

1. Maffei corrects "Scena VII" to "Scena VIII" (Verdi had written "Scena IV" for two successive scenes).
2. The final four words are cancelled, probably by Maffei.

Scena VIIII
Macbet incalzato da Macduff

Macduff   T'ho giunto alfin carnefice
          De' figli miei!
Macbet   Fatato
          Son io! non può traffiggermi
          Chi dalla donna è nato.
Macduff   * Nato io non son, ma tolto
          Dall'alvo io fui.
Macbet   Che ascolto....

(*Combattono. Macbet cade
ferito*)

V¹   Macduff   Nato io non son, ma tolto
                Fui dal materno sen.
      Macbet   * Tutto m'inganna! oh stolto!   (*brandendo la spada*)
                Tu non tradirmi almeno!

(*Combattono. Macbet cade
ferito*)

M   Macbeth   Misero me! che ascolto?
                Ah! tu mi resti almen!

(*Combattono. Macbet
cade ferito*¹)

---

1. M cancels "ferito"

[17v]

V   *Scena Ultima*
      *I precedenti. Malcolmo seguito da soldati inglesi i quali
      si trascinano dietro prigionieri quelli di Macbet*
      Malcol.   Vittoria!...ove s'è fitto
                L'usurpator?

337

Macduff		Trafitto![1]	(*accennando*[2])
Macbet		* Maledetto chi s'affida	(*alzandosi*[3] *da terra*)
		Ne' presagi dell'inferno!...	
		Mille oppressi alzar le grida...	
		Mi colpì[4] lo sdegno eterno....	
		Muojo...al cielo...al mondo in ira	
		Vil corona!...e sol per te!...	(*muore*)

V[1]	Macbet	Mal per me che m'affidai
		Nei presagi dell'inferno!
		Tutto il sangue ch'io versai
		Grida in faccia dell'eterno![5]
		Sulla fronte maledetta
		Folgorò[6] la sua vendetta.
		Muojo...al cielo...al mondo in ira
		Vil corona!...e sol per te!

Macduff	Scozia afflitta, omai respira!
	Or Malcolmo è il tuo buon re![7]

[18r-v blank]

1. Apparently the line was originally an *endecasillabo* beginning with "L'usurpator" and ending with "trafitto," for the "t" was at first lower case. Macduff's words preceding "trafitto" were crossed out and cannot be reconstructed.

2. M: (accennando Macbeth)

3. M: (alzandosi a stento)

4. V[1]: Mi atterrò

5. There follow two cancelled and illegible lines.

6. M: Sfolgorò

7. M: il nostro re!

THE 1865 LIBRETTO DRAFTS

In addition to Verdi's correspondence from 1864–65, other source material relevant to the revision of *Macbeth* can be found at Sant'Agata. We are grateful to Francesco Degrada for contributing his initial transcriptions of these documents and convey his gratitude to Dr. Gabriella Carrara-Verdi for making these sources available to him and for valuable assistance. We add our own thanks to her for allowing us to reproduce this material here.

Verdi wrote out these "lines to be added to the libretto of *Macbeth*" on the back of a draft of a letter of recommendation for Piave. The text of these snippets is virtually identical to the text that Piave later transcribed into a printed Ricordi libretto of *Macbeth I* (see following item) and, with a few minor exceptions, to the text Verdi set to music. In this final stage Lenosse became an "araldo"—since Lenox had only this one line there was little point in giving him a name—and Verdi reverted to the simple announcement "La Regina," crossed out on the page shown above.[1]

1. Two other changes may be relegated to a footnote. (i) In both the 1847 and the 1865 versions, Verdi set the line "Che fate voi misteriose donne"; the omission of the "voi" in both Verdi's jottings shown here and in the line as transcribed by Piave is probably an oversight, as it renders the line unmetrical. (ii) The word "fuggiro!" (in Macbeth's first line after the chorus) was replaced by "svaniro" in the text that Verdi set to music.

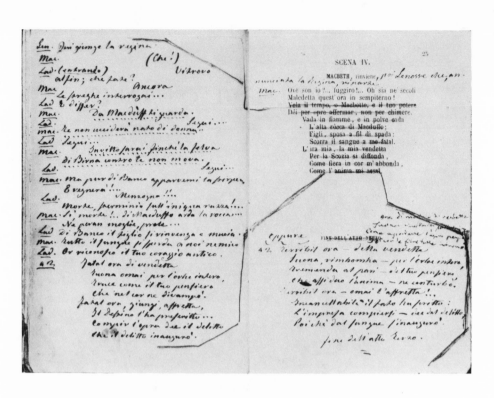

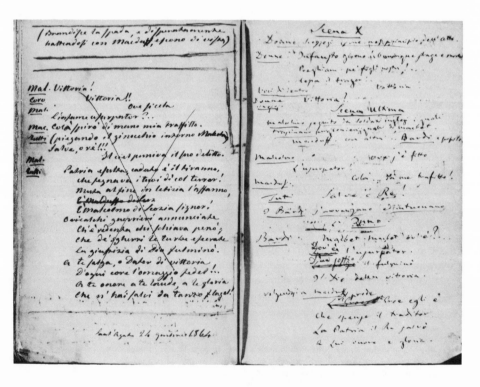

Verdi and Piave transcribed all the revised text into a printed Ricordi libretto of *Macbeth* I.[2] This copy, probably provided by Ricordi for the purpose, has a blank page facing every page of printed text. After transcribing his text for the final chorus, Piave wrote "Sant'Agata 24 gennaio 1864" (*recte* 1865). The other scenes must have been copied earlier, however—the first one shown here must precede Verdi's ca.13 January 1865 letter, for by then Verdi had already rejected the quatrains in *ottonario* meter (beginning "Fatal ora di vendetta"—bottom of the left-hand page). Everything but the quatrain in Verdi's hand (right-hand side, middle of the page) was written by Piave. The recitative lines are virtually identical to those appearing in the definitive libretto and score of *Macbeth II*; for transcriptions of Piave's rejected *versi lirici* see the notes to the ca.13 January 1865 letter.

The libretto also includes the text of Lady Macbeth's new aria in Act II (see the notes to the letters of ca.18 and of 20 December 1864), Macbeth's lines after the Act III ballet (see "Versi da aggiungere," p. 339), and the end of Act IV (see the notes to Verdi's 28 January 1865 letter and the following transcription).

The lower illustration shows the end of Act IV as Piave and Verdi apparently conceived it as of 24 January 1865. On 28 January 1865, Verdi sent Piave another version to replace it, and he also copied this new version into the libretto (right-hand page of the reproduction). For the sketches leading to this stage, see the next item; for a transcription of this text (and of the subsequent corrections made even later), see the 28 January 1865 letter. A transcription of Piave's lines on the left hand page follows.

[Mac.   Cielo!]
(Brandisce la spada, e disperatamente battendosi con Macduff, escono di vista)

Mal.   Vittoria!

Coro.   Vittoria!!

Mal.   Ove si cela
l'infame usurpator?...

Mac.   Colà spirò di mano mia trafitto.

Tutti   (piegando il ginocchio intorno Malcolmo)
Salve, o rè!!!

Mal.   Il ciel puniva il suo delitto.

Tutti   Patria esulta, caduto è il tiranno,
        che segnava i tuoi dì col terror!
        Muta alfine in letizia l'affanno,
        È Malcolmo di Scozia signor![3]

      Oricalchi guerrieri annunciate
        Ch'è redenta chi schiava penò,
        Che de' sgherri le turbe esecrate
        la giustizia di Dio fulminò.

      A te salga, o Dator di vittoria
        D'ogni core l'omaggio fedel!...
        A te onore, a te laude, a te gloria
        Che n'hai salvi da tanto flagel!

      Sant'Agata 24 gennaio 1864 [*recte* 1865]

---

2. "MACBETH / Melodramma in quattro parti di F. M. Piave / Musica del M.º Cav. Giuseppe Verdi / Ufficiale della Legion d'Onore / [decoration] / Milano / Regio Stabilimento Nazionale / Tito di Gio: Ricordi." On page 7 the date "7-64" is printed.

3. Piave wrote "E Macduffo di Scoz[ia]" before noting his slip.

SKETCHES FOR THE INNO DI VITTORIA

These sketches appear on the same sheet as the draft of a letter from Verdi to Tito Ricordi, dated "Busseto Sant'Agata 22 Gennaio 1865." The text labelled "G" is in Giuseppina's hand; that labelled "V," in Verdi's. Because of the difficulty in deciphering the manuscript, the reconstruction of the text and especially of the order in which the various layers were written must be regarded as conjectural. The transcription is considered quatrain by quatrain, numbered 1 to 7, followed by an eighth, unused stanza.

— 1 —

G   [Bardi]   Macbet Macbet ov'è?
Sparì l'usurpator
Lo spense l'anniento[4]
Il Dio della vittoria[5]

4. V: il fulminò

5. With the correction, this stanza is identical to its counterpart in Verdi's 28 January 1865 letter and in the text Verdi copied into the printed *Macbeth I* libretto. (However, further changes were subsequently made in the libretto.)

— 2 —

V Plaudiam al nuovo Re[6]
Che spense il traditor[7]
La patria a noi[8] salvò
A Lui fia[?] gloria[9]

6. V[1]: L'Eroe L'Eroe tu se'
   V[2]: L'Eroe Macduff tu se'
   V[3]: L'Eroe Macduff Egli è

7. After this line Verdi has written and cancelled:
   Sien grazie al ciel [illegible]

8. V[1]: il Re

9. V[1]: A Lui onor e gloria
   V[2]: Suonate [a fresh start, immediately cancelled]
   V[3]: s'innalz'inno [di] gloria
   V[4]: A Lui onore e gloria

It is not clear how the following long line, transcribed below the quatrain, was meant to fit in: "S'innalz'un canto a Lui che ci salvò" (cancelled and replaced by "Cantiam. la patria il Re che a noi salvò." In any event, the image of singing was not used until a later stanza; with the exception of a minor change in the first line, the corrected version of this quatrain corresponds to that found in Verdi's 28 January 1865 letter.

— 3 —

V Macbet Macbet ov'è
Sparì l'usurpator!
Cessate il duol! Lo spense[10]
Il Dio della vittoria[11]

10. V[1]: Lo spense il fulminò

11. The corrected version is identical to the first stanza; it is not repeated in either the letter or libretto.

— 4 —

V [donne] Salgan mie grazie a te
Gran Dio vendicator
In gaudio il duol cangiò
A te lode a te gloria[12]

G donne Salgan mie grazie a te
Gran Dio vendicator
Chi l'empio eliminò[13]
Onore s'abbia e gloria[14]

12. Verdi probably planned to start this quatrain with the line "Ciascuno confida in te," which is written in ink, like the previous quatrain. The present quatrain, however, written "through" it, is in pencil, as is the unused opening couplet at the top of the following page: "Fidenti [illegible] in me / Per voi cessò il terror."

13. V[1]: A chi ci liberò

14. V[1]: Inni cantiam di gloria; the variously corrected version of the quatrain, written out again in ink at foot of the second page, is identical with its counterpart in Verdi's 28 January 1865 letter.

— 5 —

G	[Malcolmo]	Servi fidate in me Avrete gloria e amor Un Dio l'eroe guidò A Lui donò vittoria.
G[1]		Popol confida in me Ti darò pace e amor[15] Splenderà[16]
V		Popol confida in me Risorga il prisco onor A Lui che si[?] salvò Onore, laude, e gloria[17]

15. V[1]: Ora tu avrai amor [possibly pace e amor; neither reading is metrical]
    V[2]: Pace [?] darovvi e amor
    V[3]: Risorga il prisco onor

16. Giuseppina breaks off after this incomplete line.

17. This version of the quatrain, assembled at the very end of the draft, was abandoned before Verdi's 28 January 1865 letter.

— 6 —

V [Soldati?] Grande Macduff tu sei
Spegnesti[18]

V[1] Ah si l'eroe Egli è![19]
Che spense il traditor
La patria il Re salvo [*sic*]
A Lui onore è [*sic*] gloria[20]

18. Verdi breaks off after this incomplete line.

19. The change may have occurred in two stages.

20. The corrected quatrain is identical to the soldiers' stanza in the 28 January letter.

— 7 —

V Fidi ciascun[21] in me
Pace darogli [?] e amor[22]
Giorno novel schiarò
Il dio della vittoria[23]

— 8 —

V Siate fida
Un dio ci liberò
A Lui onore e gloria[24]

21. Verdi began "Fidi in s" but changed to "Fidi ciascun" immediately.

22. Verdi began the second line "Avrete pace" but broke off and began again.

23. This stanza may have been intended as a second quatrain for Malcolm or a replacement for the one beginning "Popol confida in me." It was discarded before Verdi's January 28 letter.

24. An unused fragment of another stanza

A NOTE ON SHAKESPEARE'S *MACBETH*

August Wilhelm Schlegel

To Carlo Rusconi's translation of Shakespeare's Macbeth (Turin, 1838), the principal source of Verdi's libretto, was appended the following "Nota al Macbeth" taken from August Wilhelm Schlegel's celebrated and influential Course of Lectures on Dramatic Art and Literature, delivered in Vienna in 1808 and published, with additions, in 1809 and 1811. Schlegel's lectures were published in Italian translation, by Giovanni Gherardini, in 1817. Rusconi similarly appended observations by Schlegel to his translations of Romeo and Juliet, The Tempest, and Othello—which, together with Julius Caesar, make up the first volume of his "Complete Shakespeare," in which Macbeth is the first play.

The English translation of Schlegel below is based on that of John Black, revised by A. J. W. Morrison (London: Henry G. Bohn, 1846), but has here been revised again to represent in English what Verdi read in Italian. The extent to which it influenced his thinking about Macbeth will be evident to any reader of this volume. See, in particular, DEGRADA and the preface to the Ricordi "standard" libretto which follows this note.

This is how one of the best German critics expresses himself about *Macbeth:*

Of *Macbeth* I have already spoken once in passing, and who could exhaust the praises of this sublime work? Since *The Eumenides* of Aeschylus, nothing so grand and terrible has ever been written. The witches are not, it is true, infernal divinities, and are not intended to be: they are ignoble and vulgar instruments of hell. A German poet,[1] therefore, went strangely astray, when he sought to give them tragic dignity and transformed them into mongrel beings, a mixture of fates, furies and enchantresses. No man can lay hand on Shakespeare without bearing the penalty of his audacity: the bad is radically odious, and to endeavor to ennoble it, is to violate the laws of propriety. Hence, in my opinion, Dante, and even Tasso, have been much more successful in their portraiture of daemons than Milton. Whether the age of Elizabeth still believed in ghosts and witches, is a matter of perfect indifference for the justification of the use which in *Hamlet* and *Macbeth* Shakespeare has made of popular traditions. No superstition can be preserved and diffused through many centuries and among diverse people without having a foundation in human nature; and on this the poet builds. He calls up from their hidden abysses that dread of the unknown, that secret presage of a dark side of nature and of a world of spirits. In this manner he is in some degree like both the portrayer and the philosopher of superstition; that is, not like the philosopher who denies and turns it into ridicule, but what is still rarer among men, like a thinker who distinctly exhibits its origin in so many opinions at once so disagreeable and yet so natural.

---

1. Schiller, whose adaptation of *Macbeth* was first performed at Weimar in 1800. Goethe, the stage director and designer of this famous production, also worked over the text. In this version, Macbeth was "a consistently noble figure, a guiltless victim of fate, which was personified by the three witches, played by men in classic robes," with songs "suggestive of Greek odes." The Schiller *Macbeth* was published in 1801, and Andrea Maffei's Italian translation of it in 1863. It has on occasion been claimed that Schiller's conception influenced Verdi's; and that claim has also been disallowed (see pp. 146-47, and 353-55). For this influential Schiller production and its revivals, see Marvin Carlson, *Goethe and the Weimar Theatre* (Ithaca, 1978).

If Shakespeare had ventured to make arbitrary changes in these popular traditions, he would have forfeited his right to them, and his most ingenious inventions would have seemed mere idle fancies. His picture of the witches has a certain magical quality: he has created for them a particular language, which, although composed of the usual elements, still seems to be a collection of formulae of incantation. The accumulation of rhymes, and the rhythmus of the verse, form, as it were, the hollow music of the nocturnal dances of these tenebrous beings. He has been abused for using the names of disgusting objects; but who has ever imagined that the magic kettle of the witches was filled with agreeable aromatics? That would be kin, as the poet says, to desiring that hell should give good counsel. These repulsive things, from which the imagination shrinks, are here emblems of the hostile powers which ferment in nature's breast; and the repugnance of our senses is outweighed by the mental horror. With one another the witches discourse like women of the very lowest class; for this was the class to which witches were ordinarily supposed to belong: when, however, they address Macbeth they assume a loftier tone: their predictions, which they either themselves pronounce, or allow their apparitions to deliver, have all the obscure brevity, the majestic solemnity of oracles, such as have ever spread terror among mortals. We here see that these enchantresses are merely instruments; they are governed by invisible spirits, or the operation of such great and dreadful events would be above their sphere. With what intent did Shakespeare assign the same place to them in his play, which they occupy in the history of Macbeth as related in the old chronicles? A monstrous crime is committed: Duncan, a venerable old man, and the best of kings, is, in defenseless sleep, under the hospitable roof, murdered by his subject, whom he has loaded with honors and rewards. Natural motives alone seem inadequate to explain such a deed, or the perpetrator must have been portrayed as the blackest and most hardened of villains. Shakespeare wished to exhibit a more sublime picture: he portrayed a noble but ambitious hero, yielding to a deep-laid hellish temptation, and in whom all the crimes to which, in order to secure the fruits of his first crime, he is impelled by necessity, cannot altogether eradicate the stamp of native heroism. Duncan's death is fully Macbeth's responsibility; but what is more hateful about it falls on the heads of those who instigated the horrid action. The first idea comes from those beings whose whole activity is guided toward wickedness. The witches surprise Macbeth in the intoxication of glory, after a battle in which he was victorious; they dazzle his eyes by exhibiting to him as the work of fate a vision of splendors that he can attain by a path of crime; and they gain credence for their words by the immediate fulfillment of an earlier prediction. The opportunity of murdering the King immediately offers; Lady Macbeth conjures her husband not to let it slip. She urges him on with a fiery eloquence, which has at command all those sophisms that can throw a false splendor over such a crime; and Macbeth, not master of himself, commits it in a tumult of fascination. Repentance immediately follows, nay even precedes the deed, and the stings of conscience leave him rest neither night nor day. But he is now fairly entangled in the snares of hell; truly frightful is it to behold that same Macbeth, who once as a warrior could spurn at death, now that he dreads the prospect of the life to come, clinging with growing anxiety to his earthly existence the more miserable it becomes, and pitilessly removing out of the way whatever to his dark and suspicious mind seems to threaten danger. Although we may abhor his actions, we cannot refuse to compassionate the state of his mind. We lament the ruin of his noble qualities; and nevertheless we admire even in his last defense the struggle of a brave will with a cowardly conscience.

It seems that the Destiny of the ancients rules again in this tragedy. From the very first scene, a supernatural influence manifests itself; and the first event to which it gives rise inevitably draws all the other events in its train. Here, in particular, are those ambiguous oracles which, by their literal fulfillment, deceive those who confide in them. Yet more enlightened views than those of paganism inspired this work. The poet wished to show that the conflict of good and evil in this world can only take place by the permission of Providence, which converts the curse that individual mortals draw down on their heads into universal blessings.

At the close, the poet distributes retribution to all his characters with an accurate measure. Lady Macbeth, who of all the participators in the king's murder is the most guilty, is thrown by the terrors of her conscience into a state of incurable bodily and mental disease. She dies unlamented by her husband, with all the symptoms of despair. Macbeth is still found worthy to die the death of a hero on the field of battle. The noble Macduff, his country's liberator, is allowed the satisfaction of saving his country by punishing with his own hand the tyrant who had murdered his wife and children. Banquo, the object of Macbeth's jealousy, by an early death atones for the ambitious curiosity which prompted his wish to know his glorious descendants; but as he preserved his mind pure from the evil suggestions of the witches, his name is blessed in his race, destined to enjoy for a long succession of ages that royal dignity which Macbeth could only hold for his own brief life. In the progress of the action, this tragedy is altogether the reverse of *Hamlet*: it strides forward with terrible rapidity from the first catastrophe (Duncan's murder) to the ending; and all designs are scarcely conceived but they are put into action.

In every feature of this vigorous design we see an energetic age, in the hardy North which breeds men of iron. The precise duration of the action cannot easily be ascertained: several years perhaps, according to the history; but we know that to the imagination the most crowded time appears always the shortest; and what has here been compressed into so narrow a space—not merely external events, but the very minds of the dramatic personages—is truly prodigious.

It is as if the drags were taken from the wheels of time, and they rolled along without interruption in their descent. Nothing can equal this picture in its power to excite terror. We need only allude to the murder of Duncan, the phantom dagger that hovers before the eyes of Macbeth, the vision of Banquo at the feast, the nocturnal entry of Lady Macbeth, walking in her sleep. Such scenes stand alone; only Shakespeare could have conceived them: and if they were more often played in the theatre, the Tragic Muse would be compelled to count the head of Medusa among her attributes.

Rusconi's excerpt ends at this point, but the notice in the Ricordi libretto of Macbeth *(see next item) includes a paraphrase of what follows in Schlegel: "I wish merely to point out as a secondary circumstance the prudent dexterity of Shakespeare, who could still contrive to flatter a king by a work in every part of whose plan nevertheless the poetical views are evident. James the First drew his lineage from Banquo . . . " etc. Whoever its author may have been—Maffei seems a likely candidate—he evidently knew more of Schlegel than what appears in Rusconi.*

THE PREFACE
IN THE
RICORDI LIBRETTO

As early as spring 1848, Ricordi's printed "standard" libretto of Macbeth[1] included this preliminary note:[2]

Macbeth, Duncan's general, returning from a war in which he distinguished himself, fighting the rebels and the King of Norway, was in the intoxication of his glory surprised by witches who dazzled his eyes with a vision, presented as a prophecy, of grandeur which he could attain to only by a criminal path. Prompted by his wife, he did not delay to stain himself with the blood of the best of kings and that of a friend; he mounted the throne using the heads of a thousand victims as his footstool; but he found on the battlefield and beneath Macduff's sword his deserved punishment.

Shakespeare took the idea of his play from the Scottish chronicles that tell of the general's meeting with the witches. Taking advantage of history, like an imaginative poet, he had these extraordinary beings predict the future with the majestic solemnity that is found in all oracular pronouncements and cloaks the truth beneath the aspect of the miraculous. "Beware Macduff," the sorceresses intimate, indicating the plot that they would see woven against a gallant soldier who does not tolerate Macbeth's triumph. "Thou mayst be bloody, ferocious, no man born of woman will harm thee" they intone to his ear, meaning that he will fall at the hand of a man not born but ripped from the maternal womb; and, at last, they promise him, "Thou shalt be glorious and invincible until thou seest Birnam Wood rise up and come against thee," indicating by that a shrewd martial device of his foes, who would use the branches of the forest as a screen for a numerous force. But Shakespeare had another political intent: to flatter James I. The son of the unhappy Mary Stuart traced his origin from Banquo and was the first to unite the three crowns of England, Scotland, and Ireland; and therefore we see him pass with the visible sign of this triple power in the magic procession of the cavern, and he is promised a long series of successors.

Yet there is a section of the public that, while not supposing that tragic dignity is compromised by the specter of Ninus or of the daughter of Aristodemus, consider Lemurs and Lamias the unworthy fantasies of an uncivilized nation's drama. Whether the men of Elizabeth's age believed in spirits and magic or not is a question quite irrelevant to the use

1. Plate number 19350. Ricordi printed a libretto for theatres that were not prevented by censorship from using the "standard text." To this would be attached a sheet (four pages) with the date, name of the theatre, cast, staff, etc.

2. For discussion of this preliminary note, see DEGRADA at 158.

the English poet made of them. Certainly no superstition could maintain itself and be diffused through many centuries if it did not have a foundation in the human heart; and it was to this that the poet directed himself. From the abysses he evoked the fear of the unknown, the secret presentiment of a mysterious part of nature, of an invisible world around us. For him, the witches are instruments governed by invisible spirits; by themselves they would not be able to rise to the sphere whence they influence events no less grand than terrible.

These preliminary observations seem worth making, because there are some—those whose passion for reason blinds them, as a modern critic has put it, to the intelligence of poetic reason—who do not wish to be persuaded that a kind of poetry such as that of *Macbeth* arises from the "miraculous" (the "miraculous" of Shakespeare's times as of ours, and as of those of the greatest masters of antiquity) and becomes absurd if it is derived from any sources other than contemporary beliefs and popular traditions. [3]

---

3. Hilary Gatti ("Shakespeare nei teatri milanesi dell'ottocento," *Biblioteca di Studi Inglesi*, 12 [Bari: Adriatica, 1968], 19) considers that these comments reveal a detailed knowledge of the Shakespearean tragedy, and in the original English, as well as a knowledge of the political situation in which the drama was written, and regards the comments on the witches as the best to be found in all of nineteenth-century Italy. Unfortunately, he attributes the authorship of this prefatory note to Piave. For the preface that Piave wished to have attached to the *Macbeth* libretto, see his letter to Ricordi of 28 January 1847.

VERDI AND
THE ITALIAN TRANSLATIONS
OF SHAKESPEARE'S *MACBETH*

Andrew Porter

In his famous letter of 28 April 1865 to Léon Escudier, Verdi, accused by the Paris critics of not knowing his Shakespeare, said, "He is a favorite poet of mine, whom I have had in my hands from earliest youth and whom I read and reread constantly." He did not know English. In the bookshelf beside his bed at Sant'Agata there stood—and still stand—the Shakespeare translations of Carlo Rusconi (first published in 1838) and of Giulio Carcano (first published 1843–53). By 1847, the following Italian translations of *Macbeth* had appeared:

Opere drammatiche di Shakespeare volgarizzate [in prose] da una dama veneta [Giustina Renier Michiel] (Venice: Giacomo Costantini, 1798–1800) (The three volumes contained *Othello, Macbeth,* and *Coriolanus;* there was an earlier issue of Vol. 1, "da una cittadina veneta," in 1797.)

Macbetto, tragedia di Guglielmo Shakespeare, recata in versi italiani da Michele Leoni di Parma (Pisa: Niccolò Capurro, 1815) (In 1820 [see below], Leoni published a revised version of *Macbeth* along with the other tragedies, in which the language is less archaic, and Lady Macbeth is no longer named Margherita.[1])

Macbet, tragedia ... recata con alcune variazioni in versi italiani da W. E. Frye, inglese (Mannheim, 1827)

Tragedie di Shakespeare tradotte in endecasillabi da Michele Leoni (Verona, 1819–22)

Opere ... tradotte da Giunio Bazzoni e Giacomo Sormani (Milan: Vincenzo Ferrario, 1830)

Macbet, Tragedia di Guglielmo Shakspeare recata in italiano da Giuseppe Nicolini (Brescia: Francesco Cavalieri, 1830)

Teatro Completo di Shakespeare tradotto [in prose] da Carlo Rusconi (Padua: La Minerva, 1838)

The question of which versions were used in the making of *Macbeth* is discussed by WEAVER and DEGRADA. That Verdi himself read Shakespeare in Rusconi's prose translation becomes swiftly apparent to anyone who scans that version. (He used it again when working on his *King Lear, Otello,* and *Falstaff* librettos.) Evidence of verbal parallels, both in 1846–47 and again in 1864–65, is set out in our footnotes to Verdi's letters to Piave of 25 and 29 October, and 3 and 10 December 1846, and those of c. 13 December 1864 and mid-January 1865 (the last placed after a 10 January letter). Moreover, in the letter of mid-January 1865 Verdi urges Piave to use "his [Shakespeare's] very words" and then cites words ("Ora di morte,"

---

1. According to Lord Haile's *Annals of Scotland,* 2: 332, her name in history was Gruach.

etc.) that appear only in Rusconi, not in Shakespeare nor in any other Italian translation.

WEAVER (at 146) suggests that in versifying the composer's *selva* Piave had recourse, too, to Leoni's verse translation. Daniela Goldin ("Il *Macbeth* verdiano," 361) makes the same point:

LEONI: Un verro/A sgozzar mi recai [I.3]
RUSCONI: Ad offrire in olocausto un cinghiale
LIBRETTO: Ho sgozzato un verro [I.1]

LEONI: or pari alle tue lorde ho le mani [II.2]
RUSCONI: le mie mani rosseggiano come le tue
LIBRETTO: Le mani ho lorde anch'io [I.14]

LEONI: di doppio usbergo vo' armato [IV.1]
RUSCONI: mi sia la tua morte duplice garante di sicurezza
LIBRETTO: Doppio usbergo sarà la tua morte [III.2]

Incidentally, the first citation indicates that Piave used Leoni's later, 1820 text; in the 1815 version his First Witch kills a "majale," not a "verro." Piave also owned, or at least consulted, the Nicolini version, for he quotes from its preface in the "preliminary note" he sent to Giovanni Ricordi on 28 January 1847 (pp. 38–39). For an instance of specific recourse to Nicolini's lines, see p. 456.

In 1848, a year after the opera's first performance, Carcano published the third volume of his *Teatro scelto di Shakespeare* (Milan: Pirola, 1843–53), containing *Macbeth;* the preface is dated 4 March 1848. There are some parallels between this and the libretto, and to account for them it has been suggested that the translation was prepared much earlier and that, consulted in manuscript, it influenced Piave's versification of Verdi's sketch. Giuseppe Vecchi has pointed out to us such passages as:

RUSCONI: Oh Duncano! non udirlo questo squillo ferale, che funebre
        t'appella nel regno degli estinti. (II.1)
CARCANO: Oh! non udirlo,
        O Duncan, questo suono; egli è lo squillo
        Che ti chiama nel cielo o nell'inferno.
LIBRETTO: Non udirlo Duncano. È squillo eterno
        Che nel cielo ti chiama, o nell'inferno! (I.11)

RUSCONI: . . . rivolgila a più possente visione. (IV.1)
CARCANO: Eccone un altro, e più possente.
LIBRETTO: Ecco un altro di lui più possente (III.2)

But a simpler reading of the evidence, given the chronology, is that the libretto influenced Carcano's translation. The lines above are from his original 1848 text; he produced a revised edition in 1857–58 (Florence: le Monnier). When Adelaide Ristori and Ernesto Rossi took Shakespeare's *Macbeth* into their repertories, in the 1850s, they used a revised version of the Carcano translation brought closer to the libretto of the opera; see WEAVER at 148.

All the Italian translators seem to have had trouble with the witches' exchange at the start of IV.1:

I: Thrice the brinded Cat hath mew'd.

II: Thrice, and once the Hedge-Pigge whin'd.

III: Harpier cries, 'tis time, 'tis time.

In editions from 1709 to 1883, the First Folio's "Harpier" became "Harper." Steevens suggested "Harpy." *Rusconi* has:

I.   Tre volte il gatto-tigre ha miagolata.

II.   Tre volte ha gemuto la nottola dei sepolcri.

III. Una musica surge dalle viscere della terra, e ci dice: È tempo, è tempo!

Carcano, noting Steevens' emendation, has:

    I.   Il gatto macolato

           Tre volte miagolò,

    II.   E il porcospin l'usato

           Guair tre volte alzò.—

    III. Un arpeggìo qui sento:

           Ecco il momento.

The libretto has:

I: Tre volte miagola la gatta in fregola.

II: Tre volte l'upupa lamenta ed ulula.

III: Tre volte l'istrice guaisce al vento.

All: Questo è il momento. (III.1)

Metrically and verbally, the last line suggests, again, that Carcano remembered the libretto when he came to make his translation. As for the birds and the beasts: that unShakespearean owl has evidently flown in from Rusconi; the hedgepig, missing in Rusconi, has been adduced as evidence that the librettists must have seen the (unpublished) Carcano, but in fact the creature was already present both in Nicolini and in Leoni, who has (1820): "Tre volte/Sua lamentosa voce il riccio mise." For the variously-colored spirits of the cavern scene—and another instance of the libretto's conflating material from various translated sources—see 456. Goldin (*op. cit.,* 345-6) has the further interesting note that with their "Due vaticini compiuti or sono" (Two prophecies are now fulfilled), Verdi and Piave followed Leoni's ("Compiuti or son due vaticin") and Rusconi's ("Già due vaticinii compiuti") mistranslation of Shakespeare's "Two truths are spoken." The witches' first salutation is no prophecy but an established fact, and Macbeth's second elevation, as Thane of Cawdor, has already taken place, although he does not yet know it. Carcano, on the other hand, got it right:

    Due cose vere udii; prologo lieto

    A quel dramma regal che si natura.

In 1863, Andrea Maffei published his translation [Florence: Le Monnier] of Schiller's adaptation and translation of *Macbeth* for the Weimar stage—an adaptation that, as Verdi knew (see p. 158), Schlegel had denounced as perverse. Frits Noske has claimed that Maffei's translation must have been completed some seventeen years earlier and that, indeed, it was Verdi's principal source.[2] His arguments seem unconvincing: Verdi's view of the witches is plainly not Schiller's; and any verbal resemblances between the libretto and the 1863 Schiller translation are (especially when chronology is considered) most naturally explained by the fact of Maffei's having already worked in detail on the former. For example, the evidence of the stage direction for the Shew of Kings suggests a conclusion opposite to Noske's. The First Folio (1623) reads:

> A shew of eight Kings, and Banquo last, with a glasse in his hand.

Nine apparitions in all, then, and the mirror in Banquo's hand? But a few lines later (IV.1.119) Macbeth cries: "And yet the eight appeares, who beares a glasse." There is a crux here. Editors from Hanmer (1744) onward have emended the stage direction to accord with what Macbeth says and have placed the glass in the eighth king's hand. A usual reading of eighteenth-century editions is:

> Eight kings appear, and pass over the stage in order; the last with a glass in his hand: Banquo following.

That is what Carcano translated:

> Otto re appariscono, e passano l'uno dietro all'altro; l'ultima di essi con uno specchio in mano. Banco li segue.

But both Schiller and Rusconi[3] used a text in which Banquo, bearing the glass, *is* the eighth king (or both translators decided independently to solve the crux in this alternative way). Schiller has:

> Acht Könige erscheinen nach einander und gehen mit langsamen Schritt an Macbeth vorbei. Banquo ist der letzte, und hat einen Spiegel in der Hand.

and his Macbeth exclaims:

> Da kommt der Achte noch mit einem Spiegel.

Rusconi has:

> Otto re compariscono in fila, e passano uno dietro l'altro; l'ultimo di essi, Banquo, ha uno specchio magico in mano.

Verdi in his autograph libretto (see p. 330) followed Rusconi:

> Otto re passano l'uno dopo l'altro: l'ultimo è Banco che ha uno specchio in mano.

---

2. "Schiller e la genesi," 196–203; "Ritual Scenes," 420–21

3. In his preface, Rusconi acknowledges how helpful he found notes by, especially, Johnson, Warburton, Steevens, and Bolingbroke. Several late-eighteenth- and early-nineteenth-century editions incorporate notes by the first three. The Steevens edition of 1773 or of 1778 could have served Rusconi—but (because of his *blue* spirits; see p. 456) not the 1785 Steevens edition. Carcano, as his own ample notes make clear, also used such an edition—possibly the well-known Malone edition of 1821. But Bolingbroke is a puzzle; in the writings of the prolific Henry St. John, Viscount Bolingbroke, we have so far found nothing about *Macbeth* nor any edition of the play with notes by him.

But Maffei changed the second phrase to read:

> da ultimo vien Banco con uno specchio in mano

and this is the reading of the 1847 libretto and the first vocal scores. When Maffei made his Schiller translation, he retained his earlier phrase:

> Otto re appariscono uno dopo l'altro, passando con lenti e lunghi passi innanzi al Macbeth. Da ultimo Banco con uno specchio nel mano.

All this may seem ado about nothing, but it has practical significance for the staging of *Macbeth*: eight kings and then Banquo, or seven and then an eighth, bearing a glass, who turns out to be Banquo? That Verdi intended the second is made clear by the score. For the appearance of the final apparition there is another stage direction: "Apparisce l'ultimo re Banco che ha uno specchio in mano." In eight bars of F major, Macbeth exclaims in terror at this apparition who in his magic glass reveals further generations of kings. Then the harmony leaps to B♭ minor as Macbeth cries, "È Banco!" It is as if the eighth king suddenly lowers a glass that has hitherto concealed his features.[4]

It has been suggested[5] that Macbeth's death scene in the 1847 score ("Mal per me"; see p. 478) is based on the Faustian speech written by David Garrick for his production of the play:

> 'Tis done! the scene of life will quickly close.
> Ambition's vain, delusive dreams are fled,
> And now I wake to darkness, guilt and horror;
> I cannot bear it! Let me shake it off—
> 'Two' not be; my soul is clogg'd with blood—
> I cannot rise! I dare not ask for mercy—
> It is too late, hell drags me down; I sink,
> I sink—Oh!—my soul is lost for ever!
> Oh!

The speech appears (as an interpolation, with its author identified) in John Bell's popular edition of Shakespeare (1774), dedicated to Garrick, and again (without the fourth and fifth lines) in Mrs. Inchbald's edition (1808), representing the text that Kemble played with Mrs. Siddons. Readers may judge for themselves whether there is any significant resemblance. It should be noted, however, that Garrick's interpolation appears in none of the Italian translations that Verdi might have known.

---

4. James I, before whom, it is generally agreed, *Macbeth* is likely to have had its first performance, traced his descent from Banquo (a fact noted in the preface to the Ricordi libretto; see p. 349); the mirror may then have reflected the continuance of Banquo's royal line in the features of the present sovreign. Henry N. Paul (*The Royal Play of "Macbeth"* (New York: Macmillan, 1950; 179) and Richard Flatter (in a letter to the *Times Literary Supplement* of 23 March 1951) have proposed other ways of staging the episode (in the play). No solution matches at all points; to the suggestion that the eighth king, bearing the glass, turns out to Banquo it can be objected that—as the witches have made abundantly clear—Banquo is not a king.

5. By Godefroy (*The Dramatic Genius*, 1: 139) and by Kimbell ("The Young Verdi," p. 66)

A NOTE ON CENSORSHIP

Verdi's recurrent troubles with Italian censorship, reaching their climax with *Un ballo in maschera,* are well known. Regicide could not be represented on the Bourbon stage; nor could it be represented in Venice in 1851, when the historical protagonist of Victor Hugo's *Le Roi s'amuse* became the anonymous Duke of Mantua in *Rigoletto.* An examination of early- and mid-nineteenth-century librettos soon reveals the varieties and the extent of the censorship, political and ecclesiastical, that were imposed. *Macbeth,* an opera dealing with both regicide and the supernatural, did not pass scatheless, as the small selection of examples which follows will show.

MILAN, 1849

The expression "vil corona," as Francesco Degrada (*Il palazzo incantato,* 2, 136) has pointed out, was evidently too much for those who censored what was sung at the Regio Imperial Teatro alla Scala, where *Macbeth* had its Milanese premiere in February 1849—just six months after the Austrians, having crushed the rebellious Milanese and their allies, reentered the city. In the libretto prepared for that production, Macbeth dies exclaiming:

> Muoio al cielo ... al mondo in ira
> O mia donna ... e sol per te!

The exiles' chorus, "Patria oppressa," begins "Noi perduti!,"and "La patria tradita" becomes "La fede tradita."

PALERMO, 1852;[1] MESSINA, 1853

Regicide played no part in the *Macbeth* given in these cities of the Kingdom of the Two Sicilies. Count Walfred, "a very rich Scottish nobleman, King Duncan's first military general," is murdered by a Macbeth eager to secure that post for himself. The witches' third, prophetic greeting is:

> Salve, o premiero guerriero del re!

and their promise to Banquo is: "Non *conte,* ma di *conti* genitore!"
The letter Macbeth sends to his Lady reads "... che predisser *gran cose* al destin mio," and of course she cries "Walfredo sarà qui? qui? qui la notte?" Macbeth's last line is: "*Ambizione,* e sol per te!"

1. The "maestro di cappella e direttore," as at the Florence premiere, was Pietro Romani.

ROME, 1852

Regicide—at any rate regicide long ago, in a distant northern country—passed the ecclesiastical censor who set his imprimatur, dated 21 December 1852, to a *Macbeth* libretto printed in Rome by the Tipografia Menicanti.[2] What could not be allowed in the Holy City was any suggestion of supernatural power possessed by witches—or, for that matter, any witches at all. The opera begins with a chorus of gypsies busy with the fortune-telling cards of their "superstitious prophecies":

I	Che scovriste?...Dite su!
II	Già nel bosco è sono.
I	E tu?
III	M'era fiso nel pensier;
	Di Macbetto è quel destrier: (*additano una carta*)
	Ed il *Tre* che lo segnò
	Con tre *Regi* s'associò!
	Tanti serti predirò.
I	Trar par Banco l'*Asse* io vo...
II	Donna e rege si mostrò...

Banquo to the witches: "Who are you? From these *shores,* or from another *region?* I would call you *Scotswomen,* but that your *unfamiliar garb* forbids it." In II.1, the "spirtali donne" are "maliarde donne." "Calice" is evidently a word with sacred associations; the *brindisi* begins "Il nappo colmisi." Banquo's ghost passed muster. At the start of Act III, the witches, in a dark room, are preparing in their *pentola* a brew, recipe unspecified, which, they claim, will comfort the lovesick, make businessmen successful in their enterprises, and confer invincibility on soldiers. Macbeth is given a philter to drink; doped and duped, he sees the three prophecies appear as writings on the wall. The reasoning behind some of the other changes is hard to find: Banquo's "Studia il passo" becomes "Muova il passo." Perhaps the censor was also a literary critic. "Studia il passo" was one of the phrases mocked by the Florentine critics in 1847.

In 1853 Gioacchino Belli, the liberal dialect poet, now turned Roman censor, reported on Shakespeare's play[3] that even if Duncan were demoted to being some unspecified ruler, and "Maestà" changed to "Altezza," there would remain a benign lord betrayed in sacred hospitality and murdered by a subject fired simply by the ambition for power, "atto di malaugurato esempio in ogni tempo, ma specialmente in dì di oggi," and made still worse by "una certa misteriosa intervenzione di non umani influssi e di tenebrose idee di fato" guiding the assassin's hand. Belli continues: "the fact that even here [the savage drama] has been tolerated in music [Verdi's *Macbeth* had its Roman premiere in 1847] makes one reflect on the distance between the sung word, in which the greater part of the listener's attention is absorbed by the music, and the spoken word, which appeals directly to minds and hearts."

In Adelaide Ristori's *Studies and Memoirs* (London: W. H. Allen, 1888), p. 20, we find the following passage:

2. But *Macbeth* had its Roman premiere in September 1847 and was revived in 1849, 1850, and 1852; we have traced no 1853 performances.

3. Luigia Rivelli, "Gioacchino Belli 'Censore' e il suo spirito liberale," *Rassegna Storica del Risorgimento* 10 (1923), 388–89.

On another occasion, when *Macbeth* was given in Rome, and one of the three witches says in the second scene of the first act: "Here I have a pilot's thumb, Wrecked as homeward he did come," the Censor cancelled the lines. "Why?" asked the manager of the company.

"Because," was the answer, "the public will probably find an allusion in them to the vessel of St. Peter, which is in danger of being submerged by the wickedness of the times."

What can be said in defense of such absurdities?

Ristori continues with examples of censors' interference in *Luisa Miller* and *Norma*.

PALERMO, 1853

One of the most ingenious transformations of *Macbeth* was Professor Giuseppe Bozzo's, into *Saul,* an "azione sacra da cantarsi nell'oratorio de' PP. della Congregazione di San Filippo Neri." The libretto was printed in Palermo in 1853; Verdi is named as composer. Into this new story many of Piave's and Maffei's lines are taken unaltered or little changed. When Saul and Abner enter the Israelite camp, the former can exclaim, "Giorno non vidi mai sì fiero e bello!" Micol, Saul's daughter, reads a letter from David, her betrothed ("Nel dì della vittoria io sarò teco") and breaks into "Vieni! T'affretta! Arrendermi/Vo'al nobile tuo core ... Davidde sarà qui? qui? qui fra poco?/Or tutti sorgete—miei spirti abbattuti," etc. Saul kills Abimelech, the chief Levite, whom he suspects of promoting David as king. In place of the assassins' chorus, David's followers sing:

> Chi v'impose unirvi a noi?
> Fu Davidde...Ed a che far?
> Dobbiam Saule allegrar.
> Quando? dove?...Insiem con voi.

But Abner arrives filled with gloomy presentiment: "Studia il passo ciascuno ...In notte eguale Achimelech,/Qui presso, a morte andò." The *brindisi* begins "S'innalzi un cantice/Di puro affetto,/Nasca il diletto,/Cessi il dolor"; but then Abimelech's ghost appears to Saul and blights the party. In the next scene, Saul consults the Witch of Endor and her companions; they call up the Shade of Samuel, who prophesies Saul's downfall. Saul sings "Vada in fiamme, in polve cada/D'Israele il campo armato." In the Israelite camp, David sings "Oh, la celeste mano," and is joined by Jonathan: "Dove siam? Che giorno è questo?" The sleepwalking scene becomes a dialogue between Micol and Abner; she reproaches him for deserting Saul in phrases partly familiar:

> Tremi tu?...Non parli ancor?
> Tu premier non corri a morte?
> Oh vergogna!...Orsù, t'affretta.

In a final battle against the Philistines, Saul sees Jonathan slain. His dying speech begins, "Mal per me che abbandonai/Il sentier d'eterno amore" and ends "Figlio, ahi figlio, io son con te."

MACBETTO: BALLO MIMICO
IN CINQUE ATTI (EXCERPT)
Luigi Henry

In the words of David R. B. Kimbell:

[*Many*] *of the great Shakespearian tragedies, though not, as far as I know,* Macbeth *itself, had been given operatic settings of sorts well before Verdi, and a substantial number of Shakespearian ballets were produced in Italian opera-houses. Nonetheless, Shakespeare's impact on the Italian theater, his impact as a dramatic force, had as yet been minimal. Verdi's* Macbeth, *far from being just one example of a general trend, is the first Italian opera that is Shakespearian in any meaningful sense of the word. In all the other cases the resemblance of the opera to the play in terms of plot and characterization is tenuous in the extreme.*[1]

As an example, Kimbell cites Luigi Henry's five-act ballet Macbetto, *premiered during La Scala's 1830 Carnival season.*[2] *We present here translated excerpts from the printed libretto*[3]—*the most interesting part of Henry's* Avvertimento, *or prefatory note (excluding only the customary appeals for the public's favor) and the complete scenario.*

PREFACE

In order to depart from the costumes of the Middle Ages or the Age of Chivalry, which are seen on the stage almost everyday, I thought it well to choose the subject of *Macbeth,* the setting of which is Scottish. And since we no longer live in times when people believed in sorcery, and since the human heart takes an interest only in verisimilar events, I considered it appropriate to avoid the Marvelous, but without altering the basic plot. I retained the *Witches* because they have a role in the development of the action, and I avoided the

---

1. "The Young Verdi and Shakespeare," p. 62.

2. Probably February 20, 1830, according to Giampiero Tintori's chronology in Carlo Gatti, *Il Teatro alla Scala nella storia e nell'arte (1778-1963)* (Milan: Ricordi, 1964) 2: 181. Louis Henry (Versailles, 1784–Naples, 1836) made his debut as a dancer in 1803, as a choreographer in 1805. After 1808, when he joined La Scala as *primo ballerino,* he worked mainly in Milan, Naples and Vienna. *Macbeth* was the third of his Shakespeare ballets—he had choreographed an *Otello* in 1808 (Naples) and a *Hamlet* in 1816 (Paris). (See *Enciclopedia dello Spettacolo,* s.v. Henry, Louis.)

3. Professor Giuseppe Vecchi kindly provided us with a xerox of the copy in the Civico Museo Bibliografico Musicale of Bologna. The title page reads as follows: "Macbetto / Ballo mimico in cinque atti / di composizione / del Signor Luigi Henry / da rappresentarsi / nell'I. R. Teatro alla Scala / Il Carnevale del 1830 / Milano / per Antonio Fontana / M.DCCC.XXX." Henry is listed as "Inventore e Compositore de' Balli Grandi"; Cesare Pugni is credited with the music of *Macbetto,* "except for the pas."
   Our translation of Act I of the scenario is based upon Kimbell's.

apparitions and visions, for, if I had decided to retain them, I would have presented *Walter Scott*'s witches rather than Shakespeare's. If I were to seem guilty in a certain sense toward the latter, let me offer as a justification my desire to win for myself the good will of the Public, which does not seem to enjoy that type of entertainment...

ACT I
MOUNTAINOUS COUNTRY WITH A STREAM
SCENE WITH MOUNTAINS AND A STREAM

Duncan, King of Scotland, is attending the warlike sports of his son [Malcolm], whose education is entrusted to the bards. The young prince is ignorant of his birth and believes himself to be the son of an ordinary Scot. — The witches, who have knowledge of the secret, want to take advantage of it to obtain substantial rewards; they offer some gifts to Duncan, which he refuses to accept. — The presence of these Megaeras always bodes some disaster in the area. [Henry's footnote: A Scottish superstition that Walter Scott often mentions.] A distant sound of hunting is heard, and Duncan departs, followed by his attendants. — The witches vow vengeance on the King. A terrible storm breaks, which they make use of to show themselves under a veil of mystery to Macbeth, who took part in the hunting sports.—Things cannot be seen except by the illumination provided by the lightning and thunderbolts. Macbeth perceives a crown and a dagger. — A witch tells him: *You will be King*—and disappears, followed by her companions. Macbeth, terror-struck, follows them.

ACT II
GALLERY IN MACBETH'S CASTLE

Duncan's arrival at the castle and his reception. Lady Macbeth, at the instigation of the witches, insinuates the poison of ambition into her husband's heart. He yields to the urging of his wife and kills Duncan, asleep in an adjoining apartment. All this was foreseen by the witches, and the suspicion of such an atrocious assassination falls upon two warriors who were standing guard over him. — Macbeth, in accordance with the Scottish custom, is acclaimed King by his warriors.

ACT III
THE BARDS' GROTTO[4]

Macduff, persuaded that Macbeth is the guilty one, betakes himself to the Bards and informs them of Duncan's death. All the Scots gather; the secret of Malcolm's birth is revealed to him, and vowing to avenge the death of his father, he leaves with the plan of attacking Macbeth.

---

4. It is probably only a coincidence that Verdi introduced Bards in the "Victory Hymn" in the 1865 revision of his opera.

ACT IV
AN UNDERGROUND PLACE

The witches, summoned by Macbeth, seem to foresee danger and want to withdraw, but one of them expresses the necessity of learning what Macbeth demands of them. — He wants to know if his son will wear the royal diadem. The witches, reluctant to respond, hesitate, and because of this Macbeth flies into a rage and threatens to kill them if they ever were to divulge the fatal secret. Lady Macbeth, who comes in search of her husband[5] to lead him to their coronation, saves the witches from death.

A BANQUETING HALL

Banquet and festivity — Macbeth's imagined visions and the universal joy. He believes himself pursued by Duncan's specter, and flees in terror.

ACT V
MACBETH'S BEDROOM

Lady Macbeth (sleepwalking), believing that she is on her way to kill Duncan, strikes her own son. The child's cries attract his father, who recognizes the error and succumbs to the weight of his own remorse. A warrior comes on to inform him of Malcolm's arrival. Macbeth regains all his fury, and departs to repel his enemy.

OUTSIDE MACBETH'S CASTLE,
ON THE COAST

Tumult, attack, defense — Macbeth falls beneath the blows of the victorious Malcolm. Tableau and end.

---

5. Providing precedent (of a sort) for the Lady's arrival at the close of the corresponding scene in *Macbeth II*.

TWO GREAT LADIES

ADELAIDE RISTORI

Verdi in his first letter to Escudier of 11 March 1865 (p. 110, published for the first time in this volume) refers to the interpretation of the sleepwalking scene given by the celebrated Italian actress Adelaide Ristori. Ristori was celebrated in the role of Lady Macbeth; in 1882 she played it, in English, at Drury Lane, and she often included the sleepwalking scene in recital programs. Her Memoirs and Artistic Studies (*English translation by G. Mantellini; New York: Doubleday, Page, 1907*) *contain a chapter on her psychological and physical interpretation of the character, from which we excerpt (pp. 171–74) the following passages about the effects that Verdi refers to.*

In the fifth act Lady Macbeth appears only in a scene of short duration, but which is the most marvellous one among all the philosophical conceptions of the author, and it offers to the actress a very difficult study of interpretation.

This woman, this colossus of both physical and moral force, who with one single word had the faculty of imaging and causing the execution of deeds of hellish character—there she is, now reduced to her own shadow which, like the bony carcass left bare by a vulture, is eaten up by the remorse preying on her mind. In her trouble she becomes so thoroughly unconscious of herself as to reveal in her sleep her tremendous, wicked secret. But what do I say "in her sleep"? It is like a fever which, rising to her brain, softens it. The physical suffering taking hold of her mind with the recollection of the evil of which she has been the cause masters and regulates all her actions, causing her, spasmodically, to give different directions to her thoughts. . .

The true rendering of this artificial and double manifestation and the fusing of these effects without falling either into exaggeration or into the fantastic at every change of countenance, of gesture, of voice, all demanded from me a most exhaustive study. I enter the stage with the looks of an automaton, dragging my feet as if they wore leaden shoes. I mechanically place my lamp upon the table, taking care that all my movements are slow and intercepted by my chilled nerves. With a fixed eye which looks but does not see, my eyelids wide open, a difficult mode of breathing, I constantly show the nervous agitation produced by the derangement of my brain. It was necessary to clearly express that Lady Macbeth was a woman in the grasp of a moral disease whose effects and whose manifestations were moved by a terrible cause.

Having placed the lamp upon the table, I advance as far as the footlights, pretending to see on my hands still some spots of blood, and while rubbing them I make the motion of one who takes in the palms of his hands a certain quantity of water in order to wash them. I am very careful with this motion, which I repeat at various moments. After this I say:

> Yet here's a spot. Out damned spot! out, I say!

Then listening, I say softly:

> One: two: why, then 't is time to do 't.

Then, as if answering:

> Hell is murky!—Fie, my Lord, fie! a soldier, and afraid? What need you fear? Who knows it, when none can call our power to account.

And at this place, returning to the cause of my delirium:

> Yet who would have thought the old man to have had so much blood in him?

And I show here that I am struck by the colour of blood in which it seems to me as if I had dipped my hands. Returning to my manifestation of delirium, I add:

> The Thane of Fife had a wife: where is she now?

And looking again at my hands with an expression between rage and sadness:

> What, will these hands ne'er be clean?

With a convulsive motion I rub them again. Then, always a prey to my delirium, in a bitter tone, and speaking excitedly, I pretend to whisper in Macbeth's ear:

> No more o' that my lord, no more o' that; you mar all with this starting.

Then coming back to my first idea, I smell my hands, pretending they smell of blood, and I break forth with passion:

> Here's the smell of the blood still: all the perfumes of
> Arabia will not sweeten this little hand. Oh! oh, oh!

And I make these exclamations as if an internal shudder convulsed my heart and caused me to breathe with difficulty, after which I remain with my head thrown back, breathing slowly, as if in deep lethargy...

I took much care never to forget that the woman who spoke was in troubled sleep; and during this scene, between one thought and another, I would emit a long, deep and painful sigh.

The following verses:

> To bed, to bed! there's knocking at the gate:
> Come, come, come, come, give me your hand.
> What's done cannot be undone. To bed, to bed, to bed!

I speak these words in an insistent tone, as if it were a thing that should be done quickly; then, frightened, fancying that they knock at the door of the castle and come to surprise us, I show great emotion, a greater fear, as if I found it necessary to hide ourselves quickly in our own rooms. I start in that direction, inviting Macbeth to follow me, saying in a very imperative and furious tone: "Come, come, come! . . ." Then, simulating the act of grasping his hand, I show that I am dragging him with great pain, and disappear from the sight of the audience, saying in a suffocating voice: "To bed, to bed, to bed! . . .[1]"

1. But the great Italian actress Eleonora Duse remarked that Ristori's "breathing with difficulty"—the *rantolo* or death rattle that Verdi refers to—sounded to *her* as if the somnambulistic Lady were snoring in her sleep! See note 2 to Verdi's letter of 11 March 1865.

PAULINE VIARDOT

The great mezzo-soprano Pauline Viardot was the first Lady Macbeth in the British Isles. For Willard Beale's touring troupe, with Francesco Graziani as Macbeth, she sang the role in Dublin in 1859 and 1860, again in Manchester the latter year. A letter that she wrote to Luigi Arditi, the conductor of the Dublin production, casts interesting light on performing practices of the time. The original Italian appears in facsimile in Arditi's My Reminiscences *(London: Skeffington, 1896), pp. 58–61.*

Caro Maestro   15 March 1859

Here are the transpositions I make in the part of Lady Macbeth. The most difficult one that will necessitate certain changes in the instrumentation, will be that of the *Cavatina*. The recitative in D♭, the andante, "Vieni, t'affretta" in B♭, and the allegro "Or tutti sorgete" in D♭, consequently the whole scene will be a minor third lower. That's not bad! All the rest of the act as written. The *cabaletta* "Trionfai" is not sung.

In Act II, the banquet scene requires a transition from the last bars of the chorus that finishes with the words "Come ci detta il cor" to join it to the *brindisi* in A♭. The allegro is done as written in F (after the scene with the cutthroat). For the second verse of the *brindisi* a downward transposition of a tone, five bars before the *brindisi*, is achieved by putting an A♭ in the preceding F chord:

And we are all set for A♭.

After the repeat of the *brindisi*, a transition must be introduced to reach the seventh bar of the allegro agitato, where we find ourselves back in F.

Or one could go straight to the bar of Macbeth's "Va!," thus cutting the six previous bars.

The sleepwalking scene a tone lower—that is to say, the ritornello and recitative in E♭ minor, and the andante in B major. I fancy I see your orchestra making faces at the horrible sight of the *six flats* ♭♭♭♭♭♭ and the *five sharps* ♯♯♯♯♯! Dear maestro, you must have the parts of these three numbers copied, because the orchestra we'll have likes to transport/transpose [*trasportare*]...only the public.

I happen to own the Ricordi vocal score from which Arditi conducted [A. P.] . It is marked up in accordance with Viardot's instructions; other indications show that, for example, she delivered the reprise of the brindisi *with an emphatic break after each of the first two lines—as if Lady Macbeth were having to summon all her energy to continue the song. The long, interesting Irish* Daily Express *review of the piece and its performance is reprinted in* The Musical World *for 16 April 1859, p. 247. ("Of Madame Viardot, too much cannot be said. Not even Ristori could equal her.") The production also gave rise to an incident recalled in several nineteenth-century memoirs. This is T. W. Beale's version of it, from his* The Light of Other Days *(London: R. Bentley & Son, 1890), pp. 290-91:*

The sleep-walking scene jeopardised the result of the first representation of the opera at the Theatre Royal, Dublin. It is introduced by a singularly characteristic symphony, during which the violoncellos and double basses give forth much beautiful although lugubrious music. The house is darkened. The scene on the stage represents the door of Lady Macbeth's sleeping apartment. A nurse and doctor are seated at the door, a small table stands between them, and upon the table is a bottle of physic with the conventional long label of days gone by attached to it. The crowded audience has sat through three acts of new music, and is naturally rather tired. The 'cellos and double basses are groaning on; we are anxiously waiting the rentrée of Lady Macbeth, when a voice in the gallery calls out to the well-known leader of the band, 'Ah! hurry now, Mr. Levey! tell us, is it a boy or a girl?' Viardot delayed her appearance a few minutes in order to allow the commotion this singular inquiry caused to tone down.

REVIEWS
and Other
Published Commentary

There are several reasons for reading the 1847 reviews of *Macbeth* beyond that of discovering how nineteenth-century critics dealt with an important new work by a prominent composer and what they thought of it. Verdi considered the abilities and disabilities of his cast when composing the piece, and so it is worth learning all we can about the voice, style, art, and appearance of Marietta Barbieri-Nini and of Felice Varesi. Verdi supervised the production himself. The critics on the spot provide us with scraps of information about the rehearsals and even about the creation of the work: for example, Enrico Montazio's claim (No. 14) that it was the inadequacy of the leading tenor, Angelo Brunacci, which led to the addition, only after rehearsals had started, of a second tenor voice, Malcolm's, to the *cabaletta* of Macduff's aria.

Furthermore, the reviewers of a premiere took care to report the audience's reception of the individual numbers of a score; indeed, the accurate reporting of public reaction was considered a prime responsibility of a nineteenth-century Italian critic. It is interesting to note that when Verdi revised *Macbeth* for Paris, he altered none of the three numbers—the opening witches' chorus, the *primo tempo* of the Act I duet, and the Act II murderers' chorus—that are reported as having been generally successful in 1847.

Besides evaluating the performance and reporting the audience reception, the reviewers of a new opera provided extensive descriptions of the piece, in part narrative and factual and in part (though often in small part) critical. The observations of a Casamorata or a Basevi (see pp. 421–25) have an inherent value independent of their historical interest as primary sources. In some other cases, we read the critics to discover their prejudices and limitations and only then, by cautious extrapolation, to assess those of Verdi's wider audience. For instance, there is an almost unanimous condemnation of the "Northern" supernatural happenings in *Macbeth*—a phenomenon connected with the particular nature of Italian "Romanticism." Another example: it is at once fascinating and reassuring to find that while many of the critics praised the ingenious orchestration and variation technique of the assassins' chorus, they were as puzzled as we are by its character. Verdi's staccato, sotto voce conspiratorial style—the cat-like tread of men stealing upon their foe—may have been a wholly personal convention rather than one understood and accepted by all his contemporaries and so often derided by ours.

The Florence reviews are followed by those of some other early productions, especially those (e.g. at La Fenice and La Scala) that would have been influential in determining the success of the opera; and by a few "atrocity stories" that illustrate what could happen to a work once launched and beyond its composer's control.

Verdi did not travel to Paris to supervise the production of the revised version, and he did not have a firsthand knowledge of the Théâtre-Lyrique cast. But he did convey his intentions about certain specific issues to Léon Escudier; and the reviews in Escudier's *L'Art Musical* make it all too clear that he and Léon Carvalho, the director of the Théâtre-

Lyrique, ignored them. Moreover, since little attention was paid to the revision in Italy—it is often difficult to tell from a later Italian account which version was performed—the Paris reviews are the best source of contemporary comment specifically about *Macbeth II*. In addition, they reflect, when taken as a whole, the French lack of understanding of what Verdi really was about. For Paris, he composed some of his most ambitious and elevated music, as if in recurrent attempts to make the superior musical and scenic resources of the French theatres serve a nobler end than that of spectacular entertainment. His wry comments on the Paris reviews of *Macbeth* (see p. 119) reflect his recurrent disillusionment; yet within a year he was, with *Don Carlos,* composing for Paris again.

Verdi's feeling of not being understood was not, of course, confined to the French assessment of his works. The famous later complaint—of "stupid criticism and praise more stupid still! Not a single elevated or artistic idea! No one has wished to point out my intentions"—refers to the Italian reception of *La forza, Don Carlos,* and *Aida.* But it sums up much that he had often said before. These collected *Macbeth* reviews provide a cross-section of what criticism was like at the mid-century.

The full texts are now lodged in the archive of the AIVS, and there anyone who wishes may plow through them all, in the original languages. Reproducing them in full would have meant recounting the plot of *Macbeth* move by move and number by number over and over again. In making this selection, we have tried to include any particularly interesting points while in general insuring that most points of view are represented and that the distribution of space and emphasis gives a reasonably fair picture of the work's reception. We are indebted to H. Robert Cohen, Marcello Conati, Ursula Günther, and Leonardo Pinzauti for contributing copies of the reviews, and to Piero Weiss for the English translations.

Macbeth I:

THE FLORENCE PREMIERE, 1847,
AND SOME LATER
ITALIAN PRODUCTIONS

— 1 —

C. Mellini's "scene-setting" essay "Concerning Maestro Giuseppe Verdi's Musical Style: General Observations" appeared in Enrico Montazio's Rivista, *a big Florentine paper, about two weeks in advance of the* Macbeth *premiere. Mellini's view of Verdi as "worthy successor of the great masters of the Italian school" was not unusual even then.*

... Now, has Verdi brought about a new revolution in music? No. He is to be considered as an inspired, beneficent genius, the reconciler of many virtues, which unite to form a whole of absolute goodness, worthy of the universal admiration it has earned. When any art has succeeded in producing its most sublime, incomparable examples, the path to decadence lies already open before it, and along that path crowd ill-advised imitators, intent on overdoing the forms of some of the excellent models which they choose to imitate. There is only one expedient, then, suited to put a stop to the fatal decadence, and it consists in knowing how to cull the best qualities wherever they might be, thus forming an original manner, though it be borrowed from others. For that, one needs intellects who, though they may not be more elevated, are certainly more educated and learned than the great inventors ever were. To this class of superior artists belongs, as an example, the excellent, incomparable school of the Caracci which for two centuries continued the classical glories of Italian painting, else doomed to die with Correggio and Titian. To the same class belongs the music of Verdi. He is original in many of his melodies, but not so much so that he does not show, in this branch, that he has copied Bellini; treats the recitative well, but in no wise differently from the way it was treated by Bellini and Donizetti; sometimes, in the instrumentation, he is vigorous like Mercadante, sometimes fluent like Donizetti, sometimes simple, like Bellini himself; in the concerted pieces he is more imposing than novel; in the overtures, more graceful than uncommon; in the choruses, more magnificent than surprising; in some trios, more magical than profound. He does, however, show he possesses great qualities of musical learning, which he does not like to flaunt at the expense of dramatic expression, and in this he acts wisely. Some of his melodies are of a sweet, ethereal simplicity and breathe that noble candor which only the great masters know how to infuse into their thoughts. This quality in itself should be sufficient to silence the loud chatter of many detractors, but their blind incompetence encourages them only too much to persist, even battling against the universal consensus. Blessed is he who knows not his own ignorance.

A great advantage of Verdi, and a wholly Italian one, is the mellifluous quality of his style, the fluency of his vein, and the native loveliness of his inspirations, which begin, continue, and resolve with marvelous spontaneity, and such a flavor of novelty, in flights that are unexpected, indefinable, and not at all forced, that we could not wish for more from any other of the great masters. Oh how well he succeeds at times with certain instrumental supports and underlinings that buttress the vocal part and give it a new effect! This is not an uncommon device, but Verdi makes use of it in a rare, precious, and entirely personal manner. . . .

But a very substantial virtue of the music of Verdi, which, wisely and coolly considered, could convert many of his opponents, is the universality of his style. Triumphs, tourneys, ceremonies, exequies, conspiracies, amorous dialogues, festive banquets, elegant balls, scenes of terror and alarm, magnanimous acts, glorious deeds—all these he knows how to treat worthily, and how to impress on each its peculiar character, at times with strokes of not only a great master, but a great man. This precious attribute is not only a good quality, but a cause for pride. It has always, and with good reason, been affirmed that Rossini generally succeeds better in the festive, gay vein, Bellini in the affecting and passionate, Mercadante in the grave, Meyerbeer in the fantastic, Donizetti in *adagios*, Pacini in *cabalettas*. Until now, I could not, nor perhaps could others, indicate precisely toward which of these Verdi in fact inclines and in which he is in fact deficient. This quality in itself makes him a dramatic composer of the utmost importance, for it reveals him to us devoid of any inclination that might lead him astray from the true path of the accurate interpretation of the affections.

We have already said that Verdi did not, nor was obliged to, nor could, bring about a new revolution in theatrical music, which Rossini did, marvelously, some thirty years ago, and which, in his turn, Bellini did some fifteen years ago. We have touched on Mercadante without toppling him from the chair whence he can teach, if not all, then the greater part of composers. We have remembered Donizetti without having deprived him of the honor of being proclaimed the Ovid of Italian music. We have spoken, and we shall speak, of Verdi as of one who, in a very difficult period, has known how to open for himself a path to fine successes, something we have seen denied to many worthy talents who have made so many vain attempts. . . . But there are many who accuse Verdi of reminiscences and of scant originality. This is the field in which the criticism of listeners, even inexperienced ones, is wont to roam with all kinds of strictures, against which no composer has ever been proof. . . . Verdi has purely melodic forms that are essentially his

own, as had Rossini and Bellini. The same cannot be said of Mercadante, of Donizetti, and of other eminent composers who may well be original in entire pieces, periods, or even phrases, but not in the forms. And note that by *melodic forms* I do not here mean an entire melody or *cantilena,* but certain fleeting moments which, in music, are nevertheless of great importance and constitute, if I may so express myself, the profile of a theme. Verdi, too, has certain ensemble effects that are essentially his own. True, he does not stint his use of these forms and these effects, and this may well be the cause of the accusations against him of frequent reminiscences. Similarly, he sins in abusing *syncopations,* in answering a theme too often by the same turn of phrase (*modulando per quella medesima via*), in having the chorus sing too often in unison, and in showing himself hopelessly enamored of certain endings peculiar to himself, but of less than perfect coinage.

For the rest, he is a most worthy orchestrator and a various and appropriate accompanist. Verdi's instrumentation, if the rigid observer will forgive him a certain unnecessarily variegated and flowery manner, may be considered a continuous marvel of beautiful effects. The care he takes in weaving his score is singular, elaborating it as he does with no less bravura than constant diligence, so much so that it seems impossible that he should be able, in so short a time, to produce works so well-wrought that they would seem to be the fruit of lengthy study. In this way he serves well both the public and his own reputation.

But there is no lack of detractors who accuse Verdi of being a corruptor of good taste; no lack of those who date from him a period of decadence in dramatic music; finally, there is no lack of those (and these are the largest group) who blame him as a lacerator of ears, because of the instrumental din, as a waster of singing voices because of the *tessitura* of his parts and because of the nature of the *cantabiles,* which are too showy in their declamation. Now, the Lord be praised, these very same complaints were constantly being droned by the numberless opponents of Rossini in the days when that great genius was active; nor did they subside until the great genius began to slumber. . . . For which reason the wisest course is to be cautious both in praising someone to the skies and in utterly condemning him. . . .

"Estetica Musicale. Intorno allo Stile Musicale di Maestro Giuseppe Verdi: Osservazioni Generali." *La Rivista* (Florence), 27 February 1847

— 2 —

This letter, dated Florence 13 March and published in Ricordi's Gazzetta Musicale di Milano, *reports Varesi's indisposition and the consequent postponement of the premiere. As noted at 137–39, Florence had an extraordinarily active concert life—a lengthy passage omitted here discusses three instrumental concerts occurring within the span of four days—and was also a center for the publication of* musica classica, *an ill-defined term evoking music from beyond the Alps, especially instrumental music.*

Yesterday evening at La Pergola we had thought to have the first performance of *Macbeth*, the new opera composed expressly for that theater by Verdi:. . . . but a sudden illness having overtaken Varesi, who is entrusted with the principal part, as it had caused the general rehearsal to be interrupted on the preceding night of Thursday, so did it bring about on Friday the postponement to a later date of the eagerly-awaited opera, whose music is already being talked about in the most flattering terms by those who have obtained the favor of being admitted to the rehearsals and by the orchestral musicians who are to perform in it. It is hoped

the public's expectations will be fulfilled tomorrow evening.

The flow of concerts continues unabated. . . . Also the editor Passerai of this city has undertaken to bring out by subscription a monthly periodical of sacred music by classical authors; a motet by Michael Haydn has already been published, and now Joseph Haydn's Mass in B flat with orchestra and obbligato organ is in press. The edition is in full score, neat, and very inexpensive: three noteworthy attributes.

(from the *Carteggio Particolare* section of the
Gazzetta Musicale, 21 March 1847)

— 3 —

Vincenzo Meini's 15 March communication to La Moda *is mainly intended as an account of "how our public received Verdi's new opera" at the premiere. We have cut much of Meini's description of the plot.*

. . . . The opera begins with a *preludio* which goes through various themes that will be heard again later; next comes a chorus of witches divided into three clusters or groups, and it is well-wrought, and artfully developed so as to bring out that fantastic element which those bizarre, supernatural creatures so often awaken in our spirits. The audience gave vent to clamorous signs of approval, and after copious, unanimous, prolonged applause for the composer, the number was encored. . . . The witches *evanesce* [a dig at Piave's "Vanîr!"], and there follows a duet which was rather coldly received. The duet of Macbeth (Varesi) and Banco (Benedetti) finished, here you have the witches once more with another chorus, not as good as the first, after which the maestro was once again summoned forth. Lady Macbeth makes her entrance reading a letter from her husband, in which he informs her of the oc-

currence and of the witches' prediction; here, as you may guess, we have the lady's cavatina. . . . This piece of music in three movements was crowned with the most emphatic applause, which was shared by the acclaimed Barbieri and by Verdi, both most worthy of this, and of even a more festive (if possible) and more jubilant reception. . . . After an excellent scene of delirium, well played and declaimed by Varesi, [Macbeth] enters the royal apartment, and poor Duncano is done for. Meanwhile, Lady Macbeth, who has been looking out, enters and meets her homicidal husband, who has already consummated the crime. And here, what with the assassin's remorse, his fear of his guilt, and his commotion in narrating the courtiers' prayers (they prayed at court in those days), what with the contrast, in short, between Macbeth's passions and Lady Macbeth's sarcasm—she derides those aberrations, that childishness—Maestro Verdi has created a duet as new and sublime as it is inspired by a rare genius and by an imagination that reveals the great spirit that is sometimes imbued with images worthy of his fame and of the homage paid to him by all. In my estimation, this piece alone would be sufficient to cause one to foretell for its author, were he a novice, an extraordinary musical potential. And see what magic is wrought by beauty, when it assumes the impress and character that are most suitable! Though the music does not titillate the ears, either by means of popular tunefulness or din, or by means of that false glittering pomp acquired by instrumental combinations, nevertheless it moved the whole audience to what is known as enthusiasm, and after prolonged applause and calls for the maestro, it had to be repeated. When I say that Verdi, at this point, has rivaled Shakespeare himself in the realm of the sublime, I believe I have said all that can be said in his praise; he did not, unhappily, approach him in the terrifying apparition of Banco's ghost at the banquet, an unique scene, as Gioberti puts it, of sublime terror....

The stretta of the duet was coldly received.... The finale opens with unaccompanied voices, and seemed a well-designed and well-worked out composition. But here I cannot remember how the public received it, and so I shall jump ahead....

... Lady Macbeth ... sings (I think) an allegro with all the vigor and energy of which Barbieri's lungs are capable. Endless calls and applause. [The] chorus of cutthroats ... is classical, beautiful, original, well-thought-out, and novel, both in the instrumental combination and the vocal part. Immense applause; the piece repeated. Banco's *romanza,* which to me

seemed lovely, passed unnoticed. Banco too is dispatched, and that is that. The banquet scene ... was coldly received. Nor can I understand how Shakespeare's sublime *terribilità* at this supremely dramatic point failed to inspire in Verdi something comparable to the *finale* of Semiramide.... [For Meini's discussion of Act III, see CONATI at 233.]

Act IV opens with a chorus of Scotsmen led by Macduff, intent on reconquering the fatherland, or rather the throne Macbeth usurped from him [sic]. The chorus is grandiose and beautiful; beautiful, too, the largo in the aria of Macduff (Brunacci), lord of Jiffe [sic]. The *cabaletta* of that piece ends with the two tenors (Malcolm, Duncan's son, signor Rossi) alternating with the entire chorus; and nonetheless the public did not take to it. Not that the poor Macduff did not wave his arms about, jump up and down as if spring-driven, strut like a wagtail, to put the public on notice that he was present and willing, for they had not yet become aware of him. But all to no avail. Nothing helped to remove him from the category of supporting actors (*seconde parti*) to which he seems to have been purposely relegated, together with Banco. The somnambulism of Lady Macbeth, racked with remorse, is a masterpiece full of effect and musical philosophy.[1] And the public received it and rewarded it with incessant applause. A *romanza* by Macbeth, who, on the point of engaging the enemy, laments his coming misfortune, is delicate, passionate, and was heard with great pleasure, hugely applauded, and excellently expressed by Varesi. Both the artist and the maestro received much applause....

> "Il *Macbeth* di Verdi alla Pergola" (letter dated Florence, 15 March 1847), in *La Moda: Giornale di Mode e Teatri,* 20 March 1847

---

1 A catchword for learnedness—evoking images of canon and fugue and modulations to distant keys—and high seriousness.

—— 4 ——

"A libretto need only bear the name of this poor devil [Piave] for the poetry to be judged bad, even before reading it" (Verdi's 11 April 1857 letter to Tito Ricordi). "D. J." 's unsolicited contribution to Antonio Calvi's Ricoglitore, another Florentine periodical, is typical of the Florentine critics in its attacks on Piave, but unusual for its censure of Verdi's music.

.... The author [of the libretto] is Piave, and the choice (to tell the truth) does scant justice to the maestro's discrimination, for that poet-librettist has but seldom chosen, or been able, to present the public with estimable works; hence, given that precedent, little of value could be expected of him: and now, as we read the book of *Macbeth,* we might almost be inclined to believe that *abissus abissum invocat;* and, although the general report here in Florence is that maestro Verdi is fanatically partial to this libretto, I, to avoid taxing him with bad taste or poor judgment, refuse to believe it. [For the conclusion of this paragraph see CONATI at 232.]

The Florentine Public, which may almost be termed Verdian, and which crowned his first three operas[2] with clamorous applause, and applauded and cheered various pieces in the other ones too, was not inclined, in its wisdom, to give itself up entirely to enthusiasm upon hearing *Macbeth* for the first time, except at the witches' chorus in the *introduzione* of Act I, a portion of the duet for soprano and bass in the same act, and a chorus of hired assassins in Act II; here, the whole public burst into unanimous and plentiful applause, nor was it long ere many requested that it should be repeated, and the maestro, amid spontaneous, clamorous applause, was called and appeared many times on the stage. In Act III, a very long one, even his admirers failed to applaud, and there was only silence, interrupted occasionally by some hissing ... Act IV, too, was coldly received, except for some fleeting applause, and at curtain fall the task of applauding and of calling the maestro to the stage fell to his isolated devotees, while the Public, not finding itself satisfied with having spent six hours at the theater to hear the musical composition of *Macbeth,* had quite other things in mind than applauding its author.

...Barbieri, for her part, did what she could, but it would seem the maestro was not too inspired over her role; her *cavatina,* in effect, drew no sighs, though she sang it with a will. Her sleepwalking scene, in the last act, made no effect; although the music here is fine, it lost all its effectiveness because of its sheer length. Varese [*sic*] did his very best to impart some prominence to the role entrusted to him by the maestro, but was he successful? And it will be nothing short of miraculous if the worthy Varese or anyone else can survive three nights of singing so high-pitched and fatiguing a role without suffering from sinister effects in the long run. Consequently, we may conclude generally that maestro Verdi's new opera may well, commercially speaking, go round the theatrical world but will with difficulty maintain itself in the repertory, since neither its music nor its poetry appeal to the senses, to the mind, to the heart—in the first place, because there is a lack of *cantabiles;* second, because maestro Verdi's usual effects are wanting; third, because we only rarely come upon so-called musical philosophy in it, whereas the fantastic songs of the witches and all their spells are applicable to any other sort of song, and the accompaniments are ever the same, thus being guilty of monotony, whence those beauties which emerge here and there are far from sufficient, in their entirety, to impart eminent artistic value and theatrical life to maestro Verdi's *Macbeth.*

This is not the expression of an individual opinion, but of a public which with reason admires and enthusiastically applauds various operas by the same composer....

D. J.'s report originally appeared in Antonio Calvi's *Ricoglitore* and was reprinted in *Bazar* of Milan (24 March 1847 number), our source.

1. Earlier that year, for example, the Florentine critics had roasted Piave's libretto for *Tutti amanti,* an opera by Carlo Romani produced at the Pergola. A letter from Florence published in the 7 February 1847 number of Ricordi's *Gazzetta Musicale* sarcastically referred to their criticisms as the "critical-philological-aesthetic-dramatic observations" of "our arch-knowledgeable theatrical chroniclers."

2. I.e., *Nabucco, Lombardi,* and *Ernani; Oberto* and *Giorno di regno,* which had not yet been performed in Florence, were sometimes regarded as juvenilia (Basevi, for example, begins his discussion with *Nabucco*).

—— 5–6 ——

The following two items are from F. Regli's apparently pro-Verdian theatrical journal, Il Pirata *(Milan).*

We have a packet of letters before our eyes, and they all concur in saying that the first two acts of this new creation of Verdi's are marvelous: the others, too, are said to be splendid, but the opinion is that they will have a much better reception in the future. . . .

Il Pirata, 19 March 1847

Despite reports to the contrary, written out of partisanship or ignorance, the celebrated Verdi's *Macbeth* continues to enjoy a total and enduring success. The second performance evoked indescribable enthusiasm: the illustrious composer was called forth no less than *forty times,* and, in addition, was escorted to his quarters by a vast number of people, amidst acclamations and hurrahs. Both on the first night and on the second, *three pieces were repeated,* viz., a *Witches' Chorus,* a duet by Barbieri-Nini and Varesi, and a *Chorus of Cutthroats.* It is claimed that this (and no longer *Nabucco*) is the illustrious Composer's masterpiece. He has unfolded a genre which, until now, was not thought within his reach: it contains pieces which Meyerbeer would be pleased to have composed. To the provinces the opera will pose problems, for it demands much sumptuous scenery; but there is a remedy for everything, and *Macbet* will no doubt be seen everywhere. Tenors will be less than pleased but will have to resign themselves—it will be reckoned against the many times when the public was not pleased with them. . . .

Unsigned and undated communication from
Florence, printed in Il Pirata, 23 March 1847

—— 7–8 ——

The reports of Luigi Casamorata and Enrico Montazio suggest that the work was received more warmly at its second performance. Both articles are designed as reports of the work's reception—"for the historical record," as Casamorata expressed it—to be followed by more detailed critical examination (see Nos. 13–15).

Casamorata:

Verdi's long-awaited, long-wished-for opera *Macbeth* was finally produced at La Pergola last Sunday night: the crowd of spectators, jammed into every nook and cranny of the theater, the long wait, the overly-great expectation concerning that favorite maestro's new creation—all this contributed perhaps toward reducing the evening's applause, which was more scanty than not during Acts III and IV and which, if not totally wanting during Acts I and II, did not, however, come up to expectation, when we consider the virtues that embellish these two acts. Nor, in speaking thus, do we mean to say that the public remained silent; far from it: for, besides the applause for the singers, the maestro was called out not less than *twenty* times, and several pieces had to be repeated. The favorite things were:—the *introduzione,* the *primo tempo* of the Lady's *cavatina,* a duet between her and the baritone, the largo of the first-act finale, a men's chorus in the second act, and the Act II finale. A factor in the public's coolness towards the third act may have been the Satanic nature of the spectacle, and much incongruousness and deficiency in the scenic representation. In the last act, applause was accorded especially to a *romanza* of the baritone and to the lady's sleepwalking scene, where a vocal line characterized by fine declamation is underpinned by instrumentation of a novel and elaborate workmanship. As for the execution, Barbieri-Nini was excellent; Varesi very intelligent, although his vocal resources suffered somewhat from his recent illness; orchestra, supporting parts, choruses, in a word the *ensemble,* very good.

Good, too, the second performance last night, in which the public suddenly passed from the restraint of the first night to a furor of plaudits, with the result that not one piece went by without its share of vigorous applause, not excluding those which, on the previous night, had been heard with at best a sense of indifference by a part of the public; the whole third act was an instance. The calls for the maestro were endless, and a crowd of his warmest supporters and friends followed his carriage, applauding, from the theater to his dwelling; where, once he had arrived, he was repeatedly obliged to emerge on the balcony and show himself, thanking his well-wishers.

All this for the *historical* record; for to hazard a critical examination of this *Macbeth* after only two hearings would be an impudent audacity: Verdi's work is serious, and it deserves to be treated seriously and with mature deliberation by the critics: we shall attempt to do this in due time. . . .

> "Recenti Notizie di Firenze: Macbeth di Verdi, Prudent, Bazzini." Casamorata's communication, which deals with concerts as well as with *Macbeth*, is dated Florence, March 16, and appears in the March 21 issue of the *Gazzetta Musicale di Milano*.

Montazio:

On Sunday the 14th and Monday the 15th March we had the first two performances of this grand musical work, staged with great care and with uncommon [scenic] apparatus. The public gave vent neither to fanaticism nor to enthusiasm: it judged fairly. The illustrious maestro was called out on the stage approximately thirty times on the first night, more than forty times on the second, since greater attentiveness led to a better appreciation of the admirable beauty of certain pieces which had not been justly appraised before or had re-mained unobserved because of the variegated splendor of the harmonies.—Barbieri surpassed herself. The others spared no effort in support of the splendid achievements of that sovereign artist. The choruses had never before sung with such fervor the conspicuous part entrusted to them, thus nobly expiating their ancient, recent, and frequent sins. The orchestra proved worthy of their outstanding conductor and deserve high praise. *Macbeth,* if so imposing a work may be judged after but two performances, seems to us, in its musical philosophy and in the richness and beauty of its instrumentation, one of the best, indeed perhaps the finest and most accomplished of Verdi's operas. We shall speak of it at length in the next number of the *Rivista*. Meanwhile, much to the credit of the maestro and of the young persons who promoted the flattering ovation, we can inform our distant readers that on Monday night the illustrious Verdi was escorted to the doors of his hotel by a cheering swarm of Florence's finest youth, who had awaited his exit from the Teatro della Pergola, where the production of *Macbeth* must surely form one of its most splendid and honorable events.

> *Rivista di Firenze,* March 17, reprinted in the March 21 number of the *Gazetta Musicale* di Milano

— 9 —

In his 12 April 1847 letter Muzio reported that all the French newspapers except one had praised Macbeth; *the exception is probably Alessandro Gagliardi's review in the* Revue et Gazette Musicale *of March 28. It is noteworthy that even a critic as hostile to Verdi as Gagliardi regards him as the undisputed successor to Rossini, Donizetti, and Bellini.*

I believe, my ancient friend (as Panurge said to Friar Jean des Enteaumures), I have already told you that in the matter of expenditure the Florentines are in the habit of thinking twice, and that they are highly economical or even highly parsimonious, the latter epithet being permissible without straining polite language; but we must, in all justice, allow that, at least, they are not overly particular and that, though they pay little, they are content with little too. And here we have the reason why, in one of the most illustrious, most populous, and, above all, most frequented capitals of the Peninsula, a new opera written by a renowned master is a rarity occurring not more often than the jubilee year, that is, four times in a century. Today, however, the Florentines will have waited for only fifteen years or so; for, unless I am mistaken, it was 1832 or thereabouts when they enjoyed the first performance of the score of *La Parisina,* written by that excellent Donizetti. . . .

Will the *Macbeth* by the currently modish composer be equally fortunate? I wish it may be so, for his sake; for we must not wish anyone ill luck. I had never seen Verdi; I have found myself in his company quite often during the two or three weeks he has been here to mount his new work, and, before I speak to you of his piece, I should like to tell you something about his physiognomy. . . . Let's line up the heads of the four Italian composers who have wielded the scepter in recent times: Rossini, Donizetti, Bellini, and finally Verdi. Just look at that habitually jovial face, with its pure lines, wide-open eyes, elevated forehead, characterized above all by a most amiable, though inexplicably mocking, mouth. Then call to mind the handsome face of Donizetti, its broad and pronounced lines, the nobility of his earnest look and the frankness of his laughter; thence to the tender and melancholy visage of poor Bellini—and follow, along a parallel line, their way of composing. Have you done? Now we shall pass on to Verdi. Alas! just as his music has qualities peculiar to him, but few of those that enhance [the music of] his three illustrious precursors, so the appearance of his face is very different indeed. Its traits are pronounced, but reveal reflection rather than imagination. He is lean, spare, and yellow; it is only too evident that abandon and spontaneity have never been his bent; his sad and preoccupied air matches his afflicted and tormented music; he is a ploughman who works an unyielding soil and is constantly worrying about the harvest. And yet the successes Verdi has obtained, which have fallen off only very recently, ought to inspire him with confidence and courage. Or does he already feel his vein is exhausted, and is his rule coming to an end? Rossini resigned in the midst of the most brilliant and uncontested glory that any musician can ever have hoped to attain; Donizetti went mad; Bellini died; might it be Verdi's fate to be simply dethroned? I don't know, but for the moment he may compose and sleep undisturbed, for, to this day, there is no one to be seen either on the steps of his throne or elsewhere who will dispute his crown. . . .

I must first of all tell you that in all the time that horrible librettos have been heard in Italy (and that is a long time indeed), none I know of has been worse than *Macbeth*'s. Not only is the drama's structure deplorable; it is impossible to imagine more ridiculous poetry. The only sign of good judgment on the part of the librettist was that he did not name himself, at least in the printed libretto. The appearance of such balderdash is even more surprising if we consider it was intended for the Italian city with the best-preserved literary tradition, a city where the language is still generally respected.

There is no overture; ever since Bellini exempted himself from writing one (and it was well he did so, for his talent did not lean that way), the majority of composers have taken it easy in that respect; it is quicker, and thus one is rid of a rather unpleasant piece of drudgery. For, in overtures, a popular lady singer cannot make a feeble or trivial aria bearable. In them, the shouting we have become accustomed to calling "dramatic expression" has no place whatever. All the composer has at his disposal is an orchestra, more often than not a bad one, and, although in Italy they pay little enough attention to the orchestral music that introduces a work, it is nevertheless annoying to begin by cutting a poor figure. No more overtures, then, they say nowadays; and they add that Rossini himself didn't take the trouble to write one for *Mosè*. Stop a minute; just be good enough to give us an *introduzione* like the one in that work, and we will exempt you from *overtures*.

In *Macbeth*, there was much, and, in my opinion, quite undeserved applause for a little orchestral introduction that is as insignificant as you please. It precedes the witches' chorus, which opens the scene. This chorus, with which the author apparently expected to make a great effect, was, as I see it, wrongly conceived. Macbeth takes the witches very seriously; therefore, they should not be made to sing twaddle that is comical and, consequently, out of place in such a somber tale. When Macbeth (baritone) and Banquo (bass) come to consult the witches, I cannot imagine why Verdi, who on other occasions has shown dramatic sense, did not take more advantage of the scene—for example, of the witches' threefold greeting. . . .

The witches withdraw, and some messengers of the King enter and announce to Macbeth that he has been made thane of Cawdor. The entrance is treated in a straightforward manner but does not live up to its promise, for it merely leads into a duet *a parte* between Macbeth and Banquo, and it is cold and colorless. The witches reenter to sing a chorus in unison: it makes a meager effect. And, frankly, you must forgive me if I find it a little strange that twenty women (witches at that) should be there, on the stage, singing only one part. Lady Macbeth appears, reading a letter. Although this obbligato recitative appears to be written with care, it does not rise above the ordinary and leads into an aria that is rather short of ideas, although sung perfectly by Barbieri, concerning whose talent more later; this scene made an effect, and rightly so. The arrival of King Duncan, a mute role, is announced by "rustic" music, says the libretto; nevertheless, it is performed by military instruments. . . . This piece is exceedingly vulgar, and the only rustic thing about it is that it is written in 6/8. When Macbeth has been induced by his culpable spouse to kill the King, he sings, before resolving himself to commit the crime, a declaimed aria which, I am forced to confess, seemed to me very sorry indeed and lacking in variety, despite the numerous images introduced into this recital by the poet, after the example of Shakespeare. Having done the deed, Macbeth reenters the stage and, in a new duet with his wife, describes its circumstances and already feels the promptings of remorse. The melody is extremely felicitous [in the passage beginning at Ricordi 61.2.1]. . . . All this duet, which, by the way, is quite short, would be entirely deserving of praise, did it not conclude with a little allegro more appropriate to vaudeville and to *chansonnette* than to elevated lyric tragedy. The news of the King's death is then announced. General amazement and first-act *finale*, where we come upon some truly beautiful things. There is, above all, one of those effects, here managed very well indeed, that are always sure of success. I mean a piece for unaccompanied voices, which interrupts the din of the orchestra. . . . Excellent modulation makes this whole passage a thing of great price. It was much applauded and, in conjunction with Barbieri's performance, seemed to presage a great success for the work, despite several weak parts which this first act had already revealed to the ears and discernment of connoisseurs and impartial men.

The action of Act II revolves round the murder of Banquo. . . . It opens with a dialogue between Macbeth and his spouse, concluding with an aria in the worst possible style and taste, which, however, was well sung. Chorus of assassins sent to kill Banquo: this chorus, syllabic and dialogued, certainly has nothing of the words' terrifying character, and its whole effect rests upon an explosion of force at the words:

> Trema, o Banco! nel tuo fianco
> Sta la punta del coltel.

Banquo dead, there is a great banquet at Macbeth's, who has become king. Lady Macbeth sings some couplets to invite the guests to rejoice, but at the very moment when the new monarch is about to take his place, he finds it occupied by Banquo's ghost. This apparition is not announced by any important musical effect. Since the musician has, from the beginning, deployed all his orchestra's resources, he has none left to cope with this new and terrible situation.

The third act opens, as did the first, with a chorus of the witches, whom Macbeth has come to consult. A contrast was sought here, and when Macbeth drops in a faint, sylphs arrive and dance around him and revive him. This scene is an imitation of one in *Robert le diable*, and the music in it is a rather pronounced reminiscence of that employed by Meyerbeer on that occasion.

In the fourth act, the Scotsmen who have fled the tyranny of Macbeth revolt against him. Malcolm [*sic*], their chief, sings an aria rather better sustained [*posé*] than the rest of the work's melodies. The scene changes and takes us back to Macbeth's castle; and the composer has found some ideas for the sleepwalking scene. . . . Unhappily, by then everyone was so fatigued by what had gone before that the merits of that part of the drama were not much noticed. All that is now left is the denouement, produced, as is known, by the trickery of the soldiers arrayed against Macbeth, who advance toward him hidden behind tree branches. . . .

As you can see, the poet has more or less followed Shakespeare's play, without any changes; this poet, whom the libretto did not name, is called M. Piave on the poster: may the god who presides over poetry and the dramatic art be with him! What could a maestro, even one of the highest merit, extract from the poem of *Macbeth*? No more than M. Verdi; that is, some stretches, and at most some scenes. M. Verdi has attempted to take advantage of the occasion in order to fashion for himself a new style and even a new *manner*, as Rossini had done in *Guillaume Tell*. But even though the latter libretto was very bad, it at least fulfilled the genre's principal conditions, and the great musician was able to introduce in it a thousand new forms without being reduced to falling into grave errors, of which the principal, cruelest, and most unavoidable one for the composer is a desolating monotony. . . . Would you believe, for example, that the drama is, almost from the beginning to the end, in the minor mode, and that entire pieces are treated with almost no modulation, that the cadences occur most often in the tonic, and the half-closes in the region of that very same tonic? There is, if you will, some sophistication (*recherche*) in the details of the orchestration (*dans les petits traits de l'orchestre*), though the orchestra jumps and bustles about irrelevantly for the most part, and really serves only to put a wry face upon the situation. If only the author's ideas had the imprint of local color upon them. But no. In all

Macbeth you would not find a single phrase having the melancholy, limping turn of the airs peculiar to the mountains of Scotland, not a tiny little solo for the oboe or other instrument that might tell or remind us where we are. Compare with [Rossini's] La donna del lago, or rather do not compare, for there is nothing in common between the professional man who performs a task and the man of genius in whose brain artistic masterpieces seem to blossom forth unbidden.

We have seen how little the musician was favored by the poet; the time has come to tell you that he was rather better served by the singers. But in this regard, too, what, I ask you, is an opera without a tenor, or one, at least, in which he has but a role so secondary that it is only at the end of the work that we notice he was there? The whole drama pivots round the soprano and the baritone, performed by Marianna Barbieri-Nini (Lady Macbeth) and by Felice Varese [sic] (Macbeth). A word concerning these artists, about whom I have never had occasion to speak to you. Barbieri undertook her musical studies exceedingly late; but she is gifted with what today is an absolute necessity, a strong constitution and a strident, uncommonly powerful voice. She has learned enough to manage deftly, and sometimes even brilliantly, the pointed passages (traits en pointe) that have become the successors of sustained singing (chant posé) and prolonged passages of agility. Today, such shamelessness is applauded, and we must endure it. Barbieri has this advantage that, despite the power of her voice, she executes this sort of passage with a great deal of lightness; she is able, besides, to dominate almost without effort in ensemble pieces. Granted, she ought to make a somewhat better appearance on the stage, be a better actress, not feel obliged, though it facilitates the action of the lungs, to raise both her arms whenever her voice rises towards the top. Varese [sic] is a good baritone, who has sung on all the important stages of Italy; his singing and his bearing are, in general, suitable; but if he performs Macbeth or other works of that sort often, his voice will not last two years. Today's manner of writing, so unhappily sponsored by Verdi, leaves but few years of existence to even the best-constituted and apparently soundest voices.

A final word on the success of the production. At the first performance, the first two acts were received with much applause and frequent calls for the singers and the composer. The public was icy toward the last two, for the Florentines, though they are Verdians, cannot withstand certain impressions, and that of boredom is the most imperious of all. At the second performance, which took place on the morrow, measures had been taken to insure that the last two acts should be vigorously applauded. . . .

— 10 —

Antonio Calvi's review, written after the third performance and appearing in his Ricoglitore, confirms the favorable reception. Other passages from the review are quoted in CONATI and PINZAUTI.

The appearance of a new work by Maestro Verdi is for Italy a solemn event; and just as at the beginning of the century all Europe anxiously awaited the result of the Napoleonic wars, and after every battle the continent was crisscrossed by letters, bulletins, and dispatches, so in our less ferocious and bellicose days at every new opera by the Lombard Maestro all Italy awaits its news impatiently. That is praise indeed for the author of Nabucco, Ernani, and I lombardi, and shows that he has succeeded in making himself popular. . . . [Calvi then dissociates himself from the fanatics on both sides—see PINZAUTI at 139-40]

. . .Going back to the libretto, we shall say first of all that, as to the verses, it is pretty much like the others which the Maestro has lowered himself to set to music up to now. I shall not comment on the plot of the Drama, since that is not in any way due to the efforts of the librettist, but rather to those of that immense mind, Shakespeare; nor will I say that he who laid profane hands on it ought to have displayed better taste in the reduction, omitting many matters of lesser moment and keeping to the more essential points, that his work might seem less broken up, less composed of minute particles—even at the cost, I would almost say, of deviating somewhat from the Shakespearean plot.[1] To come at once to the verses, I shall say

1. Cf. the review in the Gazzetta Privilegiata di Venezia (No. 25), which found that too much had been omitted from the Shakespearean model.

that, according to the public notices, Signor *F. M. Piave* would seem to be their less than loving father, even though for some time there has circulated the rumor that they were the product of a noted professor [Andrea Maffei], the elegant translator of many fine works of foreign literature.

[Here C. provides a sarcastic account of the libretto, mocking Piave's diction on the way; e.g.:]

> ... *stricken by the law,*
> *Under the block he expired.*

Perhaps they should have said on the block, unless, to kill the thane of Cawdor, the block was dropped on his head, as one might do with an ox.[2]

[It is enormously revealing, however, that the vast majority of the strictures are directed at passages rendered faithfully from Shakespeare, e.g.:]

> *Now o'er the one half-world*
> *Nature seems dead. . . .*

as if we could not say the very same thing at every instant, and half the world were not always submerged in darkness. . .

Now, coming to the music, I will say it contains at least three excellent pieces. They are the Act I duet between Macbeth and his wife; where maestro Verdi has arrived at Shakspeare's sublimity and has admirably expressed with his notes the contrast between the remorse felt by Macbeth after the murder and the cold cruelty of his wife who, almost mocking him, treats his remorse as folly. A pity the allegro does not come up to the excellence of the rest! Very fine, too, and eminently *characteristic* is the cut-throats' chorus in Act II, and uncommonly well-scored for the orchestra, as is the whole opera, from beginning to end. Finally, in Act IV, wonderful and well developed is the whole of Lady Macbeth's sleepwalking scene. The finales of Acts I and II are good, as are many of the *adagios;* not so the allegros, which, with few exceptions, are rather common: a weakness we might perhaps impute to the excellent Maestro in other operas as well, for his sensitive spirit seems more attuned to sadness than to joy. . . .

There are some that criticize maestro Verdi for not having given the opera a *local* character and for having written music that is not at all reminiscent of Scotland but can be adapted to that or to any other land. Others there are who

wish he had given his characters a more *individual* quality, and to each his own characteristic musical style. It was further noticed that the absence of a tenor in the majority of the pieces deprives the maestro of one of his principal means of obtaining contrast and variety;[3] but this failing must be imputed solely to the libretto. But we shall expend no further words on this and shall, in conclusion, declare that if *Macbeth* is not the first of *Verdi's* operas in point of inspiration, it has, in our opinion, but one rival in point of artistry, and that is *Nabucco.* And indeed, the public received the opera with uncommon cordiality; many pieces had to be repeated (the first part of the duet for bass and soprano had to be done three times on the third night, a thing unheard of in the musical annals); the calls for the Maestro were without number. On the third night he was escorted to his lodgings amidst the applause of a dense crowd of people and for part of the way drawn in his carriage not by quadrupeds but by featherless bipeds; and, finally, a golden crown of no mean value presented to him on the stage will ever remind him of the high esteem in which the Florentines hold his merits.

The performance was almost entirely praiseworthy. *Barbieri* was superlative, incomparable; *Varesi*, though not in voice on the first night, yet lived up to his deserved fame and showed himself an artist second to few. *Bernabei* [*recte* Brunacci] was able to reap applause in his rather inconsiderable part. The choruses good nearly always, the orchestra excellent, directed by the worthy *Biagi*. I have nothing left to say.

P.S. The present article was finished when the post brought me the following letter, which I append, leaving its diction and spelling untouched. I am not sure whether to attribute it to one of Verdi's friends or to one of his enemies.

I hope you will not do like those fanatical and venal persons to praise what deserves censure. The opera by Verdi pufformed yesterday in the evening at La Pergola is pure —. So be sure to say in your article it was a triumph for the maestro because he was called out twenty-five times; those who called for him were his satellites; persons paid to do it. Let my warning serve for your guydance, meanwhile good day. Florence 15 March

"Prima rappresentazione del Macbeth del M. Verdi," *Il Ricoglitore,* March 1847

---

2. The phrase "sotto il ceppo," to which Montazio also objected, is in fact "the product of [the] noted professor"—Piave had written the perfectly reasonable "sul patibolo" (on the scaffold).

3. Neither Calvi nor Montazio notes that Macduff's role is larger than Ismaele's in *Nabucco*.

— 11 —

Letter from Florence, published in the April 4 issue of the Gazzetta Musicale.

On Thursday of last week [March 18] Verdi left this city for Milan. His *Macbeth* has every evening gained increasing favor with the public, proof of which (rather than the applause) is the progressively greater number of listeners. On Wednesday night, the eve of the popular maestro's departure from this city, after the opera's second act, a rich golden crown was publicly presented to him on the stage, where he had gone to acknowledge the applause, by Barbieri-Nini on behalf of a society of admirers, whose head was Prince Giuseppe Poniatowski. And at the end of the performance, upon his emergence from the theatre, he was as usual escorted to his quarters amid the warmest applause of his supporters, whose enthusiasm went so far that they detached the horses and pulled his carriage by hand.

The pieces in *Macbeth* that always enjoy the greatest favor are the very same ones previously mentioned in these pages; of these the following are usually requested again every evening: the witches' chorus in the *introduzione*, the cutthroats' chorus in Act II, and twice or even three times the *primo tempo* of Lady Macbeth's and Macbeth's duet in Act I. Besides, also the other pieces (now that the public is calloused to the poetry's improprieties and the defects in the staging) appear every evening more deserving of sincere praise.

Letter dated 24 March 1847, published in the
Gazzetta Musicale di Milano, 4 April 1847

— 12 —

Letter written after the close of the season.

The performances of *Macbeth* brought the Lenten season to an end last night on the boards of La Pergola, this largest of our theatres; and they did so amidst the same din of applause that accompanied that fortunate opera every evening of the season. The repetition of various pieces was, as usual, both requested and granted, among which we cite the *primo tempo* of the duet, "Fatal mia donna," etc., which was repeated four times. It is the general wish that the management should revive this favorite opera during the coming spring season, thus satisfying the desires of the public, which was disappointed by the paucity of performances (nine all told) caused by the shortness of time remaining this season.

Letter dated March 27, published in the
Gazzetta Musicale di Milano, 4 April 1847

Montazio dedicated the March 27 issue of La Rivista di Firenze *entirely to Verdi. We give no more than a sample of two of Montazio's verbose articles.*

— 13 —

Montazio's "Macbeth: Profanation in Four Acts by F. M. Piave" is the fiercest of the attacks on the Macbeth libretto. Like Calvi (No. 10 above), Montazio inadvertently blamed Piave for the libretto's very fidelity to Shakespeare. Furthermore, a number of the passages Montazio attacked were actually by Maffei (see Maffei's 11 April 1847 letter to Verdi and Verdi's letter to Ricordi written exactly ten years later). Montazio's discussion of the opening of Act I and of the sleepwalking scene will suffice to show his method and style.

With all the respect due to William Shakespeare and to all the ancient and illustrious martyrs of genius who unknowingly have been [made] champions of modern Romanticism, and before I undertake to bone the baroque carcass of this new Balaam's ass brought forth by the fecund mind of Piave, I feel it necessary to declare solemnly that, except in marionette shows, in the particular labors of Stenterello [the Florentine, dialect-speaking mask in commedia dell'arte productions], and in certain other low exhibitions of the arena, I consider the fantastic element, with all its witches, apparitions, soothsayings, sabbaths, wires, trapdoors, Bengal lights, phantasms, gnomes, sylphs, undines, *willis,* etc., etc., to be incompatible with our times, our habits, our ways, our audiences, our theatres, and most of all our [theatrical] machinists. . . .

This libretto is a faithful copy of Shakespeare's drama of the same name—indeed at first sight it might be taken for its very counterpart; however, when I saw with what care the librettist made every pathetic situation ridiculous, parodied every maxim, exaggerated every exaggeration, mutilating whatever might serve as accessory, context, explanation, excuse to the principal scenes of the Shakespearian drama, I decided to grace it with the title you see above. . . .

The first scene opens in a wood, which is perhaps one of Gianni's least infelicitous canvases in recent times, and in this wood appear three *clusters* of witches, played (let it be said once and for all) egregiously in all respects by La Pergola's lady choristers.

Those dames are kind enough to inform us that they have just slaughtered a pig, proof that the sabbath doings of witches are more innocuous than is commonly believed, except perhaps to members of the porcine world. It is true that one of the ladies announces *a sailor's wife has crossed her thought,* upon hearing which news each one of her respectable sisters promises to belabor the poor wife, one by arousing a *norther,* another by *raising the billows,* another by dragging the husband over shoals (the libretto says *ore shoals* [*pele secche*]), another, finally and to be done with it, by drowning him outright. . . .

After this fine opening we hear the sound of the drum announcing the arrival of Macbeth, who in fact enters, not with a drummer, but with Banquo; being perhaps accustomed to having the drummer protect the rear, rather than sending him ahead. I advise journalists in general to adopt this salutary habit. . . .

Macbeth, having done battle (mind you, it is a purely Baconian induction that prompts me to say he has done battle, for the libretto breathes not a word about it), was in the equally salutary habit of dropping in at a wineshop, for he is to all appearances a bit tight as he enters, mistaking the lightning for the sun, the darkness of the mysterious forest for a splendidly bright sky; whereupon, with the aplomb of an open-air lotto barker, he announces he has never before seen a day so *fierce* and *beautiful.* Banquo, less drunk than he, wastes no time with exclamations; instead he

examines those ladies' equivocal countenances and asks them whether they are of this world or of another *region*—for you must know that, to librettists, *worlds* are *regions,* a more resounding name and one richer in rhymes. To Banquo (poor wretch!), who is no great expert on women, it would seem these are women, but he is afraid to make a faux pas, for he has noticed their dirty beards. Banquo had little schooling, or he wouldn't have been so reluctant to call them women without further ado. The witches boldly tell both men's fortunes, and, having properly confused them in order to prove they are women after all, they "evanesce," which verb, *vanire,* is younger brother to the verb *fremire* and a host of other original, cockeyed verbs with which the Piavesque vocabulary overflows. . . .

At last the end is in sight. Lady Macbeth is suffering—suffering from *somnambulism,* so the libretto seems to imply, and a physician and a lady are waiting for her to walk on asleep and reveal her private affairs to them, presumably so that they can tattle about her. And in fact Lady Macbeth walks on, in the attire that is de rigueur for sleepwalkers and with the inevitable lamp in her hand—for every stage somnambulist must carry a light, not to light her way (for she sees nothing) but to light others'. Lady Macbeth being a queen, she could not *bear in her hand* the traditional small lantern; and so she has a sort of torch, which makes one dwell apprehensively on the risk to her eyes of watering and to her bed of catching fire, for we learn from the two spies that this is *the lamp she always keeps by her bed.* In order not to remain idle, Lady Macbeth abandons herself to all the whims of somnambulism: she *rubs her hands thinking to wash herself* but is obsessed with the thought she *will never clean it,* and since one of her obsessions is to reform grammar, she apostrophizes her *little hand, to whom* [!] *all Arabia will not clean up again.* Once started on the path of malapropisms, it is a demonstrated, documented fact that Piave never stops at the first one; therefore after the *little hand* (*piccol mano*) he makes Lady Macbeth tell her husband to *put on the cloths of night* (a fine costume for next Carnival's masquerade!) and to *spruce up.* A most felicitous image and a most felicitous expression! . . . . To avoid further malapropisms, Lady Macbeth then goes to bed, there to finish her slumbers. . . .

—— 14 ——

In his discussion of the opera—"Macbeth and the Music of Fantasy"—Montazio sets aside his vituperative tone, although some of his comments are nonetheless highly negative. (A long disquisition on the fantastic and on Act III is not included in these excerpts, since Montazio's attitude is discussed in CONATI *and* PINZAUTI.*)*

At the time of his journey to Rome, Verdi had contracted an obligation to write an opera for the Teatro di Apollo [there]. A shift in that theatrical management put this latest work of Verdi's under the control of Alessandro Lanari; and through a concatenation of events whose recital would be idle, Florence was enabled to witness its first performances at her greatest theatre.

The subject had been chosen by Verdi himself; it was he who sketched out the plot, slavishly modeled after Shakespeare's drama *Macbeth;* the versification of this plot was entrusted to Verdi's usual librettist, the most trivial Piave. But his verses were found so awkward and nonsensical that the same hand that had applied soothing plasters to *Attila* [i.e., Maffei] took the vain trouble of patching up here and there this rent and Harlequinesque tunic of Piave's. A vain labor, we were saying, since the few tolerable verses we chance on at rare intervals in this ridiculous farrago only serve to throw into relief the absurdities and resounding malapropisms with which it is covered and encrusted. Whence derives much harm to the music: the total absence of a poetic concept made an expressive and characteristic musical concept difficult, nay almost impossible; the absurdity of many senseless phrases provoked frequent laughter in the audience and greatly jeopardized the success of a good many pieces. But then the composer was faced with other obstacles, besides those presented by the strange and heterogeneous poem, if indeed Piave's play upon words may be termed a poem. The gravest difficulties were also exhibited by the subject, in which the fantastic element stands out in bold contrast and the variegated hues of domestic and popular affections are eclipsed by that dominant coloring.

. . .

As for the fantastic side, let us declare it openly: Verdi is still far from attaining to the high level of idealism reached by Weber, Mozart, Beethowen [*sic*], and, among the living, Mayerbeer [*sic*]. Whether it was a fear of inadvertently plagiarizing one of those lofty masters, or a resolve to remain at the opposite extreme of the model of the fantastic genre set up by those fanciful composers, or again that he lacked the time to develop his conceptions; in short, whatever the reason that may be adduced on Verdi's behalf, we may assert anything we like, except that here, in the purely fantastic portion of the Shakespearean poem set by Verdi, we have an example of fantastic grandeur, of characteristic harmony.

It is true that the brief prelude that precedes Act I gives brilliant promise of fantastic inspirations; but we do not meet with them in the course of the Opera.

Well-wrought yet graceful, varied though cast in a single movement, rich in excellent passages for the full orchestra is this prelude, which revolves mainly round the themes of Act III; and this prelude is magnificently joined by the first part of the witches' chorus, which opens Act I. The second part of this chorus, which accompanies a fanciful round dance, is an easy, graceful, very popular tune; and so, from the very first night of *Macbeth*'s run, it has invariably been encored. This magnificent chorus is followed by a very well orchestrated recitative, which brings us to a *duettino* with chorus between the two basses (Macbeth and Banquo); this is very rich in harmonies that fit the meaning of the words; yet it belongs to the usual group of musical effects to which Verdi has given his name and which characterize his style, not so much through their originality as through their constant use.

The brief witches' chorus that follows the departure of the two Scottish generals has a sufficient stamp of originality about it and matches the fanciful subject; and yet it passed by unnoticed by the audience.

The recitative of the soprano (Lady Macbeth) is of rare beauty; but it is not fully matched by the *adagio*, let alone by the allegro, a most complicated *cabaletta* in three movements, though the first is touched with a certain characteristic tinge that distantly hints of the dark and covetous cravings which Macbeth's ambitious consort is turning over in her mind. Wholly impregnated with marvelous harmonies is the ensuing recitative of Macbeth, on the point of killing the sleeping monarch, and it is a fitting introduction to one of the most inspired, sublime, dramatic, original pieces which ever issued forth from the Maestro's imagination—I refer to the *duettino* for soprano and bass that precedes the *finale*. The energetic, vibrant expression, full of passionate melody with which this marvelous duet is replete from beginning to end is indescribable, as is the impression it made upon the listeners, who were not content with calling for two encores of it every night—an extremely rare event in our theatres, occurring only when enthusiasm reaches the highest degree of over-stimulation. If nothing else in Verdi's opera were really good, beautiful, well-wrought, and masterly besides this magical duet, and the dramatic scene of Lady Macbeth in Act IV, these would be sufficient—and we affirm it without fear of being accused of exaggeration—to place *Macbeth* among Verdi's most original and beautiful works. Here every phrase is accentuated with supreme mastery: each syllable has its expression, each note awakens an echo in the listener's heart: a shudder seizes him involuntarily: a cry of fearful astonishment all but escapes his quivering lips: the harmony, which here attains that perilous limit of imitative music beyond which Parody and the Grotesque lie in wait with a sneer, so identifies itself with the sentiments expressed by the words, with the situations set in motion by the events, that it would be easy to deduce the dramatic import of both these scenes from the mere music; and the spectator, confused, palpitating, stunned, would find himself unable, at the conclusion of these miraculous creations, to applaud the wizard who worked those wonders, were he not prompted by the lively desire to delight once more in these sovereign melodies which plunged him into an ecstasy of admiration. To deny the presence of genius in these gigantic inspirations is an absurdity, a folly, like denying the sun's light, the warmth of fire. This dramatic boldness, this beauty of form and conception the *stretta* could not wholly match; though by no means to be disdained, it is yet nevertheless of a common cut and possibly even not perfectly original, being reminiscent, upon close examination, of certain phrases in a theme of *La Straniera*. . . .

The most characteristic and applauded piece in Act II is the cutthroats' chorus, which is always encored. It is a piece original in its make-up, magically orchestrated, and to a large extent accompanied only by the kettledrums which, in the ritornello, are joined by an indistinct and confused murmuring of instruments that marvelously conveys the idea of the fierce intentions motivating those murderers, while at the same time it gradually engenders a secret terror in the minds of the listeners.[1] Banquo's little *romanza*, which follows the chorus, appeared to us—perhaps owing to the scarcity of vocal resources in the executant (Benedetti)—to be quite insignificant.

The second part of this second act unhappily bears the mark of the precipitous pace at which the Maestro undoubtedly was obliged to deliver it to the performers, without having the opportunity of examining it carefully. Had he been able to do so, I have no hesitation in believing that, but for the *finale*, the Maestro would have decided to throw back that unfinished and merely sketched creation into the crucible of his glowing imagination, in order to infuse in it greater originality, and one more appropriate to the dramatic situation: the only [situation], perhaps, that offered an element of beauty and imagination to the musician, and the only one, by a strange fatality, which he failed to seize and render with his usual mastery. Macbeth's banquet, which is attended by the shade of Banquo, invisible to all except his slayer, is undeniably more dramatically fantastic and replete with terrible majesty than any other moment in the entire drama of Shakespeare. If Verdi did not make it altogether commonplace, he nonetheless neglected to represent by musical means the amazement of the guests, the terrible menace implicit in that mute apparition, which music alone could have worthily interpreted. Verdi saw the loftiness of the conception to which he could and should raise himself, but on the other hand he also saw the stipulations in the contract that bound him to the Impresario; and, satisfied he had already done enough in this work for his own fame and triumph, he wrote no longer masterfully, but commercially. In any case, this long segment of Verdi's work is not to be considered worthless; if the musician did not attain to the ideal beauty to which the situation seemed bound to impel him, if the gourmet listener sighs at the

---

1. Many writers praised the music *per se* of the murderers' chorus, but Montazio seems to be alone in defending its dramatic appropriateness. It seems, then, that Verdi's contemporaries, as well as twentieth-century critics, were puzzled by Verdi's "conspiracy style"—the convention is a personal one.

memory of the matchless *finale* in *Semiramide*, which Verdi now had a splendid opportunity of confronting with a worthy pendant, he nevertheless was able to infuse much grace and vivacity into a *brindisi*, with which Lady Macbeth opens the banquet; and graceful, too, is the accompaniment of the first portion of this scene, though it seems to us (perhaps it is an indiscreet observation) that it should be performed more quietly by the orchestra, which vastly dominates the singing. The *finale* of this act, as we observed earlier, is not only one of the finest pieces in the opera, but perhaps to be ranked among the most elaborate and rich in majestic harmonic combinations thus far composed by Verdi. . . .

[In Act IV], the tenor's *adagio* appears to us to be of fine workmanship, and the allegro with Choruses is Donizettian—a very effective, though not very original, piece; which, once an aria, had to be made into a duet during the opera's rehearsals, when it was realized that the tenor's vocal insufficiency prevented him from being heard with his voice alone. . . .

—— 15 ——

L. F. Casamorata's detailed essay on Macbeth *appeared in six installments in Ricordi's* Gazzetta Musicale di Milano *between April 11 and June 2. His comments rival Basevi's in interest; his remarks on the music, supported with musical examples, are more "technical" than any of the other Italian or French reviews consulted; and so we have reproduced, though by no means all of it, at any rate a good deal.*

We promised the readers of these pages a detailed essay on *Macbeth,* a new opera by Giuseppe Verdi; we will now keep that promise.—A short notice and general considerations on the book, a detailed examination of each piece of music, general considerations regarding the latter—this the order in which we shall proceed.

I

The subject of the book is such that it can be sketched in a few words: *Macbeth,* instigated and abetted by his wife, violates the code of hospitality and kills his king and cousin Duncan in order to usurp the crown at the expense of the latter's sons. Add to this main misdeed a series of accessory and secondary misdeeds, perpetrated to insure the fruits of the first one; add the recourse, on the part of the protagonist, to magic arts, to sorcery, in order to obtain counsel and help in his misdoings: and we have said everything on this matter. And in fact, there is in this drama, an absolute lack of any mild or gentle affection, of any generous passion that might comfort the spectator's oppressed spirits: not even pity comes to his aid to vary his sensations; whom should he pity, if King Duncan himself, Macbeth's victim, is known to him only by name and, just barely, by sight? . . . . One may therefore well ask what evil spirit advised Verdi to choose this subject, than which it is difficult to imagine a less musical one or one less suitable for music, at least with any good effect. Granted it is dramatic, granted it is tragic and suitable for tragedy; the portrayal of two odious characters (a man in whom the heat of depraved ambition, opposed by superstitious fears, is accompanied by weak cowardice;[1] a woman as wicked as he, ambitious and revoltingly cynical); that portrayal, I was saying, can offer grounds favorable to the unfolding of the poet's imitative faculties and engage, if not the heart, at least the intellect of the audience; for it is the function of poetry to speak in equal measure to the intellect and to the heart; but unhappy music, which only addresses herself to the heart—what is she to make of all this?—Somber, dismal, invariable, and unvaried hues, from beginning to end: this is the only result possible.

But is not recourse to the supernatural sufficient to spread so much variety over the subject that the listener's pleasure, if not his intellect, will be catered to?—Let us see.

The supernatural, or, as they said in former times, the *machine,* can be introduced into drama as either a real or a fantastic element; as either a principal or a secondary element. The supernatural is a real element in the drama when superhuman beings intervene in it, and when the spectators for whom the drama is intended believe in their existence; it is a fan-

1. I say this with regard to *Macbeth* as he appears in the opera; for in the English tragedy from which the libretto is drawn, the ugliness of his character is at least in part compensated for by his indomitable courage, which, in the words of a famous critic [Schlegel—see pp. 347–48] saves him, if not the sympathy, at least the partial esteem of the spectators [Casamorata's note].

tastic element when the drama includes beings in whose existence, or in the possibility of whose existence, the viewers have no faith;—it is a principal element when it serves directly to tie the knot or develop the action; it is an accessory when it does not serve that purpose directly or necessarily, so that, even if it is removed, the action would take place and proceed unchanged. Now the only supernatural element that is truly capable of moving the spectators is the first, which, being connected to religious sentiments and beliefs, is as respectable as they; and it must not be squandered on subjects that are not grand and noble. On the contrary, if the second type is to interest the spectator, then the latter must be well-furnished with imagination—an imagination so easily impressionable that it can rise effortlessly to the level of the poet's fantasy. But in times of dominant skepticism on the one hand, of positivism on the other, as, in truth, are our times; in times in which faith is so cool, and imagination reserved almost exclusively for financial speculations, this source of interest has lost much of the efficacy that distinguished it in the past. Besides it is easy to see that *supernaturally real* or *fantastic* are expressions to which I resort, as it were, approximatively and which need to be interpreted broadly; their meaning is entirely contingent on the degree of intellectual development ŏr the quality of the religious beliefs of the spectators: thus, that which is supernaturally real for Christians (angels, devils, the souls of the blessed and the damned, etc., etc.) is supernaturally fantastic to the followers of other religions; and, on the contrary, that which is real for the latter (divinities, spirits, and genii of the Greek and Egyptian heathenism, of Brahmism, Buddhism, Islam, Druidism, etc., etc.) is fantastic to Christians. . . .

However, one may have recourse to the fantastic supernatural, if not as a means of stimulating interest, then at least as a means of making abstract verities materially sensible, or to provide varied delight; and it may be treated as a principal element or as an accessory. To that end, one may fruitfully borrow from all sorts of theogonies and mythologies, and especially from those beings (fairies, witches, lemures, etc., etc.) in the existence of whom all Europe, even the Christians, once believed and in whom, thank Heaven, today surely no person, no matter how ignorant, places his faith. The first of these two ways of employing the supernatural, in other words *allegory*, is rather antithetical to music because of its excessive coldness, although Meyerbeer, in *Robert le diable*, succeeded with it not long ago. The second can be useful, however, for it offers occasion to vary the hues of the musical painting. And to the last-mentioned end the author of the present *Macbeth* seems to have had recourse to the supernatural; but to tell the truth, it seems that in fact the attempt has wholly failed: for what effective variety could be expected from fleeing the horrible reality of the characters of *Macbeth* and his wife only to plunge into the midst of the disgusting fantasy of those lurid, bearded witches, who amuse themselves by "killing swine" and making "hell-broths" by boiling "fingers of birth-strangled babes?" It is true that, besides the witches, help has been sought in our case from undines and sylphs, graceful and gentle images; but to what purpose, seeing that no sooner have they appeared in Act III than they vanish at once? For the rest, let no one put forward as an excuse the example of Shakespeare, from whom the libretto is drawn, because Shakespeare wrote his *Macbeth* at a time and for a nation in which the belief in witches and witchcraft was still general; at a time closely proximate to that in which King James himself wrote and published a serious treatise on witchcraft; at a time in which the parliament approved, and the king sanctioned, a minutely detailed law condemning witches to death, repealed only in modern times; he wrote, finally, for a nation in whose popular poetry witchcraft occupies a good two-thirds of the substructure: this kind of supernatural, then, was to him a real, not a fantastic element of his drama.[2]

But to conclude our promised observations on the book as a whole, it should be noted that not only the plot but the elocution derives from the English tragedy of the same name; note

---

2. Many critics have reproached Shakespeare himself for those lurid witches; and Johnson, defending him, says at bottom little else than that in his day it was necessary to put credulity on guard against false prophecies, given *due consideration for the state of public opinion*. Steevens, for his part, praising the author for those witches, rests his argument solely on this, that witchcraft is deeply rooted in the popular poetry of England [Casamorata's note]. This argument allows Casamorata to avoid censuring the immortal Shakespeare for his use of the fantastic, but does it not also imply that Casamorata and his enlightened contemporaries would need to reject the original play along with the belief in witches?

well, though, that with regard to the first both the cuts and the amplifications have given rise to gigantic incongruities; and that, with regard to the second, the literal translation into bad lines and abominable language of the English Euripides' elocution, which is by turns concise, verbose, imaginative, severe, etc., etc., has resulted in blithering nonsense. . . .

Here is an example of incongruity due to the amplification of Shakespeare's plan. . . . The cutthroats ambush Banquo in the nighttime and kill him; but his son escapes with the servant, who has dropped the light, which has gone out, so that the two cannot be pursued in the dark. But in the libretto the three cutthroats are replaced by a chorus, with the resulting incongruity and improbability that some thirty well-prepared people are incapable of killing an old man and a boy, especially since in the libretto the servant's help and the incident of the extinguished light are missing.

Another most unfortunate addition or amplification, among others, is the toast which, in the banqueting scene, the proud Lady Macbeth, now queen, sings while going round the room with her glass like a bacchante before sitting down at the table. That a young, mindless soldier like Orsini should sing a toast at a discreetly ambiguous feast such as Negroni's, in *Lucrezia Borgia,* may pass; but that one should be sung by a Lady, a Lady Macbeth, and a Lady Macbeth become queen, it seems incredible that a human mind should even conceive: even so, one might suffer it if only she sang it seated at the table, like Orsini!

Now, to have an idea of the beauty of the elocution, it is enough to open the book at random and see what has become of the following concept of Shakespeare:

. . . oftentimes, to win us to our harm,
The instruments of darkness tell us truths;
Win us with honest trifles, to betray us
In deepest consequence.[3]

thus rendered in Italian:

Ma spesso l'empio spirto d'inferno
Parla, e c'inganna, veraci detti,
E ne abbandona poi maledetti
Su quell'abisso che ci scavò. . . .

II

Having expended sufficient words in considering, from a general point of view, the book that forms the subject of Verdi's latest musical work, it is time to busy ourselves with the music: let us begin, then, with a description, as brief as possible, yet detailed, of each of the pieces that make up the opera.

A brief prelude opens the opera: it consists of a linking of some of the principal themes in the opera itself, yet, in addition to its fine instrumentation, it has the merit of presenting good workmanship and a logical structure.

. . . The Witches' choruses in this *introduzione* are all fine and make a very popular effect, but in some parts lack character, perhaps; rather than to the lurid sorceresses who sing them, they would at times be more appropriate to blithe and graceful dancing peasant girls. The duet between Macbeth and Banquo (baritone and bass) that intersects this introduction is very good; it distinguishes itself with some effective points, though it offers no novelties in its melody or structure.

After the introduction, the scene shifts from a wood to the interior of Macbeth's castle. His wife reads a letter in which he tells her of the witches' predictions, which have partially come true. Moved by immoderate ambition, she shows herself ready to have recourse to any means whatever, no matter how wicked, so that the prediction that promised the crown of Scotland to her husband might also come true. All this serves as subject to a recitative and to the first section of a *cavatina*. The [recitative opening Act II] is beautiful; and so is the [*primo tempo*] in which some delicious, and even novel, effects stand out. Furthermore, all of this singing part is most characteristic and appropriate to the harshness of the character's personality.[4]—A servant announces to Lady Macbeth that the King, accompanied by her husband, is about to arrive at the castle, where he will spend the whole night: at this news, she is immediately struck with the thought of killing the King, that her husband might usurp his crown, and her *cavatina* concludes with an invocation to the infernal furies in the form of a *cabaletta*. This *cabaletta* is, in essence, nothing much, offers

---

3. In footnotes to this and the other three quotations from Shakespeare, Casamorata gives literal prose renderings in Italian. His most extended example consists of all of Lady Macbeth's lines in the sleepwalking scene, a passage written by Maffei.

4. In the recitative that precedes this *cavatina* the composer has fallen into the error of substituting the spoken word for the sung in the reading of Macbeth's letter; an error greater than any that can be conceived, in opposition

nothing new, reminds us, perhaps, of some other, familiar *cabalettas;* but taken as a whole, it flows spontaneously, is easy to listen to, and offers the singer an opportunity of displaying her vocal resources to good advantage.

Enter Macbeth; immediately, his wife makes the most of the occasion in order to instill into his mind the sanguinary thought that besets her: his reaction is uncertain, but he shows he is not totally averse to the infamous suggestion. The gradual approach of rustic music announces the King's arrival. The couple go to meet him, introduce him onto the stage together with his son Malcolm, Banquo, Macduff, and many other gentlemen, and forthwith send him and all the others to bed unsupped, not without a great show of bows, curtsies, and gestures of all kinds (for this whole scene is in dumb show), an effect so bizarre and comical, that the audience's laughter could only be contained by the freshness of the lovely music, called "rustic" [*villereccia*] in the libretto, but which, in fact, has nothing rustic about it except the six-beat measure.

Once the King has retired, the night deepens, and Macbeth, agitated by the thought of the crime which he is considering, paces about near the King's chamber, frightened by sanguinary visions, beset with remorse, devoured by ambition; all at once he is resolved, and he enters the chamber to kill the King. [The dagger monologue], an instrumental and, for the most part, measured recitative, is (it seems to me) one of the finest pieces of dramatic musical declamation to have come from Verdi's pen: especially fine is its instrumentation, particularly certain heavy progressions in the middle of the harmony rendered by low clarinets, bassoons, etc. etc. There are also certain long-held notes in the clarinet which make an eminently dramatic effect. Why, then, was this piece allowed to pass almost unnoticed, not only by the public at large, but even by the maestro's warmest admirers?—Who can guess?

When Macbeth has entered Duncan's chamber, Lady Macbeth appears on the stage,

anxious to know what her husband has done: he returns with bloody hands and dagger, and reports the crime has been consummated. His disorientation, fears, and remorse, her derisive cynicism form the subject of a duet, the *primo tempo* of which has been received with frenetic applause at every performance and has had to be repeated two, even three times, so great is the feeling in it, so evident and true to life the double musical-dramatic imitation. The same reception has not been granted the *tempo di mezzo* of this duet, though not devoid of real virtues; much less the final *tempo*, which was rather coldly passed over. Nor wrongly so, indeed, for if the first part is well-wrought, it also awakens distinct reminiscences, while in all the rest the composer, for love of simplicity and truth of expression, has grazed the style of opera buffa.

... The *finale* begins with an agitato, at the point where Macduff comes out of the King's chamber: in this first section one notices a fine ostinato progression in the orchestra and much vitality, but in essence it does not rise above the common run of such pieces. At the moment when Banquo announces the King's death, all burst forth in a very dramatic transport of despair, which is followed by a prayer without instrumental accompaniment, in which the solo concerted voices are very well alternated with the masses of the chorus; the conception is fine, and it results from the combination of all the parts, rather than from the melody of one of them; fine, too, their distribution, and fine the modulations through which they proceed till at last they join again with the orchestra, and, now in unison, now divided into distinct parts, weave some ensemble periods that lead to a warm and vigorous, though brief, peroration. From the moment when Banquo announces the King's death, the movement takes on the form of an andante and maintains it essentially until the end, though at the conclusion the time takes on a different form. The whole of this piece is one of the finest that have been written for the theatre in a long time. There is only one thing

---

to the canons of good sense and musical imitation, even though examples are not lacking of great masters who have acted in the same fashion. To expend words in order to demonstrate the irrationality of this practice would, I believe, be out of place here, especially since I have done so in these pages on former occasions, more particularly in Vol. II, No. 49.

Fortunately, however, the singer (Nini-Barbieri, to whom the composer owes a debt of gratitude for the intelligence, bravura, and zeal with which she plays the role of Lady Macbeth) had the good sense this time to correct the composer's error, substituting on her own initiative song for declamation in the reading [of the letter] [Casamorata's note]. In his 31 January 1847 letter to Barbieri-Nini, after she had apparently complained about speaking the lines, Verdi expressed his willingness to set the letter in recitative.

Example 1

spar - ve il   sol, la not-te_or re - - gni   scel - le - ra-ta_in san-gui-na - - ta

in which the author merits some reproach, and it might be an error of judgment were it not perhaps an oversight caused by too blind an adherence to the librettist. Macbeth and his wife burst out with imprecations, together with the others, against the King's unknown assassin, pray for divine vengeance upon him, implore God for assistance in discovering him. Now, in the poet's defense, it might be said he did this intending that those two should speak thus, dissembling astutely lest they betray themselves; very well: now there is no doubt at all that, were the play to be spoken, the two actors playing Macbeth and his wife should evince their hidden motivation with those lines, with that *jeu* (the French would say); a *jeu* wholly different from that of the rest, who pray and imprecate sincerely, not out of design. And the composer, whose notes should correspond to the tone of the declamation, ought in that case to have assigned to those two characters a melody that, though it affected to agree with that of the others, differed from it in proportion as their dramatic intention was different. But this Verdi has not done; on the contrary, he has fused their voices into the undifferentiated mass of all the other voices.

[In Act II].... [the murderers' chorus is] most effective; the voices begin together with the orchestra; then they are left by it to continue by themselves; the kettledrums, however, accompany sotto voce.[5] Then the orchestra reenters, and with a forte comes to rest upon the dominant; and on that same dominant the violas introduce a subdued pedal in the middle register, above which the voices reproduce the same strain they sang first with the kettledrums, now enriched, however, by a delicate and beautifully imagined play of instruments. This is drawn out to the end, which is effected by a brief peroration in the guise of a decrescendo.—This piece is deliciously worked out; it leaves something to be desired, however, on the side of character, since it lacks (it seems to me) the

expression of that cold and indifferent savagery which is proper to these hired ruffians. But what we cannot forgive Verdi is the very strange way in which the words are set under the melody, so that they seem to have been forced into wedlock with an already existing tune. Here is how they sound beneath the notes: "Spar-ve il sol-la-not-te or-re-e-gni scel-le-ra-ta in-san-gui-na-a-ta, etc." [See music example 1.]

All of [the Act II] *finale* is generally well-made, but in essence it presents no remarkably good or novel features: it is not devoid, nonetheless, of finely-wrought points or *details*, as the saying goes. The opening march is remarkable for a certain sense of effort or oppression that freezes all its verve, with fine dramatic perceptiveness: in the final andante (for this act, too, ends with an andante), if the conception is not as lofty as in that of the first act, the characters of Macbeth and his wife are, on the contrary, well-defined and differentiated from all the others. For the rest, I believe the effect of this whole piece would gain a great deal if one were to shorten by one-half the piece before the andante, by cutting one statement of the *brindisi* and one apparition of the ghost; it seems in truth impossible that one should formulate such a wish apropos the music of Verdi, who by instinct has always had the gift of being relatively brief, and of sensing the point at which pieces really ought to end!

Act III [opens in the] Grotto of the witches.—The witches are gathered round a magic cauldron, attending to their sorcery; this is the subject of a rather good chorus, in which the beginning is characteristic, and especially one strain, where we hear an odd, but (from the point of view of expression) perfectly appropriate fluctuation from one key and mode to another;[6] now and then, however, the expression becomes wholly rustic, particularly at the peroration.—Macbeth comes to the witches in order to learn his future destiny; to that end,

---

5. I wish the composer had not, in a way, anticipated the effect of those drums alone with the voices by using them in more or less the same manner in the prayer of the first finale [Casamorata's note].

6. Casamorata must mean the passage beginning "Tu, rospo venefico" (*Ricordi*, p. 184), which, like the opening, presents successive phrases on i, III, and v of the tonic, E minor.

various spirits and apparitions are summoned ... All this portion is treated partly in the manner of recitative, partly metrically; but, to tell the truth, it offers little that is remarkable. At the last of the revelations, Macbeth starts and faints: the witches summon undines and sylphs, who, dancing around him, recall him to his senses and vanish: this provides the occasion for a ballet and, simultaneously, a charming chorus, which, however, reminds us a little, both as to the idea and the instrumentation, of the Druid priestesses' chorus in Act III of *Attila*, at first; and, later, of the "temptation by drunkenness" in *Robert le diable.*—The king, having come to, rants and raves, and a similar *cabaletta* (a rather common one, however) concludes this act, which, frankly speaking, is the least praiseworthy act of the opera. Its music, it would almost seem, was neglected by the author, who placed his trust wholly in the spectacle; if this is so, we must say he acted unwisely, for, once a fantastic subject had been chosen, the fantastic side was the main one, and so not to be neglected on any account. Meanwhile, an expedient way of alleviating (if not removing) the ills that beset this act would be to make considerable cuts in it; in this regard, besides reducing the number of apparitions, it might not be a bad thing to suppress all of the final *cabaletta*, ending with the chorus and ballet of the sylphs; or, were one to retain it, it might be well to add to it a men's chorus, for it would be an easy thing to do, if one were to imagine that Macbeth's attendants had come after him, just as in the tragedy Lennox comes looking for him; that might serve to heighten the effect of the concluding piece.

Act IV [opens with] a fine chorus, whose first melody in particular, in the minor mode, breathes the most melancholy gloom: this piece was perhaps not applauded as much as it should have been because in the second part, with the passage into the major mode, the Public felt it recognized a resemblance to a famous chorus in another opera by the same master ... a war hymn sung alternately by Macduff, Malcolm, and the chorus brings the scene to an end. This hymn is a sort of polonaise, really common in conception, but having the usual advantage of lucidity and a certain momentum capable of keeping an audience attentive.

... [The sleepwalking] scene consists of a continuous rhythmical declamation, broken from time to time by brief stretches of melodious singing; it is accompanied by an instru-

mental process [andamento] that is almost constantly ostinato, borne mainly by the muted strings and the basset horn [corno-bassetto; Casamorata means the English horn]. The tragically somber coloring of this whole piece, the excellence of its execution, the feeling that dominates the sung part, the artistry of the instrumentation, all contribute to making this one of the pieces that do the greatest honor to the young maestro from Parma.

Another hall in the Castle.—It is day: Macbeth, abandoned by nearly all his followers, laments his situation: recitative, of the commonest sort; *romanza*, its melody well-conceived and carried out, and breathing an appropriate sadness. [Casamorata characterizes the following section, up to Macbeth's exit, as "well-made, but without any special musical interest."]

[... The remainder] is treated, musically speaking, in a very perfunctory way; and the composer in so doing acted wisely, for by now it was best not to detain the audience much longer; yet Macbeth's musical agony does not lack an appropriately dramatic dark coloring. Some have maintained that in a dying man's mouth the imprecations preceding his death were unseemly; if Macbeth died exhausted and worn out by illness, the criticism would be indubitably just; but as he dies a sudden death, in the fullness of his strength, stimulated even by the battle, by rage and anger, that shouting before his death may be considered not unreasonable, nor unnatural, hence the criticism is not valid.

III

... It has been said by many that *Macbeth* is deficient in song, or, put differently, that it lacks melodies.—Is this true?—I do not think so: on the contrary, I think there are melodies in it—many melodies—though there not too conspicuous ones, for they are all, or nearly all, of the same kind more or less, for they are all wholly syllabic. This is, I believe, an undeniable and undenied fact; let us now see why it is so, and whether the maestro ought to be praised by us or not for having proceeded in this manner.

It is in the nature of song that it adapts itself to the genius, to the taste, to the character of the languages spoken by the different nations: this indeed is why the song of all those peoples who speak languages whose sounds are open, whose articulation is lovely, bases itself characteristically upon vocalization [i.e., a melismatic style of setting texts to music] while, on the contrary, it is principally and characteristically syllabic with nations who speak languages whose sounds are somber, muffled, or nasal, whose articulation is harsh and violent. The Italian language belongs to the former; it has always been a salient characteristic of Italian song that it is vocalized. On the contrary, it is a fundamental characteristic of the song of the nations beyond the Alps, who speak languages to be classed in the latter of the above categories, that they are principally syllabic. . . .

. . . This being so, it is certainly an odd thing for all to see how the modern Italian musical school, following those who most preach nationality in everything, who always march with the national colors aloft, thinking it is carrying out an *Italian* musical reform plunges itself into a system which is in fact peculiar to the foreign schools! And the system I mean consists in the virtually total banishment of vocalized songs and the all but exclusive adoption of syllabic songs on the part of the modern Italian dramatic composers; a banishment and adoption which, because they are total, deserve to be thoroughly rebuked, inasmuch as they replace a rich arsenal of means with a far poorer one, a source of the most varied effects with one producing much the same effect all the time. . . .

Unhappily, it seems to me that all of today's young Italian composers, more or less, are guilty of the above-mentioned sin, and Verdi at least as much as the others; and perhaps more than the others in this *Macbeth* of his: now the accusation of monotony directed, not wholly unjustly, against this work is indeed a consequence of that. . . .

But it must be said, for truth's sake, that if the efficient cause of the error is the tendency of the modern Italian school, the immediate cause of it in the present work of Verdi is the nature of the libretto which he has had to set to music this time. [There follows a long and interesting general discussion of the kinds and forms of verse drama apt for setting.]

. . . Let, then, modern musical poets be frankly and fearlessly lyrical when they need to be so, that is, *when they write for music;* and let composers take care not to choose librettos that are not lyrically written. Let Verdi do the same; for had he done so on the present occasion, he would have had opportunities for intermixing with his syllabic songs major vocalized songs, as beautiful as many that he has composed, and

their effect in *Macbeth* would have been even greater. It would have been the more desirable here besides, to lighten the harm unavoidably done to the music by the absence in the drama of the more musical and music-able passions and by the fact that it hinges upon one of the passions most antithetical to music, cold ambition.

. . . From what I have already said separately on each piece in the opera, it is easy to infer my thinking on [the subject of characteristic expression]. Not being able to rest my judgment on proof, by the very nature of things, I prefer to limit myself to reporting that the general opinion in Florence . . . was that the characteristic expression was far from being attained in the whole fantastic part [of the work], . . . On the other hand, in the non-fantastic portion of the opera—especially with regard to *Lady Macbeth*—the character, it seems to me, is very well observed. . . .

It truly grieves me to have to reprove Verdi for a certain negligence that from time to time disfigures his work. It consists sometimes in the division or contraction of diphthongs in a manner opposite to the metrical requirement of the verse, as, for instance, by making "pa-tri-a" a three-syllable word, "po-tei" a two-syllable word; and so forth, when in fact they should contain two and three syllables respectively; it consists at other times in shifting the tonic accents of the words, as, for example, in "aconitò," "crepuscolò," "nascerè," "sentò," etc., in lieu of "acònito," "crepùscolo," "nàscere," "sènto," etc.; it consists sometimes in a lack of syllabic and rhythmic correspondence between the song and the words, so much so that it would seem the former was imagined with not the least thought of the latter, and the latter driven by force beneath the former by hook or by crook: here are some examples of all this: [He quotes the witches' "ed il nostro oracolo gli parlerà" (*Ricordi* 32.3.3–4); Macbeth's "in cor m'abbonda come l'anima m'assal," from "Vada in fiamme" (506.5–507.1.1 in this volume); and the cutthroats' chorus, Ex. 1]; it consists at times in a lack of correspondence between the phrasing of the music and that of the words, which constitutes an ugly offense of false musical declamation, as in the following example:

[See Example 2, overleaf]

where the harmony ought to enter by way of support at the substantive "pensier," the main

Example 2

word in the sentence, and not at the adjective "cruento," which is an accessory in it. An even more pronounced example:

[See Example 3, below]

where the adjective "inaridita," in the poem already a little too distant from the noun "vita" and the verb "sento," on which (with the verb "essere" understood) it depends, is wholly cut off from them by the music and treated as if it had a meaning of its own, isolated and absolute. But the following example, from the largo (a fine piece, incidentally) of the tenor's aria in Act III, may serve as fuller and incontestable proof of what I mean in this regard. [Casamorata quotes the vocal line and figured bass of *Ricordi* 251.3.3–252.2.1.] There is no need of taste or of too nice an intelligence to notice that the musical declamation of these words, from the point of view both of emphasis and of prosody, is wholly false, while on the other hand it would have cost but a modicum of trouble to render it utterly irreproachable, as can be seen

[See Example 4, opposite]

At times that negligence consists in a lack of correspondence between the voice and the accompaniment, as when the latter resolves (onto a unison) an appoggiatura ahead of, or behind, the former [Casamorata's example corresponds to Ricordi 250.4.1–3 (transposed up a third—though without the required key signature), but unfortunately his whole point is based upon a corrupt text that resolves the accompaniment on the *second* sixteenth in measure 2]; or when it [the voice] resolves an appoggiatura at the very moment when the accompaniment strikes it [Macbeth's "Lo sono ed audace s'io guardo

tal cosa"; 494.1.1–4 in this volume]; or when the voice and the accompaniment collide at minimal intervals, examples of which may be seen in the seventh and thirteenth bars of the *Andante assai sostenuto* of the sleepwalking scene (for the rest very beautiful); here the voice attacks A flat and B flat, while in both cases the basset horn leaps to a B double-flat against those sounds; a most repugnant clash, and one having no justification, which could easily have been avoided by means of changes so minimal in the vocal part, that its character would surely not have suffered any alteration.

It consists, finally, in the treatment of harmony (though only rarely) in such a negligent way, in the jotting down of parts with such a lack of unequivocal intention, that at times they seem to be butting each other: here is an example of this, in which the C, doubling the fundamental bass of a dominant seventh chord, seems astonished at finding itself in close contact with the D flat, the minor ninth of the same bass [487.1.3–5 of this volume].

Here is another example, in which a dominant pedal point in the treble is difficult to execute and makes a disagreeable effect, for no other reason than that the chords placed under it are too full and too closely spaced [Casamorata's quotation corresponds to Ricordi 40.3.2–40.4.1 (beat 1 only)]. The effect would have been better if the third and fourth chord had been treated thus:

[See Example 5, opposite]

especially because in this way one would have avoided the poor resolution of the D flat to the A flat [instead of to C] from the second inversion of the chord of the diminished seventh to the dominant in the root position. But it is even

Example 3

Example 4

pos-sa a co-lui le brac - cia del tuo per-do - no a - prir; a lui le

brac - cia a lui le brac - cia del tuo per do - no a - prir.

worse when this negligence is found in those very passages where the composer meant to display some degree of workmanship: here is an example from the second part of the famous first-act duet [482.3-483.1 of this volume]. Seeing that counterpoint of the soprano against the melody of the baritone, especially in the second bar [482.3-4], one may truly assert in all candor that the harshness of the effect is equal to the shoddiness of the workmanship.

Some may think, perhaps, that I have lingered too long on these observations; the defects I have indicated may seem small sins, too venial to deserve such particular critical notice; and I agree they are not so great that they need to, or are able to, influence the general judgment to be passed on the opera, especially in view of the real qualities with which it is indubitably adorned. But just because it is beautiful, it is a pity the author neglected those measures which might have made it lovelier, with a minimum of trouble, with only a few more hours' work. Nor let anyone attempt to excuse him by adducing the example, unfortunately widespread, of the slipshod way in which many, and not the least, of our composers are accustomed to treat the art in our midst: that proves nothing. Granted those sins I have pointed out above are of the slightest consequence; but, pray, when a poem, or a discourse, is of great worth, any defects we should notice in the punctuation, in the spelling would also be considered very slight; yet what man of letters, whether he be great or of no account, would not blush at being reprimanded for such faults?

But as I am pouring from the bitter cup of criticism, I will empty it all at once. Would it have been a bad thing for the young maestro to try to infuse more variety into the accompaniments of his opera?—I know very well that Italian singing requires freedom, and that this freedom too often is hampered by the shackles of obbligato counterpoints and by the play of real parts in the accompaniment: but to tell the truth, the modern abuse of unisons ties it down even more. Besides, cannot a middle way be found between excessive rigor and inordinate relaxation?—Some artifice which, without obscuring or hindering the melody, should be somewhat more significant than a mere accompaniment of arpeggiated or repeated notes, varied at most by some redoubling on the first weak beat, or on the weak part of strong beats in the manner of a polonaise? And in *Macbeth,* to tell the truth, there is hardly an accompaniment not thus conceived: I say "hardly," because there are a few which are highly elaborated and of such a quality as to demonstrate that, when the maestro so wishes, he does not lack this ability.

Having begun by telling at great length what seemed to me less well done in *Macbeth,* I am now impelled by my last remark to discuss what, though well done, could be done better still. In this regard I beg leave to ask whether, for a true lover of the art, it is not painful to observe, sometimes, in the works of the young maestro from Parma how perfection is only grazed, when with a trifle it might have been wholly attained; how some small additional

Example 5

che tar - di che tar - di

*C. has

393

Example 6

thing has been neglected, which might wholly have satisfied the artists without in the least damaging the wished-for popular success. To make my idea more comprehensible, I choose an example at random from the final allegro [i.e. the *cabaletta*] of the soprano's *cavatina* in Act I. After the repeat of the *cabaletta,* the piece ends with a brief peroration in which the perfect cadence is conveyed by a bass passage over which the upper parts sustain the harmony of the tonic major triad [*Ricordi,* p. 48.1.1–3 (first beat only)]. Now, it should be noted that that passage is entirely new at that point and bears no resemblance, whether melodic or rhythmic, to the rest of that allegro. See now how easily this defect in musical logic could have been averted at least in part by taking advantage of the motif advanced by the voice in the course of the final cadence:[7]

[See Example 6, above]

An analogous observation could be made to some extent concerning the orchestral tutti that separates the *cabaletta* in this piece from its repeat, for it also, though not quite so much, lacks a clear relationship to the rest. In truth, why, in order to express a sole poetic concept underlying the words, must the music employ several wholly disparate ideas?[8]

I trust no one will do me the injustice of believing I think highly of the artifice I proposed above: Heaven forbid I should be so puerile! On the contrary, I consider it pretty crude, and had recourse to it only to give a concrete illustration of my meaning: but for the rest, when a tiny artifice that costs nothing, harms nothing, can lend greater correctness, greater perfection to your work, why, O composers, do you wish to neglect it? The vogue for themes, for the way in which they are presented and adorned, changes, unhappily, every five years, and as it changes, music's popularity mostly fades away: but the art of deriving accessory ideas from the principal one, of properly tying together the different parts of a composition, of preserving the diversity of those parts within the unity of the whole, remains always the same, and it alone is capable of keeping alive, at least in the esteem of artists, a composition, though the composer be dead and buried. Witness Mozart's *Don Giovanni,* shining still, after so many years, with a success which, if not popular, is at least general with all persons of taste, whereas with so many more modern works, once applauded to the skies by the multitudes, the very titles are now unknown. Say now, O composers, do you think that correctness, that elegance of form, of workmanship, had no share in that result?—As for myself, I believe candidly they may be credited with a good half of it. I know well enough that these are useless considerations for those composers who content themselves, when they write, with doing only as much as is required in order to pocket the salary for their work: but I also know that Verdi is not, the Lord be praised, of their number; I esteem him as an artist, and a most noble artist; that is why I here speak of him to artists in all artistic freedom.

Having exhausted whatever there was of bitterness in what the ungrateful duty of a critic obliged me to say ... I cannot help but offer my congratulations in seeing Verdi, in this *Macbeth* of his, cast off the fetters of certain preestablished forms, the serfdom of certain, as

7. Ten years later Verdi complained that the violas and cellos in Italian orchestras were almost always *razze di cani* (*Abbiati* 2, 413); it is interesting to contemplate how the cellos and basses would fare with Casamorata's suggested revision.

8. Verdi knows well, when he wishes to, how to practice the art of linking ideas; an ingenious example of this is in the final *cabaletta* in Act III, where the return to the forte is accompanied by a progression derived from a fragment of instrumental melody that served to introduce the return itself [507.3 and 506.2.2 ff., respectively]. It is a pity, however, that the good intention at that point is in fact lost through a miscalculation of the relative strength of the instruments [Casamorata's note].

it were, mechanical means of producing effects, to whose use he seemed to have committed himself forever in the works following his first theatrical essays. Now, in truth, with all the freedom of a composer who has gained full self-assurance, he proceeds openly and boldly in casting his work, and, while preserving intact his own individual artistic profile, he now adopts a formula, now prefers another; now organizes his pieces this way, now that, depending on the dictates of his inspiration or the objects of his designs; depending on what he feels the economy of the drama or the purely musical effect may require.

And this artistic individuality of his is now more pronounced; not that he ever lacked one, for, on the contrary, this was always one of his foremost virtues; but, though he has always known how to develop and, especially, conclude his ideas in a manner entirely his own and characteristic, it was rare that the ideas in themselves, formerly, should not be traceable to other works for their genesis. But in *Macbeth,* except for a few coincidences, rather than reminiscences, to which I have already alluded ... the case is in truth otherwise. That, to my mind, is no small merit in this day and age.

Another remark I must make concerns a matter of the highest current interest: I mean, the instrumentation. If Verdi has always deserved the highest praise in this field, he deserves as much now for his *Macbeth,* in which he has come even closer to perfection. It is truly pitiful to see how often composers who conceive their works excellently in the abstract, who can trace lovely melodies, develop and work them out well, who do not lack the fecundity to imagine a rich variety of accompaniments for them, in the end miss the effect totally, their good intentions lost through the fault of an unhappy instrumentation.... Now this is not the case with Verdi, nor was it even at the beginning of his musical career. But while he has never failed in obtaining brilliant effects, he had not, before now, been able always to guard himself against an excess of force, the more damaging in that, thanks to his intimate knowledge of instruments, he knows how to use them so that they will deliver to the full all their sonority. Now, among the good qualities of *Macbeth* there is indubitably that of a great and wise economy in this matter. Among many other pieces, one can cite as an example the scena and duet in Act I, the cutthroats' chorus in Act II, and the sleep-walking scene in Act IV.

And continuing on the same topic, I shall also note that Verdi, in the past, was somewhat prone to fall into the universal modern sin: the abuse of doublings in the instrumentation. And here, too, I notice with pleasure that a most noteworthy improvement has taken place in his *Macbeth....*

Now, to conclude this lengthy discourse of mine, and before I lapse into silence, I must express my congratulations to all artists and to the art itself at the thought that Verdi is at the moment summoned personally across the Alps and the sea to sustain Italy's musical honor, of which in his preceding works, and especially in this recent *Macbeth,* he has luminously proved himself a most powerful champion. For the sake of his honor and that of the art I wish him, in this honorable contest, a propitious fate and remain confident that we shall see him return to the fatherland, his brow wreathed with a new, most noble garland.

> L. F. Casamorata's essay on *Macbeth,* serialized in six numbers of the *Gazzetta Musicale di Milano,* from 11 April to 2 June 1847

— 16 —

Maestro Verdi's grand Opera MACBETH, which has already reappeared at the above-mentioned Theatre on four nights of the current season ... has elicited even greater enthusiasm than at its first production.

> Notice from the Imperial and Royal Teatro della Pergola published in the June 15 number of *Gazzetta di Firenze*

— 17 —

... La Pergola continues happily with *Macbeth.* Last night's performance was a benefit for [Augustina] Boccabadati; between the acts of *Macbeth* the young artist sang, as beautifully as ever, the scene in *Giovanna d'Arco* she had sung before at the Filarmonica.

> published in the June 25 number of the *Gazzetta Musicale di Milano*

—— 18 ——

From Montazio's "Chronicle of the Florence Theaters"

... Macbeth has been making its reappearance for several nights now on the boards of La Pergola, minus the *Barbieri's* organ, minus a wee portion of the chorus, minus a wee portion of goodwill in the orchestra, and in every other respect similar, very similar to the *Macbeth* of four months ago.—Augustina Boccabadati worked the miracle of ameliorating the general regret at the absence of the Barbieri's mighty voice, and where her voice is insufficient she finds a way of winning the public's favor by means of intelligent and animated acting, which with Barbieri had always been an impossible wish. That swarm of obstinate anti-Verdians who ascribed wholly to Barbieri the triumph Verdi gained with Macbeth have been made to look like monkeys seeing him elicit the same

applause as usual and confirm the original opinions of the impartial, even with the collaboration of a less than sublime singer and the test of perilous and recent comparisons.

Achille de Bassini has lived up to his name [i.e., the Achilles of Little Basses] and has sustained with his accustomed valor the ponderous weight of the title part. Only at some few dramatic points should we like to see him not so preoccupied with singing as to neglect his acting and show himself cold and insensible in those very scanty situations where the perfidious librettist inadvertently let slip out words and actions that drew forth a fertile spark from the bosom of the composer.

Montazio, in *Rivista di Firenze,* 23 June 1847

—— 19 ——

Letter of Melchiorre Balbi dated Padua, 12 August 1847, two days after the season closed with Macbeth

How much this opera was appreciated let that public tell which on that evening demanded to hear no less than five times the *primo tempo* of the duet between *Macbeth* and his spouse, performed marvelously well by the celebrated

Barbieri-Nini and the equally worthy, valiant Collini. Everything in this opera pleases! ... The singers, the chorus, the orchestra please extremely ...

Gazzetta Musicale di Milano, 18 August 1847

—— 20 ——

The principal review of the Padua production was that written by G. Stefani (Caffè Pedrocchi, 1 August 1847). His views are generally similar to those of Montazio, whom he frequently cites with approval; these echoes of Montazio's articles excerpted above need not be presented again here.

[Stefani predictably begins with an attack on the libretto and] all the ridiculous, insipid phrases, all the grammatical blunders, all the newly-coined words and the verbs that are the property of the authors, not to mention the other colossal oddities with which this bastard work is encrusted." ... How Signor Verdi can have become enamored of [Piave's libretto] I know not: perhaps the need of a fantastic subject, an acquaintance with Shakespeare's original, the new and terrible situations, the total absence of the inevitable loves, angers, revenges, jealousies with which the other dramas overflow, while here ambition rules as the sole dominant passion—perhaps all these seduced him (poor man!), exposing his music to the risk

of falling at any moment because of the ridiculous accompaniment of the words!

[After decrying fanatics who are excessive in either praising or condemning the work, Stefani continues.]

In some of Macbeth's pieces (Verdi) has attempted a totally new genre, and he has succeeded; in many others, it must be confessed, he not only does not approach the grandness and originality of the former, but falls so far behind that these seem made by a professional notegatherer, simply to increase the number of bars, rather than by an exacting high priest of the art. There are some who say that when, in a score, there are two or three truly masterly pieces, it is well not to sift into the rest too minutely. Not true, say I; maestro Verdi's reputation is such that it alone suffices to induce the two most formidable devourers of Italian music, the Signori Ricordi and Lucca, to pay a king's ransom for each product that emerges from his creative mind; and he can afford to remain at home for months on end, studying his subject in depth and informing his works, from top to bottom, with that originality and philosophy which, when he so wishes, he knows how to employ and of which we have the most convincing proofs in this very score.

... [Lady Macbeth's] very beautiful recitative, [is] followed by an *adagio* which is too reminiscent of other, happier inspirations in *Nabucco* and *I lombardi*. The *cabaletta*, in three sections, has nothing good about it except one solitary phrase, which conveys extraordinarily well the thought, "Tu notte ne avvolgi di tenebra immota" (*And pall thee in the dunnest smoke of hell*): the rest is straw, ill-woven.

Now move aside, ye reeking critics, and doff your hats to the most dramatic, most inspired, most sublime scene to have emerged in a long time from the musical storehouse of Italy's Euterpe. There's no exaggeration in my words: I call to witness first of all the sonorous yell emitted by 1400 throats which followed the *primo tempo* of the duet for soprano and baritone, the piece of which I speak; secondly, the irresistible need for an encore; finally, the state of overexcitement that suddenly, like an electric current, invaded every listener, from the cold cynic to the most possessed Verdian enthusiast.

... Macbeth preludes with a recitative filled with philosophical beauties: each note, each syllable expresses the fearful sentiments of the regicide; and the verse (it is good, for all that), "or l'assassino—Come fantasma per l'ombre si striscia" is marvelously well-translated in a musical phrase of the imitative kind, tenebrous and close. Enter Lady Macbeth, who encourages her anguished consort, who has already killed Duncan.... The hurried and supremely expressive melody that accompanies the words, "Nel sonno udii che oravano" etc., and the wife's artfully light and ornate reply, in which, with warbled simpering, she tries to pacify her crazed husband, are inspirations of a kind to touch your every fiber and send a shudder through your whole frame. The rest of the duet, too, maintains the same original imprint: from the first bar to the last, the instruments graze their notes mezza voce: all the violins have their mutes: indeed, a single cry might

awaken the courtiers sleeping round about: it was high time a little common sense penetrated the theatre. A precipitous *cabaletta*, lasting just a few minutes, not new but well-suited to the circumstances, closes this stupendous and masterly piece of work. You gentlemen who are detractors of the new, tell me now where, 'midst the scrap iron of your emasculated cantilenas, you can find a scene like this one, containing such dramatic clarity and the power to engulf you in a state of feverish enthusiasm. And then you would deny the presence of genius in Verdi!

After so much beauty and novelty of form and conception it was hard to find, in the further course of the score, another piece that should equal or approach that magnificent duet. Therefore it seems to me that, placed as it is in the first part, it damages the subsequent effect of the drama; for the soul, profoundly agitated by that vigorous shock, can only be capable of weaker sensations thereafter; and every other beauty appears to fade by comparison....

The banquet scene ... would call for greater originality.... and for greater relevance to the eminently dramatic situation in Shakespeare's work—there is too great a discrepancy between the terrible and broken utterances of Macbeth and the jovial toast intoned by his wily spouse. The former do not rise to the height of the conception, while the latter, though popular and graceful, is too vivacious and bouncy; and it reminds us of our good [old] fathers' simple and primitive tunes with guitar accompaniment. It seems to me that Verdi has neglected the culminating point of the action which calls for a more accomplished and mature development....

Now we have arrived at the capital scene of the whole opera, but for the first-act duet. Attention, gentlemen, to the exquisite beauties of this masterly piece (I act the charlatan this time, because I thought that on the first night it was somewhat neglected). It is a scene that awakens horror. Fear, remorse invade the soul of the regicide's accomplice. She sleepwalks, and in her delirium utters terrifying things: every note expresses a feeling: the piece as a whole departs from the common rule, from which Verdi gradually emancipates himself: it is not a recitative, not an aria, nor a *romanza*; but a free musical translation, highly philosophical, of the thoughts that pass like shadows through the queen's deranged mind; it is a bloody and terrible recollection of the murder; the music itself and the action bring it to mind. The public, after the last note has sounded, remains as it were stupefied by the novelty of the conception; which, once understood, cannot fail to elicit a torrent of applause, pouring truly from the heart, which is deeply stirred. The baritone's *romanza* which follows is of a very simple cast that demands in performance an impassioned style of singing, the style of the worthy Colini. After this, good night! Everyone may return to his home, unless he wishes to listen to the *rata-tatat* of drums and martial trumpets, which is drawn out longer than necessary, and to a *recitativo cantabile* of Macbeth, mortally wounded, which Verdi might well have spared himself. Verdi is the man who should by now be banishing these prolonged and screaming songs of the dying, as well as other things that lack common sense. This ended, the curtain falls. . . .

Maestro Verdi's opera owes much of its fame to the stupendous performance of signora Barbieri–Nini, the drama's heroine. She, by the spell of her all-powerful voice, captivates the emotions, the soul, the spirit of the listener. She sings, and a thousand spectators sit open-mouthed, listening to the purest, most winning, most natural timbre, and forget all about daggers, witches, cauldrons, and ridiculous ascents and descents of royal phantasms. In the first-act duet and in the sleepwalking scene she also acts dramatically and conserves admirably that treasure of a voice which at other times she expends too generously. We have need of her songs; let her then economize, for our sake as well as for hers. . . .

— 21 —

After a production in Lucca (with Tadolini as Lady Macbeth), the opera was next done in Rome. For a complaint about cuts taken in this production see No. 25.

Verdi's *Macbeth* was produced at the Teatro Argentina on the twelfth of this month. The outcome was excellent, for the music and singers pleased in the highest degree. Even Act III, which elsewhere has met with less approbation than the other acts, was most fortunate here. The pieces that won the greatest ovations were, in Act I, the soprano's *cavatina*, the duet of the soprano and baritone, and the *finale*; in Act II, the soprano's *cavatina*, the cutthroats' chorus, the *brindisi*; in Act III, the baritone's two pieces; in Act IV, the sleepwalking scene. . . .

Gazzetta Musicale di Milano, 22 September 1847

— 22 —

A report on the Venice (La Fenice) production, of 26 December 1847

Verdi's *Macbeth* has pleased. . . . And this is due, in the first place, to the merits of the music, in the second to those of the performance, entrusted, for the title role, to Varesi, for whom in fact this opera was written.

The pieces in the score that were best-liked were principally the concerted numbers, especially the sextet. The solos and the duets were also enjoyed, but not, I think, as much as the music deserved: the cause of this may well have been the voice of signora de La Grange, who, though a good performer, is not endowed with the vocal resources requisite for the performance of the dramatic role of Lady Macbeth. The sleepwalking scene, which is after all a sublime piece, did not obtain the effect it had elsewhere. . . . The tenor, signor Palma, was also well-liked in his Aria, whose *cabaletta* was in fact demanded again.[1]

Letter dated Venice, December 27, published in the *Gazzetta Musicale di Milano*, 29 December 1847

1. For "Folchetto's" report of a patriotic demonstration triggered by Palma's performance (and costume), see p. 420.

The avowed conservatism of the review of this production in the Gazzetta Privilegiata di Venezia *(29 December 1847) is rather refreshing after the pretentiousness of some of the Florentine critics.*

The opera, or better the libretto, has this disadvantage, that the events in it—rather strange ones, to tell the truth—are so clustered, so piled up on top of each other, that anyone attempting to follow them closely is left quite breathless. To confine the vast tableau of the Shakespearean drama within the meager limits of an opera, it was necessary to omit many incidents accessory to the action, incidents whose function it was to prepare it or make it believable: the beauties of the dialogue and of the passions were lost or could not be saved: so that all that was left was a vain and puerile phantasmagoria that leaves the mind and heart utterly unmoved. The poetry, as always, is neglected: though here and there we find a good line, whoever its author might be.

As for the music, the opera is certainly one of Verdi's best and at its first appearance caused a great stir in Florence, and later also in Padua. It does not, however, contain the same great quantity of beautiful vocal melodies we admire in his other works. One might even think the valiant maestro meant, with it, to respond in advance to the accusations of the French papers, which charge Italian music with paying little or no attention to dramatic expression and with considering it an accessory or secondary matter, when to combat this unjust attack it would be enough to quote a single aria in *Otello* [Rossini's], [of 1816] viz., "L'ira di avverso fato," and the whole magnificent third act of that opera, a masterpiece made up of the most magnificent harmonies from beginning to end. Verdi has here indeed decided to make song secondary to the expression and has put all his study into certain special instrumental effects, which, while they doubtless deserve the praise, nay, the acclaim, of experts, are on the whole lost [upon the audience]. This is known as the philosophy of the art: but this type of philosophy is not always accompanied by pleasure when it strays from the beauties of song and when harmony lords it over the vocal part. Nor do we mean by this that the new score is lacking in those qualities: only, they are in short supply, in proportion to the quantity of the pieces. Nevertheless, the duet between Lady Macbeth and her husband is a magnificent creation which not only conveys, by means of the

harmonic language, the situation of the characters, but is also rich in the loveliest, most novel themes in each of its several sections. Another piece equally perfect, both in its invention and in the workmanship of its execution, is Macbeth's final aria [i.e., "Pietà, rispetto"]. In both those places the maestro's muse rose to the sublimest heights of the art, and they are above all criticism. Much skill has also gone into all the witches' choruses: they are perfectly in character, and the orchestra, with its grave and singular chords, marvelously adapts itself to the temper of those fantastic creatures and to their mysterious responses. Fine, too, for their melody are the [prima] donna's *cavatina*, sung with excellent bravura by Lagrange, and the first-act *finale*. From the point of view of its theme and the ingenious interweaving of its parts, the same might also have been said of the second-act *finale*; however, it lacks appositeness and suitability, and the cheery elegance of the tune answers but poorly to [the meaning of] the words and to the terrifying impression remaining at that point from Banquo's apparition. For the rest, the opera is a display of science, applied to making evident, through music's eloquence, the various incidents in the dialogue and action; this can only be appreciated to the full by professionals. Thus, both at the first and at the second performances, Lady Macbeth's *brindisi* and sleepwalking scene went by unnoticed, though the latter made such a sensation elsewhere. As for the *brindisi*, the only singularity that draws attention is that it takes place before dinner and away from the table, and Lady Macbeth is so little in awe of her guests that she even turns her back on them. But as everything in this world, and so also in the theatre, is subject to the whims of fortune, the piece which without question made the biggest success was that poor, common *cabaletta* of the chorus . . . beginning with the words, "La patria tradita," with all that follows; so much so that, at both of these first performances, it was asked for, and graciously granted, again.

But in point of fact, to be properly appreciated the opera would seem to require a different sort of performance. Lagrange sings in a way that few other *virtuose* can equal; she has a voice that is true and very fresh, excellent schooling, and an even better manner of singing; she was educated in it by no less a man than the one and only *Rossini*, who is very proud and complimentary of his pupil; but the part of Lady Macbeth does not suit her as well as many another part . . .

—— 24 ——

Macbeth reached the stage of La Scala in February 1849; while calling it "a triumph on Milan's greatest stage," the Gazzetta di Milano *review is mixed.*

The tenor has only a very slender part: his aria is left absolutely for the end and is also among the maestro's least favored and studied pieces; which notwithstanding, *Palma* recited it so nicely that he made it seem beautiful and earned much applause, which was redoubled at the choral cabaletta that was repeated, in which he participates, together with the second bass. [In the score Malcolm's role is assigned to a tenor.] . . .

The opera and the ballet [*I filibustieri* by Galzerani] are staged with all magnificence: one might in fact almost say that the impresario, Lasino, was afraid of being thought a miser and therefore was lavish with gold and silver, even unto the Scottish highlanders' costumes. The scenery is a match to the rest of the decorations, and the park in the opera and the garden in the ballet would merit praise from even the most finical, and surely do great honor to Bertoia. . . . If our memory does not fail us, the poem is by Piave, though the libretto does not tell us so. But since, in a sort of proem, care was taken not only to inform us of the subject's origin and theme, but to forestall the judgment of those *few in whom a passion for reasoning blinds* [by asserting] that thus, and only thus, could the present opera [melodramma] be treated; far from belonging to the number of those in whom a passion for reasoning blinds, we content ourselves with saying that we do not feel the poem is at all times wedded in proportionate union with the marvelous of the initial conception, but that, in exchange, it abounds with notable dramatic situations and with that magical theatrical effectiveness which interests, seduces, and diverts the multitudes.

. . . The valiant author of the most acclaimed modern operatic works has attempted with *Macbeth* a new path, to separate himself from the crowd of composers, placing himself third with Meyerbeer and Rossini in the immense field of the fantastic and the marvelous. That he has been entirely successful nobody will maintain; on the other hand, nobody will deny that, though he was not well-served by the poem, maestro Verdi has in this vigorous work given proof of a many-sided imagination and of an ability more worthy of being envied than easy to imitate. And if not all the music is completely suited to the dominant idea and to the drama's end result, there are nevertheless pieces that decidedly do honor to the skill and imagination of the valiant maestro Verdi and which the public listened to and applauded with deference and even with enthusiasm, namely the witches' chorus in the *introduzione*, the prima donna's *cavatina*, the duet for soprano and bass in the first act, a cutthroats' chorus in the second act, the lovely accompaniments to the magic spells, . . . the sleepwalking scene in the last act and various other things. And if the opera, divided into four acts, were not guilty of excessive length, and if it did not exact an Herculean lung-power from the protagonist and the soprano, too, and if the totality of the musical work presented us with a lesser dearth of cantabiles, *Macbeth* would already find itself in the number of the most popular operas which grace the modern [melodrammatico] dramatic repertoire. . . .

From the opera's title, where it is styled "fantastic," it is easy to infer that its production requires machines, scenery, and costumes of unusual complexity, ingenious and magical; and the public was able to ascertain that the requirements were not met by the reality. . . .

Gazzetta di Milano, 25 February 1849; no reviews from the Gazzetta Musicale di Milano or other Milanese theatrical journals are available, for the Austrians had shut them down upon retaking the city the previous summer.

—— 25–27 ——

Three atrocity stories:
September 1847, Teatro Argentina (Rome):

The six performances of *Macbeth* given so far at the Teatro Argentina have been received with ever-growing enthusiasm and have attracted packed houses. Not a *cavatina* or duet, not an aria or concerted piece, not a chorus, whether of witches, cutthroats, or refugees, has gone without its nightly tribute of reiterated and unanimous ovations. The highly original chorus of the cutthroats in the second act is constantly repeated every night, and if the same is not required of the magnificent duet between Macbeth and his wife, of the magical final quartet in the second act, of the sublime sleepwalking scene, it is only because of the Herculean labor that would entail for the two principal performers, already overwhelmingly burdened with their task. This may be the reason why the administration of the Opera has thought good to amputate Verdi's splendid work here and there, even before the public could pass judgment on the intrinsic value of these pieces and on the effect they might have produced. We should have been resigned if these amputations (reprehensible in any case when practiced on operas by celebrated composers, unbeknown to them and perhaps against their wishes) had had as their sole object the removing and alleviation of a burden exceeding the respective strengths of the two principal actors, as one might say of many passages in the scene of Macbeth in the grotto, of the repetition in his *cabaletta*, of the recitative between Macbeth and Macduff before the fight, of the entire scene with Macbeth at the end of the action; but to have taken away, for example, the repetition of the *brindisi* in the second-act banquet, the three stanzas that form the first section of the sorceresses' chorus in the introduction of the third act, and various other pieces that fatigued no one and that perhaps contained qualities and beauties unknown to the anatomical knife of the operators, seems to us at the very least a discourteous and indelicate thing.

Reprinted from the *Rivista* (Rome), in the *Gazzetta Musicale di Milano*, 6 October 1847

A report about the Fenice production, dated 22 January 1848:

Thursday night it was decided to inject some variety into the performance at the Opera by substituting for Acts I and IV of Macbeth (for the act, that is, which contains the best piece in the Opera [the duet] and for the one that contains the most applauded piece [the *cabaletta* of Macduff's aria] Act III of *Maria di Rohan*. . . . The result was pretty successful.[1]

Communication signed M-ni, *Il Caffè Pedrocchi* (Padua), 30 January 1848

Production of the Teatro Carcano (Milan), October-November 1850:

. . . of signor Guerra [Macduff] we cannot speak, since his part in this score is rather slight and he himself cuts it further by frequently omitting his aria.

In the banquet scene was added a ballet by maestro Panizza, who also transferred the march from the stage to the orchestra. Although this new ballet is found tolerable, nonetheless we shall always condemn the introduction of other men's music into the scores of famous composers, just as we declare ourselves in principle irreconcilably opposed to the liberty, not to say audacity, of tampering in any way with the works of our composers, whether for theatrical expediency or for any other reason.

Gazzetta Musicale di Milano, 3 November 1850

---

1. A quarter century later, Verdi (piling it on) complained that the soprano Antonietta Fricci "didn't [in *Don Carlos*] shy away from taking out several pieces from her part to insert in it now an act from the *Ugonotti*, now an act *from Macbeth!!* . . ." (*Abbiati* 3, 716).

Interlude: The Abortive
Théâtre-Italien Production

In 1858, the Théâtre-Italien, in Paris, planned a production of *Macbeth*, with a grand cast (announced in the October 31 issue of *La France Musicale*): Giulia Grisi—Bellini's first Adalgisa (1831) and Elvira (1835), a famous Norma, Paris's reigning Italian prima donna from 1832 to ca. 1850 and London's from 1832 until her farewell in 1861—as Lady Macbeth; Francesco Graziani as Macbeth; his brother Lodovico as Macduff; and Angelini as Banquo. It didn't come off. We are indebted to Marcello Conati for his transcription of the following notices.

Madame Grisi will make her return in November, in *Macbeth*, which they plan to stage with great sumptuousness.

La France Musicale, 19 September 1858

The chorus is about to be taught its music.

Ibid., 10 October 1858

The choruses of Verdi's *Macbeth* are in rehearsal. According to all indications, this great work will not be performed before December.

Ibid., 31 October 1858

Verdi's *Macbeth*, which, as we have announced, was being prepared, will not be given this winter. It is a firm decision, for which we thank the director of the Théâtre-Italien, who recognized that for so elevated a work other interpreters than Madame Grisi and the Graziani brothers were needed.

Ibid., 21 November 1858

Macbeth II:

THE PARIS PREMIERE, 1865

—— 1–2 ——

Two notices appearing in Léon Escudier's L'Art Musical *before the premiere. The first should be read in the light of* GÜNTHER *(especially at 179–80), which shows that Escudier was frantically attempting to bolster the tenor part, against Verdi's wishes, and that the work was after all staged in five acts, again against Verdi's wishes.*

... M. Carvalho ... requested M. Monjauze to interpret the part of Macduff, which is not one of the chief roles in the work; but this did not deter M. Monjauze; for artists of his caliber there are no minor roles; besides, Macduff has some effective pieces to sing, and we are con-

vinced M. Monjauze will be able to make the most of them.

Some newspapers have erroneously ascribed five acts to Verdi's work; *Macbeth* has only four acts.

L'Art Musical, 16 March 1865

At the Théâtre Lyrique, the first performance of *Macbeth,* grand opera in four acts and ten tableaux, music by Verdi, which was to have taken place last Monday [April 10] has had to be postponed till Wednesday, April 19. The scenery, which is very important in this grand work, could not be completed in time.

The Théâtre Lyrique is all the rage; *The Magic Flute* is drawing a considerable crowd four times a week. Yesterday, Wednesday, there was a general rehearsal of *Macbeth;* another general rehearsal will take place the day after tomorrow, Saturday. On Sunday will be performed *Violetta,* with Mlle. Nilsson and MM. Monjauze and Lutz; Monday and Tuesday, *Magic Flute,* and Wednesday will see the first performance of *Macbeth.*

L'Art Musical, 13 April 1865

--- 3 ---

Most writers commented on the divergence in style between the new and old pieces with many, like Smith, finding that Verdi's youthful "chaleur" and exaggeration had been tempered. Less common were complaints about a lack of stylistic unity or complaints that the early pieces were superior to the revised ones (No. 6). Smith's praise of the performance is typical of the reviews; his reservations about Rey-Balla's acting are uncommon.

... When he [first composed *Macbeth*], Verdi was still at that stage in which one might often blame the warmth and energy of his style for a certain savage roughness, which he has since moderated considerably. ... The score which we have just heard finds itself on the borderline of the two periods and two styles. There is, in several of *Macbeth's* pieces, something of that exaggerated vigor that brings to mind *Nabucco, Ernani, I lombardi,* but there are also pieces of an extreme refinement, of a lightness that is full of grace, and we should be tempted to believe that these were newly written.

Let us hasten to declare that the first act of *Macbeth* made an excellent effect; that the introduction, the witches' choruses, the duet of Macbeth and Banquo, the orchestral music that accompanies the King's entrance deserved unstinting praise. Lady Macbeth's grand aria and the duet which she sings with her husband are also highly remarkable; the *finale,* which follows Duncan's death, was called for again and repeated to universal applause. ...

Mme. Rey-Balla, who undertook [the role of Lady Macbeth], is a former student of our Paris Conservatoire; it was not possible to engage her at the time she finished her studies, and so she went off to the provinces, where she always occupied one of the front ranks. She comes back to us now having lost some of her youth but, in exchange, having gained more experience. Her voice has lost none of its strength, of which it has plenty; she triumphs with assurance over the greatest difficulties; repeatedly, the emphatic *bravos* bore witness to the success obtained by this singer.

One might wish that the actress were at the same level, and that her face indicated better the sentiments which one must suppose agitated her soul. That criticism cannot be directed at Ismaël, whose face, on the contrary, speaks with eloquence; perhaps an excess of warmth and effort was a hindrance to his voice, which lacked color and precision the other day.

Monjauze has reaped the reward of his dedication. The part of Macduff, though not in his line, brought him a success that greatly benefited the work. Petit put a great deal of intelligence and talent into the part of Banquo living and Banquo dead.

In sum, this interpretation of *Macbeth* in no way harmed the cause of the composer or of the theatre. The orchestra deserves particular mention on account of its conductor, M. Deloffre, and of several musicians, whose names we wish we could mention.

As for the scenery and costumes, need we say that M. Carvalho took the opportunity of distinguishing himself, both from the point of view of historical accuracy and from that of pictorial effect? The ten tableaux that succeed each other in *Macbeth,* by their at times savage horror, at times strange magnificence, may well contend for the prize in this curious exhibition.

Paul Smith, in *Revue et Gazette Musicale de Paris,* 23 April 1865

—— 4 ——

From A. Hennette's rather curious review—he thought Lady Macbeth's cavatina "le morceau capitale de l'ouvrage" and found the Act I duet lacking in originality—we reproduce only comments on the Act II finale, a remark about the decor, and his overall evaluation of the reception.

... The capital scene in the third [*recte*, second] act is that of the banquet: Ismaël is splendid in it. It is thrilling to see him convey, by turns, now self-assurance, now terror, as Banquo's ghost appears or withdraws.

Here, the composer has too patently exaggerated the alternation. The joy he wishes to express is depicted in too vulgar a fashion, by means of music that would be more appropriate in a ballet: the transition is almost shocking in its abruptness. In this banquet scene, Monjauze has a *brindisi*, which he sings with much warmth and taste. He was applauded,

though not enough, for this piece merits the honor of being encored.

... The scenery for [the cauldron scene], depicting a ruined manor in a forest, is extremely beautiful; it is a pity that the action which it frames should be so deficient from the point of view of the impression it makes. ...

... The work was received with a good deal of benevolence by the first-night public. It did not, however, fully live up to the general expectation.

A. Hennette, in *Revue et Gazette des Théâtres*, 23 April 1865.

—— 5 ——

Comments about the first night reception, from Marie Escudier's La France Musicale.

... [Rey-Balla] carried away the whole house with her first-act aria, and she was obliged to encore the celebrated *brindisi* in Act II, which she sang with a brio and charm not to be described.

The choruses play a very important part in Verdi's opera, and it has long been a well-known fact that few composers treat the choral masses with as much grandeur as that illustrious

master. The first-act chorus had to be repeated; it is certainly very beautiful, though we very much prefer the conspiracy chorus in Act II, as well as that which so movingly closes Act III, that which serves as an introduction to Act V, and especially the dance chorus, whose beauties the public has not yet fully grasped. ...

Marie Escudier, in *La France Musicale*, 23 April 1865

—— 6 ——

If Léon Escudier dared to send this review to Verdi, it may have been the one that led the composer to protest that he knew Shakespeare well.

A new chapter has been added, as of yesterday, to the book which might be entitled *On the Dangers of Re-Inspiration*. Verdi, at the Théâtre Lyrique, has disappointed his admirers. The interpretation of his hybrid *Macbeth* is excellent and will possibly impart a semblance of life to it, but the French dilettante who is familiar with the *original* score, and above all anyone who has heard this at times lofty inspiration in Italy will always regret that a master should have dared to lay a fatal hand on a work typical of his youth. The muse is still a virgin, and she shies away from him who, after a first, forgotten kiss, comes to her with such strange embraces.

Ten pieces, deemed remarkable by all, have passed from the old *Macbeth* to the new, and the seven or eight pieces that have been added are far from reaching as *high* an average. The soprano *cavatinas* in Acts I and II[1] and the work's final chorus are lifeless and without character; the "black swan" expires before his last song. The whole of the second act is mediocre: there is much dancing in it, amid weighty accompaniments. The introductory chorus in Act IV is just as thick and colorless, and as for the famous *fugue* in Act V, it passed almost unnoticed, at half past twelve in the morning, amid general tedium! ...

1. The Act I *cavatina* remains untouched from the 1847 version; note also Ferry's curious volte-face about those two pieces three paragraphs later.

Mulier formosa desinit in piscem[2]

Let us express a regret. . . .Toward the end of the Calzado administration, certain difficulties that arose between that impresario and the publisher Escudier prevented Paris from becoming acquainted with the first *Macbeth,* which would, at the time, have been interpreted by Mme. Penco, Tamberlick, and Graziani. The success, with such artists, would undoubtedly have attained grandiose proportions; the master's work would have been consecrated, and the Théâtre-Lyrique, in its passion for adapting foreign works, so deadly to our national art, would have limited itself to translating the first *Macbeth,* which is superior to this *Macbeth,* dipped in I know not what fountain of youth, where it has acquired wrinkles, and whose two finest scenes Viardot and Graziani made popular among us.

Let us not hesitate to reveal our entire thought: to M. Bagier falls the task and the honor of giving us the real *Macbeth* next year, and we should be content to hear it from the great artists named Mme. Charton-Demeur, Agnesi, and Fraschini!

It is only a wish. Let us analyze the "new" work: After a short, choral introduction, there is an agreeable duet for baritone and bass, then a fine soprano *cavatina* and the famous duet for soprano and baritone, which has always been considered the best duet Verdi has ever written. Act I ends with a septet with chorus, treated on a large scale, but already tainted by a slight revision.[3]—In Act II we have another soprano *cavatina,* quite fetching; a cutthroats' chorus reminiscent, for its situation, of the chorus in the second act of *Lucrezia,* yet far inferior to it; a touching bass aria in a good style; finally, the *brindisi* sung by the soprano and taken up by the tenor and chorus, a *brindisi* full of verve and fashioned with skill. The trio that ends this act and whose dominant phrase was alternatively sung by the baritone, the tenor, and the soprano, is worked out quite broadly, but made diffuse by its prolixity.

Let us dispense, today, with dwelling on the witches' choruses, the sylphs' dances, the incantations and apparitions with which the whole work is filled. We yawned at them till our jaws ached, just as we did during the hunting scene in the *Troyens* or the symphonic dream in [Gounod's] *La Nonne sanglante.* In the chaos of this act, there floated to the surface only some passages for the violins and the cellos, the recitatives for baritone, and a magnificent sally of Lady Macbeth.

A monotonous exiles' chorus opens Act IV; then comes an aria with chorus for the tenor, worthy of the inspirations in *Trovatore;* at last, the grand sleepwalking scene, long a classic in the Italian repertoire. From Act V there emerges an aria for baritone with a sort of curtailed chorus: it is not as good as that for the tenor. Shakespeare, whether in light or shadow, often eludes M. Verdi; here, the maestro is neither profound nor human: "He has no children?" I demand an echo to this sublime cry and I seek the ineffable accent of anxiety and doubt with which Macbeth receives the crushing news of the death of the woman who shared in his act of violence upon the royal person. The music of the *finale* suggests a melodrama by Nicolet. . . . and it does not rise to a height sufficient to envelop the brutal denouement in a luminous aura.

Paul Ferry, in *La Comédie,* 23 April 1865

2. Horace, *Ars poetica,* line 4 (slightly garbled): "Desinat in piscem mulier formosa superne" (in Jacob Fuchs's translation, "A black, disgusting fish below, on top a lovely girl")

3. This number is in fact identical in both versions.

—— 7 ——

L'Art Musical, Léon Escudier's magazine, can be relied upon to say nothing but good about the work and the performance. The most interesting part of the long review are these Byzantine justifications for his and Carvalho's blatant disregard of Verdi's wishes.

The first librettist of Verdi's operas is the composer himself. He chooses the subject, draws up the scenario, decides on the form of the pieces; the man of letters only furnishes the verses—and still! It is not always because of the beauty of the versification that the majority of the poems set by Verdi shine. This does not trouble the composer. He points out, not without reason, that it is the dramatic situations rather than pretty phrases which inspire the musician. . . .

There was, in the earlier score, one regrettable point. One might apply to it Horace's phrase: *Desinit in piscem . . . formosa superne.* The fourth act, which in the Italian version was the last, had nothing truly remarkable to offer but the sublime sleepwalking monologue of Lady

Macbeth. It was a great deal, regarded both as a dramatic situation and as a piece of music, but it was not enough to constitute an act of an opera, especially not a final act. A tenor aria (which was generally, and wrongly, entrusted to an artist of inferior rank), some bits of recitative, and a final ensemble piece that was neither a chorus proper nor a *finale*, were not sufficient to set this act in relief and lend it the necessary importance; and the proof is that the public was often seen to quit the theatre after the sleepwalking scene, in part because everything else seemed of secondary importance, in part to retain the impression made by this inimitable passage.

In the French score, this act, which by itself was not self-sufficient, has so been amplified, enriched, strengthened, that it became necessary to divide it and cut it in two. The result has been an opera in five acts with excellent proportions. Furthermore, the effect produced by the sleepwalking aria of Lady Macbeth is no longer weakened by the pieces that follow, because the curtain falls most appropriately at the end of this aria, leaving the public vividly impressed. ....[1]

... On the subject of changes, we must mention that which consists in having the tenor repeat the *brindisi* in the Act II banquet; in the Italian version this *brindisi* is sung twice by Lady Macbeth. The composer, in this instance, yielded to considerations of *convenienze teatrali*, as the Italians say; though he has always defied them, luckily for the logic and success of his works ... So much the worse for the hurt feelings, more or less, of Their Majesties the prima donnas and Their Highnesses the first tenors!

In Italy, the role of Macduff not being important enough or, rather, not flattering enough for a worthy tenor to *deign* to play it, it was entrusted to a second tenor. Such a one would have been hard put to it to compete with the prima donna by repeating, rivaling her, one of the most melodious and, surely, most brilliant pieces in the opera. In France, that same tenor role, better understood and better cultivated, could be entrusted to an artist of talent. It is therefore not surprising that, for the sake of variety, he should be given the repetition of the *brindisi* sung the first time by the soprano. Possibly the dramatic logic suffers somewhat in consequence, but that logic so often yields to musical requirements that it would be really childish to quibble with the composer over a change whose effect is so captivating.[2]

That dramatic logic might also have suffered a little because of the addition of a ballet in the third act, but the remarkable beauty of the music completely exonerates the authors; one might even congratulate them for having had the strange notion of inserting dances, not in the banquet scene—which would have been quite natural, since dancing there is in it [!?]— but in the witches' cave. In the Italian score, there was only the disheveled round of the old sorceresses—which cannot be considered a dance—and the aerial fluttering of the sylphs accompanied by the silvery tinkling of harps. It was enough. But everyone knows that in France no opera is complete without a divertissement. If, therefore, the public is fond of seeing ballerinas gamboling in a witches' cave, let them enjoy it. Luckily—we repeat—the music is so original, so well-cadenced, so beautifully picturesque that one may well suffer the insertion of this *ballabile*, even closing one's eyes and forgetting Shakespeare. ...

We must indeed do justice to M. Carvalho, who makes his theatre an international stage, on which all the masterpieces of the art— French, Italian, German—meet with the noblest, most intelligent hospitality.

This eclecticism has so often brought him good luck! It will not fail him now this time either. *"All hail, Macbeth!" "Salut, Macbeth!"* "Ralph," in *L'Art Musical*, 27 April 1865

1. Cf. d'Ortigue's comments, No. 10 below.

2. See GÜNTHER at 179–80.

—— 8 ——

Ruelle's comments are interesting primarily for their opposition to Verdi on nationalistic grounds (rarely made so explicit).

I announced Macbeth to you a week ago, and today I can tell you about it, for the Théâtre-Lyrique performed it on Friday; it gave the premiere of this famous *Macbeth*. Like many, I foresaw a success, yet my conviction was not very deep; I dreaded the piece, which, as you know, is unusually monotonous. I also asked myself whether the number of pieces done over by M. Verdi would be sufficient, and especially whether these new pieces would be remarkable enough to impart to the score so much merit that audiences who have applauded *Rigoletto* would applaud it. I attended the first performance and was persuaded that my fears were well-founded. The first act provoked enthusiasm; its *finale* was encored; same success in the second, and the *brindisi* encored; cooling off at the third; some empty seats at the fourth; many more empty seats at the fifth.[1] The audience were fatigued, enervated by the uniformity of the scenic apparatus (oeuvre scénique), and the music had not succeeded in holding their interest to the point of keeping them back. That is what I saw. It may be that it will shortly turn into a success—experience teaches us not to pledge the future—and yet I do not much hope so. For there are here some capital causes. *Macbeth* is a magnificent drama; it is the least musical subject in the world. It lacks variety; heartfelt poetry, sentiment, contrasts are not there. For a composer, it was an arid, ungrateful subject. M. Verdi, as ill-luck would have it, was not served inordinately well by his imagination: I consider this to be one of his weakest works. The things he has done over are not superb. *Rigoletto* is infinitely superior; even *Violetta,* which has nothing extraordinary about it, is preferable to *Macbeth.* To reveal my thinking completely, I should dare to say that this ill-success, should the subsequent evenings confirm it, will have been a misfortune justly deserved and, from a certain point of view, an excellent thing. M. Carvalho was wrong to produce three Verdi operas in one year; I do not believe that it was for this that he was granted a subsidy, so much the more since the last of these operas will probably prevent the performance of the work that won the competition of the *prix de Rome;* so much for the administration. From a general point of view, I say it will be an excellent thing and I believe I am right in saying so. For some years now, Verdi's music has been flooding the provinces; these acidulated, pungent dishes have made the public demanding by giving it an excessive appetite for gross emotions; and the *opéra comique,* that amiable genre, French par excellence, which our authors have the wit to wish to cultivate, has come down considerably in the general opinion. If *Macbeth* obtains a great success, the provinces will want nothing but *Macbeth,* to the great detriment of our musicians, who will exhaust themselves to produce well-wrought works only to see them fail through the indifference of a blasé, satiated public. I admire Verdi's beautiful works, but I dread their influence. This master, more than any other, should be severely scolded, mercilessly criticized whenever he is inferior to himself. I therefore repeat as forcefully as possible, and in good conscience, that *Macbeth* is inferior to the majority of Verdi's other works and that the Lyrique is thoroughly to be blamed for producing it to the detriment of the works it has pigeonholed. The interpretation is excellent. . . .

Jules Ruelle, in *Le Guide Musical,* 27 April 1865

1. Cf. a notice about the second performance in Escudier's *L'Art Musical,* 27 April 1865: "Despite the late hour at which the performance ends, not a single spectator thought of leaving his seat."

—— 9 ——

Lasalle, with many others, brought up the lack of love and Verdi's temerity in choosing "un sujet intraduisible."

Only the attraction of the impossible can have impelled M. Verdi to attempt twice a musical translation of *Macbeth.* The somber legend, immortalized by Shakespeare, presents the composer with this difficulty—the sentiment of love is absent from it. Now the verb "to love" is conjugated to the seven notes of the scale, and music, of all languages, being the only one that allows two living beings to speak at the same time without confusion, is for that very reason the most appropriate language for love. . . .

These heroes in Shakespeare have the stature of giants, and I cannot help admiring them; but transferred to the operatic stage where they can express their passions only in song, they strike me as a howling menagerie. Either one or the other: either the music will convey the sentiments that agitate them, and it will jar; or it will remain within the limits acceptable to the ear, and then it will be insufficient.

One may rest assured that M. Verdi has accumulated in his score all the sonorous procedures which are so familiar to him. The unison, which is the most ancient of all, he uses with prodigality, as if he were proud of having invented it. The instrumentation, that is to say the combination of orchestral colors, is also not too praiseworthy in *Macbeth:* it does not present a great variety of effects, unless one is to consider it a novelty that a drumroll announces Macbeth's entrance on several occasions. Note that this is not some antique instrument restored expressly for the sake of local color, but an ordinary drum, a real army drum reminiscent rather of the parade ground than of the mists of medieval Scotland.

As for the melodic invention, the opera of *Macbeth* has singularly disappointed our expectations. We do not find in it that firmness of design which distinguishes the melodies of *Trovatore, Rigoletto,* and *La traviata.* And yet, see how wrongheaded we are: contrary to the opinion of many experts, the scene we liked best was that of the apparitions in Act III. Not that it is written with that feeling for the picturesque of which Weber knew the secret, not that it produces the shuddering sensation peculiar to the nuns' scene in *Robert le diable,* but at least it has the merit of a great unity of style. . . .

Albert de Lasalle, in *Le Monde Illustré,*
29 April 1865.

—— 10 ——

Joseph D'Ortigue, Berlioz's successor at the Journal des Débats, *devoted more than half of his review to attacking Piave's libretto. Much of this has been omitted here, since it is based upon Basevi's account (see pp. 421–25). This review is also discussed, with some inaccuracies, in Schmidgall,* Literature as Opera, *pp. 211–14.*

The beautiful and terrible drama by Shakespeare has been disfigured, lacerated, dislocated, shattered by an Italian librettist, il signor Piave. In his hands, and, unfortunately, also in the hands of the French librettists, the most dramatic subject has become the subject of a vulgar melodrama, the marvelous has given way to the grotesque, the fantastic to shadow-theatre tricks. What is this legion of witches (we ought rather to say fishwives) instead of the three created by Shakespeare? What's the meaning of their fantastic doings, their ridiculous dances? Is the great name of Shakespeare to be evoked only so the finest conceptions of his genius can be delivered up to the hilarity of the public? Beware: one trifles with that giant only at one's peril. One thought only to borrow one of his subjects, but what music, and above all what Italian music, will be capable of encompassing it? . . .

If Verdi's fantastic coloring is borrowed and somewhat gross, we must say, on the other hand, that in the course of his opera he has found some profound and vigorous accents. The witches' greeting to Macbeth, in Act I, produces a great effect. Duncan's arrival is signaled by a fanfare of horns reminiscent of Gessler's in *Guillaume Tell.* The whole scene that precedes and accompanies the murder is treated vigorously. The orchestra is filled with agitation and anxiety, and it is somber and terrible to the words spoken by Macbeth when the murder is consummated. There follows a fine aria by Banquo. The *finale* opens with a grandiose chorus, expressive of indignation and amazement. Sometimes we hear cries, but they are dramatic cries. The unaccompanied ensemble, in which, if I am not mistaken, only the kettledrum plays in the orchestra, is a masterpiece. I cannot say as much for the *stretta,* whose effect is vulgar and violent.

Act II opens with a good aria in two movements by Lady Macbeth. It is followed by a cutthroats' chorus which seems to me one of the best pieces in the opera. The violas have muted groups of low notes in it, while the kettledrums, tuned now in thirds, now in fourths, play not the part of supporting instruments, but of principal ones. After that, the royal banquet scene seems as pale as it is noisy. Lady Macbeth's *cavatina* [the *brindisi*] is cut after the pattern of all *cavatinas.* It is not in the least improved by being taken up later by Macduff. The chorus that closes this scene is equally rich in commonplaces.

In Act III, one must limit oneself to pointing out a chorus that follows the first witches' chorus (the latter lacking both in profile and in character) and a very graceful little chorus in A, [*recte,* G] supported by pizzicati, which is combined with the dances.

I will note in Act IV an excellent introductory chorus in which the instrumentation is remarkable. The violins' upper fifth laid bare has a singular effect. I will pass over Macduff's aria, which has no prominent features, to mention the sleepwalking scene, whose ritornello, highly developed, is very fine. During this scene the oboes [*recte* English horn] give vent to a lament so raw in its expression that it becomes unbearable, giving rise to a sensation of physical pain. It has been asked what realism in music might be: here it is. This act ends with an aria by Macbeth and a brilliant chorus intoned by the people when, through Macbeth's death, they are delivered from an unbearable and hateful oppression.

Of these four acts, it is unhappily the first which contains the most remarkable and most numerous beauties. But what ever entered the librettists' minds when they cut Act IV in two, separating the two parts with an intermission which might have got by at eight o'clock but is intolerable at half past eleven, and began the second part with an uncommonly long aria by Macbeth?

Here is the reason. Monjauze had an aria in the first half; and so it became necessary for Ismaël to have one in the second. Besides, it takes time to prepare the scenery for the *finale*.

Thus it happened that, what with all these fine considerations for the importance of a set and the need to satisfy the artists' self-esteem, one risked compromising the success of an opera. A great part of the public, seeing that the liberty is taken of adding a fifth act to the four that were announced, loses its patience and departs, leaving the house more or less empty for the proclamation of the authors' names.

The event of the evening was Mme. Rey-Balla's debut in the role of Lady Macbeth. This singer is experienced; she knows the stage; she possesses a voice having considerable range and power, a little fatigued, but thoroughly dramatic. Her success was very great. Ismaël sings the part of Macbeth with talent, but he forces and thickens his voice excessively. Is it the singer's fault? Is it the composer's? Perhaps it is the fault of both. Monjauze was roundly applauded in the part of Macduff, and Petit lent a terrifying aspect to the role of Banquo.

The usual praises and congratulations to the choruses, the orchestra, and their able and conscientious conductor, M. Deloffre.

Joseph d'Ortigue, *Journal des Débats*, 29 April 1865

—— 11 ——

Even the press friendly to Verdi, such as Marie Escudier's La France Musicale, *admitted that the work was not a popular success.*

... Taken as a whole, the score of *Macbeth*, as it has been produced at the Théâtre-Lyrique, is a work of the highest order, both instrumentally and melodically. Why is it, however, that at first hearing the public seemed possessed with a feeling other than boundless admiration? The cause of this effect, in our opinion, is to be sought nowhere but in the subject itself. *Macbeth* is assuredly one of Shakespeare's capital works; but sublime as are the horrors through which the drama's characters move, the imagination tires of following this long procession of

corpses, figments ... of the imagination, and finally [it is] not an agreeable spectacle to contemplate when not a ray of hope or of love ever pierces the chaos of abominations and crimes.

Nonetheless, one should not insist on this point too much, for one might, with reason, point out to us dramas every bit as lugubrious as *Macbeth* which have successfully been transplanted to the lyric stage, witness *Il trovatore, Lucrezia, Rigoletto, Otello*. ...

Marie Escudier, *La France Musicale*, 30 April 1865

—— 12 ——

From Les Modes Parisiennes, *a fashion magazine*

... It's Banquo's ghost here, Duncan's ghost there; then one shade, two shades, ten shades; they issue forth from all trapdoors, enveloped in white shrouds. I make no mention of the witches and sorcerers assembled round the cauldron where spells are cast and where they have all the appearance of being engaged in seasoning their stew.

Instead of being content with eliciting those apparitions in the old-fashioned melodramatic way, why was not recourse had to the new magical procedures, which make shades impalpable? The effect would have been more arresting.

The ensemble is treated without abrupt violence or lugubrious cries; the music is written with skill and sufficiently inspired.

A witches' chorus was warmly received; so were the first-act *finale*, very energetic and highly colored; Lady Macbeth's aria, encrusted with manly embellishments; the joyful themes of the ballet; the *brindisi;* the sleepwalking scene, where all is terror and repentance; Macbeth's romance; Macduff's war song, as rousing as a boot-and-saddle trumpet call; the final chorus, a bold conception.

Who other than Verdi could have approached this terrifying subject? He loves peaks, bogs, precipices, savage vistas, all that is harsh and tormented.[1] And so he chooses poems in accord with his ideas, like *Il trovatore, Ernani, Rigoletto, I lombardi,* and *Macbeth,* which outstrips them for somberness of color.

He is the Eugène Delacroix of music, with his qualities and faults.

A debutante, Madame Rey-Balla, played Lady Macbeth, and I vow she plays her well.

She has the right bearing and accent. Tragedienne to the tips of her fingers, she sings with an ardor, I would even say with a fury, that is moving. Her tense voice provokes a shudder when she implacably identifies the victims that must be sacrificed. Her talent affirmed itself from the very first. . . .

I know of no establishment that can rival the Théâtre-Lyrique in the careful distribution of a piece, down to its smallest detail. Add to this the corps de ballet, composed of charming and perfectly disciplined ballerinas, ten tableaux painted by able scene-painters, an irreproachable mise-en-scène, well-drilled choruses, an orchestra conducted with intelligence, and you will comprehend the work's artistic success. I say "artistic" advisedly; because the uninitiated will surely complain over the absence of dialogue and comic elements.[2]

Les Modes Parisiennes, 6 May 1865.

1. "Verdi, the man of contrasts, of rages, of action, passions, and tumult" is the description proposed by the *Journal des Demoiselles,* July 1865.

2. From this and other passages not cited here, one gathers that many of the magazine's readers were familiar with neither the genre of serious opera nor the Shakespeare play.

— 13 —

The allusions to German influence found in Paul Bernard's review were repeated two years later about Don Carlos—*for Verdi's annoyed reaction then, see his 31 January 1847 letter, Note 2.*

The new score of *Macbeth* offers without question beauties of the first rank. The symphonic introduction that precedes the sleepwalking scene, the Act I duet between Macbeth and Macduff [*recte,* Banquo], the grand duet of crime, the *brindisi,* which toured the world before reaching Paris, a very fine chorus of exiles, the aria of Macbeth before the battle, and two superb ensembles within the framework of the *finales* in Acts I and II: here, surely, is sufficient ground for admiration from the connoisseurs. To be sure, here and there a delicate ear might detect some flaws: a witches' chorus at the rise of the curtain, beginning in the minor in a highly-colored fashion, ends in a major movement of questionable character. Some of the warlike themes, some of the festive songs lack distinction, style, and perplex the listener, suddenly leading him far from the blue lakes of old Scotland and the grand traditions of the Middle Ages. But it must not be forgotten that the dramatic art of Italy is less concerned than is ours with what we call local color; and if

human passion will but cry out in a melody or laugh in a song, more often than not that is all that is needed to give life to opera from Milan to Naples. Let us not require a school to give more than it need to.

On the day when maestro Verdi writes an absolutely French opera, we will be entitled to exact from him the Swiss scent that elates us in *Guillaume Tell,* the hues of chivalry that dazzle us in *Robert le diable,* that medieval vigor that overflows in *La Juive.* But today let us not forget we have to judge the merits of a score of Italian origin, with only its melodies, writ large and vigorously impassioned—a genre, for the rest, which has numerous successes to its credit and numerous devotees, both in France and in Italy.

. . . For the final tableau, the composer has written a fine, very active scenic fugue, and a grandly conceived victory chorus. In the fugue especially, M. Verdi has abandoned his old manner, all dash and spontaneity; he has wished to prove that he knew how to handle the orchestra and counterpoint, and he has doubly succeeded. ... Let us mention in these new pages certain of the Master's tendencies already noted in his latest works, principally in *La forza del destino*. It would seem that the laurels that grow in dreamy, learned Germany rob M. Verdi of his sleep. Yet those he gathered on Italian soil were glorious enough to have satisfied him. All in all, it is with the ancient beauties of the old score of *Macbeth* that the principal effects were obtained at the Théâtre Lyrique. Let us nonetheless be thankful to M. Verdi for his recent efforts, for genius has not the right to stop in its progress; but let us still greet in him the spontaneous creator, the passionate melodist, the man of dramatic sentiment, the true composer, finally, of the joys and sorrows of earthly existence. That is his path, and that will always be his triumph.

Paul Bernard, "Les Deux Macbeth," in *Le Ménestrel,* 7 May 1865

—— 14 ——

De Villars's long article in L'Art Musical, *probably commissioned by Escudier, aims to counter all the objections to* Macbeth *made by other reviewers. The two excerpts presented here are typical.*

Shakespeare's poem has been followed with respect by the librettists. It begins with the fantastic part and the witches' prediction. The complaint has been voiced that, to begin with, the composer did not preserve the fateful number of the three witches. But what meddling is this? You wish to deprive the musician of the resources of the choral masses and the power of harmony. You always bring scissors to art—leave it its wings. Is it really so difficult to imagine the monotony and inevitable tedium of a constant trio of witches? You need only recollect the three Anabaptists in *Le Prophète;* they were short of inspiring. ... To the best of my knowledge, Aeschylus did not reduce the number of Eumenides in his *Oresteia* ... nor did Gluck in his *Iphigénie en Tauride*. ...The composer, owing to the very nature of his art, can therefore change Shakespeare's fantastic trinity into a chorus. ...

... The composer has been blamed for having Lady Macbeth sing a *brindisi:* a strange misconception. The *brindisi* is indicated by the poet himself. Macbeth says:

Love and health to all;
Then I'll sit down. Give me some wine; fill full.
I drink to the general joy o' the whole table.

—— 15 ——

It is a result of tact and sense of appropriateness that caused the musician to assign the musical toast to Lady Macbeth. The development of Macbeth's few words through melodic means was specially suited to the supple and imperturbable character of his wife, and the *brindisi* which she sings, with audacious nonchalance, is not only *not* dramatic contradiction, but is in full accord with the original character. If one wishes to be persuaded that the composer did not write this drinking song of Lady Macbeth's fortuitously, one need only set it side by side with that in *La traviata*, comparing the rhythm and character. One will appreciate the great distance that separates the *terrible* Queen of Scotland from the lovable Parisian sinner. During the ritornello of the *brindisi*, Macbeth converses with the assassins: the original harmony is altered and here takes on harrowing and characteristic hues.

The apparition of Banquo's bloody corpse fills Macbeth's spirit with dread and contrasts with the festive singing. This juxtaposition of light and shade is twice employed, and the scene concludes with one of those general depictions in which music so excels. ...

F. de Villars, "Shakespeare et Verdi: à propos de *Macbeth* et de quelques critiques," in *L'Art Musical,* 11 May 1865

Escudier's account of the enthusiastic reception of Macbeth *is at odds with the box-office receipts, the only criterion of success that Verdi accepted (and with* blague *such as the following, one understands Verdi's insistence on an objective criterion). The work was not revived in Paris during Verdi's lifetime.*

... The last nights of *Macbeth* were magnificent, and it was impossible to satisfy the demand for seats. ... As these artists will take their leave at the end of this month, the performances of Verdi's opera will of necessity be broken off; the last three will take place tomorrow (Friday), Sunday, and next Wednesday. But the music of *Macbeth*, whose success grows at every hearing, will be taken up again grandly at the beginning of next season, with the same cast.

L'Art Musical, 25 May 1865

—— 16 ——

From the Journal des Demoiselles *(July 1865) the second half of the review, after familiar objections to the difficulties posed by the subject. It is noteworthy how often lists of the best pieces included Duncan's march.*

... One of the opera's great difficulties was the three witches. ...Three witches, in the middle of a deserted heath, illuminated by the twilight's last rays, flinging enigmatic sayings to Macbeth, to the accompaniment of bizarre and mysterious gestures, might strike the imagination. Thirty witches and thirty sorcerers [*sic*] declaiming musical phrases make no appeal to it whatever. At the second incantation, when one sees so many specters appearing in succession, the chorus of witches was doubled by a chorus of ballerinas whose costume is not in the least infernal, and who might as well grace the salon of the king of Scotland as the somber cave where one watches their maneuvers.

There are some excellent pieces, from a musical point of view; for instance [the march accompanying Duncan's entrance, Macbeth's dagger soliloquy, the following duet, and] finally the ensemble piece that concludes Act I, in which the vocal parts are distributed with the skill peculiar to the Italian master. All this is worthy of Verdi.

Act II is less rich; the scene in which Banquo's ghost appears to Macbeth seemed weakly done to us. But the composer redresses the balance with brilliance in the *finale*, where, to the particular qualities he displays in such cases, Verdi has joined a more novel form and a more original character. The sleepwalking aria, sung by Lady Macbeth, is in a grand style and of an energetic, terrifying expressiveness. It is assuredly the most remarkable, the finest thing in the score. If everything else were of that strength, *Macbeth* would have to be considered one of the works in which the master has shown his utmost genius. That, however, is not the case. There are in it many weak pieces, of lusterless hue, of a doubtful originality, whose vocal violence and noisy instrumentation cannot hide their weakness. Be that as it may, there are some great pages in this work, and the Théâtre-Lyrique should be proud of having added it to its repertoire.

Journal des Demoiselles, July 1865

FIVE *FIGURINI* (COSTUME DESIGNS) FOR *MACBETH*

DESIGNED BY FOCOSI
(CURTI, "COLORITORE"; VASSALLI, LITHOGRAPHER)

In the last numbers of the 1846 volume of the *Gazzetta musicale di Milano* Giovanni Ricordi offered bonuses to those subscribing for the entire following year. The gifts to the "signori Associati" included "about 200 pages of music"—the *Antologia Classica Musicale* (the scores chosen for 1847 were Palestrina's Pope Marcellus Mass, Pergolesi's *La serva padrona*, Mozart's G-minor quartet for piano and strings, and Beethoven's *Coriolan* Overture)[1] and "many of the best pieces, vocal or instrumental, of the most esteemed modern composers" (e.g., E. Golinelli's *Souvenir de Macbeth de Verdi pour piano*, distributed to subscribers on 26 May 1847)—and a collection of lithographed and colored *Figurini* for at least one opera. The *Figurini* are discussed in the *Gazzetta*, 20 December 1846 (the English translation here is by Piero Weiss):

... Our industrious editor-owner will also, within the coming year, reactivate a system of publications which he gave up some time ago and, it seems to us, wrongly so. He will from time to time publish the so-called *Figurini* of the latest and most successful operas—that is, the wardrobe costumes of the principal characters in the above-mentioned operas. But there is a difference between the present publication and that which he issued formerly;[2] for then, such *figurini* were but the copies of those adopted in those theatres where a score was performed for the first time, and so were only approximately faithful to the costume of the period, because in Italy, especially, the traditions of history are not very much respected. But now, Ricordi is most worthily thinking of turning this publication into an artistic object of some sort: for, besides entrusting them to our best artists for the execution, he will commission persons to supervise the work, in order that these *figurini* may turn out in perfect conformity with the most genuine historical traditions. There is little doubt that, with the passing of time, a publication so well conceived will also benefit the manner in which theatrical performances are produced in Italy; for it will encourage the taking of precautions, rather more than is at present the habit, against nonsense and anachronisms. Well, then: we have spoken of this publication because Ricordi invites us to announce that he will deem it an honor to regale his Subscribers with the collected principal *figurini* of at least one opera in the coming year.

The *figurini* will be executed in lithograph by the most expert artists: and they will also be colored, for the sake of greater clarity, and furnished with suitable descriptions. ...

---

1. So, while *musica classica* may have been especially cultivated in Florence, it seems not to have been completely neglected elsewhere.

2. The Brera Library in Milan has a collection of more than 150 *figurini* issued by Ricordi probably during the early 1830s. The composers represented include Bellini (four operas), Rossini (two operas), Donizetti, and Vaccai (one opera each). (call number ZBB-V-48.)

It is of course tempting to relate Ricordi's comments to Verdi's growing concern about the staging of his operas, but there is no evidence that Ricordi had *Macbeth* or even Verdi in mind specifically at the time. In any event, it was not until the 30 June 1847 number of the *Gazzetta* that Ricordi announced that the *figurini* to be distributed would be those of Verdi's *Macbeth*. (One week later, Lucca's first issue of *L'Italia musicale* promised "disegni rappresentanti scene, o figurini di costumi teatrali"—five *figurini* from Verdi's *I masnadieri* were in fact issued between November 24 and December 22.)[3]

Ricordi's distinction between the purposes of the older and newer *figurini* is somewhat daunting. Since we all are probably more interested in the actual costumes and sets of the premiere performance—whether they were historically accurate or not—rather than the state of knowledge, in mid-nineteenth century Italy, of eleventh-century Scottish fashion, we would have preferred the policy of the older *figurini*. Nonetheless, since both Ricordi and Verdi were committed to the ideal of historically-accurate costumes and were both involved in preparations for the production, the actual costumes were probably close in spirit to those in Focosi's figurini (see COHEN at 191–95).

The *"libroni"* in the Ricordi archives (see pp. 302–03) give for each of the five *figurini* issued in 1847[4] a "data della stampa" as well as a later date, the "epoca della pubblicazione," the latter being the date of the number of the *Gazzetta* with which the lithograph was included.[5] In each case the number of colored copies drawn was 400; since Ricordi also offered the illustrations for sale, the number of "signori Associati" must have been even smaller than that. An average of 504 "copie stampate" (i.e., black and white) were also drawn. The five *figurini*, followed by the "data della stampa" and then the date of publication in the *Gazzetta* are as follows:

1. Macbeth in costume di Guerriero, e Guerrieri Scozzesi	8 October	3 November
2. Macbeth in costume da Re, Paggio e Sicario	14 November	8 December
3. Lady Macbeth in costume da Regina, e Ancelle	14 November	8 December
4. Strega	December 1847	22 December
5. Lady Macbeth nel Sonnambulismo, Medico ed Ancella	December 1847	22 December

Reproduced below are the articles of Antonio Piazza that appeared in the *Gazzetta* to announce the publication of the *figurini*; Piazza—the librettist of Verdi's *Oberto*, it will be remembered—has interesting comments about the contemporary Italian libretto, as well as about the *figurini* whose appearance occasioned these articles. The translations are by Piero Weiss.

—D.R.

3. Since separately issued illustrations often get separated from the bound periodicals, it is worth noting that the Brera's run of *L'Italia Musicale* has all but the first of the *figurini*.

4. The *libroni* list a final *Macbeth* illustration designed by Focosi, that of the "Scena della Caverna" (III, 1); it may well be identical to the illustration on the title page of the piano-vocal score. There is no information about the date and number of copies drawn, but the previous catalog entry, an illustration for *Luisa Miller*, is dated November 1850.

5. The *libroni* list the prices as .8 franc for "copie stampate" and 1.30 francs for colored copies; however, according to an advertisement in the 29 December 1847 issue of *GMM*, they were not sold separately. The prices for the set of five were Fr. 4 (in nero) and Fr. 6.50 (in colore). The advertisement, incidentally, notes that the *figurini* will be useful to impresarios and costumiers.

REGARDING THE COLORED LITHOGRAPH
OF *MACBETH*

Now that Italian literature is increasingly ceasing to be original; now that our poets can find their inspiration only in the works of Shakspeare, Schiller, Byron, Lamartine, whom they freely translate, slavishly imitate, or impudently plagiarize; now that a few poetic exceptions in our fatherland hang their lyre on the wall of their home to avoid being compared or confused with so many modelers of alien thoughts, what wonder if on the Italian lyrical stage no original spirit is ever greeted who is capable of composing a good libretto all by himself, without having continual recourse to French, English, or German productions?

The profession of the librettist has therefore fallen into disrepute, since it is entrusted to sacrilegious and mercenary hands that mutilate, alter, and spoil the dramatic masterpieces of other nations, calling down upon us quite rightly both hisses and laughter from abroad. The French papers notably have more than once derided the haughtiness that makes us constantly repeat the rancid old adage, *that we have been masters to the world,* [adding] that we are still, in pleasant literature, most extraordinary, meaning "gross." Yet, when an operatic book is wanted, see how Hugo, Scribe, Delavigne, Schiller, and recently again Shakspeare are taken in hand, despoiled, violated.

Macbeth
Costume di Guerriero

Of course, we do not mean to bundle all modern librettists together; the world knows them and knows how to distinguish amongst them; however, if there is diversity in the form, there is always uniformity in the system. Be the verses good or bad, the merchandise that is brought to the impresarios' market is always foreign.

Some tell us of the need to give the public, desirous of violent shocks, situations that are eminently dramatic. Agreed, if only to spare the public the inconvenience of sleeping in bad seats at the theater. ... But is it possible there are no brains amongst us who, applying invention to any given point in history, could spin a drama unaided and find scenes of lively interest, situations moving to pity, compassion, or terror? Is it absolutely indispensable always to have recourse to foreign drama, and to treat with such a want of Christian charity the artistic luminaries of the French, the Germans, the English, and the Spanish?

There is no doubt that two great models for a librettist are Shakspeare and Schiller; the first especially, who lived in a strangely stormy period, his days filled with ghosts, blind kings, ambitious men punished, unhappy women, with whom to link by means of fiction the realities of the past with those of the future. But, we repeat, in times such as these of great poetic and literary pretensions, ours is an unhappy condition in that we are always staging subjects and words of works that are not our own.

Maestro Verdi has set to music a Macbeth, whose *figurino* our *Gazzetta* is distributing today, in accordance with its pledge. We feel repugnance at saying that this is the Macbeth of the supreme poet who was born between the religious revolution initiated by Henry VIII and the political revolution that was about to end under the unhappy Charles I; of that star which shone in the firmament of Europe at the same time as Camoens, Tasso, Ercilla, Lopez [*sic*] de Vega, Calderon; of that *bagatellier* who created English drama, without losing it while he created it, as Voltaire wrongly accused him of doing; of that shadow, finally, of the Middle Ages who (to borrow Chateaubriand's expression) rose over the world like the nocturnal star at the very moment when the Middle Ages were finally descending amongst the dead. Portentous centuries, opened by Alighieri and closed by Shakspeare! ...

Yes, we find it hard to say this is the Macbeth of the author of *Hamlet, King Lear, Julius Caesar,* and we cannot find any argument to justify this plundering of works by the great in order to furnish rhymed and almost conventional words for our modern composers to set to music.

Heaven forbid we should confuse the imitative work of the poet, though laundered at second hand, with the original work of Verdi. The manly beauties of this score have no need of new encomia, and we feel justly saddened that, while Milan has been summoned before any other city to *admire the figurino* of Macbeth, executed by the worthy Focosi, she should be relegated amongst the last to hear the much-applauded musical inspirations of the author of *Nabucco.* ...

Many praiseworthy Italians have turned into our tongue, some in verse, some in prose, all or a part of the tragedies of the supreme English poet, whom Alexandre Dumas called *the greatest creator, after God:* Michele Leoni, Gaetano Barbieri, Virginio Soncini, Giacomo Sormani, Giunio Bazzoni, Carlo Rusconi, and most recently Giulio Carcano. *Macbeth* has been translated in verse by Giuseppe Nicolini, a distinguished mind, who succeeded in overcoming those difficulties which are naturally encountered in reproducing into our *versi sciolti* Shakspeare's dramatic dialogue; for, as one of our poets has said, he is an author who now puts on the buskins, now wears slippers. Later, this very same *Macbeth* was to be reduced to ariettas and little duets!. ...

Should we say a few critical words, in speaking of Focosi's drawing, concerning the character presented to us in warlike dress, with plumed helmet, the hilt of his sword tightly grasped in his left hand whilst his right points to we know not what? Heaven forfend! We have been voluble enough in discharging our duty of *describing a figurino*, which has in fact provided us with the occasion to express some opinions which not all our readers will perhaps share with us.[1] Which, after all, does not much matter, for there is no writing or prescription that will serve as a universal panacea.

Whoever will look at the lithograph which Signor Giovanni Ricordi is having distributed today to his numerous Subscribers will find a theater *card* and nothing else; he will imagine Macbeth in the process of performing an *entrance aria*, surrounded by the members of the chorus, possibly singing out of tune or with a voice affected by a cold, perhaps even in the act of letting out one of those famous *shouts* that nowadays are so fashionable and make such a marvelous effect on the majority of the spectators....

Gazzetta Musicale di Milano, 3 November 1847

FURTHER *FIGURINI* FOR *MACBETH*

When the publisher of the *Gazzetta Musicale,* intent on giving it a bent [*colorito*] that should justify the title and wishing assiduously to offer it to Italy as an exact account of contemporary music, also decided to add a series of theatrical *figurini* to the musical pieces he regularly sends out to his Subscribers, his particular aim was to be useful in this respect, too, to the lyrical and operatic stages of the peninsula, on which have been seen, and are still seen (especially at some distance from the capitals) anachronisms, errors, confusion of costume and habits, whether to humor the whims of the singers (the prima donnas especially), or for economy's sake, now adapting the Oriental robe to the Medieval gown, now moulding the Roman peplum to a Crusader's shoulders.

Anyone who has been to Paris and has visited those theaters has seen with what scrupulous exactitude the artists present themselves on the stage, dressed according to the customs of the period in which the event they are acting takes place. Histories are consulted, galleries visited, ancient paintings examined; and those who do so collect with painstaking research whatever is needed to take us faithfully and clearly back to a period possibly five or six centuries remote from us.

In a letter recently written by Verdi from the capital of France, the distinguished maestro cannot praise enough the magnificent, surprising, and, for him, novel exactitude of the scenery and costumes.

It might perhaps be a useful undertaking on the part of anyone willing to assume it, and profitable to artists, to collect in Milan (as has always been done in Paris) all the *figurini* of the comic, tragic, or musical productions, as they are presented on our stages, and to append to such a gallery some brief but pithy description, devoting also some words of admiration to those artists who should have singularly distinguished themselves in this or that role.

The *Gazzetta Musicale* has for its part begun to correct the errors that might be committed in the costuming of the new works of our musical theatre, spreading amongst the

1. Giuseppe Giusti surely would have agreed—see his letter of 19 March 1847 to Verdi.

public diligent and well-colored engravings of the characters in those works, in accordance with the precise usage of the times of the event represented. If these engravings will not provide sufficient matter for compiling a gallery, such as the one we would wish some adventuresome undertaker to produce, they will at least serve for a guide to avert the usual gross blunders and as a defense to the provinces in refusing to accept wrong or inexact deliveries from the tailoring establishments of the capital.

Today we are once again with *Macbeth*, concerning whom we have already discoursed in our No. 44. The two little *cards* show, respectively, Macbeth, in kingly costume, a page, and a cutthroat; and Lady Macbeth, in queenly costume, with handmaids. Before the end of the year, the *Gazzetta Musicale* will publish some other *figurini* of *Macbeth*, which, with those already published, will form a collection sufficient for the mise-en-scène of this opera by our Verdi, whose genius and good fortune make him one of the strongest pillars of the Italian lyrical theater.

Gazzetta Musicale di Milano, 8 December 1847

LAST *FIGURINI* FOR *MACBETH*

We have come to the last *figurini* of this great historical personage, to whom a supreme poet, better than his own royal deeds, has furnished an unfavorable but yet undying celebrity; for it is sometimes a privilege of poetry, persecuted and unhappy, to send on to the furthest posterity those very persons whom an obscure and dishonorable life would justly have condemned to oblivion.

If the name of Verdi is not of the same merit as that of Shakspeare, it is however certain that the celebrated Italian maestro has contributed to the popularity amongst us of the name of that foreigner, just as Rossini once made immortal in the peninsula that of the count Ory. . . .

In the second *little card* one may see a witch amidst her mystical invocations and nocturnal sabbaths. These disgusting creatures, in league with the devil, have a thousand times come to the aid of folk tales and poetic inventions, since the people and poets always feel a preference for the marvelous and strange. The Italians have put these female monsters on the stage with greater sobriety than the French and English; the Germans have, on the contrary, made exaggerated use of them at times.

The scene of Shakspeare's witches is famous in the annals of dramatic literature; and Verdi, with his musical notes, has simply sustained this foreign celebrity, making it, so to speak, indigenous amongst us.

We really have no idea what historical foundation underlies the dress of the fantastic creatures of whom we speak; we are pretty certain the *figurini* of Parisian mode never influenced it with its voluble prescriptions, and Mme. Alexandrine would faint away at the sight of the strange toilette of this witch in *Macbeth*. A Bedouin mantle with a fire-red

Strega

Lady Macbeth
nel Sonnambulismo.

hood; a robe embroidered, at its lower extremity, with little monsters; a broad belt and buckle, and, hanging from it, the type of Imperial purse to which fashion writers of the time gave the name of *ridicule* [*recte réticule*]; the footgear of the Hottentots [i.e., none at all], a cane or magic wand in the right hand, and on her chin the pointed beard of the Arabs: there you have the portrait of a witch most unlike those who once made famous on the stage of La Scala both *Il noce di Benevento* and the name of Viganò.[1]

Gazzetta Musicale di Milano, 22 December 1847

1. *Il noce di Benevento* (25 April 1812) was the seventh of the nine ballets Salvatore Viganò produced in his first season (1811–12) as ballet-master at La Scala; it was revived in 1813 and in 1822; one of the leading characters is Martinazza, *strega benefica*.

A NOTE BY "FOLCHETTO"[1]

Macbeth is a special opera, which has sometimes been harmed by the lack of a leading-tenor role but which has always had a great success in Italy. A great singer, Barbieri-Nini, taking the title role has often transformed this success into true enthusiasm. *Macbeth* was given in Venice shortly before the 1848 Revolution, and become the occasion of tumultuous scenes at the Fenice. A Spanish tenor, a great liberal, Palma, came on in Act III to sing the famous aria "La patria tradita ..." with the tricolor cockade in his hat, and he sang it with such ardor that the public were inflamed and took it upon themselves to become the chorus and give vent to "seditious" cries. That aria in so stirringly patriotic a presentation seemed to become the match that would touch off the gunpowder. The affair became so serious that it once resulted in the Imperial Royal Grenadiers' being called out. More than likely, that aria figured largely in the reports that the police of the time sent to Vienna about every littlest incident. It is not widely known that those two stanzas are by Andrea Maffei.[2] Verdi had begged Maffei to write a libretto for him, but he, not yet knowing how to adapt himself to the numerous cuts the composer would inevitably want, warded him off. Nevertheless, to show good will to Verdi, and also to Piave, he wrote not only "La patria tradita" but also the words of the witches' choruses that are found in *Macbeth*, for which Verdi devised music that is admirable, expressive, picturesque beyond words. Anyone who reread these choruses of Maffei's would see the contrast between his poetry, lively and picturesquely faithful to the original, and the rest, perfunctorily done by Piave.

Macbeth was first performed in Florence. ... This was the first occasion on which Verdi received a public tribute of admiration in the form of a golden laurel crown, each leaf of which bore the title of one of his operas. ...[3]

1. From *Giuseppe Verdi: Vita aneddotica di Arturo Pougin con note ed aggiunte di Folchetto* [Jacopo Caponi] (Milan: Ricordi, 1881), 54–55. *Caveat lector!* Although Verdi was sent proofs of this publication, he was unable or unwilling to correct all its inaccuracies.

2. There is no supporting evidence for this; see Verdi's letter of 11 April 1857 to Ricordi, DEGRADA, and the manuscript libretto (p. 333).

3. Cf. Verdi's letter of 26 March 1847

MACBETH, FROM *STUDIO SULLE OPERE DI GIUSEPPE VERDI*

by *Abramo Basevi*
Translated by *Edward Schneider*[1]

On the example of various celebrated transalpine masters, Verdi determined to set a fantastic or pagan supernatural subject. Neither the success of Meyerbeer or Weber in this genre of music, nor a certain aversion on the part of Italian composers to setting this sort of extraordinary plot served to make Verdi avoid the dangerous risk. I say dangerous because the fantastic genre, of transalpine birth and character, requires music appropriate to its nature, and so, the Italian composer must abandon the beaten paths which he knows well to venture into a labyrinth in which the Northern genius may safely wander without becoming lost.

Piave took no great trouble to seek for a fantastic subject which would best suit the Italian genius, but, casting his eye over the tragedies of Shakespeare, chose *Macbeth*. In this tragedy we do not find that sort of fantasy which is inoffensive to our fastidious minds: that in which, under an extraordinary, supernatural exterior, is hidden some wise dogma or an embodiment of human vices or virtues. The witches and magical deeds of *Macbeth* are today without significance and utterly ridiculous to us. Still, if we subtly consider this creation of Shakespeare's great mind, we can see that—under a thick veil it is true—the witches represent the force of destiny. But what is destiny if not the effect of a force which knows no obstacles? And what is this force in the present case if not the ambition of Macbeth, fed by his wife, and not strongly enough combatted by his virtue? Did Piave understand this? It really seems not.

But Piave made another enormous mistake in choosing a drama in which love plays no part. Neither Meyerbeer nor Weber fell into this error in *Robert le diable, Der Freischütz,* or *Oberon*. Love is the emotion which is best suited to music; of this Nature herself can be our teacher, for we observe not only that many species of animals give forth more often and more richly with their song in mating season, but also that species mute at other times then acquire voices.

We will not waste our time in noting all the inconsistencies, the gracelessness and the blunders in this wretched libretto of Piave's. I am sure that my readers will gladly bear with me in this. I shall give only a brief résumé of the plot: Macbeth, general to the King of Scotland, encounters a group of witches, from whom he learns that he is destined for the Scottish throne, but that his successors will be descended from the line of Banquo. He reveals the witches' predictions to his wife who, cruel and ambitious above all else, convinces him to murder King Duncan to hasten the desired events. Macbeth secretly murders the

1. Copyright © 1978 Edward Schneider

king to whom he is giving hospitality under his very roof. Brought in this way to the throne, and not content with that alone, he lays an ambush for Banquo with the intent of killing him together with his son. The assassins are unable to do more than murder Banquo. The enormity of the crime weighs heavily on Macbeth and his Lady. Meanwhile, from all sides, the oppressed populace moves against the usurper, who loses his life in the conflict.

Verdi's new opera appeared in Florence at the Teatro della Pergola in March 1847. It had a good reception, but more out of regard for its composer than for the sake of the music, which never more than half pleased. The opera had the same luck in other principal theatres. This shows not only that the judgment made by the Florentines was sound, but also that the execution of the work—in a manner less than common for the Italians—left nothing to be desired. While there might have been difficulties for some orchestras, that of the Pergola overcame them as it had all others. Where a Pietro Romani is the conductor and musical director of the theatre, and where the orchestra has an Alamanno Biagi for a leader, there may be no fear with regard to the perfect execution of the music. My words are confirmed by the great success which *Robert le diable*, *Les Huguenots*, and *Le Prophète* had on the stage of the Pergola, where they were performed for the first time in Italy.

As soon as we hear the first section of the witches' chorus in the introduction we have a just idea of how Verdi comprehended these imaginary beings. He saw in them nothing but ugly old women, bizarre, spiteful, and crazy. On these lines Verdi has written his music which, for that reason, lacks what is most important, that is, sufficient expression of supernatural and evil power as to stir up disgust and horror in us. Verdi had nothing in mind if not Mercadante's famous chorus of sorceresses, in which model the same shortcomings are found. The music of the witches' dance, in major, is built on a graceful melody, but it is even less well adapted to the witches than the preceding piece in minor. But it is not all the fault of the composer if the character of the witches is not well colored; this must also be blamed on the poet who, to tell the truth, presents them to us as more mad than evil. In fact, in the first scene (where Shakespeare's three witches have, with great improbability, become three *groups* of witches) the second group says, in the singular, "ho sgozzato un verro" (I have slaughtered a boar) which is utterly ridiculous and mad coming from a group of witches. In the English tragedy we find the opposite, that a single witch has gone about "killing swine," which is more sinister than silly. Also, Piave makes his third group of witches brood about a seaman's wife, who wishes them in Hell, don't ask me why; then, for vengeance, they want to make her husband, who is on the high seas, fall prey to the waves. Shakespeare, on the other hand, has nothing to do with brooding, and puts the aforesaid threat into the mouth of a single witch—not madly and without cause, but as vengeance for the sailor's wife having denied her some chestnuts. Verdi then exaggerates this madness with his music, as when in the second scene the witches say, "Macbeth e Banco vivano!" and then disappear.

The following duet between Macbeth and Banquo (baritone and bass) is finely conceived. Macbeth's solo is grand and solemn when he is seized by horror at the contemplation of shedding the blood of his king in order to usurp the throne in fulfillment of the witches' prophecy. That phrase is notable for being a long idea in one sweep, continued without becoming forced or abstruse for twelve bars by means of frequent chord changes with harmonies distant from the home key. The change from C to D flat at measure 21 of this number is bold. The movement from one key to another unrelated key, by means of a unison instead of complete chords, must be used carefully, and only when it yields a fine effect. Mozart, in the Act II finale [measures 116-18] of *Don Giovanni,* goes from the key of D to the key of F by means of the single note of E. In Rossini's *Guillaume Tell,* in the duet between Arnold and Guillaume, the cantilena "Ah Matilda" (in G flat) is begun by the tenor after the orchestra, leaving the chord of B-flat seventh, has played a unison B natural and then a C, so that the singer, taking up the succeeding D flat, suddenly finds himself in the key of G flat.

The chorus of witches, sung when they return to the stage, is well written but has the defects already noted.

The *cavatina* of Lady Macbeth (soprano) is full of energy, with the old Verdian stamp. The andantino is proud and grandiose. The employment of high notes (or screaming) is here abused according to the taste of those times. In the allegro we find one of those customary impetuous phrases on the words "Qual petto percuota." Note the first period of this *cabaletta,* for, while it is composed of the usual two phrases, the second phrase is longer than the first, in contravention of the usual symmetrical structure. Donizetti supplies us with a similar example in the *cabaletta* from *Anna Bolena* "Nel veder la tua costanza." Fine in its melody though not in its character is the rustic music which announces the arrival of the king; its disappearance into the distance is most effective.

The duet for Macbeth and his wife is the culminating number of the opera. Macbeth's recitative which precedes it is notable for its expression and for certain instrumental combinations. The *tempo d'attacco* of this duet, which begins "Fatal mia donna," is the finest part. It is a true flash of Verdian genius, and must be numbered amongst the most beautiful creations of the "Swan of Busseto." Macbeth's terror at his sin, his remorse when he tells of his inability to repeat the word "amen," and finally, the contrast with the evil indifference of his wife, could perhaps not be better interpreted in music. Splendidly daring, impossible to anyone but a great genius, is the lively cantilena—almost in the style of opera buffa—on Lady Macbeth's words "Follie, follie, etc." This cantilena does not destroy the scene's horrific quality, but rather increases it, bathing it in a blood-red light. The melody does not contribute as much to this as the simple but effective instrumentation. The second violins, muted, have a sort of murmur over which the first violins and the English horn double the voice. Other instruments join later, always with magical effect. Verdi, in this opera, reaped much profit from the use of the woodwinds, a section which has fantastic qualities or, rather, is appropriate to the depiction of the fantastic—as is shown by Weber, Meyerbeer, etc. The ⅜ andantino which comes afterward is singular in form, and the bass's phrase "Com'angeli d'ira" is majestic. The remainder of the duet is quite mediocre.

The first *finale* has a grandiose character which is most suitable to the amazement and indignation which has been aroused in everyone toward the assassination of King Duncan. Its design and color bring to mind the composer of *Nabucodonosor* and *I lombardi.* This first act ends without a *stretta;* for this we must laud Verdi, because with his authority he has contributed to the destruction of one of those bonds by which Italian composers think themselves entwined, one does not understand just why. I do not want to malign *strette;* some by Rossini and Pacini show us their best aspect. With the second-act soprano aria "Trionfai secura alfine," Verdi himself offers us an exaggeration of his own system—an exaggeration of the kind to which we have become accustomed in the works of his imitators.

The chorus of assassins has some nice chiaroscuro effects, but it contains little or no expressiveness. I must praise the change in orchestration upon the repetition of the motive in this piece, which is placed in better relief over a quickly moving figure in the violas. It is time to free ourselves from da capos pure and simple. The tympani are used with great craft in this piece, not merely as reinforcing but as essential instruments.

The entire banquet scene until the end of the act is very well constructed. A brisk instrumental part with a broken, leaping rhythm like that of German dance and band music is repeated several times through the entire scene, serving also for a parlante. The *brindisi* is somewhat trivial. Afterward, the oboe repeats the motive, while the clarinet and the bassoon descend by semitones, giving a most praiseworthy sombre color to this scene; this serves for a brief parlante dialogue between Macbeth and an assassin. Contrast between a motive and its accompaniment was first used, and with great effect, by Gluck, in *Iphigénie en Tauride,* where Oreste sings a motive suited to the words "Le calme rentre dans mon coeur" while the accompaniment is dark and agitated. The players at the first rehearsal tried to sweeten this accompaniment, which they judged to be contradictory to what Oreste was saying, but Gluck, (as related by Mme. de Staël in *De L'Allemagne*) nearly losing his temper, exclaimed, "Pay no attention to Oreste; he is not at all calm; he is lying!" In the largo of the *finale,* "Sangue a me," there are eighteen chord changes in the space of eight bars, used with such taste and shrewdness that the melody does not cease to be infectious. Sixteen measures immediately follow where, with great expression, the soprano alternates with the others. Then a lovely concerted section of twenty-two measures begins, accompanied with triplets, which contrasts well with the preceding material and which ends the act. The crescendo on the motive "Biechi arcani, etc.," especially from the point at which Macbeth enters with the words "Il velame del futuro," gives me occasion to bring to the attention of the student a particular melodic procedure: in the indicated passage you will note that the rhythm which is begun by the bass in the first two quarters of the measure is continued by the soprano in the last two, and it remains thus for three measures with harmonies which change in order to keep the listener in anxiety and make him desire the resolution which occurs later with a forte in the fourth measure. This is followed by a fortissimo in the following measure where the melodic thought finds its fulfillment. This is another example of the *effect of anxiety* upon which I dwelled in the last chapter.

The witches' chorus which opens the third act is long and, with the exception of a few bars at the beginning, characterless. The end, in the major, by no means expresses the fierce joy of these evil beings, or even approaches doing so. See how Meyerbeer was well able to fit music to demonic joy in the celebrated "Valse Infernale" of *Robert le diable.*

The apparition scene is unworthy of the name of Verdi; it lacks a concept, an order, even an effect. And almost as proof of the composer's inattention to the search for new harmonic, melodic, and rhythmic combinations, the scene ends, when Macbeth sings "Oh mio terror! dell'ultimo," with one of those old, old rhythms, as used six times in *Attila*—a rhythm which in the course of the opera of *Macbeth* we find also in these pieces: "Oh, qual'orrenda notte," and "Come dal ciel precipita"

The chorus "Ondine e Silfidi" is graceful and most appropriate. Some points in this piece remind us of a dance movement in *Robert le diable.*

The third finale, "Vada in fiamme," is extremely vulgar.

The chorus "Patria oppressa" with which the fourth act begins is characterized by its gravity, and it produces a certain effect which is not, however, novel; the rhythm itself is old-fashioned. The *adagio* as well as the allegro of Macduff's aria also have a very old-fashioned rhythm—and are moreover without effect.

With Lady Macbeth's sleepwalking scene Verdi wished to recoup, and he wrote a piece which, if it does not please the ear, certainly gratifies the mind. The carefully-wrought accompaniment is dominated by a hollow tinge; from time to time a sort of lament is heard in the English horn which somehow echoes the inner cries of the conscience.

Macbeth's aria, which comes next, presents nothing of note; I shall say only that there too a very old rhythm is used. At this, I should like to mention that rhythm constitutes so great a part of melody that it is unjust to give the name of an original writer to one who forms new motives upon old rhythms, altering only the notes. The much-praised memorability of many Italian arias comes in great part from the antiquity of their rhythms.

Would you like a recipe for the composition of facile, catchy melodies? Take an old rhythm from amongst the clearest examples. It does not take much work to adapt new notes to it, for there are some nearly fixed rules for the choice of a pleasant succession of notes, such as those which recommend leaps of a rising fourth, a major sixth, a third, or a fifth descending, etc., etc. With regard to the way in which the piece unfolds—its form—copy directly, as from a pattern, the one in vogue at the moment, without taking the trouble to introduce the least modification. For the harmonies, you have those of the key of the piece, and where you wish to make other graceful modulations, there are the appropriate rules. It is in this manner that many pieces of music claiming the title of "new" are created. The dilettanti then go to the theatre and cry, "Lovely, lovely! *This* is immediately comprehensible music—it's certainly not to study that one goes to the theatre!" These foolish judgments fly from mouth to mouth; if they were to be heeded by anyone truly touched by the sacred spark of genius, the art of music would be quickly dragged down to its final stages of corruption.

As the poetry of modern languages, content with a handful of accents, places no importance on the contrast between long and short syllables, music must take the best possible advantage of rhythmic richness. One of the principal causes of rhythmic uniformity is the lack of variety in the meters used in modern dramatic poetry. Fine examples of the needed variety may be found by anyone in the poetry of Chiabrera, Parini, Monti, etc.[2] The dramatic poet must cherish this variety, for otherwise musical rhythm will perforce continue to be as impoverished as it is at present.

2. Gabriello Chiabrera (1552–1638) diplomat and poet who wrote libretti for intermezzi; Vincenzo Monti (1754–1828), poet to the papal court and translator of the *Iliad* (1786); Giuseppe Parini (1729–1799), ordained priest and satirical poet.

Appendices

A HUNDRED YEARS OF *MACBETH*

Annals compiled by Tom Kaufman and others

The 1847 *Macbeth*, as everyone knows, was a successful opera. But just how widely and how frequently it was performed may come as a surprise to anyone scanning these annals. Within a year of its Florence premiere, *Macbeth* had reached some eleven cities and three countries. By the end of 1857, there had been 187 or more productions; by the end of 1865, the year of the revised version, 310 or more. Even after *Macbeth II* had been published, *Macbeth I* continued to be performed. The first Italian performance definitely of *Macbeth II* which we have traced is the Scala production of 28 January 1874. It is a reasonable assumption that in the Spanish and Portuguese productions of 1866–68 with Rey-Balla (who created the revised role in 1865) as Lady Macbeth she, at least, used the revised version. But precise evidence is lacking. The libretto for the 1866 Barcelona performance, with Rey-Balla, presents the first version, including "Trionfai." Among other librettos in the AIVS archive, those for Turin 1867, Florence 1870, Busseto 1877, and Parma 1881 are all of *Macbeth I*, and there is a Ricordi *Macbeth I* libretto blind-stamped as late as 1890. The first production specifically identified as *Macbeth* "*nuovo*" in the royalty statements Ricordi sent to Verdi is that of Modena 1874 (immediately after its Italian premiere at La Scala). Thereafter, when Ricordi sent out performing material, it was in all likelihood of the revised version; but performances of *Macbeth I* from existing material continued to be frequent.

So far as we know, this is the first attempt to trace the performance history of a nineteenth-century opera in such detail. Until similar annals are compiled for other works, it must remain an individualized, not a perspective, picture of *Macbeth's* wide dissemination. The picture is certainly not complete, but Tom Kaufman, the principal author of this chapter, suggests that for the nineteenth century it includes perhaps eighty to ninety per cent of the *Macbeth* productions in major cities or with major artists. The likeliest omissions are those of productions in provincial towns in South America and Eastern Europe, and German productions in the 1930s. Among Verdi's early operas, Mr. Kaufman's researches suggest, *Macbeth* was less popular than *I due Foscari* and *Ernani*, but more popular than *Attila* and *I masnadieri*, and far more so than *Giovanna d'Arco*. Other operas of the 1840s which were performed more often than *Macbeth* are Donizetti's *Poliuto* (given perhaps twice as often), *La favorite*, and *Maria di Rohan* and Pacini's *Saffo*. Donizetti's *Lucrezia Borgia* (1833) and Petrella's *Jone* (1859) also surpass it; Donizetti's *Anna Bolena* (1830) does not.

Macbeth held many of the world's stages for three decades, until 1877; then the listings grow thinner. In the postwar Verdi "boom," *Macbeth II* has become the repertory opera that *Macbeth I* once was. We chose 1947 as a convenient centenary terminus: the numerous modern productions can be traced in the annual indexes of the magazine *Opera*. After 1947, we have recorded only the five modern revivals of *Macbeth I*.

The first draft of these annals was assembled by Amy Aaron, from the principal published sources and from information supplied by Martin Chusid, Marcello Conati, Giorgio Gualerzi, Tom Kaufman, and others. The listings were then enormously expanded and refined by Mr. Kaufman, working from published opera-house *cronache* (which vary widely in the amount of information they present and are not always reliable) and from the many nineteenth-century theatre journals, notably *Fama; France Musicale; Gazzetta Musicale di Milano; Gazzetta Musicale di Napoli; *Gazzetta dei Teatri; Italia Musicale; *Mondo Artistico; Revue et Gazette Musicale; *Teatri, Arti e Letteratura;* and *Trovatore.* (Those marked with an asterisk were particularly useful.) Newspapers provided further evidence for such things as the Manchester performance of 1860, probably the English premiere, and the two Boston stagings. The casts were then checked, wherever possible, against those shown in the librettos printed for individual productions. The AIVS archive has a particularly rich collection of these (several other collections, too, were consulted), and Dr. Chusid spent long hours in confirmation and correction. Irreconcilable information is recorded in footnotes. Librettos, which were printed in advance, can be misleading (see Parma 1862), unless a previous owner has penciled in last-minute cast changes or, as in the case of the AIVS copy of a libretto for Venice 1865, a paste-over slip has held firm through many decades. On the other hand, critics sometimes get names wrong. That these *Macbeth* annals are certainly incomplete and imperfect, all of us who have worked on them know only too well. Additions, amplifications, and corrections will be welcome. But readers are urged to cite the exact source of any new information they may send us. Music history has too long been bedevilled by uncritical acceptance of what the papers said. Reviews—and the cross-checking provided by multiple reviews—probably give the surest indication of who actually sang in any performance, and from them the greatest part of our listings has been compiled. Edoardo Arnosi, of Buenos Aires, Don L. Hixon, of Irvine, California, Lim Lai, of San Francisco, Marius Sotropa, of Cluj Napoca, Rumania, and Giuseppe Biglia and Oscar Strona, both of Turin, provided some specialized information. Janet Bone, of the Morris County Library, New Jersey, helped to secure many of the books and journals that made possible the preparation of the annals; and Judith Stein brought scholarly order to a mass of information typed or written on many different pieces of paper.

Conductors, stage directors, and (except in Paris) scenic designers did not assume the dominant and individual roles that they do in operatic life today. The Letters section of this volume shows clearly enough the extent to which the preparation of the 1847 premiere was a collaborative enterprise in which the composer, the librettist, the Florence impresario, his house conductor, and others all played a part. *Macbeth* was generally treated as a grand spectacular opera; in early librettos, many credits are given. (See the facsimile at p. 471.) Even the "inventor of the artificial chemical fires" for the Messina staging of 1853 can be named. But in the 1865 Paris libretto, no designers are mentioned—rather surprisingly—although eighteen dancers are. (But see COHEN at p. 182-98 on this subject.) If we had included columns for "conductor,"[1] stage director, and designers[2] they would have remained largely blank except in the cases where actual librettos have been examined. But productions of *Macbeth* known to have been directed by Verdi himself and those directed by his pupil Emanuele Muzio or by Angelo Mariani are footnoted as such.

An asterisk against a singer's name indicates that she or he was a member of the original 1847 or 1865 casts. A slash between singers' names indicates that the second took over the role during the run. Among variant spellings we have tried to use the most common. Singers (e.g. Marcellina Lotti, Antonietta Fricci) who later in their careers joined husbands' names (-Della Santa, -Baraldi) to theirs continue to be listed as at their first entry. Theatres are listed by their names at the date of the performance concerned. The language of non-Italian performances, when known, is specified. Performances of which only the year, season, or month is known are given an approximate placing among the precisely established dates. Some differences in dating from those in Loewenberg's *Annals* are deliberate. At the end of the chronology, there is an index by countries and towns.

—A.P.

1. Or "conductors." The libretto for the Palermo 1852 performance, e.g., lists, in addition to Pietro Romani as "maestro di Cappella Compositore e Direttore," a "maestro al Cembalo e supplimento al Direttore," a "maestro direttore e istruttore dei Cori," "primo Violino e Direttore dell'Orchestra," and "Violino concertino e supplimento al Direttore."

2. Three designers are specified, by scene, for the production mentioned in the preceding note.

Date	City	Theatre	Lady Macbeth	Macbeth	Banquo	Macduff
1847						
March 14	Florence	Pergola	Barbieri-Nini*	Varesi*	Benedetti*	Brunacci*
June 9	Florence	Pergola	A. Boccabadati	De Bassini	Benedetti*?	Borioni
July 29	Padua	Nuovo	Barbieri-Nini*	Colini	Euzet	Lanner
Aug 29	Lucca	Giglio	Tadolini	Gorin	Benedetti*	Brunacci*
Sept 12	Rome	Argentina	A. Boccabadati	Gnone	Sottovia	Lucchesi
Oct 9	Leghorn	Avvalorati	Evers	Gorin	Benedetti*	Brunacci*
Dec 26	Venice	Fenice	De La Grange	Varesi*	Rigio	Palma
Dec 26	Lodi[1]	Sociale	Giuseppina Brambilla	Lovati	Gandini	Belleni
Dec 30	Verona	Filarmonico	Evers	De Bassini		Borioni

1. Conducted by Emanuele Muzio

Date	City	Theatre	Lady Macbeth	Macbeth	Banquo	Macduff
1848						
Feb 12	Mantua[1]	Sociale	Gruitz	Valli	Torre	Mercuriali
Feb 20	Madrid[2]	Circo	Bosio	Morelli		Calzolari
Feb 26	Budapest	Nemzeti Szinhaz	Schodel	Reina		
April	Reggio Emilia	Comunale	Gabussi	De Bassini	Benedetti*	Pancani
May 4	Ancona	Muse	Arrigotti	Fiori	Manfredi	Miraglia
May 13	Genoa	Carlo Felice	De Giuli-Borsi	Gnone	Bianchi	Roppa
July 1	Barcelona	Liceo[3]	Salvini-Donatelli	G. Ferri	Silingardi	Bozzetti
Aug 13	Fermo	Aquila	Gresti	Fiori	Manfredi	Banti
Oct 4	Constantinople	Naum[4]	Medori	Bencich	Nanni	Ademollo
Oct	Valencia	Ciudad	Callinari	De Gironella	Segara	Font
Nov 15	Trieste	Grande[5]	Barbieri-Nini*	De Bassini	Giacomelli	Pavesi
Dec	Madrid	Museo	Rocca-Alessandri	Saez	Echeverria	
Dec 26	Brescia	Grande				

1. Conducted by Emanuele Muzio
2. Although this is the earliest staging listed by Carmena y Millan: *Cronica de la opera italiani en Madrid desde el año 1738 hasta neustros dias* (Madrid, 1878), a letter from Madrid dated 8 January 1848 and published in *La France Musicale* early that year refers to an earlier success of *Macbeth* in Madrid. This suggests that the Madrid premiere took place sometime in late 1847, possibly with Bosio and Morelli Ponti, who were singing in Madrid that season.
3. An earlier performance probably took place in the autumn of 1847, perhaps at the Teatro de Santa Cruz (cf. *Gazzetta Musicale di Milano*, 1847).
4. Inauguration of a new theatre, and probably conducted by Angelo Mariani
5. The libretto specifies eighteen male and twenty female choristers; Luigi Ricci was "mastro direttore della musica."

1849

Date	City	Theatre				
Jan 1	Warsaw[1]	Wielki	De Giuli-Borsi	Colini		Miraglia
Jan 10	Rome[2]	Argentina	Gresti	Fiori	Benedetti*	Volpini
Jan 13	Lisbon	S. Carlos	Tadolini	Badiali	Arati	Agresti
Jan 22	Naples	S. Carlo	Grutz	Gnone	Scalese	Ferretti
Feb 24	Milan	Scala	Rocca-Alessandri?	Giraldoni?		Cuzzani?
March 21	Madrid	Circo[3]	Servoli	Crivelli	Poggiali	Bianchi
March 31	Malta	Manoel	Gresti	Fiori	Benedetti*	Volpini
July	Oporto	S. João	Tadolini	Badiali	Arati	Agresti
Aug?	Naples	S. Carlo	Leva	Donelli	Righi	
Sept 15	Corfu	S. Giacomo	Gresti	Fiori	Benedetti*	Baldanza
Nov 4	Lisbon	S. Carlos	Bovay-Pizzigati	Pizzigati	Dall'Asta	Stecchi-Bottardi
Nov 7	Bologna	Comunale	Hasseldt	Staudigl		Kreutzer
Dec 11	Vienna[4]	Kärntnerthor	Bosio	Badiali	D. Coletti	Lorini
Dec 19	Havana	Tacon	Basseggio	Gorin	Della Costa[5]	Petrovich
Dec 26	Trieste	Grande	Salvini-Donatelli	Ferrario	Goré	Bozzetti
Dec 26	Parma[6]	Regio	Bovay-Pizzigati	Pizzigati	Aliprandi?	Silvestri
Dec 26	Mantua	Sociale				

1. According to *Loeuenberg*, Polish translation by J. Jasiński.

2. Probably supervised by Verdi; see Ricordi's letter of 19 January 1849.

3. The specific cast is not known; however, during the spring season of 1849 the roster of singers at the Circo di Madrid included the baritones Ansotegui and Giraldoni, the sopranos Rocca Alessandri and DeRossi, and the tenors Cuzzani and Castigliano.

4. In German. A performance in Italian, with Barbieri-Nini as Lady Macbeth, had been announced for the season of spring, 1848, at the Kärntnerthor. Strong anti-Italian feeling in Vienna at the time, however, caused the entire season to be canceled.

5. The libretto lists Perrone, but Della Costa was reviewed.

6. For the costume designs for this production, see COHEN at 191–95.

1849–50	Temesvar					

1850

Date	City	Theatre				
Jan 27	Warsaw	Wielki	Evers	Gassier	Fedrighini	Cuzzani
Feb 2	Genoa	Carlo Felice	Vittadini	Mancusi	Euzet	Alzamora/Gonzalez
April	Trapani	S. Ferdinando				
April 2	Madrid	Circo				

Date	City	Theater				
April 24	New York[1]	Niblo's Garden	Bosio	Badiali	D. Coletti	Lorini
May 15	Rome	Argentina	De Giuli-Borsi	Colini	Lanzoni	Pagnoni
May 28	Boston	Howard Atheneum	Bosio	Badiali	D. Coletti	Lorini
June 8	Forli	Comunale	Albertini	Colini	Consoli	Marcucci
July 17	Sinigaglia	Fenice	Barbieri-Nini*	Colini	Della Costa	Biondi
Aug	Budapest[2]	Nemzeti Szinhaz	De La Grange?			
Aug 7	New York	Castle Garden	Bosio	Badiali	D. Coletti	Lorini
Oct ?	Logrono		Mas-Porcell	C. Ferri		
Oct 3	Bologna[3]	Comunale	Barbieri-Nini*	G. Ferri	Contedini	Biondi
Oct 26	Milan	Carcano	Gariboldi-Bassi	Bartolucci	Pons	Guerra
Oct 29	Havana	Tacon	Bosio	Badiali	Coletti	Bellini
Nov?	Burgos		Mas-Porcell	C. Ferri		
Dec 23	Hanover[4]	Hoftheater				
Dec 25	Turin	Regio	Barbieri-Nini*	G. Ferri	Vajro	Palmieri
Dec 26	Modena	Comunale	Alaimo	Zacchi	Poggiali	Bernabei[5]

1. United States premiere
2. According to *Loewenberg*, Hungarian translation by B. Egressy; but if the principals were Italians, they probably sang in Italian.
3. Conducted by Verdi
4. In German
5. Reviews indicate that—as often happened when a celebrated tenor took the role of Macduff—Bernabei sang the *Alzira* cabaletta.

Date	City	Theater				
1850-51	Temesvar		Caspani	Rossi-Corsi	Bailini	Bianchi
	Vercelli	Civico				
1851						
Feb 3	Oporto	S. João	Bianchi	Prattico	Baillou	Gamboggi
Feb 6	Verona	Filarmonico	Gariboldi-Bassi	Gorin	Nanni	Ceresa
April 21	Vienna	Kärntnerthor	Gruitz	De Bassini	Manfredi	Bordas
May 15	Barcelona	Liceo	De Giuli-Borsi	Gassier	Rodas	Font
June 9	Trento	Sociale	Castagnola	Bartolucci	Padovani	Palmieri
Summer	Oporto	S. João				
July 15	Warsaw[1]	Wielki	Mansui	Assoni	Casali	
Aug 23	Brescia	Grande	Spezia	Corsi	Nanni	Piccinnini
Sept 13	Trieste	Grande	Gruitz	G. Ferri		Pozzolini

Date	City	Theatre				
Sept 18	Alicante	Principal	Villò	Sermattei	Gallo–Tomba	Volpini
Sept 27	Venice	S. Benedetto	A. Boccabadati	Steller	Ghini	Scannavino
Oct 14	Rovigo	Sociale	Bovay–Pizzigati	Pizzigati		Galvani
Oct 23	Seville	S. Fernando	Bianchi	Prattico		
Nov 29	Milan	Carcano	Castagnola	Walter		Calbot
Dec 26	Genoa	Carlo Felice	Albertini	Bencich	Panzini	Gentili
Dec 26	Pisa	Ravvivati	Bovay–Pizzigati	Pizzigati	Lanzoni	Chiesi
Dec 26	Florence	Alfieri	Mauri–Venturi	Barili	Bertani	Pellegrini

1. The Macbeths sang in Italian, the rest in Polish.

1851–52

Carnival	Siena	Rinnovati				

1852

Date	City	Theatre				
Jan?	Malaga	Real	Cattinari	Cresci?	Martorell?	Barba
Jan 2	Madrid	Scala	Gruitz	Fiori	Padovani–Polli	Musiani
Jan 20	Milan	Nazionale	Gariboldi–Bassi	Crivelli		
Feb	Turin	Apollo	Alaimo	Crivelli	Lanzoni	Chiesi
Feb 10	Rome	Floridi	Medori	De Bassini	Morelli	
March 7	Leghorn	Kärntnerthor	Zecchini	De Lauro	Capurri	Vergini
March 21	Vienna	Provisorio[1]	Campagna	Storti	Topai	Pellegrini
March 25	Rio de Janeiro	Civico	Gruitz	Crivelli	Lanzoni	
April 12	Fiume	Comunale	Normanni	Della Santa	Walin	Strandberg
April 24	Ferrara	Royal[2]	Campagna	Storti	Topai	Pellegrini
April 29	Stockholm	Comunale	Evers	Corsi	Nanni	Ferlotti
May	Ljubljana	Wielki				
June 27	Faenza	Riccardi[3]	Lotti	Fiori	Dalbesio	Musiani
July 24	Warsaw	Mauroner	Ruggero–Antonioli	Storti	Topai	Pellegrini
Aug 7	Bergamo	Nuovo Comunale	Peruzzi	Mattioli	Dolcibene	Ferlotti
Aug 14	Trieste	Comunale	Finetti–Battocchi	Coliva		Badolachi
Aug 28	Cesena	Italiano	Normanni	Della Santa		
Sept 18	Lugo					
Sept 21	Stockholm					
Nov	Odessa[4]		Basseggio	Zacchi	Benedetti*	Volta

Date	City	Theatre				
Nov 13	Turin	Nazionale	Soss	Olivari	Olara	Neri
Nov 23	Rio de Janiero	Provisorio	Zecchini	De Lauro	Nanni	Pompeani
Dec 13	Palermo	Carolino	Marcolini	Barili[5]		Miserocchi
Dec 26?	Padua	Concordi	Sass	Rossi–Corsi	Puccini	Lucchesi
Dec 26	Terni	Comunale	A. Boccabadati	Buti	Puccini	

1. Inauguration of the new theatre
2. Probably in Italian, contrary to *Loewenberg*
3. The opera was probably staged in the 1849–50 season at the Teatro di Società.
4. In Italian, as *Galmar Ben*
5. Ottavio Tiby: *Il Real Teatro Carolino e l'ottocento musicale Palermitano* (Florence, 1957) lists Filippo Colini in the title role (pp. 221–22); but the libretto lists Barili, and *La France Musicale* (1853, p. 19) confirms that he sang the role.

1853

Date	City	Theatre				
Feb 1	Munich[1]		Gaziello–Brambilla	Giani	Celli	Viotti
March 28	Zagreb	S. Benedetto	Barbieri–Nini*	Fiori	Ghini	Miserocchi
Lent	Venice	Oratorio of St Philip Neri[2]				
	Palermo					
April 2	Messina	S. Elisabetta	A. Boccabadati	Walter	Lazzari	Russo
June 12	Warsaw	Wielki	Rywaska	Zacchi?		
Aug	Odessa	Italiano	Cortesi	Morelli		
Aug 13	Perugia	Civico	Finetti–Battocchi	Barili	Capriles	Orlandi
Aug 14	Macerata	Condomini	Alaimo	Monari	Boccolini	Conti
Aug 15	Città di Castello	Nuovo[3]	Monge	Mancusi		Lelmi
Oct 25	Savona	Ventidio Basso	Gruitz	Bencich	Laura Boccolini	
Oct 29	Ascoli Piceno	Comunale	Alaimo	Giorgi–Pacini?	Contedini?	Conti
Nov	Catania	San Felipe	Forti–Babacci?	Ribas	Tati	Lelmi
Nov 17	Montevideo	Royal	Edelvira	Cima?	Grossi?	Guglielmini
Dec	Copenhagen		Gaziello–Brambilla			Allegri?

1. In German (if it actually took place)
2. As *Saul*, an *azione sacra*, libretto by Giuseppe Bozzo. See p. 358.
3. Inauguration of new theatre

432

1854

Date	City	Theater				
Jan 6	Milan	Scala	Gariboldi	Corsi	Negrini	Stefani
Jan 24	Madrid	Real	Basseggio	Varesi*	Baillou	Denti
March	Oporto	S. João	Giordano	Gorin	Cervini	Bisaccia
March 8	Constantinople	Naum	Foroni-Conti	Mattioli	Manfredi	Guidotti
March 12	Florence	Pergola	Barbieri-Nini*	Crivelli	Mitrovich	
March 21	Buenos Aires	Argentino	Edelvira	Rivas	Tati	Guglielmini
Spring	Lübeck?					
May 13	Rome	Argentina	De Giuli-Borsi	Colini		Conti
May 13	Warsaw	Wielki	Ortolani?	Buti?		
July 9	Milan	Carcano	Marcolini	Prattico	Llorens	Monti
Aug	Odessa	Italiano	Gordosa?	Ferlotti		
Sept 22	Urbino	Raffaele Sanzio	Barbieri-Nini*	Steller		Galletti
Nov 4	Buenos Aires	Argentino	Edelvira	Casanova		
Dec 6	Palermo	Carolino	Lotti	Fiori	Garcia	Graziani
Dec 16	St. Petersburg[1]	Imperial	Tedesco	De Bassini		A. Bettini

1. In Italian, as *Sivardo il Sassone*

1854–55

Date	City	Theater				
Carnival	Barcelona	Liceo		Varesi*	Rodas	
	Temesvar					

1855

Date	City	Theater				
Jan 13	Ferrara	Comunale	Gresti-Codeglia	Fagotti	Capriles	Cruciani
Feb 10	Venice	Fenice	Barbieri-Nini*	Corsi	Nanni	Toffanari
April 28	Ravenna	Alighieri	De Giuli-Borsi	Morelli	Atry	Testa
May 2	Lisbon	S. Carlos	Castellan	Bartolini	Manfredi	Swift
May 12	Montevideo	Nacional	Vera-Lorini	Cima	Figari	Comelli
May 24	Fabriano	Camurio	Basseggio	Cresci	Rinaldini	Chierici-Severini
June 14	Santiago	Republica	Olivieri	Luisia	Olivieri	Rossi-Guerra
Sept 23	Lisbon	S. Carlos	Alaimo	Bartolini	Celestino	Braham
Oct 13	St. Petersburg	Imperial	Lotti	De Bassini	Tagliafico	A. Bettini
Nov 11	Udine	Sociale	Murio-Celli	Prattico	Echeverria	Scannavino
Nov 14	Alessandria	Civico	Gordosa	Giraldoni	Gandini	Ferlotti

Date	City	Theatre				
Nov 15	Warsaw	Nacionale	Ponti-dell'Armi	Coliva	Gianetti	Lorini
Dec 5	Bucharest	Sociale	Della Valle/ Bellocchio	Busi	Llorens[1]	Badalucchi
Dec 26	Novara					
Dec 26	Leghorn	Rossini	Gruitz	Proni	Sottovia	Piccinnini
Dec 26	Como	Sociale	Orecchia	Zacchi	Bisi	Negri
Dec 26	Piacenza	Comunale	Arrigotti[2]	Massiani	Mirandola	Rossi-Guerra
Dec 28	Valparaiso	Victoria	Olivieri	Luisia		

1. The libretto lists Maccani, the Novara *Cronaca* Llorens.
2. Librettos list Carmela Marziali, but Arrigotti is reviewed in *Fama* (1856), 12.

1856

Date	City	Theatre				
Jan-Feb	Pressburg		Mansui	Giannini	Ruiz?	Petrovich
Feb	Jassy	Reale	Zecchini	Mattioni	Contedini	Neri
	Athens		Borsi-De Leurie	Olivari	Della Costa	Serazzi
Feb 26	Constantinople	Naum	Bendazzi	Ferri	Romanelli	Cappello
March	Genoa	Carlo Felice	Lotti	Buti	Müller?	Dobrski
March 27	Warsaw	Wielki	Babacci?	Grandi?		
Spring	Santander		Ermini	Fabbricatore	Tovajera	Bertolini
May 3	Pavia	Comunativo	Edelvira	Bastoggi		Guglielmini
July 29	Santiago	Republica	Weisser	Coliva		Lanner
Aug 12	Badia Polesine	Sociale	Fumagelli	Fumagelli?	Gardini	Petrovich
Sept 13	Bassano	Sociale?				
Sept 22	Graz[1]					
Oct 13	St. Petersburg	Imperial	Lotti	De Bassini	Tagliafico/Polonini	A. Bettini
Dec	Athens	Reale	Ortolani-Brignoli	Crivelli		Bruni
Dec 13	Brünn					
Dec 26	Mantua	Sociale	Barbieri-Nini*	Orlandi	Ghini?	
Dec 26	Arezzo	Petrarca	Ballerini	Padovani-Polli	Foci	Bertolini
Dec 27	Cremona	Concordia	Weisser	Coliva	Garcia	
Dec 27	Ancona	Muse	Vaccari	Antico	Fiorani	Z. Bettini

1. Announced, but it is not known whether it actually took place

1857

Date	City	Theatre	Provenzali	Fabbricatore		
Jan	Pistoia		Casali	Barili		Bianchi
Jan	Zagreb		Angelini	Storti		Guglielmini
Jan 10	Mexico City	Nacional	Edelvira	Lanzoni		Lorini
Feb 1	Messina	S. Elisabetta	Ponti-dell'Armi	Bertolini		Petrovich
Feb 6	Valparaiso	Victoria	Marzioli	Walter?	Casali	Tesi
March	Bucharest	Nacional	Berini?	Cresci	Bruscoli	Luise
May	Zara	Nobile	Ruppini	Casanova	Maccani[1]	Bianchi
May 9	Warsaw	Wielki	La Grua	Gnone	Pons	
June 11	Florence	Pagliano	Cattinari	Squarcia	Gariboldi	
July?	Buenos Aires	Colón	Angelini	Barili	Llorens	
Aug 1	Milan	Carcano	Cortesi	Bertolini	Gariboldi	
Nov 14	Alessandria	Civico	Speranza	Bellini?	Rossi-Galli?	
Dec 1	Mexico City	Nacional	Morazzoni?	Fiori	Celli	
Dec 26?	Brescia	Grande	Galletti-Gianoli		Contadini	
Dec 26	Vercelli	Civico				Tartini?
Dec 26	Pesaro	Rossini				Svampa

1. The libretto lists Della Costa, but Maccani is reviewed in *Fama* (1857), 164.

1858

Date	City	Theatre	Provenzali	Fabbricatore		
Jan?	Buenos Aires	Colón	La Grua	Casanova	Farina	Bichi?
Jan?	Vicenza		Arrigotti	Sacconi		
Feb	Odessa	Municipale	Orecchia	Sermattei	Rossi	Cappello
Feb	Trieste	Grande	Angelini	Orlandi	Benedetti*	Massimiliani
Feb 6	Turin	Regio	Alaimo	Pizzicati	Nanni?	Errani
Mar 2	Barcelona	Liceo	Barbieri-Nini*	Bencich	Figari	Lorini
March 15	Rio de Janeiro	Lirico Fluminense	Vera-Lorini	Reina		Cruciani
March	Constantinople	Naum	Borsi-De Leurie	Corti		
Spring	Odessa		Orecchia?	Marra		
May–June	Palma de Majorca	Principale	Pirola	Dal Negro	Sottovia	Pozzo
June	Civitavecchia	Trajano				
July 31	Viterbo	Unione?	Ponti-dell'Armi	Giannini		
Aug 4	Imola	Comunale	De Montelio	Orlandi	Della Costa	Minocchi
Sept 8	Cagliari	Civico	Melada			

Date	City	Theatre	Morandini	Fagotti	Cornago	Sarti
Oct 7	Milan	Scala				
Oct 15	Asti	Civico				
Oct 28	Mexico City	Nacional	Cortesi	Ottaviani?	Gainnelli?	Sacchero
Nov	Pernambuco		Pinelli-Sacchero	Mari-Cornia	Capponi	Giusti
Nov	Bucharest	Nacional	Zenoni	Steller		
Nov	Corfu	S. Giacomo	Mollo	Giotti		
Nov 3	Alexandria	Europeo	Pellini	Fabbricatore	Romerio?	Molini
Nov 20	Madrid	Real	De Giuli-Borsi	Bartolini	Llorens	Luise
Dec 5	Bogota[1]		Olivieri	Luisia	Mirandola	Rossi-Guerra

1. This fascinating company made an extended tour of South America from c. 1853 until 1860 (when it created *I masnadieri* in New York) and had already sung *Macbeth* in Santiago (see June 1855) and in Valparaiso (see Dec. 1855). It reached Lima in Spring 1856, making its debut with *Attila*, and is very likely to have sung *Macbeth* there in April. We then lose track of the company until it appears in Bogota in 1858; Guayaquil and Quito were the most likely previous stops; and again *Macbeth* was probably given. It is known to have sung in Caracas (but there is no positive record of a *Macbeth* there), Mendoza, Port au Prince, Mayaguez, Santo Domingo, and other Caribbean cities, and is likely to have sung in Cordova, Rosario, Panama, Asunción, Cartagena, Medellín, and elsewhere. It is equally likely that it gave *Macbeth* in some if not all of these towns.

1859

Date	City	Theatre	Morandini	Fagotti	Cornago	Sarti
Jan 11	Venice	S. Benedetto	Morazzoni-Dordoni?	Bellini		
March 30	Dublin	Royal	Viardot	Graziani	Lanzoni	Corsi
April 4	Lisbon	S. Carlos	Tedesco	Cresci	Rossi	Mercuriali
April	Rio	Lirico Fluminense	De La Grange	Arnaud	Didot	
Aug	Bahia		Gavetti-Reggiani			
Nov?	Malta	Manoel		Tournerie		
Dec 18	Lisbon	S. Carlos	Lotti	Bartolini	Cappello	Falco

1860

Date	City	Theatre	Morandini	Fagotti	Cornago	Sarti
Feb 8	Palermo	Carolino	Bendazzi	Bencich	Lanzoni	Sirchia
Feb 29	Montevideo	Solis[1]				
March 8	Amsterdam	National	Devries	Marra	Bianchi	Danieli
April	Valladolid		Micheli	Padovani		
Spring	Melbourne	Prince of Wales	Bianchi	Coulon	Grossi?	Bianchi
July 5	Sydney	S. Carlo	Bianchi	Coulon	Grossi	Bianchi
Aug 5	Naples[2]	Royal	Ruggero-Antonioli	Guicciardi	Arati	Morelli
Sept 11	Dublin[3]	Nazionale	Viardot	Graziani	Ciampi	Luise
Oct	Turin		Bazzurri	Grandi	Da Neri	Cancelli

Date	City	Theatre				
Oct 2	Manchester[4]	Royal	Viardot	Ciampi	Fallar?	Luise
Oct 8	Liverpool	Royal	Viardot	Ciampi?	Fallar	Luise
Oct 6	Rome	Apollo	Ponti-dell'Armi	Carboni	Laterza	Zacometti
Nov	Lucera	Maria Teresa Isabella	Schenardi	Corona		Mariannini
Dec?	Bucharest	Nacional	Lezniewska	Steller		
Dec?	Lucca	Pantera	Banti	Busi		

1. Announced, but it is not known whether it actually took place.
2. Cesare De Sanctis reported to Verdi that the choruses were very good; the men, all young, numbered 120 (*Carteggi 1*, 81).
3. Sung by a touring company, which may have also been given it elsewhere
4. Probably the first performance in England. T. W. Beale, *The Light of Other Days*, 2 vols (London, 1890) mistakenly quotes a review in the *Manchester Herald* as 1859, exactly one year off.

1861

Date	City	Theatre				
Jan 10	Havana	Tacon	Lotti	Cresci		
Feb	Valencia	Principal	Zenoni	Morelli	Rossi	Viani
Feb	Bari	Piccinni	Finelli-Banti	Sansone	Boccabadati	Cantoni
Mar	Bucharest	Nacional	Lesniewska	Steller		
March 15	Linz[1]					
May 9	Milan	S. Radegonda	Beringeri	Viganotti		
June	Naples	S. Carlo	Galletti-Gianoli	De Bassini	Laterza?	Cruciani
June–July	Genoa	Doria	Alba	Viganotti	Tagliapietra	Savelli
Summer	Lecce	Paisiello				
Sept 13	Tiflis	Italiano	T. Stolz	Baraldi		
Autumn	Asti		Morandini	Grandi	Cornago	Mariotti
Oct	Trieste	Grande	Csillag	Fagotti	Bremond	Bazzoli
Autumn	Valencia	Principal	Edelvira	Morelli	Segri-Segarra	Padovani
Nov	Smyrna	Cammarano[2]	Ottonelli-Bresciani	Sutter	Dondi?	Alvisi? Manaresi?
Nov	Bucharest	Nacional	Cattinari	Reina	Llorens	Giorgetti
Nov 13	Turin	Vitt. Eman.	Abbadia			Pardini
Dec 26?	Crema		Abbadia	Archinti?	Siriotti	Zappa?
Dec 26	Brescia	Grande	Morandini	Grandi	Bernasconi?	Panseri
Dec 28	Spoleto	Nobile	Censi	Giacomelli	Chierici	Severini

1. In German

1862

Date	City	Theatre				
Jan 6	Buenos Aires	Colón	Parodi	Walter	Cornago	Bertolini[1]
Feb 6	Parma	Regio	Borsi-De Leurie	Storti	Nerini	Sindacci
Feb 16	Havana[2]	Tacon	Basseggio	G. Ferri	Filiberti	Minetti
March 12	Bologna	Comunale	De Ruda	Panerai	Medini	Dei
March?	Florence	Pergola	De Ruda	Cresci	Tagliapetra	Cervari
April	Oporto	S. João	Alba	Viganotti		Cruciani?
May	Fiume	Civico		Grandi		
	Ferrara	Comunale	Zenoni	Storti	Giannoli	Bicchielli
June 28	Trieste	Mauroner	Zangheri	Grandi		
Aug 13	Siena	Rinnovati	Banti	Crivelli		
Nov 5	Genoa	Paganini	De Giuli-Borsi	Pizzigati	Lari	Pozzolini
Nov 28	San Francisco	Maguire's	Bianchi	Gregg	Grossi	Bianchi
Dec	Malaga		Albertini	Lanzoni		
Dec 3	Havana	Tacon	Medori	Bellini	Biacchi	Minetti
Dec 7	Lisbon	S. Carlos	Lotti	Orlandi	Antonucci	Fillippi
Dec 9	Constantinople	Naum	Cattinari	Mari	Benedetti*	

1. The libretto lists Nicoli, but *Il Trovatore* (15 Jan. 1862), supp. p. 1, shows that Bertolini took over at the last minute.
2. Conducted by Emanuele Muzio

1863

Date	City	Theatre				
?	Budapest		Carina	Furedi	Fiorini	Niccoli
Jan 29	Milan	Scala	Devries	Saccomanno	Ruiz?	Mea? Dell'Armi?
Feb	Jerez		Ponti-dell'Armi	Massiani?	Lazzaro	
Feb 24	Messina	Vitt. Eman.	Beltramelli	Prattico	Medina?	
Feb–March	Reggio–Calabria		Bruni?	Zanetti?	Ruiz	
April	Granada		Ponti-dell'Armi	Giorgi-Pacini	Poli	
May 6	Turin	Vitt. Eman.	Ravina	Rossi	Caprile	Aurelli
May 8	Chieti	Marrucino	Dordoni	Pioni	Grossi	Caserini
May 25	San Francisco	Metropolitan	Bianchi	Fellini	Anselmi	Bianchi
June 29	Trieste	Mauroner	Lanzi	Dal Negro		
Summer	Porto Alegre	S. Pedro				
Aug 29?	Fano	Fortuna	Majo	Storti	Gasparoni	
Autumn	Rome	Argentina	Carozzi-Zucchi	Boccolini	Gennari	
Oct	Valencia	Principal	Majo	Varvaro	Mitrovich?	Agretti-Spagnuoli

Oct 21	New York	Acad. of Music	Medori	Bellini	D. Coletti	Lotti
Nov	Bari	Piccinni	Angelini	Bartolucci	Anselmi	
Dec?	Palma de Majorca		Chiaramonte	Gnone	Lanzoni	Galletti
Dec	Alicante	Principal	Peruzzi	Bachi-Perego	Garcia	Marelli
Dec 9	Philadelphia	Acad. of Music	Medori	Bellini	D. Coletti	Lotti
Dec 26	Foggia	Dauno		Sansone? Morghen?	Pisani	
Dec 29	Barcelona	Liceo	La Grua	Squarcia	Selva	
1864						
Jan 13	Boston	Boston Theatre	Medori	Bellini	Weinlich	Lotti
Feb	Bucharest	Nacional	Gianfredi	Mari		Urio
Feb	Corfu	S. Giacomo	Bellati			
Feb 9	Naples	S. Carlo	Gavetti-Reggiani	De Bassini		
Feb 14	Valparaiso	Victoria	Manzini	Bertolini	De Antoni	De Antoni
March 2	New York	Academy	Medori	Bellini	Weinlich	Lotti
March	San Fernando		Ponti-dell'Armi	Buti		
Spring?	Buenos Aires	Colón	Mollo	Celestino		
Spring	Kharkov		Noel-Guidi	Giannini		
June 11	Padua	Sociale	Cattinari	Giotti	Manfredi	Gottardi
Oct	Alicante	Principal	Cattinari	Prattico	Reduzzi	Villa
Oct 20	Florence	Pagliano	Medori	Mazzanti	Dobbelz	
Nov	Salerno	Flora				
Nov 30	Bari	Piccinni	Casimir-Ney	Capurro		
Dec	Tiflis	Imperial	Zacconi	Coliva		
1865						
Jan	Trieste	Comunale	Borsi-De Leurie	Orlandi	Rossi	Sinigaglia
Jan	Leghorn	Goldoni	Baratti	Mazzanti	Lari	
Jan	Perugia	Civico	Dunord			
Feb?	Puerto Mahon	Coliseo	Contarini	Crotti		
Feb	Barcelona	Liceo	Cattinari	Colonnese		Ordinas
Feb 22	Genoa[1]	Carlo Felice	Salvini-Donatelli	Cotogni	Milesi	De Azula
March	Palermo	Bellini	Stolz	Storti	Ruiz	
March	Bucharest	Nacional	Kapp Young	Cottone		Coy
Spring	Kharkov		Cattinari			

April 21 (*Macbeth II* premiere) Paris[2]	Lyrique	Rey-Balla*	Ismaël*	Petit*	Monjauze*
July 22 Madrid	Rossini	La Grua	Squarcia	Giordoni	Ruiz
Aug 12 Bergamo	Riccardi	Abbadia	Guglielmini	De Giuli	Bachetti
Nov Mexico City	Nacional	Plodowska	Padilla	Cornago	
Dec Zaragozza		Ruggero–Antonioli	Bartolami	Rodas	
Dec Valladolid	Lopez de Vega	Ruggero–Antonioli	Bartolami	Rodas	
Dec 26 Venice	S. Benedetto	Spezia	Aldighieri	Vecchi	Niccoli

1. For the elaborate machinery devised for this production, see Verdi's letter to Escudier of 11 March 1865.
2. French translation by Nuitter and Beaumont

1866

Spring Kharkov		Paganini	Bartolini	Marinozzi	
April 11 Madrid	Real	Rey-Balla*	Merly	Rodas	Toffanari
May 8 Barcelona	Principal	Rey-Balla*	Cotogni	Petit*	Ciarlini
Oct Palermo	S. Cecilia	Siebs	Bacchi-Perego		
Oct Alessandria		De Zorzi	Viganotti	Di Benedetto	
Oct Casalmonferrato					
Oct 5 Lisbon	S. Carlos	Rey-Balla*	Squarcia	Ordinas	Marini
Dec? Malaga	Principe Alfonso	Spezia	Aldighieri	Garcia	
Dec 25 Cagliari	Civico	Banti	Sutter	De Giuli	Guerrieri

1867

Jan 24 Messina	Vitt. Eman.	Noel–Guidi	Laurence		Lazzari
Feb? Palermo	Bellini	Siebs	Bacchi-Perego?		D'Antoni?
Feb Constantinople			Cottone		
Feb 3 Rome	Apollo	Pozzoni	Cotogni	Milesi	De Azula
Feb 14 Smyrna		Scheggi	Orsi	Savoldelli	
Feb 25 Madrid	Real	Lotti	De Bassini	Medini	Palermi
March 2 Turin	Regio	Fricci	Cima	Bremond	Tagliazucchi
Aug? Adria		Luzzi–Feralli	Valle	Galvani	
Aug 20 Cento		Majo	Bachi-Perego	Mazzarini	Mariotti
Sept 22 Este		Borsi–De Leurie	Valle	Galvani	Vanzan
Oct Verona	Ristori	Luzzi–Feralli	Giotti	Galvani	
Nov Barcelona	Lico	Rey-Balla*	Storti	Rodas	Negre
Nov Venice	S. Samuel				
Nov Malaga	Principe Alfonso	Spezia	Aldighieri	Rossi–Galli	Zenari
Dec? Cadiz	Principal	La Grua	Mari	Coulon	Utili
			De Dominici	Gasparini	

1867–68	Guatemala City	Nacional	Cellini	Petrilli		Stefani
1868						
Jan 18	Turin	Vitt. Eman.	Gordosa	Guglielmini		
March	Tiflis	Imperial	Arancio-Guerrini	Storti	Manfredi?	Bronzini?
April	Seville	S. Fernando	Rey-Balla*	Mari	Reduzzi	Sinigaglia
April	Malta	Reale	Bianchi-Montaldo	Burgia	Grimelli	Masato
Oct 6	Lisbon	S. Carlos	Rey-Balla*	Merly	Galvani	Sinigaglia
Oct 21	Voghera	Sociale	Mosconi	Marziali	Scolara	Rinaldini
Nov	Gibraltar		Gordosa	Mari		
Nov 7	Udine	Minerva	Baratti	Cesari	Kaschmann[1]	
Nov 7	Treviso	Garibaldi	Scheggi	Grandi/Laurence		
Dec 26?	Piacenza	Comunale	Davidof	Guglielmini	Costa	Liverani
Dec 26	Milan	Carcano	Ademoli	Carboni	Manni	

1. The review in *Il trovatore* does not give a Christian name; the great baritone Giuseppe Kaschmann studied in Udine before making his official debut in Zagreb, 1869, and this Banquo may represent an earlier, previously unrecorded, appearance.

1869		Nacional	Cellini	Petrilli		Stefani
1869						
Jan?	Odessa	Municipale	Bianchi-Montaldo	Bachi-Perego		
Jan?	Leghorn		Scheggi			
Jan 28	Madrid	Real	La Grua	Boccolini		Rosnati
Spring	Pau		Ferlotti	Otto		
May	Barcelona	Liceo	Giovannoni-Zacchi	Squarcia		Garibay
June	Alicante	Principal	Gordosa	Mari	Reduzzi	
Aug 21	Vicenza	Eretenio	Fricci	Sparapani		Capponi
Oct?	Santiago		Pezzoli			
Oct 25	Rome	Argentina	Blume	Bertolasi		
Nov	Valencia	Principal	Ponti-dell'Armi	Varvaro		
Nov 10	St. Petersburg	Imperial	Fricci	Graziani	Bagagiolo	A. Bettini
Nov 12	Lisbon	S. Carlos	Giovannoni-Zacchi/Benza	Merly	Marchetti	Maurelli
Dec	Tiflis		Arancio-Guerrini	Storti	Manfredi	

Date	City	Theater				
Dec	Malta	Reale	Bossi	Butti	Del Riccio	Pugi
Dec	Athens		Monari	Carboni		Panseri
Dec 26	Cuneo		Engedi	Bastianelli		
Dec 26	Rimini		Antonietta Brambilla	Morelli	Bratiano	Giannini[1]

1. Giannini sang the *cabaletta* from *Alzira*.

Date	City	Theater				
1870						
Jan 26	Florence	Pergola	Giovannoni	Sparapani	Fiorini	Casarini
March	Oporto	S. João	Benza	Spallazzi	Marchetti	
April 20	Seville	S. Fernando	C. Marchisio	Boccolini	Milesi	Vistarini
May 3	Buenos Aires	Colón	Ronzi-Checchi	Celestino?	Ordinas	Sinigaglia
Sept 11	S. Sebastian	Kursaal	Ruggero-Antonioli	Varvaro		
Nov 28	Valencia	Principal	Ruggero-Antonioli	Varvaro		
Nov 23	Bologna	Comunale	Fricci	Storti	Cesaro	Manfredi
1871						
Jan?	Piacenza	Comunale	Hovertol	Carta	Morotto	Casari
Feb 8	Novara	Sociale	De Zorzi	Gambetti	Del Fabbro	Biondini
Feb 12	Havana	Tacon	Pelegatti-Visconti	Mari	Ruiz?	
March 9	Zaragozza	Principale	Ruggero-Antonioli	Faentini-Galassi	Marconi	Vanzetti
April	Barcelona	Liceo	Marziali-Passerini	Merly	Marconi	
April 29	Valladolid	Calderon	Ruggero-Antonioli	Faentini-Galassi	Llorens	Vanzetti
May 6	Reggio Emilia	Municipale	Bianchi-Montaldi	Bertolasi	Morotto	Patierno
May 11	Mexico City	Nacional	Pelegatti-Visconti	Mari	Maffei	Verati
July 22	Turin	Alfieri	Antonietta Brambilla	Brambilla	Vaguer	Alegiani
Sept 9	Conegliano	Accademia	Ronzi-Checchi	Cesari		
Sept 23	Varese	Sociale	Kottas	Bertolini		
Oct	Gerona		Ruggero-Antonioli	Prattico?		
Oct 18	Genoa	Doria	Antonietta Brambilla	Burgio	Romanelli	Torri-Lazari
Oct 29?	Odessa	Municipale	Giovannoni-Zacchi	Parboni	Rossi-Galli	Benfratelli
Nov 15	Lisbon	S. Carlos	Fricci	Cotogni	Gasperini	Sinigaglia

1872

Date	City	Theatre				
Jan?	Guatemala City		Bernardi?	Petrilli	Zuchelli	Bossi
Feb 8	Venice	Fenice	Majo	Silenzi		
Feb 15?	Verona	Nuovo	Marvaldi	Toledo		
March	Valencia	Principal	Spitzer	Mazzoli		
April 3	Madrid	Zarzuela	Fricci	Quintili-Leoni	Del Fabbro	Fabbri
April 3	Adelaide	Royal	Zenoni	Coliva	Dondi	Coy
April 6	Barletta	Comunale	Cattinari	Parboni	Loparco	De Santis
April 14	Guadalajara		Degollado	Visconti	Ottaviani	
Spring	Melbourne		Zenoni	Coliva		
June	Seville	S. Fernando	Fricci	Boccolini	Maini	
July 16	Buenos Aires	Opera	Marziali-Passerini	Guadagnini	Ruiz	Aragon
Sept 5	Florence	Pagliano	Papini	Borgioli	Mirabella	Falciai
Oct 15	Sydney[1]	Victoria	Zenoni	Coliva	Benso	Coy
Nov	Patras		Urbani?	Mastriani		
Nov	Novi			Murri		Tavella
Nov 27	Messina	Vitt. Eman.	Creny	Faentini-Galassi	Lazzaro	Byron
Dec 4	Auckland[2]	Choral Hall	Zenoni	Coliva	Dondi	Coy
Dec?	Leghorn	Rossini	Ronzi-Checci	Valle	Fradelloni	Falciai

1. The review in the *Sydney Morning Herald* states that the opera had been given years ago in an abridged version without chorus or orchestra.

2. The opera was probably given also in Wellington, Christchurch, and Dunedin, the stops of the touring company after Melbourne, Sydney, and Auckland. An advertisement in the Auckland *Southern Cross* refers to twenty performances of *Macbeth*, "Verdi's greatest opera," given in Melbourne and Sydney.

1873

Date	City	Theatre				
Jan	Trieste	Grande	Bendazzi	Valle	Nerini	Giussani
Jan 20	Havana	Tacon	Bulli-Paoli	Mari		
Jan 28	Barcelona	Liceo	Ponti-dell'Armi	Toledo		
March	Pisa	Verdi	Guadagnini	Tirini	Del Fabbro	Fabbri
April	Salerno		Marvaldi	Parboni	Di Jorio	Panzetta
April	Genoa	Nazionale	Kottas	Parolini	Rossi-Castagnola	Falciai
July 8	Buenos Aires	Opera	Marziali-Passerini	Guadagnini	Maffei	Bardi
Dec	Cagliari	Civico	Bartoletti	Massera	De Serini	Minotti

1874

Date	City	Theatre				
Jan 28	Milan	Scala	Fricci	Pandolfini	Padovani	Cesi
(probably *Macbeth* II Italian premiere)						
March 25	Modena	Aliprandi	Antonietta Brambilla	Cabella	Giordano	
May?	Barcelona	Novedades	Vogri	Borgioli		
May	Zaragozza	Principal	Vogri	Borgioli		
Aug	Oaxaca		D'Aponte	Petrilli	Mancini?[1]	Coranzzani[1]

1. Mancini and Coranzzani appeared in a benefit concert in Oaxaca on 26 June 1874 at which Act 1 of *Macbeth* was performed; D'Aponte and Petrilli sang the main roles.

1875

Date	City	Theatre				
Jan 16	Modena	Comunale	Pantaleoni	Bertolini	Sovoldelli	Byron
Jan	Noto			Pogliani		
March	Caltanisetta		Fusini-Rosanoff	Bertolini		
March 6	Florence	Principe Umberto	Mocoroa	Valle	Monti	Fattorini
March 20	Catania	Comunale	Pitarch	Capocci	Pinto	Manfrini
April 3	Turin	Balbo	Tati	Corti	Belfiore	Cesaro
April 9	Mexico City	Principal	Visconti	Petrilli	Visconti	Donati
May?	Rome	Capranica	Pogliani	Ciotti		
June	Constantinople					
Sept?	Barcelona	Novedades	Kottas	Parboni	Buzzi	
Oct 30	Rome	Argentina	Ferlotti-Danchini	Pogliani	D'Ottari	
Dec 26?	Pistoia	Arena	Sabaini-Constantini	Cresci	Paolicchi	Tesi

1876

Date	City	Theatre				
Jan	Corfu	Comunale	Bellariva	Bergamaschi	Mancini	Bardi
April 22	Barcelona	Principal	Fricci	Boccolini	Gasperini	Giraud
June 24	Buenos Aires	Colón	Wiziak	Storti	Lombardelli	Ambrosi
Summer	Guatemala		Potentini			
Sept	Santiago	Municipal	Bulli-Paoli	Guadagnini	Maffei?	Milani?
Oct?	Alba		Boccabianca			
Oct 14	Treviso	Comunale	Nandori	Lalloni	Galvani	Pugi
Oct 29	Lisbon	S. Carlos	Fricci	Aldighieri	Della Costa	Bieletto
Dec	Nice	Municipal	Potentini	Cresci	Gianoli	Boganini
Dec	Pau		Mosconi	Varvaro		

1877

Date	City	Theatre				
Jan	Padua	Concordia	Bossi	Noto	Della Torre	Milani
Jan 20	Valparaiso	Victoria	Bulli-Paoli	Guadagnini	Maffei	
Feb 19	Palermo	Circo	Baratti	Farina	Cesaro	Carnelli
March	Gorizia		Ciuti	Valcheri	Furlan	
March	Santander					
April	Brescia	Grande	Gerbi	De Giorgio	Leoni?	
April 15	Seville	S. Fernando	Pozzoni	Pachilla?		
April 28	Naples	Mercadante	Saverthal	Noto		Astori
May 18	Montevideo	Solis	Potentini	Lalloni	Nerini	Parmisini
June	San Juan	Municipal	D'Aponte	Petrilli	Monti	Graziani?
June 2	Venice	Goldoni	Mocoroa	Colonna	Atienza	Piffer
June 17	Buenos Aires	Colon	Fricci	Mendioroz	Furlan	Ambrosi
July	Sondrio		Drog	Giannini	Lombardelli	
Aug	Milan	Dal Verme	Erba	Valle		Damiani
Aug?	Ponce	Perla	D'Aponte	Petrilli	Panari	
Aug 16	Rio de Janeiro	Pedro II	Fricci	Mendioroz	Lombardelli?	Ambrosi
Aug 23	Busseto	Verdi	Bellot	Burgio	Rossi-Castagnola	Adami
Sept 28	Venice	Malibran	Bossi	Barbieri	Corti	Damiani
Autumn	Porto Alegre	S. Pedro	Potentini	Lalloni		
Dec 12	Havana	Tacon	Wiziak	Storti		

1878

Date	City	Theatre				
Jan	Alexandria	Rossini	Flavio-Concetti	Cresci	Contedini	Ferrari
Jan 12	Florence	Pagliano	Nandori	Priani	Campello	Turchetti
Feb	Tiflis	Imperial	Bossi	Masi	Mancini?	Deliliers?
March 2	Naples	Bellini	Creny	Quintili-Leoni	Vecchioni	Cesari
March 12	Genoa	Carlo Felice	Tabacchi	Athos-Caldani	Bagagiolo	Pizzorni
Oct 25?	Turin	Vitt. Eman.	Erba	De Anna	Silveri	Sanguineta
Nov 20	Berlin[1]	Kroll	Boy-Gilbert	Medica	Povoleri	Bertocchi
Nov 26	Lisbon	S. Carlos	De Giuli-Borsi	Aldighieri	Della Costa	Bieletto

1. The *Neue Berliner Musik Zeitung* of Nov. 28, 1878 (p. 381) has a brief review of the performance and the work, although it mentions neither cast nor date; these are found in the *Neue Preussische Zeitung* of 20 and 23 Nov. 1878.

1879						
Feb 13	Genoa	C. Felice	Barbieri-Angeli	Barbieri	Rapp	Colombana
Dec 25	Lucca	Pantera	Colombini	Carisio		Papeschi
Aug 27?	Venice	Malibran	Bossi	Barbieri	Conti	Damiani
Nov	Smyrna		Fochi	De Giorgi		
1880						
Jan	Casalmorferrato		Rinaldini	Cavaratti		
Feb 12	Parma	Reggio	Conti-Moroni	Medini	Roveri	
March	Barcelona	Novedades	Vogri?	Quintili-Leoni		
March	Barcelona	Liceo	Fossa	Bianchi		
Oct 3?	Vigevano	Cagnomi	Nandori	Laban/Toledo	Coda	Paterlini
Dec 26?	Brescia	Grande	Mery/Nandori	Conti	De Serini	Pugi
Dec 26	Bergamo	Società	Ilari		Sertori	Doerfles
1881						
Carnival	Chioggia	Garibaldi	Ilari	Noto	Aquilina	Turchetto
Jan	Malta	Reale	Cristino	Isamat		
Jan	Girgenti		Davidoff	Caravatti		
Jan 5	Constantinople	Concordia	Creny	Majocchi		
Jan 26	Cremona	Concordia	Rastelli/Raggi	Lentini	Sales?	Donati
Feb 6?	Fermo	Dell'Aquila	Spettrino	Medini	Graziani	Bardi
Feb 12	Parma	Regio	Conti-Foroni	Gambetti	Roveri	Labruna
July	Smyrna		Fochi		Grommi	
1882						
Jan 7	Turin	Regio	Giunti-Barbera	Barbieri	Migliara	Bello
Jan 12	Bari	Piccinni	Pozzi-Ferrari	Gnaccarini		
Aug	Santiago	Municipale	Wiziak	Lalloni		
Aug 27?	Athens	Olimpico	Martinez	De Giorgio		
Oct 6	Trieste	Politeama	Aimo	Medini	Graziosi	Lorini
Oct 24	Lisbon	S. Carlos	Vanda Miller	Aldighieri	Navarini	Piazza
Dec 26	Lodi		Pagliani	Felini	Pro	

Date	Place	Theatre				
1883						
Jan 13	Verona	Filarmonico	Bossi / Giunti-Barbera (on Jan 25)	Medini / Cottone (on Jan 25)	Fradelloni	Garulli
Lent	Salerno					
August	Barcelona	Buen Ritiro	Castiglioni	Blasi / Ponsini		
1884						
Jan	Seville	S. Fernando				
March 30	Zaragozza		Martinez	Viganotti / Gnaccarini		
1885						
March	Barcelona	Buen Ritiro		Pelz		
March	Trapani	Garibaldi	Giunti-Barbera	Blasi		
Spring	Acquila					
July 8	Athens	Olimpo	Giannetti	De Giorgio	Dadò	
Aug	Castel San Pietro		Cavazza	Gnaccarini	Scarneo	Elias
Dec 25	Ferrara	Comunale	Stefanini	Barbieri	Pizzolotti	Vanni
1886						
May 13	Zagreb[1]					
Dec?	Galari		Giannetti			
1887						
March	Bologna	Brunetti	Nosari	Gnaccarini	Borucchia	Barbieri
Aug?	Volterra	Fiacco	Parodi	Casini	Paltrinieri	Brandaglia
Dec 10	Oporto	S. João	Caligaris-Marti	Verdini	Serra	
Dec 25	Crema		Nicelli	Melossi	Francalancia	
1888						
March	Oviedo		Caligaris-Marti	Verdini	Resplendino	Onet
Dec 25?	Fossano		De Vecchi	Sacco		

1. In Croatian [Loewenberg], translation by I. Trnski

Date	City	Theater				
1889 March 16	Genoa	Politeama	Buzzolla	Fari	Lucenti	Asti
1890 Jan 8 Feb 1	Pavia Cagliari	Fraschini	Marco Ilari	Broggi Pacini	Lopez Bardossi	
1894 Feb 11 March Spring	Messina Palermo Tortona	Vitt. Emanuele Politeama Garibaldi	Stinco-Palermini Caligaris-Marti Aimo	Barbieri Pacini Alberti	Chiossone Tos	Benfratelli
1898[1]						
1901 Oct 30	Treviso	Comunale	Caligaris-Marti	Gnaccarini	Spoto	Spadoni
1903 Dec 18	Lisbon	S. Carlos	Bianchini-Cappelli	Pacini	Mansueto	
1904 Nov 8	Florence	Verdi	Chelotti	Pacini	Bernardi	
1905 Feb 1 Feb 24 May 6 May	Madrid Lisbon Seville Malaga	Real S. Carlos S. Fernando Cervantes	De Lerma Bianchini-Cappelli De Vila De Vila	Pacini Arangeli Blanchard Blanchard	Possato Mariani	Gennari
1911 March 11	Rome	Costanzi	Gagliardi	Battistini/Kasch- mann	Gaudio	Sala

1. The former owner of a *Macbeth I* libretto now in Andrew Porter's possession has penciled opposite the cast page, "Costanzi [Rome] /1898/Marconi/Medea Borelli/(pesante)." But there is no record of this performance in the Costanzi *cronache* or in the periodicals of the time.

1921						
Oct 15	Stockholm[1]					

1. Swedish translation by H. Key

1928						
April 21	Zurich[1]					
	Dresden[2]		Burckhardt	Burg	Bader	

1. German translation by Georg Göhler, also used for the subsequent Dresden, Berlin, Hamburg, Vienna, Munich, and Prague productions; and see the following note.

2. There were several more German productions of *Macbeth* in succeeding years than those whose details we have been able to establish. Wilhelm Altmann's statistical tables in the *Allgemeine Musik-Zeitung* 61 (1934), 438 and 498, and 62 (1935), 536 and 552 give the following totals of *Macbeth* performances on German stages: 1929–30, eight; 1930–31, twenty; 1931–32, forty-seven; 1932–33, twenty-four; 1933–34, thirty-seven; 1934–35, (six productions), thirty-seven. In 1931–32, Verdi was the opera composer most often performed in Germany, with a total of 1420 performances; Wagner came second, with 1385.

1931						
Oct 18	Berlin	Stadttheater	Bindernagel/Onegin	Reinmar	Tappolet	Noort

1932						
Oct 1	Zurich		Pauly			
Dec 26	Rome	Reale	Scacciati	Franci	Vaghi	De Gaviria-Mazziotti

1933						
April 6	Vienna	Staatsoper	Pauly/Runger	Ahlersmayer	Marowski	Wolf
	Hamburg	Stadttheater	Kalter			

1934						
April 28	Vienna	Staatsoper	Ranczac	Rehkemper	Weber	Gerlach
Dec 12	Munich	National Theater				

1935						
Dec	Wuppertal	Stadttheater	Höngen			
	Prague					

	City	Theater				
1935–36	Hamburg	Stadttheater	Kalter			
1938 May 21 Dec 26	Glyndebourne[1] Milan	 Scala	 Schwartz Jacobo/Cigna	 Valentino Sved	 Franklin Pasero	 Lloyd Parmeggiani
1939 June 2 June 23	Glyndebourne Buenos Aires	 Colón	 Grandi Spani	 Valentino Sved	 Franklin Vaghi/Baronti	 Lloyd Mastronardi
1941 Oct 24	New York[1]	44th Street	Kirk	Walters	Silva	Marshall
1942	Hamburg	Stadttheater				
1943 April 4	Vienna	Staatsoper	Höngen	Schöffler/ Ahlersmayer	Alsen	Witt
1947 Aug 24	Stockholm Edinburgh	Royal King's	Nilsson Grandi	Björling Valentino	Tajo/Brannigan	Midgley

1. British premiere of *Macbeth II*

1. U.S. premiere of *Macbeth II*. New Opera Company; Fritz Busch conducted, Hans Busch directed; Martha Lipton was the Lady-in-waiting.

TWENTIETH-CENTURY REVIVALS OF *MACBETH* I

1969
| March 31 | Boston | Shubert | Kuhse | Paskalis | Estes | Novoa |

1976
| Feb 18 | London[1] | Collegiate | Jacques | Summers | Lawrence | Blackwell |

1977
| Nov | Louisville, Ky[2] | Macauley | Hunt | Fazah | Gaal | Khanzadian |

1978
| July 25 | London | Albert Hall (Prom) | Hunter | Glossop | Tomlinson | Collins |

1981
| March 15 (concert performance) | Stony Brook | Fine Arts Center | Fiske | Stith | Ramirez | Manno |

1. English translation by Nell and John Moody.
2. The production was given at the Regional Arts Center, Centre College, Danville, on November 11, as part of the Fifth Verdi Congress; English translation by Andrew Porter.

INDEX BY COUNTRY AND CITY

As in Loewenberg's Annals of Opera, *the borders are those in effect between 1920 and 1934. Thus Fiume is under Italy, although it was part of Hungary in the nineteenth century and is now in Yugoslavia. Any attempt to take shifting borders into account would have meant a mass of cross-references. The exception is Zara, listed under Yugoslavia, although it was Italian between the two World Wars; the reason is that, while Fiume was contiguous with Italy, Zara was an Italian enclave within Yugoslavia.*

Crema, 1861, 1887
Cremona, 1856, 1867, 1881
Cuneo, 1869
Este, 1867
Fabriano, 1855
Faenza, 1852
Fano, 1863
Fermo, 1848, 1881
Ferrara, 1852, 1855, 1862, 1885
Fiume, 1852, 1862
Florence, 1847 (2), 1851, 1854, 1857, 1862, 1864,
    1870, 1872, 1875, 1878, 1904
Foggia, 1863
Forli, 1850
Fossano, 1888
Genoa, 1848, 1850, 1851, 1856, 1861, 1862, 1865,
    1871, 1873, 1878, 1879, 1889
Girgenti, 1881
Gorizia, 1877
Imola, 1858
Lecce, 1861
Leghorn, 1847, 1852, 1855, 1865, 1869, 1872
Lodi, 1847, 1882
Lucca, 1847, 1860–61, 1879
Lucera, 1860
Lugo, 1852
Macerata, 1853
Mantua, 1847, 1849, 1856
Messina, 1853, 1857, 1863, 1867, 1872, 1894
Milan, 1849, 1850, 1851, 1852, 1854 (2), 1857,
    1858, 1861, 1863, 1868, 1872, 1874, 1877, 1938
Modena, 1850, 1874 (2)
Naples, 1849 (2), 1860, 1861, 1864, 1877, 1878
Noto, 1875
Novara, 1855, 1871
Novi, 1872
Padua, 1847, 1852, 1864, 1877
Palermo, 1852, 1853, 1854, 1860, 1865, 1866,
    1867, 1877, 1894
Parma, 1849, 1862, 1881
Pavia, 1856, 1890
Perugia, 1853, 1865
Pesaro, 1857
Piacenza, 1855, 1868, 1871
Pisa, 1851, 1873
Pistoia, 1857, 1875
Ravenna, 1855
Reggio Calabria, 1863
Reggio Emilia, 1848, 1871
Rimini, 1869
Rome, 1847, 1849, 1850, 1852, 1854, 1860, 1863,
    1867, 1869, 1875 (2), 1911, 1932
Rovigo, 1851
Salerno, 1864, 1873, 1883
Savona, 1853

Siena, 1851–52, 1862
Sinigaglia, 1850
Sondrio, 1877
Spoleto, 1861
Terni, 1852
Tortona, 1894
Trapani, 1850, 1885
Trento, 1851
Treviso, 1868, 1876, 1901
Trieste, 1848, 1849, 1851, 1852, 1858, 1861, 1862,
    1863, 1865, 1873, 1882
Turin, 1850, 1852 (2), 1858, 1860, 1861, 1863,
    1867, 1868, 1871, 1875, 1878, 1882
Udine, 1855, 1868
Urbino, 1854
Varese, 1871
Venice, 1847, 1851, 1853, 1855, 1859, 1865, 1867,
    1871, 1872, 1877 (2), 1879
Vercelli, 1850–51, 1857
Verona, 1847, 1851, 1867, 1872, 1882–83
Vicenza, 1858, 1869
Vigevano, 1880
Viterbo, 1858
Voghera, 1868
Volterra, 1887
Malta
    La Valletta, 1848, 1859, 1868, 1869, 1881
Mexico
    Guadalajara, 1872
    Mexico City, 1857 (2), 1858, 1865, 1871, 1875
    Oaxaca, 1874
Netherlands
    Amsterdam, 1860
New Zealand
    Auckland, 1872
Poland
    Warsaw, 1848, 1850, 1851, 1852, 1853, 1854,
        1855, 1856, 1857
Portugal
    Lisbon, 1848, 1849 (2), 1855 (2), 1859 (2), 1862,
        1866, 1868, 1869, 1871, 1876, 1878, 1882, 1903
    Oporto, 1849, 1851 (2), 1854, 1862, 1870, 1887
Puerto Rico
    Ponce, 1877
    San Juan, 1877
Rumania
    Bucharest, 1855, 1857, 1858, 1860, 1861 (2), 1864,
        1865
    Galati, 1866
    Jassy, 1856
    Temesvar, 1849–50, 1850–51, 1854–55
Russia
    Kharkov, 1864, 1865, 1866
    Odessa, 1852, 1853, 1854, 1856 (2), 1858, 1869,
        1871

St. Petersburg, 1854, 1855, 1856, 1869
Tiflis, 1861, 1864, 1868, 1869, 1878
Spain
  Alicante, 1851, 1863, 1864, 1869
  Barcelona, 1848, 1851, 1854–55, 1858, 1863, 1864,
    1865, 1866, 1867, 1869, 1871, 1872, 1873, 1874,
    1875, 1876, 1880 (2), 1885
  Burgos, 1850
  Cadiz, 1867
  Gerona, 1871
  Granada, 1863
  Jerez, 1863
  Logrono, 1850
  Madrid, 1848 (2), 1849, 1850, 1852, 1854, 1858,
    1865, 1866, 1867, 1869, 1872, 1905
  Malaga, 1852, 1862, 1866, 1867
  Oviedo, 1888
  Palma de Majorca, 1858, 1863
  Puerto Mahan, 1865
  San Fernando, 1864
  San Sebastian, 1870
  Santander, 1856, 1877
  Seville, 1851, 1868, 1870, 1872, 1877, 1884
  Valencia, 1848, 1861 (2), 1863, 1869, 1870, 1872

  Valladolid, 1860, 1865, 1871
  Zaragozza, 1865, 1871, 1874, 1884
Sweden
  Stockholm, 1852 (2), 1921, 1947
Switzerland
  Zurich, 1928, 1932
Turkey
  Constantinople, 1848, 1854, 1856, 1858, 1862,
    1867, 1875, 1881
  Smyrna, 1861, 1867, 1879, 1881
United States
  Boston, 1850, 1864, 1969
  Danville, Ky., 1977
  Louisville, Ky., 1977
  New York, 1850 (2), 1863, 1864, 1941
  Philadelphia, 1863
  San Francisco, 1862, 1863
  Stony Brook, L.I., 1981
Uruguay
  Montevideo, 1853, 1855, 1860, 1877
Yugoslavia
  Lubljana, 1852
  Zagreb, 1853, 1857, 1886
  Zara, 1857

OTHER MUSIC FOR *MACBETH*

Music written for or based on Shakespeare's plays is considered in Phyllis Hartnoll, ed.: Shakespeare in
Music *(London: Macmillan, 1964), referred to below as H. Winton Dean's long chapter on "Shakespeare
and Opera" is especially rewarding. There is a catalog of operas and other music based on the plays, incidental
music, and settings of Shakespeare. Christopher Wilson's* Shakespeare and Music *(London: The Stage,
1922; Da Capo reprint, 1977), referred to below as* **W.***, contains some interesting commentary.*

—— 1 ——

Incidental Music: In its presumed original
form—*i.e.*, before interpolations from Middleton's *The Witch*—Shakespeare's *Macbeth* called
for little incidental music. The direction
"Flourish" appears five times: for Duncan's entrance and for his exit in I.4, and thrice in the
final scene—at Malcolm's entry; after the general cry "Hail, King of Scotland!"; and at the
very end, after Malcolm has invited his subjects
to attend his coronation at Scone. John H.
Long[1] notes an apparently deliberate intention

of reserving flourishes to distinguish true royalty from the usurper. Macbeth is not accorded
a flourish; in III.1 the entrance of "Macbeth as
King" is heralded by a "Senit." For the rest: in
I.6 "Hoboyes" welcome Duncan to Macbeth's
castle and I.7 accompany the preparations for
the banquet in his honor. In IV.1, the Witches'
cauldron sinks to the sound of "Hoboyes."
"Drum" is specified in the initial stage directions of V.2,4,5, and 6.

    But the Middleton additions, possibly intro-

1. John H. Long: *Shakespeare's Use of Music: The Histories and Tragedies* (Gainsville: University of Florida Press,
1971), p. 183

duced at the Globe in 1611[2], bring more music. In III.5 (the Witches' meeting on the heath with Hecate), there is a "Song within, *Come away, come away, &c.*"; and IV.1 (the Witches' cavern scene) calls for both "Musique and a Song, *Black Spirits, &c.*"–the charm song ordered by Hecate to consolidate the spell in the brew–and, at the Witches' departure, "Musicke. The Witches Dance, and vanish."[3]

With the Middleton interpolations and then with further musical additions (notably a musical finale to close Act II) introduced by Davenant in the 1660s, *Macbeth* became what Pepys could describe as "a most excellent play in all respects, but especially in divertisement, though it be a deep tragedy" (7 January 1666–67) and as "one of the best plays for a stage, and variety of dancing and musique, that I ever saw" (19 April 1667). Matthew Locke is known to have composed music for Davenant's production of the mid-1660s; the Dorset Gardens production of 1673, put on by his widow, was described as "being in the nature of an Opera."[4] John Eccles wrote *Macbeth* music in *ca.* 1695 for the Lincoln Inn Fields theatre, and in 1702 Drury Lane put on a new *Macbeth* with music by the popular bass Richard Leveridge (who continued to sing in *Macbeth* at Drury Lane, then Lincoln's Inn, then Covent Garden, into the 1740s; his role was Hecate). In 1770, Boyce published *The Original Songs Airs & Chorusses which were introduced into the Tragedy of Macbeth in Score Composed by Matthew Locke*, dedicating the publication to Garrick. This is the "Famous Music from *Macbeth*" that retained its popularity and accompanied most productions well into the nineteenth century.

Burney declared that its "rude, wild excellence cannot be surpassed."[5] George Hogarth called it "one of the noblest and most beautiful works that ever was produced by an English musician."[6] In *ca.* 1785, it was reattributed to Purcell. Today, it is generally ascribed to Leveridge.[7]

The authorship of the Famous Music and the extent to which the seventeenth- and eighteenth-century *Macbeth* composers borrowed numbers from earlier scores are topics that have been much discussed but are scarcely of Verdian relevance. What is significant is that *Macbeth* entered the nineteenth century as an "operatic" play rich in music. Introducing her edition of it (1808), Mrs. Inchbald begins: "In this grand tragic opera is combined that which is terrific, sublime, infernal."[8] And the following is from a writer of 1812 who objects to the prominence given to the music but (as Roger Fiske, in whose article we found the passage, observes) does not consider omitting it:

The score, or more, of vocal performers who are brought on in russet cloaks, and drawn up in rank for full ten minutes in front of the stage, are intruders ... fatal to the whole course of ideas that should attend us in this part of the play. The men are mostly comedians, as well as singers; and, whatever they may intend, their countenances, as soon as they are recognized, throw an air of burlesque upon the whole. The women, who are generally pretty enough to *bewitch* us in a sense very different from Shakespeare's, are often employed in laughing with each other, and sometimes with the audience, at their dresses, which they think frightful, but which, in fact, conceal neither their bright eyes, nor rosy lips, nor, scarcely, their neat silk stockings. Now all this interruption to the solemn influence of the scene may be avoided by an easy alter-

---

2. Simon Forman in his "Book of Plaies" (GB-Ob) cites an evidently spectacular revival of *Macbeth* at the Globe (Macbeth and Banquo entered on horseback) for 1610 [1611]; see Bartholomeusz, *Macbeth and the Players*, p. 3–4.

3. For the original music of *The Witch* (*ca.*1609), presumably taken over into the amplified *Macbeth*, and probably by Robert Johnson, see J. Cutts: "The Original Music of Middleton's *The Witch*," *Shakespeare Quarterly* 7 (Spring 1965), 203–9; and Long, *Shakespeare's* pp. 184–200.

It has been proposed (*Macbeth*, ed. J. Dover Wilson, Cambridge University Press, 1957; xxvii) that music from Ben Jonson's *The Masque of Queens* (1609) was taken into *The Witch*; Jonson's description of his witches' dancing may prove suggestive to a modern director of Verdi's *Macbeth* (*The Masque of Queens* [London: The King's Printers, 1930], p. 30; cit. from Long, *Shakespeare's*, pp. 190–91) "*At which, with a strange and sodayne musique, they fell into a magicall Daunce full of preposterous change, and gesticulation, but most applying to their property: who, at their meetings, do all things contrary to the custome of men, dancing back to back, hip to hip, their hands joyn'd, and making their circles backward, to the left hand, with strange phantastique motions of their heads and bodyes.*"

4. John Downes [for many years the Dorset Gardens prompter]: *Roscius Anglicanus* (London, 1708), 33

5. *A General History of Music*, ed. F. Mercer, 2 (London: 1935), p. 643

6. *Memories of the Musical Drama* (London: 1838), p. 129

7. See Robert E. Moore, "The Music to *Macbeth*," *Musical Quarterly* 47 (1961), 22–40; and Roger Fiske, "The *Macbeth* Music," *Music & Letters* 45 (1964), 114–25.

8. *The British Theatre*, 4 (London: Longman, etc., 1808)

ation in the performance. The fine words of the incantations (partly Shakespeare's and partly Middleton's), the highly-appropriate music of Locke, the harmony of our best voices may all be preserved ... by stationing the whole chorus behind the scenes, partly on the ground and partly aloft ... and the music would indisputably be heard with an effect more suitable to the occasion.[9]

The text of the "operatic finales" of Acts II and III and of the infernal divertimento in Act IV appear in many editions of the play from 1764 (the so-called "first quarto") and 1765 (the much-rewritten Davenant version) onward. For although Middleton's *The Witch* was published only in the late eighteenth century, the songs from it were evidently familiar, and in most eighteenth-century editions the song incipits of the First Folio are expanded. From Rave (1709) to Steevens (1778), the witches sang about their cauldron:

Black spirits and white,
Blue spirits and gray,
Mingle, mingle, mingle,
You that mingle may.

But in 1779 Steevens discovered *The Witch*, with its "charme Song, about a Vessell"; Middleton's spirits are black, white, *red*, and gray, and in his 1785 edition Steevens made them so. Among the Italian translations (for an account of them, see pp. 351-55), Leoni, evidently working from a pre-1785 text, has:

Spirti neri, spirti bianchi,
Spirti azzurri, e spirti grigi,
Mescolate. De' prodigi
Ha tal arte il germe in sè.

Likewise Rusconi (1838):

Spirti neri e bianchi, spirti azzurri e grigi, fondete,
fondete, fondete, voi che mescolar sapete.

But Carcano (1848) used a post-1785 version:

Spiritelli—farfarelli
Bianchi e neri—rossi e bigi
   Che mescer sapete,
   Mescete, mescete.

The 1847 libretto has:

E voi, Spirti
Negri e candidi,
Rossi e ceruli
Rimescete!
Voi che mescere
Ben sapete,
Rimescete!
Rimescete!

Spirits both red and blue (and none gray)! The appearance in the opera of these red spirits, missing in both Leoni and Rusconi, have led to a presumption that the librettists must have had access to a manuscript version of the not-yet-published Carcano translation. But, in printed black and white, these red spirits already had an Italian habitation closer at hand: Piave also had recourse to the Nicolini translation (see his letter to Ricordi of 28 January 1847), and there he would have found:

Spirti bianchi, spirti neri,
Spirti rossi, spirti bigi,
Voi che l'arte ne sapete,
Rimescete, rimescete.

Nicolini is evidently responsible for not only the red spirits but also the meter and wording of the subsequent lines.[10]

In 1744, Garrick produced *Macbeth* in a text with much Shakespeare restored and with Davenant removed—except for the Witches' musical scenes. (He also added a death scene for Macbeth; see p. 000.) At a Lyceum production of 1875, the Famous Music was abandoned for the first time, according to Irving, who in 1888 commissioned a new score from Sullivan.[11] A list of composers who have written incidental music for *Macbeth* appears at H.259; notable among them are Milhaud, Spohr, and Walton. To that list may be added Oscar de Lagoanère, whose music (for Jean Richepin's version, at the Théâtre de la Porte St. Martin, 1884) was published in vocal score.

—— 2 ——

Operas: A "pantomime" by F. Asplmayr, *Leben und Tod des Königs Macbeth*, appeared in Vienna in 1777.[12] In 1819, a Sadler's Wells pantomime,

9. Baker, *Biographia Dramatica* (1812), iv.2

10. We are grateful to Nati H. Krivatsy, of the Folger Shakespeare Library, and to O. W. Neighbour, of the British Library, for help in conjuring up these particular red spirits and for checking other readings in the Leoni and Nicolini translations.

11. Fiske, "The *Macbeth* music," 117–18

12. Stephanie the Younger's adaptation of *Macbeth* had appeared in Vienna in 1772. Duncan (Macbeth's uncle) is

by J. Whitaker, was entitled *The Weird Sisters, or the Thane and the Throne*. The earliest opera appears to be Hippolyte Chélard's *Macbeth* (Paris: Opéra, 1827; three acts), with a libretto by Rouget de Lisle, author of the *Marseillaise*. It failed after five performances (the only number that pleased, it seems, was a trio for the witches; their names were Elsie, Groëme, and Nona), but had more success when Chélard revived it in Munich in 1828; a five-act version appeared in Weimar in 1861. An account of Chélard's *Macbeth* appears in Allwyn Charles Keys: *Les Adaptations musicales de Shakespeare en France* (Paris: Sirey, 1933), 115–24. Dean (*H*.156–58) remarks, justly, that the music "shows a lively sense of the theatre but an incongruously mixed style derived from Rossini, Spontini, Weber, and Spohr. It veers abruptly between skittish coloratura and the utmost chromatic succulence." Schröder-Devrient sang Lady Macbeth in the London production, 1832.

Wilhelm Taubert's *Macbeth*, libretto by F. Eggers, appeared at the Berlin Opera in 1857 (*H*.158, *W*.58–59). An amusing account of Lauro Rossi's *Biorn* (London: Queen's, 1877) is given in Joseph Bennett's *Forty Years of Music* (London: Methuen, 1908), 264–67. The action is transferred to Norway, Lady Macbeth is named Editha, and the witches become norns. Bennett quotes some of Frank Marshall's libretto, among them the lines of Editha's ladies-in-waiting when she enters reading the letter:

If we only had a letter
We might ponder o'er it too

and their plaint at serving a somnambulistic mistress:

When shall we know the sweet delight
Of sleeping well for one whole night?

Ernst Bloch's *Macbeth* (Paris: Opéra-Comique, 1910) is a distinguished opera (*H*.161–63, *W*.59–62, and A. Porter, *A Musical Season* (New York, Viking, 1974), 266–72). There are also *Macbeth* operas by Nicholas Gatty and by Lawrence Collingwood (London: Sadler's Wells, 1934).

Keys (*Les Adaptations*, 215–17) mentions the following pieces, unlisted in *H*.: *Les Visions de Macbeth, ou les Sorcières d'Écosse*, "mélodrame en trois actes" by Augustin H[apdé], Paris: a

Boulevard theatre, 1817; *Les Deux Macbeth, ou l'apothèose de Ducis*, "impromptu mêlé de chant et de danses" by D[ubois], Paris: Gaîté, 1817 (in the fourth scene, a Haydn symphony is played; "*Bard*: I know this air. *Scotsman*: Who doesn't know it? It sends us to sleep every night."); *Macbeth, ou les Sorcières de la forêt*, "pantomime en quatre actes à grand spectacle," music arranged by Othon, Paris: Cirque Olympique, 1817; and *Macbeth*, "mélodrame en cinq actes avec un prologue" by L. A. Piccinni, libretto by Victor Ducange and Anicet Bourgeois, after Shakespeare, Paris: Porte St. Martin, 1829 (Lady Macbeth has the last lines, to her husband: "You lacked audacity. Now our throne is the scaffold").

The greatest composer to have embarked on a *Macbeth* opera was, of course, Beethoven. His sketch (1808) for a D-minor witches' chorus, into which the overture was to have led directly, is in Nottebohm: *Zweite Beethoveniana* (Leipzig: Rieter-Biedermann, 1887), 225–27. The librettist, Heinrich von Collin, completed only the first act.

—— 3 ——

Concert music: Notable among the instrumental pieces based on *Macbeth* are R. L. Pearsall's overture (1839), with deliberately archaizing passages to match the Famous Music (which is quoted from); the symphonic poem, op. 54 (1859), by H. H. Pierson, another English composer much esteemed in Germany (the score carries extensive quotations from the play); and Richard Strauss's tone poem, op. 23, (1890). Smetana composed a piano piece, *Macbeth and the Witches* (1859). The Intermezzo in the third of Schumann's *Noveletten*, op. 21 (1838), was first published with the epigraph "When shall we three meet again?" And the third of Grieg's *Lyric Pieces* (Set I, 1867), called "Watchman's Song," depicts—in far from drunken fashion—the Porter. "Incredibly," Fiske writes (*H*. 222), "a bawdy old Scotsman . . . has become an honest son of the soil singing a stirring Presbyterian hymn." But Grieg evidently knew his *Macbeth* in Schiller's adaptation (see p. 147), where the Porter sings two strophes, beginning "The gloomy night is past

---

the ghost, appearing to Macbeth and to Banquo, who assisted in his murder seventeen years earlier. Fleance is in love with Goneril, Macduff's daughter. In a mad scene, Lady Macbeth, reenacting the murder of Duncan, stabs her husband by mistake, and at the close she falls on his body while the palace is consumed by flames.

and gone,/The lark sings clear; I see the dawn," and "Let songs of praise and thanks be swelling/To God who watches o'er this dwelling." Many other pieces are listed in *H.* 259–60, as are the vocal settings—mainly of the witches' songs. To them may be added G. F. Malipiero's *Preludio e morte di Macbeth* (1958), for baritone and orchestra.　　　　—A.P.

MACBETH ON RECORDS

The 1865 *Macbeth* is well served on records by two complete modern sets, both made in 1976: one on Deutsche Grammophon, with Shirley Verrett as Lady Macbeth, Piero Cappuccilli as Macbeth, Nicolai Ghiaurov as Banquo, Placido Domingo as Macduff, and Claudio Abbado conducting the chorus and orchestra of La Scala; the other on Angel, with Fiorenza Cossotto, Sherrill Milnes, Ruggero Raimondi, José Carreras, and Riccardo Muti conducting the Ambrosian Opera Chorus and the New Philharmonia Orchestra. The choice is effectively between these two; earlier versions have their points of interest, but only one of them (a London Records set conducted by Lamberto Gardelli, with Elena Souliotis as an inadequate heroine) is complete. The Deutsche Grammophon follows the common practice of inserting Macbeth's "Mal per me" into the final scene; the Angel has an 1847 "appendix" consisting of Lady Macbeth's "Trionfai," Macbeth's "Vada in fiamme," and his "Mal per me." The rival merits of the two sets are discussed in detail by Conrad L. Osborne in *High Fidelity* reviews (January and May 1977), reprinted in *Records in Review 1978* (Great Barrington, 1978, pp. 354–60). These and other *Macbeth* recordings are considered by Harold Rosenthal in a chapter of *Opera on Record* (ed. Alan Blyth; London, 1979) 201–207.

Four sets that illustrate the performing history of the opera in recent decades are: 1) A Urania version in German, resulting from the Verdi cycle that Karl Böhm and the Vienna State Opera put on in 1943, for the composer's 130th birthday; Elisabeth Höngen is the heroine, Mathieu Ahlersmeyer the hero. 2) An abridged version on Royale, labeled with a fictitious cast ("Inge Camphausen," etc.) but in fact representing the Glyndebourne 1952 production with Dorothy Dow and Marko Rothmüller, Vittorio Gui conducting. 3) A Cetra Opera Live set of La Scala's 1952 *Macbeth* with Maria Callas and Enzo Mascherini, Victor de Sabata conducting. 4) An RCA set based on the Metropolitan's 1959 production with Leonard Warren in the title role; Callas and Dimitri Mitropoulos were the intended heroine and conductor, but Callas withdrew and Mitropoulos died; Leonie Rysanek and Erich Leinsdorf took their places. An earlier London Records set, conducted by Thomas Schippers, with Birgit Nilsson and Giuseppe Taddei, presents Schippers' own "version" of the score.

The most important historical issue is the "Pietà, rispetto, amore" of Mattia Battistini (1856–1928), the great turn-of-the-century baritone. It was recorded in Milan in 1912, the year after Battistini sang the role in Rome (G&T 052369, H.M.V. DB 199). Verdi recommended Battistini for the Bologna premiere of the revised *Boccanegra* in 1881 (see *Abbiati* 4, 167–68, 299). Macduff's aria was recorded by Caruso in 1916 (Victor 88558, several modern reissues). More recent discs of note are Margherita Grandi's "La luce langue" and sleepwalking scene, with Beecham as conductor, recorded in 1947–48 (H.M.V. DB 6739–40)—Grandi was the heroine of Glyndebourne's 1939 *Macbeth* and of its 1948 revival—and Callas's studio performances of "Vieni t'affretta ... Or tutti sorgete," "La luce langue," and the sleepwalking scene, made in 1958, for Angel. The BBC 1978 Prom performance of the 1847 *Macbeth*, with Rita Hunter and Peter Glossop, conductor John Mattheson, has been issued on the pirate label Voce.

Silvi's *Fantasia Brillante* on themes from *Macbeth*, together with flute-and-piano pieces derived from *La traviata*, *Il trovatore*, *Don Carlos*, *Rigoletto*, and *Aida*, by various composers, is recorded by Severino Gazzelloni and Bruno Canino on Dischi Ricordi RCL 27049.　　　—A.P.

Glossary

Not all foreign-language (i.e., italicized) terms are glossed, but only those with a particular application to the subject of this book; additional meanings not relevant to the book are omitted. The terms are generally given in the singular.

adagio   Generic term for a slow movement usually of an aria, duet, or other small ensemble. *Concertato* or *largo concertato* is the term usually preferred for large ensembles with chorus, such as "Schiudi, inferno" and "Sangue a me," from the Act I and II *finales*, respectively. *Andante* is sometimes used in the same sense.

brindisi   a drinking song or toast.

cabaletta   The (usually) fast concluding *tempo* [*q.v.*] of an aria or duet. (The term *stretta* is sometimes used with duets and generally preferred with larger ensembles and choruses.) While some *cabalette* are in moderate tempo, they are at least faster than the *adagio* heard earlier. Among the features generally ascribed to *cabalette* are repetitiousness (in the solo *cabaletta* there is usually a repeat of the entire vocal part), simple accompaniment patterns, sharply rhythmicized melody, and, compared to the *adagio*, a simpler, more immediately-grasped nature. These features allow *cabalette* to be recognized as such even when they appear as independent, single *tempo* numbers (e.g., "Trionfai" and "Vada in fiamme,"—see pp. 488–91 and 504–08).

canzone   A song, usually one that would be sung even within a spoken drama.

cavatina   An aria, almost invariably including both an *adagio* and *cabaletta*, sung by a character at his or her entrance (e.g., Lady Macbeth's *cavatina* in Act I).

concertato   See *adagio*.

copisteria   The office where manuscript orchestral scores and manuscript performance materials (including the singers' parts, when a piano-vocal score was not yet in print) were prepared.

decasillabo   A line in which the final accent falls upon the ninth syllable (see *Metrics*).

doppio (*quinario*, *settenario*, etc.)   See *Metrics*.

duettino   A duet consisting of a single static movement (usually the *adagio*).

endecasillabo   A line in which the final accent falls upon the tenth syllable (see *Metrics*).

finale   1) Adj. meaning final, i.e., closing an act (as in the Scena e Duetto *Finale* that concludes Act III of *Rigoletto*); 2) n. a usually complex unit, involving soloists and chorus, and consisting of kinetic and static sections, concluding an act (as in Acts I and II of *Macbeth*; a more striking example, however, is the Act II *finale* of *La traviata* which includes the entire scene at Flora's house).

gran scena   A term not used in Verdi's autographs; it indicates numbers that include long, elaborate recitative sections, such as Lucia's mad scene or Linda di Chamounix's *gran scena del delirio*.

introduzione   A multi-movement complex, usually including solo (or small ensemble) and choral sections, opening Act I. In the *Macbeth* autograph Verdi labels as "Introduzione", and gives a single number to everything between the Prelude and Lady Macbeth's *cavatina*, although Ricordi published it as three distinct "pezzi staccati" (separate pieces) for commercial reasons.

largo concertato   See *adagio*.

libroni   See pp. 302–03.

Metrics   Lines (*versi*) of Italian poetry are classified by the position of the final accent:

1. *piano*—accent on penultimate syllable, e.g., *Scendea-mi vo-ceal cò-re*
2. *sdrucciolo*—accent on antepenultimate syllable, e.g., *Fu quel-loil pri-mo pàl-pi-to*
3. *tronco*—accent on final syllable, e.g., *D'a-mor che mi be-ò*

Although these three lines differ in the number of syllables (seven, eight, and six respectively), they are all classified as metrical *settenario* lines and may coexist in a single stanza; in fact, these three lines are lines 4–6 of Ernani's "Come rugiada al cespite" (from his Act I *cavatina*). Since lines may be *sdruccioli* or *tronchi* rather than the more common *piani*, it is misleading to define *verso settenario* as a seven-syllable line, rather than as a line in which the final accent falls upon the sixth syllable. (There are further "rules" governing the placement of other accents—not all possible combinations and permutations are allowable—but these cannot be considered here.) Naturally, the principle discussed here applies to other meters as well. The "double meters," such as *doppi quinari*, can be thought of as a series of lines of which only even-numbered lines rhyme. The lines are generally set beside one another in pairs, often with a dash separating them. The "new" composite line will often have a caesura in the middle, but the articulation will be weaker than if there were a rhyme. The difference between a *doppio quinario* and a *decasillabo* is simply explained: the *doppio quinario* has an obligatory accent on the fourth syllable of each *quinario* unit—i.e., on the fourth and, depending on the type of the first *quinario*, eighth, ninth, or even tenth syllable. The *decasillabo* will generally have accents on the third, sixth, and ninth syllables—a very different rhythm.

ottonario   A line in which the final accent falls on the seventh syllable (see *Metrics*).

pezzo concertato   see *adagio*.

quinario   A line in which the final accent falls on the fourth syllable (see *Metrics*).

recitative verse   Lines intended to be set as *recitative;* generally unrhymed, freely alternating *settenario* and *endecasillabo* (and less frequently, *quinario*) lines; cf. *versi lirici*

romanza (French, *romance*)   An aria consisting of an *adagio* (usually with preceding *scena*) i.e., lacking a *cabaletta* (such pieces may simply be labeled aria *tout court*).

scena   In Verdi's usage, usually a recitative, as in the *Scene e Duetto* of Act I, where the *scena* is Macbeth's dagger monologue. More rarely in Verdi's autographs, it means simply a scene or number, as in English one might refer to Banquo's scene (*Scena Banco*) or, in *Forza*, the Inn Scene (*Scena Osteria*).

sdrucciolo   See *Metrics*.

selva   A scenario or prose draft of a libretto.

senario   A line in which the final accent falls upon the fifth syllable (see *Metrics*).

settanario   A line which the final accent falls upon the sixth syllable (see *Metrics*).

stretta.   See *cabaletta.*

strofetta   Literally, a little strophe (or stanza); usually equivalent to a quatrain.

tempo   Movement or section set to *versi lirici* (a *recitative* section would not be called a *tempo*); the *primo tempo* is the first such section in a number (e.g., "Fatal mia donna") and usually its incipit is used to refer to the number as a whole, as in the index of Ricordi scores; the *tempo di mezzo* is the section between the *adagio* and *cabaletta* or *stretta* (e.g., the section beginning "Il pugnal là riportate" in the same duet); it serves to provide a stimulus for the change of emotion and musical character between those two sections.

tempo di mezzo   See *tempo.*

tinta   The musical mood or character; *Stimmung.*

tronco   See *Metrics.*

versi lirici   Rhymed lines in a single meter; the lines may be organized into symmetrical stanzas (as in the *adagio* and *cabaletta* of the Act I duet of Macbeth and Lady Macbeth) or may be free in that respect; individual lines may be divided among different characters (as in the *tempo di mezzo* of the same duet).

verso   Line of poetry (see *Metrics*).

Personalia

ARRIVABENE, Count APPRANDINO (1805–1887). Italian writer and patriot. Frequented Countess Maffei's salon. Close friend of Verdi. Their rich correspondence has been published.

BARBIERI-NINI, MARIANNA (ca. 1820–1887). Italian soprano. Debut 1840, Scala. Created role of Lucrezia in *I due Foscari*, Teatro Argentino, Rome, 1844; Lady Macbeth in *Macbeth*, Teatro della Pergola, Florence, 1847; Gulnara in *Il corsaro*, Gran Teatro, Trieste, 1848.

BAREZZI, ANTONIO (1798–1867). Busseto merchant and music lover. Verdi's patron, father of Verdi's first wife, Margherita. In Verdi's own words, Barezzi was his "secondo padre." *Macbeth* is dedicated to him.

BASEVI, ABRAMO (1818–1885). After practicing medicine in Florence, Basevi dedicated himself to music. He composed two operas (*Enrico Howard* was premiered in Florence in 1847), but turned to music history and criticism. Founded the journal *Armonia* and the *Mattinate Beethoveniane* (which became the *Società del Quartetto*, an important institution in the revival of interest in instrumental music). Best known for his *Studio sulle opere di Giuseppe Verdi*, but works also include two harmony manuals, and a study of Beethoven's Opus 18 quartets.

CAPPONI, Marchese GINO (1792–1876). Florentine statesman of moderate views, writer (especially interested in education), and member of many Florentine intellectual and philanthropic groups. Blind from 1840.

CARCANO, GIULIO (1812–1884). Author in almost all genres, friend of Verdi, the Maffeis, and Manzoni, translator of all of Shakespeare's plays into verse (beginning with *King Lear*, published in 1843; his *Macbeth* was published in 1848, the year after Verdi's opera). From 1844, he was vice-librarian at the Brera in Milan, but, having held an important position in the provisional government formed after the "Cinque giornate" in 1848, went into exile after the Austrians recaptured the city. He held various positions in the government after his return in 1859.

CARVALHO (CARVAILLE), LÉON (1825–1897). French baritone and impresario, manager of Théâtre-Lyrique (1856–60, 1862–68). Presented *Rigoletto*, *Traviata*, and the revised *Macbeth* (1865). Stage director at the Opéra, 1869–75; director of the Opéra-Comique, 1876–87. Married to soprano Marie (Caroline) Miolan.

CASAMORATA, LUIGI FERDINANDO (1807–1881). Florentine music critic, writer (on political subjects as well as music), and composer (at least one opera, but mainly sacred and instrumental music). A frequent contributor to Ricordi's *Gazzetta Musicale di Milano* (in 1847–48 his "Studio biografico-bibliografico intorno ai musicisti toscani" appeared there). In the 1860s he co-founded and became director of the Istituto Musicale of Florence (now the Florence Conservatory).

DE BASSINI, ACHILLE (1819–1881). Italian baritone. Debut ca. 1837. Created roles of Francesco in *Foscari*, Argentina, Rome, 1844; Seid in *Corsaro*, Teatro Grande, Trieste, 1848; Miller in *Luisa Miller*, San Carlo, Naples, 1849; Melitone in *Forza*, Imperial Theater, St. Petersburg, 1862. Repertory included *Nabucco*, *Alzira*, *Ernani*, *Lombardi*, *Masnadieri* (Italian premiere).

DUPRÉ, GIOVANNI (1817–1882). Italian sculptor. Knew Verdi in Florence in 1847 and made a cast of his right hand (later carved in marble). Wrote *Memoirs* with amusing Verdi anecdotes.

ESCUDIER, LÉON (1821–1881). French publisher, author, impresario and agent, for many years in collaboration with his brother MARIE (1819–80). Published most of Verdi's operas in France, first at the Bureau Central de Musique, later under his own name. Important correspondence with Verdi. With his brother, founded *La France Musicale* in 1838. Manager of the Théâtre-Italien after 1874, where he mounted the French premiere of *Aida*.

FRASCHINI, GAETANO (1816–1887). Italian tenor. Created Zamoro in *Alzira*, San Carlo, Naples, 1845; Corrado in *Corsaro*, Teatro Grande, Trieste, 1848; Arrigo in *Battaglia*, Argentina, Rome, 1849; title role in *Stiffelio*, Teatro Grande, Trieste, 1850; and Riccardo in *Ballo*, Apollo, Rome, 1859. Also sang in *Traviata* (Théâtre-Italien, 1863) with great success. Verdi began *Masnadieri* with Fraschini in mind and thought of the tenor as late as 1870 for Radamès in *Aida*. Sang nearly all of Verdi's tenor roles and was much admired by the composer.

GIUSTI, GIUSEPPE (1809–1850). Italian poet. Florentine. Verdi was given a letter of introduction to him in 1847, and through him met prominent Florentines such as Gino Capponi (q.v.) and Baron Bettino Ricasoli. Giusti referred to Verdi in one of his most famous poems and wrote the composer a well-known letter (19 March 1847), after the premiere of *Macbeth*, advising him to stick to Italian themes.

ISMAEL (ISMAËL, ISMAIEL) JAMMES, JEAN-VITAL (1827–?). French baritone. Debut in Nantes, 1843, aged 16; at the Théâtre-Lyrique, 1863 (in Bizet's *Les Pêcheurs de perles*). Sang title roles in French-language opening of *Rigoletto*, 1864, and *Macbeth*, 1865. Still singing in Monte Carlo in 1879.

LANARI, ALESSANDRO (1790–1862). Italian impresario, a key figure in Italian operatic history. Close friend of Giuseppina Strepponi during her active career in

461

the theater. Impresario at Senigallia 1837–43 (where he met Strepponi). Manager of Teatro della Pergola, Florence, from 1823–28, 1830–35, 1839–48 (when he commissioned *Macbeth*), and later in the 1860's. Extensive correspondence with Verdi, Strepponi, and others (largely unpublished).

LOEWE (LÖWE), SOFIA (SOPHIE JOHANNA) (1816?–1866). German soprano from a family of actors. Scala debut in 1841, after success in Germany and London. Created Elvira in *Ernani*, Fenice, Venice, 1844, and Odabella in *Attila*, Fenice, Venice, 17 March 1846. Was to have sung Lady Macbeth but cancelled and was replaced by Barbieri-Nini (q.v.). Repertory included *Lombardi* and *Alzira* (Verdi wrote an aria for her in this opera, performed in Venice, 1845).

LUCCA, FRANCESCO (1802–1872) and Giovannina Strazza (1814–1894). Music publisher, Ricordi's chief rival in Italy until Ricordi acquired the Lucca firm in 1888. Lucca published three of Verdi's operas: *Attila*, *I masnadieri* and *Il corsaro*—but after the last (1848), Verdi dealt exclusively with Ricordi in Italy.

MAFFEI, ANDREA (1798–1885). Italian poet, translator. Close friend of Verdi from the 1840s. Verdi set several Maffei poems as songs. Made revisions of *Macbeth* libretto and wrote some scenes at Verdi's request. Provided libretto for *Masnadieri*. Husband of Clara Maffei (q.v.).

MAFFEI, Countess CLARA (CLARINA), born Carrara Spinelli (1814–1886). Italian patriot and intellectual. Close friend of Verdi from the early 1840s. Friend of Mazzini and Cavour, as well as of many writers and musicians whom she entertained in her Milanese salon. Introduced Verdi to Manzoni (1868). After legal separation from Maffei, she was the lifelong friend of the patriot-statesman-writer Carlo Tenca. Their correspondence has been published.

MANARA, LUCIANO (1825–1849). Italian patriot, fought in the Milanese insurrection (*cinque Giornate*), an officer in the Piedmontese army, and then with Garibaldi; killed in the defense of the Roman Republic.

MONJAUZE, JULES SÉBASTIEN (1824–1877). Debut as an actor at the French theater in St. Petersburg, then the Odéon, Paris. Debut as a tenor, Paris, 1855. Sang in first French-language performances of *Rigoletto*, 1863, and *Macbeth*, Théâtre-Lyrique, Paris, 1865, as Macduff. Repertory included Rodolphe (Alfredo) in *Violetta* (*Traviata*).

MORIANI, NAPOLEONE (1808–1878). Italian tenor. Debut Pavia, 1833. Popular singer throughout the 1840s, known as the "tenore della bella morte" for his moving death scenes. Repertory included *Ernani*, *Lombardi*, *Attila* (Verdi wrote a new aria for Act III, sung by Moriani, carnival season, Milan, 1846–47). Believed by Frank Walker to be the father of Giuseppina Strepponi's illegitimate children.

MONTAZIO, ENRICO (1816–1886). Italian journalist. Editor of *Rivista di Firenze*. Adversely criticized Maffei's libretto of *Masnadieri*. Born Enrico Valtancoli, changed his name, made infamous by his father's having informed on his Masonic brothers. Giusti's "A Enrico Montazio" is a violent attack on the journalist.

MUZIO, EMANUELE (1825–1890). Italian composer and conductor. Verdi's principal pupil, whose studies were aided also by Antonio Barezzi. A fellow native of Busseto, Muzio remained with Verdi for some years, acting as his amanuensis and companion. Later conducted Verdi's operas throughout Europe and in America (including U.S. premieres of *Vêpres*, New York, 1859 and *Aida*, New York, 1873). Conducted the production of *Rigoletto* for the opening of the Cairo Opera House, 1869.

PIAZZA, ANTONIO. Italian journalist. Presumably wrote original libretto of *Oberto*, subsequently refashioned by Solera, and perhaps by Verdi himself.

PIAVE, FRANCESCO MARIA (1810–1876). Italian librettist. Joined staff of La Fenice as librettist and stage manager in 1844. Wrote his first libretto, *Ernani*, for Verdi, and became his most constant collaborator. In 1859 moved to Milan to stage productions at La Scala and teach. Paralyzed in 1869. Verdi contributed to his family's support. Wrote librettos of *Ernani*, *Foscari*, *Macbeth*, *Corsaro*, *Stiffelio*, *Rigoletto*, *Traviata*, *Boccanegra*, *Aroldo*, *Forza*, and completed Solera's *Attila*. Important correspondence with Verdi.

REY-BALLA, AMÉLIE (ca.1835–1889). French soprano. Sang Lady Macbeth, Théâtre-Lyrique, Paris, 1865. Sang at La Scala, 1870. Retired in 1872. Wife of composer Jean-Étienne Rey.

RICORDI family. Italian music publishers.

GIOVANNI (1785–1853) established the Stamperia di Musica in Milan 1808 and began publishing piano-vocal scores of successful operas. By 1844 the firm had published works of Verdi, as well as operas of Rossini, Bellini, and Donizetti. In 1842 Giovanni founded *La Gazzetta Musicale di Milano*, which continued publication until 1902.

TITO (1811–1888), son of Giovanni, worked for his father from 1825 until his death. In 1864 he established the Clausetti firm in Naples, and in 1887 took over the catalogs of Guidi of Florence and Del Monaco of Naples. Was an accomplished amateur pianist.

GIULIO (1840–1912), his son, entered the family firm in 1863, took over the *Gazzetta* in 1866, and gradually supplanted his father in the handling of the firm's never easy relations with Verdi. In 1888, Ricordi took over the firm of Lucca, their chief Italian rival, and Giulio assumed the management. Giulio was also a writer, painter, and (under the name of J. Burgmein) composer. He compiled the production manuals, published by Ricordi, for *Aida*, the revised *Boccanegra,* and *Otello.* He recognized the talent of the young Puccini and persuaded the firm to support the composer until he was successfully launched.

Verdi wrote about 1500 letters, not all published as yet, to the firm of Ricordi from 1843 to his death.

ROMANI, PIETRO (1791–1877). *Maestro e direttore dell'opere* of Florence's Pergola Theatre. Also composer of at least two operas, ballet music, and "insert numbers" (such as "Manca un foglio," composed for Bartolo in the 1816 Florence production of Rossini's *Barbiere*).

RUSCONI, CARLO (1812–1889). Author of political essays and historical novels, best remembered for his history (1849) of the Roman republic (in which he had held office) and his translations of Byron and Shakespeare. His prose translation of the complete Shakespeare, published in 1838, was Verdi's principal source for all his Shakespeare operas (including *Re Lear*).

STREPPONI, GIUSEPPINA (CLELIA MARIA JOSEPHA) (1815–1897). Italian soprano. Verdi's second wife.

Debut 1834. Immediately successful, a leading singer for the next decade, after which her voice declined sharply. Created Abigaille in *Nabucco,* Scala, Milan, 1842. Also sang Elvira in *Ernani.* After her retirement from the stage in 1846, she moved to Paris where she sang in concert, (mostly Verdi's music), taught, and probably began living with Verdi there in 1847. They married in 1859. Left voluminous correspondence and important notebooks (only partially published).

TADOLINI, EUGENIA (1809–?). Italian soprano. Debut Florence, 1828. Created title role of *Alzira,* San Carlo, Naples, 1845. Repertory included *Ernani* (Vienna premiere, 1844), *Macbeth,* and *Attila.*

VARESI, FELICE (1813–1889). Italian baritone. Debut 1834. Created title role in *Macbeth,* Pergola, Florence, 1847; title role in *Rigoletto,* Fenice, Venice, 1851; role of Germont in *Traviata,* Fenice, 1853. Repertory also included *Ernani, Foscari, Luisa Miller, Corsaro, Masnadieri.* Artist of unusual intelligence (which Verdi respected) and—though not handsome—a convincing and versatile actor.

Bibliography

Alpert, Clifford. "Verdi's use of the minor second interval in *Macbeth*." *The Opera Journal* (fall 1971), 11–14

Badacsonyi, George. "Verdi's two *Macbeths*." *Opera* 27 (1976), 108–13

Baldini, Gabriele. *Abitare la battaglia*. Milan: Garzanti, 1970. In English, as *The Story of Giuseppe Verdi*. Translated by Roger Parker. Cambridge: Cambridge University Press, 1980

Barblan, Guglielmo. "Il *Macbeth* e la crisi verdiana nel nome di Shakespeare." *English Miscellany* 15 (Rome, 1964), 313–35

Bartholomeusz, Dennis. *Macbeth and the Players*. Cambridge: Cambridge University Press, 1964

Basevi, Abramo. *Macbeth*. In *Studio sulle opere di Giuseppe Verdi*. Chapter 8. Florence: Tofani, 1859. Translation by EDWARD SCHNEIDER at 421–25

Budden, Julian. *The Operas of Verdi* 1 (London: Cassell, 1973), pp. 267–312

Dean, Winton. "Shakespeare and Opera." In *Shakespeare in Music*, edited by Phyllis Hartnoll, pp. 156–63. London: Macmillan, 1964

De Angelis, Marcello. *Le carte dell'impresario: melodramma e costume teatrale nell'Ottocento*. Florence: Sansoni, 1982

Degrada, Francesco. "Lettura del *Macbeth* di Verdi." *Studi Musicali* 6 (1977), 207–67. Also in *Il palazzo incantato* 2. (Fiesole: Discanto, 1979), pp. 79–141

Gerhartz, Leo Karl. *Die Auseinandersetzungen des jungen Giuseppe Verdi mit dem literarischen Drama; ein Beitrag zur szenischen Strukturbestimmung der Oper*. Berliner Studien zur Musikwissenschaft. Berlin: Merseburger, 1968, pp. 82–193, 465–75

Godefroy, Vincent. *The Dramatic Genius of Verdi* 1 (London: Gollancz, 1975), pp. 101–41

Goldin, Daniela. "Il *Macbeth* verdiano: genesi e linguaggio di un libretto." *Analecta Musicologica* 19 (1979), 336–72

Hughes, Spike. *Famous Verdi Operas*. London: Hale, 1968, pp. 37–81

Kimbell, David. "The Young Verdi and Shakespeare." *Proceedings of the Royal Musical Association* 101 (1974–75), 59–73

_____ *Verdi in the Age of Italian Romanticism*. Cambridge: Cambridge University Press, pp. 169–89, 363–84, 516–80

Lawton, David. "Tonality and Drama in Verdi's Early Operas," University of California, Berkeley, dissertation (1973) and David Rosen. "Verdi's Non-Definitive Revisions: The Early Operas." In *Atti del 3° congresso internazionale di studi verdiani (Milan, 1972)*. Parma: Istituto di Studi Verdiani, 1974, pp. 189–237

Mila, Massimo. *La giovinezza di Verdi*. Turin: ERI, 1974, pp. 253–79

Noske, Frits. "Verdi and the musical figure of death." In *Atti del 3° congresso internazionale di studi verdiani (Milano, 1972)*. Parma: Istituto di Studi Verdiani, 1974, pp. 349–86. Reprinted in *The Signifier and the Signified*. The Hague: Nijhoff, 1977, pp. 171–214

_____ "Ritual Scenes in Verdi's Operas," *Music & Letters* 54 (1973), 415–39. Reprinted in *The Signifier and the Signified*. The Hague: Nijhoff, 1977, pp. 241–70

_____ "Schiller e la genesi del *Macbeth* verdiano." *Nuova Rivista Musicale Italiana* 10 (1976), 196–203

Osthoff, Wolfgang. "Die beiden Fassungen von Verdis *Macbeth*." *Archiv für Musikwissenschaft* 29 (1972), 17–44

Praz, Mario. "Come Shakespeare è letto in Italia." *Ricerche Anglo-Italiane* (Rome: 1944), pp. 169–96

Quartetto Milanese Ottocentesco: lettere di Giuseppe Verdi, Giuseppina Strepponi, Clara Maffei, Carlo Tenca, e di altri personaggi del mondo politico e artistico dell'epoca. Edited by Laura Perrotta Gruppi. Rome: Archivi Edizioni, 1974.

Schlegel, August Wilhelm. *Corso di letteratura drammatica; traduzione italiana*. Translated by Giovanni Gherardini. 3 vols. Milan, 1817

Schmidgall, Gary. *Literature as Opera*. New York: Oxford, 1977, pp. 182–215

Varesi, Giulia Cora. "L'interpretazione del *Macbeth*." *Nuova Antologia* 281 (1932), 433–40

Walker, Frank. *The Man Verdi*. London: Dent, 1962

Weaver, William. "Verdi the Playgoer." *Musical Newsletter* 6 (1976), 3–8, 24

A Table of Revisions¹ and a Concordance of Four Piano-Vocal Scores

		First Version		Revised Version	
Number, title,² Incipit	Nature of the Revisions³	Ricordi (obl.) Plate nos. 19621–43	Bureau Central Plate no. B.C. 1027	Ricordi Plate no. 42311	Schirmer Plate no. 46438
ACT I					
1. Preludio		Pp. 5-7⁴	Pp. 1-2	Pp. 1-3	Pp. 1-3
2. Introduzione "Che faceste? Dite su! [Choro]		8-19	4-14	4-15	4-15
3. Scena e Duetto [Macbeth, Banquo]		20-30	15-24	16-26	16-26
4. Coro di Streghe—Stretta dell'Introduzione		30-37	25-31	27-34	27-37
5. Scena e Cavatina [Lady Macbeth] "Vieni! t'affretta" "Or tutti sorgete"		38-52	33-44	35-48	38-53
6. Scena e Marcia [Lady Macbeth, Macbeth]		53-56	45-48	49-53	54-58
7. Scena e Duetto [Macbeth, Lady Macbeth] "Fatal mia donna" **"non parti d'udire"**	Retouched	57-66.3.4 **66.3.5-73**	49-58.2.2 **58.2.3-65**	54-63.3.4 **63.45-71**	59-68.4.4 **68.45-76**
8. Scena e Sestetto—Finale 1		74-100	66-98	72-106	77-111

ACT II

9. Scena ed Aria [Lady Macbeth]					
"Perchè mi sfuggi?"					
"[Al venir di questa] notte"	Retouched	101–104.1.1[4]	99–101.4.3	107–110.1.1	112–115.1.1
"Trionfai" (1847)	Replaced	104.1.2–104.2.4	101.4.4–102.2.1	110.12–110.2	115.12–115.2
"La luce langue" (1865)	New text and music	104.2.5–109	102.2.2–106	110.3–115	115.3–120
10. Coro di Sicarj		110–116	107–113	116–122	121–128
10½. Gran Scena [Banquo]		117–120	114–117	123–127	129–133
11. Convito e Brindisi nel					
Finale II					
"Si colmi il calice"		121–131	118–127	128–138	134–147.4
12. Apparizione e replica					
del Brindisi					
"Che ti scosta"		132–133.3.3	128–129.5.1	139–140.4.5	147.5–149.4.3
"Di voi chi ciò fece?"	Significant revisions	133.3.4–138.1.2	129.5.2–133.2.4	140.4.6–144.4.4	149.4.4–154.1.4
"Voi siete demente"	Retouched	138.1.3–138.4.1	133.2.5–133.5.4	144.5–145.4.2	154.15–155.2.2
"Si colmi il calice"		138.4.1–143.2.1	133.5.5–136.3.3	145.4.3–150.2.1	155.2.3–161.2.1
"Fiammeggian quell'ossa"	Retouched	143.2.2–145.3.6	136.3.4–138.4	150.2.2–152.3	161.2.2–163.3
"La vita riprendo"		145.3–147	138.4–139	152.2–154.1	163.4–165.1
13. Quartetto—Finale II		148–162	140–152	154.2–179	165.2–191

ACT III

14. Introduzione–Incantesimo					
"Tre volte miagolò"		163-174.2.5[4]	153-163.1	180-190.1.4	192-204.2.4
Final statement of "rimescete, voi che mescer ben sapete rimescete"	**Retouched and slightly abridged**	**174.2.6-177**	**162.2-165**	**190.1.5-192**	**204.2.5-207**
Ballet (1865 only)	**Completely new**	**178-192**		**193-208**	**208-223**
15. **Gran Scena delle Apparizioni**	**Significantly revised**	193-201	**166-178**	**209-225**	**224-240**
16. Coro e Ballabile			179-185	226-233	241-250
17. **Gran Scena–Finale III**					
"Ove son io"	**Significantly revised**	**202-202.2.2**	**186-186.2**	**234-234.2**	**250-250.2**
"Vada in fiamme" [Macbeth] (1847)	**Replaced**	**202.2.3-206**	**186.3-190**	**234.3-241**	**250.3-257**
"Ora di morte" [Macbeth, Lady Macbeth] (1865)	**New text and music**				

ACT IV

18. Introduzione—Coro di profughi scozzesi "Patria oppressa"	**New music**	**207–213⁴**	**191–198**	**242–248**	**258–264**
19. Scena ed Aria [Macduff] "Oh figli"	**Retouched**	**214–214.2.1**	**199–199.2.1**	**249–249.2.1**	**265–265.2.1**
"Ah la paterna mano"		214.2.2–219.2	199.2.2–203.3.2	249.2.2–254	265.2.2–270
"La patria tradita"	**Enriched accompaniment and new coda**	**219.3–229**	**203.3.3–210**	**255–261**	**271–277**
20. Gran Scena del Sonnambulismo "Una macchia" [Lady Macbeth]		230–240	211–222	262–274	278–290
21. Scena ed Aria [Macbeth] "Pietà, rispetto, amor"		241–245	223–227	275–279	291–296
22. Scena e Battaglia "Ella è morta"	**Significantly revised**	**246–246.3.1**	**228–228.3.1**	**280**	**297**
"È morta la regina"	**Rewritten**	**246.3.2–254**	**228.3.2–235**	**281–289**	**298–306**
23. Scena e morte di Macbeth "Mal per me" [Macbeth] (1847)	**Replaced**	**255–257**	**236–238**	**290–302**	**307–320**
Inno di Vittoria (1865)	**New text and music**				

1. Revisions are indicated by bold face type.
2. From the Ricordi p.-v. score Pl. no. 19621-43 (Bur. Central almost identical) except Ballet and Inno di Vittoria from Ricordi Pl. no. 43211
3. Unless otherwise noted, revisions refer only to the music.
4. Page numbers are inclusive. An entry such as "110.1.2-110.2" is to be interpreted as follows: "From p. 110, first brace, second measure, up to and including the second brace on p. 110."

MARTIN CHUSID

THE 1847
LIBRETTO

MACBETH

Da rappresentarsi nell' I. e R. Teatro

IN VIA DELLA PERGOLA

LA QUARESIMA DELL'ANNO 1847.

Sotto la Protezione di S. A. I. e R.

LEOPOLDO II.

GRANDUCA DI TOSCANA

ec. ec. ec.

ORIGINALE

FIRENZE
Tipografia di G. Galletti
in Via delle Terme

Tanto la Musica che la Poesia del presente Libretto sono proprietà dell' editore Sig. GIOVANNI RICORDI di Milano, cessionario del Sig. ALESSANDRO LANARI.

ORCHESTRA.

Maestro e Direttore dell' Opere Sig. PIETRO ROMANI
Sostituto Sig. CARLO ROMANI

Capo e Direttore di Orchestra Sig. ALAMANNO BIAGI
all' Attual Servizio di S. A. I. E R.

Primo Violino, e Supplemento Sig. GAETANO BRUSCAGLI
Primo Violino di Concerto Sig. RANIERI MANGANI
Primo Violino de Balli Sig. CARLO FERRANTI

Primo Violino dei Secondi	Sig. LUIGI PECORI
Primo Violoncello	Sig. GUGLIELMO PASQUINI al Servizio di S. A. I. e R.
Primo Contrabbasso	Sig. CARLO CAMPOSTRINI al Servizio di S. A. I. e R.
1. Contrabb. dei Balli e Suppl.°	Sig. CARLO BECATTINI
1.° Violoncello e Suppl.	Sig. EGISTO PONTECCHI
Prime Viole	(Sig. TOMMASO TINTI (Sig. FRANCESCO MINIATI
Primo Oboe	Sig. EGISTO MOSELL al Servizio di S. A. I. e R.
Primo Clarinetto Concertista	Sig. GIOVANNI BIMBONI al Servizio di S. A. I. e R.
Altro Primo e Supplim.	Sig. GIOVACCHINO GORDINI
Primo Flauto ed Ottavino	Sig. CARLO ALESSANDRI
Primo Corno di 1ma. Coppia	(Sig. FRANCESCO PAOLI (al Servizio di S. A. I. e R.
1.° Corno di 2da. Coppia	Sig. LEOPOLDO BRASCHI
Primi Fagotti	(Sig. PIETRO LUCHINI (Sig. CARLO CHAPUY
Primo Trombone di Concerto	Sig. GIOVACCHINO BIMBONI al Servizio di S. A. I. e R.
ed in sua assenza il	Sig. STANISLAO BELLUCCI
Primo Trombone	Sig. DEMETRIO CHIAVACCINI
Oficleide	Sig. FERDINANDO BARBADORO
Prima Tromba	Sig. PIETRO MATTIOZZI
Timpanista	Sig ANTONIO PRATESI al Servizio di S. A. I. e R.

Suggeritore Sig. LORENZO CARRARESI
Copista della Musica Sig. FRANCESCO MINIATI
Scenografo Sig. GIOVANNI GIANNI
Figurista e Costumista Sig. ODOARDO CIABATTI
Macchinista e Illuminatore Sig. COSIMO CANOVETTI
Il Vestiario e gli Attrezzi sono di proprietà dell'Impresa
e diretti, il primo dal Sig. VINCENZIO BATISTINI, il 2.di dal Sig. STOCCHI.
Calzolajo Sig. FRANCESCO SACCHI
Caffettiere del Teatro Sig. ANDREA LANDINI.

PERSONAGGI

DUNCANO, Re di Scozia
N. N.

MACBETH }
BANCO } Generali dell' esercito del Re Duncano
Sig. Felice Varesi.
Sig. Niccola Benedetti.

LADY MACBETH, moglie di Macbeth
Sig. Marianna Barbieri Nini.
Cantante di Camera di S. A. I. e R. il GRANDUCA DI TOSCANA, e Cantante di Camera, e Cappella di S. M. l'ARCIDUCHESSA e DUCHESSA DI PARMA.

DAMA di Lady Macbeth
Sig. Faustina Piombanti.

MACDUFF, nobile Scozzese Signore di Fiff
Sig. Angelo Brunacci.

MALCOLM, figlio di Duncano
Sig. Francesco Rossi.

FLEANZIO, figlio di Banco
N. N.

Domestico di Macbeth
N. N.

Medico
Sig. Giuseppe Romanelli.

Sicario
Sig. Giuseppe Bertini.

Tre Apparizioni

L' Ombra di Banco.

CORI, E COMPARSE DI

Streghe, Messaggeri del Re, Nobili e Profughi Scozzesi, Sicarj, Soldati Inglesi, Spiriti Aerei.

La Scena è in Iscozia, e massimamente al Castello di Macbeth. Sul principio dell' Atto quarto è tra il confine di Scozia, e d' Inghilterra.

La Musica è di GIUSEPPE VERDI.

ATTO PRIMO

BOSCO

Tre Crocchi di Streghe appariscono l'un dopo l'altro fra lampi, e tuoni.

SCENA PRIMA

I.	**C**he faceste? dite su!
II.	Ho sgozzato un verro.
I.	E tu?
III.	M'è frullata nel pensier
	La mogliera d'un nocchier;
	Al dimòn la mi cacciò...
	Ma lo sposo che salpò
	Col suo legno affogherò.
I.	Un rovajo io ti darò...
II.	I marosi io leverò...
III.	Pe le secche io lo trarrò. *(odesi un tamburo)*
Tutte	Un tamburo! Che sarà?
	Vien Macbetto. Eccolo quà!

(Si confondono insieme e intrecciano una ridda.)

Le sorelle vagabonde
Van per l'aria, van sull'onde,
Sanno un circolo intrecciar
Che comprende e terra, e mar.

SCENA II.

MACBETH e BANCO. *Le precedenti.*

Mac. Giorno non vidi mai sì fiero, e bello!
Ban. Nè tanto glorioso!
Mac. (*s'avvede delle Streghe*) Oh, chi saranno
Costor?

[page 6]

Ban. Chi siete voi? Di questo mondo,
O d'altra regïone?
Dirvi donne vorrei, ma lo mi vieta
Quella sordida barba.
Mac. Or via parlate!
Streghe I. Salve, o Macbetto, di Glamis Sire!
II. Salve, o Macbetto, di Caudor Sire!
III. Salve, o Macbetto, di Scozia Re!
(*Macbeth trema*)

Banco (a Macbeth)
Tremar vi fanno così lieti auguri?
(*alle Streg.*) Favellate a me pur, se non v'è scuro,
Creature fantastiche, il futuro.
Streghe I. Salve!
II. Salve?
III. Salve!
I. Men sarai di Macbetto e pur maggiore!
II. Non quanto lui, ma più di lui felice!
III. Non Re, ma di Monarchi genitore!
Tutte Macbetto e Banco vivano!
Banco, e Macbetto vivano! (*spariscono*)
Mac. Vanìr!... Saranno i figli tuoi sovrani.
Ban. E tu Re pria di loro.
Ban. e Mac. Accenti arcani!

SCENA III.

Messaggeri del Re. I precedenti.

Mess. Pro Macbetto! Il tuo signore
Sir t'elesse di Caudore.
Mac. Ma quel Sire ancor vi regge!
Mess. No! percosso dalla legge
Sotto il ceppo egli spirò.
Ban. (Ah, l'inferno il ver parlò!)
Mac. (fra sè) Due vaticini compiuti or sono...
Mi si promette dal terzo un trono...
Ma perchè sento rizzarsi il crine?
Pensier di sangue, d'onde sei nato?...

[page 7]

Alla corona che m'offre il fato
La man rapace non alzerò.
Ban. (fra sè) Oh, come s'empie costui d'orgoglio
Nella speranza d'un regio soglio!
Ma spesso l'empio Spirto d'inferno
Parla, e c'inganna, veraci detti,
E ne abbandona poi maledetti
Su quell'abisso che ci scavò.
Mess. (Perchè sì freddo n'udì Macbetto?
Perchè l'aspetto — non serenò?)
(*Tutti partono*)

SCENA IV.

Le Streghe (ritornano.)

S'allontanarono! — N'accozzeremo
Quando di fulmini — lo scroscio udreme.
S'allontanarono — fuggiam!... s'attenda
Le sorti a compiere — nella Tregenda.
Macbetto riedere — vedrem colà,
E il nostro oracolo — gli parlerà. (*partono*)

SCENA V.

Atrio nel Castello di Macbeth, che mette in altre stanze.

LADY MACBETH, *leggendo una lettera.*

» Nel dì della vittoria io le incontrai...
» Stupito io n'era per le udite cose;
» Quando i Nunzj del Re mi salutaro
» Sir di Caudor, vaticinio uscito
» Dalle veggenti stesse
» Che predissero un serto al capo mio.
» Racchiudi in cor questo segreto. Addio.
Ambizioso spirto
Tu sei Macbetto... alla grandezza aneli,
Ma sarai tu malvagio?
Pien di misfatti è il calle

[page 8]

Della potenza, e mal per lui che il piede
Dubitoso vi pone, e retrocede!
Vieni! t'affretta! accendere
Vò quel tuo freddo core!
L'audace impresa a compiere
Io ti darò valore;
Di Scozia a te promettono
Le profetesse il trono...
Che tardi? accetta il dono
Ascendivi a regnar.

SCENA VI.

Un Servo, e la precedente.

Ser. Al cader della sera il Re quì giunge.
Lady Che di? Macbetto è seco?
Ser. Ei l'accompagna.
La nuova, o donna, è certa.
Lady Trovi accoglienza, quale un Re si merta.

SCENA VII.

LADY MACBETH *sola.*

Duncano sarà quì?... quì? quì la notte?...
Or tutti sorgete —, ministri infernali,
Che al sangue incorate — spingete i mortali!
Tu notte ne avvolgi — di tènebra immota;
Qual petto percota — non vegga il pugnal.

SCENA VIII.

MACBETH, *e la precedente.*

Mac. Oh donna mia!
Lady Caudore?
Mac. Fra poco il Re vedrai...
Lady Ripartirà?
Mac. Domani.
Lady Mai non ci rechi il sole un tal domani.

9

Mac. Che parli?
Lady   E non intendi?
Mac. Intendo, intendo!
Lady   Or bene?...
Mac. E se fallisse il colpo?
Lady Non fallirà... se tu non tremi. *(lieti suoni che a poco a poco si accostano)*
Mac.   Il Re!
Lady Lieto or lo vieni ad incontrar con me. *(partono)*

SCENA IX.

Musica villereccia, la quale avanzandosi a poco a poco annuncia l'arrivo del Re. Egli trapassa accompagnato da BANCO, MACDUFF, MALCOLM, MACBETH, LADY MACBETH, *e seguito.*

SCENA X.

Notte.

MACBETH, *ed un servo.*

Sappia la sposa mia, che pronta appena
La mia tazza notturna,
Vò che un tocco di squilla a me lo avvisi.
        (il servo parte)

SCENA XI.

MACBETH *solo.*

Mi si affaccia un pugnal?! L'else a me volta?
Se larva non sei tu ch'io ti brandisca...
Mi sfuggi... eppur ti veggo! A me precorri
Sul confuso cammin che nella mente
Di seguir disegnava!... Orrenda immago!...
Solco sanguigno la tua lama irriga!...
Ma nulla esiste ancora... Il sol cruento
Mio pensier le dà forma, e come vera
Mi presenta allo sguardo una chimera.
Sulla metà del mondo

10

Or morta è la natura: or l'assassino,
Come fantasma per l'ombre si striscia,
Or consuman le streghe i lor misteri.
Immobil terra! a passi miei sta muta...
        (un tocco di squillo)
Non udirlo, Duncano! È squillo eterno
Che nel cielo ti chiama, o nell'inferno.
        (Entra nelle stanze del Re.)

SCENA XII.

LADY MACBETH.

Lady Regna il sonno su tutti... Oh qual lamento!
     Risponde il gufo al suo lugubre addio!
Mac. *(di dentro)* Chi v'ha?
Lady   Ch'ei fosse di letargo uscito
     Pria del colpo mortal?

SCENA XIII.

La Precedente. MACBETH, *(stravolto con un pugnale in mano.)*

Mac.   Tutto è finito!
     Fatal mia donna! un mormore
     Com'io, non intendesti?
Lady Del gufo udii lo stridere...
     Testè che mai dicesti?
Mac. Di! nella stanza attigua
     Chi dorme?
Lady   Il regal figlio...
Mac. *(guardandosi le mani)*
     O vista, o vista orribile!
Lady Storna da questo il ciglio...
Mac. Nel sonno udii che oravano
     I Cortigiani, e: *Dio*
     Sempre ne assista, ei dissero;
     Amen dir volli anch'io,

     Ma la parola indocile
     Gelò su' labbri miei.
Lady Follia!
Mac.   Perchè ripetere
     Quell'*Amen* non potei?
Lady Follia, follia che sperdono
     I primi rai del dì.
Mac. Allor questa voce m'intesi nel petto:
     Avrai per guanciali sol vepri, o Macbetto!
     Il sonno per sempre, Glamis, uccidesti!
     Non v'è che vigilia, Caudore, per te!
Lady Ma dimmi, altra voce non parti d'udire?
     Sei vano, o Macbetto, ma privo d'ardire:
     Glamis, a mezz'opra vacilli, t'arresti,
     Fanciul vanitoso, Caudore te se'.
Mac. Vendetta, tuonarmi com' Angeli d'ira,
     Udrò di Duncano le sante virtù.
Lady (Quell'animo trema, combatte, delira...
     Chi mai lo direbbe l'invitto che fu!)
     Il pugnal là riportate...
     Le sue guardie insanguinate...
     Che l'accusa in lor ricada.
Mac. Io colà?... non posso entrar!
Lady Dammi il ferro. *(strappa dalle mani di Macbeth il pugnale, ed entra nelle stanze del Re.)*

SCENA XIV.

MACBETH *solo.*

     (Bussano forte alla porta del Castello)
Mac.   Ogni romore
     Mi spaventa! *(si guarda le mani)* O questa mano!...
     Non potrebbe l'Oceàno
     Queste mani a me lavar!

SCENA XV.

LADY MACBETH, *e il precedente.*

Lady Vè! le mani ho lorde anch'io.
     Poco spruzzo, e monde son.

     L'opra anch'essa andrà in obblio...
        (battono di nuovo)
Mac. Odi tu? raddoppia il suon!
Lady Vieni altrove! ogni sospetto
     Rimoviam dall'uccisor;
     Torna in te! fa cor, Macbetto,
     Non ti vinca un vil timor.
Mac. Deh potessi il mio delitto
     Dalla mente cancellar!
     Deh, sapessi, o Re trafitto,
     L'alto sonno a te spezzar! *(Macbeth è trascinato via da Lady.)*

SCENA XVI.

MACDUFF, *e* BANCO.

Macd. Di svegliarlo per tempo il Re m'impose;
     E di già tarda è l'ora.
     Quì m'attendete, o Banco. *(entra nelle stanze del Re)*

SCENA XVII.

BANCO *solo.*

Oh qual orrenda notte!
Per l'aer cieco lamentose voci,
Voci s'udian di morte...
Gemea cupo l'augel de' tristi auguri,
E si sentì della terra il tremore...

SCENA XVIII.

MACDUFF, *e* BANCO.

Macd. Orrore! orrore! orrore!
Ban. Che avvenne mai?
Macd.   Là dentro
     Contemplate voi stesso... io dir nol posso!...
     Correte!... olà!... tutti corrte! tutti! *(Banco entra nella Stanza del Re.)*
     O delitto! o delitto! o tradimento!

SCENA XIX.

MACBETH, LADY MACBETH, MALCOLM, MACDUFF, BANCO,
Dama di Lady , Servi.

Lady , Mac. Qual subito scompiglio !
Ban.   Oh noi perduti !
Tutti Che fu ? parlate ! che seguì di strano ?
Ban. È morto assassinato il Re Duncano ! !

(*Stupore universale*)

Tutti   Schiudi, inferno la bocca , ed inghiotti
     Nel tuo grembo l' intero creato;
     Sull' ignoto assassino esecrato
     Le tue fiamme discendano, o ciel.
     O gran Dio, che ne'cuori penetri,
     Tu ne assisti, in te solo fidiamo,
     Da te lume , consiglio cerchiamo
     A squarciar delle tènebre il vel !
     L' ira tua formidabile e pronta
     Colga l' empio , o fatal punitor.
     E vi stampa sul volto l' impronta
     Che stampasti sul primo uccisor.

FINE DELL' ATTO PRIMO.

ATTO SECONDO

SCENA PRIMA

Stanza nel Castello.

MACBETH *pensoso , seguito da* LADY MACBETH.

Lady Perchè mi sfuggi, e fiso
     Ti veggo ognora in un pensier profondo ?
     Il fatto è irreparabile ! Veraci
     Parlàr le Maliarde , e Re tu sei.
     Il figlio di Duncàn , per l' improvvisa
     Sua fuga in Inghilterra,
     Parricida fu detto , e vuoto il soglio
     A te la lasciò.
Mac.   Ma te spirtali donne
     Banco padre di Regi han profetato ...
     Dunque i suoi figli regneran ? Duncano
     Per costor sarà spento ?
Lady   Egli , e suo figlio
     Vivono è ver ...
Mac.   Ma vita
     Immortale non hanno ...
Lady   Ah sì, non l'hanno !
Mac. Forz' è che scorra un altro sangue, o donna !
Lady Dove ? Quando ?
Mac.   Al venir di questa notte.
Lady Immoto sarai tu nel tuo disegno ?
Mac. Banco ! l' eternità, t' apre il tuo regno.
           (*parte precipitoso*)

SCENA II.

LADY *sola.*

Trionfai ! securi alfine
Premerem di Scozia il trono

Or disfido il lampo , il tuono
     Le sue basi a rovesciar.
     Tra misfatti ha l'opra il fine
     Se un misfatto le fu culla,
     La regal corona è nulla,
     Se può in capo vacillar !

SCENA III.

Parco. In lontananza il Castello di Macbeth.
Coro di Sicarj.

I.   Chi v' impose unirvi a noi ?
II.   Fu Macbetto.
I.   Ed a che far ?
II.   Dobbiam Banco trucidar.
I.   Quando ? ... dove ? ...
II.   Insiem con voi.
     Con suo figlio qui verrà.
I.   Rimanete ... or bene stà.
Tutti Sparve il sol ! ... la notte or regni
     Scellerata — insanguinata.
     Cieca notte, affretta e spegni
     Ogni lume in terra, e in ciel.
     L'ora è presso ! ... or n' occultiamo
     Nel silenzio lo aspettiamo.
     Trema, o Banco ! — nel tuo fianco
     Sta la punta del coltel !

SCENA IV.

BANCO , FLEANZIO.

Ban. Studia il passo, o mio figlio... usciam da queste
     Tenèbre ... un senso ignoto
     Nascer mi sento in petto
     Pien di tristo presagio e di sospetto.
     Come dal ciel precipita
     L'ombra più sempre oscura !
     In notte ugual trafissero
     Duncano il mio signor.

Mille affannose immagini
     M' annunciano sventura ,
     E il mio pensiero ingombrano
     Di larve e di terror.
        (*si perdono nel parco*)
    (*Voce di Banco entro la scena*)
Oimè !... Fuggi, mio figlio !... o tradimento !...
(*Fleanzio attraversa la scena inseguito da un Sicario.*)

SCENA V.

Magnifica Sala. Mensa imbandita.
MACBETH, LADY MACBETH, *Dama di Lady Macbeth, Dame,*

Coro Salve, o Re !
Mac.   Voi pur salvete,
     Nobilissimi Signori,
Coro Salve , o donna !
Lady   Ricevete
     La mercè de'vostri onori.
Mac. Prenda ciascun l'orrevole
     Seggio al suo grado eretto.
     Pago son' io d' accogliere
     Tali ospiti a banchetto.
     La mia consorte assidasi
     Nel trono a lei sortito ,
     Ma pria le piaccia un brindisi
     Sciogliere a vostr' onor.
Lady Al tuo reale invito
     Son pronta, o mio Signor.
Coro E tu n'udrai rispondere
     Come ci detta il cor.
Lady Si colmi il calice
     Di vino eletto,
     Nasca il diletto
     Muoja il dolor.
     Da noi s'involino
     Gli odj, e gli sdegni ,
     Folleggi, e regni
     Qui solo amor.

Gustiamo il balsamo
D'ogni ferita
Che nova vita
Ridona al cor.
Tut. (*ripet.*) Cacciam le torbide
Cure dal petto,
Nasca il diletto
Muoja il dolor.

SCENA VI.

I precedenti. Un Sicario si offaccia ad un uscio
laterale. MACBETH *gli si fa presso.*

Mac. Tu di sangue hai brutto il volto.
Sic. È di Banco
Mac. Il vero ascolto ?
Sic. Sì.
Mac. Ma il figlio ?
Sic. Nè sfuggì !
Mac. Cielo !. e Banco ?
Sic. Egli morì.
(*Macbeth fa cenno al Sicario, che parte.*)

SCENA VII.

I precedenti meno il Sicario.

Lady Che ti scosta, o Re mio sposo,
Dalla gioja del banchetto ? ...
Mac. Banco falla ! il valoroso
Chiuderebbe il serto eletto
A quant' avvi di più degno
Nell' intero nostro Regno.
Lady Venir disse, e ci mancò.
Mac. In sua vece io sederò.
(*Macbeth fa per sedere. Lo Spettro di Banco, veduto*
solo da lui, ne occupa il posto.)

atterrito) Di voi chi ciò fece ?
Tutti Che parli ?
Mac. (*allo spettro*) Non dirmi,
Non dirmi ch'io fossi ! ... le ciocche cruente
Non scuotermi incontro ...
Tutti (*sorgono*) Macbetto è soffrente !
Partiamo ...
Lady Restate ! Gli è morbo fugace...
(*piano a Macbeth*)
E un uomo voi siete ?
Mac. Lo sono ed audace
S'io guardo tal cosa che al demone istesso
Porrebbe spavento... là... là... nol ravvisi ?
(*allo spett.*) Oh poi che le chiome scrollar t'è concesso,
Favella ! il sepolcro può render gli uccisi?
(*l'Ombra sparisce*)
Lady (*piano a Mac.*) Voi siete demente !
Mac. Quest'occhi l'han visto...
Lady (*forte*) Sedete, o mio sposo ! Ogni ospite è tristo.
Svegliate la gioja !
Mac. Ciascun mi perdoni
Il brindisi lieto di nuovo risoni,
Nè Banco obbliate, che lungi è tuttor.
Lady Si colmi il calice
Di vino eletto,
Nasca il diletto
Muoja il dolor.
Da noi s'involino
Gli odj, e gli sdegni
Folleggi, e regni
Qui solo amor.
Gustiamo il balsamo
D' ogni ferita
Che nova vita
Ridona al cor.
Tutti (*ripet.*) Vuotiam per l'inclito
Banco i bicchieri !
Fior de' Guerrieri
Di Scozia onor, (*riappare lo spettro*)

19

Mac. Va, spirto d'abisso !... Spalanca una fossa,
O terra, e l'ingoja... Fiammeggian quell'ossa !
Quel sangue fumante mi sbalza nel volto !
Quel guardo a me volto — trafiggemi il cor !
Tutti Sventura ! terrore !
Mac. Quant'altri, io pur oso ! ...
Diventa pur tigre, lion minaccioso
M'abbranca... Macbetto tremar non vedrai,
Conoscer potrai — s'io provi timor ...
Ma fuggi !... deh fuggi fantasma tremendo !
(*l'Ombra sparisce*)
La vita riprendo ! (*Vergogna, Signor !*)
Lady (*piano a Mac.*)
Mac. Sangue a me quell'ombra chiede
E l' avrà, l'avrà, lo giuro !
Il velame del futuro
Alle Streghe io squarcierò.
Lady (*a Mac.*) Spirto imbelle ! il tuo spavento
Vane larve t' ha creato.
Il delitto è consumato;
Chi morì tornar non può.
Macb.(*fra sè*) Biechi arcani ! ... s'abbandoni
Questa terra; or ch'ella è retta
Da una mano maledetta
Viver solo il reo vi può.
Tutti Biechi arcani ! sgomentato
Da fantasmi egli ha parlato !
Uno speco di ladroni
Questa terra diventò.

FINE DELL'ATTO SECONDO.

ATTO TERZO

Un'oscura Caverna: nel mezzo una Caldaja che bolle. Tuon
e Lampi.

SCENA PRIMA

Streghe.

I.   Tre volte miagola la gatta in collera,
II.   Tre volte l'upupa lamenta ed ulula,
III.   Tre volte l'istrice guaisce al vento.
Questo è il momento.
Tutte Su via ! sollecite giriam la pentola,
Mesciamvi in circolo possenti intingoli;
Sirocchie, all'opra ! l'acqua già fuma
Crepita, e spuma.
I.   Tu rospo venefico
Che suggi l'aconito,
Tu vepre, tu radica
Sbarbata al crepuscolo,
Và, cuoci e gorgoglia
Nel vaso infernal.
II.   Tu lingua di vipera
Tu pelo di nottola,
Tu sangue di scimia,
Tu dente di bòttolo,
Và, bolli e t'avvoltola
Nel brodo infernal.
III.   Tu dito d'un pargolo
Strozzato nel nascere,
Tu labbro d'un tartaro,
Tu cor d'un eretico,
Và dentro, e consolida
La polta infernal.

21

Tutte (*dansando intorno*)
> E voi Spirti
> Negri e candidi ,
> Rossi e ceruli ,
> Rimescete !
> Voi che mescere
> Ben sapete
> Rimescete ?
> Rimescete !

SCENA II.

MACBETH. *Le precedenti.*

Mac. Che fate voi misterïose donne ?
Stre. Un' opra senza nome.
Mac. Per quest' opra infernale io vi scongiuro !
> Ch'io sappia il mio destin, se cielo, e terra
> Dovessero innovar l'antica guerra.
Stre. Dalle incognite Posse udir lo vuoi ,
> Cui ministre obbediamo, ovver da noi ?
Mao. Evocatele pur, se del futuro
> Mi possono chiarir l' enigma oscuro.
Stre. Dalle basse, e dall'alte dimore ,
> Spirti erranti, salite, scendete !
(*scoppia un fulmine, e sorge da terra un capo coperto*
d' elmo.)
Mac. Dimmi o spirto...
Stre.   T'ha letto nel core;
> Taci, e n' odi le voci segrete.
(*Apparizione*)
> O Macbetto! Macbetto! Macbetto!
> Da Macduffo ti guarda prudente.
Mac. Tu m'afforzi l'interno sospetto !
> Solo un motto...   (*sparisce.*)
Stre.   Richieste non vuole.
> Ecco un'altro di lui più possente.
(*Tuona: apparisce un fanciullo insanguinato*)
> Taci, e n' odi le occulte parole.

22

(*Apparizione*)
> O Macbetto! Macbetto! Macbetto!
> Esser puoi sanguinario , feroce
> Nessun nato di donna ti nuoce. (*sparisce*)
Mac. La tua vita, Macduffo perdono...
> Nò!... morrai! sul regale mio petto
> Doppio usbergo sarà la tua morte.
(*Tuoni e lampi: sorge un fanciullo coronato che porta*
un' arboscello.)
> Ma che avvisa quel lampo, quel tuono?...
> Un fanciullo col serto dei Re !
Stre. Taci, ed odi.
(*Apparizione*)   Sta d' animo forte
> Glorïoso invincibil sarai
> Fin che il bosco di Birna vedrai
> Ravviarsi, e venir contra te. (*sparisce*)
Mac. Lieto augurio ! Per magica possa
> Selva alcuna fin or non fu mossa.
> Or mi dite ! Salire al mio soglio
> La progenie di Banco dovrà ?
Stre. Non cercarlo !
Mac.   Lo voglio ! lo voglio !
> O su voi la mia spada cada !
> (*La caldaja cala sotterra*)
> La caldaja è scomparsa ? perchè ?
> (*Suono sotterraneo di cornamusa.*)
> Qual concento ! Parlate ! Che v'è ?
Stre. I.   Apparite !
    II.   Apparite !
    III.   Apparite !
Tutte Poi qual nebbia di nuovo sparite
(*Otto Re passano uno dopo l' altro. Da ultimo viene*
Banco con uno specchio in mano.)
Mac. (*al primo*)
> Fuggi, o regal fantasima,
> Che Banco a me rammenti !
> La tua corona è folgore,
> Gli occhi mi fai roventi !

(*al secondo*) Via, spaventosa immagine,
> Che il crin di bende hai cinto !
(*agli altri*) Ed altri ancor ne sorgono?...
> Un terzo?... un quarto?... un quinto?
> O mio terror !... dell'ultimo
> Splende uno speglio in mano,
> E nuovi Re s'attergano
> Dentro al cristallo arcano...
> E Banco !... ahi vista orribile !
> Ridendo a me gli addita?
> Muori fatal progenie!...   (*trae la*
spada, s' avventa agli spettri , poi si arretra)
> Ah ! che non hai tu vita !
(*alle Streghe*) Vivran costor?
Streg.   Vivranno.
Mac.   O me perduto !
                     (*perde i sensi*)
Streg. Ei svenne !... Aerei spirti,
> Ridonate la mente al Re svenuto !
(*Scendono gli spiriti, e mentre danzano intorno a*
Macbeth, le Streghe cantano il seguente)

SCENA III.
Coro.

> Ondine , e Silfidi
> Dall'ali candide
> Su quella pallida
> Fronte spirate.
> Tessete in vortice
> Carole armoniche ,
> E sensi , ed anima
> Gli confortate.   (*Spiriti, e Streghe*
>   *spariscono*)

SCENA IV.
MACBETH (*rinviene*)

Ove son'io?... fuggiro !... Oh sia ne'secoli
Maledetta quest' ora in sempiterno !

24

> Vola il tempo, o Macbetto, e il tuo potere
> Dei per opre affermar , non per chimere.
> Vada in fiamme, e in polve cada
> L'alta rocca di Macduffo !
> Figli , sposa a fil di spada :
> Scorra il sangue a me fátal.
> L' ira mia, la mia vendetta
> Per la Scozia si diffonda,
> Come fiera in cor m'abbonda
> Come l'anima mi assal.

FINE DELL' ATTO TERZO.

ATTO QUARTO

Luogo deserto ai confini della Scozia, e dell' Inghilterra.
In distanza la foresta di Birnam.

Profughi Scozzesi, uomini, donne, fanciulli.
MACDUFF *in disparte addolorato.*

SCENA PRIMA.

Coro.

Patria oppressa! il dolce nome
Nò, di madre aver non puoi,
Or che tutta a' figli tuoi
Sei conversa in un avel!
D' orfanelli, e di piangenti
Chi lo sposo, e chi la prole
Al venir del nuovo Sole
S' alza un grido e fere il Ciel,
A quel grido il Ciel risponde
Quasi voglia impietosito
Propagar per l' infinito,
Patria oppressa, il tuo dolor.
Suona a morto ognor la squilla,
Ma nessuno audace è tanto
Che pur doni un vano pianto
A chi soffre, ed a chi muor.

Macd. O figli, o figli miei! da quel tiranno
Tutti uccisi voi foste, e insiem con voi
La madre sventurata!... E fra gli artigli
Di quel tigre io lasciai la madre, e i figli?
Oh, la paterna mano
Non vi fu scudo, o cari,
Dai perfidi sicari
Che a morte vi ferir!

E me fuggiasco, occulto
Voi chiamavate invano
Coll' ultimo singulto
Coll' ultimo respir.
Trammi al tiranno in faccia
Signore! e s'ei mi sfugge
Possa a colui le braccia
Del tuo perdono aprir.

SCENA II.

Al suono di tamburo entra MALCOLM *conducendo molti soldati inglesi.*

Mal. Dove siam? che bosco è quello?
Coro La foresta di Birnamo.
Mal. Svelga ognuno, e porti un ramo,
Che lo asconda, innanzi a sè.
(a Macd.) Ti conforti la vendetta.
Macd. Non l'avrò... di fig'i è privo!
Mal. Chi non odia il suol nativo
Prenda l' armi, e segua me.
(Malcolm, e Macduff impugnano le spade)
Tutti La Patria tradita
Piangendo ne invita!
Fratelli! gli oppressi
Corriamo a salvar.
Già l' ira divina
Sull' empio ruina;
Gli orribili eccessi
L' Eterno stancâr.

SCENA III.

Scena nel Castello di Macbeth, come nell' Atto Primo.

Notte.

MEDICO, e DAMA *di Lady Macbeth.*

Med. Vegliammo invan due notti.
Dama In questa apparirà.

Med. Di che parlava
Nel sonno suo?
Dam. Ridirlo
Non debbo ad uom che viva... Eccola!...

SCENA IV.

LADY MACBETH, *e precedenti.*

Med. Un lume
Recasi in man?
Dam. La lampada che sempre
Si tiene a canto al letto.
Med. Oh come gli occhi
Spalanca!
Dam. E pur non vede.
Med. Perchè sfrega la man?
Dam. Lavarsi crede!
Lady Una macchia è quì tuttora...
Via, ti dico, o maledetta!...
Una... due... gli è questa l'ora!
Tremi tu?... non osi entrar!
Un guerrier così codardo?
Oh vergogna!... orsù t'affretta!...
Chi poteva in quel vegliardo
Tanto sangue immaginar?
Med. Che parlò?...
Lady Di Fiffe il Sire
Sposo e padre or or non era?...
Che n' avvenne?... e mai pulire
Queste mani io non saprò?...
Dam. e Med. Oh terror!...
Lady Di sangue umano
Sa quì sempre... Arabia intera
Rimondar si piccol mano
Co' suoi balsami non può.
Oimè!...
Med. Geme?
Lady I panni indossa

Della notte... or via ti sbratta!...
Banco è spento, e dalla fossa
Chi morì non surse ancor.
Med. Questo a presso?...
Lady A letto, a letto...
Sfar non puoi la cosa fatta...
Batte alcuno!... andiam, Macbetto,
Non t'accusi il tuo pallor.
Dam. e Med. Ah di lei, pietà, Signor!

SCENA V.

Sala nel Castello.

MACBETH.

Perfidi! All'Anglo contra me v'unite!
Le potenze presaghe han profetato
« Esser puoi sanguinario, feroce
« Nessun nato di donna ti muoce. »
Nò, non temo di voi, nè del fanciullo
Che vi conduce! Raffermar sul Trono
Questo assalto mi debbe,
O sbalzarmi per sempre... Eppur la vita
Sento nelle mie fibbre inaridita!
Pietà, rispetto, amore,
Conforto ai dì cadenti
Non spargeran d'un fiore
La tua canuta età.
Nè sul tuo regio sasso
Sperar soavi accenti:
Sol la bestemmia, ahi lasso!
La nenia tua sarà.

Grida interne
Ella è morta!
Mac. Qual gemito?

29

SCENA VI.

Dama della Regina, e MACBETH.

Dama   È morta
    La Regina ! . . .
Mac. *(pensoso)*   La vita!... che importa ?...
    È il racconto d'un povero idiota ;
    Vento e suono che nulla dinota !

                                    (*Dama parte*)

SCENA VII.

Coro di Guerrieri, e MACBETH.

Coro Sire! ah Sire !
Mac.   Che fu?... quali nuove ?
Coro La foresta di Birna si muove !
Mac. *(attonito.)*
        M'hai deluso presagio infernale !...
            Quì l'usbergo, la spada il pugnale !
            Prodi all'armi! La morte, o la gloria.
Coro   Dunque all'armi! sì, morte, o vittoria.
    Suono interno di trombe. Intanto la scena si muta,
    e presenta una vasta pianura. Il fondo è occupato
    da soldati inglesi, i quali lentamente si avanzano,
    portando ciascheduno una fronda innansi a sè.

SCENA VIII.

MALCOLM, MACDUFF e *Soldati.*

Mal. Via le fronde, e mano all'armi !
        Mi seguite !   *(Mal. Macd. e Soldati part.)*
Grida di dentro. All' armi ! all'armi !
        (*di dentro odesi il fragore della battaglia*)

SCENA IX.

MACBETH *incalsato da* MACDUFF.

Macd.   T' ho giunto alfin carnefice
        De' figli miei !

30

Mac.   .   Fatato
        Son' io ! non puoi trafiggermi,
        Tu d' una donna nato.
Macd.   Nato io non son, ma tolto
        Fui dal materno sen.
Mac.   Misero me ! che ascolto !
        Ah ! tu mi resti almen ! *(brandendo la spada)*
                (*combattono, Macbeth cade*)

SCENA ULTIMA.

I precedenti. MALCOLM *seguito da soldati inglesi, i*
quali si trascinano dietro prigionieri quelli di Macbeth.

Mal.   Vittoria !... ove s' è fitto
        L'usurpator ?
Macd. *(accennando Mac.)* Trafitto !
Mac. (*alzandosi a stento da terra*)
        Mal per me che m' affidai
        Ne' presagi dell'inferno ! . . .
        Tutto il sangue ch' io versai
        Grida in faccia dell'Eterno ! . . .
        Sulla fronte . . . maledetta . . .
        Sfolgorò . . . la sua vendetta ! . . .
        Muojo . . . al Cielo . . . al mondo in ira,
        Vil corona ! . . . e sol per te !   *(muore)*
Macd.   Scozia afflitta, ormai respira !
Tutti   Or Malcolmo è il nostro Re.

PAGES

from the
1847 MACBETH
Piano-Vocal Score

The following pages present, in piano-vocal score, the principal episodes of the 1847 *Macbeth* that in 1865 were revised and recomposed. The plates are basically those of the 1847 Bureau Central Score (plate number B.C.1027), and bear their pagination, but both the music and the text have been newly edited: the pages are taken from the edition of the 1847 *Macbeth* which David Lawton prepared, from the autograph and other primary sources, for the Danville production. They are reproduced by his permission and that of G. Ricordi & C. To facilitate comparisons, points of departure from the familiar, revised *Macbeth* are indicated by page references to the current Ricordi piano-vocal score (plate number 42311), shown as [R.63], etc. See the Table of Revisions and a Concordance of Four Piano-Vocal Scores at 463-6.

Act I, Scene 12, Lady Macbeth–Macbeth duet (excerpt)

60

Act II, Scene 1, Lady Macbeth's aria ("Trionfai!")

Repeat measures 74 to 101 (as 113 to 140), and continue:

[105]

106

A.

130

[R.141]

132

Act III, Scene 2, the Apparitions Scene (excerpt)

172

[R.217]

173

178

Act III, Scene 4, Macbeth's aria ("Vada in fiamme")

186

[R.234]

* mm. 494-5: voice: this reading follows the autograph.
The earliest piano-vocal scores (Ricordi, pl. no. 19637, p. 206,
and Bureau Central, pl. no. 1027, p. 190) and most manuscript
full scores have:

494 -sal m'assal, m'assal, m'assal, m'assal

Act IV, Scene 1, The Exiles' Chorus ("Patria oppressa!")

194

Act IV, Scene 10, Macbeth's Death Scene ("*Mal per me*")

FINE DELL'OPERA

Index: Names and Works

Entries preceded with an asterisk (*) are included in the Personalia section at pp. 461–63. Boldface page numbers indicate primary sources (e.g., excerpts from the writings of a critic) and italics indicate pages of special importance in an extended series of references. Indexing of Reviews and Other Published Commentary and the Appendices is schematic.

Index: Verdi's Macbeth